REAL ESTATE INVESTMENT AND ACQUISITION WORKBOOK

SECOND EDITION

HOWARD A. ZUCKERMAN

PRENTICE HALL
Paramus, New Jersey 07652

Library of Congress Cataloging-in-Publication Data

Zuckerman, Howard A.
  Real estate investment and acquisition workbook.
  Includes index.
    1. Real estate investment.   I. Lewis, Stephen E.
II. Title.
HD1382.5.Z83 1989 332.63'24 88-32382
ISBN 0-13-628637-2 (c); 0-13-649435-8 (p)

Printed in the United States of America

10 9 8 7 6 5 4 3 2 1   10 9 8 7 6 5 4 3 2 1
ISBN 0-13-628637-2 (c)   ISBN 0-13-649435-8 (p)

This publication is designed to provide accurate and authoritative information in regard to the subject matter covered. It is sold with the understanding that the publisher is not engaged in rendering legal, accounting, or other professional service. If legal advice or other expert assistance is required, the services of a competent professional person should be sought.

—From the Declaration of Principles jointly adopted by a Committee of the American Bar Association and a Committee of Publishers and Associations.

ISBN 0-13-628637-2

9 780136 286370   90000

ATTENTION: CORPORATIONS AND SCHOOLS

Prentice Hall books are available at quantity discounts with bulk purchase for educational, business, or sales promotional use. For information, please write to: Prentice Hall Special Sales, 240 Frisch Court, Paramus, New Jersey 07652. Please supply: title of book, ISBN, quantity, how the book will be used, date needed.

PRENTICE HALL
Paramus, NJ 07652
A Simon & Schuster Company

On the World Wide Web at http://www.phdirect.com

Prentice Hall International (UK) Limited, *London*
Prentice Hall of Australia Pty. Limited, *Sydney*
Prentice Hall Canada, Inc., *Toronto*
Prentice Hall Hispanoamericana, S.A., *Mexico*
Prentice Hall of India Private Limited, *New Delhi*
Prentice Hall of Japan, Inc., *Tokyo*
Simon & Schuster Asia Pte. Ltd., *Singapore*
Editora Prentice Hall do Brasil, Ltda., *Rio de Janeiro*

For my wife and partner, Amy,
my three children, Lindsey, Carley, and Adam
my parents and sister

To the memory of Dr. James A. Graaskamp;
may his legacy continue with
the thousands of students he taught

ACKNOWLEDGMENTS

This book entailed a long process of sifting through old files and notebooks to try to detail, in a manner that the reader should be able to walk through, the real estate acquisition process. Many long hours were put in at my trusty computer to compile this book and the subsequent revision.

I would like to give special thanks to my wife and children, who had to live with me coming home late at night and sneaking away to finish this book.

I would also like to thank the following individuals for contributing the new chapters to this book.

- Chapter 2:   James R. Ziegelbauer

- Chapter 6:   Byron Taylor

- Chapter 14:   Thomas Hanszen

I would like to thank the following individuals for contributing various sections and review of this book.

- Chapter 7:   Douglas Thorton

- Chapter 8:   Alvin Arnold

- Chapter 16:   Ronald Dean

- Chapter 16:   Michael Uhler

In addition, special thanks go to the memory of Dr. James A. Graaskamp, Professor of Real Estate at the University of Wisconsin, who taught me many years ago the basic concepts of real estate and the value of "sticktoitiveness."

Howard A. Zuckerman

ABOUT THE AUTHOR

Howard A. Zuckerman is President of The Seville Companies, a real estate acquisition and development firm in Atlanta, Georgia. Since 1976, Mr. Zuckerman has been active in the acquisition, development, financing, and equity placement of income-producing properties valued at over $500,000,000.

His experience covers a wide range of real estate: syndication of new and existing residential and commercial properties; the development, construction, management, leasing, and resale of residential and commercial properties; and brokerage of residential and commercial properties throughout the Sun Belt. These activities have involved single-family homes, apartments, offices, shopping centers, and mini-warehouses.

The author's scholastic background includes an undergraduate degree in Marketing at Ohio State University and a Masters of Science in Real Estate Urban Land Economics and Appraisal at the University of Wisconsin.

Mr. Zuckerman's other business affiliations, past and present, include memberships in local and regional real estate trade groups, including Real Estate Securities and Syndication Institute (RESSI), the National Association of Realtors (NAR), the National Association of Home Builders, the National Mini-Storage Institute, National Association of Real Estate Trusts, and the Urban Land Institute (ULI).

Mr. Zuckerman has been the subject of numerous articles in regional and national trade and business publications and has been included in *Who's Who in Real Estate* and *Who's Who in Finance and Industry.*

Mr. Zuckerman is the author of:

* *The Real Estate Development Workbook & Manual* (published by Prentice Hall, Fall 1991)

* *Real Estate Wealthbuilding: How to Make Money in Real Estate* (published by Dearborn Publishing Co., Fall 1991)

* *The Real Estate Workout Deskbook* (published by Probus Publishing Co., April 1992)

* *Problem Real Estate* (published by Probus Publishing Co., October 1992)

* *Real Estate Exchange: Using Tax-Deferred Exchange in Real Estate Investment Management* (published by Probus Publishing Co., July 1993)

Mr. Zuckerman is the editor of:

* *Real Estate Workout & Asset* Newsletter (published monthly by West Group)

* *Capital Sources for Real Estate* Newsletter (published monthly by West Group)

* *Real Estate Development & Asset Management* Newsletter (published monthly by West Group)

ABOUT THE CONTRIBUTORS

James R. Ziegelbauer is a partner in the Atlanta, Goergia office of Price Waterhouse and is the Southeast Region Real Estate Tax Services Group Leader. He received his BS/BA from Marquette University and his MBA from the University of Chicago.

Mr. Ziegelbauer has been active in the real estate industry for over 20 years and has been a leading tax partner in the Southeastern Real Estate Group for over eight years. For the past 15 years, he has been actively involved in the formation and operation of numerous investments in the U.S. by investors from other countries. The vast majority of his international client base consists of wealthy individuals and companies seeking to diversify their investment portfolio into quality U.S. real estate.

He is a member of the American Institute of Certified Public Accountants, Georgia Society of Certified Public Accountants, International Council of Shopping Centers and the Urban Land Institute.

Byron Taylor, President of TVG, Inc. and TVG Environmental, Inc., brings to his work a solid background in both environmental engineering and commercial real estate. His concept for TVG—combining the two areas—created the first firm of its type in the country. With Master's degrees in Business Administration and Environmental Engineering, his work experience includes posts as an engineer for the EPA, as a manufacturer of pollution control equipment, and with the United States Air Force Reserve. Mr. Taylor also has more than ten years' experience in the field of commercial real estate. He is a member of the Society of Industrial and Office Realtors, the Building Owners and Managers Association, and the Society of American Military Engineers. A popular speaker and teacher and author of many articles, he has become an internationally recognized authority on asbestos and hazardous waste detection and remediation in commercial properties.

Douglas D. Thorton, CPA., graduated from the University of Georgia in 1974 with a BA in accounting. He joined Jones and Kolb in 1980 and has done extensive work in the area of real estate and has experience in auditing, accounting and taxation of real estate ventures. Jones and Kolb is an Atlanta, GA firm founded in 1976 and services approximately 100 real estate related clients.

Alvin L. Arnold is a managing consultant with BDO Seidman, an international accounting and consulting firm. He specializes in originating, writing, and editing real estate and real estate-related publications.

Mr. Arnold originated and, since 1968, has written the semimonthly newsletter, *The Mortgage and Real Estate Executives Report.* He also originated and for many years was executive editor of Real Estate Review. He is the author of *Real Estate Transactions: Structure and Analysis; Real Estate Investor's Deskbook; Modern Real Estate and Mortgage Forms; Modern Ownership and Investment Forms; Real Estate Syndication Manual;* and *Construction and Development Financing.* He is coauthor of *Real Estate Leasing Manual; Managing Corporate Real Estate;* and *Tax-Deferred Real Estate Exchanges.*

Mr. Arnold is a member of the New York State bar, and has taught real estate courses at the Real Estate Institute of New York University and the Graduate School of Business, Long Island University. He is a graduate of Cornell University and Harvard Law School.

Thomas Hanszen is a Director with the Real Estate Consulting Practice of KPMG Peat Marwick LLP. With an extensive background in many aspects of the real estate industry, he has national responsibility for real estate information and process improvement services. During the last nine years he has focused heavily in the real estate systems area, assisting large banking and insurance institutions and real estate companies in developing and implementing MIS solutions and business/process re-engineering. Mr. Hanszen was responsible for bringing technology to bear as a primary tool in the due diligence of real estate loan pools and securitization, thereby bringing the transaction costs down significantly. He was responsible for negotiations with all domestic providers of Licenses Information for the Teleres service, data collections and assisted with product development activities.

Mr. Hanszen has a Bachelor's and a Master's degree from Texas A&M University in College Station, Texas and completed the graduate real estate program at A&M.

Ronald Dean has been active as both a principal and consultant in all aspects of the investment real estate industry for over 27 years. He has been involved as either developer, consultant, broker, asset manager or property manager on properties valued at over $6.5 billion, performing analysis, acquisition, leasing, management, and sales of all forms of commercial real estate at both the property and portfolio levels.

In January 1996 Mr. Dean decided to combine his experience in commercial real estate with his knowledge of computer-based financial analysis and investment modeling systems by becoming Managing Director of ARGUS Financial Software, the world's leading developer of analytical software for the commercial real estate industry. He has implemented new market penetration techniques and product enhancements, dramatically increasing sales revenues to historical highs. His most recent emphasis has been on the design of new product features, open data integration with other products, business development for strategic accounts and the international expansion of ARGUS.

A graduate of Yeshiva University, McGill University in Montreal, and the University of Houston, Mr. Dean is a member of real estate trade group advisory boards. He is frequently called upon to speak to national commercial real estate organization about technology issues. His comments and editorial content can often be read in a variety of national real estate trade publications such as *National Real Estate Investor, Real Estate Forum* and *Commercial Property News*. His depth of real estate experience and proficiency in a number of computer applications has enabled Mr. Dean to develop analytical/data management tools and procedures that are in use by major international property services firms today.

Michael P. Uhler is a graduate of the McIntire School of Commerce at the University of Virginia where he earned a Bachelor of Science degree in Finance and Management Information Systems. Accomplishments during undergraduate studies included making the Dean's Honor List and winning the Pettit Finance Case Competition. Mr. Uhler is currently pursuing a Master in Business Administration at Georgia State University.

Since 1986, Mr. Uhler has been active as a fee appraiser with Pritchett, Ball & Wise, Inc. in Atlanta, Georgia and as a consultant with Arnold S. Tesh Advisors in Washington, D.C. Mr. Uhler is now employed as a Senior Commercial Property Analyst with Holliday Fenoglio L.P., a leading national real estate investment banking firm and a subsidiary of AMRESCO, Inc. Mr. Uhler lives in Atlanta, Georgia.

*H*OW THIS WORKBOOK WILL HELP YOU ACQUIRE SUCCESSFUL AND PROFITABLE REAL ESTATE INVESTMENTS

This workbook provides all the information you need to prepare yourself for successful real estate investing.

It offers a comprehensive guide for the analysis and acquisition of income-producing real estate, for existing properties as well as properties to be built. In this workbook you will find the tools you need to be successful—ready-to-use forms, checklists, sample contracts, and model reports and letters to use during the various stages of acquiring income properties. Whether you're a first-time purchaser or a professional buyer, you'll find this a handy reference that leads you step-by-step through all the major processes involved in acquisition, including:

- How to find investment properties and recognize profitable purchases

- How to finance your purchase and where to look for income sources

- How to correspond with investment partners and keep accurate records

- Eight ways to measure a property's value before you invest

- Strategies for negotiating a successful real estate acquisition

- When and how to dispose of the property

In addition, the Appendixes are packed with checklists and financial tables for your ready use and has an extensive glossary of the words and phrases most commonly used in real estate.

The sample forms and outlines that are included in this workbook can be used as is or modified for your own individual needs. They are designed to help you quickly analyze and recall the necessary information about your purchase. The two case studies in Chapter 12 show how some of these forms are used and completed.

There are no guarantees in real estate; many factors are at work over which the investor has no control. Your chances for success will increase dramatically when you prepare for your investment properly and thoroughly. By using this workbook, you will be ready to make intelligent acquisition decisions—decisions that will play a crucial role in attaining your goal of making a profitable real estate investment.

CONTENTS

Chapter 7

Chapter 8

HOW TO PREPARE YOURSELF FOR REAL ESTATE OWNERSHIP: ANALYZING THE RISKS AND BENEFITS

Before embarking on any type of investment, whether it be real estate or the stock market, the wise investor should look at the risk factors associated with that particular investment. Real estate shares many risks in common with other investment vehicles, but there is one overriding consideration that sets real estate apart: real estate is more difficult to buy and sell than stocks, bonds, or precious metals.

In other words, the extra risk you take when you invest in real estate is that you may have to end up living with a bad decision longer than with other types of investments—perhaps for years. If you see a stock heading in the wrong direction, you can sell out overnight. With real estate, you may be forced to hold onto a property far longer, and every day it will cost you money to hold onto that mistake.

Further, the homework involved is far more complex. You might buy stocks on the recommendation of your broker, or gems based on an appraisal. But in real estate the decision is based on many long hours of research into numerous factors such as market conditions, financial conditions and the physical shape of the property. With the stakes as high as they are, extra care must be taken.

FOUR MAJOR REAL ESTATE RISKS TO CONSIDER BEFORE INVESTING

Financial Risk

As in all types of investments, there is a possibility that part or all of the investment may be lost. Let's say an investor purchased a $100,000 rental property with a $10,000 down payment. His projected rental income at $1,250 a month, and his monthly mortgage, taxes, insurance, and maintenance would be $1,150 a month. He was looking forward to a $100 a month positive cash flow, and the anticipated increase in value of the property over a period of years.

He successfully rented the property, but after a few months, his tenant suffered a financial setback and was forced to move out early. He could not re-rent the property quickly, and had to pay the entire $1,150 a month out of his own pocket. After six months, his cash reserves were depleted, and he was forced to sell the property for $92,000 to get out from under this unexpected financial strain. So, on top of losing a majority of his initial $10,000 investment (he sold the property at an $8,000 loss), he was out an additional $6,900 from the six months he had to carry the property on his own. Thus, he lost a total of $14,900 in less than a year.

Opportunity Risk

There is also the risk associated with losing the opportunity to invest your money elsewhere. In the above example, the investor lost much more than his $10,000 investment. He lost the opportunity of putting that additional $6,900 in some other investment; and he lost the opportunity of investing his projected $100 a month cash flow somewhere else.

Inflationary Risk

An added factor of inflation in the economy can further erode an investor's return of initial capital. Let's look at the investor in the above example. What if inflation had been at ten percent during the period he owned the rental property?

By the time he sold his property at an $8,000 loss, the value of each dollar he received was actually less than the value of each dollar he put into the deal. This, of course, adds insult to injury, further increasing the size of his actual loss.

Liquidity Risk

Since real estate is not a liquid investment, as are stocks and government bonds, the investor may have to hold on to a real estate investment for a longer period than originally intended. In the above example, our investor decided to sell his property shortly after losing his tenant. But due to the illiquidity of real estate, he could not immediately find a buyer. He could not cut his losses as quickly as he wanted, nor could he have freed up monies for more attractive investment opportunities. Thus, he lost the opportunity to recoup his losses.

FOUR CASH BENEFITS OF REAL ESTATE ACQUISITION

There is no investment that is 100 percent risk free. The eventual reward from the investment is associated with the risk that is taken. The investor should analyze his financial situation and determine the amount of funds he will have available for investing. He should look at his short-term and long-term needs. Although real estate is illiquid, the benefits of ownership can often outweigh the disadvantages.

While tax reform has reduced the tax benefits of real estate ownership, such ownership still allows the investor to shelter his current cash flow from the property. So, for example, if you get a 10 percent cash flow on your investment, you will be able to shelter all, or a majority, of that income. This would not hold true for income received from most other types of investment.

Here, then, are some of the major benefits of real estate ownership.

Increased Cash Flow

In any type of business, income is received for a product or a service, and expenses are then paid out. The remaining funds represent the cash flow associated with the business. In real estate, the rental income is received from the tenant and then the expenses are paid out. Since the majority of real estate will have a mortgage, the debt service (monthly mortgage payment) on this mortgage is also paid from the rental income. The funds that are available after all these expenses are paid is the cash flow.

Remember our investor with the $100,000 rental property? As long as he was receiving that $1,250 per month rent, and his monthly expenses were $1,150 he was realizing a $100 per month cash flow.

Lower Tax Payments

A major advantage of owning real estate is that while you may, in fact, make money on a property in a given year, you can show a loss for tax purposes, thus paying little or no tax on the money you "made."

Although your property may be actually increasing in value (appreciating), the Internal Revenue Service allows investment property to be treated as if it loses value each year (depreciates). Thus, each year, a certain amount of depreciation may be used to help offset income you have received through cash flow. In addition, interest payments are also deductible. If the total depreciation you are allowed, plus the interest payments you may deduct, are greater than the cash flow you received during the year, the property will show a "paper loss" for tax purposes.

Let's go back to our investor, and assume he had not lost his tenant. He would have had $100 cash flow a month, or $1,200 for the year. But, with depreciation and interest deductions totaling $1,250 per month, he would have shown a paper loss of $50 per month, or $600 for the year.

So, in the early years of ownership, real estate will actually show a taxable loss on paper, even though the property might be throwing off a positive cash flow. This tax loss will then shelter the positive cash flow for the investment.

Equity Buildup

As mentioned above, the majority of real estate has a mortgage placed on it. The majority of these mortgages are amortizing mortgages; that is, they are scheduled to be paid off over a predetermined time period. Every mortgage payment that the investor makes, usually on a monthly basis, will include not only the interest due on the outstanding loan balance but will also include a payment to reduce the loan balance. The portion of the loan balance that has been paid down is known as equity buildup. If our investor in the previous example had held the property for five years and had paid down the balance on his $90,000 mortgage to $85,000, $5,000 would have been then the equity buildup. Most mortgages are set up to pay the interest first on the outstanding loan balance and then to pay a reduction in the principal. The monthly payments will have large interest payments in the early years. As time passes, the majority of the payment will be applied to the principal payments.

Capital Appreciation

Capital appreciation is realized by the investor upon resale of the property. This capital appreciation the investor receives is known as the profit. Once a profit is achieved on the sale of the property, the Internal Revenue Service will be waiting to take its fair share as the taxes due.

Given the $100,000 purchase price, if our investor held his property for five years and sold it for $120,000, he would have realized capital appreciation of $20,000.

SUMMARIZING THE RISKS AND BENEFITS

Here, then, are the major risks and benefits associated with real estate ownership.

TABLE 1-1
Risk/Benefit Analysis

DISADVANTAGES	ADVANTAGES
Financial Risk	Cash Flow
Opportunity Risk	Tax Benefits
Inflationary Risk	Equity Buildup
Liquidity Risk	Capital Appreciation

Although there is great risk associated with real estate investment, history has shown that owning property has been a good hedge against inflation and a potential source of personal wealth. In fact, in *Forbes* magazine's annual listing of both America's and the world's wealthiest individuals, real estate ownership was listed as the prime source of that wealth more often than any other occupation.

The investor who has weighed all of the risks and benefits of owning property and has concluded that the benefits outweigh the risks will be ready to consider what types of property and other investment criteria will guide the investment decision.

DECIDING WHAT TO BUY:
KEY TYPES OF REAL ESTATE PROPERTIES

The first step in any deal is to determine your investment criteria. It is a process of considering various alternatives and choosing the most desirable opportunity. As in any investment decision, the investor must determine what to buy before deciding how to buy it.

The investor's level of experience in real estate dictates the number of choices available. The beginning investor will not want to tackle a complicated shopping center deal. Conversely, a large, sophisticated investor will not want to be involved in small rental properties.

Residential

Residential properties providing living quarters to individual tenants. These properties are available on a rental or for sale basis and are further divided into the following ten categories.

1. Single-family homes: Individual houses to be rented to a tenant.

2. Duplex, triplex, quadraplex: Two, three or four units that are attached, and are rented to tenants.

3. Mobile homes: Prefabricated homes that are rented to tenants, either in a single or double width.

4. Lot rentals: An investor can receive rental income from lots that mobile homes or recreational vehicles can be placed on.

5. Multi-family apartments: Properties with five or more rental units.

   a. Garden style: One- to three-level apartment buildings.

   b. Townhouse: Properties that contain multi-level units attached in rows.

   c. Mid-Rise: Three to six stories, with an elevator.

   d. High-Rise: Over six stories, with an elevator.

6. For sale housing: Homes developed or purchased by an investor for immediate resale.

   a. Single family

   b. Condominium: Ownership of an individual residential unit in a multi-unit building. The owner gets an undivided ownership interest in the unit and an undivided interest in the common areas, including the lobby, hallways, stairways, exterior sitework.

   c. Cooperative: A type of ownership whereby the owners of a building are stockholders in a corporation that owns the real estate. Each shareholder then gets a proprietary lease to his unit.

7. Conversions of multi-family projects from rental to for sale

   a. Condominium

   b. Cooperative

8. Resort: Investing in vacation property to rent or to sell. This includes:

   a. Single family

   b. Condominium

   c. Time share: A form of ownership in which the property is owned by several parties. Each owner has the ownership rights to the property for a specific time period.

9. Retirement housing: independent housing that is either rented or sold to the retirement market. This includes pure rental communities, nursing home facilities or congregate care facilities, or assisted living facilities.

10. Rehabilitation: Renovating residential property, upgrading it to meet current market demands.

    a. Historic renovation. Renovation of a building that has been certified as an historic property.

Commercial

Commercial properties provide space for businesses. The major categories are listed below.

1. Retail: Properties that are rented to tenants who sell goods directly to the public.

   a. Strip center: A retail center with a straight line of stores.

   b. Neighborhood center: A small shopping center with a supermarket or drug store, typically having up to 50,000 square feet of rental space.

   c. Power center: A center with over 150,000 square feet and includes two to four large retail tenants.

   d. Community center: A medium-size center, with about 50 stores and up to 150,000 square feet of rental space.

   e. Regional center: A large center, usually enclosed, with two to five department stores and from 400,000 to 1,000,000 square feet of rental space.

   f. Super regional center: A large regional center, with 750,000 to 2,000,000 square feet of rental space.

   g. Theme center: A retail center designed around a common theme.

      1. Off-price center: A retail center that caters to tenants that offer merchandise at discount prices.

      2. Factory outlet: A retail center that caters to manufacturers who sell their goods directly to the public.

      3. Fashion oriented: A retail center that deals in high-priced, high-fashion merchandise.

      4. Car care centers: A retail center that caters to tenants who deal in the automobile aftermarket business.

2. Office: Buildings that are rented to non-retail commercial users. These buildings are designed as garden, mid-rise or high-rise structures.

3. Business park: A group of rental buildings designed for office and warehouse users.

4. Warehouse: Buildings that provide rental space to users of bulk storage.

   a. Light industrial: Buildings that cater to storage users.

   b. Heavy industrial: Buildings that cater to manufacturers.

5. Mini-warehouse: Buildings designed to rent space to small storage users. Usually 25 square feet to 500 square feet.

6. Lodging: Properties that lease living space to individuals on a daily basis or longer. These properties can have price ranges from budget to mid-range to luxury. They could be marketed toward the transient, resort, convention, or commercial user.

   a. Motel: A property in which a renter can park his automobile adjacent to his rental unit. This type of property is usually a garden-type building with few amenities.

   b. Hotel: A property which is higher quality, with more amenities than a motel. These properties can be garden style, mid-rise or high-rise in design. They usually contain such amenities as food and beverage service, conference areas or health facilities.

   c. Suites: A lodging property that offers a living area and a bedroom area.

7. Multi-use: Properties that combine two or more of the following uses: residential, commercial (retail or office), or lodging.

8. Condominium: Commercial properties that are either converted or developed to be sold to the individual users. These can be either retail, office or industrial properties.

9. Recycling: Upgrading a property for the purpose of changing its present use, that is converting an old industrial building to a retail or office property, or for historic renovation.

10. Single purpose buildings: Properties designed for a specific purpose, for example a theater or bowling alley.

Raw Land

The purchase of land with no existing building improvements. This land could be zoned or rezoned for residential, commercial, industrial, or agricultural use. This land could be bought for eventual development or resale.

Distressed Property

Distressed property is any type of real estate that is having severe financial problems. These are normally caused by poor market conditions: over-building, high local unemployment, high interest rates, or a general slowdown in the local economy. The results of these problems will cause the property to lose occupancy and thus reduce cash flow. With this reduction the maintenance and services of the property will, in turn, decrease.

In many cases property becomes distressed property because of poor management controls and care which, in turn, will cause the loss of tenants due to poor curb appeal, services, and maintenance.

You can spot a distressed property by first looking for apparent vacancies and visible deferred maintenance. While some would consider such properties eyesores or losers, the shrewd investor can visualize opportunity. It takes imagination and the ability to look beyond the dirt, grime, and disrepair to visualize a potential financial opportunity. Depending on the circumstances, the purchaser might be able to visualize a totally new use for the property.

Of course, in order to take full advantage of such an opportunity, the property has to be purchased for the right price and terms. In negotiating for a distressed property, the purchaser should be prepared with a marketing, management, and financial game plan. In other words, a potential purchaser should have a clear idea of how to turn the property around to make a profit. Since the property probably has a negative cash flow, the purchaser should also be prepared with the necessary cash reserves to carry the property until it turns around. The funding of the negative cash flow can be handled through the raising of additional equity, the negotiating of a reduced debt service payment, or in some cases a reduction in the tax bill by the local taxing authority.

LAND PLAY—A SPECULATIVE PURCHASE FOR EXPERIENCED INVESTORS ONLY

In a land play, a property is purchased with the idea that within a relatively short period of time the existing property improvements will be torn down and a new property of "higher and better use" will be rebuilt in its place. Such acquisitions are highly specula-

tive in nature and therefore should only be considered by an experienced and sophisticated investor.

There are several reasons for this. For example, an investor may be purchasing a parking lot with the intent of building an office structure at a future date. However, the property must first be rezoned. There is no guarantee that this can be done. Further, rezoning can
take a long time. By the time the property is rezoned, there may be an oversupply of office
space on the market. Even if there is sufficient demand for office space, financing might not
be available. And, of course, you may not be able to rent the building once it is built.

So why take the risk? Because the rewards on this type of speculative investment
can be great. You might be able to resell that parking lot to another end-user or specula-
tor at a much higher price within a short period of time.

These types of deals can be purchased with either a positive or negative cash flow
already in place. If there is a negative cash flow, these funds are figured into the holding
costs of the property.

There are many varieties of land play. Common examples are as follows:

1. Purchase of a piece of land, development of a parking lot for a period of time and
   construction of an office building on the property.

2. Purchase of a mini-warehouse with the idea of rezoning for a higher commercial use
   at a later date.

3. Purchase of an older shopping center with the idea of rezoning to an office building.

4. Purchase of an entire neighborhood with the idea of rezoning the total tract as commercial. In urbanized areas of the country, where land is at a premium, this phenomenon has taken place.

BEFORE YOU INVEST:
EIGHT WAYS TO MEASURE A PROPERTY'S VALUE

The fact that investors have different tastes, levels of experience, and amounts of money
available for investment determines what each will invest in. These decisions will be
based on the equity involved and the experience of the investor. Additionally, each investor has different profit motives and yield expectations. The final decision to invest
rests with the individual investor, but a good attorney and accountant should be involved in the decision making process. The following are the various criteria that should
be determined prior to making an investment decision.

1. Age of Property

   Once you have determined the type of property that you want to invest in, you
   should set up criteria for the age of this property. Some investors will only invest in
   to-be-built properties, while others want properties that are under five years old.
   Other investors specialize in older properties that are in need of renovation or total
   recycling of their present use.

   Bear in mind that older properties, while often presenting great opportunities, generally require a good deal of construction knowledge. Therefore, the beginning in-

vestor should concentrate on properties that require minimal amounts of cosmetic repairs, that is, "facelifting," as opposed to complex structural repairs.

The more experienced investor with construction knowledge will not mind tackling older projects that require structural as well as cosmetic repairs.

2. Location

The old saying "LOCATION, LOCATION, LOCATION" is of the utmost importance. When analyzing markets, you move from the macro to the micro, that is, from the big picture to the small, local picture. In other words, the investor should first determine the part of the country in which to invest. Then this should be further broken down to the state, the city, and the submarket within the city.

Certain investors will start with a set of demographic requirements, such as population, income average, employment growth trends, traffic counts (number of cars passing a certain area each day) and area vacancy rates. Demographic information can be obtained from national companies, such as Urban Decision Systems and National Decision Systems, while traffic count information can be obtained from either local or state traffic departments.

The building site itself should be further evaluated for ease of access, proximity to community services, and traffic flow.

3. Size of the Investment

Each investor has a different sized pocketbook. The investor has to determine the amount of equity there is to invest. The purchase price of the deal will vary with each investor, depending on the equity and the leverage (use of borrowed funds) available. Just as an individual should never gamble all assets in Las Vegas, the real estate investor should never put at risk more money than she can afford to lose or tie up for an indefinite period of time in a nonliquid investment.

4. Tenant Profile

Each investor has personal criteria for tenant profile. Some residential investors will only acquire white collar properties while others only want to deal with blue collar. Many times the purchase price and terms will dictate the type of tenancy available. Some commercial purchasers only want "Fortune 500" type tenants, while others will settle for local tenants.

5. Construction of Building

As individuals have different tastes in consumer goods, so do investors. Some investors will only invest in brick apartment units because the maintenance costs of brick exteriors are less than those of wooden exteriors. Other investors want only buildings with a pitched roof as opposed to a built-up flat roof. Many investors want only apartment units with individual utility meters as opposed to a master meter for the whole building. Many times these preferences in the type of construction have come from past experiences. Once an investor has had problems with a flat roof, any investment in another property with this type of roof is unlikely.

Landscaping is also a criterion when acquiring property. Investors who are image conscious want a lush and well maintained appearance. Investors who are looking to enhance or create maximum value may look for a run-down property. If this run-down or distressed property can be purchased at a bargain price, the investor can increase the value by renovating the exterior as well as the interior of the property. By doing this, the investor can upgrade the image of the property and thus attract a better class of tenant, who will in turn pay a higher rental rate. Remember, the more income generated from a property, the higher its value.

6. Holding Period

Any investor should determine the holding period for each investment. Some want to acquire property, fix the property up, raise the rents, and resell as quickly as possible. Others want to invest for the long haul. Insurance companies and pension funds have large sums of money to invest every year, preferably in property for a minimum of ten years. Many limited partnerships project that they will invest for a ten-year period.

Although investors originally project a certain holding period, they very often change their criteria during this time. Resale decisions are made for many reasons. Some investors resell because they are running out of working capital and they do not want to recapitalize the deal. Others sell because they are in need of cash. The reduction of the tax benefits is a major reason that tax oriented limited partnerships resell. In the fifth to seventh year their depreciation deductions are reduced, and therefore the cash flow that was sheltered now will not be. Other reasons include disagreements between the partners.

7. Quality of Property

The quality of real estate varies as much as the types of properties themselves. Each investor must determine the quality he is willing and able to pay for. The higher the quality, the higher the price. Typically, the lower-quality properties have lower prices. Ironically, these can offer the greatest opportunities for profit.

The beginning investor should be looking for a property that is a "Class B" property or lower, as defined below. These properties will require some tender loving care, but will have the greatest profit-making potential.

Class A Property

Class A property is investment grade, "picture postcard" properties. They are in the choicest locations with the best tenancy. However, they often command the highest prices. Many times these properties are priced and sold for more than they are worth on an economic basis. With high demand for these properties by large insurance companies, pension funds or banks, the prices are usually bid up very high.

Class B Property

Class B properties are "bread and butter." They are still in excellent locations, but their tenants are not of the same quality as those found in Class A properties. In an office building, a Class A property will have the regional office of a Fortune 500 company as a tenant, while the Class B building will have a local company. Also, a Class B property might be an older one in a market catering to the newer buildings. The rental rates might be lower than they should be due to older leases. Usually, these buildings can be acquired at a better price and terms than the Class A properties. For example, similar buildings may sell at different prices due to the quality of the tenants. Where owners of Class A buildings can demand all cash from buyers, owners of Class B properties might receive a lower price or be asked to take back mortgages for the buyer.

Class C Property

These are "turnaround" properties. Usually, they are mismanaged or have run out of funds. For example, they will have unusually high vacancy rates and deferred maintenance. This deferred maintenance can include roofs that have not been repaired or outdated mechanical systems. By using some creativity and "tender loving care" (relatively inexpensive cosmetic repairs that can dramatically improve the outward appearance of the property), the investor might be able to turn the property around and create a very nice profit. You might find an older, neglected shopping center, provide a new facade and some different tenants, and thereby be able to collect higher rents from both the existing and new tenants. There is little doubt such properties offer the highest returns, but they are also more labor intensive.

Class D Property

Class D properties are the "dogs" and should not have been built in the first place. They could be properties in poor locations, poorly designed or poorly built. Or, there may simply be no market for this kind of property at any price. Even with all the money in the world, it would be difficult to increase its potential value. There is a big difference between these properties and those that offer opportunity. A property that is on the wrong side of town cannot be moved, and thus may never attract the kind of tenants needed to make it a success. A poorly designed building that cannot be changed structurally will hinder its chances of attracting quality tenants. Additionally, it might cost so much to correct the inherent construction flaws in a poorly constructed project that it becomes financially unfeasible. When you hear these dogs "bark," run the other way!

Triple Net Leased Property

Triple net leased property is a building with a long term "triple-net lease." With a strong tenant and a long-term lease in place (with yearly escalations), this type of investment could be a gem. Triple net leases are those in which the tenant pays not only the rent but also all the expenses for the property. With this type of investment, all the investor has to do is collect the rent checks and pay the mortgage. The tenant takes care of the daily problems. With this type of lease in hand and a quality tenant the value of the property should definitely increase.

8. Return on Investment

Investor need to determine up front the kind of return they are looking for. For each investor, expectations will vary, as will the complexity of the tools for measuring that return. There are five main methods for measuring the return on investment. They are: cash flow, tax loss ratio, resale yield on invested capital, resale yield on total purchase price and internal rate of return. For the purpose of illustrating how these various returns work in the first year of ownership, the following example is used:

Assumptions:

Property type:	Office Building
$ 90,000	Purchase Price
$ 10,000	Down payment
$ 80,000	Mortgage (30 years, 10 percent interest rate)
$ 10,000	Land Value
$ 80,000	Depreciable Basis
31.5	Number of Years to Depreciate Asset
99.4 %	Percent of Principal Balance Remaining on Loan After First Year
$120,000	Resale Price—Fifth Year

Operating Proforma:

$18,000	Gross Potential Income
($900)	5 Percent Vacancy
$17,100	Effective Gross Income
($ 7,700)	Operating Expenses
$ 9,400	Net Operating Income
($ 8,424)	Debt Service
$ 976	Cash Flow

Cash Flow Return

Current cash flow is the money that comes to the bottom line after all the bills are paid.

Some investors are seeking higher return on equity invested than others. Cash flow depends on many factors. In a tight rental market where demand exceeds supply, investors can achieve higher rental rates. In high inflationary periods, the costs of operating a property can increase dramatically and thus reduce cash flow. Financing is also a very important factor in its determination. If rates are high, more dollars are used to service the debt.

Some investors may be looking to achieve a 10 percent return on equity. Others might settle for a lower cash flow return. In the example above, the investor who puts up a $10,000 down payment would need $1,000 per year cash flow return to meet that goal. In the example, however, this return only came to 9.76 percent.

$$\frac{\$976 \quad \text{Cash Flow}}{\$10,000 \quad \text{Down payment}} = 9.76\,\%$$

The reasons why some investors are willing to take a lower return are many. Some might have purchased the property with capital appreciation in mind. This could be the Class C type property in which, with creative thinking and aggressive management, the investor might be able to greatly increase the property's value. Others might have purchased the property as a land play. The foreign investor might be willing to take a lower return than an American investor due to the fact that returns might be lower in his native country, and his money is safer invested in America than in a less stable country. These investors usually invest for a much longer term.

Tax Loss Ratio

Another investment return measurement is the tax loss ratio. This is calculated by dividing the total taxable income or loss by the current investment contribution. Taking the figures from the above example, the following exercise is used to calculate this tax loss ratio.

$ 9,400	Net Operating Income
$ (8,374)	Interest—Year One ($8,424 x 99.4 %)
$ (2,540)	Depreciation—Year One ($80,000/31.5 Year)
(1,514)	Taxable Income (Loss)
$ 1,514	Taxable Loss = 15.14 %
$10,000	Down payment

Thus, the tax loss ratio for the first year was 15.14 percent. If the investor had contributed equity over a longer period of time as opposed to having invested the full amount up front, there would have been a higher tax loss ratio. For example, if the down-payment was $10,000, but only $5,000 was put up at closing with the remaining $5,000 paid twelve months after closing, the tax loss ratio for the first year would be twice the 15.14 percent or 30.28 percent.

$1,514	Taxable Loss = 30.28 %
$5,000	Down-payment—Year One

Tax losses are created through the depreciation of the property. Even though properties have historically appreciated through inflation and increased rental rates, the U.S. tax codes have permitted the owners of property to depreciate these owned assets. In the last few years this depreciation schedule has had numerous changes; therefore, investors have already altered their investment criteria. The highly leveraged tax shelter deals of the early 1980s will be taken over by the economic cash flow deals in the future. These reductions in the depreciation schedules will force investors to look for their returns in cash flow. Since tax laws are both political and economic they are always subject to change. Because of the liberal tax codes of the early 1980s many types of properties throughout the United States have been overbuilt. Many were built, not with the market demand for the space in mind but because of demand by investors for these properties. Due to the new codes, the tax benefits will be looked at as the "icing on the cake."

Resale Yield on Invested Capital

The resale yield on invested capital is a measurement of the total profit divided by the total capital investment or total property cost. In the example, the investor put up $10,000 and resold the property for $120,000 five years later. This was a $30,000 profit. The resale yield was 300 percent on the original capital investment, or 60 percent per year.

$120,000	Sales Price
$ 90,000	Original Price
$ 30,000	Profit
$ 30,000	Profit = 300 %
$ 10,000	Down-payment
300 %	Total Yield = 60 %/Year
5	Number of Years

Resale Yield on Total Purchase Price

The resale yield on total purchase price is a measurement of the total profit divided by the original purchase price. In our example, the investor made $30,000 on the original $90,000 purchase price. This return is 33.3 percent or 6.66 percent per year.

$$\frac{\$ 30,000}{\$ 90,000} = 33.33 \%$$

33.3 %	Total Yield = 6.66 %
5	Number of Years

Internal Rate of Return

Many sophisticated investors will use the internal rate of return method to project and calculate an overall return on their investment. By taking the current operations of the property, they can project their future return by using assumptions about the future performance of the property and the economy, and thus project their future return. This rate calculates the dollars invested, when invested, and gives a return based on when the cash flow and the anticipated resale cash flow proceeds are received. This yardstick can also calculate the return after taxes. This return can then be used to compare various investment opportunities. Remember, since the formula for this return uses assumptions, it is only as good as the assumptions used. Therefore, the astute investor must project both high and low returns, or best-case and worst-case scenarios.

INVESTMENT CRITERIA FORM

Investment Criteria Checklist. This form is designed to update the investor's investment criteria.

FORM 1–1 INVESTMENT CRITERIA CHECKLIST

Prepared by _____
Date Prepared _____

TYPE PROPERTY:

RESIDENTIAL:		WAREHOUSE BUILDINGS:		LODGING:	
SINGLE FAMILY	____	LIGHT INDUSTRIAL	____	MOTEL	____
DUPLEX-QUADRAPLEX	____	HEAVY INDUSTRIAL	____	HOTEL	____
MULTI-FAMILY	____	MINI-WAREHOUSE:	____	SINGLE PURPOSE BUILDINGS:	
MOBILE HOME	____	LODGING:		_____	____
CONDOMINIUM	____	MOTEL	____	_____	____
COOPERATIVE	____	HOTEL	____	_____	____
CONVERSION	____	MULTI-USE PROPERTIES:		_____	____
RETIREMENT HOUSING	____	RESIDENTIAL/RETAIL	____	_____	____
REHABILITATION	____	RESIDENTIAL/OFFICE	____	RAW LAND:	
NURSING HOME	____	OFFICE/HOTEL	____	RESIDENTIAL	____
COMMERCIAL:		OFFICE/RETAIL	____	RETAIL	____
RETAIL:		RES/OFF/RETAIL/HOTEL	____	OFFICE	____
STRIP CENTER	____	CONDOMINIUM:		INDUSTRIAL	____
NEIGHBORHOOD CENTER	____	RESIDENTIAL	____	AGRICULTURAL	____
COMMUNITY CENTER	____	OFFICE	____	DISTRESSED PROPERTY:	
REGIONAL CENTER	____	RETAIL	____	RESIDENTIAL	____
SUPER REGIONAL CENTER	____	INDUSTRIAL	____	RETAIL	____
THEME CENTER:		RECYCLING:		OFFICE	____
OFF-PRICE CENTER	____	RESIDENTIAL	____	INDUSTRIAL	____
FACTORY OUTLET	____	OFFICE	____	LODGING	____
FASHION CENTER	____	RETAIL	____	LAND PLAY	____
CAR CARE CENTER	____	INDUSTRIAL	____		
OFFICE BUILDING:	____				
BUSINESS PARKS:	____				

LOCATION: _____   AGE OF PROPERTY: ____   HOLDING PERIOD: ____

INVESTMENT VEHICLE:				SIZE OF INVESTMENT:		INVESTMENT QUALITY:	
SOLE OWNERSHIP	____	JT. TENANCY	____	NUMBER UNITS	____	CLASS A	____
LTD. PARTN'P	____	CORPORATION	____	SQUARE FOOTAGE	____	CLASS B	____
GEN. PARTN'P	____	SUBCHAPTER S	____	EQUITY	____	CLASS C	____
TENANTS-COMMON	____	REIT	____	MAX. PRICE	____	CLASS D	____
						TRIPLE NET PROPERTIES	____

TENANT PROFILE:

RESIDENTIAL:		OFFICE:		RETAIL:		INDUSTRIAL:		LODGING:	
WHITE COLLAR	____	FORTUNE 500	____	ANCHORED:	____	FORTUNE 500:	____	BUSINESS:	____
BLUE COLLAR	____	FORTUNE 1000	____	LOCALS	____	FORTUNE 1000	____	CONVENTION:	____
ALL ADULT	____	REGIONAL	____			REGIONAL	____	FAMILY:	____
FAMILY	____	LOCAL	____			LOCAL	____	RESORT:	____

TYPE CONSTRUCTION:

RESIDENTIAL:				COMMERCIAL:			
STICK BUILT	____	UTILITY SYSTEM:		STICK BUILT	____	UTILITY SYSTEM:	
MASONRY	____	2 PIPE	____	MASONRY	____	2 PIPE	____
ONE LEVEL	____	4 PIPE	____	TILT UP	____	4 PIPE	____
2-3 STORY WALK UP	____	MASTER METER	____	LIGHT STEEL	____	MASTER METER	____
MID RISE	____	INDIVIDUAL METER	____	CONCRETE	____	INDIVIDUAL METER	____
HIGH RISE	____	ROOF SYSTEM:		STEEL	____	ROOF SYSTEM:	
		FLAT	____	LOW RISE	____	FLAT	____
		PITCHED	____	MID RISE	____	PITCHED	____
				HIGH RISE	____		

RETURN ON INVESTMENT:				BUYING PRICE RANGE:	
CASH FLOW	____ %	RESALE YIELD ON PURCH. PRICE	____ %	GROSS RENT MULTIPLIER	____
TAX LOSSES	____ %	INTERNAL RATE OF RETURN	____ %	CAP RATE	____
RESALE YIELD ON CAPITAL	____ %			PRICE/SQ.FT.	____
				PRICE/UNIT	____

*T*HE TAX RAMIFICATIONS INVOLVED IN REAL ESTATE

James R. Ziegelbauer
Partner, Southeast Region Real Estate Services Group Leader
Price Waterhouse

TAX RAMIFICATIONS TO THE OWNER OF REAL ESTATE

Acquisition of Real Estate

FORM OF OWNERSHIP ENTITY

Historically there have been four basic structural forms that can be employed as the vehicle for real estate ownership. These are direct ownership, regular or "C" corporation, the flow through or "S" corporation, and the partnership. Recently, thirty-six state governments have also permitted the use of a new type of entity known as the Limited Liability Company, LLC. Finally, the Real Estate Investment Trust, REIT, which was widely used in the 1970s, has regained popularity in the 1990s. Each structural type can be the best or worst, depending on the tax posture and business needs of the owner. In this section we will analyze the characteristics of each type of ownership as a guide in the choice of ownership form.

Direct Ownership

Direct ownership of real estate is clearly the simplest structure available. With direct ownership, all of the characteristics of the property flow directly to the owner's income tax return. The income earned is taxed only once in the owner's return. Losses also flow directly into the owner's return and may be available to offset other income, subject to the passive loss rules discussed later in this chapter. Administrative costs are minimized with direct ownership, since no separate tax return filings are required for this type.

The principal downside of direct ownership is the fact that the owner's liability cannot be limited in this form. Although insurance can mitigate this risk, it cannot be absolutely limited, as is generally possible with all of the other ownership forms. For this reason, direct ownership is rarely employed by the real estate owner/operator.

Regular or "C" Corporation

A corporation is generally considered to be legally separate and distinct from its owners. A stockholder's legal liability for losses is generally limited to the investment in the corporation. Ownership of a regular or "C" corporation can also be organized in a very flexible manner. Multiple classes of stock can be utilized to reflect the owners' varied interests in vote, investment and return. Control of the corporation can be vested in whatever group of officers and directors that the stockholders set forth. But for the impact of taxes, the corporate form would likely be utilized for virtually all real estate investment and business endeavors.

Regular corporations are subject to income taxes on a basis completely separate from their owners. Federal corporate income tax rates are graduated, starting at 15% for taxable income up to $50,000, 25% for taxable income from $50,000 up to $75,000, 34% for taxable income over $75,000, but less than $10 million, and 35% for taxable income in excess of $10 million. States also generally tax corporate income at rates varying from 6% to 12%. Currently individuals can be taxed at a maximum Federal tax rate of 39.6%; however, the phase-out of personal exemptions and the floor on itemized deductions can create an even higher effective marginal tax rate. Virtually all states also tax the income of individuals at rates roughly similar to the corporate rate structure. In short, income tax rates on corporate income are generally lower than the tax that would be paid by an individual on an identical amount of income. This disparity in tax rates has led some to conclude that the regular corporate form may be the most desirable taxwise.

The tax trap with a regular corporation is the concept of double taxation. When a corporation distributes income to its individual stockholders in the form of a dividend, a second level of income tax is imposed on the individual owner. Generally, whether or not a distribution from a corporation will be treated as a dividend depends on the corporation's accumulated earnings and profits, as well as those in the year of distribution. With rental real estate, it is not uncommon for distributions of cash during the operating years of the project to be largely treated as tax-free returns of capital, since depreciation, a non-cash deduction, will shield some or all of the cash flow. These early tax-free returns do reduce the stockholders' basis in stock. Any distributions received in excess of the stockholders' investment are generally treated as a capital gain, subject to individual tax, but at a lower 28% rate. Even if one were to assume that all distributions in excess of the stockholders' investment were only subject to the 28% capital gains tax rate, the cumulative tax paid with the regular corporate structure would be nearly 53%. This added layer of tax generally makes the regular corporate form unacceptable to the individual owner of rental real estate.

Utilization of this form, however, can still be advantageous for some owners. Public companies are usually regular corporations, since by law it is difficult to take on any other form. Real estate investment by public companies is usually undertaken in the form of a subsidiary of the public parent corporation, in order to shield the parent and other members of the group from liability. Regular corporations are also generally the vehicle of choice for the non-U.S.-based owner of U.S. real estate. The tax law currently forbids foreign investors from being shareholders in S corporations. Also, unlike their U.S.-based counterparts, foreign investors generally are permitted to liquidate with no second level of income tax. As a result, combined tax rates for the foreign investor are usually slightly lower when a corporation is employed as the ownership vehicle.

Flow Through or "S" Corporation

An alternative to the regular, or "C" corporation status for a business, is the flow through or "S" Corporation. Its advantage is the avoidance of double taxation on earnings, while still being allowed the other benefits of the corporate form, like limited liability. The mechanism employed by Congress to permit this is to treat the S Corporation as merely a conduit through to the stockholder for all items of income, deduction, credit or loss. There is a limit, however, to the amount of losses under this form; generally they are only allowed to the extent of the stockholders' direct investment in the corporation. This limitation often comes into play in a leveraged rental real estate investment, where tax losses are the norm during the operating years, due to depreciation.

There are certain eligibility requirements that must be met in order to successfully achieve S corporation status. Generally, there can be no more than 75 shareholders who may be individuals, electing small business trusts, qualified retirement plan trusts, and regular corporations. All shareholders must be U.S. residents, and finally, only one class of stock may be issued. There is no limitation on the size of the corporation, or the amount of revenue it can generate and still be eligible. Also, an election must be made and consented to by all shareholders. To be effective for the current year, the election must be made by the 15th day of the third month of the year. Elections made after that date will be effective for the following tax year. Once the election is made, it will not be terminated unless revoked by a majority of stockholders, or one or more of the other eligibility requirements is no longer met.

One such requirement which can easily be inadvertently violated with real estate investments is the "one class of stock" prerequisite. A potential violation exists where a corporation has little equity capital in comparison to its debt, a condition referred to as "thin capitalization." Under these circumstances, the IRS may determine that the debt investment is in reality equity, reclassifying it as such under general principles of tax law. The reclassification would generally create a new class of stock, automatically terminating the S corporation election.

At its best, the S corporation is an excellent vehicle for eliminating the corporate level of tax, while limiting the liability of its owners. At its worst, the S corporation is very limited in its ability to pass through losses to its owners. Also, the single class of stock requirement makes it extremely difficult to "fit" the disparate returns of various classes of owners into the structure. For example, in a typical real estate investment the developer owner will often receive a "carried interest," representing the value he adds to the project. Money investors in the deal will generally want a preferred return on their capital. These varied returns are virtually impossible to structure in the S corporation environment. Finally, the stock ownership requirement eliminates large classes of potential real estate investors from being S corporation participants. Other corporations, foreign entities, pension funds, and any other non-individuals cannot be S corporation shareholders. As a result, this form has only very limited applicability as a rental real estate investment vehicle.

Partnership

A partnership is probably the most flexible form of real estate ownership. There is no limit on the type of entity which can be a partner in a partnership. There is also no limit on the number of partners. Under this form, the varied interests of the ownership groups can be taken into account with little risk of disallowance by the taxing authorities. Special allocations of income and loss are permitted to take account of the economic interest of the money partners and the carried interest of the developer partner. The number and magnitude of these special allocations are also generally not limited, provided they have "substantial economic effect."

The partnership entity itself is not subject to income taxation. Like an S corporation, a partnership is a pass-thru entity, avoiding the double taxation of income present in the typical C corporation. The mechanism employed by Congress to permit this is to treat the partnership as merely a conduit through to the partners for all items of income, deduction, credit or loss. However, unlike an S corporation, where deduction of losses is limited to the shareholders' investment, the partners in a partnership are generally permitted to add partnership level debts to the base for losses.

Typically, a partnership is formed when a number of individuals contribute money, property, or services in exchange for an interest. Formation itself is a non-taxable event; no gain or loss is usually recognized to the partnership, or to the respective partners. The partnership receives a carry-over basis in the property contributed and each partner's basis in the interest received in exchange is equivalent to the basis of the property contributed. In the case of services, the partner's basis of the contribution is zero; likewise, the basis in the partnership interest received by the contributing partner is zero. If property subject to a liability is contributed to a partnership, the contributing partner is deemed to have received a cash distribution equivalent to the amount by which the other partners have assumed responsibility for the debt.

Because a partnership is merely a conduit entity, the initial basis a partner receives in the partnership will be adjusted for the pass-thru of items of income or loss from the partnership itself. Both taxable and non-taxable income serve to increase a partner's basis in the partnership interest, as will any further contributions by the partner. A reduction in a partner's basis will occur upon the pass-thru of losses and non-capitalizable non-deductible expenses, as well as for distributions of cash and property. Distributions by a partnership are either liquidating (current), or non-liquidating.

Distributions are, in general, not taxable to the distributee partner and can be in the nature of cash or property. No gain will be recognized upon a non-liquidating distribution, unless the distribution includes cash in excess of the partner's adjusted basis in the partnership immediately prior to the distribution. Loss can never be recognized on a non-liquidating distribution. A partner would not recognize gain on a property-only distribution. While a distribution of cash that exceeds a partner's adjusted basis in the partnership triggers gain recognition, a distribution of property in excess of a partner's adjusted basis results in a downward adjustment to the basis of the property distributed. If a distribution is made to a foreign partner, there are applicable federal withholding requirements. The exact requirements will differ if there is a treaty involved. Similarly, individual states have withholding requirements for distributions to non-resident partners.

Unlike an S corporation, where pass-thru losses are limited to the shareholders' investment, in a partnership losses are allowed to be deducted up to an amount equal to the sum of the partner's investment plus the partner's share of partnership liabilities. A partner's share of qualified nonrecourse liabilities is generally determined by an agreement among the partners. A partner's share of recourse liabilities is equal to that partner's share of the risk associated with the liability, i.e. the extent to which a partner could be required to make the lender whole in the event of loss. Qualified nonrecourse liabilities are generally those loans secured only by partnership assets and made by a bank or other financial institution, where the institution is not also a partner in the partnership. A recourse liability is one where the lender can look to the assets of the individual partner or partners in addition to his partnership level security.

The increase in tax basis permitted to partners is one of the key advantages of the partnership form. Losses during the operating years of a venture are generally not limited due to the use of leverage. Also, there is an increased opportunity for cash distributions either from operations or refinancings before triggering gain recognition.

Limited Liability Company (LLC)

The LLC is a hybrid company that has recently become popular as a real estate acquisition entity. An LLC offers the type of liability protection afforded shareholders in a corporation and the form of taxation made available to partnerships. It appears to be the best of both worlds. The LLC provides the limited liability of an S Corporation along with the flexible ownership structure and basis advantages for loss flow through of a partnership. The LLC is a creation of state law. To date, all 50 states have adopted LLC statutes. If an LLC operates in more than one state, it must take care that it does not run afoul of the LLC statute in the other state(s). A major additional current limitation of the LLC is that the U.S. Congress has not legislated its approval of the LLC as a viable entity. When considering an LLC as an ownership form, the owner should take the U.S. Congress' propensity for new revenue sources into account before moving further down that road. Despite this limitation, the IRS has made numerous pronouncements approving the LLCs created by the various state statutes.

Real Estate Investment Trust (REIT)

REITs were born in the U.S. Congress as a vehicle for facilitating investments in U.S. real estate by smaller investors. Congress believed that the more traditional forms for real estate investment did not readily fit the small investor. Partnerships composed of many small investors proved unwieldy from the standpoint of administrative cost. Regular corporations forced a second level of taxation, which placed them at a competitive disadvantage with their "flow through" counterparts. S Corporations could only have 75 shareholders, which knocked out the small investor. A new entity was needed. The REIT was their answer.

A REIT is treated as a regular corporation for all purposes of the U.S. Tax Code, except one. It is allowed a deduction for dividends paid, which effectively allows it to escape the corporate level income tax in its entirety, if it so chooses. In order to qualify as a REIT a number of complex mechanical rules must be strictly adhered to, one of which is that the REIT must have at least 100 shareholders. The complexity of the mechanical rules raises the administrative costs of conducting business in the REIT form. As a result, REITs tend to be large in size so its cost can be spread over a much larger base, to where it can be competitive in the marketplace. Most REITs are publicly traded, so the small investor can readily participate.

In the beginning, REITs typically invested in real estate mortgages. The reason this type of investment came into vogue was that the original REIT rules required the REIT to be a very passive investor. It could not manage or develop the actual real estate. It could only passively own it, or lend to others who actually owned the properties. In the 1970s REITs raised large amounts of capital in the marketplace. Many were "captives" of the real estate developer, and they frankly did not make good investment decisions. The real estate recession of the late 1970s caused these REITs to lose large sums of money for their shareholders. As a result, many went out of existence, or converted to much smaller, privately held entities. Very few survived.

Congress, perhaps seeing the error of its ways, revised the REIT rules several years ago, to allow the REIT much more active participation in the actual underlying real estate. This change, combined with the shortage of capital from traditional sources and the liquidity available with a public company, caused the REIT to gain a new popularity in the 1990s. In 1992 and 1993 the number of new REIT offerings virtually swamped the new issue equities markets. This trend is likely to continue as long as the REIT market allows current owners the ability to finance their products more cheaply than the traditional debt and equity markets.

CAPITAL STRUCTURE

Whatever the entity chosen to acquire real estate, it should be capitalized with sufficient equity as well as debt in order to have the capital structure respected for tax purposes. As previously mentioned, an S Corporation that is capitalized with too little equity could inadvertently terminate its S election. A capital structure with sufficient equity capital is also important in other types of entities. The thin capitalization rules can also affect a C corporation. If debt is reclassified as equity, it could result in double taxation, as the interest payment could be considered a dividend. Also, corporate partners that are not sufficiently capitalized could lose their limited liability status.

Foreign owners of real estate must be particularly mindful of the level of debt utilized in their ownership structure. Complex rules known as "earnings stripping" apply to the foreign owner. These rules provide a statutory mechanical limit to the amount of interest expense which can be deducted for U.S. tax purposes. The U.S.-based investor has a similar risk, but it is not mechanically codified as is true with the foreign owner. Also, earnings stripping comes into play at a much lower debt level than would normally apply to a U.S.- based investor. While the rules are beyond the scope of this text, the foreign investor can expect them to apply any time the debt level in the overall investment equals or exceeds 1.5 times the level of equity invested. That level of debt is generally exceeded in nearly all real estate investments.

ISSUES UNIQUE TO DEVELOPERS

Start-up and Other Costs

There are four distinct phases of a real estate project for tax purposes. Costs incurred are treated differently in each of these phases. These are (1) pre-development, (2) construction, (3) operations, and (4) disposition. During pre-development, costs such as site investigation, soil testing, preliminary engineering, architect's fees, etc. are incurred. If the project proceeds to the construction phase, these costs must be capitalized as part of the construction costs. Often, the pre-development costs are incurred by a development company and then "purchased" by the actual entity that will hold the real estate. If the project is abandoned, these costs are written off fully at that time.

During construction, direct and indirect construction costs will be incurred, as well as preliminary marketing, leasing, accounting, and tax fees. Costs of direct and indirect construction, including interest expense incurred during the construction period, are required to be capitalized. Costs such as marketing and tax fees that would normally be deducted (except that the business of renting property has not yet begun) are referred to as "start up" costs. These costs are capitalized and amortized over a sixty-month period beginning in the month that business begins (the month that the project is first held out for rent). An election must be made in the tax return in the year the start up costs are incurred in order to use the five-year amortization period. Once business has begun, all ordinary and necessary business expenses are deductible, while any fixed asset additions must continue to be capitalized. Disposition related costs generally must be offset against the sales proceeds received in the transaction and may not be separately deducted.

Environmental Costs

Environmental concerns have added a tremendous burden to the real estate developer. The cost of environmental clean-up has skyrocketed, as has its potential liability.

Toxic waste removal, asbestos abatement and other forms of environmental clean-up have become common to the real estate industry. From a tax perspective, the key question is whether these costs are deductible expenses or must be capitalized to either the building or, worse, the land.

Currently, there is little guidance as to the correct tax treatment of environmental clean-up costs. There is an IRS/Treasury Task Force for the purpose of issuing guidance in this matter; however, it has not indicated when that guidance will come. In the meantime, the IRS appears to be taking the approach that most of these costs should be capitalized. Justification for currently deducting these costs lies in the premise that the cost is more in the nature of a repair, rather than a cost that adds value or increases the useful life of the asset. A further complication is whether the costs must be capitalized to land, which is not depreciable, or to buildings or land improvements which have depreciable lives of 39 years and 15 years respectively. Obviously, the developer would argue that the clean-up costs should be considered as part of the cost of a depreciable asset. Each situation will have to be examined in order to determine the correct treatment. Until Congress acts, the treatment of these costs is in jeopardy. Their proliferation has made direct Congressional action necessary, especially if the industry is to successfully deal with the environmental issue.

Other Development Costs

Direct development costs such as the bricks and concrete that are used in a structure are capitalized and depreciated over a 39-year life. However, there are other development costs such as development fees, financing costs, and pre-development costs incurred during the pre-development and construction phases that do not directly belong to the land or building structure. These costs are either allocated to the building and improvements as an indirect cost of construction, or specifically capitalized to be amortized over a specified time period. For example, loan costs are amortized over the life of the loan, and leasing costs are amortized over the life of the lease once business begins. During the construction period, loan cost amortization is required to be capitalized as an indirect construction cost under the rules of Code Section 263A.

Cost Segregation

As indicated previously, different components of a real estate project have specific depreciable or amortizable lives. These include: land which is not depreciable; buildings and tenant improvements—39 years; land improvements—15 years; personal property (signs and equipment)—7 years; loan costs—life of loan; leasing costs—life of lease; and start-up costs—60 months. The shorter the life of the asset, the greater the acceleration of tax deductions. Therefore, it is important that pre-development, direct and indirect construction costs and other development costs be segregated into their proper categories. Unfortunately, all too often real estate owners allocate the entire cost to land and building which costs the owner valuable tax deductions.

Land improvements are those which are not part of the actual building structure, but that add value to the land. These include finish grading, paving, sidewalks, landscaping, roads, retaining walls, drainage facilities, etc. Land improvements also include a pro-rata amount of the indirect costs incurred on the project. Construction period interest and taxes, development fees, architects' fees, etc. can be partially allocated to land improvements.

Ownership and Operation of Real Estate

The ownership and capital structure of real estate is critically important to the successful tax posture of the investment. No less important are the choices that the owner must consider over the operational life of the investment. Failure to properly access these operational choices can cause the owner to prepay or overpay the proper tax liability. This section deals with these numerous tax issues and decisions related to the ownership and operation of real estate.

ACCOUNTING METHODS

A threshold question is the selection of the overall method of accounting for the investment. Regardless of the structural form chosen by a real estate owner, taxable income must be computed in accordance with the regular method of accounting that the taxpayer uses in keeping his books. That is, a method or system must be maintained whereby the amounts of income, gains, losses, deductions and credits are determined as well as the timing of when those items must be realized and recognized. The term "method of accounting" includes not only the overall method itself but also the accounting treatment of any specific item. There are two common overall methods and several hybrid methods of accounting that may be chosen. The basic premise is that the one chosen must clearly reflect income and be consistently applied and utilized.

Cash Method

The cash basis of accounting is perhaps the easiest method to understand. Under this approach, income is generally reported in the year that it is actually (or constructively) received. Deductions are generally taken for the year in which they are actually paid, unless taking the deduction in a subsequent period would more clearly reflect income. Also, certain expenses must be recognized in subsequent periods based on their specified treatment as outlined in the law. For example, if an expenditure results in the creation of an asset which has a useful life that extends beyond the end of the tax year, the deduction can only be taken over that time period.

The cash method is mandatory where there are only cash transactions. On the other hand, use of the cash method is prohibited for certain types of entities. C corporations may not use the cash method for real estate investments unless they have annual gross receipts of less than $5,000,000. Similarly, partnerships who have a C corporation as a partner are generally restricted from using the cash method. In addition, tax shelters and charitable trusts are also prohibited from using this method.

Accrual Method

The advantage of the cash method of accounting is its simplicity. Its disadvantage for use with real estate is that it usually results in a delay in deducting expenses, while not allowing a similar delay in income recognition. This occurs because rentals are typically received "on time," while payment of project expenses may be deferred for days, weeks, or months. This phenomenon is why the most commonly utilized method of accounting for investments in real estate is the accrual basis.

Under the accrual method, income is recognized when all the events that determine the right to receive it have occurred. It is not the actual receipt but the right to receive that causes income to be recognized. Generally, taxpayers' right to income is fixed when it is unconditionally due to them or they have performed their part of the contract. Similarly, accrual basis taxpayers are entitled to deductions in the year in which all the events have occurred that establish the liability of the taxpayer and the amount of deduction is determinable with reasonable accuracy.

Hybrid Methods

As stated earlier, an accounting method may also apply to the treatment of specific items. Thus a combination of specific methods may be utilized by the taxpayer in computing taxable income. Also, a taxpayer engaged in more than one business is authorized to use a different method for each trade or business. In order to do this, a taxpayer must elect a different method and must be able to show that a different business must exist. However, any "hybrid" method must meet the general requirement that it clearly reflects income.

Deferred Income

For a cash basis taxpayer, the receipt of an amount for future goods or services is taxable when received since the establishment of a liability for future performance is not recorded under this method. Unfortunately for accrual basis taxpayers, the same rule generally applies and income must be recognized upon receipt. An exception to this rule exists under either method if there are restrictions on the use of such payments. This recognition of income when received represents one of the major differences between book and taxable income. Most real estate owners who receive rent payments in advance must recognize them in the year in which they are received. The income tax regulations specifically provide that amounts received for advance rents are recognizable as income when received but amounts received as refundable deposits are not considered income. A deposit that guarantees the customer's payment of amounts owed to a creditor is considered an advance payment and cannot be deferred while a deposit that secures property is a true security deposit and not an advance payment.

Prepaid Expenses and "Economic Performance"

Cash basis taxpayers may deduct prepaid expenses in the year they are paid in certain circumstances. A distinction is made between expenditures that are considered capital in nature and those that may be currently deducted. If a payment creates an asset that has a useful life which extends beyond that tax year, the expenditure, or a portion of it, may not currently be deductible. If a payment is made for an item that is considered to be capital in nature, a deferral and a charge-off for depreciation or amortization is taken over the life of the item. For example, if a cash basis taxpayer leases a building and pays a specific amount at the beginning of the lease term and a certain amount each month, the amount paid up-front is not deductible when paid but over the life of the lease.

An accrual basis taxpayer is not allowed a deduction until the "all-events" test is met, regardless of when actual payment is made. Under this test, an expense is deductible in the tax year in which (1) all of the events have occurred that determine the fact of liability, and (2) the amount of the liability can be determined with reasonable accuracy. A liability cannot be established any earlier than the time that economic performance occurs. For a liability that requires a payment for property or services, economic performance occurs as that property or those services are provided. If the liability arises out of the use of property, economic performance occurs as the property is being used. However, if it can reasonably be expected that the property will be provided or used, or the services will be performed within 3 1/2 months after the payment, then the deduction may be taken in the year in which it is paid.

As seems true with virtually all tax rules, there are some exceptions to the economic performance rules. First, a payment is considered to meet the economic performance rules under the following circumstances: (1) a liability to another person which arises out of workers' compensation, tort, or breach of contract, (2) rebates and refunds, (3) awards, prizes, and jackpots, (4) insurance, warranty and service contracts, and (5) taxes other than creditable foreign taxes. Additionally, there is an exception relating to items that are recurring in nature, for example, if they can reasonably be expected to be incurred from one tax year to the next. Under this exception, an item is treated as incurred during the tax year if (1) the all-events test, without economic performance, is met, (2) the economic performance test is met within the shorter of 8 1/2 months or a reasonable time after the close of such year, (3) the item is recurring in nature and similar items are consistently treated as incurred in the year in which the all-events test is met, and (4) either the item is not material or the accrual of the item results in a better matching against the income to which it relates.

DEPRECIATION AND AMORTIZATION

When a real estate owner purchases or develops an item to be used in the trade or business, it must first be determined whether the item is an expense item to be deducted in the current year or a capital expenditure. A capital expenditure occurs if an asset is created that has a useful life which exceeds one year. When a capital asset is purchased or developed, its cost is booked as an asset on the company's balance sheet and a deduction for its use each year is taken as depreciation or amortization, assuming the asset is considered depreciable property. Depreciation usually refers to the annual deduction for the use of tangible property treated as a capitalized asset, while amortization refers to the use of intangible property treated as a capitalized asset. Under the new tax laws effective 1/1/97, there is a phased-in increase in the amount of qualified business property that may be expensed rather than capitalized and depreciated. The phase-in starts at $18,000 for 1997 and increases each year up to $25,000 in 2003 and thereafter.

Property, including real, personal and intangible, is considered depreciable or amortizable property if it (1) is used in a trade or business or is held for the production of income, (2) has an exhaustible useful life that can be determined with reasonable accuracy, and (3) is not inventory, stock in trade, or property held for investment, such as stocks or bonds. Land is not considered depreciable property since it isn't considered exhaustible. Land improvements, such as parking lots, loading docks, etc., do qualify as depreciable assets, since they have a limited useful life.

The owner of the property is usually the taxpayer who is allowed the depreciation deduction. In the case of leased property, the lessee is treated as the owner and may take the depreciation deductions on any improvements he makes to the leased property. In that case, the depreciable life is still the life of the underlying asset, even if the lease term is shorter. If at the end of the lease, the improvement is not fully depreciated and the lessee does not retain the improvement, the lessee may take a loss on the remaining unrecovered basis of the property. Importantly, in that case, the owner typically may take ownership of the asset with no income recognition at the end of the lease, despite the fact that it may have a remaining life and value. However, if the improvements are intended to be a substitute for rent payments, then the lessor recognizes gross income to the extent of the fair market value of the improvements in the year they were made.

If a lessee is required to replace property by the end of the lease term, the lessor is not entitled to the depreciation deduction.

Depreciable Lives

The tax code has assigned useful lives to property. Most personal property is either 5-or 7-year property, land improvements are generally 15-year property, residential real property (buildings and their structural components) is considered 27.5-year property, and non-residential real property is considered 31.5-year property if placed in service before 1993. For years after 1993, non-residential real property has a useful life of 39 years. Accordingly, it is more advantageous to classify property as personal since the useful life is much shorter than real property and thereby the cost of the asset will be recovered more quickly.

Depreciation Methods

There are several types of depreciation methods allowable for tax purposes. The most common methods include the straight-line method, the modified accelerated cost recovery system (MACRS) and the accelerated cost recovery system (ACRS). The date the asset is placed in service determines the appropriate method.

The straight-line depreciation method allows a taxpayer to write off the cost of an asset equally over its useful life. Real property must be depreciated using this method. Personal property may be depreciated under this method but results in the same deduction each year.

The MACRS method generally uses the 150% declining balance method with an appropriate switch to straight-line to maximize the deduction over the life of the asset. This results in more depreciation being allowed in the earlier years; however, this method can only be used for assets placed in service after 1987. The IRS has developed tables listing the applicable percentages to be used for each class of property. (See Chart 2.1 below which details common types of property, their useful lives, and each year's depreciation percentage.)

The ACRS method is used for assets placed in service between 1981 and 1986. This method applies a statutory percentage (which is generally based on the 200% declining balance method) to the cost of the asset based upon its appropriate class life.

Corporate and high-income noncorporate taxpayers who use MACRS depreciation for property placed in service after 1986 must also calculate depreciation for alternative minimum tax (AMT) purposes. The alternative minimum tax rules were enacted to ensure that at least a minimum amount of income tax is paid. Basically, AMT for a tax year is the excess of the tentative minimum tax over the regular tax liability. AMT is calculated on alternative minimum taxable income which is regular taxable income plus or minus tax preference items and AMT adjustments. The depreciation adjustment is typically the largest difference between regular and AMT income. Under the AMT rules, depreciation must be recomputed using the 150% declining balance method based on the alternative depreciation system class lives which are generally longer than the class lives under the MACRS method. The difference between the depreciation calculated under this method and that calculated under MACRS is the AMT adjustment. There is also an AMT adjustment when property is sold, which is the difference between the gain or loss recognized when the adjusted basis is computed under the AMT depreciation rules and the MACRS rules. There is also an AMT preference item relating to nonrecovery real property placed in service prior to 1987. The preference amount is the excess of accelerated depreciation taken for regular tax purposes over straight-line depreciation.

CHART 2.1

GENERAL DEPRECIATION SYSTEM
APPLICABLE DEPRECIATION METHOD: STRAIGHT LINE
APPLICABLE RECOVERY PERIOD: 27.5 YEARS
APPLICABLE CONVENTION: MID-MONTH

IF THE RECOVERY YEAR IS:

AND THE MONTH IN THE FIRST RECOVERY YEAR THE PROPERTY IS PLACED IN SERVICE IS:

THE DEPRECIATION RATE IS:

If the Recovery Year Is:	1	2	3	4	5	6	7	8	9	10	11	12
15	3.636	3.636	3.636	3.636	3.636	3.636	3.637	3.637	3.637	3.637	3.637	3.637
16	3.637	3.637	3.637	3.637	3.637	3.637	3.636	3.636	3.636	3.636	3.636	3.636
17	3.636	3.636	3.636	3.636	3.636	3.636	3.637	3.637	3.637	3.637	3.637	3.637
18	3.637	3.637	3.637	3.637	3.637	3.637	3.636	3.636	3.636	3.636	3.636	3.636
19	3.636	3.636	3.636	3.636	3.636	3.636	3.637	3.637	3.637	3.637	3.637	3.637
20	3.637	3.637	3.637	3.637	3.637	3.637	3.636	3.636	3.636	3.636	3.636	3.636
21	3.636	3.636	3.636	3.636	3.636	3.636	3.637	3.637	3.637	3.637	3.637	3.637
22	3.637	3.637	3.637	3.637	3.637	3.637	3.636	3.636	3.636	3.636	3.636	3.636
23	3.636	3.636	3.636	3.636	3.636	3.636	3.637	3.637	3.637	3.637	3.637	3.637
24	3.637	3.637	3.637	3.637	3.637	3.637	3.636	3.636	3.636	3.636	3.636	3.636
25	3.636	3.636	3.636	3.636	3.636	3.636	3.637	3.637	3.637	3.637	3.637	3.637
26	3.637	3.637	3.637	3.637	3.637	3.637	3.636	3.636	3.636	3.636	3.636	3.636
27	3.636	3.636	3.636	3.636	3.636	3.636	3.637	3.637	3.637	3.637	3.637	3.637
28	1.970	2.273	2.576	2.879	3.182	3.485	3.636	3.636	3.636	3.636	3.636	3.636
29	0.000	0.000	0.000	0.000	0.000	0.000	0.152	0.455	0.758	1.061	1.364	1.667

GENERAL DEPRECIATION SYSTEM
APPLICABLE DEPRECIATION METHOD: STRAIGHT LINE
APPLICABLE RECOVERY PERIOD: 31.5 YEARS
APPLICABLE CONVENTION: MID-MONTH

IF THE RECOVERY YEAR IS:

AND THE MONTH IN THE FIRST RECOVERY YEAR THE PROPERTY IS PLACED IN SERVICE IS:

THE DEPRECIATION RATE IS:

If the Recovery Year Is:	1	2	3	4	5	6	7	8	9	10	11	12
1	3.042	2.778	2.513	2.249	1.984	1.720	1.455	1.190	0.926	0.661	0.397	0.132
2	3.175	3.175	3.175	3.175	3.175	3.175	3.175	3.175	3.175	3.175	3.175	3.175
3	3.175	3.175	3.175	3.175	3.175	3.175	3.175	3.175	3.175	3.175	3.175	3.175
4	3.175	3.175	3.175	3.175	3.175	3.175	3.175	3.175	3.175	3.175	3.175	3.175
5	3.175	3.175	3.175	3.175	3.175	3.175	3.175	3.175	3.175	3.175	3.175	3.175
6	3.175	3.175	3.175	3.175	3.175	3.175	3.175	3.175	3.175	3.175	3.175	3.175
7	3.175	3.175	3.175	3.175	3.175	3.175	3.175	3.175	3.175	3.175	3.175	3.175
8	3.175	3.174	3.175	3.174	3.175	3.174	3.175	3.175	3.175	3.175	3.175	3.175
9	3.174	3.175	3.174	3.175	3.174	3.175	3.174	3.175	3.174	3.175	3.174	3.175
10	3.175	3.174	3.175	3.174	3.175	3.174	3.175	3.174	3.175	3.174	3.175	3.174

IF THE RECOVERY YEAR IS:	AND THE MONTH IN THE FIRST RECOVERY YEAR THE PROPERTY IS PLACED IN SERVICE IS:											
	1	2	3	4	5	6	7	8	9	10	11	12
	THE DEPRECIATION RATE IS:											
11	3.174	3.175	3.174	3.175	3.174	3.175	3.174	3.175	3.174	3.175	3.174	3.175
12	3.175	3.174	3.175	3.174	3.175	3.174	3.175	3.174	3.175	3.174	3.175	3.174
13	3.174	3.175	3.174	3.175	3.174	3.175	3.174	3.175	3.174	3.175	3.174	3.175
14	3.175	3.174	3.175	3.174	3.175	3.174	3.175	3.174	3.175	3.174	3.175	3.174
15	3.174	3.175	3.174	3.175	3.174	3.175	3.174	3.175	3.174	3.175	3.174	3.175
16	3.175	3.174	3.175	3.174	3.175	3.174	3.175	3.174	3.175	3.174	3.175	3.174
17	3.174	3.175	3.174	3.175	3.174	3.175	3.174	3.175	3.174	3.175	3.174	3.175
18	3.175	3.174	3.175	3.174	3.175	3.174	3.175	3.174	3.175	3.174	3.175	3.174
19	3.174	3.175	3.174	3.175	3.174	3.175	3.174	3.175	3.174	3.175	3.174	3.175
20	3.175	3.174	3.175	3.174	3.175	3.174	3.175	3.174	3.175	3.174	3.175	3.174
21	3.174	3.175	3.174	3.175	3.174	3.175	3.174	3.175	3.174	3.175	3.174	3.175
22	3.175	3.174	3.175	3.174	3.175	3.174	3.175	3.174	3.175	3.174	3.175	3.174
23	3.174	3.175	3.174	3.175	3.174	3.175	3.174	3.175	3.174	3.175	3.174	3.175
24	3.175	3.174	3.175	3.174	3.175	3.174	3.175	3.174	3.175	3.174	3.175	3.174
25	3.174	3.175	3.174	3.175	3.174	3.175	3.174	3.175	3.174	3.175	3.174	3.175
26	3.175	3.174	3.175	3.174	3.175	3.174	3.175	3.174	3.175	3.174	3.175	3.174
27	3.174	3.175	3.174	3.175	3.174	3.175	3.174	3.175	3.174	3.175	3.174	3.175
28	3.175	3.174	3.175	3.174	3.175	3.174	3.175	3.174	3.175	3.174	3.175	3.174
29	3.174	3.175	3.174	3.175	3.174	3.175	3.174	3.175	3.174	3.175	3.174	3.175
30	3.175	3.174	3.175	3.174	3.175	3.174	3.175	3.174	3.175	3.174	3.175	3.174
31	3.174	3.175	3.174	3.175	3.174	3.175	3.174	3.175	3.174	3.175	3.174	3.175
32	1.720	1.984	2.249	2.513	2.778	3.042	3.175	3.174	3.175	3.174	3.175	3.174
33	0.000	0.000	0.000	0.000	0.000	0.000	0.132	0.397	0.661	0.926	1.190	1.455

GENERAL DEPRECIATION SYSTEM
APPLICABLE DEPRECIATION METHOD: STRAIGHT LINE
APPLICABLE RECOVERY PERIOD: 31.5 YEARS
APPLICABLE CONVENTION: MID-MONTH

IF THE RECOVERY YEAR IS:	AND THE MONTH IN THE FIRST RECOVERY YEAR THE PROPERTY IS PLACED IN SERVICE IS:											
	1	2	3	4	5	6	7	8	9	10	11	12
	THE DEPRECIATION RATE IS:											
1	2.461	2.247	2.033	1.819	1.605	1.391	1.177	0.963	0.749	0.535	0.321	0.107
2–39	2.564	2.564	2.564	2.564	2.564	2.564	2.564	2.564	2.564	2.564	2.564	2.564
40	0.107	0.321	0.535	0.749	0.963	1.177	1.391	1.605	1.819	2.033	2.247	2.461

[IRS Pub. 534 (for 1994 returns), p. 49]
[Note: Depreciation computed under Table 7A for the first or last recovery year for this property varies slightly from depreciation computed without such table because of the manner to which it was constructed by the IRS.—CCH.]

Disposition of Depreciable Property

When depreciable property is disposed of, the depreciation recapture rules may apply. For personal property, known as Section 1245 property, any gain is taxed as ordinary income to the extent of all depreciation or amortization previously taken. The amount treated as ordinary income is the excess of the lower of (1) the property's recomputed basis or (2) the amount realized or fair market value over the property's adjusted basis. The property's recomputed basis is the property's adjusted basis plus previously allowed or allowable depreciation or amortization. For real property, Section 1250 property, the amount treated as ordinary income is the lower of the excess of post-1969 depreciation over that which would have been available under the straight line method. A more detailed discussion of the tax ramifications on the disposal of assets is included in a later section.

Amortization

Intangible assets are generally amortizable. The following intangibles are known as Section 197 assets if placed in service after August 10, 1993 and are amortizable over 15 years using the straight line method: (1) goodwill, going concern and covenants not to compete; (2) workforce in place; (3) information base; (4) know-how; (5) any customer-based intangible; (6) any supplier-based intangible; (7) any license, permit, or other right granted by a governmental agency; and (8) any franchise, trademark, or trade name. For any of these intangibles placed in service before August 10, 1993, the amortizable life was its useful life if it could be determined. However, goodwill and going concern were not amortizable, since they do not have a definite useful life.

From a practical point of view, the acquisition of real estate does not generally include amortizable intangibles. Generally the purchase price is allocated to the underlying assets and any excess purchase price would be allocated to land which is not amortizable or depreciable. However, two amortizable intangibles commonly found are start-up costs and organizational costs. These two intangibles are generally amortized over a period of 60 months.

LEASE INDUCEMENTS

Often real estate owners will offer inducements to entice potential lessees into long-term leases. Examples include rent holidays, cash payments made to tenants, moving allowances, lease buyouts, and build-out allowances. Both the lessor and the lessee must look at the tax aspects of each type of inducement since they may produce unintended results. The tax effect of a given inducement may affect the lessor, the lessee, both or neither and may be favorable, unfavorable, or neutral.

Rent Holidays

Rent holidays include free or reduced rents for a portion of the lease term. The most common inducement is having a period of free rent at the inception of the lease. The tax advantage (and economic disadvantage) for the lessor is that gross income is generally not recognized during this period of no rent. Obviously, the downside is that the lessor has no cash flow. Another potential problem could exist if the lessor is subject to the passive activity loss rules as discussed below. Since the lessor will recognize less income, a loss could be sustained or increased that is deemed non-deductible by the passive loss rules.

Cash Payments

Cash payments to tenants are often used as lease inducements. Normally, a cash payment would be income to the tenant in the year in which it is received but the lessor would not be allowed a deduction. Instead, the lessor would capitalize and amortize the payment over the term of the lease. If the lease contains options to renew, usually they are ignored in determining the lease term unless they are such that the option is certain to be exercised. This type of incentive is less favorable to both the landlord and the tenant than a rent holiday from both a tax and cash flow point of view.

In some cases, a lessor will agree to pay the moving expenses of a tenant. Whether the payment is made directly to the moving company or reimbursed to the tenant, the tax treatment should be the same as for a cash payment. This inducement is more favorable to the tenant than a cash payment since a business deduction is allowed for the moving expenses to offset the income recognized. The landlord must still amortize the cost of this item over the lease term.

A lessor may agree to buy out or take over a potential tenant's existing lease. If the lessor pays a lump sum to have the tenant released from the existing lease, the tax result is that the potential tenant will recognize income regardless of whether the amount is paid to the tenant who then pays off the existing lease, or the amount is paid directly by the lessor to the former lessor. The tenant would again be allowed an offsetting rent deduction. The lessor will treat the payment as a lease inducement payment which would be capitalized and amortized over the term of the tenant's new lease. If the existing lease is assigned to the lessor who then subleases it, the tenant should not recognize income and the lessor will have a new passive activity. However, if the tenant subleases the existing space to the new lessor, then the tenant has the passive activity.

Tenant Improvements

Finally, a lessor may offer a potential tenant the option of finishing the leased space for an allowance of a certain amount per square foot. Under one approach, the improvements would be considered to be owned by the lessor who is allowed the depreciation deduction over the useful life of the asset. If the improvement is abandoned or destroyed at the end of the lease term, any unrecovered basis may be written off. Otherwise, the asset is continued to be depreciated over its remaining useful life. The tenant should not recognize income as a result of this type of inducement even if the payment is made directly to the tenant. However, if the tenant has the option of taking cash in lieu of spending the money on improvements, immediate income recognition results. The tenant will then be treated as the owner of the improvements purchased, depreciable over the asset's life. The lessor's payment will be treated as a cash payment, amortizable by the lessor over the life of the lease. This result is very bad for the tenant, but good for the landlord. Unfortunately, this part of the tax law is probably the most misunderstood in the real estate industry. All too often, tenants do not pick up the income or the depreciation; landlords do not treat the asset as theirs, and amortize the cost over the lease term.

OTHER EXPENSE ISSUES

Real Estate Taxes

Local, state, and foreign real property taxes associated with a trade or business are deductible as ordinary and necessary business expenses. Real property taxes are those levied on interests in real property and are for the general public welfare. Taxes are generally deductible only by the person or entity on whom they are imposed. In other words, if a taxpayer voluntarily pays taxes on behalf of another taxpayer, the deduction is disallowed. For example, a shareholder may not deduct real estate taxes paid for a corporation in which he is a shareholder.

A cash basis taxpayer is allowed a deduction for real estate taxes in the year in which they are paid. An accrual basis taxpayer generally deducts taxes in the year in which all events have occurred which determine the fact of the liability, economic performance has occurred, and the amount is determinable. This is consistent with the economic performance rules previously discussed. There are two elections which could be made in order to take the deduction before making an actual payment. The first is to elect to accrue the property taxes which are related to a definite period of time ratably over that period. The second is to adopt the recurring item exception, discussed above, under which the deduction may be accrued on the lien or assessment date. A taxpayer must look at his tax year as well as the tax year and lien date of the jurisdiction in which the real property is located in order to determine which method is most beneficial.

Repairs and Maintenance

Expenditures made to keep property in efficient operating condition and which do not add to the property's value or prolong its useful life are generally deductible as repairs. Any improvement that materially adds to the value or utility of the property or appreciably prolongs its useful life must be capitalized. In addition, expenditures as part of a general plan of reconditioning, renovating, improving or altering property must be capitalized even though certain portions, if standing alone, would constitute a repair. Examples of repairs include repainting, mending leaks, and plastering. However, the installation of a new roof is considered a capitalizable asset that must be depreciated over its useful life.

RULES ASSOCIATED WITH THE DEDUCTIBILITY OF REAL ESTATE LOSSES

At-Risk Rules

Generally, a taxpayer may only deduct losses incurred in a trade or business or for the production of income up to the amount that the taxpayer is financially "at risk" with respect to the activity. These rules apply to individuals and certain closely held corporations. Two activities which are not subject to the at-risk rules are: (1) the holding of real estate placed in service before January 1, 1987 and (2) the leasing of equipment by closely held corporations.

The rules were designed to prevent taxpayers from offsetting trade, business, or professional income with losses from investments in activities which are largely financed by nonrecourse debt for which the taxpayer was not personally liable. If an activity sustains a loss, a taxpayer must first determine the amount of the loss allowed under the at-risk rules. Any loss that passes through the at-risk limitation must then also survive the passive activity loss rules, described later, in order to be currently deductible.

Under the at-risk rules, a loss is limited to the amount of the taxpayer's cash contributions and the adjusted basis of property contributed plus a personally allocable share of any debt in which the taxpayer is liable. Personal liability usually exists if the taxpayer is the ultimate obligator and there is no recourse against other parties. Accordingly, nonrecourse financing, guaranteed debt and similar arrangements are not considered to be at-risk. A taxpayer's at-risk basis is decreased in subsequent years by losses incurred in previous years. The converse is true for income recognized.

Partners in a partnership are also subject to the at-risk rules. The amount of losses deductible by a partner is limited to the amounts at risk in the activity, which does not include any portion of a partnership liability for which the partner has no personal liability. However, most partners are personally liable for partnership liabilities since this form of ownership does not offer limited liability. This is not true if limited partners are involved. Since an S corporation provides limited liability with respect to its liabilities to its shareholders, its debt generally is not considered to be at-risk.

An important exception is provided for qualified nonrecourse debt. That is, certain nonrecourse debt is considered to be an amount at-risk if it is qualified. Qualified nonrecourse debt is either debt obtained from a commercial lender or a related party. If a related party is the lender, then the terms must be such as would be provided to an unrelated third party and is secured only by real estate used in the activity.

Passive Activity Losses

A passive activity is one that involves the conduct of a trade or business in which the taxpayer does not materially participate. All rental activities are considered passive, regardless of taxpayer participation. However, there are special rules for rental activities, which are discussed later in this chapter. The passive activity rules only apply to individuals, estates, trusts and personal service corporations. There is also a rule that applies to certain closely held C corporations. If a partnership or S corporation is involved in a passive activity, then the activity retains its passive status in the hands of the partner or shareholder.

A taxpayer is considered to materially participate in an activity if one of the following tests is satisfied:

1. the taxpayer participates more than 500 hours,

2. participation by the taxpayer constitutes substantially all of the participation in the activity,

3. the taxpayer participates for more than 100 hours and this participation is not less than the participation of any other individual,

4. the activity is a "significant participation activity" (as defined below) and the taxpayer's participation in all such activities exceeds 500 hours,

5. the taxpayer materially participated in the activity for any 5 years of the 10 years that preceded the current tax year,

6. the activity is a "personal service activity" (as defined below) and the taxpayer materially participated in the activity for any 3 years preceding the current tax year, or

7. the taxpayer satisfies a facts and circumstances test that requires evidence to show participation on a regular, continuous, and substantial basis.

A significant participation activity is one in which a taxpayer participates for more than 100 hours but does not materially participate. Thus, a taxpayer will not be subject to the passive activity rules if total hours of participation in at least two significant participation activities exceeds 500 hours.

A personal service activity involves the performance of personal services in (1) the field of health, engineering, architecture, accounting, actuarial services, the performing arts, or consulting, or (2) any other trade or business in which capital is not a material income-producing factor.

A limited partner is not treated as materially participating in any activity of a limited partnership unless she would be treated as materially participating under items (1), (5), or (6) above if she were not a limited partner.

Under the passive activity rules, generally losses sustained by a passive activity cannot be used to offset any other type of income except income from other passive activities. In addition, any credits generated by passive activities are also limited to the tax generated by the passive activities. Any disallowed losses are suspended and carried forward to the next succeeding tax year. Upon the disposition of the entire interest in the passive activity, the losses are then allowed in full: first, against passive activity income and then against non-passive types of income including wages, interest, or dividends.

A passive activity loss for a tax year is sustained if the total losses (including prior year unallowed losses) from all passive activities exceed the total income from all passive activities. Where a taxpayer's disallowed passive losses are derived from more than one activity, a ratable portion of the loss (if any) from each passive activity is disallowed. In other words, only a ratable portion of each activity's loss is used to offset income from other passive activities. Any unused losses are then carried forward. A taxpayer must track suspended losses and credits from each activity each year.

There are special rules which relate to real estate activities. A "rental activity" is defined as one where payments are made principally for the use of tangible property. However, if any of the following are met, then the activity will not be treated as a rental activity:

1. the average period in which a customer uses the property is 7 days or less

2. the average period in which a customer uses the property is 30 days or less and the owner provides significant personal services

3. the owner provides extraordinary personal services (the average period of customer use is disregarded)

4. the rental of tangible personal property is incidental to the nonrental activity of the owner

5. the property is made available during defined business hours for nonexclusive use by various customers

6. the property is provided for use in a partnership, S corporation, or joint venture activity of a nonrental nature by the taxpayer owning an interest

Under the exception for rental real estate, an individual, or estate for up to two years following the individual's death, may utilize up to $25,000 of passive activity losses to offset income from nonpassive sources if the individual is an active participant in the activity. The taxpayer must own a minimum of a 10% interest in the activity in order to utilize this exception. To be considered an active participant, an individual must make management decisions or arrange for or provide services in a significant and bona fide sense. The taxpayer does not have to maintain regular or continuous involvement in the operation of the activity, but must maintain the right to exercise discretion and judgment in management decisions.

The $25,000 amount is reduced (but not below $0) by 50% of the amount by which the taxpayer's adjusted gross income exceeds $100,000. This amount is completely phased out when adjusted gross income exceeds $150,000. For purposes of this exception, adjusted gross income is determined without regard to social security benefits, qualified U.S. savings bonds, qualified retirement contributions, and passive activity losses. For married taxpayers who file separately, the reduction amount is $12,500 and is reduced when adjusted gross income reaches $50,000.

There is also an exception to the general passive activity rules for individuals who are considered real estate professionals beginning after 1993. If the individual qualifies for the exception, then the activity is not treated as being passive. Thus, any loss sustained by the activity can be used to offset other types of income. To qualify for this exception, the following two requirements must be met:

1. more than one-half of the personal services performed in trades or businesses by the taxpayer during the year must involve real property trades or businesses in which the taxpayer materially participates, and

2. the taxpayer must perform more than 750 hours of service during the year in real property trades or businesses in which the taxpayer materially participates.

If the taxpayer files a joint return with his/her spouse, the two requirements must be satisfied by one spouse. Under this exception each rental real estate activity is treated as a separate activity unless the taxpayer elects to treat all interests in real estate as one activity.

A closely held C corporation can qualify for this exception if more than 50% of its gross receipts for the tax year are derived from real property trades or businesses in which it materially participates. Services performed as an employee are disregarded unless the employee is a more-than-5%-owner of the employer.

A real property trade or business is defined as any real property development, redevelopment, construction, reconstruction, acquisition, conversion, rental, operation, management, leasing or brokerage trade or business.

REPORTING REQUIREMENTS

Corporations

U.S. corporations must file an income tax return, Form 1120, by the 15th day of the third month following the tax year end. If the corporation is foreign and is considered to have effectively connected income with the U.S., it is required to file Form 1120F. Generally, the ownership and rental of real property is considered effectively connected income with the U.S. In addition, if a corporation is controlled by a foreign person, Form 5472 must be filed.

Dividend distributions to U.S. shareholders are not subject to withholding. The shareholder, however, must report the dividend as income on an individual income tax return. Dividend distributions to nonresident aliens and foreign corporations are subject to withholding at a flat rate of 30% unless reduced by an applicable tax treaty.

Partnerships

Partnerships report their income and deductions on Form 1065, which is due by the 15th day of the fourth month following the tax year end. Each partner is given a Schedule K-1 which reports his share of the partnership activity. If the partnership is engaged in a passive activity, that information is reported separately to the partner. If the partner sustains losses with regard to the passive activities, he files Form 6198 to determine his loss under the at-risk rules, and Form 8582 to determine the losses which are currently deductible under the passive activity rules on his individual return.

Distributions from partnerships are generally not taxable if the partner has significant basis in the activity. Thus, there is no withholding on partnership distributions. However, if there is a foreign partner, the partnership must withhold tax at the highest rate of U.S. tax to which the foreign partner is subject on the foreign partner's allocable share of effectively connected U.S. taxable income. The partnership must withhold a 30% tax on a foreign partner's allocable share of taxable items that are not effectively connected with its U.S. trade or business unless a tax treaty in effect allows a lower withholding percentage.

S Corporations

S Corporations must file Form 1120S to report income and deductions. The form is due by the 15th day of the third month following the tax year end. Each shareholder is given a K-1 which reports her allocable share of the corporation's activity. As with a partnership, if an S corporation is involved in a passive activity, then the shareholder must determine if any losses from the activities are limited under the at-risk and/or passive activity rules.

Distributions from the S Corporation also are not generally taxable if the shareholder has significant basis. The withholding requirements of an S Corporation are generally the same as for a partnership.

Disposition of Real Estate

NATURE OF GAIN OR LOSS

Generally, a gain or loss is recognized upon the disposition of real estate. Its character is determined by the type of real estate and the purpose for which it is held: personal use, trade or business use, or investment. Gains on the sale of real estate held for any of these three purposes are fully taxable. On the other hand, losses recognized on personal use assets are not deductible. Losses on the remaining two types of property are deductible but subject to certain limitations.

The character of the gain or loss (capital vs. ordinary) also differs depending on what use the property is held for and the taxpayer who sells it. Determining the character is important since the applicable tax rates are different. If the property is disposed of by an investor who is holding the property for investment purposes, the resulting gain or loss will be a capital gain or loss. The capital loss is subject to different limitations depending on the taxpayer.

However, if a dealer who holds the property primarily for sale to customers disposes of the property, the resulting gain or loss is generally classified as ordinary, and any loss will be fully deductible. To determine whether a taxpayer is a dealer, several factors must be considered: the nature of the taxpayer's business, taxpayer's purpose in holding the property, length of time the property was held, and frequency of sales. Real estate brokers are not usually real estate dealers because they sell real estate on behalf of someone else. Case law has shown that holding property for many years indicates an investment purpose. The disposition of land held for investment purposes will generate capital gains or losses. Real estate dealers can hold land for investment purposes as well as for use in a trade or business.

The depreciation recapture rules also dictate the character of gain or loss on disposal. Depreciation recapture can occur when depreciable property held for trade or business purposes has been disposed of for tax purposes. Depreciation recapture refers to the conversion of capital gain into ordinary income. This recapture supersedes any other rule that would characterize the nature of the gain or loss recognized.

In addition, the character of a gain or loss will be decided by whether the property is considered Section 1231 property which refers to depreciable property used in a trade or business that is considered long term. If an asset is held for more than one year, the holding period is considered to be long term, otherwise it is treated as short term. This determination is important for the proper classification of gain or loss recognized by taxpayers holding property for use in a trade or business. This does not include either property which would properly be included in the taxpayer's inventory at the close of the taxable year or property held primarily for sale to customers in the ordinary course of trade or business. Net Section 1231 gains are treated as long-term capital gains, while net Section 1231 losses are treated as ordinary losses. This creates the best of both worlds.

TIMING OF GAIN OR LOSS

Annual gains and losses are aggregated based on their character. Capital gains and losses are netted together to determine whether there is an overall gain or loss. Generally, the gain or loss is recognized in the tax year of the sale. However, if the net result is a loss, the amount of loss currently deductible is dependent on the type of ownership structure chosen. Noncorporate taxpayers are allowed to offset up to $3,000 of ordinary income. Corporate taxpayers are not allowed to offset any ordinary income with capital losses. Corporations may carry a capital loss back to the preceding 3 years and then forward for 5 years; individuals may carry over a capital loss until it is exhausted.

INSTALLMENT SALES

If the terms of a sale agreement are such that the sales price is not received in one tax year, then the installment sales rules may apply. Generally, nondealers who sell real property must report gain on the installment method when they are to receive at least one payment after the close of the tax year in which the disposition occurs. Dealers in real property are generally not allowed to use the installment method.

An interest charge will be imposed on receivables with a face amount greater than $5,000,000 at the close of the taxable year. This interest charge is calculated by multiplying the "applicable percentage" of the deferred tax liability by the underpayment rate in effect for the month in which the taxable year ends. The applicable percentage is determined by dividing the amount of the aggregate face amount of the obligations outstanding at the close of the taxable year in excess of $5,000,000 by the aggregate face amount of such obligations arising in and outstanding at the close of the taxable year. This percentage remains fixed for the life of the obligations. The taxpayer takes this interest into account when determining the interest deduction allowable for the taxable year. The maximum tax rate is important because it determines the interest charge. The deferred tax liability is calculated by applying the outstanding obligation at the close of the taxable year by the maximum tax rate. Therefore, as tax rates fluctuate, so does the interest charge.

If property that has been depreciated is sold in an installment sale, the seller must report all "recapture income" in the year of disposition. The installment sale rules apply only to the gain in excess of the amount recaptured as ordinary income under the depreciation recapture rules. The recapture income is the income that would be converted to ordinary income under the rules previously discussed if all payments were received in the year of disposition.

TAX DEFERRED EXCHANGES

Generally when an exchange of property occurs, there is a taxable event whereby a gain or loss is recognized by the taxpayer. However, in certain cases, the tax consequences of an exchange are not immediately recognized, but rather deferred. Like-kind exchanges are such an example.

Gain or loss realized on a like-kind exchange is deferred. A like-kind exchange occurs when there is an exchange of property held for productive use in a trade or business for property of a like-kind to be held either for productive use in a trade or business or for investment. There are certain criteria that must be met for an exchange to be classified as "like-kind," such as:

a. There must be an exchange of like-kind property;

b. The property given up and the property received must both be held for productive use in a trade or business or for investment;

c. The property cannot be property held primarily for sale or other excluded property.

A like-kind exchange occurs only when property of one kind or class is exchanged for property of the same kind or class. Personal property is considered a kind or class and real property is considered another type or class. Therefore, personal property exchanged for real property would not qualify as a like-kind exchange.

"Like-kind" refers to the nature or character of the property and not to its grade or quality. Thus, if unimproved real estate was exchanged for improved real estate, the exchange would qualify for like-kind exchange treatment because the grade or quality of the two kinds or classes of property is immaterial.

To qualify for like-kind exchange treatment, the property exchanged must be held for productive use in a trade or business or for investment purposes. Property held for personal purposes, such as the family car, would not qualify. Productive trade or business property could be exchanged for investment property. Likewise, investment property could be exchanged for property held for productive use in a trade or business.

Certain types of property do not qualify for like-kind exchange treatment. These types include stock in trade, other property held primarily for sale, other securities or evidences of indebtedness or interest, partnership interests, certificates of trust or beneficial interests, or choses in action. Such properties are not considered held for productive use in a trade or business or for investment purposes.

The basis of the like-kind property received is determined by reference to the adjusted basis of the property given up. The presence of "boot" will also affect the basis of the acquired property. "Boot" refers to money or other non-like kind property given or received in the transaction. The basis of the acquired property is calculated by adding to the adjusted basis of the old property any boot given plus any gain recognized, and subtracting any boot received as well as any loss recognized.

TAX RAMIFICATIONS TO THE REAL ESTATE SERVICE COMPANY

Form of Ownership

For tax and liability reasons, the best form of ownership for the real estate service company is usually an S corporation. Limited liability companies may also be a good choice if they continue to be accepted by the IRS. The reason for these forms of ownership is that the service company is usually an income generator. A pass-through entity, unlike a corporation, allows the income to be taxed only at the shareholder level. A corporation is usually necessary for liability purposes. Partnerships usually do not provide sufficient liability protection for the service company.

Method of Accounting

Under normal tax accounting principles, brokerage income, leasing commissions and management fees are taxed at the time they are earned for an accrual basis taxpayer, and at the time cash is received for a tax basis taxpayer. The method of accounting chosen by the service company can provide a deferral of taxes. Usually the cash method of accounting provides the greatest deferral for the service company. In most cases, income is not recognized until the cash is actually received. An accrual basis taxpayer picks up income as it is earned. For example, a customer pays the December, 1994 management fee on January 1, 1995. The service company using the cash method of accounting would pick up the income in 1995. The accrual method company would pick up the income in 1994. Of course the same is true for expenses. A service company considering the cash method of accounting must weigh the benefits of not recognizing cash until collected against not deducting expenses until paid.

Alternatives to Straight Commission-Based Compensation

Often, compensation for services does not come in the form of a cash commission or fee. Ownership positions in lieu of a cash commission are sometimes used as compensation for the real estate service company. The tax consequences of ownership positions can differ from those for commission-based compensation. Generally, receipt of a partnership interest in exchange for services is considered a taxable event to the provider of the services. The value of those services and thus the amount of taxable income depends on the fair market value of the partnership interest. While an interest in the capital of a partnership may have immediate value, a future profits interest only is much harder to value. This is a complicated area of taxation and usually turns into a facts and circumstances situation. The service company should be aware that taking a partnership interest instead of a fee does not guarantee tax deferral.

TAX RAMIFICATIONS FOR THE REAL ESTATE TENANT

Lease Inducement Payments

In the current leasing market, landlords are often prepared to offer various inducements to a potential tenant. These inducements can take many different forms. Typically, more than one type of inducement is offered, and the tax consequences of the entire package must be assessed.

Prospective tenants must be aware that if they receive incentives in the form of cash payments they will likely end up having to recognize large amounts of income in the year the lease commences with no offsetting deductions in that year. The cash payments could be used for moving expenses, build-out costs, personal property purchases, or simply a signing bonus. It is highly recommended that the landlord and tenant set out unambiguously in the lease the intended tax responsibility to be assumed by each party, with a particular focus on who will take ownership of tenant improvements and personal property that has been acquired with cash incentives.

The tax consequences of cash payments for tenant improvements are contingent upon who is deemed to have ownership of the improvements. If it is the landlord, then the tenant will not have to recognize any income as a result of receiving the cash inducement. Additionally, the tenant will have no basis in the improvements for depreciation purposes.

If, however, the deal is structured to give ownership of the assets to the tenant, then the cash payment by the landlord would be included in the tenant's income in the year or years deemed received. As the owner of the assets, the tenant would be entitled to take depreciation on the improvements. If, at a later date, the lease terminates before the improvements are fully depreciated, then the tenant will be entitled to write off the undepreciated balance at that time.

Tenant improvements made after December 31, 1986, regardless of whether they are owned by the lessor or the lessee, must be depreciated in accordance with the MACRS rules discussed in a previous section. Generally, MACRS would dictate that such leasehold improvements constitute nonresidential "real" property and must be depreciated using the straight-line method over 39.5 years if placed in service after May 13, 1993 and over 31.5 years if placed in service prior to that date. Prior to 1987, leasehold improvements could be amortized over the term of the lease, if it was shorter than the asset recovery period.

Any improvement that is demolished receives special treatment. The undepreciated balance is usually deductible as a loss upon demolition.

Rental Arrangements

In the "good old days" of real estate (before the 1986 Tax Reform Act) savvy real estate owners often would structure their leases with heavy initial free rental periods, low early year rentals, and substantial escalations in the last years of the lease. These types of leases were intended to produce two desired results. First, it was hoped that a buyer would agree to capitalize the higher-than-market end of lease rental rate into a future sales price. Second, since tax losses earned a 50% tax benefit and gains only cost 28%, there was a tremendous incentive to "sell" these properties before the leases ran out, effectively selling that higher end of lease rental stream at capital gains tax rates.

Congress got wise to the game in 1984. They added Section 467 to the Tax Code, which severely restricted the ability to get any tax benefit from structuring leases in this manner. This section was designed to target leases involving total payment for the use of property in excess of $250,000 and which provide for deferred or "escalating" rental amounts. It also applies to certain leaseback transactions and long-term agreements. It effectively places the lessor and the lessee on the accrual basis with respect to the lease, irrespective of the taxpayer's accounting method.

The lessee will be required to treat as an expense, for any taxable year, the sum of the rent accrued under this section plus any interest that is due on amounts taken into account previously which still remain unpaid at the end of the year. The amount of accrued rent under section 467 will generally be in accordance with the allocation of the rents payable per the rental agreement. If the agreement does not provide an allocation, then a constant rent amount ("leveled amount") to be accrued each period must be calculated as outlined in the section. The other instances where such a leveling of the rent payments is required is with regard to certain leaseback transactions and long-term agreements that do not fall under the "safe harbor" provisions provided by the section.

Section 467 also prevents the conversion of ordinary income attributable to future unrealized rental income into capital gain which is taxed at the favorable 28% rate. The future unrealized rental income would have arisen as a consequence of a rental agreement providing for escalating payments. The portion of the gain that must be recaptured as ordinary income, in a manner similar to that required under Sections 1245 and 1250 which were discussed earlier, is generally the excess of the amount that would have been taken into account if the rent had been leveled over the amount actually taken into account in accordance with the rental agreement.

In some cases this section can be used to the taxpayer's advantage. This would be the case when the deduction to the tenant is accelerated at the same time that passive income to the landlord is being generated which can be used to offset any other excess passive losses the landlord may have previously generated.

Build to Suit

Another type of rental arrangement is known as "build to suit." As discussed earlier, a common component of an inducement package is an allowance of a certain amount to be used to "customize" the leased space in a manner that meets the needs of the prospective tenant. The degree of control and supervision that the landlord has over the tenant improvements is generally outlined in the agreement and can vary significantly. As previously mentioned, the goal of the tenant should be to have the landlord considered the "owner" of the improvements. If this occurs, the tenant will not be required to recognize any income as a result of receiving the cash inducement. Therefore, the rental agreement should be structured with this goal in mind. For example, the landlord's control and supervision of the assets should be significant, the risk of loss should be with the landlord, and the depreciation of the improvements should be taken by the landlord.

Joint Venture with the Developer

An offer of equity participation with the possibility of future appreciation is an alternative to an escalated rent agreement, a cash payment or other inducement, all of which provide immediate benefits. In some limited circumstances this might seem like an appealing alternative; however, the uncertainty, risk and increased complexity of such an arrangement may cause this option to be not viable. Generally, if the equity interest to be obtained is relatively small, this will likely be the case since the costs will far exceed the benefits.

It would seem that a joint venture would only be a profitable alternative in cases where the lease term exceeds fifteen years plus renewal options, the reputation of the landlord/partner is solid, the occupancy rate and the location of the leased property are favorable, and the financing is being provided by a solvent lender. Otherwise, the tenant could end up paying high rent for undesirable space and, possibly, if listed as a guarantor on any part of the debt, could end up making good on the guarantee as well.

As previously discussed, another consideration would be the effect of the passive activity rules on the losses that would likely be generated in the early years. If the tenant does not have other sources of passive income, the losses will not be utilizable until the equity interest is disposed of. On the flip side, if the leased property generates income, the tenant would be required to pick up a share of the income currently, regardless of whether or not a distribution is received.

Sale or Leaseback Transactions

The desired tax result to a seller engaging in a sale-leaseback transaction occurs in two steps. First, the seller realizes gain or loss on the sale. Following the sale, lease payments to the purchaser by the seller are fully deductible. Each step has its own significant advantages and disadvantages for the seller.

As a result of the sale itself, the seller has gained access to 100% of the cash value of any equity in the asset and without running up against any previous borrowing restrictions imposed. In addition, the seller will enjoy a greater deduction for payments made on the property. The fully allowable deduction for rent payments will presumably exceed the deduction for the interest only portion of a mortgage payment. The cost of the entire real estate parcel will also be meted out between building and land. Depreciation is allowed on the building, or improvement, segment only; therefore, the depreciation deduction allowable solely on the building portion of the real estate parcel will be exceeded by the fully deductible rental payments.

However, there are disadvantages which must be weighed against the benefit of equity cash-out and higher deductions for the same property. First, the seller must consider the fact that giving up the bundle of ownership rights to the purchaser means that the seller can no longer benefit from any future appreciation in the property. This can be avoided up-front, however, by negotiating a bargain purchase price in the lease.

Another problem to consider is that the seller will likely be locked into a long-term contract agreement. While the property may no longer satisfy any needs after some time has passed, the seller may still be locked in, either due to a liquidated damages clause in the lease, or a similar provision. A sub-lease provision would be useful in this instance.

There are significant tax advantages available to the buyer-lessor in the context of a sale-leaseback. The buyer-lessee will be entitled to the receipt of rental payments. If the buyer-lessor has a mortgage on the property, any interest payments will be deductible. Furthermore, as the owner of the real property, the buyer is entitled to a depreciation deduction and to any credits, such as the rehabilitation credit, available on the property. Absent a bargain purchase element in the lease, the buyer-lessor also participates in enjoyment of appreciation in the property.

A significant danger in the sale-leaseback arena is the potential for the Internal Revenue Service to re-characterize the agreement as something other than a sale-leaseback arrangement. In many instances, it is likely that the Service will find the sale-leaseback is nothing more than a financing arrangement, especially if the bargain purchase price is low in comparison to the expected value of the asset at the end of the lease term. The issue arises because the very nature of the deal often is indeed a financing arrangement wherein the rental payments are geared to generate an expected rate of return compensating the lessor for the use of the property (a rental element) and for the time value of money (an interest element).

As a result of the re-characterization, the purchaser-lessor would be treated as a lender receiving interest payments. The seller-lessee would be treated as the owner with corresponding interest payments to the purchaser-lessor. The significant tax advantages of this arrangement would be lost.

OTHER TAX ISSUES

Foreclosures and Workouts

The late 1980s saw an unprecedented number of foreclosure and workout situations. An important consideration in almost all of these is the tax implications to the owners of the property. Many workouts were hampered by the potential tax liability to the owners as a result of the workout. Foreclosures can also result in a tax problem for the owner of foreclosed property.

The tax problem inherent in these cases stems from the general tax principle that any transfer of property is considered a sale, and any gain on the transaction is triggered at that time. Also, cancellation of indebtedness is considered income to the debtor. In a foreclosure where the debt on the property is recourse to the debtor, the property is considered to be sold for its fair market value. The balance of any remaining debt is considered cancelled. In most nonrecourse debt situations, fair market value is not considered and the property is considered sold for the amount of the debt. In either case, if the owners have used tax losses from the property to shelter other income, these losses must be recaptured as income. Note that if the losses did not shelter other income, they should be preserved in the form of passive loss carryovers or net operating losses.

Section 108 of the Code provides important exceptions to the general cancellation of indebtedness rule when a taxpayer is insolvent (the fair market value of assets is less than liabilities immediately before the discharge) or is in bankruptcy. In these situations, cancellation of debt is excluded from income. Any amount excluded reduces the taxpayer's tax attributes such as net operating losses, capital loss carryovers, passive loss carryovers, basis in remaining assets and credits. In an insolvency case, cancellation of debt income is excluded to the extent of the insolvency. In other words, the most cancellation of debt that can be included in the insolvent taxpayer's income is net worth after the discharge.

Section 108 can provide a tremendous benefit to insolvent or bankrupt taxpayers by deferring or eliminating the tax liability that they might be unable to pay as a result of their financial conditions. It allows much more flexibility and planning opportunities in structuring workouts by taking the tax dollars out of the equation. Additionally, the Revenue Reconciliation Act of 1993 allows solvent taxpayers to elect to reduce the basis in their depreciable property rather than recognize cancellation of debt income on certain real property indebtedness.

Recent Trends Toward "Securitization"

As previously discussed, a real estate investment trust (REIT) is the most common vehicle for taking a real estate company public. It is a classification specifically created by the tax code for real estate activities. Its main advantage is that it eliminates the "double" taxation of corporations by allowing the entity a deduction for dividends paid to its shareholders. However, the qualifications and requirements to order to qualify as a REIT are complex and would only benefit very large real estate developers.

It is often difficult for real estate developers to raise large amounts of cash without mortgaging the real estate property. A REIT is able to provide liquidity to both the company as well as the owners through the sale of both debt and equity. The sale of shares in the REIT provides equity while debt is issued through the bond market. This is known as "securitization" and allows cash to be raised from investors rather than from a commercial lender. Investors are willing to invest in REITs where there are many real estate activities and the portfolio of real estate is diversified. These REITs are able to obtain a favorable bond rating similar to those of industrial bonds.

One of the main disadvantages to the owners of a real estate company who employ securitization is the fact that the debt is nonrecourse. Generally, nonrecourse debt does not create basis to the owner unless it is "qualified nonrecourse debt." Nonrecourse debt is generally considered to be qualified only if it is issued by a commercial lender or a related party under terms that would be provided to an unrelated third party and is secured by the real estate used in the activity. In most cases, securitization is not considered to be qualified. Accordingly, the owners have no basis in the debt for purposes of applying the at-risk basis rules discussed above.

A major disadvantage is that the debt holder only has recourse against the entity and does not have the benefit of obtaining the underlying assets as would a debtor who has recourse debt. In comparison, the investor is similar to holders of industrial bonds. However, this type of investment offers the advantage of liquidity in that the investment can be traded on the open market. This makes securitization more advantageous than the traditional method since many small investors can participate.

STRATEGIES FOR NEGOTIATING A SUCCESSFUL REAL ESTATE ACQUISITION

Finding a good real estate deal is as difficult as finding the proverbial needle in the haystack. If you pay attention to detail and do your homework properly, you might still have to look at a hundred deals to find the one you would like to negotiate on, and negotiate on ten deals to actually close one deal.

All this searching and examining is necessary because not every deal that comes across your desk will meet your criteria. Even if a deal does meet those criteria and you begin negotiating, there is no guarantee that you will end up with the property. The seller may be negotiating with another potential buyer and take that offer instead. Or, additional research may convince you to abandon the deal. This could happen for several reasons. You may be uncomfortable with the seller himself; this will come from a "sixth sense" you will develop about people through experience. Or, you may find a better deal, deal "B," while you are negotiating on deal "A," and you only have enough money to go into one deal.

As you acquire more experience, you will be able to react to opportunities more quickly, and seize them to make profits. You will also be able to anticipate potential roadblocks and avoid being bogged down in pursuits that will waste your time, energy, and financial resources. However, it will never be easy; if it were, everyone would be doing it. And, since it is that weeding out process that requires that you look at so many properties, it is the "hunt" that takes the greatest amount of time and work.

It is important to realize that in the real world, the functions of search, analysis, negotiation, and structuring a deal are not so neatly delineated. Nor do they proceed in a specific chronological order. Once you have done a preliminary analysis, you will probably contact the seller to feel him out, which, of course, is part of the negotiating process. You may also be investigating possible ways to structure the deal. But final negotiations and structuring of the deal will not take place until you have completed your preliminary analysis and are satisfied that you have left no stone unturned. For this reason, we have arranged this chapter in the order indicated above.

FINDING THE DEAL: WHERE TO LOOK FOR PROFITABLE INVESTMENT OPPORTUNITIES

Once you have decided on what type of property to invest in and what type of returns you are seeking, you must go out and find that "perfect" deal. The following are various sources that could aid in your search.

Real Estate Brokers

There are brokers who specialize in various types of properties. Your objective as an investor is to identify those who can find what you are looking for. You should interview several to determine their market knowledge and should discuss with them your investment criteria. Using a broker will cost you a fee, but you will usually get your money's worth. A good broker can help you find a deal that may not be on the open market.

Local and National Newspapers

Most local and national newspapers have a classified or business section that lists various properties for sale. You can either advertise for what you are looking for, or you can look in the classified section for what is currently on the market. You never know what "gems" you can find this way.

Trade Magazines

Throughout the real estate industry there are local, regional, and national trade publications on various segments of the real estate market. These carry advertisements from sellers, buyers and brokers. Depending on how active you plan to be, you will want to compile a list of these sellers or even subscribe to these publications. Among them are:

1. *National Real Estate Investor*
2. *Shopping Center World*
3. *Real Estate Forum*
4. *Commercial Property News*
5. *Commercial Real Estate South*
6. *National Mall Monitor*
7. *Multi Housing News*
8. *Professional Builder*
9. *Real Estate Today*
10. *Real Estate Times*

Local Banking Community

The local banking community is another good source of leads. Local bankers might have knowledge of who is looking to sell or who might have to sell. Frequently they have a portfolio of "real estate owned" (REO) properties that have been taken back through foreclosure. Since bankers are not in the business of owning property, they would much rather sell to a new and capable buyer. This might be a way to acquire property with much better terms than if purchased under different circumstances. Since bankers are not in the real estate business, this might be a way to find your leads without paying a real estate commission.

Local Federal Housing Administration (FHA) Office

Another source of potential deals is contacting your local FHA office. These offices could tell you when the next sales auction will take place.

Auction Companies and Foreclosure Reports

Auction companies are also a good source of leads. Either contact these companies directly or watch for announcements in the press. These companies specialize in selling unwanted property. Not all of the properties are distressed. Many times people sell through auction companies in order to facilitate a quick and clean sale.

   The investor should check for any pending foreclosures in the local paper or legal newspaper. In addition, there may be periodic foreclosure auctions in the area where properties can be bought very cheaply.

Title Companies

Many times a local title company will have knowledge of properties that are currently for sale or will be for sale in the near future.

Attorneys and Accountants

In many instances, local attorneys and accountants will have clients who are thinking about selling their property.

Estate Sales

Investors should check on estate sales. Many times property that is bought in an estate sale can be purchased at bargain prices. Many families might not realize the value of the property or might want to have a quick sale to pay the estate taxes that are due.

Business Associates and Friends

Tell your business associates and friends you are interested in investing in real estate. They might have heard of someone who knows someone who wants to sell.

Property Management Companies

Since management is their game, property management companies might have some good leads on who is looking to sell their property. They are hoping that if you purchase this property, they would have a shot at the management or at least they could pick up a fee for the referral.

Drive an Area

Another method for finding deals is to just drive through an area and decide what you would like to buy. Once you have compiled this list, go to the local tax department and research the records for the ownership of these properties. Then contact the owners to see if they are interested in selling their property. It is important to stay in contact with these property owners. They might not be interested in selling today, but if they put you on the list of potential buyers, they might call back in the future with a desire to sell. People have many reasons to sell. They may have been transferred, lost their jobs, divorced, had a death in the family, undergone a change in financial status or simply decided it's time to sell.

Letters to Property Owners and Real Estate Brokers

An investor should develop a form letter that lists investment criteria and send these letters out on a regular basis to local property owners and to the real estate brokerage community.

Even after you have established a solid network of sources, there is no guarantee that deals will come quickly and easily. Do not get frustrated. The main idea is to expose yourself to as many potential deals as possible. You may have to look at 100 deals to get five worth negotiating on. Even then you may only be able to acquire one property. You must then use the "Babe Ruth Theory" which says that even though Babe Ruth hit the most home runs, he struck out the most times. But remember he hit those home runs because he was persistent and he took the most swings.

ANALYZING THE DEAL:
KEY FACTORS FOR DETERMINING PROFIT

There are many factors involved in analyzing a potential deal. These factors are critical, because in order to make a future profit the investor must "buy the property right." An investor who overpays for the property up front will reduce any future chances of seeing a profit. The ideal time to make a "future" profit is when the property is initially purchased. This can only be achieved if all of the pertinent information concerning the subject property and competitive properties has been thoroughly gathered and analyzed. This process involves extensive research into all areas of the property, including its construction, marketing, and financial aspects. Only after this research and analysis will the investor be able to determine what is considered to be the true value of the property.

In analyzing the deal, the investor should contact any and all knowledgeable individuals who might be able to share some insight. Some of these individuals will be extremely helpful to the investor at no charge; others will not share any information at all, and others may charge for their information. Consider the following people as good sources:

- Real estate agents
- Appraisers
- County officials
- Bankers
- Mortgage brokers
- General contractors
- Architects/engineers
- Property owners

How to Calculate a Preliminary Financial Analysis

With either a broad range of experience or just starting out, the investor should rely on several financial benchmarks to decide about whether to proceed with a potential deal.

Some basic yardsticks for calculating value are: price per square foot, price per unit, gross rent multiplier, and capitalization rate. Each type of property has a range of values that other investors are paying currently in the marketplace.

It is important to check with market sources such as brokers, appraisers, and other buyers to establish the range for the type of property you are looking at in that particular location. It should be remembered that these yardsticks, used individually, can be inaccurate. They are a good method of quickly screening properties, but they should be thoroughly reviewed and compared on an "apples to apples" basis. If the asking price of the property does not fit within that range, you can save yourself a lot of wasted time; don't pursue the deal unless there are other factors that justify "overpaying" for a property. These could include certain seller guarantees, additional land, or a property that is underrented but can be improved in a short period of time.

The chart below illustrates the following analysis of these yardsticks.

	PROPERTY A	PROPERTY B
Number of Units	100	100
One Bedroom Units	100	-0-
Square Footage/Unit	600	-0-
Two Bedroom Units	-0-	100
Square Footage/Unit	-0-	700
Total Square Footage	60,000	70,000
Sales Price	$3,000,000	$3,000,000
Capital Expenditures	-0-	$100,000
Average Rental Rate-1 BR	$400	-0-
Average Rental Rate-2 BR	-0-	$450
Gross Potential Income	$480,000	$540,000
Vacancy Factor	5%	5%
Expense Factor (% EGI)	42%	40%
Net Operating Income	$264,480	$307,800

PRICE PER SQUARE FOOT

The price per square foot method of assessing value is calculated by dividing the sales price by the total square footage. This method can, however, be distorted due to the fact that different investors measure square footage differently. Some investors use gross square footage measurements while others use net measurements. In computing gross square footage, measurements are taken from the outside wall measurements, while the net square footage is the interior heated space. Some residential properties have basement space which can, if computed in this total measurement, greatly reduce the price per square foot calculation.

Let's look at two "identical" duplexes. The seller of Duplex A is claiming that the units have 1,000 square feet of heated space per unit, while the seller of Duplex B is claiming those units have 1,100 square feet per unit. Assuming a $100,000 asking price for Duplex A and $105,000 for Duplex B, it appears that Duplex A is selling for $50.00 a square foot, while Duplex B is selling for $47.73 a square foot. The inexperienced investor would say Duplex B has a better price. After careful scrutiny, however, the investor would find out that Duplex B actually had 980 square feet per unit. Thus, it is selling for $53.57 per square foot on an "apples to apples" basis. Assuming that all other factors were equal, Duplex A would be a better buy.

FIRST ANALYSIS

	DUPLEX A	DUPLEX B
Square footage/unit	1,000	1,100
Total duplex square footage	2,000	2,200
Asking price	$100,000	$105,000
Price/square foot	$50.00	$47.73

SECOND ANALYSIS

	DUPLEX A	DUPLEX B
Square footage/unit	1,000	980
Total duplex square footage	2,000	1,960
Asking price	$100,000	$105,000
Price/square foot	$50.00	$53.57

Be aware that analyzing the price per square foot for two similar properties will not always give you the complete picture you need to choose one over the other. Some residential properties will have different mixes of unit size, and this will also throw off the price per square foot comparison.

Another factor that could distort the price per unit is any initial capital expenditure added to the property just after the closing. Examples of capital expenditures added at closing could be a tennis court or a new roof. This dollar amount should be added to the sales price to determine the adjusted sales price.

For example, an investor may be looking at two adjacent apartment projects, both having 100 units. Property A has all one-bedroom units at 600 square feet each, or a total of 60,000 square feet. Property B has all one-bedroom units of 700 square feet each, or 70,000 square feet. Both properties are priced at $3,000,000. So, while both 100 unit properties have an asking price of $3 million, Property B looks like the better buy, with a lower cost per square foot.

	PROPERTY A	PROPERTY B
Number of units	100	100
One bedroom units	100	-0-
Square footage/unit	600	-0-
Two bedroom units	-0-	100
Square footage/unit	-0-	700
Total square footage	60,000	70,000
Sales price	$3,000,000	$3,000,000
Capital expenditures	-0-	$100,000
Price/square foot	$50.00	$42.86
Adjusted price/square foot	$50.00	$44.29

But the equation is still incomplete, because investors must look at more than just this one benchmark. They must also look at the price per unit costs and the rent and expense levels of these two projects to get a true picture of their relative merits and values.

If investors are going to compare any investment to others using this method, they should take great care in getting the facts and trying to compare properties on an "apples to apples" basis.

PRICE PER UNIT

The price per unit method is calculated by dividing the sales price by the total number of units. This benchmark, like price per square foot, needs to be carefully examined because calculation results can be distorted.

For example, two residential properties can have the same number of units but one property can have all one-bedrooms while the other property will have all two-bedrooms. In the example used, both properties are priced at $30,000 per unit.

Once again, the price per unit can be distorted if any capital expenditures are added to the property at closing.

	PROPERTY A	PROPERTY B
Number of units	100	100
One bedroom units	100	-0-
Square footage/unit	600	-0-
Two bedroom units	-0-	100
Square footage/unit	-0-	700
Total square footage	60,000	70,000
Sales price	$3,000,000	$3,000,000
Capital expenditures	-0-	$100,000
Price/unit	$30,000	$30,000
Adjusted price/unit	$30,000	$31,000

It would appear that the buyer would get more bedrooms for the investment dollar in purchasing the property with all two bedrooms. To make that determination, the investor should now analyze the property cash flow.

GROSS RENT MULTIPLIER (GRM)

The gross rent multiplier (GRM) is calculated by dividing the purchase price by the gross rents. This ratio is somewhat deceptive, though, because some sellers base their rents on street rents (the rents they are currently asking on vacant units) when in reality, they should be based on actual collections plus a fair market rent for the vacancies. Additionally, some properties include all utilities and this will throw off this ratio unless an adjustment is made.

In the example, Property A has a GRM of 6.25, while Property B has a GRM of 5.56.

	PROPERTY A	PROPERTY B
Number of units	100	100
One bedroom units	100	-0-
Square footage/unit	600	-0-
Two bedroom units	-0-	100
Square footage/unit	-0-	700

	PROPERTY A	PROPERTY B
Total square footage	60,000	70,000
Sales price	$3,000,000	$3,000,000
Capital expenditures	-0-	$100,000
Average rental rate- 1 BR	$400	-0-
Average rental rate- 2 BR	-0-	$450
Gross potential income	$480,000	$540,000
Gross rent multiplier (GRM)	6.25	5.56

The investor should note that the gross rent multiplier could be distorted by the fact that the property being analyzed includes all utility payments or can include some units that are furnished as well as any capital expenditures. This extra revenue will cause the GRM to be lower than it would have been had that property been analyzed without this extra revenue.

To make an "apples to apples" comparison between both properties, the investor should deduct from the gross rent an amount equal to the extra utility cost paid by the owner or the furniture revenue generated by a furnished unit. This new "net" figure should then be used as an adjusted gross rent number to obtain the GRM.

	PROPERTY A	PROPERTY B
Number of units	100	100
One-bedroom units	100	-0-
Square footage/unit	600	-0-
Two-bedroom units	-0-	100
Square footage/unit	-0-	700
Total square footage	60,000	70,000
Sales price	$3,000,000	$3,000,000
Capital expenditures	-0-	$100,000
Average rental rate- 1 BR*	$400	-0-
Average rental rate- 2 BR	-0-	$450
Gross potential income	$480,000	$540,000
Gross rent multiplier	6.25	5.56
Gross potential income	$480,000	$540,000
Less: utility cost	($22,800)	-0-
Adjusted gross income	$457,200	$540,000
Adjusted sales price	$3,000,000	$3,100,000
Gross rent multiplier	6.56	5.74

*This unit includes $20/month for utilities.

CAPITALIZATION RATE

The capitalization rate is a ratio that is calculated by dividing the net operating income (the cash flow available after expenses are deducted from the revenue) by the value of the property. Using this ratio, the investor must be careful and totally scrutinize the rent collections and the expenses.

	PROPERTY A	PROPERTY B
Number of units	100	100
One-bedroom units	100	-0-
Square footage/unit	600	-0-
Two-bedroom units	-0-	100
Square footage/unit	-0-	700
Total square footage	60,000	70,000
Sales price	$3,000,000	$3,000,000
Capital expenditures	-0-	$100,000
Average rental rate- 1 BR	$400	-0-
Average rental rate- 2 BR	-0-	$450
Gross potential income	$480,000	$540,000
Vacancy factor	5%	5%
Expense factor (%EGI)	42%	40%
Net operating income	$264,480	$307,800
Capitalization rate	8.88	10.26

What the current owner or broker is representing as actual income and expenses may be inaccurate. The investor should investigate all revenue and expense figures. Many times the revenue includes money that is projected and is not currently being collected. The expenses might not reflect costs that should be included or may include capital expenditures. The following examples show that Property A's Expense Factor went from the original 42 percent of the effective gross income to 44 percent due to the management fee being increased from 3 percent to 5 percent. If capital expenditures are needed for the property they should be added to the sales price. The following example shows what happens when the analysis is completed.

	PROPERTY A	PROPERTY B
Number of units	100	100
One-bedroom units	100	-0-
Square footage/unit	600	-0-
Two-bedroom units	-0-	100
Square footage/unit	-0-	700
Total square footage	60,000	70,000
Sales price	$3,000,000	$3,000,000
Capital expenditures	-0-	$100,000
Average rental rate- 1 BR	$400	-0-
Average rental rate- 2 BR	-0-	$450
Gross potential income	$480,000	$540,000
Vacancy factor	5%	5%
Expense factor (%EGI)	44%	40%
Net operating income	$255,360	$307,800
Capitalization rate	8.51	10.26
Adjusted capitalization rate	8.51	9.99

In summary, the investor should not look at any of these yardsticks in a vacuum, but should analyze them, and in terms of each other, to obtain the clearest possible picture of the value of the property being considered. If the property falls into the acceptable range, as found in the market for that property type, the investor should proceed with further physical analysis of the property.

How to Figure Your Break-even Occupancy Rate

The investor should also consider at what occupancy rate the property will break even. This is done by adding all of the operating expenses plus the current debt service and dividing this figure by the gross potential income. Since the expenses will not vary in this analysis, the only factor that will cause the occupancy rate to fluctuate up or down will be the current debt service payment. The debt service payment, assuming that the interest rates are constant, will only vary depending on the amount of the mortgage that is being paid off. Following are three examples of how this break-even rate can fluctuate. Although operating expenses are made up of fixed expenses and variable expenses, these examples do not take into consideration that certain variable expenses are reduced when occupancy is reduced. If this were taken into consideration, it would somewhat reduce the break-even occupancy rate in these three examples.

As can be seen by this analysis, the greater the leverage (the use of borrowed funds) the higher the break-even occupancy. This will also increase the future percentage of return. Table 3.1 also illustrates that if the market shifts downward, the property is more likely headed toward the area of negative cash flow.

TABLE 3.1
Break-even Occupancy

Assumptions:

Property value	$3,000,000
Gross revenue	$480,000
Operating expenses	$191,520

Abbreviations:

Positive cash flow	PCF	Operating expenses	OE
Negative cash flow	NCF	Breakeven point	BP
Gross revenues	GR		

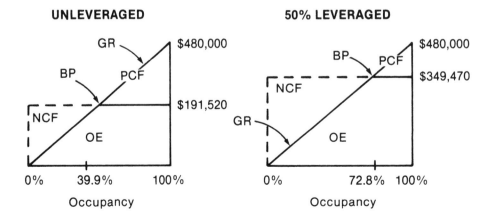

Assumptions:		Assumptions:	
Loan to value ratio	-0-	Loan to value ratio	50%
Loan amount	-0-	Loan amount	$1,500,000
Loan constant	-0-	Loan constant	10.53
Loan payment	-0-	Loan payment	$157,950
Break-even occupancy	39.9%	Break-even occupancy	72.8%

75% LEVERAGED

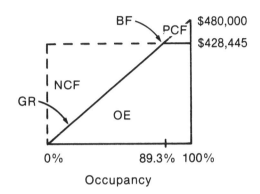

Occupancy

Assumptions:	
Loan to value ratio	75%
Loan amount	$2,250,000
Loan constant	10.53
Loan payment	$236,925
Break-even occupancy	89.3%

Deal Terms and Conditions: Why a Buyer May Want to Pay More for a Property

How the deal is financially structured is critical to the value the investor places on the real estate. Investors who pay all cash will seek those deals in which the price is significantly lower than those deals in which leverage (the use of borrowed funds) is used. Just like the old science equation of the man using the fulcrum to lift a heavy object, borrowed funds give the investor the needed leverage to lift or acquire larger properties than might be possible if the investor was paying all cash. For example, an investor who has $100,000 to invest can either purchase a $100,000 piece of property on an all cash basis, or can borrow additional funds using that $100,000 as the down-payment. If the investor can secure an 80% loan to value, the $100,000 down-payment will enable the investor to purchase a $500,000 property through the use of leverage. The cash flow from the property will be used to pay the debt service (monthly payments to pay the principal and interest due on the mortgage) on the borrowed funds.

Other factors in determining the value of real estate are the terms and conditions that are available. A property might be worth more or less depending on the terms and conditions of the deal. The following are reasons why an investor might pay more for a property. In some cases, the purchaser can negotiate one or more of these terms and conditions without paying a premium price. This is generally a function of the negotiating ability of the purchaser and the motivation of the seller.

1. *Low down-payment.* By leveraging the property the purchaser is able to get more property with less cash out of pocket.

2. *Split funding.* Paying the down payment in more than one installment enables the investor to buy a property that has a down payment that is greater than the cash available at that time, and might enable payment for it out of cash flow. Using the above example of an investor purchasing a $500,000 property, the investor might be able to pay the $100,000 down-payment over a twenty-four month period, paying $25,000 every six months.

    a. *Split funding of the down-payment with no interest on the outstanding balance, or interest at a below-market rate.* The seller who is reluctant to wait for the twenty-four month period might charge the purchaser interest on the outstanding balance, in exchange for stretching out the down-payment period.

3. *Long-term seller financing.* If the seller provides mortgage financing at below-market interest rates, this might enable the buyer to purchase a property that might otherwise be unfinanceable by conventional lending sources. Using the above example, let's say the investor was able to pay the $100,000 down-payment to the seller, but due to currently available high interest rates the purchaser might only be able to obtain a $300,000 mortgage. At this point the buyer can negotiate a $100,000 second mortgage on the property from the seller. In some cases, the seller might even take back the entire $400,000 mortgage personally at possibly a lower interest rate than can be obtained by local banks.

4. *Seller taking part of the down-payment as a deductible fee to the purchaser.* A down-payment, in and of itself, is not tax deductible. If, however, part of that down-payment were paid as a legitimate fee for services rendered by the seller, that portion of the down-payment could be deducted currently, or over the period of the services rendered. In the above example, maybe the buyer was able to negotiate a $20,000 fee to be paid to the seller at closing for a management consulting fee. The purchaser is therefore now paying $480,000 to the seller, which includes $80,000 as down-payment, plus a deductible $20,000 management consulting fee.

5. *Seller taking part of the purchase price or down-payment in trade.* In our example, maybe the purchaser can trade out $30,000 of the down-payment for rendering some services to the seller. In this case the seller must check the tax ramifications of this type of transaction with an accountant.

6. *Seller guaranteeing a certain occupancy or rental income level.* In our example, to reduce some of the financial risk, the purchaser might be able to negotiate for the seller to "guarantee" a certain occupancy or rental income level. For example, the seller might guarantee that for a period of one year after closing, if the occupancy drops below 95 percent or if the rent level drops below specified dollars, the seller will make up the difference to the purchaser. The purchaser, guaranteed some financial stability for this time period that would relieve the risk, might be willing to pay a somewhat higher price for the property.

7. *Seller guaranteeing a master lease on the property for a specified time period.* Seller will guarantee rent on the entire property. This example takes paragraph 6 above to a higher degree of sophistication. In this example, the seller, in order to obtain a

higher-than-market price for the property, will give the purchaser a "master lease" (a lease for the entire property for a specified time period) for a negotiated term with periodic rent increases. Once again, by using this method, the purchaser is reducing the financial risk and thus might be willing to pay the seller a premium price.

8. *Seller offering a guaranteed buyback (purchaser has the right to make the seller buy back the property if certain conditions are not met) in a specified time period.* In the example above, the purchaser might be able to negotiate a guaranteed buyback of the property at a predetermined price at some time in the future. This buyback price can ensure the purchaser of at least a break-even or a guaranteed profit, thus once again reducing the financial risk.

9. *Seller guaranteeing a specified cash return during a specified time period.* Using our example, the purchaser might be able to negotiate a 10 percent return on equity for a specific time period.

10. *Seller guaranteeing a "no negative cash flow" on the property for a specified time period.* Using our example, the purchaser might be able to negotiate that if the property has a negative cash flow during a predetermined time period, the seller will make up this difference to the purchaser.

11. *Seller guaranteeing a construction cost guarantee (the seller is taking the risks of the construction costs) on a to-be-built property.* The purchaser of a to-be-built property might be able to negotiate so that the seller would guarantee the construction costs would not exceed a certain dollar amount.

All of these terms and conditions should be carefully evaluated. By splitting the down-payment over installments or having the seller take back a mortgage at below-market interest rates, the real price of the property is discounted. For example, a purchaser who pays the seller $100,000 over a twenty-four month period, with no interest on the remaining balance, is not *really* paying $100,000. Due to the time value of money, that $100,000 might only "cost" the investor $90,000, because the investor would have deposited the remaining balance in the bank where interest would have accrued.

Other terms and conditions may have more intangible benefits, such as the guarantees. These guarantees are hard to put an exact dollar value on. When researching prices paid for comparable properties in the market area, the investor should try to verify whether these properties were sold with any of the above conditions.

Tips on Investigating the Property's Location

Location, location, and location are three important criteria for analyzing property. The investor should physically investigate the property's location, study the area's past history, and research what is going to happen to the area in the future. If the area has been run down, is it on an upturn? Are future road changes going to affect the visibility of or access to the property? The investor should check with various sources when analyzing a location. He should discuss the property's location with local county officials, bankers, real estate agents, business owners, appraisers, and other knowledgeable individuals who might have an opinion on the property's location. Check with the local zoning department to see if there are any impending zoning changes that would enhance or hurt your potential acquisition. The investor should also check the distances to other comparable properties. If you have an excellent location, time has proven you are going to get capital appreciation.

If you have a poor location, you might have to wait a long time for the market to come to you. There are also some locations that may never get better, and which you will simply want to avoid.

Also, check out the traffic counts adjacent to your property. Traffic counts, which tell how many vehicles pass the property on an average day, can be obtained from either the local county traffic department or the state Department of Transportation (DOT). If the counts are low, you may have a difficult time bringing new business to your property. A high traffic count can increase the value.

How to Conduct a Successful Market Study

Market conditions are crucial to analyzing any deal. Once you have decided on the type of property that you want to purchase, you should carefully check out the market conditions and demand for that type of property. See if you can obtain any market studies from local real estate brokers, property owners, county officials, or local appraisers. If these studies are not readily available, you might have to do your own market study (see Chapter 5) which should include the following:

- A verification of the rent or sales levels for the competition by unit type
- The lease and term option periods available
- Who pays utilities
- Age of the property
- Square footage of unit types
- Type of construction
- Condition of the comparable properties
- Occupancy history for the subject property as well as for the competition
- The features and amenities offered by the competition
- The customary security deposits received by the competition
- The leasing commissions paid to outside agents by the competition
- The target market for current tenants

Check out the pending building permits and potential new construction projects for the area that your property is located in. To find this information, contact the local building and zoning department. Just because your property is located in a 95-percent occupied market does not mean that you are on easy street. The fact that this market is tight could cause a lot of new construction that will not only drive the occupancy levels down but will cause rent concessions and lower rental rates.

If you decide to invest in an oversupplied market, you should plan on having a large contingency of working capital to help you ride out an overbuilt market. If your buying criteria are for a short-term holding period, you may not want to invest in this type of market.

Timing: Four Cycles That Affect When You Should Buy Property

Timing is extremely critical in buying property. The general rule, "buy low, sell high" applies to real estate as it does to any type of investment. Once again, the best time to make your future profit is when the property is bought.

The following four cycles of timing are predicated on a market with "classic" conditions and economic ebb and flow. They assume that the economic base of the area is sufficiently stable to enable it to recover from hard times, and that there is a continual need for additional residential and commercial properties. These cycles will vary in duration and severity depending on many outside and intangible forces. Many markets may have submarkets that behave differently during the same period; the northside of the city could be booming at the same time the southside is in the doldrums. Nevertheless, the ability to recognize these cycles can give the investor the added edge in making informed investment decisions.

Down Cycle

Your ability to "buy low" in real estate necessitates being able to identify its four major cycles. In a "down" cycle, the market conditions include high vacancies, rent concessions (reduced rental rates or free rent), and little new construction. An investor who buys during this period should be prepared to wait out the cycle before selling at a profit. While purchasing during this period will enable an investor to buy at bargain prices, such an investor should be prepared with extra cash to hold the property until the market is back on an "up" cycle. The negative factors that have caused this down cycle, and that have enabled the purchaser to buy the property at a bargain price, will also likely cause the property to suffer in cash flow, because it is harder to rent property during a down cycle. The astute investor will have cash reserves available to sustain this period of reduced or negative cash flow.

TABLE 3.2
Market Cycles

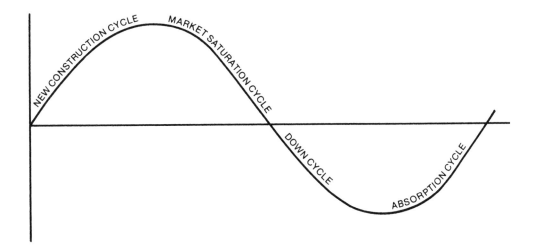

Absorption Cycle

Due to the lack of new construction resulting from the down cycle, the market forces of supply and demand start to take effect. What the market will now go through is the absorption of the overbuilt inventory of space. As the excess inventory is absorbed, the rental rates will start to climb back up and rental concessions will decrease. At this time, new construction activity will start to take place due to the increase of new demand and a shortage of supply.

New Construction Cycle

The cycle that follows will see new demand in the market, with the supply of available space decreasing. At this time, developers will be tripping over themselves to build product to satisfy this demand. Rent levels will increase, as will prices that investors are willing to pay for property. This is because during a recovery cycle, the rate of inflation usually increases, and with that increase come higher construction costs. In order for developers to realize their desired profit margins, they must pass along these increased costs in the form of higher rents or sales prices. The greater demand for property during this cycle enables the developers to obtain these higher prices.

Market Saturation Cycle

The fourth cycle appears after the market has peaked and starts to slide downward. Occupancy levels will start to decrease, rent concessions will begin to reappear, and construction activity will grind to a halt. At this point, the market has gone full cycle.

The best time to buy property is either during a "down" cycle or when the cycle is on the way up, not when it has peaked or is on its way down.

What to Look for When Reviewing Tenant Leases

Since investment properties are based on a current and projected income stream, the investor should carefully evaluate all the tenant leases. The following information should be reviewed and verified to determine the likelihood of the property performing as projected.

Tenant History

The type of tenants is extremely important to a successful purchaser. The rent roll, copy of each lease, and the rental application should be carefully checked out. Verify the payment history and the credit of each lessee. A property is more valuable with reliable tenants. A tenant who does not pay on time will cause nothing but headaches.

Lease Terms

Carefully analyze the lease terms and conditions. Check that the tenant is currently paying what the lease says. A cautious investor will also personally visit each tenant to verify the shape of the leased space. Confirm the expiration date of each lease. A shrewd investor does not want all the leases expiring at the same time, because the property would then be vulnerable to a dramatic increase in vacancies. Clearly, it is easier to find one new tenant every three years than to have to search for four or five all at once. Upon inspecting the lease, the investor may discover that certain tenants are paying below market rental. With good property management, you might be able to create a new cash flow opportunity by increasing the rent on such tenants.

LEASE OPTIONS

Check for all options in all leases. Options are typically one-sided, either for the tenant or the landlord. You might find out by reading the leases that the tenant has an option for a five-year period at no rent increase. This means that your property will not increase in value because the net operating income will stay level over that period of time, or it may increase in value due to increased expenses.

RENT ESCALATIONS

Check for how the operating expense increases are covered in the leases when the lease term is longer than one year. Since commercial leases are for a three to ten year period, you want to make sure that the tenant will pay for the increases in the operating expenses. The following are methods used for rent increases:

1. *Consumer Price Index (CPI) Increase.* This method will increase the yearly rental rate in proportion to this cost of living index. Many tenants will want a cap on this increase. If there is one, there should also be a floor. For example, a lease might be based on the CPI with a floor of 5 percent and a cap of 9 percent.

2. *Flat Rate Increase.* This type of lease escalation will increase the yearly rental rate by a predetermined dollar amount. For example, a lease might have a set 5 percent per year increase over the base rate.

3. *Operating Cost Passthrough.* This method will pass on the cost of any increases in operating expenses over a specified amount. For example, the lease might say that all costs over a $3.00 per square foot base rate will be passed on to the tenant.

4. *Percentage Leases.* Many retail leases base their increases in the yearly rental on a percentage of gross income of the tenant over a specified dollar amount. This method enables the landlord to share in the success of the tenants. The actual collections of these tenants should be carefully screened, because an understatement of these revenues can cost the investor lost revenue. For example, a clothing shop might have a $12.00 per square foot rental rate plus 5 percent of revenue over $100,000 per year in gross revenue.

SQUARE FOOTAGE

The investor should verify the square footage used by the existing tenants. It might be discovered that a tenant with a lease for 3000 square feet actually has 3500 square feet.

COMMON AREA MAINTENANCE CHARGES

Most retail leases have a common area maintenance fee that is charged to each tenant. This charge is based on a set rate per square foot. Common area maintenance charges may include the following:

- Janitorial
- Common area utility costs
- Landscaping
- Security
- Common area maintenance costs

The investor should make sure that each tenant is paying a fair share of these costs.

SECURITY DEPOSITS

All security deposit accounts should be verified. Sellers often commingle these funds when they should be separated. Make sure that the seller has funded this account at closing. The security deposits should be used to fund deficiencies in the rental payments and for tenant damage at the end of the lease.

TENANT MIX

Check out the tenant mix. In a retail property, this mix is extremely important. You do not want competing businesses adjacent to each other. A good retail property has a good blend of businesses that complement each other.

How to Tell if Property Is Being Mismanaged

Carefully review the current management of the property. The sellers may be mismanaging it, which can create some interesting opportunities. While it is difficult to control market conditions, two "identical" properties can perform differently at the same time depending on how they are managed. Good management can help increase occupancy and decrease operating expenses, thereby yielding greater cash flow and ultimately greater profits. The following areas should be reviewed and analyzed.

MANAGEMENT CONTROLS

By setting up an organized system of management controls a property can be greatly enhanced. These controls include tenant relations and accounting controls. Since the tenant is the customer and since the "customer is king" you want to create an environment in which the tenant can prosper. A happy tenant will not only renew a lease but will pay a higher rental rate.

REVIEW MAINTENANCE POLICY

Review the maintenance history. Slow reaction time to complaints can mean unhappy tenants. In addition, if a deferred maintenance program (a scheduled program of inspection and repairs) is not currently in place, one should be instituted. This will improve the appearance of the property and enable the investor to increase rents and keep a happier tenancy. Remember, it is easier and less expensive to regularly maintain an item than it is to replace it prematurely.

REVIEW OFFICE PROCEDURES

Check out the current management's paperwork and office procedures. An unkempt office can hurt the value of a property. Tenants want and respect a clean and organized work area.

RENTAL COLLECTIONS

In reviewing the past and current rental collection policies and procedures, the investor might find out that the current management has been lax in collections. This is an area where, with good management controls, the new investor can increase the income base.

ACCOUNTS PAYABLE POLICY

The investor should review how the current management pays bills. Many suppliers and subcontractors will discount their bills if they are paid early or on time or they will add penalties if the bills are paid late. With proper accounting controls, the new investor could save money in this area and thus increase cash flow.

Leasing: Four Questions to Ask

The investor should take a good look at how the leasing of the property is being handled. Depending on the type of property being analyzed, a management company or a separate leasing company may handle the leasing of the vacant space. In residential properties, the management company will handle both functions, while in some types of commercial properties a separate company may handle the leasing of the space. The investor should seek answers to the following four questions:

1. Are the leasing agents knowledgeable about the property and the area?
2. Do they know their competition?
3. Are they aggressively seeking new leases at higher rental rates?
4. Are they being unrealistic about the rental rates?

Construction Quality: A Thirteen-Point Checklist for Determining Structural Soundness

A construction professional should be consulted to determine the quality of construction. Contact a local building, architectural, or engineering association. The property should be checked completely, both inside and out. The last thing an investor wants to happen after purchasing property is to find out that it has structural problems that need repair. This could eat up the working capital account. A good engineer can tell the investor how much money is needed to be put into the property immediately as well as how much will be needed over time. Remember, it's better to know up front what needs to be corrected than after the fact.

A structural inspection should include answers to the following:

1. Is there any lean to the building due to settlement?
2. Are there any drainage problems?
3. Is the building adequately soundproofed?
4. Are there any roof or window leaks?
5. Are the plumbing, electrical and mechanical systems all working?
6. Is the pavement or sidewalk in need of repair?
7. Does the building need gutters?
8. Does the building have termites?
9. Are the underground pipes in need of repair?

10. Does the property need to be repainted?

11. Is the landscaping in good condition?

12. Is there any asbestos that needs to be removed?

13. Has the property been checked for radon?

UTILITY SYSTEM: MASTER VERSUS INDIVIDUAL METERS

Check out the utility system. If the market for the property calls for individual meters with the tenant paying for these utilities and the subject property has a master meter with the owner paying for utilities, the investor might have an opportunity to restructure the system from a master to an individual metering system. To make this decision, the investor would need to do a study to analyze the cost to restructure the metering system versus what the payback period would be to recover these costs. If the decision is made to change the utility system, the investor should hire a qualified electrician.

The investor might also discover that the subject property has an outdated and inefficient system which might need a large sum of money to update. Then another study is required to review the cost payback period of this expenditure. It could be determined that the purchase price of the property plus the costs to upgrade the utility system might make the economics of the deal unfeasible.

Due Diligence: Twenty-two Key Areas to Review

PROPERTY MEASUREMENT

An investor should have an updated survey to determine the exact boundaries of the land area as well as the measurements of the gross and net rentable building areas. If these measurements are under the pro-forma square footage, the value of the income stream will be reduced and thus the value of the property will be reduced. For example, if the investor thinks of buying a property with 100,000 square feet, and is paying $60 per square foot (or $6 million) and then finds out through the inspection of the property that it is only 95,000 square feet, the payment then is $63.15 per square foot. This means that the investor is paying more per square foot for less square footage. Furthermore, if a property has additional land to build on, a smaller land parcel could reduce the amount of future space that could be built.

UNIT MIX

An investor who is looking to acquire a residential property should carefully analyze the unit mix. It might turn out that the apartment project has a large number of three-bedroom apartments when the market is catering to singles, who prefer efficiencies or one-bedroom units. The investor should analyze the unit mix by use of a Market Study (Chapter 5) to determine which units are in demand.

UNIT SIZE

The size of each unit in a residential property is very important. If the market is demanding 1,000 square foot, two-bedroom apartments, you do not want to have units with only 700 square feet. An investor who is purchasing an office building should be very careful that the spaces available to lease are marketable. If purchasing a retail center, the size of the retail bays (the space that is occupied by the retailer) should be considered. If the bays are too deep, retailers will not pay for this extra space. The floor size in an office building should be designed for flexibility. If large tenants need 20,000 square feet per floor and your building has 8,000 square feet per floor, you will not be able to attract those tenants.

PROPERTY REPUTATION

The investor should contact any and all knowledgeable people in the market area to determine the current and past reputation of the property. It may have a reputation that may be extremely difficult to overcome. Or, on the other hand, it could be a real opportunity. This is where a creative mind can build up a misused or mismanaged asset.

CURB APPEAL

First impressions are what sells. The investor should carefully review the curb appeal of the property. Does the property look first class, or does it look run down? Even though a property looks bad today does not mean that with some spit and polish it cannot look better tomorrow. The following items should be reviewed:

- Property entrance signage
- Property entrance landscaping
- Building exteriors
- Condition of paved surfaces
- Neatness of common areas

POLITICAL CLIMATE WITHIN THE MARKET AREA

The investor should become familiar with the local government's attitudes toward development. Some sources of information are:

- Local developers
- Local newspapers
- Local property owners

Many areas are pro-growth; others are anti-business. However, a pro-growth climate can be a double-edged sword; it could create more competition for your property.

COMMUNITY SERVICE ACCESS

In evaluating real estate, the community services available to the property should be identified. In purchasing a residential property, the investor must know that the property has access to a good school system as well as a public transportation system. Many times the availability of these services, such as the closeness to the property and the adequacy of police and fire protection, will help reduce insurance rates.

NEW COMPETITION

In analyzing the market, the investor should not only research the existing competition, but should also be aware of any new competing properties that are going to be built. To obtain this information the investor should contact the following:

- Local building and zoning departments

- Local apartment or building associations

Many times a new competitor will offer a new product at a lower rate than the current market in order to fill the property as quickly as possible. Some times, in an over-built market a competitor will go bankrupt just after finishing the property, and the bank will then lower the rental rate to fill it up. Or the bank might sell the property to a new investor, who will get attractive financing terms from the lender and thus be able to lower the rates. If a new property is able to be rented at the same price as an older property, tenants will usually leave the old for the new.

AVAILABLE LAND FOR FUTURE DEVELOPMENT

The investor should research the market for any undeveloped land in the market area that is currently zoned or can be rezoned for the same use as the subject property. Often an investor has had the market alone, only to find a new neighbor down the street competing for tenants.

In compiling this research, the investor should contact the following:

- *Local zoning departments.*

  The investor can obtain current and proposed land use maps.

- *Local utility departments.*

  Determine the availability of utilities. Even though a parcel of vacant land is zoned the same as the subject property, it might not have access to these utilities and thus not be competition.

The investor should also know the prices of available zoned land and what the density (the number of square footage or units per acre that can be built) requirements are. It could be that the density requirements have been lowered or raised. If they are raised a competitor could pay more for a parcel of land, put more square footage on the property, and thus potentially threaten the investor's property. On the other hand, the zoning density could have been lowered and thus be uneconomical for a competitor to build.

INTERIOR AND EXTERIOR DESIGN

Design is critical to the success of real estate. In reviewing the design for the subject property, the investor should contact potential or existing tenants, local architects and leasing agents. The exterior must be pleasing to the eye, since it is the first thing a prospective tenant sees, and it should make a statement. The interior floor space, be it an apartment layout or the floor layout of an office building, should be functional and efficient. The design of a residential unit should be geared towards livability. Yesterday's design might be totally out of date for today's consumer.

Check out the unit features and the amenity package (convenient services or recreational facilities available to tenants). Remember, consumer trends are always subject to change. The investor must determine whether the property has the features and amenities that are currently needed to market the property or whether extra dollars will have to be spent to add these items.

On-site Parking Availability

The availability of on-site parking is critical to the success of a property. The parking requirement is typically based on a zoning requirement of X number of spaces per 1,000 square feet of usable space or X number of spaces per living unit. In many cases, even with these requirements there is a shortage of parking spaces. This could cause a loss of potential tenants as well as existing tenants. The parking needs of both current and potential tenants should be thoroughly analyzed. It might be found that the property is in need of additional parking. The investor might then have to acquire an adjacent parcel of land to build a parking deck to meet this need. These costs will then have to be added into the acquisition costs.

Ceiling Height

The ceiling height is important to properties in which tenants must store their products. The needs of your target market should be carefully analyzed. A property that has a ceiling height of twelve feet in a market that demands sixteen to eighteen feet will have a difficult time attracting tenants.

Floor Loads

Many tenants have needs for either heavy equipment or computers. These tenants will need to be located in properties that can accommodate not only their space needs but their equipment needs. If the property is marketed toward users of heavy equipment, the floors should be capable of handling these needs.

Sprinkler System

Many businesses have products that are highly flammable. These potential tenants will be required by their insurance agents to be located in properties that either have sprinkler systems or have fire walls between certain areas. Even though the property might not need this fire protection today, a new tenant or a future fire code change could cause the building owner to spend the moneys needed for this protection.

Rail Access

Rail access is an important feature for many industrial users. An industrial building that is catering to users with a need for rail delivery must be located adjacent to a rail spur.

Loading Facilities

In most commercial properties an area that is designated for loading and unloading should be available to the tenants. These facilities should be reviewed to see that they meet the dock height requirements of the current tenants as well as of any future tenants. Without a proper loading area, a potential tenant could be lost to a competing property.

Elevators

Most buildings over two stories have elevators. They should be reviewed for size, speed, and reliability. Usually the size of the building determines their number and size. Many larger office buildings will also have a separate elevator to be used as a service elevator.

Outside Storage

Many tenants have additional needs for storage space. Residential properties often have an extra storage area built onto the balcony area or in the basement of the building. This extra storage might give the property a competitive edge over its adjacent neighbor.

Window Sizes

The size of the windows can make the difference in signing up a tenant. Retail tenants use their windows to display their merchandise, while commercial and residential tenants use their windows for viewing. In addition, if office windows are sized incorrectly, they can throw off the layout of the space for a prospective tenant.

Security

Security is an important selling point for most tenants. The security system can range from a video camera with a controlled entrance to the use of a full-time security guard or the use of guard dogs.

Utilities

Access to all necessary utilities is critical for the success of a property. An investor should confirm that all utilities, including water, sewer, telephone, cable TV, gas, and electricity, are available to the property and should also evaluate their present capacity. Many tenants have greater needs than the building standards for electrical or heating and air conditioning. These needs must be able to be met to service both existing and prospective tenants.

Building Code Violations

The investor should make sure that the property does not violate any current local building codes. Check with the local building code department.

Financial Records to Consider Before Purchasing a Property

Real Estate Property Taxes

The local real estate assessment department should be contacted to verify the past and current tax assessments and bills. Many investors calculate the most recent tax bills in their proforma and neglect to get a realistic number for the taxes. The investor should know if the tax rates will be increasing in the near future, as well as what the impact will be on the taxes due to the pending sale.

Availability of Insurance

Insurance must be available for the property. Often the insurance market for the subject property has disappeared, and a long search for a company that will cover the property could increase coverage costs. If the property is in a flood plain, special flood plain insurance will be required by the lender.

Operating Statements

The first thing that should be done in reviewing the operations of the property is to obtain from the seller the past two years' operating statements. In reviewing the revenue side of the statement, the investor should make a chart of all the current tenants with their current rental rates. (See Lease Summary Forms in Chapter 5.) If the tenant is paying any common area charges (fees assessed for areas used by all tenants, such as lobbies, corridors, and public restrooms) or percentage rents, these items should be added in. All miscellaneous income, such as late fees, vending, and telephone charges, should be carefully estimated based on past trends.

Each line item under an expense category should be analyzed and double-checked with vendors. A quick call to your insurance agent will give you a good idea of what insurance should cost for the necessary coverage. Copies of all service contracts should be reviewed. They will tell the investor the services to be performed as well as the price and terms of the contract. The local tax department can tell the investor the current tax bill as well as a projection for the upcoming year. Remember, when you purchase this property, the taxes might be substantially increased due to the higher sales price. Also check with the local utilities to see if an increase is planned for the near future.

Once you have scrutinized the expenses, it would be a good idea to have a management company check them over. Additionally, find out from the local Institute of Real Estate Management (IREM) chapter what expenses are for comparable properties. IREM has an annual book that breaks down property types into age, size, and location and shows the expenses on a per unit, square footage and percentage of the collected income basis.

MORTGAGE TERMS AND CONDITIONS

Copies of the existing mortgages on the property should be obtained. A knowledgeable investor will not only personally review these documents, but will have a good real estate attorney review them for potential pitfalls. The following items should also be reviewed:

1. *Mortgage loan balance.* The current loan balance of the loan.

2. *Mortgage rate.* The interest rate that is charged by the lender. This rate could be a fixed rate, it could increase or decrease over time, or it could have a fixed payment rate but accrue interest at a higher rate.

3. *Mortgage maturity.* The date the loan is due.

4. *Mortgage amortization.* The number of years over which the original loan balance is paid.

5. *Prepayment penalty.* The penalty that the lender charges to the borrower to pay off the loan prior to its maturity. Many lenders want to lock in the loan for a set period of time, and they will charge a percentage of the outstanding loan balance on a decreasing basis over time to enable the borrower to prepay the loan.

6. *Security for the loan.* A clause defining what property is given as security for the loan. In addition to the subject property, the lender may require additional collateral to secure the loan.

7. *Cross default clause.* A clause used by lenders whereby a default on the subject property triggers a default on other loans made by the lender to the borrower, even though those loans may not be in default.

8. *Transferability of the loan.* A clause that gives the borrower the right to transfer the property with the existing loan in place. Borrowers should want this right. Many lenders who will allow a loan to be assumed also want the right to approve the new borrower and will probably want a loan transfer fee for this right.

9. *Exculpatory language.* A clause that states whether the borrower has personal recourse to pay the loan back or whether the loan is a nonrecouse loan, in which case the borrower is not personally obligated to repay.

10. *Escrows required.* This determines if the borrower must escrow the real estate taxes and insurance premiums with the lender on a monthly basis. Lenders usually will require these escrows to assure that the borrower has paid these items. Additionally, in some states the lender makes extra profit by earning interest on these funds.

11. *Borrower's reporting requirements.* Reports and statements required by the lender, for example, weekly traffic reports, monthly cash flow statements, yearly audited statements.

12. *Closing costs.* Costs the borrower must pay to obtain the loan. In almost every case, the borrower will pay 100 percent of the closing costs, including the legal costs incurred by the lender.

13. *Late charges and grace periods.* Penalty charged by the lender if the mortgage payment is late. The date the payment is late and the date on which the penalty will start are specified.

14. *Prohibition against secondary financing.* States whether the lender will prohibit any junior mortgages on the property. Most lenders do not like to see any secondary financing. They feel it adds to the financial burden of the property.

FINANCIAL FORECASTS: HOW TO MAKE AN EDUCATED GUESS ABOUT FUTURE PROFIT

The investor who is comfortable with the current operating figures should project a five-or ten-year proforma. This is done by taking the current numbers and making a conservative assumption for increases in the rent and expenses. These assumptions should be based on past history and an educated guess for the future, which should include not only past history of rent and expense increases over the past few years, but also the anticipated performance of the economy and certain market conditions. For example, if the market is overbuilt and competition is offering rental concessions, assumptions about future rent levels will either be stable or lower than if there were a greater demand for this product type. In times of high inflation, the expenses will likely rise at a higher rate than when inflation is low.

When the inflation rate is low, it might be assumed that future expense increases will be modest. However, that is not always the case. It could be that certain fixed costs, such as insurance, could increase at a rate far greater than inflation due to other factors within that industry. The same may be true of utilities. In addition, the mortgage might have increases over the next ten years, and those figures should be included. A category for property improvements should also be included. All property will have items that will wear out or have to be replaced. Commercial property will need future dollars to renovate tenant space for new tenants. The assumptions that are made during this process are the benchmarks for evaluating the overall performance of the transaction down the road. The investor who uses aggressive assumptions will be disappointed when they do not materialize. On the other hand, very conservative projections might result in no one wanting to invest in the deal. (For an example of a financial forecast, see Chapter 7, "Ten-Year Cash Flow Forecast.")

STRUCTURING THE DEAL:
HOW TO MAKE MONEY WHEN YOU BUY A PROPERTY

After all the above information is compiled and digested, the investor should analyze the structure of the deal, remembering that money is made when you buy a property. What is meant by this statement is that if the property is bought under the wrong terms and conditions, it will not produce the desired results. If, after careful analysis of the economics of the transaction, the investor discovers that the bottom line is not as good as once thought, the choice is to either pass on the deal or go back to the seller and renegotiate the price and terms. Additionally, the investor might find out that more renovation work is required than first appeared, so that an adjustment in price would be needed.

Down-payment

The down-payment is a key ingredient to the structure of any transaction. The lower the equity (down-payment) requirement, the greater the leverage. A higher potential yield could be achieved based on this down-payment. Additionally, how it is paid is important. It might be advantageous for the investor to structure a staged down-payment.

Seller Guarantees

Guarantees could be needed in the transaction. When the original deal was structured, the investor might have thought that the property was in a healthy market with good leases. The completed analysis process may show the opposite to be true. Because of this new information, the investor is justified in going back to the seller and asking for different terms or additional guarantees. If it is discovered that the bottom line is not what was originally presented, it could be that the investor might need the seller to reduce the purchase price, reduce the mortgage rate, increase the seller financing, or lengthen the maturity of the seller financing.

Option Period

In structuring the deal, the purchaser should make sure to have a period of time in which to inspect the property and review all aspects of the transaction. This time period can be for a few days or a few months, depending on the complexity of the transaction. During this period the investor will want to keep the option money or earnest money as low as possible even though these funds are not at risk.

Financial Transactions You Can Use for Both the Buyer's and Seller's Benefit

There are many techniques to accommodate both the purchaser's and the seller's needs. The following are various types of structures that can be used.

ALL CASH

Transferring the entire purchase price in cash is the simplest type of structure that can be used. The purchaser simply negotiates the best deal at the lowest price. Many all cash buyers base their price on a predetermined capitalization rate based upon the current cash flow available. If the property can be bought within this buying range, they will purchase the property. An example would be a deal in which the purchase price is $1,000,000 and the buyer pays $1,000,000 in cash.

LEVERAGED PURCHASE

A leveraged structure uses the advantages of the existing debt, new financing, or seller financing. With leverage the purchaser is trying to obtain the maximum return on the invested equity without overburdening the property with debt. An example is paying a $100,000 down-payment on a $1,000,000 property.

SPLIT DOWN-PAYMENT

This structure utilizes the splitting of the equity requirements to the seller over a specified period of time. This technique helps to increase the leverage and the overall return as well as to enable the purchaser to close the property with a lower down-payment. Using the above example, the purchaser might pay $100,000 in four equal installments every six months.

DOWN-PAYMENT PAID AS PARTIAL FEES

Part of the down-payment may be paid to the seller as fees for services rendered. The fees will then be deductible to the purchaser over a shorter time period than available if depreciated over the life of the property. The purchase contract price for the property will not show the value of these fees paid, since the purchaser will deduct these payments as fees. By using this method, the seller must accept these fees as ordinary income. In the above example, if the purchaser paid the seller $950,000 for the property with $50,000 cash down-payment and a $50,000 fee for services rendered, the purchaser would be able to deduct the $50,000 fee over a shorter period of time than by amortizing this $50,000 over the then current depreciation schedule. As far as the seller is concerned, he has still received the $1,000,000 asking price for the property, that is, he has received $950,000 plus a fee of $50,000.

MASTER LEASE

With a master lease transaction, the investor is able to avoid many of the risks associated with real estate. In this type of deal the seller will lease the property back from the investor at a specified lease rate for a specified time period. In the above example, the seller will give the investor a master lease for $150,000 per year with an escalation rate of five percent per year to take inflation into account for a period of five years. The seller will then collect the rents and pay all the expenses.

GROUND LEASE

A ground lease enables the investor to acquire the property less the ownership of the land, which is kept by the seller or an outside third party. This type of transaction is used to increase the leverage of the deal due to a lower purchase price and thereby a lower down-payment. In addition, since land is not a depreciable asset, the purchaser gets to deduct the ground lease payment. The purchaser should make sure that the ground lease is for a long period of time, since at the end of the ground lease, the improvements on the land revert back to the owner of the land. In using the above $1,000,000 example, the purchaser could have structured the deal to buy only the building improvements for $850,000 with a $75,000 down-payment, and then lease the land for 10 percent of its current appraised value of $150,000. The ground lease could have escalations based on inflation or future appraised value. It could also have a formula for buying out the ground lease in a certain number of years.

BRIDGE LEASE

A bridge lease enables the investor to lease the property for a period of time and then purchase the property at a predetermined purchase price. For example, the investor can lease the property in the above example for $150,000 per year for a five-year term, and then, at the end of the five-year term, purchase the property for $1,200,000.

LAND CONTRACT

Under the terms of a land contract, the investor will get possession of the property, even though the seller retains the title to the property. Upon a specified loan paydown the seller will release the title to the purchaser. In the above example, the investor can pay the seller $50,000 of the down-payment but will not receive the title to the property until the full $100,000 has been paid to the seller.

LEASE WITH AN OPTION TO PURCHASE

This type of transaction is most common in single family residential properties. A purchaser might want to purchase the property but, for a number of reasons, would rather lease the property for a period of time prior to making the decision to purchase. The option could have a specific price, or it could have a price that will increase over time. It could also be structured to give the tenant the first right of refusal to purchase the property at a price equal to that of an outside offer.

Purchasing Contingencies: What to Request Be Changed Before You Agree to Buy

Many times a property will appear attractive to you, but only if certain events occur or impediments are removed. Sellers might agree to these contingencies if they are removed during a set time period. These could include all or some of the following.

ZONING

A property may be contracted for with a totally different use in mind and must be rezoned for the new use (for example, a condominium conversion).

ZONING VARIANCE

Due to a different intended property use the property may need a zoning variance to add a building or for a reduced parking requirement.

FINANCING

A new mortgage might be required and the purchaser will require time to obtain a mortgage commitment.

CONSTRUCTION INSPECTION

A purchaser may require time to conduct a thorough structural inspection.

FINANCIAL INSPECTION

Time might be needed to verify all of the financial operating statements.

INSURANCE

With the high cost of various types of property insurance, extra time might be required to find a lower insurance rate or even coverage itself.

REAL ESTATE TAXES

The current real estate taxes might be higher than other comparable properties, and the purchaser may need time to attempt to have the taxes reduced.

RAISING THE EQUITY

Since the transaction will most likely require equity, the purchaser may require ample time to raise this equity.

SELLING OFF A PIECE OF THE PROPERTY

If the property has available vacant land, the purchaser might require time to find a suitable buyer. An example might be when a buyer wants a building but does not want the majority of vacant land adjacent to the building. Such a buyer might require the deal to be contingent on selling off this parcel.

RENOVATIONS

The purchaser might need time to price certain property improvement or renovations. An example would be when the purchaser needs to obtain an estimate to repair structural damage to a property, and wants to make the deal contingent on getting the work done for a certain price.

If the above mentioned contingencies are not met, the purchaser can either call off the deal and get back the option money, or can renegotiate some of the terms and conditions of the purchase.

Transaction "Outs": When to Consider Calling the Deal Off

In structuring the deal, the purchaser should make sure that if certain events take place prior to the closing, the deal can be called off. The purchaser is justified in making such requests of the seller, because if any or all of these events occur, the property may no longer be worth what the seller was asking. The following items may be factors in deciding whether to call a deal off:

RENT ROLL

The contract might state that the property must have a certain stated rent level at closing.

OCCUPANCY LEVEL

The contract might have been conditioned upon the property having an agreed upon occupancy level.

LIEN FREE

The deal might state that at closing the property will have no liens against it. If the seller does not clear up all liens on the property prior to closing, the purchaser should have the right not to close.

CLEAR TITLE

The contract might state that at the closing the deal must have a clear title. If someone clouds the title prior to closing, the purchaser should have the right to terminate the deal.

TRANSFER OF THE EXISTING FINANCING

The deal might have been contingent upon the transferring of the existing mortgage debt. If the underlying lender decides at the last minute not to improve the deal, the purchaser should have the right to walk from the transaction.

CONDEMNATION OR RIGHT OF EMINENT DOMAIN

If the local or state government decides prior to closing to take all or part of the property, the purchaser should have the right to terminate the deal.

How a Right of Contract Assignment Clause Can Help the Purchaser Avoid Losses

Since each purchaser should try to negotiate into a deal as well as out of a deal, the purchaser should have a right of assignment clause in the contract. This clause will give the purchaser either the right to assign the contract to a new entity that will be formed prior to the closing, or to assign the contract to another unrelated party. The purchaser who has substantial moneys at risk and will be unable to close might be able to sell the contract to another party to cut losses or even to make a profit. Many sellers are reluctant to give this right, because they want to know whom they are selling their property to. A purchaser who is not able to negotiate an unlimited right of assignment should try to get this right with a "not to be unreasonably withheld" clause.

NEGOTIATING THE DEAL:
FIVE BASIC STEPS TO A SUCCESSFUL ACQUISITION

Since there are hundreds of books written on how to negotiate, this section will deal only with the basics. First and foremost in negotiating a deal is to have done your homework. This is the whole basis of this book.

Step 1: Research the Property and Have a Specific Idea of Its Use

Prior to negotiating a deal, investors should have a good idea of what they are willing to pay for the property. By researching the market the investor should know at what price similar properties are selling for in the area.

The investor should know everything there is to know about the property and its market. To get this information, a smart investor will start by investigating the facts and then setting about to analyze these facts. Remember, these decisions are based on obtaining the best available information possible.

A thorough knowledge of the mortgage market will also help in negotiating a deal. Many times a property will have to be refinanced, and knowing who will make a loan and at what rates could help expedite the negotiations.

Step 2: Verify All the Facts

A smart investor will double and triple check all this information, and will then analyze it. Remember, "garbage in, garbage out."

Step 3: Research the Seller

Another important aspect for negotiating the deal is to get to know the strengths and weaknesses of the selling party through a careful background check. You might find that the seller has hidden motives for selling, or has severe financial problems that could lead to a better bargaining position for you.

Get to know your seller. Find out where his "hot buttons" are—what turns him on and what turns him off. How you relate to a seller can eventually determine how good a deal you can negotiate.

Step 4: Have Alternative Plans

An investor who is well prepared will have a Plan A, Plan B, Plan C, and if necessary, a Plan D. Since every transaction is different and sellers are different, the investor should be able to quickly react to the seller's counter offers. The investor's counter offers should be based on a knowledge of what to pay for the property and how the deal can be structured so that both parties can obtain their desired goals.

Step 5: Avoid Getting Caught in the "Greater Fool" Theory

When looking and negotiating for property the investor should make sure not to get wrapped up in the "Greater Fool Theory," which states that there is always a bigger fool out in the marketplace who will pay more for a property. In negotiating, stick to your predetermined price and terms. Just because someone else will pay more for a property than you will does not mean that you should. Remember, that investor could either be a "bigger fool," or might have a different measurement for investment than you.

SUMMARY

The main point in analyzing any type of property is to do your homework. Never rely entirely on the seller's information or the broker's information. Use it, but do a thorough job in double-checking these facts. The financial analysis that is done up front will either make or break the transaction. Always be conservative. It is better to be pleasantly surprised than to be unprepared for the future.

DO'S AND DON'TS OF BUYING REAL ESTATE

Do's of Buying Real Estate

- Buy real estate in a neighborhood that will appreciate.
- Look for property that will have a broad appeal and marketability.
- Look for property that does not require a lot of maintenance.
- Specialize in one type of property acquisition.
- Compare prices of comparable properties to establish market value.
- Check out comparable market rents in the market area.
- Be knowledgeable of the market trends and forces in the market area.
- Make sure to have an engineer inspect the construction of the property.
- Get professional advice regarding all financial and legal aspects of the purchase.
- Ask the seller the reasons for selling the property.
- Have an adequate working capital reserve established for the unforeseen.
- Carefully review all the mortgage documents.

Don'ts of Buying Real Estate

- Do not buy a property with a negative cash flow unless you are prepared to carry the property.
- Do not buy a property with a large mortgage that is due relatively soon unless you are prepared to refinance.
- Do not buy property by using the wrong benchmark of financial analysis.
- Do not take the seller's or broker's operating numbers as undisputed fact.
- Do not invest in property in an area that only has one main employment center.
- Do not accept a contract until the total deal has been put in writing and signed by all parties.

- Do not use someone else's assumptions without first reviewing and approving.

- Do not over-leverage a property

- Do not forget to review all the service contracts, leases, and other important documents in the transaction.

- Do not forget to have the seller fully fund the security deposit account at the closing.

PROPERTY FORM

Property Log In Report

Form 3.1 is to be used to log in properties.

FORM 3-1
Property Log In Report

PREPARED BY: _____
TYPE PROPERTY: _____

DATE	PROPERTY NAME	ADDRESS	RECEIVED FROM	TEL. NO.	ASKING PRICE	GRM	PRICE/ SQ. FT.	PRICE/ UNIT	CAP. RATE	COMMENTS
				( )	$		$	$		
				( )	$		$	$		
				( )	$		$	$		
				( )	$		$	$		
				( )	$		$	$		
				( )	$		$	$		
				( )	$		$	$		
				( )	$		$	$		
				( )	$		$	$		
				( )	$		$	$		
				( )	$		$	$		
				( )	$		$	$		
				( )	$		$	$		
				( )	$		$	$		
				( )	$		$	$		
				( )	$		$	$		
				( )	$		$	$		
				( )	$		$	$		
				( )	$		$	$		
				( )	$		$	$		

*H*OW TO CONTRACT FOR THE PROPERTY: FOUR SAMPLE LEGAL DOCUMENTS THAT HELP AVOID LITIGATION

LETTER OF INTENT: YOUR FIRST OFFER TO THE SELLER

The first step in negotiating a real estate transaction is to send the seller a letter of intent. This letter should be as thorough as possible and should include all of the business points in the deal. At the end there should a place where the seller can acknowledge agreement to the terms and conditions. This letter should also include a time period for the seller to respond.

Since this is the first offer to the seller, the deal might have to be renegotiated based on this initial offer. Using this form and the attached exhibits will save you both time and money. When the final draft of the letter of intent is signed, a copy should go to the attorney who will draft the final purchase agreement.

SAMPLE LETTER OF INTENT

September 26, 19—

Mr. Martin Thomas
Vice President
Empire Development Company
1900 First Street, Suite 200
Atlanta, Georgia 30067

RE: Looking Glass Apartments
    Atlanta, Georgia
    200 Apartment Units

Dear Mr. Thomas:

Based upon the information furnished by you, I have outlined below the terms and conditions under which I would acquire the above referenced property.

1.	Purchase Price:	$6,000,000
2.	Cash Down Payment:	$2,000,000
3.	First Mortgage	
	A. Loan Amount:	$3,000,000
	B. Lender:	First Savings and Loan

C.	Interest Rate:	Ten percent per annum
D.	Term:	Ten years
E.	Amortization Period:	30 years
F.	Payment	$26,327.15 per month

Second Mortgage

A.	Loan Amount:	$1,000,000
B.	Lender:	Empire Development Company
C.	Interest Rate:	Eleven percent interest only
D.	Term:	Ten years
E.	Payment:	$9,166.67 per month
F.	Due on Sale Clause:	None
G.	Right of Transfer:	Allowed, seller cannot unreasonably withhold approval
H.	Transfer Costs:	None
I.	Escrows:	None
J.	Prepayment Penalties:	None
K.	Security of Loan:	Second Mortgage on property

4. Closing Date: January 15, 19—

5. Earnest Money: $25,000 Paid into escrow with Chicago Title Co. All interest will accrue to the Purchaser. Earnest money will go "at risk" at the end of the inspection period.

6. Inspection Period: Thirty days from the later of the execution of the purchase agreement or the delivery to the purchaser of all the items in Exhibit A.

7. Closing Costs:

A.	Title Insurance Premium	Paid by purchaser
B.	Transfer Tax:	Paid by seller
C.	Intangible Tax:	Paid by purchaser
D.	Pest Report/Bond:	Paid by seller
E.	Recording Costs:	Paid by purchaser
F.	Survey:	Paid by seller
G.	Legal Fees:	Each party pays his own

8. Closing Extension: Thirty days

A.	Additional Earnest:	$10,000 applied toward the purchase price
B.	Notice to Seller:	Seven days prior to original closing date

9. Closing Prorations: All revenue and expenses are to be prorated as of the day of closing. Any late receipts or expenses will be prorated within forty-five days after the closing.

10. Seller Warranty: Seller warrants that all mechanical and plumbing systems are in working order at the closing.

A. Rent Ready Units: Seller warrants that all vacant units as of the closing date will either be ready for occupancy, or a credit will be given to the Purchaser for a dollar amount to bring the unit to rent-ready status.

11.	Occupancy Guarantee:	Seller warrants that at closing the property will have 190 units rented with leases on terms of no less than six months.
12.	Rental Rates:	One-bedroom units no less than $350 per month
		Two-bedroom units no less than $400 per month
13.	Security Deposits:	At closing seller will turn over a fully funded account.
14.	Brokerage Commission:	Seller shall be responsible for and shall pay at its sole cost all brokerage fees and/or real estate commissions of any kind due to any third party who has dealt with the Seller. Purchaser will warrant that it has dealt with no other persons in negotiating this sale.

Add to letter of intent if purchasing a to-be-built property.

15.	Negative Cash Flow Guarantee:	Seller warrants to fund any operating deficits for a period of twenty-four months from the date of 100 percent completion as certified by the construction lender.
16.	Construction Warranty:	Seller will warrant the construction of said property for a period of twelve months after 100 percent certified completion. Seller will also warrant all plant material and ground covering for a three-month period after 100 percent certified completion.
17.	Construction Penalty:	A $10 per unit penalty will be assessed to the Seller if all the units are not 100 percent "Rent Ready" (as certified by ABC Management Co.) by November 30, 19—. This penalty will be paid to purchaser within thirty days of 100 percent completion as certified by the construction lender.
18.	Down-payment Holdback:	Purchaser will hold in escrow (all interest will accrue to the seller) the sum of $50,000 until the property is totally punched-out.
19.	Punch-out:	Purchaser will submit to seller a list of punch-out items within thirty days of certified completion. BBB Construction Management Co. will make the final, binding decision on punch-out completion.
20.	Construction Follow-up:	Purchaser requires that seller supply to purchaser all of the documentation listed in Exhibit B during the construction phase. Additionally, purchaser requires that the seller supply all the items in Exhibit C within ninety days of 100 percent completion.

Add to letter of intent if seller will manage the property.

21.	Management:	Purchaser agrees to have the seller manage the property under a twelve-month management contract for a fee of five percent of the monthly collectable income. Exhibit D is a list of items that should be supplied to the purchaser during the inspection period.

It is my intention to purchase The Looking Glass Apartments under the above stated terms and conditions. If these terms are acceptable, so please acknowledge at the bottom of this page and return this agreement within five (5) business days to the undersigned. Upon receipt of the executed letter, I shall instruct my attorneys to draft a purchase agreement.

Sincerely,

AAA Acquisition Company, Inc.

Mark Randall
President

MR/rke

Enc.

Accepted and agreed upon this _____ day of _____, 19___.

Empire Development Company

BY:_____

EXHIBIT A (FOR EXISTING PROPERTIES)

1. Copy of the complete set of working drawings and specifications: The blueprints and specifications for the subject property.

2. Copy of the zoning letter: Letter from the municipal government showing that the subject property is currently zoned for its intended use.

3. Copy of all utility letters: Letters from local utility companies showing that service is currently available to the subject property.
   a. Gas
   b. Electric
   c. Telephone
   d. Water
   e. Sewer
   f. Cable TV (if applicable)

4. As-built Survey: Current survey showing the improvements on the property. Completed by a registered engineer.

5. Copies of all current service contracts: Contracts showing the term of the contract, the monthly costs for these services, the work to be performed, and the termination penalty, if applicable.
   a. Pest Control
   b. Trash Removal

      c. Landscaping

      d. Elevator

      e. Janitorial Service

      f. Maid Service

      g. Tax Consulting

      h. Window Washing

      i. Parking Lot Sweeping

      j. Snow Removal

      k. Music

      l. Security

6. Legal description of the property.

7. Copies of all leases and rental applications.

      a. Rent roll

      b. Security deposits

8. Copies of all mortgage documents.

9. Copies of all insurance policies.

10. Copies of the last two years' operating statements.

11. Copies of the last two years' tax bills.

12. Copies of all permitted encumbrances on the property: Liens or liabilities on the subject property that should be known to the purchaser prior to closing.

13. List of all employees with current salary history.

14. Copy of the estoppel letter from the lender(s): Letter from the current lender(s) showing the current balances and terms of the mortgages. This letter will usually contain the lender's approval of this loan transfer and property sale.

15. Copy of the estoppel letter from the tenant(s): Usually obtained in commercial transactions, this letter will contain the terms and conditions of the various leases.

16. Inventory: Complete list of all inventory to be transferred with the property.

      a. Office

      b. Maintenance

      c. Pool

      d. Appliances (including all serial numbers)

      e. Mechanical (including all serial numbers)

17. Copies of all warranties:

      a. Appliances

      b. Maintenance equipment

      c. Mechanical

d. Plumbing

e. Electrical

f. Roof

g. Paving

h. Pool

i. Tennis court

j. General contractor

EXHIBIT B (TO-BE-BUILT PROPERTIES)

1. Copy of the complete set of working drawings and specifications.

2. Copy of the landscaping plan and specifications.

3. Copy of all utility letters.

4. Copy of the property survey.

5. Copy of the property topography.

6. Copy of the legal description.

7. Copy of any tenant pre-leases and applications.

8. Copies of the builder's risk policy.

9. Copy of the last two years' land tax bills.

10. Copy of any property easements or encumbrances.

11. Copy of any lender estoppels.

12. Copies of any tenant estoppel letters.

13. Copies of all development and building permits.

14. Copies of the mortgage loan documents.
    a. Construction loan
    b. Permanent loan

15. Copy of the construction contract with the construction budget.

16. Copy of the construction bond or letter of credit: A construction bond is a bond that a general contractor gives to an owner so that if the general contractor is unable to complete the construction contract, the bonding company will complete the construction.

17. Copy of the lender appraisal.

18. Copy of the list of the proposed service contracts.

19. Copy of the proposed inventory.

    a. Office

    b. Maintenance

    c. Pool

    d. Appliances

    e. Mechanical

20. Copy of the proposed construction completion schedule showing weekly progress.

21. Copy of the color board (a visual display with actual samples) for the building exteriors.

    a. Exterior facade

    b. Paint or stain

    c. Roof shingles

22. Copy of the color board for the unit interiors.

    a. Type of cabinets

    b. Type and color of appliances

    c. Drapes/blinds/window shades

    d. Countertops

    e. Floor covering

    f. Wallpaper

    g. Paint color

    h. Ceramic tile

    i. Light fixtures

    j. Plumbing fixtures

    k. Lobby walls

    l. Hallway walls

23. Listing of the insulation R-factors: These are numerical measurements of insulation efficiency.

    a. Floor

    b. Ceiling

    c. Walls

EXHIBIT C (TO-BE-BUILT PROPERTIES)

These are items needed during and after the construction process.

1. Copies of all lien waivers: Waivers signed by the various contractors stating that they have been paid for the work performed to date.

2. Copies of all weekly progress reports.

3. Copies of all construction draw requests: A construction draw request shows all of the various line items that the general contractor is drawing down on from the construction loan.

4. Copies of the lender inspection reports: Reports that the lender's engineer, architect, or construction manager will complete every time that the general contractor submits a draw request. They will either approve or disapprove the draw request. They will include an update on the progress of the construction, as well as review any problems with this construction. Will also include pictures of the construction.

5. Copies of all certificates of occupancy issued by the local building department.

6. Copy of the lender 100 percent completion certification: Letter supplied by the construction lender or representative stating that the construction is 100 percent completed according to the original plans and specifications.

7. Copies of any construction change orders. Documents that define the nature and cost of any work that deviates from the original construction plans and specifications. This document should be signed by the owner, the contractor, the inspecting construction manager, and many times the construction lender. This document should be signed prior to any of the work being completed.

8. Copy of the general contractor's completion certification: Document that the general contractor gives to the owner and the lender stating that construction has been completed in accordance with the plans and specifications.

9. List of all serial numbers: List of the serial numbers of each piece of equipment.
   a. Appliances
   b. Mechanical

10. List of all subcontractors (including addresses, telephone numbers, and contacts): This list is used by the property owner if contact with any of the original subcontractors is needed in the future.

11. List of all material reference numbers: This list will include the names of the material suppliers, their addresses, and their telephone numbers. It will also give an exact description of model names and any other reference numbers. This list will be used by the owner for future reordering.

EXHIBIT D (TO-BE-BUILT PROPERTIES)

These are items needed if the seller/developer will manage the property for the owner.

1. Market study of at least ten comparables: Market study including information on the market comparables (similar properties in the area). It will include information on the rental rates, unit types, features of the units, amenities for the property, security deposits, and real estate commissions paid.

2. Month-by-month line item analysis for the revenue and expenses (See Budget Line Item Form).

3. Written analysis of each line item: Analysis giving the backup assumptions on each line item in the budget.

4. Written report on the marketing strategy: Report defining the marketing strategy to be used to rent the subject property.

5. Sample of reporting system: Forms the management company will supply to the owner on a weekly or monthly basis.

    a. Weekly traffic reports

    b. Monthly profit and loss statements

    c. Sources and application of funds

    d. Monthly budget variance report

6. Projected absorption schedule of rent-up: Schedule detailing the monthly projections of the rent-up progress of the subject property.

PURCHASE AGREEMENT: DEFINING THE CONDITIONS FOR THE PURCHASE

Once a letter of intent has been negotiated and signed, the purchaser's attorney should prepare a purchase agreement. This document will include all of the business terms and conditions already agreed upon, and will contain the proper legal language that will define the rights and obligations of each party. Once the first draft is reviewed, both parties will then refine all the language to suit both sides. This done, each party will sign the document. If there are any future disputes in the transactions between the two parties, this document should help define their obligations. The following is an outline for a typical Purchase Agreement.

1. Sale of Property

2. Price

3. Allocation of Purchase Price

4. Closing

5. Taxes

6. Title Examination

7. Default

8. Survey

9. Prorations at Closing

10. Operation Prior to Closing

11. Construction of Units (if to-be-built)

12. Representations and Warranties

The following purchase agreement is a sample to be used for acquiring property during the construction stage.

SAMPLE RESIDENTIAL PURCHASE AGREEMENT

THIS AGREEMENT, made and entered into effective this _____day of _____, 19__, and between _____, a _____ partnership (hereinafter called "Seller") and _____, a _____ corporation (hereinafter called "Purchaser").

In consideration of the mutual terms, covenants, conditions, and agreements hereinafter contained, it is hereby agreed by and between the parties hereto as follows:

1. Sale of Property. Seller agrees to sell, convey, assign, transfer, and deliver to Purchaser, and Purchaser agrees to purchase, acquire, and take from Seller, the following described property:

A. All that real property located in the County of _____ and State of _____ more particularly described on Exhibit "A" attached hereto and made a part hereof, together with all hereditaments and appurtenances thereunto belonging or in any wise appertaining, and any and all buildings and improvements situated thereon, including but not limited to _____ individual heated and air-conditioned apartment units currently under construction on said real property and commonly known as "_____ Apartments" (hereinafter collectively called the "Subject Premises");

B. All furniture, fixtures, equipment, appliances and other items of personal property now and hereafter located upon the Subject Premises which are owned by Seller and which are or will be used or useful in connection with and for the occupancy, management, and operation of the Subject Premises, including, by way of example and not by way of limitation, oven ranges, refrigerators, dishwashers, disposals, trash compactors, sets of living room and dining room draperies on rods (it being the intent of the parties hereto that there be _____ of each of the foregoing items upon the Subject Premises on the Date of Closing or that an adjustment be made in the purchase price to enable Purchaser to replace any that are missing), heating and air conditioning units, water heaters and equipment, washers, dryers, shrubbery, swimming pool equipment, maintenance equipment and all office furniture equipment and supplies, and including, but not limited to, the property described in Exhibit B attached hereon and hereby made a part hereof;

C. Seller's copies, if any, of all original and supplemental blueprints, all documents relating to the development or construction of the Subject Premises including but not limited to plans, specifications, designs and architectural drawings ("Plans and Specifications"), operating manuals, warranties and guarantees, if any, covering the above-described buildings, improvements, furniture, fixtures, equipment, appliances and personal property, and all of the Seller's right, title, and interest in and to assignable licenses, franchises, and permits, if any relating to the operation of the Subject Premises;

D. The lessor's interest in the residential apartment leases and tenancies, if any, in existence as of Date of Closing and related to the Subject Premises all of which are set forth on Exhibit "C" attached hereto and hereby made a part hereof, as well as damage deposits, security deposits and other deposits for which Seller is accountable as of Date of Closing to tenants of the Subject Premises; and

E. The non-exclusive right to use in _____, the business and trade names "_____ Apartments" and "_____" under which the Subject Premises are to be managed and operated (the property described in subparagraphs A through E hereof sometimes hereinafter being collectively called the "Property" or the "Business").

2. <u>Price.</u> The purchase price to be paid by Purchaser to Seller for the Property shall be _____ DOLLARS ($_____), payable as follows:

A. $_____ earnest money (the "Earnest Money") shall be delivered to a title insurance company (the "Escrow Agent") acceptable to Purchaser no later than ___ p.m. on the second business day after the Effective Date of this Agreement. Escrow Agent shall hold the Earnest Money in an interest-bearing escrow account, which need not be a segregated account, and shall disburse the same in strict accordance with the terms of this Agreement. If Closing occurs, then the Earnest Money (including interest earned thereon) shall be refunded to Purchaser at Closing or, at Purchaser's election, shall be applied against the case portion of the purchase price payable at Closing. If Purchaser so desires, Seller and Escrow Agent will join in the execution of an Escrow Agreement related to said Earnest Money, provided that such Escrow Agreement is consistent with the terms and conditions of the Agreement and that said Escrow Agreement is otherwise reasonably satisfactory to Seller and Escrow Agent.

B. $_____ of the purchase price shall be payable in cash on the Date of Closing (as hereinafter defined) less a credit for Earnest Money, prorations and other adjustments, of any, as provided herein.

C. $_____ of the purchase price shall be payable on the Final Completion Date as that term is defined in Paragraph ___ of the Development Agreement to be entered into pursuant to Paragraph ___ hereof (the "Final Completion Date"). Purchaser shall deliver to Seller on the Date of Closing a nonrecourse promissory note in the amount of $_____ (The "Completion Note") representing the above described portion of the purchase price.

D. $_____ of the purchase price shall be payable in cash on the later of _____ or _____ months from the Final Completion Date and shall be represented by a nonrecourse promissory note in the amount of $_____ (the "Final Note") from Purchaser to Seller to be delivered on the Date of Closing. The Final Note shall bear interest in the total amount of $_____ which shall be due and payable on the payment in full of the Final Note.

E. The balance of the purchase price in the amount of approximately $_____ shall be represented by Purchaser taking the Subject Premises subject to a first priority lien mortgage against the Subject Premises (the "First Mortgage") which secures an indebtedness not to exceed $_____, representing the proceeds of a construction/permanent loan relating to the development of the Subject Premises (the "Construction/Permanent Loan").

The Construction/Permanent Loan shall be evidenced by that certain note, dated _____, executed by Seller payable to the order of _____ ("Lender") in the original principal amount of $_____ (the "Construction Note"), a copy of which Construction Note is attached hereto as Exhibit "D" and is hereby made a part hereof. The Consruction Note is secured by that certain Deed of Trust, dated _____, executed by Seller to _____, for the benefit of Lender, a copy of which is attached hereto as Exhibit "E" and is hereby made a part hereof (the "Construction Mortgage"). The loan evidenced by the Construction Note is referred to as the "Construction Loan"and the Construction Note, the Construction Mortgage, and the other instruments securing the Construction Note are referred to as "Construction Loan Documents." The Construction Loan shall be converted to a permanent loan to be represented by a promissory note in an amount not to exceed $_____, which shall bear interest at the rate of _____ percent per annum and shall be amortized over a period of _____ years, _____ months, with monthly payments of principal and interest not to exceed $_____ (the "Permanent Note"). The loan evidenced by the Permanent Note is referred to as the "Permanent Loan," a copy of which is attached hereto as Exhibit "F."

In the event that the amount of the Permanent Loan is less than $_____, the purchase price shall be reduced by such an amount.

3. <u>Allocation of Purchase Price.</u> The parties hereto agree that the said purchase price shall be allocated to, and will be paid in consideration of, the various components which comprise the Property as follows:

(i)   Buildings, structures, improvements and personal property $_____

(ii) Land $_____

(iii) Property described in subparagraphs 1(C), 1(D), & 1(E) $_____

      Total $_____

Seller agrees to cooperate with Purchaser, at Purchaser's request and at Purchaser's expense, in obtaining an appraisal of the market value of the Property and its component parts; provided, however, that this sale is in no way contingent upon the results of any such appraisal.

4. <u>Closing.</u> Closing shall occur at _____ A.M. at the offices of _____ or at such other location as Purchaser and Seller may agree on, or such other date upon which the parties hereto may hereafter agree (hereinafter referred to as the "Date of Closing").

The seller shall execute, where necessary, and deliver to Purchaser on the Date of Closing the following:

A. A Warranty Deed in recordable form, conveying to Purchaser good and marketable title to the Subject Premises free and clear of all liens, charges and encumbrances with the exception of those encumbrances to which Purchaser does not object under either paragraph 6 or paragraph 8 of the Agreement (the "Permitted Exceptions").

B. A Warranty Bill of Sale, in the form attached hereto as Exhibit "G" and hereby made a part hereof, covering the furniture, fixtures, equipment and personal property described in subparagraph

1B hereof and upon Exhibit "B" hereto (to the extent same have then been acquired by Seller), free and clear of all liens, charges, and encumbrances, with the exception of the Permitted Exceptions. Seller, in this capacity as Developer under the Development Agreement, will execute a supplemental bill of sale on completion (as defined in said Development Agreement) for all remaining items of said furniture, fixtures, equipment and other personal property described in said subparagraph 1B and Exhibit "B" which are not covered under said bill of sale delivered at Closing hereunder.

C. An effective assignment of the lessor's interest in and under the apartment leases and tenancies in existence as of Date of Closing, together with copies of all written lease agreements then in existence and an accounting for all damage, escrow, cleaning, pet, security, or other deposits for which Seller is accountable as of Date of Closing to tenants of the Subject Premises. The assignment of the damage, escrow, pet, cleaning, security, and other deposits shall be accomplished by Purchaser receiving a credit at closing against the cash due at closing. The damage, escrow, pet, cleaning, security and other deposits so assigned and credited to Purchaser shall be sufficient to cover the landlord's liability therefor. Seller shall indemnify, hold harmless, and defend Purchaser against any damages Purchaser may suffer as a result of any deficiency in the amount of said deposits. Seller shall deliver to Purchaser a complete list of all leases and tenancies on the Date of Closing certified by the Seller as accurate and correct.

D. An affidavit indicating that on the Date of Closing there are no outstanding, unsatisfied judgments, tax liens or bankruptcies against or involving the Seller or the Subject Premises; that there have been no service, labor, or materials furnished to the Subject Premises in connection with any construction and development thereof and related improvements thereon for which mechanic's liens have been filed of record and have not been either released of record or bonded or covered by escrow deposit sufficient to permit a title insurance company acceptable to Purchaser to commit to insure Purchaser's title to the Subject Premises without exception for any such lien, and that there are no other unrecorded interests in the Subject Premises of any kind except the lien of taxes not yet due and payable and inchoate lien rights of contractors, subcontractors, materialmen, suppliers, *et al.* who are then providing, who have provided, or who are to provide, materials and/or services in connection with any development or construction of the Subject Premises and related improvements on the Subject Premises and for whom Seller has then made reasonable provision for payment.

E. Any affidavit or document requested by the Lender to satisfy the terms and conditions of the Construction/Permanent Loan.

F. An effective assignment of the Seller's right to use the business and trade names "_____ Apartments" or "_____," and/or variants thereof and all transferable licenses, franchises, and permits, warranties, guarantees to the extent the same then exist or arise in the future in connection with the development of the Subject Premises.

G. An assignment of Seller's right, title, and interest in the Construction Loan Documents together with the consent of the Lender to such assignment.

H. An assignment by Seller and its affiliates of any right, title, and interest under that certain Purchase Agreement between _____ and _____ relating to the transfer of the partnership interest in the Seller.

I. Delivery of copies of all blueprints, plans, and specifications, related to the Subject Premises.

J. All other documents affecting title to and possession of the Business and necessary to transfer and assign the same to Purchaser, free and clear of all liens, charges, and encumbrances not hereinbefore specifically excepted.

K. A standard ALTA owner's policy of the title insurance satisfactory to the Purchaser to insure title to the Subject Premises in Purchaser's or its assign's name, free and clear of all liens, claims, and encumbrances except the Permitted Exceptions, and free from exceptions for unrecorded mechanic's liens. Seller shall deliver to the title insurance company any and all lien waivers in form and substance as the title insurance company may request from general contractors and subcontractors who have furnished skill and labor to the Subject Premises. The premium for such owner's title insurance policy shall be paid for by _____, and such policy shall be in the insured amount of $_____.

L. An estoppel certificate executed by Lender setting forth the amount of funds released to Seller under the Construction/Permanent Loan, the remaining undisturbed balance of the Construction/Permanent Loan, that the Construction Loan Documents, the Permanent Note, and the First Mortgage have not been modified as specifically described in said certification, that, to Lender's best knowledge, no default exists under the Construction/Permanent Loan, that Lender consents to the sale of the Property to a _____ corporation or limited partnership as an assignee of Purchaser and of which an affiliate of Purchaser (i.e., _____, a _____ corporation or limited partnership composed of _____) is the managing general partner, that there is then no uncured default under the Construction Loan Documents, Permanent Note, or First Mortgage by Seller, or any affiliate of Seller, that no conditions exist which would relieve the Lender of any obligation to convert the Construction Loan to the Permanent Loan, if such conversion has not occurred prior to the Date of the Closing, that Lender will exercise its best reasonable efforts to forward to Purchaser copies of all notices which it sends to Seller related to the Construction Loan that Purchaser may cure any default by Seller under the Construction/Permanent Loan if and to the extent Seller is privileged to cure same, that from and after the closing hereunder the Subject Premises will secure the Construction/Permanent Loan and such additional sums as may be advanced by Lender to protect and preserve the Subject Premises and its security interest therein, to render substituted performance for any obligation or covenant of the borrower under the Construction/Permanent Loan or other advances pursuant to and contemplated by Lender's Construction/Permanent Loan Agreement, and that the Construction Note and Construction Mortgage will cease to be operative after repayment of the Construction Note. Purchaser shall not be required to pay any costs of obtaining said consent or any expenses or fees in connection therewith.

M. A termite treatment guarantee provided at the sole cost and expense of the Seller by a licensed and bonded company reasonably acceptable to Purchaser certifying that the Subject Premises are free from termite or other wood destroying organism damage or infestation as of the Date of Closing, and that should any such damage occur during the period from the Date of Closing until five years after the Date of Closing, such company will be liable to Purchaser, or its assignee, for the full cost of repair and replacement resulting from such damage.

N. A letter from the appropriate authority in the form attached hereto as Exhibit "H" and hereby made a part hereof confirming that the Subject Premises are properly zoned for multi-family residential purposes and allow _____ units to be constructed and operated thereon. Seller shall provide and pay for all other certificates of building use and occupancy and evidence of compliance by the Property with all regulations, laws and ordinances which any lender may require in connection with the Construction/Permanent Loan.

O. An opinion of counsel for Seller in form and substance satisfactory to Purchaser that all documents hereunder have been duly and validly authorized, executed, and delivered by the Seller; that all consents (necessary to authorize the transactions contemplated hereby) under any documents to which Seller is a party or by which the Subject Premises are bound to have been obtained and that the documents hereunder vest the Seller's interest in the business or rights described in said instruments in Purchaser.

Seller shall pay the recording costs, transfer taxes, if any and any other tax on the Warranty Deed and Mortgage encumbering the Subject Premises. Each party shall pay its own attorney's fees and all its other costs and expenses in connection with the closing of this transaction. Seller agrees to deliver possession of the business to Purchaser on the Date of Closing.

Notwithstanding any contrary provision contained elsewhere in this Agreement, if any condition precedent of closing has not been satisfied on or before the Date of Closing, then the party for whose benefit the condition was imposed may waive such condition and closing shall occur. Each party agrees in good faith to use its best efforts to satisfy all conditions precedent for which it has responsibility under this Agreement.

5. Taxes. A proration of real estate taxes and personal property taxes payable with respect to the Property shall be made as of the Date of Closing. If the actual amount of said taxes is not known on the Date of Closing, taxes will be prorated on the basis of the amount of taxes payable in 19__ and shall be adjusted between the parties when the actual amount of taxes payable in 19__ is known to Purchaser and Seller. Seller shall cause all special assessments, all real estate taxes, and all personal property taxes due and payable on or before the Date of Closing, to be paid on or before the date of closing provided, however, if any special assessments are announced or imposed with respect to the Subject Premises prior to Closing, but are not due and payable until after Closing, then Seller shall make provision at Closing for payment of said assessment no later than the due date of same which provision must be reasonably satisfactory to Purchaser.

6. Title Examination. Within _____ (___) days after the effective date hereof, Seller shall provide Purchaser with a commitment for the owner's policy of title insurance described in paragraph 4(K) of this Agreement and legible copies of all exceptions thereto. Purchaser shall deliver to Seller a written statement of any objections to Seller's title, within _____ (___) days after receipt by Purchaser of said commitment and legible copies of said exceptions. Purchaser reserves the right to make additional title objections based upon the survey required pursuant to Paragraph 8 hereof, and Purchaser shall deliver a copy of said objections to Seller within _____ (___) days after receipt of the survey. If any objections to title are not timely delivered to Seller, all as herein provided, such objections shall be deemed waived, but such waiver shall not negate the obligation of Seller to convey the Subject Premises by Act of Sale, nor negate any of the warranties to be contained in the same. If any objections to title are timely delivered to Seller, all as herein provided, Seller shall give notice of its intent to cure objections and shall then be allowed until the Date of Closing to cure said objections. Seller agrees to use all reasonable efforts as may be reasonably necessary to cure said objections, including, where necessary, the expenditures of money.

7. Default. If any properly made objections to title are not cured on or before the Date of Closing or if Seller materially defaults in any of its obligations hereunder in any manner, then Purchaser may elect to (a) rescind this Agreement and receive refund of all Earnest Money, or (b) elect to consummate the transaction contemplated by this Agreement in the same manner as if there had been no title objections or defaults, in which instance Purchaser shall have the right to withhold from the purchase price an amount sufficient to cure said objections or defaults. Seller agrees that its refusal to consummate the transaction contemplated by this Purchase Agreement, if it is required to do so by the terms hereof, would cause Purchaser irreparable damages which could not be measured in money damages, and that Purchaser would be entitled to institute proceedings in any court of competent jurisdiction to enforce the performance by Seller of the terms hereof upon the Seller's refusal to consummate the transaction contemplated herein. If the Purchaser shall default in the performance of any of its obligations hereunder, the Seller shall be entitled to retain all Earnest Money, and Purchaser shall deliver to Seller copies of all surveys, inspections, evaluation, and other reports on the Subject Premises prepared by or for Purchaser, which are available to it, as and for its liquidated damages and sole remedy for said default, and not as penalty or forfeiture, actual damages being difficult or impossible to determine. In the event of Purchaser's breach, neither party shall have any remedy against the other except as specifically set forth in this subparagraph.

8. <u>Survey.</u> Within ____ (__) days after the effective date hereof, Seller shall deliver to Purchaser, at Seller's expense, a copy of a current perimeter survey of the Property. Seller shall deliver to Purchaser after closing, and at Seller's expense, an as-built survey certified to Purchaser showing all boundaries, easements and, if recorded, the deed book and page number, driveways, streets, ditches, rights-of-way indicating whether paved or unpaved, fences, power lines, buildings, improvements, encroachments, and containing a flood plain certification that the Subject Premises are not within a 100 year flood plain or in any area that has been designated by H.U.D. as a flood prone or flood hazard area, and metes and bounds legal description. Purchaser reserves the right to make written objections to title based upon said perimeter survey authorized in Paragraph 6 above. Said perimeter survey shall show the location of all building setback lines, situs of then existing easements which shall be labeled by reference to book and page recording data; the perimeter survey shall also contain a flood plain certification (that the Subject Premises are not within a 100 year flood plain or in any area that has been designated by H.U.D. as a flood prone or hazard area) and a certification that buildings in place do not violate any building setback lines or restrictions.

9. <u>Prorations at Closing.</u> All income and expenses of the Business shall be prorated on a daily basis between Seller and Purchaser as of the Date of Closing (said date of proration shall be referred to in this paragraph as the "Proration Date"). Seller shall make any and all of the payments of principal and interest due or otherwise accruing under all liens or encumbrances on or before the Date of Closing as and when due. Purchaser shall receive all income from the Business attributable to the period from and after the Proration Date and shall be responsible for all expenses of the Business attributable to the period commencing on the Proration Date. Seller shall be entitled to all income from the Business attributable to the period prior to the Proration Date. Seller agrees to pay in full on the Proration Date its prorata share of all expenses, charges, bills, or trade accounts maintained or incurred by the Seller in connection with the management or operation of the Business or otherwise accrued for the period prior to the Proration Date. Seller shall have sole responsibility for the payment of all sales taxes, excise taxes, payroll taxes, withholding taxes, or other taxes, if any, collected or payable by the Seller or its agents in connection with the management or operation of the Business for or during said period. Seller shall indemnify Purchaser against and shall hold the Purchaser harmless from any costs, expenses, penalties, or damages, including reasonable attorneys' fees, which may result from any failure by either of them to pay or cause to be paid any of the items described in this subparagraph 9. Purchaser shall use its best efforts to assist Seller in collecting all accounts receivable, including accounts receivable for rent, attributable to the period prior to the Proration Date which are outstanding on the Date of Closing. If Seller or Purchaser received any payment from a debtor under such account, said payment shall first be applied by the recipient to rent or other payments due from said debtor in connection with the Business for the period from and after the Proration Date, and the excess, if any, shall be applied to said accounts receivable. Purchaser shall have the option either of continuing all or any of the existing hazard, liability, rent loss, business interruption, and/or worker's compensation insurance upon the Business, to the extent the same is reasonably available, or of canceling and replacing any or all of said insurance. In the event of any such continuation, the premiums thereon shall be prorated to the Proration Date. If Purchaser elects to cancel and replace said insurance as of the Proration Date, the Seller shall be entitled to any refund of premiums prepaid thereon.

The closing prorations provided for in paragraphs 5 and 9 hereof shall be credited against or added to the cash payable on the Date of Closing pursuant to subparagraph 2(b) hereof. If any prorations made at closing pursuant to this paragraph prove to be inaccurate, the parties shall make an appropriate adjustment not later than _____ (___) days after the closing date.

10. <u>Operation Prior to Closing.</u> Seller agrees to continue to develop, maintain, operate, and manage the Business in the same manner between the date hereof and the Date of Closing as it currently is being managed and operated, making every reasonable effort to do nothing which might damage the reputation of the Business or its relations with its tenants. Seller agrees to enter into no material agreements or contracts and shall incur no major expenses relating to the Business prior to the Date of Closing without Purchaser's prior written consent, which consent shall not unreasonably be withheld. Purchaser and its representatives shall have the right from and after the date hereof to enter upon the

Subject Premises for the purpose(s) of examining the same and conducting such inventories, observations, tests, and investigations of the Subject Premises and the Business as it may desire, so long as Purchaser and said representatives do not unreasonably interfere with the operation of the Business. Purchaser shall indemnify, hold harmless and defend Sellers from and against any damages Seller may suffer as a direct result of actions taken by Purchaser or its representatives in connection with its entering and examining the Subject Premises. At all reasonable times prior to closing, Seller shall give Purchaser, and its counsel, accountants, and representatives, full access to all books and records with respect to the ownership, management, and operation of the Business, shall permit them to copy the same, and shall make available to Purchaser all such information concerning the same as Purchaser may reasonably request. During the term of this Agreement, Seller agrees to allow Purchaser and its representatives and accountants reasonable access to all financial operating statements, tax returns, bank statements, check stubs, deposit slips, invoices, and similar financial records of the Partnership relating to the operation of the Business. Seller shall use the form of lease attached hereto as Exhibit "K" and hereby made a part hereof, of all tenants of the Subject Premises.

11. <u>Construction of Units.</u> In connection with Seller's development of the Subject Premises, Seller agrees that _____ (____) apartment units shall be completed and rent ready to Purchaser's sole satisfaction strictly in accordance with the Plans and Specifications not later than the Date of Closing, and that certificates of occupancy shall have been issued with respect thereto. If any of such units have not been so finished by the Date of Closing, Purchaser shall be entitled to a cash credit of _____ ($_____).

12. <u>Representations and Warranties.</u> Seller represents and warrants to Purchaser that:

A. Seller has all requisite power and authority to execute this Purchase Agreement, the closing documents listed in Paragraph 4 hereof, and all other documents required to be delivered by Seller.

B. The conveyance of the Subject Premises pursuant hereto will not violate any private restriction or agreement to which Seller is a party of any applicable statute, ordinance, governmental restriction, or regulation.

C. There is no action, litigation, condemnation, or proceeding of any kind pending or threatened, involving the Subject Premises or against the Seller which materially or adversely affects the Subject Premises.

D. Upon completion of construction substantially in accordance with the Plans and Specifications, the Subject Premises may be used for the operation of a ____ unit apartment project without violating any federal, state, local, or other governmental building, zoning, health, safety, platting or other law, ordinance, or regulation, or any applicable private restriction. Seller, as provided in the Development Agreement, will be responsible for obtaining and paying for all certificates or other evidence required by any lender as to the compliance with the foregoing.

E. The following utility services are available or will be available at the site of the Subject Premises and have adequate capacity for improvements: electricity, gas, sanitary sewer, water, telephone, and cable TV, evidence of which is attached hereto as Exhibit "I."

F. The Subject Premises abut on and have direct vehicular access to a public road or have driveway access to public roads by permanent, irrevocable, appurtenant easements, which shall be conveyed to Purchaser on the Date of Closing.

G. Seller, on the Date of Closing, will have complied in all material respects with all of its obligations hereunder required to be performed by that date, unless such compliance has been waived in writing by Purchaser.

H. On the Date of Closing, Seller will own all of the Property, free and clear of all liens, charges, and encumbrances except for the Permitted Exceptions.

I. On the Date of Closing, there will be no service contracts, obligations, or liabilities, direct or contingent, relating to the Property other than those set forth on Exhibit "J" attached hereto and hereby made a part hereof (the "Permitted Contracts"), except for those which are terminable on no more than thirty days' notice, and exclusive of any contracts related to the development and construction of the _____ apartment units and related improvements on the Subject Premises pursuant to the Plans and Specifications. Exhibit "J" also includes copies of such Permitted Contracts, the Seller's interests in which obligations, leases, contracts, or commitments are to be transferred to Purchaser at closing.

J. On the Date of Closing all then existing tenant leases will comply with applicable laws of the State of _____ and will conform to the following requirements: each lease shall be in writing; shall have a minimum initial term not less than _____ (____) months and not in excess of _____ (___) months; will be in substantially the form of Exhibit "C" attached hereto and hereby made a part hereof; shall require payment of monthly rent in at least the amount specified on the Rent Schedule attached hereto as Exhibit "C" and hereby made a part hereof; and shall require the security deposits set forth on said Exhibit, provided, however, that Seller may lease units prior to the Date of Closing for any amount in excess of the applicable rent specified on Exhibit "C" without any consent from the Purchaser being required, and provided further that Purchaser's approval of any other rental rates, concessions, or of any lease terms or provisions otherwise differing from those described herein shall not be unreasonably withheld.

K. The damage, escrow, pet, security, and other deposits assigned to Purchaser are sufficient to cover any liability for such deposits.

L. Attached hereto as Exhibit "L" and hereby made a part hereof is a true and complete copy of certificates evidencing current insurance policies related to the Property. Seller will cause said policies of insurance to be kept in full force and effect through and including the Date of Closing. Seller will deliver copies of said current insurance policies to Purchaser promptly after execution hereof.

M. Upon completion of construction, all buildings and improvements contemplated by the Plans and Specifications to be built on the Subject Premises will comply and conform with all applicable state and local zoning regulations and building, fire, and safety codes and restrictions and will be located entirely within the boundary lines of the Subject Premises. None of the buildings or improvements, if any, now located on the Subject Premises are prior nonconforming structures under either the applicable zoning regulations or the applicable building codes.

N. Attached hereto as Exhibit "D" and Exhibit "E," respectively, are true and correct copies of the Construction Note and the Construction Mortgage encumbering the Subject Premises, and also attached hereto as a collective Exhibit "F" are copies of all other instruments executed in connection with the Construction/Permanent Loan. Seller represents and warrants that there are no defaults of any kind under said mortgages or no conditions which would, with the passage of time, create an event of default under such instruments.

O. On the Date of Closing, the buildings, structures, improvements, furniture, fixtures and equipment included within the Property and which have then been completed and installed will be in good operating condition; all apartments, which are then completed and for which certificates of occupancy have then been issued will be in rent-ready condition; and all mechanical, electrical, heating, air conditioning, sewer, water and plumbing systems in buildings which are then completed and for which certificates of occupancy have then been issued will be in proper working order, free from any known defects.

P. On the Date of Closing, there will be no uncured default under the Construction/Permanent Loan, that no conditions will exist which would relieve the Lender of any obligation to convert the Construction Loan to a Permanent Loan, if such conversion has not already occurred, and that there will be no defaults under any contracts or agreements relating to the construction or development of the Subject Premises.

Q. Attached hereto as Exhibit "M" is a copy of the soil test with regard to the Subject Premises as prepared by _____. Seller has no knowledge of any subterranean conditions on the Subject Premises which are not described on said Exhibit "M."

R. There are no material defects relating to the Subject Premises of which Seller has knowledge and of which Seller has not advised Purchaser in writing.

Seller hereby agrees that each of said preceding representations and warranties and of all other representations and warranties contained in this Agreement shall be true and correct in all material respects as of the Date of Closing; the truthfulness of each of said representations and warranties in all material respects shall be a condition precedent to the performance by the Purchaser of its obligations hereunder. If the Purchaser elects to close the sale in spite of a material breach of the foregoing representations and warranties by the Seller, such election shall in no way be considered a waiver or breach by the Purchaser, and any and all remedies for such breach (other than the termination of this Agreement) shall remain fully available to Purchaser. Seller shall indemnify Purchaser and its successors and assigns against and shall hold Purchaser and its successors and assigns harmless from any costs, expenses, or damages of any kind or nature, including reasonable attorneys' fees, which Purchaser may incur, whether prior to or after closing, because of any breach of any of the representations and warranties set forth in this paragraph or because of the material breach by the Seller of any other representation, warranty, condition, or provision hereof.

13. <u>Damage, Destruction and Eminent Domain</u>

A. If prior to Closing, any part of the work contemplated by the Plans and Specifications and theretofore installed on the Subject Premises (but excluding materials stored on site) are damaged or destroyed by fire, the elements, or any other destructive force or cause to the extent that repairing said damage or destruction would reasonably cost $_____ or more, Purchaser shall have the option of declaring this Purchase Agreement null and void. Within _____ (___) business days after receiving the insurance carrier's estimate of the amount of insurance payable as the result of such damage or destruction and the amount of insurance payable for lost rents, the Seller shall give written notice of such information to Purchaser. Within _____ (___) business days of any such damage or destruction, Seller shall give written notice thereof to Purchaser, within _____ (___) days after Purchaser receives from Seller the information described in the preceding sentence. Purchaser may elect to rescind this Agreement by delivering to Seller written notice of such rescission, whereupon the Earnest Money shall be promptly refunded to Purchaser. If Purchaser elects to proceed and to consummate the purchase despite said damage or destruction, or if any lesser damage or destruction has occurred, there shall be no reduction in or abatement of the purchase price, provided, however, that the purchase price shall be reduced by an amount equal to the deductible amount of any such loss which is not paid by insurance proceeds, and Seller shall assign to Purchaser the Seller's right, title, and interest in and subject to the rights of the Lender therein, all insurance proceeds payable with respect to such damage or destruction to be repaired as soon as is reasonably practicable to Purchaser's reasonable satisfaction, and closing shall not be deferred by any reason of any such destruction.

B. If, prior to Closing any judicial, administrative, or other condemnation proceedings are instituted in which a taking is proposed which exceeds $_____ in value, including any consequential damages to the Property, Purchaser shall have the option of declaring this Purchase Agreement to be null and void. Within _____ (___) business days of receipt by it of notice of the institution of any judicial, administrative, or other condemnation proceedings involving Property, Seller shall give written notice thereof to Purchaser. Within _____ (___) business days after Purchaser receives from Seller notice of such condemnation proceedings, Purchaser may elect to rescind this Agreement by delivering to Seller written notice of rescission, whereupon the Earnest Money shall be promptly refunded to Purchaser. If Purchaser elects to proceed and to consummate the purchase despite the institution of condemnation proceedings, or if it appears that the value of the proposed taking, including any consequential damages to the Property shall total $_____ or less, there shall not be reduction in or abatement of the purchase price, and Seller shall assign to the Purchaser all of the Seller's right, title, and interest in and to any award or settlement made or to be made in the condemnation proceedings, provided that any portion of the condemnation award allocable to loss of income related to the Property shall be allocated between Purchaser and Seller in a manner consistent with applicable provisions of the Development Agreement.

14. <u>Broker's Commission.</u>

A. Purchaser shall be responsible for and shall pay at its sole cost and expense, and shall indemnify and hold Seller harmless with respect to, all real estate or business brokerage fees, finder's fees, or any other fees or commissions of any kind or nature. ("Brokerage Fees") due or owing as a result of the execution or performance of this Purchase Agreement to any party who has dealt with Purchase Agreement in connection with the transaction contemplated by this Purchase Agreement. Purchaser shall indemnify Seller against, and shall hold Seller harmless with respect to any and all claims, damages, costs, or expenses of or for such Brokerage Fees and shall pay all of Seller's costs of defending any action or lawsuit brought to recover any such Brokerage Fees by any parties with whom Purchaser has dealt, including reasonable attorney's fees.

B. Seller shall be responsible for and shall pay at its sole cost and expense, and shall indemnify and hold Purchaser harmless with respect to, all real estate or business brokerage fees, finder's fees, or any other fees or commissions of any kind of nature ("Brokerage Fees") due or owing as a result of the execution or performance of this Purchase Agreement to any party who has dealt with Seller in connection with the transaction contemplated by this Purchase Agreement. Seller shall indemnify Purchaser against, and shall hold Purchaser harmless with respect to, any and all claims, damages, costs, or expenses of or for such Brokerage Fees and shall pay all of Purchaser's costs of defending any action or lawsuit brought to recover any such Brokerage Fees by any parties with whom Seller has dealt, including reasonable attorney's fees.

15. <u>Assignment.</u> Purchaser may assign its right, duties and obligations under this Purchase Agreement to any party without Seller's consent. Seller shall not assign its rights, duties, or obligations hereunder without prior written consent of Purchaser, such consent not to be unreasonably withheld.

16. <u>Survival.</u> All of the terms, covenants, conditions, representations, warranties, and agreements of the Purchase Agreement shall survive and continue in full force and effect and shall be enforceable after the Closing.

17. <u>Notices.</u> Any notice or election required or permitted to be given or served by any party hereto upon any other party may be given or served by personal delivery, by delivery by any nationally recognized air courier service, including, but not limited to Federal Express, Airborne, or Purolator, or by U.S. mails. Any mailed notice shall be in a sealed wrapper, registered or certified mail, return receipt requested, postage prepaid, properly addressed, deposited in an official U.S. mail box or post office. Notices shall be sent as follows:

If to Purchaser: _____

_____

_____

_____

Attn: _____

If to Purchaser's Attorney: _____
_____
_____
_____

Attn: _____

If to Seller: _____
_____
_____
_____

Attn: _____

If to Seller's Attorney: _____
_____
_____
_____

Attn: _____

Each notice sent by U.S. mail or air courier shall be deemed to have been given on the date of deposit of same in U.S. Mails, postage prepaid, *etc.,* or on a date of deposit of same with any aforedescribed air courier, respectively; any such mailed notice shall be deemed to have been received on the date of delivery or date of refusal to accept delivery as the case may be, as shown on the return receipt. Any party hereto may change its address for the service of notice hereunder by giving written notice of said change to the other party hereunder, in the manner above specified, which change shall be effective _____ (_____) days after receipt of such notice.

18. Captions. The paragraph headings or captions appearing in this Agreement are for convenience only, and are not a part of this Agreement, and are not to be considered in interpreting this Agreement.

19. Entire Agreement; Modification. This Agreement constitutes the entire and complete agreement between the parties hereto and supersedes any prior oral or written agreement between the parties with respect to the Property. It is expressly agreed that there are no verbal understandings or agreements which in any way change the terms, covenants, and conditions herein set forth, and that no modification of this Agreement shall be effective, unless made in writing and duly executed by the parties hereto, provided, however, a waiver of any condition or obligation need be executed by the party for whose benefit the only condition or obligation was imposed, and further provided that a copy of any such unilaterally executed waiver shall be promptly delivered to the other party hereto in accordance with the notice provisions of this Agreement.

20. Binding Effect. All covenants, agreements, warranties, and provisions of this Agreement shall be binding upon and inure to the benefit of the parties hereto and their respective heirs, executors, administrators, personal representatives, successors, and permitted assigns.

21. Controlling Law. This Agreement has been made and entered into under the laws of the State of _____, and said laws shall control the interpretation thereof.

22. Termination of Purchase Agreement. In addition to any other rights Purchaser may have under this Agreement, the parties agree as follows:

    A. Purchaser shall have until _____ in which to inspect the Subject Premises, the Plans and Specifications for the Improvements, and the Construction Loan Documents, and during which period Purchaser may, by written notice to Seller, elect to terminate this Agreement in Purchaser's sole discretion, and, in such event, all Earnest Money shall be refunded to Purchaser, and neither party shall have any further rights, duties, or obligations one to the other under this Agreement.

B. Seller shall have a period of _____ (_____) days from the effective date of this Agreement to deliver to Purchaser a certificate from the Lender which statement shall contain all information and agreements required by Paragraph 4(K) hereof, provided, however, that Seller shall remain obligated to deliver to Purchaser at closing the certificate required by Paragraph 4(K), which must be dated no sooner than _____ (___) days prior to the Date of Closing. In the event Seller is unable to timely procure and deliver this statement, as provided herein, at no cost or expense to Seller, Purchaser or Seller may unilaterally rescind this Agreement, all Earnest Money shall be refunded to Purchaser, and neither party shall have any further obligation hereunder.

23. Construction of Terms. Where appropriate, any word denoting the singular shall be deemed to denote the plural, and vice versa. Where appropriate, any word referring to one gender shall be deemed to include the other gender.

24. Improvements. The parties hereto acknowledge that _____ (_____) apartment units are currently under construction upon the Subject Premises by Seller in accordance with the Plans and Specifications. The apartment units together with all streets, utilities, amenities, personalty, and other improvements described in said Plans and Specifications are referred to in this Agreement as the "Improvements."

25. Additional Agreements. At the Closing hereunder, Purchaser, or its assigns, and Seller or its affiliates, shall enter into the following additional agreements and arrangements.

A. Purchaser and Seller shall enter into a Cash Flow Guaranty Agreement in the form of Exhibit "N" pursuant to which Purchaser shall pay to Seller a fee of $_____, payable $_____ at the Date of Closing, $_____ on _____, and $_____ on the Final Completion Date.

B. Seller and Purchaser shall enter into a Development Agreement in the form attached hereto as Exhibit "O," pursuant to which Seller shall be paid a fee of $_____, payable in full on the Final Completion Date.

C. Seller and Purchaser shall enter into a Management Agreement in the form attached hereto as Exhibit "P" and hereby made a part hereof, pursuant to which Seller shall be paid a fee of

_____.

D. Seller and Purchaser shall enter into a Non Competition Agreement in the form attached hereto as Exhibit "Q" and hereby made a part hereof pursuant to which Seller shall be paid a fee of $_____ payable on _____, in consideration of a valid and enforceable covenant against competition with the Business for a period of _____ years and within a radius of _____ miles of the property.

E. Seller and Purchaser shall enter into a Maintenance Agreement in the form attached hereto as Exhibit "R" and hereby made a part hereof pursuant to which Seller shall be paid a fee of $_____, payable on _____.

26. Evidence of Completion. Purchaser and Seller agree that a letter from the Lender's inspecting architect to the effect that the construction of the improvements has reached a specified percentage of completion will constitute evidence satisfactory to Purchaser and Seller for such purpose, if same is required under this Agreement regarding said level of completion, and that such a letter from the Lender's inspecting architect with certificates of occupancy for units or buildings shall constitute evidence of 100 percent completion of such units or buildings.

27. Effective Date. The effective date of this Agreement shall be the date on which the last party to sign this Agreement executes this Agreement, which effective date shall be inserted in the introductory paragraph hereof.

IN WITNESS WHEREOF, the parties hereto have caused this instrument to be executed effective as of the day and year first written above.

<u>SELLER:</u>

Witness _____

Notarized _____

_____

By: _____

Title: _____

Corporate Seal

<u>PURCHASER:</u>

Witness _____

Notarized _____

_____

By: _____

Dated: _____

Corporate Seal

SCHEDULE OF EXHIBITS

A. Legal Description
B. Inventory
C. Rent Roll/Security Deposits/Copies of Leases
D. Construction Note
E. Construction Mortgage
F. Permanent Loan Mortgage
G. Bill of Sale
H. Zoning Letter
I. Utility Letters
J. Service Contracts
K. Form Lease
L. Insurance Policies
M. Soils Test
N. Cash Flow Guarantee Agreement
O. Development Agreement
P. Management Agreement
Q. Non Competition Agreement
R. Maintenance Agreement

DEVELOPMENT AGREEMENT: WHAT TO DO WHEN TAKING TITLE BEFORE CONSTRUCTION IS COMPLETED

If the Purchaser is buying a property that will be constructed or is currently under construction, and will take title prior to completion, a development agreement should be entered into. This document will define all the rights and obligations of the parties. The following are the areas that should be addressed.

1. Definition of the terms
   a. Completion of the property
   b. Construction loan
   c. General contractor
   d. Loan documents
   e. Plans and specifications
   f. Permanent loan
2. Development Obligations
   a. Acceptance of the general contractor
   b. Acceptance of the plans and specifications
   c. Acceptance of other pre-signature items
   d. Construction/operating projections
   e. Construction of the property
   f. Time of completion of construction
   g. Unit delivery schedule
      1. Construction penalty
   h. Proceeds of construction loan
   i. Copies of correspondence and documents to owner
   j. Reports to owner
   k. As-built survey
   l. Construction and financing costs
   m. Liens of third parties
   n. Closing permanent loan
   o. Insurance
   p. Punch list work: final completion
   q. Landscaping
   r. Grading
   s. Clean-up
   t. Debris
   u. Termite inspection
   v. Inventory
   w. Lease-up services
3. Development Representations, Covenants, and Warranties
4. Possession
5. Right to cure
6. Default; remedies

7. Warranty

8. Attorney's fees

9. Notice of claims

10. Independent contractor

11. Development fee

12. Miscellaneous

13. List of exhibits

SAMPLE RESIDENTIAL DEVELOPMENT AGREEMENT

STATE OF _____

COUNTY OF_____

THIS AGREEMENT is made and entered into as of the _____ day of _____. 19_____, by and between _____ whose address is _____ (herein referred to as "Owner"), and _____, a _____ whose address is _____ (herein referred to as the "Developer").

WITNESSETH:

WHEREAS, Developer closed a construction loan from _____ ("Lender") on _____, 19 ___, in the original principal amount of $_____ to finance the construction and development of a _____ unit residential apartment complex (the "Improvements") on a tract of land briefly described as approximately _____ acres in _____ County, _____ (the "Land"), which Land is more particularly described on Exhibit "A" attached hereto and incorporated herein by this reference, said Land, Improvements, and related personalty as described in the below defined Plans and Specifications being collectively referred to herein as the "Property";

WHEREAS, Developer commenced construction of the Improvements on or about _____, 19___;

WHEREAS, Developer, as Seller, and Owner as Purchaser, executed that certain purchase agreement, dated _____, 19___, (the "Contract"), under the terms of which Developer agreed to sell the Property to said Purchaser or to certain permitted assignees of Purchaser;

WHEREAS, Owner will close simultaneously with the execution hereof the acquisition of the Property from Developer pursuant to the Contract;

WHEREAS, Developer is required by the Contract to execute at the closing thereunder this Development Agreement as a condition precedent to consummation of the purchase of the Property by Owner;

NOW, THEREFORE, in consideration of the mutual covenants contained herein and other good and valuable considerations, the parties hereto covenant and agree as follows:

1. <u>DEFINITIONS.</u> The terms used herein shall be defined as follows:

(a) "Completion of the Property" or "Completion" shall be deemed to have occurred when all of the following have occurred: the Lender's Inspecting Architect has issued a certificate certifying that construction of the Property has been one hundred percent (100%) completed in accordance with the Plans and Specifications; and certificates of occupancy or the equivalent thereof for the entire Property have been issued by the appropriate governmental authority or authorities having jurisdiction over the Property. The term "Completion" as used in referring to the individual apartment units comprising the Property shall be deemed to have occurred following the later of the date of issuance of the certificate of occupancy for such unit or the date on which such unit is habitable and in rent-ready condition as certified by _____.

(b) "Construction Loan" shall refer to the loan for financing of the construction of the Property, as evidenced by a certain Note in the original principal amount of $_____, dated _____, 19___, executed by Developer payable to the order of Lender. The Construction Loan is secured by that certain Deed to Secure Debt and Security Agreement, dated _____, 19___, executed by Developer to _____, in favor of Lender, recorded in Book __, page __, in the office of the Clerk of _____ County, _____ and by that certain Assignment of Leases and Rents of even date therewith, also executed by Developer and recorded in Book __, page __, of said county clerk's office. Copies of said Note, Deed to Secure Debt, Assignment of Leases and Rents, and all other collateral security documents executed in connection therewith are attached hereto as Exhibit B and hereby made a part hereof.

(c) "General Contractor" shall refer to _____, a _____ corporation.

(d) "Loan Documents" shall refer to the Note, the Deed of Trust and Security Agreement, and the Assignment of Leases and Rents, together with all other instruments executed in connection therewith, as the same have been amended through the date hereof, which collectively evidence and secure the Construction Loan.

(e) "Plans and Specifications" shall be deemed to mean those drawings and specifications described in Exhibit "C" attached hereto and hereby made a part hereof.

(f) "Permanent Loan" shall refer to a first-in-lien priority mortgage loan from Lender to Developer secured by the property in the amount of $_____ to be funded by Lender pursuant to its commitment, dated _____ issued to Developer (the "Construction/Permanent Loan Commitment"), for the purpose of converting the Construction Loan. A copy of the Construction/Permanent Loan Commitment is attached hereto as Exhibit "D" and hereby made a part hereof. The term "Permanent Commitment" and "Permanent Loan" shall also refer to any commitment and loan substituted therefore, respectively, pursuant to Section 2(h) below.

(g) "Escrow Agent" shall refer to _____ whose address is _____.

(h) "Title Insurer" shall refer to _____ acting by and through _____, as its issuing agent.

2. DEVELOPMENT OBLIGATIONS

(a) Acceptance of General Contractor. Attached hereto as Exhibit "E" and hereby made a part hereof are true and correct copies of all of Developer's agreements with the General Contractor which in any manner relate to the construction of the Improvements (collectively, the "Construction Agreement"). Developer represents and warrants that: (i) the General Contractor has obtained a Completion and Performance Bond from a surety company reasonably acceptable to Owner naming Developer and Owner as joint obligees thereunder guaranteeing completion of construction of the improvements in accordance with the Plans and Specifications, all as herein provided; or (ii) that Developer has obtained from the General Contractor an unconditional letter of credit in favor of Owner in an amount not less than ten percent (10%) of the total construction cost of the Improvements provided for in the Construction Agreement.

(b) Acceptance of Plans and Specifications. Attached hereto as Exhibit "F" and hereby made a part hereof is a letter from _____, licensed professional engineers, acknowledging that said firm has reviewed the Plans and Specifications and that they are in accordance with _____. Developer represents and warrants that the Plans and Specifications are in accordance with all state and local building codes. Subject to the foregoing, Owner hereby accepts the Plans and Specifications.

(c) Acceptance of Other Pre-signature Items. Attached hereto as Exhibit "G" and hereby made a part hereof is a list of all other supportive data delivered to Owner prior to date of execution of this Agreement. Developer represents and warrants that each of said items is true, correct, and complete.

(d) Construction/Operating Projections. Developer has prepared a pro-forma analysis, a copy of which is attached hereto as Exhibit "H" and hereby made a part hereof, relating to the development and operation of the Improvements as an apartment project (the "Proforma"). The Proforma sets forth: (i) a unit completion schedule; (ii) a bimonthly completion percentage schedule; (iii) a monthly construction line-item cost schedule; (iv) a unit rent-up schedule; (v) a monthly rent-up proforma; (vi) a line item income and expense analysis; and (vii) a rental and marketing plan (each of the foregoing items being attached hereto as Exhibits "H-1" through "H-7" and hereby made a part hereof). Developer represents and warrants that it alone owns all rights in and to the Proforma, and that this Agreement may be performed without infringing upon any plans, trade or service marks, any other proprietary information, and any other rights of third parties.

(e) Construction of the Property. Developer, at its sole expenses, shall construct (or cause to be constructed by the General Contractor) the Improvements on the Land in strict accordance with the Plans and Specifications and all state and local building codes, OSHA rules and regulations, and any and all other applicable laws and regulations and with applicable requirements of the Construction Loan and Permanent Loan and shall procure and install therein all personalty required by the Plans and Specifications and shall cause Completion to timely occur. Developer shall obtain at its sole cost and expense all permits and necessary government approvals required for the construction and operation of the Improvements as an apartment project. All construction work shall be performed in a good and workmanlike manner so that the Improvements, when complete, shall be constructed in accordance with industry standards and the other requirements of this Agreement. Developer, at its sole expense, shall obtain from all contractors and other third parties performing work or rendering services relating to the Improvements written guarantees from such parties that all work performed by them shall reflect good workmanship, shall meet all industry standards, and shall be in compliance with this Agreement, all applicable building codes, OSHA rules and regulations, and other applicable laws. Developer shall, as between Developer and Owner, bear all risks of cost overruns and contingencies, including, by way of illustration and not by way of limitation, weather delays, unforeseen soil or subterranean conditions, strikes, lockouts, delays of all kinds whatsoever, increase in prices of materials and labor, and damage to work in progress by fire or other catastrophe. Developer will not agree to any modification of the Plans and Specifications without Owner's prior written consent, provided, however, such consent shall not be required for nonmaterial changes or any change whose expense is agreed in advance to be borne by Owner. "Nonmaterial changes" as used in the preceding sentence shall be deemed to refer to changes which are nonstructural in nature, which result in cost reduction without a decrease in quality of materials used, or which involve costs increases not in excess of $_____ per change order. All change orders in excess of $_____ shall be signed by Owner and shall be in the form of Exhibit "I" attached hereto and hereby made a part hereof. In all events Owner's approval shall not be unreasonably withheld. Notwithstanding any contrary provision of this Section 2(d), Developer shall submit to Owner copies of all proposed change orders in advance regardless of whether Owner is required to sign or has the right under this Section to approve same, and Owner shall have a reasonable time in which to review such order. If Developer permits material changes in the Plans and Specifications without Owner's prior approval as above required, then Developer shall be solely responsible for all cost increases resulting therefrom. Developer shall within seven (7) days of their issuance deliver all certificates of occupancy obtained for the Improvements, and in addition Developer shall, not later than thirty (30) days following the Initial Completion Date, as hereinafter defined, execute a Bill of Sale with general warranty of title to Owner for the personalty required by the Plans and Specifications and an assignment of all warranties and guarantees, covering all property and equipment installed pursuant to the Plans and Specifications (setting forth serial numbers of all items of property or equipment bearing such numbers), and all the personalty and/or services of third parties performing work or rendering services relating to the Property.

(f) Time of Completion of Construction. Developer shall cause Completion of construction of the Improvements strictly in accordance with the Plans and Specifications, including any required off-site improvements, no later than the maturity date of the Construction Loan, the latest permissible funding date under the Construction/Permanent Loan Commitment or _____, whichever shall first occur (the "Funding Date"). The ___ units currently under construction on the Land will be delivered as specified in Section 2(a) below. Said Funding Date for the Property as a whole and the Required Completion Dates (as described below) for delivery of groups of units shall be extended for periods equal to time of delays caused by acts of God, fire, riots, or any other events which Developer reasonably could not have prevented (other than the normal risks of construction work or weather delays, work stoppages, labor disputes, etc.) provided, however, that in no event will such Funding Date, or any Required Completion Date for any of the units, be extended beyond the maturity date of the Construction Loan as the same may be extended, or the expiration date of the Construction/Permanent Loan Commitment, as the same may be extended.

(g) Unit Delivery Schedule. Subject to Developer's right to extensions for the reasons described in Section 2(f) above, the Developer shall effect Completion of the _____ apartment units on the following schedule:

Number of Units To Be Completed	Required Completion Date
_____ Units	_____
_____ Units	_____
_____ Units	_____
_____ Units	_____
_____ Units	_____
_____ Total	

If Developer fails to effect Completion of any unit by the applicable Required Completion Date, as the same may be extended pursuant to Section 2(f) above, then Developer shall pay Owner a penalty of $_____ per diem for such unit from said Required Completion Date, as the same may be extended as aforesaid, until the date on which Completion of such unit is effected. All past due amounts shall bear interest at the rate of ____ percent per annum. All such penalties shall be payable, without interest, by Developer not later than thirty (30) days after Completion of the last unit. Notwithstanding the foregoing if completion of all units does not take place in the calendar year in which the latest Required Delivery Date is to occur an interim payment shall be made on December 20 of such year for all units on which penalties are accruing. Such interim payment shall not relieve the Developer of its obligation to pay all penalties which accrue thereafter.

(h) Proceeds of Construction Loan. Developer shall be entitled to draw down and receive proceeds of the Construction Loan disbursed by Lender in accordance with the terms of the Loan Documents; and neither Developer nor Owner shall agree to any modification of the Loan Documents without the prior written consent of the other party hereto. Developer shall comply with all of the terms and provisions of the Loan Documents, except to the extent that compliance therewith is waived in writing by Lender and by Owner, Owner hereby agreeing not to unreasonably withhold its consent to any such waiver by the Lender. All Construction Loan draw requests shall be delivered to Owner not less than five (5) days before their submission to Lender. All amounts drawn under the Loan Documents shall be held in a joint bank account established by Developer and Owner. Owner shall be an authorized signatory on such account, but shall not draw upon said account unless Developer is in default hereunder.

(i) Copies of Correspondence and Documents to Owner. Developer shall submit to Owner copies of all draw requests and all supporting documentation (as may be required by Lender) at the same time Developer submits the same to Lender. Developer shall forward to Owner copies of correspondence to or from Lender related to the Property.

(j) Reports to Owner. During the construction of the Improvements, Developer shall, at the times indicated hereinbelow, furnish to the Owner the following:

(i) On the first and fifteenth day of each month prior to the Funding Date, a bimonthly Completion Schedule in the form of Exhibit "J" attached hereto and hereby made a part hereof;

(ii) On Friday of each week during the construction period, a "Bar Chart" in the form of Exhibit "K" attached hereto and hereby made a part hereof;

(iii) Not later than ten (10) days following the end of each calendar month during the Construction period, a cash flow statement covering the previous month in the form of Exhibit "L" attached hereto and hereby made a part hereof;

(iv) Not later than two (2) days following receipt, copies of all inspection reports of Lender; and

(v) Not later than five (5) days following each month (or earlier if more frequent draws are requested), copies of all lien waivers submitted by the General Contractor.

(k) As-built Survey. Not later than ten (10) days following Completion of the Property, the Developer shall furnish to the Owner an as-built survey at Developer's sole expense. Such survey shall comply with all survey requirements of Owner and Lender and shall be certified to Owner, Lender, Developer and Title Insurer, to Lender's and Owner's satisfaction.

(l) Construction and Financing Costs. Developer shall be fully and completely responsible for achieving Completion of the Property at its sole expense and for paying, without seeking reimbursement thereof from Owner, all costs associated with such Completion to the extent such funds are not available from the proceeds of the Construction Loan and/or the Permanent Loan, including, without limitation, the actual costs of construction, Construction Loan interest, and any carrying or financing charges in connection with the Construction Loan, appraisal fees, surveys, taxes, title insurance associated with the Loan Documents, and all other costs or changes required to achieve Completion of the Property. Developer hereby agrees to indemnify Owner and hold Owner harmless from all costs, expenses, penalties or damages relating to the completion of the property.

(m) Liens of Third Parties. If any lien in connection with the construction and/or development of the Property of any type is filed against the Property or any portion thereof, Developer shall cause the same to be released or bonded by a surety company acceptable to the Title Insurer within five (5) days of the date on which such lien is filed or such shorter period as may be required by Lender, or shall make a cash deposit with Title Insurer in such amount as may be reasonably required by Title Insurer as precondition to its insuring title to the Property without any exception for any such lien, and Developer hereby agrees to indemnify and hold Owner harmless with respect to any such lien. Upon completion, Developer shall deliver to Owner an affidavit sufficient under _____ law to extinguish any lien rights which may exist in favor of materialmen, suppliers and contractors.

(n) Closing Permanent Loan. (To be supplied following review of the loan documents.)

(o) Insurance. Developer shall maintain during the terms hereof, at Developer's sole expense, the following types of insurance:

(i) Builder's Risk Insurance. Builder's risk and other hazard insurance as Lender may reasonably require, provided such insurance is available, with standard noncontributing mortgagee clauses and standard subrogation clauses, such insurance to be in such amounts and form and by such companies as shall be approved by Lender, shall name the Owner as an additional named insured, and original signed copies of such policies, together with appropriate endorsements thereto, evidence of payment of premiums thereon, and written agreement by the insurer or insurers therein to give Owner ten (10) days prior written notice of intent to cancel, shall be delivered to owner after Owner's request therefor. Developer will maintain said insurance coverage in full force and effect at all times until the Completion of the Property or the obtaining of the insurance described in the immediately following subparagraph (ii).

(ii) Hazard Insurance. Fire and extended coverage insurance and such other hazard insurance as Lender may reasonably require, provided such insurance is available, with standard subrogation clauses, such insurance to be in such amount and form and by such companies as shall be approved by the Lender, and originally signed copies of such policies, together with appropriate endorsements thereto, evidence of payment of premiums thereon, and written agreement by the insurer or insurers therein to give Owner ten (10) days prior written notice of intention to cancel, shall be promptly delivered to Owner after Owner's request therefor; Developer will obtain such insurance immediately upon Completion of the Property, provided that at all times the Property shall be covered by the insurance described in either Section 2 (o) (i) or this Section 2 (o) (ii).

(iii) Public Liability and Worker's Compensation Insurance. A certificate from an insurance company indicating that Owner and Developer are covered by public liability insurance and a certificate from an insurance company indicating that Developer is covered by worker's compensation insurance, both of which certificates must be reasonably satisfactory to Developer, both as to form and content and must contain the written agreement of the insurer(s) to give Owner ten (10) days prior written notice of its intention to cancel.

(p) "Punch List" work: Final Completion. (a) Within seven (7) days of Completion of the Property, representatives of Developer and Owner shall meet and conduct a joint inspection of the Property and the Improvements. Based upon such inspections, Owner shall prepare and deliver to Developer a written "punch list" of all matters to be completed before the Property and Improvements have been fully completed in accordance with the Plans and Specifications. Developer shall complete all of such items to Owner's sole satisfaction within _____ (___) days thereafter (the date on which all such items shall have been completed shall be hereinafter referred to as the "Final Completion Date"). (b) Pending completion of all punch list items, Owner may withhold $_____ from amounts payable to Developer on the Final Completion Date pursuant to the Agreements described in Paragraph ____ of that certain Purchase Agreement, dated _____, 19___, between Owner and Developer. Such amount plus all interest accrued thereto during the hold-back period shall be paid to Developer not later than five (5) days following completion of all punch list items to the satisfaction of Owner. (c) Not later than _____ (____) days following the Final Completion Date of each of the following items, Developer shall deliver to Owner each of the following items:

    (i)   Compaction studies of the soil on the Property;

    (ii)   Concrete strength tests for each pour;

    (iii) Compaction studies of all soils underneath concrete slabs;

    (iv) Compaction studies of all paving; and

    (v)   Asphalt/concrete driveway composition test.

(q) Landscaping. Attached hereto as Exhibit "M" and hereby made a part hereof are the plans for the landscaping of the Property. Developer shall initiate and continue all landscaping maintenance as soon as any landscaping work is completed, irrespective of the status of construction of the Improvements. Of the total construction cost of the Improvements, Developer shall allocate an allowance of $_____ per apartment unit to be applied to the purchase and installation of grass, plant materials, and the labor costs incurred in connection therewith (but not for the cost of grading, landscaping ties, and site preparation, which shall be borne by the General Contractor). In performing its duties under this paragraph, Developer shall during the months of _____ through _____ cut the grass, trim all shrubs and beds, and take such other maintenance steps as Owner shall request at not less than weekly intervals. During the months of _____ through _____ said maintenance services shall be performed at intervals of not less than every _____ days. Developer shall water all landscaped areas at such intervals as Owner shall request, and shall keep a written record of all landscaping services performed pursuant to this Paragraph. In addition, Developer shall warrant all landscaping and plans for a period of one (1) year following the later of the Final Completion Date or the date on which all drainage or erosion problems discovered during said one year period are definitely corrected.

(r) Grading. Developer will cause surface of yard of graded areas immediately adjacent to the sidewalks to be at approximately the same elevation as the top surface of such sidewalks.

(s) Clean-up. Developer, upon Completion of the work under this Agreement, shall remove from the Property all waste material or rubbish brought thereon in connection with construction of the Improvements, as well as all tools, scaffolding, and surplus construction materials and shall leave all improvements in "broom-clean" condition.

(t) Debris. Not later than the Final Completion Date, Developer shall remove all debris from all surface areas. Developer shall repair or restore all areas used for the burial of debris if such work is required for a period of _____ months following the Final Completion Date.

(u) Termite Inspection. Developer shall furnish, at its sole cost and expense, a termite inspection report certifying that the Property is free from damage and/or infestation by termites and other wood destroying insects.

(v) Inventory. On the Final Completion Date, Developer shall deliver to Owner possession of all the items of personal property set forth in Exhibit "N" attached hereto and hereby made a part hereof. To the extent that the personal property delivered does not meet the requirements of said Exhibit, Owner shall be entitled to a cash credit of $_____ to be paid on the Final Completion Date.

(w) Lease-up Services. Developer agrees to use its best efforts to lease the units to tenants when and as they are completed and habitable. As units become available for occupancy, Developer shall use its best efforts to lease the same pursuant to written leases having an original term of six months, calling for security deposits of at least $_____ for a one-bedroom unit, $_____ for a two-bedroom unit, and $_____ for a three-bedroom unit; and having a monthly rent of $_____, $_____ and $_____ for one, two, and three-bedroom units respectively. Developer may elect not to collect a security deposit for newly leased units, in which event Developer shall pay to Owner on the Final Completion Date, a sum equal to the total amount of all security deposits which were not collected by Developer. All security deposits actually collected by Developer on Owner's behalf and not refunded to tenants shall also be turned over to Developer or its designee on the Final Completion Date.

3. <u>DEVELOPMENT, REPRESENTATIONS, COVENANTS AND WARRANTIES.</u> Developer hereby represents, covenants, and warrants that:

(a) Developer shall not effect, consent to, acquiesce in or approve any change order with respect to the Plans and Specifications without the prior written approval of Owner other than nonmaterial change orders as the same are defined in Section 2(e) hereinabove. Developer shall deliver to Owner a copy of any proposed material change order together with such other information as may be reasonably required for Owner to understand the reasons for and the nature of the change order. Any such change order shall be deemed approved by Owner unless Owner gives written notice of its disapproval within five (5) business days after receipt of the proposed change order. The Owner shall pay the expense of effecting any change order required by the Owner to the extent that the same results in an increase in construction costs. Developer shall also deliver to Owner copies of all nonmaterial change orders promptly after execution of same.

(b) Developer will maintain accurate records for all costs and expenses in connection with construction and development of the Property, including, without limitation, labor, materials, taxes, fees and other expenses incurred by it. Such records will be available to the Owner for review and reproduction at any reasonable time.

(c) Developer warrants that the improvements will, on Completion, comply with all applicable legal and building requirements, and Developer shall exercise its best reasonable efforts to insure that all work performed in connection with the development of the Property will comply with all state and local building requirements.

4. <u>POSSESSION.</u> As of the date hereof, as between Owner and Developer, Owner is entitled to full right of possession of the Property, provided, however, that Developer, its agents, representatives, and its business invitees, shall have and are hereby granted a license to come upon the Land for the purpose of performing any and all of Developer's obligations under this Agreement and under all other agreements of even date between Owner and Developer and related to the Property.

5. <u>RIGHT TO CURE.</u> As a condition precedent to exercising any remedy hereunder, under any instrument executed in connection herewith or otherwise available at law or in equity after the occurrence of any default by Developer under this Agreement, Owner shall give Developer written notice of such default and Developer shall be privileged to cure any such default within ten (10) days after receipt by Developer of written notice of such default from Owner in the case of any monetary default, or within thirty (30) days after receipt by Developer of written notice of such default from Owner in the case of any nonmonetary default, provided, however, in the case of any nonmonetary default which cannot be fully cured within said 30 day period, then Developer shall have been deemed to have cured such default if Developer commences appropriate curative action within said 30 day period and diligently prosecutes the same to completion thereafter. Notwithstanding the foregoing, the curative period under this Section 5 shall in no effect extend beyond the expiration of any curative or grace period provided for in the Loan Documents in the case of any default hereunder which is also a default hereunder, and is declared to be a default under the Loan Documents.

6. <u>DEFAULT; REMEDIES.</u> In the event of any default of Developer's obligations hereunder, and upon the expiration of any cure period provided for in paragraph 5 hereof, Owner may at its sole option, elect any or all of the remedies set forth below:

(a) Owner may assume Developer's role and take full charge of Completion of the Improvements and shall charge back to Developer any and all expenses incurred by Owner in connection therewith;

(b) Owner may set off against amounts otherwise due Developer from Owner any payments provided for under this Agreement or under that certain Purchase Agreement dated _____, 19___, between Developer, as Seller, and Owner, as Purchaser, and all agreements entered into pursuant thereto.

The election by Owner to exercise any of the foregoing remedies shall not relieve Developer of any liability to Owner arising from any breach of Developer's obligations under this Agreement and all damages suffered by Owner as a consequence thereof.

7. <u>WARRANTY.</u> Developer will correct, complete, repair, replace, or cause the corrections, completion, repair, or replacement of any defective condition or materials or workmanship in or on the Improvements and landscaping identified and reasonably requested by Owner in writing delivered to Developer within one (1) year after later of the Final Completion Date or the date on which all of the punchlist items have been completed pursuant to paragraph 2(p) hereof. Upon Completion, Developer shall also assign and deliver to Owner all operating manuals, warranties, and guarantees of or pertaining to appliances, water heaters, furnaces, air conditioners, roofs, paving, and any other items to which Developer is then entitled from any contractor, subcontractor, materialman, supplier, etc.

8. <u>ATTORNEY'S FEES.</u> In the event of any breach hereunder by either party hereto, each party shall be responsible for paying his own attorney's fees.

9. <u>NOTICE OF CLAIMS.</u> If either party hereto claims compensation for any damages alleged to have been sustained by reason of any default under this Agreement by the other party hereto, the former shall exercise its best efforts to promptly notify the alleged defaulting party of such alleged default; provided, however, the failure to so notify the alleged defaulting party shall not constitute a waiver or any claim or cause of action.

10. <u>INDEPENDENT CONTRACTOR.</u> Developer shall be an independent contractor for all purposes during the construction of the Improvements, and all persons engaged in carrying out any of the Developer's obligations hereunder shall be the servants of the Developer or its subcontractors and not the servants or agents of the Owner. Developer shall indemnify and hold harmless Owner for worker's compensation and employment taxes and any and all claims of Developer's employees with respect thereto. The Owner shall not direct, supervise or control the work of the subcontractors and shall make all complaints or comments or requests for correction regarding same to Developer. Developer will indemnify the Owner and save it harmless from any and all liability to Developer's employees or any other third parties for personal injuries, property damage, or loss of life or property resulting from or in any way connected with the performance of this Agreement; provided, however, that the foregoing indemnification shall not apply to injuries or loss of life or damages to persons or property, the principal cause of which is the negligence of the Owner, its employees or agents except to the extent that insurance is available to cover said liabilities.

11. <u>DEVELOPMENT FEE.</u> In consideration of the services to be rendered hereunder by Developer, Owner shall pay Developer a development fee of $_____, which fee shall be payable in full on the Final Completion Date.

12. <u>MISCELLANEOUS.</u>

(a) This agreement constitutes the entire agreement between the parties hereto regarding the subject matter hereof, and it is understood and agreed that all undertakings and agreements heretofore made between these parties regarding the subject matter hereof are merged herein. This Agreement may not be changed orally, but only by an agreement in writing signed by the Owner and Developer. The parties hereto acknowledge that certain other agreements and instruments have been executed of even date herewith in connection with the sale of the Property by the Developer to Owner, which other agreements and instruments are listed on Exhibit "D" attached hereto and incorporated herein by this reference (the "Other Agreements"), but that such Other Agreements do not pertain to the matters covered by this Agreement.

(b) This Agreement shall be governed by and in accordance with the laws of the State of _____.

(c) Notices given pursuant to this Agreement shall be in writing, delivered in person by any nationally recognized courier service, such as, but not limited to, Federal Express, Airborne, or Purolator or by registered or certified mail, return receipt requested, addressed to the mailing addresses given herein, or such other address as shall have been specified in writing to the party giving notice. Mailed notices, if sent in the manner specified in the preceding sentence, shall be deemed to have been given upon date of deposit in U.S. Mail and to have been received on the date of delivery of or refusal of delivery, as the case may be, as shown on the return receipt. Notices transmitted via courier shall be deemed to have been given on date of deposit of such notice with such courier and to have been delivered upon date of delivery to address of addressee.

(d) Except as otherwise specified herein, the provisions of this Agreement shall inure to the benefit of and shall be binding upon the parties hereto and their respective heirs, successors and assigns and the legal representatives of their estates, as the case may apply.

IN WITNESS WHEREOF, the parties hereto have caused this Agreement to be signed and sealed by their duly authorized and acting officers as of the date first above written.

OWNER:

Witness _____

_____

A _____ Corporation

Notarized _____

By: _____

Title: _____

Corporate Seal

DEVELOPER:

Witness _____

_____

A _____ Corporation

Notarized _____

By: _____

Title: _____

Corporate Seal

SCHEDULE OF EXHIBITS

   A. Legal Description
   B. Construction Loan Documents
   C. Plans and Specifications
   D. Permanent Loan Documents
   E. AIA Construction Contract
   F. Plans and Specifications Letter from Engineering
   G. Supportive Data Prior to Contract Signing
   H. Construction/Operating Cost Projections
      1. Unit Completion Schedule
      2. Bimonthly Completion Percentage Schedule
      3. Construction Line Item Per Month Cost Schedule
      4. Unit Rent-up Schedule
      5. Month-by-Month Rent-up Proforma

6. Line Item Income and Expense Analysis

7. Rental Marketing Strategy

I. Change Orders

J. Completion Schedule (Biweekly)

K. Weekly Bar Chart

L. Monthly Construction Cash Flow by Line Item

M. Landscape Plans and Specification

N. Inventory

MANAGEMENT CONTRACT: HOW TO CONTRACT ON A TO-BE-BUILT PROPERTY

If the Purchaser is going to use a third party to manage the property, usually either the seller or a fee management company, a management contract should be negotiated and signed. This contract will spell out the rights and obligations of each party. The Purchaser who is contracting with the seller to manage the property during the rent-up period should make sure that the following items are included in the contract.

1. Establishment of Agency and Rental Responsibility

   a. Exclusive agency

   b. Terms of agreement

   c. Renting of development

   d. Agent orientation

2. Services to be Performed by Agent

   a. Agent acceptance of construction (if to-be-built)

   b. Preparation of annual budget

   c. Employment of on-site personnel

   d. Service contracts

   e. Maintenance and repair of the development

   f. Landscaping (if to-be-built)

   g. Apartment unit preparation

   h. Insurance

   i. Collection of moneys

   j. Agent disbursements

   k. Miscellaneous

      1. Records

      2. Monthly reports

      3. Annual report

      4. Notices from mortgagees

      5. Resident complaints

      6. Returns required by law

      7. Compliance with legal requirements

      8. Claims for tax abatements and eminent domain awards

  3. Relationship of Agent to Owner

    a. Compensation of agent

    b. Major repairs

    c. Agent's affiliates and subsidiaries

    d. Use and maintenance of development

    e. Separation of owner's moneys

    f. Expense of owner

    g. Termination

    h. Management start-up and market study agreement (if seller-management deal)

    i. Definition of gross income

    j. Assignment, etc.

  4. General Provisions

    a. Notices

    b. Entire agreement

    c. Successors and assigns

    d. Interpretation

    e. Qualification

    f. No recording

    g. No waiver

    h. Severability

    i. Captions and headings

  5. Exhibits

    a. Ground maintenance yearly program

    b. Property management checklist

SAMPLE MANAGEMENT AGREEMENT

THIS AGREEMENT made as of the ____ day of _____, 19____, between _____ (hereinafter called "Owner"), and _____, an _____ corporation, having its principal office at _____ (hereinafter called "Agent").

ARTICLE I

Establishment of Agency and Rental Responsibility

1.1 <u>Exclusive Agency.</u> Owner hereby appoints Agent, and Agent hereby accepts appointment, on the terms and conditions hereinafter provided as sole and exclusive renting and management agent of the apartment project known as _____, which, together with the land on which it is erected, is hereinafter referred to as the "Development."

1.2 <u>Term of Agreement.</u> This Agreement shall be in effect for a period of _____ (_____) year(s) beginning on _____ (or if under construction the term shall begin upon Substantial Completion of construction) and ending _____ (_____) years(s) thereafter and continuing thereafter for a like term, unless on or before _____ (_____) days prior to the expiration of any such period or any extension thereof, either party thereto shall notify the other in writing that it elects to terminate this Agreement, in which case this Agreement shall be thereby terminated on the last day of such period.

1.3 <u>Renting of Development.</u> Agent shall use its best efforts to lease vacant space and to keep the Development fully rented to desirable residents. Subject to reimbursement by Owner, Agent shall advertise the Development, or portions thereof, prepare and secure advertising signs, space plans, circular matter, and other forms of advertising. All inquiries for any leases or renewals or agreements for the rental of the Development, or portions thereof, shall be referred to Agent, and all negotiations connected therewith shall be conducted solely by or under the direction of Agent. Standard lease forms, renewal forms, and other agreement forms shall have the prior approval of Owner, and apartment units in the Development shall be leased to tenants meeting the following criteria: (a) each tenant shall have a monthly income equal to or greater than _____ (___) times the then current rental rate of the apartment unit; (b) each tenant shall furnish evidence that he has not been evicted from any prior residence; and (c) each tenant shall have a satisfactory credit record as evidenced by a credit report from any independent credit agency or a credit agency to which Agent belongs; in either case, said agency shall be approved by Owner. Agent shall not lease units of the Development for terms of less than _____ months or more than _____ months. At all times during the term hereof, Agent shall not grant to tenants concessions having a value of more than _____ months free rent for leases having a term of more ____ months. Subject to the foregoing and to compliance with the approved rental rates referred to in the Development Agreement dated _____, 19___, between Owner and Agent (the "Development Agreement"), or as otherwise determined by Owner, the use of approved forms and conformance with such credit and other criteria, Agent is authorized to execute, deliver, and renew leases on behalf of Owner.

1.4 <u>Agent Orientation.</u> In order to facilitate efficient operation, Agent will inform itself with respect to the layout, construction, location, character, plan, and operation of the lighting, heating, plumbing, and ventilating systems, as well as elevators, if any, and other mechanical equipment and systems in the Development. Copies of guarantees and warranties pertinent to the equipment of the Development and in force at the time of execution of this Agreement shall be furnished to Agent who will be responsible for their safekeeping. Agent will further be responsible for copies of construction plans and "as built" drawings furnished to it by Owner.

ARTICLE II

Services to be Performed by Agent

2.1 <u>Agent Acceptance of Construction.</u> Agent shall immediately ascertain the general condition of the Development and, if the accommodations there afforded have yet to be occupied for the first time, establish liaison with the general contractor to facilitate the completion by it of corrective work as yet to be done. Not later than _____ (___) days following the date hereof, Agent shall cause an inventory to be taken of all personal property including, but not limited to, appliances, furniture, office equipment, material, supplies, maintenance tools, spare parts and supplies, and any other major equipment or material belonging to the Development. A written report of the foregoing items shall be given to the Owner, and such report shall be an acknowledgment that Agent accepts delivery and responsibility for the listed equipment. Subsequent reports of unfinished corrective work shall be furnished to Owner, on a monthly basis, until all such work has been corrected on the open items allowed by Owner.

2.2 <u>Preparation of Annual Budget.</u> Not less than _____ (_____) days prior to the occupancy of any units in the Development, and thereafter at least _____ (_____) days before the beginning of each calendar year, Agent shall prepare and deliver to Owner an operating budget in preliminary draft form setting forth an itemized statement (with a detailed line item analysis) of the estimated monthly receipts and disbursements for the new year, based upon a proposed rent schedule (herein called the "Rent Schedule") included therein, and taking into account the general condition of the Development. At the same time the proposed operating budget is submitted, Agent shall also submit a plan for capital expenditures and major repairs which will be required during the next year. Such list shall describe work to be done, location, necessity, estimated cost, and the month of the year in which it is to be done. Following receipt of these documents, Owner shall respond promptly, indicating its approval or changes to be made. Not later than _____ (____) days after submission, and following approval of the new budget and the list of capital expenditures and repair work to be done, Agent shall submit the final approved budget, management plan, capital expenditure and repair lists which shall be and will constitute a standard to which Agent shall use best efforts to adhere in the operation of the Development.

2.3 <u>Employment of On-site Personnel.</u> On the basis of the budget referred to in Section 2.2, Agent shall investigate, hire, pay, supervise, and discharge the personnel necessary to be employed in order to properly maintain and operate the Development. Such personnel shall in every instance be deemed employees of Agent or independent contractors and not employees of Owner, who shall have no right to supervise or direct such employees, or independent contractors, but may require Agent to discharge or remove from employment at the Development such employees as Owner reasonably deems unsatisfactory. Agent and all personnel of Agent who handle or who are responsible for the handling of Owner's moneys shall, without expense to Owner, be bonded in favor of owner by a fidelity bond, if available, acceptable both to Agent and Owner, in an amount of not less than _____ (____) times the gross monthly rent roll of the Development and in a company acceptable to Agent and Owner. All salaries, wages and other compensation of personnel employed by Agent hereunder, including so-called fringe benefits, medical and health insurance, pension plans, social security taxes, workman's compensation insurance, and the like shall be deemed to be reimbursable expenses of Agent as evidenced by payrolls certified by Agent in such form and manner as may be required by Owner and delivered with the monthly reports referred to in Section 2.11b. Agent understands and agrees that its relationship to Owner is that of independent contractor and that it will not represent to anyone that Its relationship to Owner is other than that of independent contractor.

2.4 <u>Service Contracts.</u> Subject to approval by Owner and in any event not later than _____ (____) days from the date hereof, Agent shall make in the Owner's name contracts for water, electricity, gas, fuel, oil, telephone, vermin extermination, trash removal, and other necessary services, or such of them as Owner shall deem advisable. Agent shall also place orders in Agent's name for such equipment, tools, appliances, materials and supplies as are necessary to properly maintain the Development, subject to limitations of the current budget approved by the Owner. When taking bids or issuing purchase orders, Agent shall act at all times under the direction of Owner and shall be under a duty to secure for and credit to Owner any discounts, commissions or rebates obtainable as a result of such purchases.

2.5 <u>Maintenance and Repair of the Development.</u> Agent shall maintain the buildings, appurtenances, and grounds of the Development in accordance with industry standards for first-class apartments in the local area, including within such maintenance, without limitation thereof, interior and exterior cleaning, painting and decorating, plumbing, carpentry, and such other normal maintenance and repair work as may be desirable, subject to limitations of the current budget approved by Owner and any other reasonable limitations imposed by Owner in addition to those contained within such a budget. For any one item of repair or replacement, the expense incurred shall not exceed the sum of $_____ unless specifically authorized by Owner, or unless authorized by the approved management plan, excepting, however, that emergency repairs immediately necessary for the preservation and safety of the Development or to avoid the suspension of any service to the Development or danger to life or property may be made by Agent. Notwithstanding this authority as to emergency repairs, it is understood and agreed that Agent will confer immediately with Owner regarding every such expenditure and will furnish a complete written report as soon as possible. In any case where repair or replacement expense exceeds $1,500.00 for any one item, Agent shall secure written bids from at least three competent bidders and shall award the work under a written contract to the lowest qualified bidder. In the case of capital expenditures and repair work which have been approved as part of the approved management plan, such bids, if not already in hand, shall be secured before work is commenced.

2.6 <u>Landscaping.</u> From and after the date hereof Manager shall at owner's expense initiate and/or continue all landscape maintenance required for the Property. In performance of its duties under this Paragraph, Manager shall perform the landscaping maintenance program set forth in Exhibit "A" attached hereto and hereby made a part hereof. Manager shall water all landscaped areas at such intervals as Owner shall request. Manager shall keep written records specifying in reasonable detail all maintenance services performed pursuant to this Paragraph.

2.7 <u>Apartment Unit Preparation.</u> Manager shall restore all vacant units to rent-ready condition within _____ (____) days following vacation of such units by tenants, unless the Manager's post move-out inspection reveals that major items of equipment or materials must be replaced or repaired and such replacement or repair cannot be accomplished within _____ (____) days, in which event such unit shall be restored as soon as is reasonably practicable. In that connection, Manager shall clean all drapes and carpets, confirm that the plumbing, electricity, and all equipment, fixtures, and appliances are in good repair and proper working order and perform all touch-up painting and minor repairs required to place such unit in rent-ready condition.

2.8 <u>Insurance.</u> Until such time as construction of the improvements is 100 percent complete, as certified by the holder of the first mortgage on the Development, Agent shall maintain insurance pursuant to Paragraph _____ of the Development Agreement. After such time as described in the preceding sentence, Agent shall, unless otherwise directed by Owner, at the expense of the Owner, cause to be placed and kept in force all forms of insurance required by law and as communicated to Agent by Owner, including, but not limited to, workman's compensation insurance, public liability and property damage insurance, fire and extended coverage insurance, rent loss insurance, and such other reasonable protection as directed by Owner. All insurance coverage shall be placed with such companies, in such amounts, and with such beneficial interests appearing therein as shall be acceptable to Owner and otherwise be in conformity with the requirements of any mortgage of the Development. Such insurance shall include: comprehensive general liability insurance including personal injury liability and contractual liability, with minimum limits of at least $_____ for bodily injury and $_____ for property damage, or $_____ combined single limit for bodily injury or property damage. Agent is to be named in such policy as an additional insured; such policy is to be endorsed to provide _____ (_____) days written notice to Agent prior to any cancellation, and Agent is to be supplied with a copy of the policy. Agent shall promptly investigate and make a full written report to Owner as to all accidents, claims for damage relating to the ownership, operation, and maintenance of the Development, and any damage or destruction to the Development and the estimated cost of repair thereof, and shall prepare for approval by Owner any and all reports required by any insurance company in connection therewith. All such reports shall be filed with Owner promptly, and any report not so filed within ten days after the occurrence of any such accident, claim, damage or destruction shall be noted in the monthly report delivered to Owner pursuant to Section 2.11(b). Agent is authorized to settle any and all claims against insurance companies not in excess of $_____, arising out of any policies, including the execution of proofs of loss, the adjustment of losses, signing of receipts, and the collection of money. If the claim is greater than $_____, Agent shall not act without the approval of Owner.

2.9 <u>Collection of Moneys.</u> Agent shall collect all rent and other charges due from residents, from lessees of other nondwelling facilities in the Development, from concessionaires in consequence of the authorized operation of facilities in the Development maintained primarily for the benefit of residents and otherwise due Owner with respect to the Development in the ordinary course of business. Owner authorizes Agent to request, demand, collect, receive, and receipt for all such rent and other charges and to institute legal proceedings in the name of, and as an expense reimbursable by, Owner for the collections thereof and for the dispossession of residents and other persons from the Development, and such expense may include the engaging of counsel for any such matter. All moneys collected by Agent shall be forthwith deposited in the separate bank account referred to in the first sentence of Section 3.5.

2.10 <u>Agent Disbursements.</u> Agent shall, from the funds collected and deposited, cause to be disbursed regularly and punctually (1) the amounts reimbursable to Agent under Sections 2.3, 2.4, 2.5, 2.8, and 2.9 hereof; and (2) the amount required to be paid monthly pursuant to any mortgage of the Development, including therein amounts due under any mortgage for interest, amortization of principal, and for allocation to reserves or escrow funds; (3) the amount of all real estate taxes and other impositions levied by appropriate authorities which, if not escrowed with any mortgagee, shall be paid before interest begins to accrue thereon; and (4) amounts otherwise due and payable as operating expenses of the Development authorized to be incurred under the terms of this Agreement, including Agent's compensation. After disbursement as herein specified, any balance remaining shall be disbursed or transferred as generally or specifically directed from time to time by Owner. Notwithstanding the foregoing, until such time as the Negative Cash Flow Guarantee Agreement of even date herewith, between _____ and Owner (hereinafter the "Negative Cash Flow Guarantee"), is terminated, Agent shall make collections and disbursements, in accordance with the terms of the Negative Cash Flow Guarantee, and in accordance therewith any cash flow deficiencies shall be paid by _____, and any balance remaining after all disbursements shall be paid to _____.

    2.11 <u>Miscellaneous.</u>

    (a) <u>Records.</u> Agent shall maintain at its principal place of business in _____ a comprehensive system of office records, books, and accounts in a manner satisfactory to Owner. Owner and others designated by it shall have at all times access to such records, accounts, and books and to all vouchers, files and all other material pertaining to the Development and this Agreement, all of which Agent agrees to keep safe, available, and separate from any records not having to do with the Development. Agent shall furnish Owner with copies of all such documents and records upon written request from Owner.

Such records shall include, without limitation, separate repair records and copies of work orders for each unit and, with respect to each tenant, a file containing:

    (i)   A signed and fully completed tenant application showing such tenant's previous address, such tenant's current employment, and setting forth all of such tenant's bank accounts;

    (ii) A credit report for such tenant;

    (iii) An executed copy of the lease agreement with such tenant;

    (iv) All correspondence with or relating to such tenants; and

    (v) Copies of all repair records and work orders for such unit.

    (b) <u>Monthly Reports.</u> On or before the _____th day of each month, Agent shall render to owner the following reports pertaining to the previous month's activity:

    (i)   Balance sheet;

    (ii) Cash flow statement;

    (iii) Capital improvement status report (shall only be submitted if Agent receives a written request by Owner);

    (iv) Listing of accounts payable;

    (v) Report of tenant arrears, vacancies, and moneys retained in any custodial accounts as of the end of the previous month; and

    (vi) Report in letter form, commenting on important operational features which are not apparent from the financial reports, forecasts of changes in operations or physical conditions, and significant variances from the approved management plan.

For purposes of this section, a fiscal month shall mean the period beginning on the first day of each calendar month, and ending on the last day of the calendar month.

    (c) <u>Quarterly Reports.</u> On or before the _____ day of the end of each quarter, Agent shall render to Owner the following reports pertaining to the previous quarter's activity:

    (i)   Complete market studies of at least _____ (____) market comparables.

    (ii) Complete traffic, move out, and advertising budget analysis for the past quarter.

(d) <u>Annual Report.</u> Within _____ (___) days after the end of each calendar year, Agent shall deliver to Owner a profit and loss statement showing the results of operations for that year and a balance sheet for the Development as of the end of that year.

(e) <u>Notices from Mortgagees.</u> All notices from any mortgagee claiming any default in any mortgage on the Development, and any other notice from any mortgagee not of a routine nature, shall be forthwith delivered by Agent to Owner. Owner shall also be kept informed at all times of communications from mortgagees concerning assignments of mortgages, extension of debt service moratoriums, and other matters of a similar nature.

(f) <u>Resident Complaints.</u> Agent shall maintain businesslike relationships with residents of the units in the Development, whose service requests shall be received, logged, and considered in systematic fashion in order to show the action taken with respect to each. Complaints of a serious nature shall, after thorough investigation, be reported to Owner with appropriate recommendation.

(g) <u>Returns Required by Law.</u> Agent shall execute and file punctually when due all notices, forms, reports, and returns required by law relating to the employment of personnel and to the operation of the Development, excluding federal, state, and local income tax returns.

(h) <u>Compliance with Legal Requirements.</u> Agent shall take such action as may be necessary to comply with any and all orders or requirements affecting the Development by any federal, state, county, or municipal authority having jurisdiction thereover, and orders of the board of fire underwriters or other similar bodies, subject to the same limitation contained in Section 2.5 of this Article in connection with the making of repairs and alterations. Agent shall promptly, and in no event later than seventy-two (72) hours from the time of its receipt, notify Owner in writing of all such orders and notices or requirements. Agent shall cause any such order or requirement to be complied with, provided the cost does not exceed $_____ without Owner's approval; provided, however, Agent shall not take any such action as long as Owner has given notice to agent it is contesting, or as has affirmed its intention to contest, and promptly institutes proceedings contesting any such order or requirement. Notwithstanding the foregoing, if the failure to comply promptly with any such order or requirement would or might expose Agent to criminal liability, Agent shall have the right to terminate this Agreement as provided in Paragraph 3.7 hereof if it believes it is subject to criminal liability.

(i) <u>Claims for Tax Abatements and Eminent Domain Awards.</u> When requested by Owner from time to time, Agent shall, without charge or reimbursement, except for out-of-pocket expenses, render advice and assistance to Owner in the negotiation and prosecution of all claims for the abatement of property and other taxes affecting the Development and for awards for taking by eminent domain affecting the Development.

(j) Agent shall provide Owner with all items specified on Exhibit "B," attached hereto and hereby made a part hereof, at the intervals indicated thereon.

ARTICLE III

Relationship of Agent to Owner

3.1 <u>Compensation of Agent.</u> Owner agrees to pay the Agent for all services performed under this Agreement a fee computed and payable monthly in the amount of _____ percent (___%) of the "gross income," as hereinafter defined, for the month in question. Such fee shall be due and payable on or before the _____th day of each month with respect to gross income received during the immediately preceding month. The management fee payable hereunder shall not commence to accrue or to be payable until such time as the Negative Cash Flow Guarantee has terminated and is no longer in force or effect.

3.2 <u>Major Repairs.</u> Agent agrees that all work in the making of any and all major repairs, improvements, additions, or alterations costing more than $_____ that cannot be handled by employees of Agent shall be done under written bid and under written contract made with the prior approval of Owner, as provided in Section 2.5 hereof.

3.3 <u>Agent's Affiliates and Subsidiaries.</u> In performing work at the Development, Agent may, from time to time, deal with certain of its affiliated or subsidiary organizations as independent contractors. The amounts payable to any such related entity shall not be greater than would have been paid under an arm's-length contract with a nonrelated entity. The provisions of Section 2.5 and 3.2 are applicable to all transactions with Agent's affiliated and subsidiary organizations. It shall be expressly communicated by Agent to Owner when contractors that are subsidiaries or affiliates of Agent are used in performing work at the Development.

3.4 <u>Use and maintenance of Development.</u> Agent agrees not to knowingly permit the use of the Development for any purpose which might void any policy of insurance held by Owner or which might render any loss thereunder uncollectible, or which would be in violation of any government restriction. It shall be the duty of Agent at all times during the terms of this Agreement to operate and maintain the Development according to the highest standards achievable consistent with such plan of Owner as communicated to Agent from Owner from time to time. Full compliance by the residents with the terms and conditions of their respective leases and rules and regulations shall be secured and, to this end, Agent shall see that all residents are informed with respect to such rules, and notices as may be promulgated and communicated to Agent by Owner. Agent shall be expected to perform such other acts and deeds as are reasonable, necessary, and proper in the discharge of its duties under this Agreement.

3.5 <u>Separation of Owner's Moneys.</u> Agent shall establish and maintain in a bank acceptable to Owner, and in a manner to indicate the custodial nature thereof, a separate bank account as Agent of Owner for the deposit of moneys of Owner from the ownership and operation of the Development. Agent shall also establish such other special bank accounts as may be required by Owner. Funds may be disbursed to cover authorized Development expenditures from Development accounts upon the signature of Agent. All payments to be made by Agent hereunder shall be made by check drawn on an account established pursuant to this Section 3.5, except petty cash items not exceeding $_____ which may be paid from a fund to be maintained by Agent for such purposes. Agent shall not be obligated to make any advance to or for the account of Owner or to pay any sums, except out of funds held in any account maintained under this Section 3.5, nor shall Agent be obligated to incur any liability or obligation for the account of Owner without assurance that the necessary funds for the discharge thereof will be provided. No provision of this Section 3.5 shall be deemed or construed to diminish or modify any obligations of Agent pursuant to that Negative Cash Flow Guarantee Agreement of even date between Owner and Agent.

3.6 <u>Expenses of Owner.</u> Everything done by Agent under the provisions of Article II shall be done as the agent of Owner, and all obligations or expenses incurred thereunder shall be for the account of, on behalf of, and at the expense of Owner, except as otherwise specifically provided in Article II and except that Owner shall not be obligated to reimburse Agent for any expenses for office equipment or office supplies by Agent for any overhead expenses of Agent, for any salaries of any executives of Agent (other than the Manager resident at the Development), or for any salaries or wages allocable to time spent on projects other than the Development.

3.7 <u>Termination.</u> This Agreement may be terminated without prejudice by either party upon at least _____ (___) days' prior written notice to the other party. If either party shall default in the performance of any of its obligations hereunder, and such default shall continue for _____ (___) days after written notice from the other party designating such default, or either party shall make any assignment for the benefit of creditors, or there shall be filed by or against either party any petition for adjudication as a bankrupt or for reorganization, or an arrangement, or for any relief under any bankruptcy law or any insolvency act, either party may terminate this Agreement by written notice at any time thereafter while such default or other events shall be continuing; and thereupon this Agreement shall forthwith terminate and, if termination shall occur, through default of Owner, Agent shall be due full compensation for its fees for the actual time of its management involvement with the Development plus _____ (___) days' termination fee based on the previous (___) days' collections. Termination of this Agreement under any of the foregoing provisions shall not release Agent from liability for failure to perform any of the duties or obligations of Agent as expressed herein and required to be performed prior to such termination. Upon such termination, Agent shall forthwith (1) surrender and deliver up to Owner the Development and all rents and income of the Development and other moneys of Owner on hand and in any bank account; (2)

deliver to Owner as received any moneys due Owner under this Agreement but received after such termination; (3) deliver to Owner all materials and supplies, keys, documents, and such other accountings, papers and records pertaining to this Agreement as Owner shall request; and (4) assign such existing contracts relating to the operation and maintenance of the Development as Owner shall require, provided that Owner shall agree to assume all liability thereunder accruing after the termination of this Agreement. Within _____ (___) days after such termination, Agent shall deliver to Owner the written report required by Section 2.11b for any period not covered by such a report at time of termination, and within _____ (___) days after any such termination, Agent shall deliver to Owner, as required by Section 2.11c, the profit and loss statement for the calendar year or portion thereof ending on the date of termination and the balance sheet for the Development certified by the Agent as of the date of termination.

3.8 <u>Management Start-up and Market Study Agreement.</u> Agent will receive from the Owner a fee of $_____ as compensation for management start-up services, and a fee of $_____ as compensation for market study services. Such services shall include but not be limited to: preparation of rental collection procedures, arranging communication procedures with tenants, installation of performance monitoring systems for the Development, determining the bookkeeping and other financial recordkeeping systems most appropriate for the Development, consulting with Owner with respect to the form and content of tenant leases, assisting in the retention of suppliers, and supervising required or desired maintenance and capital improvements. The $_____ management start-up fee shall be due and payable in full on _____ and the $_____ market study fee shall be due and payable on the earlier of _____, or (___) days from the Completion Date. The Completion Date shall mean the date on which the development of the Property has been completed and the last Certificate of Occupancy evidencing 100 percent completion of all units comprising the Property has been issued.

3.9 <u>Definition of "Gross Income."</u> As used in this Agreement, the term "gross income" shall mean all amounts actually collected by Agent as rents or other charges for use and occupancy of the Development, but shall exclude income derived from interest on investments or otherwise, proceeds of claims on accounts of insurance policies, abatement of taxes, awards arising out of takings by eminent domain and discounts, and dividends on insurance policies.

3.10 <u>Assignment.</u> Agent shall not, without Owner's prior written approval, which Owner may in its discretion withhold, assign any of its rights or obligations under this Agreement, whether by operation of law or otherwise, or permit any change in the identity of the person or persons who are in effective control of the management of Agent's business, or make any subcontract with respect to the performance of any of its obligations hereunder, or delegate any of its duties hereunder. Owner may assign its rights and obligations to any successor in title to the Development and, upon such assignment, shall be relieved of all liability accruing after the effective date of such assignment.

ARTICLE IV

General Provisions

4.1 <u>Notices.</u> All notices required or permitted by this Agreement shall be in writing and shall be sent by registered or certified mail, addressed, in the case of Owner to:

_____
_____
_____
_____

with copy to:

_____
_____
_____
_____

or to such other addresses as shall, from time to time, be designated by written notice by either party to the other party as herein provided.

4.2 <u>Entire Agreement.</u> This Agreement shall constitute the entire Agreement between the parties hereto, and no modification thereof shall be effective unless made by supplemental agreement in writing executed by the parties hereto.

4.3 <u>Successors and Assigns.</u> At all times this Agreement will inure to the benefit and constitute a binding obligation upon each of the parties hereto and their respective successors and, where permitted, their assigns.

4.4 <u>Interpretation.</u> This Agreement is made under and pursuant to and shall be construed under, and the rights, duties and obligations of the parties shall be determined and enforced in accordance with the laws of the State of _____. This is of the essence of this Agreement.

4.5 <u>Qualification.</u> Agent represents and warrants that Agent is and shall at all times during the term of this Agreement be duly licensed by the State of _____ to engage in or perform all of the services required under this Agreement and is duly qualified as a foreign corporation under the laws of the State of _____.

4.6 <u>No Recording.</u> This Agreement shall not be deemed at any time to be a lease or an interest in real estate or a lien of any nature against the Development. This Agreement shall not be placed of record by either party on the records of the county in which the Development is located.

4.7 <u>No Waiver.</u> No failure of Owner to exercise any power given to Owner hereunder or to insist upon strict compliance by Agent with its obligations hereunder, and no custom or practice of the parties at variance with the terms hereof shall constitute a waiver of the right of Owner to demand exact compliance with the terms hereof.

4.8 <u>Severability.</u> If any provision of this Agreement, or the application thereof to any circumstances, should be held to be invalid or unenforceable, the validity and enforceability of the remaining provisions of this Agreement or the application thereof to any other circumstances shall not be affected thereby.

4.9 <u>Captions and Headings.</u> The captions and headings through this Agreement are for convenience of reference only, and the words contained therein shall in no way be held or deemed to define, limit, describe, explain, modify, amplify, or add to the interpretation, construction of meaning of any provisions of or the scope or intent of this Agreement, nor in any way affect this Agreement.

IN WITNESS WHEREOF, the parties have executed this Agreement as of the day and year first above written.

OWNER:

Witness _____   _____

A _____

Notarized _____   By: _____

Title: _____

Attest: _____

Corporate Seal

AGENT:

Witness _____   _____

A _____

Notarized _____   By: _____

Title: _____

Attest: _____

Corporate Seal

SCHEDULE OF EXHIBITS

A. Grounds Maintenance Yearly Program
B. Property Management Checklist

EXHIBIT A
GROUND MAINTENANCE
YEARLY PROGRAM

A. Lawn Maintenance

1. Mowing of all turf areas every _____ to _____ days, _____ through _____, as needed there-after.

2. Scalping and dethatching of turf areas _____ through _____.

3. Trimming of secondary turf areas, and power edging of concrete surfaces bimonthly during growing season.

4. Aerating, overseeding all Fescue turf areas and seeding of bare areas in turf; Fescue turf _____ through _____. Bermuda turf _____ through _____.

5. Fertilization of Fescue turf areas, _____, _____ and _____; Bermuda turf areas, _____, _____ and _____.

6. Pre-emergent weed control applied to all turf areas, _____ through _____, and _____ through _____. Post-emergent, as needed.

7. Pre-emergent weed control applied to all mulch areas, _____ through _____, and _____ through _____.

8. Soil analysis annually in _____.

9. Application of lime to all turf areas in _____.

B. Tree, Shrub and Shrub Bed Maintenance

1. Shrubbery will be trimmed to present a good appearance in conjunction with the landscape, _____ through _____.

2. Selective and corrective pruning to all shrubs _____ through _____, forsythia shaped in _____. Azaleas selectively pruned before _____, one or two weeks post bloom drop, preferred.

3. Pruning of deciduous trees _____ through _____, low hanging limbs as needed.

4. Pruning of crepe myrtles, back to major stems in _____.

5. Mulching shrub beds, _____ through _____; _____ through _____.

6. Fertilize ornamental trees and shrubbery, _____, _____ and _____. Azaleas one extra application the first of _____.

7. Insect disease and fungus control on shrubs and ornamental trees as needed.

C. General Maintenance

1. Complete policing of all landscape areas weekly.

2. Leaf removal from all landscaped areas every _____ to _____ days, _____ through _____.

3. Picking up of and/or blowing and vacuuming of all streets, curbs, and sidewalks weekly.

4. Raking (dragging) and policing of any beach areas weekly during the swimming season.

EXHIBIT B
PROPERTY MANAGEMENT CHECKLIST

1. Send administrative service department copies of the following items:
   a. Sample lease form
   b. Rules and regulations
   c. Pet agreements
   d. Application forms
   e. Unit inspection form
   f. Employment/business verification form.
   g. Late rent reminder letter
   h. Maintenance notification letter
   i. Transfer of utilities letter
   j. Tenant file folder

2. Administrative services department will supply the property management firm with the following reports:
   a. Weekly traffic
   b. Site inspection
   c. Profit and loss statement
   d. Market comparables

3. The following item will be supplied to the administrative services department on a weekly basis (by Tuesday):
   a. Traffic report

4. The following items will be supplied to the administrative services department on a monthly basis (by the tenth of the month):
   a. Cash flow statement (either on computer or manual)
   b. Rent roll
   c. Security deposits
   d. Accounts receivable/payable
   e. Variance report
   f. Profit and loss statement
   g. List of all checks written for that month
   h. Check for the prior month's administrative service fee

5. The following items will be supplied to the administrative services department no later than November 1 of each year:
   a. Budget for the next year
      1. Written analysis of each line item

b. Capital expenditure budget for the following year

    1. Written analysis of each line item

c. Updated copy of the inventory

6. The following items will be supplied to the administrative services department on January 1, April 1, July 1, and October 1 of each year:

  a. Quarterly comparable report

  b. Summary of the weekly traffic reports

7. The following items will be set up prior to the property closing:

  a. Checkbook—property operating account

  b. Money market account—property operating account

  c. Money market account—security deposit escrow account

NOTE: Both the owner and management company should have authority to sign checks.

8. Prior to closing the management company will supply the owner with a completed site inspection outline.

9. The management company should receive a copy of the post-closing memorandum within one week of closing.

10. Each year, thirty days prior to the insurance anniversary date, the management company will rebid with three companies the insurance policies and submit them to the administrative service department.

11. All the following correspondence should be copied and sent to the administrative service department:

  a. Lender

  b. Real estate taxes

  c. Insurance

  d. Legal

12. All capital expenditure items over $1,500.00 will require three bids.

13. All capital expenditure and negative cash flow requests will be made in writing three days prior to funding.

SUMMARY

Although legal documents are only as good as the word of the parties, a well-written document will help avoid many future problems. Typically, when a problem does arise, both parties will first refer to the agreed upon documents for an answer. If no clear-cut answer or solution exists, both parties should then consult their respective legal counsel. During this process both parties should try to work out their problems prior to any expensive and prolonged litigation. If no settlement can be reached, the final solution will then be rendered by the court system.

When drafting all agreements between parties, all pertinent business points should be considered and addressed. The more complete the initial letter of intent, the easier it will be to draft and negotiate the final documents. It must be remembered and understood that these documents outline the total understanding of the deal structure, and if drafted properly they will also be used many years after the closing.

It is imperative that all legal documents be reviewed by a competent attorney who specializes in that particular area of law.

GUIDELINE FOR THOROUGHLY INSPECTING THE PROPERTY PRIOR TO ITS PURCHASE

THE INSPECTION PERIOD: WHY IT PAYS TO BE THOROUGH

Few of us would consider buying a car before first test driving it. Since most real estate transactions involve far more money, it only makes sense that the investor go through a thorough "tire-kicking" process prior to making the final commitment. The inspection period or "free look period" is used for this purpose. When negotiating the purchase of any property, be sure to negotiate the inspection period for as long as is comfortably needed to do all the necessary homework. This time period can be used to completely analyze the property as well as to test the market for the debt and equity that will be needed to complete a transaction. This time period should start at the execution of the purchase agreement and should expire upon a specific date or within a predetermined time period after receipt of all the required information requested by the purchaser. During this period any earnest money that is required should be put with a title company or neutral third party with instructions that if the purchaser decides not to proceed with the transaction, all the earnest money, or that portion of the money that was negotiated for this inspection period, should be released to the purchaser. Once this period has expired, all earnest money will then "go at risk," that is, if the purchaser is unable to complete the transaction through no fault of the seller, this earnest money will then be earned by the seller as liquidated damages.

Determining the Length of the Inspection Period

The length of the inspection period and size of the earnest money are both negotiated items. It is in the best interest of the purchaser to get the longest inspection period possible with the least amount of earnest money. The length of time for this period is a function of the demand for the property. If there is a waiting line to purchase the property, the seller will want to give the purchaser the shortest period of time needed to review the property. Indeed, in some cases a seller will not want to give a "free look" at the property. The seller may tell the purchaser to do any homework prior to contracting, and when satisfied, then sign the contract. This process is very risky. First, the purchaser may spend a lot of time and money without controlling the property, only to find that another investor has tied it up. Second, because of the sense of urgency placed by the seller, the purchaser may miss some important facts regarding the economics or the physical aspects of the property and may discover these facts too late. Another function in this time equation is the complexity of the transaction. If the deal is the purchase of a duplex, it should only take a few days to inspect the property as opposed to a few months if the deal is a major mixed-use development or a new construction project.

How to Structure the Earnest Money Deposit

Earnest money is a deposit required as a show of good faith by the purchaser, indicating interest in the acquisition of the property. Many sellers want enough money so that if the purchaser defaults, the seller will at least be compensated for the time and opportunity value that the property lost during the period of time the deposit was held.

The size of the earnest money deposit is also a function of the size of the deal. The larger the transaction, the larger the earnest money required. There are many ways to structure the earnest money. One way is to put up some of the money at the execution of the contract, with the balance at the end of the inspection period. Another method would be to use a note to be paid upon default. By using this method, the purchaser's cash or credit will not be used. Each purchaser should decide in advance on the amount of earnest money that he or she will be willing to risk if the deal falls through. The purchaser will have to look at the "risk reward ratio," that is, how much money the purchaser would make on this transaction versus the amount of money that might be lost.

THE PROPERTY INSPECTION TEAM—HOW EXPERTS CAN HELP IN COMPILING THE INFORMATION YOU NEED

During the inspection period, the purchaser should assemble a team of experts to thoroughly assist a decision in this transaction. This team will analyze the information and make recommendations. It should work together to compile a complete report on the property. The results could be positive for a "go ahead," they could show that the investor would be better off "passing" on the deal, or they might reveal new factors that would cause the investor to renegotiate the transaction. The cost for this team might be the best dollars the investor could spend. It is better to spend this money up front than to find out later that a mistake was made. Make sure to negotiate a fee structure with each team member in advance. This will avoid conflicts at a later date.

Using a Management Company Productively

A well qualified management company, whether owned by the purchaser or a third party management firm, should completely analyze the physical and financial aspects of the property. The following outline should help in this analysis.

MANAGEMENT INSPECTION OUTLINE

1. Property Information
   a. Name/address/telephone of the property
   b. Information regarding current management
      1. Current management company/address/telephone
      2. Current resident manager/address/telephone

    c. Information regarding the leasing company

        1. Current leasing company/address/telephone

        2. Current leasing agent/address/telephone

    d. Building information

        1. Number of buildings

        2. Phasing of buildings

        3. Age of buildings

        4. Number of floors in each building

        5. Total number of units or total gross and net square footage in each building or property

    e. Unit information

        1. Number of units or gross and net square footage in each unit or on each floor

        2. Mix of units—number of each type of unit

        3. Description of the interiors

    f. Site information

        1. Total acreage

        2. Current zoning classification

        3. Density of the property in number of units per acre or square footage per acre

        4. Number of parking spaces

    g. Amenity information

        1. Description of amenities

    h. Construction description

        1. Type of construction

            (a) Stick built

            (b) Masonry

            (c) Steel

        2. Utility system

        3. Roof

        4. Exterior facade

        5. Landscaping

        6. Floor system

        7. Elevators

        8. Foundations

        9. Security systems

       10. Restrooms

11. Interior walls

12. Framing

13. Fire system

14. Problem areas

2. Property Location Description

    a. Neighborhood description

    b. Area demographics

        1. Number of people

        2. Number of households

        3. Description of households

            (a) Income

            (b) Age

            (c) Marital status

        4. Buying power of area

    c. Traffic patterns of area

    d. Distance to support facilities

        1. Schools

        2. Shopping

        3. Houses of worship

    e. Description of the area's growth trends

    f. Description of local government

    g. Description of area employment trends

3. Location Maps

    a. State

    b. City

    c. County

    d. Neighborhood

    e. Site plan of property

4. Tenant Information (See Lease Summary Forms)

    a. Roster of all tenants

        1. Unit address

        2. Lease term

        3. Type unit or number of gross or net square footage

        4. Rental rate

            (a) Who pays what utilities

            (b) Common area maintenance charges

           (c) Percentage clause

           (d) Rent escalation/anniversary date

           (e) Parking rental rates

      5. Options

           (a) Option rate

           (b) Option period

      6. Security deposit

5. Tenant Profile

  a. Residential

      1. Length of occupancy

      2. Type of employment

           (a) White collar

           (b) Blue collar

      3. Size of family

      4. Marital status

      5. Number of children

      6. Age of adults

      7. Age of children

      8. Income of household

      9. Rental payment history

  b. Commercial

      1. Type of business

      2. Length of occupancy

      3. Rental payment history

6. Current Rental Policies

  a. Security deposit

  b. Pet policy

  c. Parking policy

  d. Office hours

  e. Building hours

7. Security of Property

  a. Description of security for the property

8. Exterior Building Inspection

  a. (See Site and Exterior Building Inspection Form)

9. Interior Building Inspection

  a. (See Interior Building Inspection Form)

10. Utility Deposits (See Utility Deposit Form)
    a. List of each utility deposit
    b. Address of each utility deposit
    c. Amount of each deposit

11. Insurance Coverage
    a. List of current coverage and premiums

12. Real Estate Taxes
    a. Current assessment for real and personal property
    b. Millage rates and breakdown

13. Service Contracts (See Service Contract Form)
    a. List of each service contract
    b. Address of each service contract
    c. Contact person for each service contract
    d. Term of each service contract
    e. Amount of each service contract

14. Occupancy History
    a. Past two year history by month
    b. Current/leased occupancy
    c. Projected rent-up absorption

15. Budget Forecasts (See Budget Forms)
    a. Month-by-month budget projections for the next twelve months or until 95 percent rent-up is achieved
        1. Written analysis of each line item

16. Capital Expenditure Budget (See Capital Expenditure Budget Forms)
    a. Month-by-month budget projections
        1. Written analysis of each line item

17. Deferred Maintenance Program
    a. Description of the proposed deferred maintenance program

18. Staff Analysis (See Staff Analysis Form)
    a. Interviews with staff and comments
    b. Comments on current management record keeping
    c. Comments on current maintenance procedures

19. Inventory (See Inventory Form)
    a. Listing of all current property
    b. Proposed new inventory, timing and cost estimates

20. Photographs of the Subject Property
    a. Typical elevations
    b. Entrance
    c. Amenities
       1. Pool
       2. Tennis court
       3. Playground
       4. Clubhouse
       5. Laundry facilities
    d. Typical unit interior
       1. Kitchen
       2. Bathroom
       3. Living areas
    e. Building lobby area and typical hallway
    f. Clubhouse interior
    g. Aerial of property
    h. Signage
    i. Typical landscaping
    j. Typical parking area
    k. Refuse removal area
    l. Areas in need of repair
    m. Renderings (if to-be-built)

21. Floor Plans

22. Market Comparables
    a. Market comparables (See Market Comparable Forms)
    b. Summary of comparables (See Market Summary Forms)

INSURANCE COVERAGE: TWENTY-FIVE KEY QUESTIONS

In preparing its report, the management company will need to review the current insurance coverage. In many cases it is either too low or too high. The management company should seek answers to the following questions when bidding out new insurance coverage.

There are four qualifying questions that should be asked initially when shopping for the best insurance policy.

1. Does the insurance company insure this type of property?

2. Will it insure in this location?

3. Can it insure for the proposed amount of coverage?

4. What property information is needed to quote this coverage?

If the answers to these questions are acceptable, then proceed to the following questions.

5. How much coverage does the insurance company recommend for the property?

6. Is this amount sufficient to totally replace the property or only the mortgage?

7. What is the premium for this coverage?

8. What is the term of this coverage?

9. What deductible amounts are available?

10. What deductible amounts are recommended?

11. Is contents coverage included?

    a. If so, what amount of coverage is included?

    b. If not, what amount is needed, and what is the premium?

    c. What is the deductible for this coverage?

12. Is rent loss insurance included?

    a. If so, what amount of coverage is included?

    b. If not, what amount is needed and what is the premium?

    c. What is the maximum time period covered?

13. What is the payment schedule for these premiums?

14. Are these rates projected to increase or decrease in the near future?

15. Is an updated appraisal required by the insurance company?

16. Is boiler/machinery coverage needed?

    a. If so, what are the liability limits needed?

    b. What is the premium for this coverage?

17. Is vehicle insurance available?

    a. If so, what coverage is needed?

    b. What is the premium for this coverage?

18. Is workman's compensation insurance available?

    a. If so, what coverage is needed?

    b. What is the premium for this coverage?

19. Is fidelity insurance available?

    a. If so, what coverage is needed?

    b. What is the premium for this coverage?

20. Is property manager's errors and omission insurance available?

    a. If so, what coverage is needed?

    b. What is the premium for this coverage?

21. Is utility bond coverage available?

    a. If so, what are the requirements?

    b. What is the premium for this coverage?

22. Are tenant security deposit bonds available?

    a. If so, what are the limits needed?

    b. What is the premium for this coverage?

23. Is group life, and hospitalization insurance available for the property employees?

    a. If so, what coverage is available?

    b. What is the premium for this coverage?

    c. What is the deductible for this coverage?

24. Is flood insurance available?

    a. If so, what is the coverage?

    b. What is the premium for this coverage?

    c. What is the deductible for this coverage?

25. Whose names should be added to the policy as insured?

REAL ESTATE TAXES: NINETEEN QUESTIONS TO ASK

The management company should carefully review the current real estate taxes as well as what the projected real estate taxes will be after the proposed closing of the transaction.

In order to obtain this information the management company should contact the local taxing authority and ask the following questions.

1. What is the current tax assessment and tax bill for the property?

2. What were the last three years' tax assessments and tax bills?

3. Does the tax bill include the personal property or will the personal property be taxed separately?

4. What is the current personal property tax assessment and bill?

5. If the property is "to-be-built," what is the current land assessment and tax bill?

6. What is the assessment ratio used by the local tax department?

7. Does the local taxing authority tax differently for residential and commercial properties?

8. What is the homestead exemption allowed, if any?

9. When was the last property reassessment, and when will the next reassessment be?

10. What are the past and current millage rates?

11. How is the millage rate broken down?

12. Will the millage rate increase this year?

13. When does the tax bill come out?

14. When is the tax bill due?

  a. Can this tax bill be paid in installments?

15. Is there a penalty for late payment?

  a. If so, how much is this penalty?

16. Is there a discount for early payment?

  a. If so, how much is this discount?

17. To whom are the taxes paid?

18. How are tax appeals handled?

19. Is there a local tax consultant?

Marketing the Property

The marketing company, which in many cases might be the management company, should report on how it plans to market the property. It should comment on the rent-up absorption, what rent levels it wants to obtain, how it can market against the competition, and what real estate commissions should be paid to attract outside real estate agents. Its report should also mention if any rent concessions are needed. This report should review the current marketing program and then detail its analysis of how the marketing should take place in the future. It should review the current signage, brochures, model suite and common area decor. If a new target market is sought for the property, the report should detail plans to reach this new market. Additionally, this report should set out the marketing budget. The following is a checklist for this report:

1. Marketing strategy

  a. Target market

2. Marketing budget

3. Competitive market study

4. Advertising strategy

5. Review of current signage

6. Review of current model

7. Review of brochures and direct mail programs

8. Review of real estate agent program and commission schedule

9. Review of current rent rates

10. Review of rent concession program

11. Review of public relations program

HOW TO PREPARE A MARKET STUDY ANALYSIS

In evaluating a potential property, the current market comparables should be carefully studied. The marketing company that completes this study should first compile a list of properties that are competitive with the subject property. In order to determine if the properties are qualified comparables, it should first determine if these properties are of similar building type, if they are marketed toward a similar target market as the subject property, and if they are in the particular market location as the subject property. Each market has its own particular set of characteristics and locational boundaries. Depending on these boundaries, some comparables might be five miles from the subject property while others might be just down the street. Two-story garden apartment properties should not be compared with high-rise luxury properties. Class A office properties should not be compared with Class C.

To obtain its list of potential comparables, the marketing company should start by driving the area adjacent to the subject property and listing those properties that appear similar. Additional properties can be obtained when interviewing the managers of those properties. The yellow pages, local real estate boards, banks, appraisers are other sources to be used in completing this list.

With this list in hand, the marketing company should then start compiling the data necessary for the market analysis. The market study comparable forms located at the end of this chapter can be used in compiling this information.

Since no two properties are exactly alike, certain adjustments might need to be made to this data. These include adjustments for utilities, features, and amenities. Since some properties have the tenant paying for all or some of the utilities while others do not, this adjustment figure is needed for a better comparison. These adjustment factors should be available from the local utility companies. Additionally, some properties have more "bells and whistles," or features and amenities. A cost factor should be added or subtracted for these items. These cost figures are very subjective and leave the most room for error in this analysis. It is assumed that a tenant will pay extra for these items.

To be complete, this study should contain photographs of each comparable property as well as photographs of the subject property. These can be used when rating each property as well as for future reference.

HOW TO RATE YOUR PROSPECTIVE PROPERTY AGAINST OTHERS

As mentioned above, each property should be rated as to how it compares to the subject property. The following items can be used in this comparison:

- Location within the market area
- Curb appeal
- Exterior design
- Unit design
- Quality of tenancy
- Quality of management
- Traffic count
- Accessibility of site

- Features of units

- Amenities of property

To be consistent when rating comparable properties, each one should be measured against the subject property.

There are many methods for gathering the information needed for this study. The easiest is to contact either the manager or the owner of the property and indicate that you are preparing a market study and you are requesting some market information. Many times this approach will work, but sometimes information might need to be traded to induce answers to the various questions. Other times, no information will be given at all. Since this information is vital to the study, you will need to use other methods to fill in the blanks.

TIPS ON VERIFYING OCCUPANCY AND RENT

The questions that are most often not answered or answered incorrectly are those that pertain to the current occupancy levels and any rent concessions being offered. Other methods that can be used to verify occupancy levels are:

1. Contact the local postman who can verify the number of tenants in the property.

2. Check with the local utility companies—electric, gas, and water. They should have current knowledge of what units are occupied.

3. Walk or drive by each unit and look into the window to see if the space is occupied.

Other methods to verify rent levels and rent concessions are:

1. Have a business associate or a friend contact the manager or property owner to inquire about renting space. Since all managers and property owners want to rent their vacant or soon-to-be-vacant space, they should be only too willing to give a run down on the rental rates as well as what concessions that they might give. Sometimes this process might have to be repeated many times to compile the necessary information.

2. Review the real estate classified section of the local newspaper. Properties often advertise their concessions to the public.

HOW TO OBTAIN INFORMATION ON THE UNIT MIX, SQUARE FOOTAGE, AND AGE OF THE PROPERTY

If the information regarding the unit mix, square footage, and age of the property is not known by the manager, the following methods can be used to obtain this information:

1. Contact the local building department. Many times they file the original building plans for the property. These files will show the unit mix as well as the date of construction.

2. Contact the local tax assessment department. In order to assess the property properly, this information should be in the files.

Once this information is compiled and verified, the data should then be correlated and analyzed to form an opinion regarding the market conditions.

WHAT TO INCLUDE IN YOUR MARKET DATA

The information that should be used for this market study is as follows:

1. Name of the comparable property

2. Rating of the comparable property

3. Distance to the subject property

4. Age of the property

5. Square footage

6. Rental rate

7. Utilities paid by tenant

8. Utility rental adjustment

9. Features of the unit

10. Amenities of the property

11. Features, amenities rental adjustment

12. Adjusted rent per square foot

13. Number of units

14. Occupancy of units

HOW GRAPHING CAN HELP YOU ANALYZE YOUR MARKET STUDY DATA

In order to better analyze this data, the information should be graphed to give the reader a visual picture of the market conditions. The information to be plotted will include the square footage and the current adjusted rental rate. Once this data is plotted, a line should be drawn that intersects the average of this data. The properties that are above this line will show the LOW SIDE of the market while the properties below are the HIGH SIDE of the market.

Figure 5.1 shows how this process takes place when analyzing a one bedroom, one bath apartment property.

Based on the market data shown in the above example, it can readily be seen that the subject property is on the low side of the market. This example shows three other properties with the same "5" rating that are located on the high side of the market. This graph indicates that the subject property has room to increase rents by up to $20 per month without going over the average line. It can also be seen from this graph that Mill Creek, with a "4" rating, should reduce its rental rates to come back in line with the market. Although its adjusted rental rate is $.44 per square foot while the average adjusted rate is $.49 per square foot, its "4" rating means that this property should reduce its rent to increase its occupancy level.

The same graphing technique used in the above example could also be used to illustrate various unit types on one graph. The graphing of all this data would then show the relative strengths and weaknesses of the various unit types in that particular market.

TABLE 5-1
Sample Market Study Summary

Subject Property: Foxfire Downs
Subject Location: Atlanta, Georgia
Type Property: Garden Apartment
Subject Unit: One-Bedroom, One-Bath

Code/ Rating	Name	Distance to Subj. (Miles)	Age	Sq. Ft.	Rental Rate	Utilities Paid By Tenant	Utility Adjust.*	Features**	Amenities***	Features/ Amenities Adjust.	Adjust. Rent	Adjust. Rent/ Sq. Ft.	No. Units	Occupied Units	% Occupied
NP-5	Knotty Pines	1	3	550	$300.00	+E	$0.00	WP, UC,DW,C, P/B	SP,TC	$5.00	$305.00	$0.55	48	42	87.50%
OP-5	Oaks Place	.5	5	620	$320.00	+E	$0.00	WP, UC,DW,C, P/B	SP,TC,CH		$320.00	$0.52	36	35	97.22%
SP-5	Spring Village	1.25	2.5	650	$325.00	+E	$0.00	WP, UC,DW,C, P/B	SP,TC,CH		$325.00	$0.50	40	38	95.00%
ML-6	Meadow Lake	3	1	575	$290.00	+E	$23.00	WP, UC,DW,C, P/B	SP,TC,CH		$313.00	$0.54	28	26	92.86%
MC-4	Mill Creek	2.2	4	725	$325.00	+E	$0.00	WP, UC,DW,C, P/B	SP,TC,CH		$325.00	$0.45	32	24	75.00%
TA-8	The Arbors	3.2	3	620	$330.00	+E	$0.00	WP, UC,DW,C, P/B	SP,CH	$5.00	$335.00	$0.54	12	12	100.00%
PC-3	Pebble Creek	1.5	4	680	$300.00	+E	$0.00	WP, UC,DW,C, P/B	SP,TC,CH		$300.00	$0.44	52	46	88.46%
TV-3	The Village	2	1.5	585	$295.00	+E	$0.00	WP, UC,DW,C, P/B	SP,TC,CH		$295.00	$0.50	24	20	83.33%
SUB-5	Foxfire Downs	2	2	650	300.00	+E	$0.00	WP, UC,DW,C, P/B	SP,TC,CH		$300.00	$0.46	28	28	100.00%
AVG.				630.20							$311.41				90.33%
TOTAL				189,060							$93,424.00		300	271	

*Utility adjustment–$.04/sq. ft.

**Features:
WP–Wallpaper–$5.00
UC–Utility connections–$10.00
C–Carpet–$30.00
P/B–Patio/balcony–$10.00
DW–Dishwasher–$5.00
***Amenities:
SP–Swimming pool–$10.00
TC–Tennis court–$5.00
CH–Clubhouse–$5.00

142

FIGURE 5.1
Market Graphing
One Bedroom, One Bathroom—Garden Units

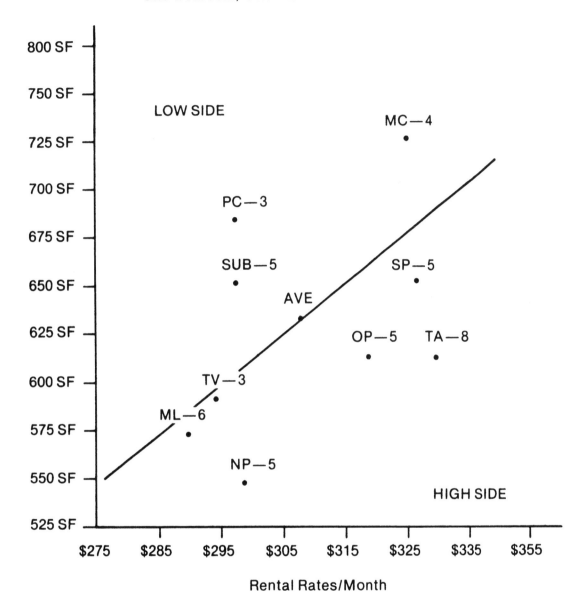

Rental Rates/Month

This process should be used when looking for properties that might be undervalued. The same process that was used in this example could be used to analyze total markets as well as various submarkets. It can show an investor what properties have the best chance of increasing their rental rates and thus increasing their potential values. Once this market analysis is complete, the investor can use this information to search for potential properties to acquire.

How the Architect, Engineer, and Construction Manager Can Tell You About the Property's Physical Structure

Since all real estate involves some type of construction, whether it is a to-be-built property or an existing piece of real estate, a knowledgeable architect, engineer, or construction manager should be consulted to review the physical structure. Although a good management company can detect visual problems, you need the construction expert to analyze the more complicated aspects of the property.

If the property is to-be-built, an architect who is knowledgeable in that type of development should review the plans and specifications. The architect's report will list any items that are missing from the property, as well as those included but that might not be needed. Moreover, the architect in reviewing the specifications might discover that there could be other cost savings.

An engineer should review the structural aspects of the property. Depending on its complexity, the engineer might have to bring in other outside experts who specialize in areas such as roofing, plumbing, mechanical or electrical systems, and elevators.

If the property is a to-be-built property, the construction manager should review the construction schedule, costs, and progress. The construction manager should wave a red flag when there appears to be a problem.

The completed report should state any current problems and any potential future problems. A detailed cost analysis should accompany this report, including bids to repair any problem items. For any items that may need repair in the future, the investor should add an inflation factor.

The following checklist gives an outline of items that should be reviewed by these construction specialists to make sure that they are included in the property and that they are in adequate, functional condition.

CONSTRUCTION CHECKLIST

I. Review of preliminary and final working drawings and specifications to evaluate the overall adequacy of:

Site

1. Site plan
   a. Siting of improvements
      1. Relation to topography
      2. Relation to view
      3. Relation to sun
   b. Grading plan
   c. Traffic flow
      1. Vehicle
      2. Pedestrian
      3. Emergency vehicles
2. Soils tests
   a. Soils test

3. Drainage control
   a. Erosion control
   b. Retention areas
      1. Design
      2. Capacity
      3. Condition
      4. Screening
   c. Location of catch basins
   d. Condition

4. Utilities
   a. Location of meters
      1. Water
      2. Sewer
      3. Electric
      4. Gas
      5. Telephone
      6. Cable TV

5. Retaining Walls
   a. Location
   b. Type of materials
   c. Condition

6. Paving
   a. Type of material
   b. Condition

7. Curb and Gutter
   a. Type of curb
   b. Condition

8. Sidewalks
   a. Type of material
   b. Condition
   c. Handicap access

9. Fire hydrants
   a. Location

10. Dumpster
    a. Location
    b. Design

      c. Screening

      d. Truck access

      e. Condition

11. Parking

      a. Location to buildings

      b. Number of spaces

      c. Handicap parking

         1. Number of spaces

         2. Location

      d. Striping

      e. Bumper guards

      f. Condition

12. Fencing

      a. Location

      b. Type of material

      c. Design

      d. Condition

13. Exterior lighting

      a. Review location

      b. Review design

      c. Review condition (if existing)

      d. Review times when lighting is in use

      e. Review size of lights

14. Mail boxes

      a. Location

      b. Design

      c. Condition

15. Signage

      a. Entrance sign

         1. Location of signage

         2. Type of material

         3. Design

         4. Lighting

         5. Condition

      b. Guest parking

        1. Location of signage

        2. Type of material

        3. Design

        4. Condition

    c. Office

        1. Location of signage

        2. Type of material

        3. Design

        4. Condition

    d. Model unit

        1. Location of signage

        2. Type of signage

        3. Design

        4. Condition

    e. Miscellaneous signage

        1. Location signage

        2. Type of signage

        3. Type of material

        4. Design

        5. Condition

16. Landscaping

    a. Landscaping plan

    b. Plant materials

        1. Quality of materials

        2. Sizing of materials

    c. Maintenance schedule

    d. Condition

17. Irrigation system

    a. Irrigation design

    b. Watering schedule

    c. Condition

Exterior Buildings

1. Building exterior

    a. Materials

    b. Warranty

    c. Durability

     d. Color selection

     e. Condition

2. Roofing

     a. Type of roof

     b. Material selection

     c. Color selection

     d. Flashing

     e. Roof bond

     f. Warranty

     g. Condition

3. Address signage

     a. Material

     b. Location

     c. Design

     d. Color selection

     e. Condition

4. Exterior lighting

     a. Location

          1. Building

          2. Unit entrances

          3. Breezeways

          4. Handicap

     b. Photo-cells and timers

     c. Design

     d. Material

     e. Condition

5. Air conditioner condensers

     a. Location

     b. Screening of units

     c. Size of units

     d. Warranty

     e. Condition

6. Exterior stairways and walkways

     a. Location

     b. Material

          1. Steps

          2. Railings

  c. Handicap access

  d. Condition

 7. Doorbells

  a. Location

  b. Condition

 8. Unit entrance doors

  a. Type of door

  b. Peephole

  c. Condition

 9. Roof access

  a. Location

  b. Condition

10. Roof overhang

  a. Design

  b. Condition

11. Gutters and downspouts

  a. Location

  b. Design

  c. Splashblocks

  d. Roof diverters

  e. Condition

12. Hose bibs

  a. Location

  b. Condition

13. Windows

  a. Location

  b. Materials

  c. Design

  d. Condition

Interior Buildings

 1. Foundation plans

  a. Design

  b. Type of materials

  c. Condition

 2. Floor plan

  a. Floor plan for traffic flow

3. Flooring
   a. Floor system
   b. Type of material
      1. Residential
         (a) Kitchen
         (b) Bathroom
         (c) Utility area
         (d) Foyer
         (e) Living areas
      2. Commercial
   c. Condition

4. Wall and ceiling areas
   a. Location
   b. Type of material
      1. Paint
      2. Wallpaper
   c. Design
   d. Condition

5. Heating, ventilation, and air conditioning (HVAC)
   a. Design
   b. Capacity
   c. Material
   d. Warranty
   e. Condition

6. Hot water heater
   a. Location
   b. Capacity
   c. Design
   d. Warranty
   e. Condition

7. Kitchen
   a. Design
   b. Appliances
      1. Type of appliances
         (a) Refrigerator
         (b) Oven

              (c) Dishwasher

              (d) Disposal

              (e) Washer

              (f) Dryer

              (g) Trash compactor

              (h) Microwave

        2. Inventory

        3. Color selection

        4. Warranties

        5. Condition

     c. Review cabinets

        1. Material

        2. Quality

        3. Color selection

        4. Design

        5. Hardware

        6. Condition

     d. Review plumbing

        1. Materials

        2. Design

        3. Sink/hardware

        4. Condition

  8. Smoke detectors

     a. Location

     b. Type

        1. Electric

        2. Battery

     c. Condition

  9. Bathroom

     a. Bathtub

        1. Material

        2. Design

        3. Condition

     b. Stall shower

        1. Material

        2. Design

        3. Condition

  c. Cabinets
    1. Material
    2. Design
    3. Color selection
    4. Condition
  d. Mirror
    1. Location
    2. Size
    3. Condition
  e. Medicine cabinets
    1. Location
    2. Size
    3. Condition
  f. Countertops
    1. Style
    2. Size
    3. Condition
  g. Sink
    1. Style
    2. Color
    3. Condition
  h. Commode
    1. Style
    2. Color
    3. Condition
  i. Hardware
    1. Style
    2. Color
    3. Condition
  j. Handicap facilities
    1. Code compliance
10. Insulation and soundproofing
  a. Specifications
    1. Floors
    2. Exterior walls
    3. Ceilings
  b. Condition

11. Electrical
    a. Location of electrical outlets
    b. Location of switches
    c. Location of panel boxes
    d. Location of telephone outlets
    e. Lighting fixtures
    f. Electrical capacity
    g. Light sizes
    h. Condition

12. Cable TV
    a. Location
    b. Condition

13. Window coverings
    a. Material
    b. Design
    c. Color
    d. Condition

14. Fireplaces
    a. Location
    b. Design
    c. Type of material
    d. Condition

15. Trimwork
    a. Location
        1. Ceiling molding
        2. Chair rail molding
        3. Door casing
        4. Window casing
        5. Floor molding

16. Mechanical Utility System
    a. Heating system
        1. Electric
        2. Gas
            (a) Location of supply and return ducts
    b. Water heating system
        1. Electric
        2. Gas

    c. Air conditioning system

       1. Electric

       2. Gas

    d. Cooking

       1. Electric

       2. Gas

    e. Clothes dryer

       1. Electric

       2. Gas

    f. Condition of systems

17. Plumbing

    a. Water pressure capacity

18. Utility room

    a. Location

    b. Appliances

       1. Washer

       2. Dryer

    c. Sink

    d. Condition

19. Doors

    a. Location

    b. Material

    c. Color

    d. Condition

20. Closets

    a. Location

    b. Shelving

    c. Lighting

    d. Size

    e. Condition

21. Parking Area

    a. Garage

    b. Carport

    c. Parking deck

       1. Location

       2. Design

       3. Materials

       4. Condition

22. Janitor's area (commercial property)

    a. Location

    b. Condition

23. Mechanical Area (commercial property)

    a. Location

    b. Equipment

    c. Condition

24. Elevators

    a. Location

    b. Design

    c. Specifications

    d. Condition

25. Common areas

    a. Location

       1. Lobby

       2. Hallways

       3. Stairways

    b. Design

    c. Color selection

    d. Material

    e. Condition

26. Fire Protection

    a. Location

    b. Design

    c. Condition

27. Security

    a. Location

    b. Design

    c. Specifications

    d. Condition

Amenity Package

1. Clubhouse

    a. Location

    b. Design

      c. Material

      d. Color selection

      e. Mechanical

      f. Plumbing

      g. Electrical

      h. Furniture, fixtures, and equipment

      i. Condition

2. Laundry facilities

      a. Location

      b. Design

      c. Plumbing

      d. Mechanical

      e. Electrical

      f. Color selection

      g. Interior finish

      h. Equipment

      i. Condition

3. Public restrooms

      a. Location

      b. Design

      c. Fixtures

      d. Color selection

      e. Cabinets

      f. Electrical

      g. Mechanical systems

      h. Plumbing

      i. Hardware

      j. Condition

4. Office

      a. Location

      b. Design

      c. Color selection

      d. Interior finish materials

      e. Electrical

      f. Mechanical systems

      g. Plumbing

      h. Condition

5. Pool
   a. Location
   b. Design
   c. Specifications
   d. Decking area
      1. Material
      2. Size
   e. Inventory
   f. Pool equipment room
   g. Diving board
   h. Condition

6. Tennis court
   a. Location
   b. Design
   c. Lighting
   d. Fencing
   e. Materials
   f. Condition

7. Playground Area
   a. Location
   b. Design
   c. Lighting
   d. Inventory
   e. Materials
   f. Fencing
   g. Condition

8. Lake area
   a. Location
   b. Design
   c. Condition

II. Review of the plans to determine:

1. Gross/net leasable square footage

2. The number and type of units

3. The size of each unit

4. The number of parking spaces

III. Review and verify the plans and specifications to make sure that they comply with all local zoning and building codes, in addition to being sufficient for issuance of a building permit and certificate of occupancy.

IV. Prepare an independent cost analysis, by trade, of direct construction costs for comparison with the cost breakdown estimates submitted by the contractor. Determine whether or not:

1. The project can be completed for the dollars indicated.

2. There are any "front loaded" costs.

3. There are any incorrect or underestimated costs.

V. Determine whether or not the project can be completed in the indicated time frame.

VI. Review the construction contracts and any other agreements or material pertinent to the project.

VII. Draft a report for the investor/owner summarizing the findings and highlighting the following:

1. Completeness of the plans and specifications

2. Unusual features and/or construction techniques employed

3. Cost estimates

4. Time schedules

5. Recommendations for correcting any deficiencies

CHECKLIST FOR USE AFTER CONSTRUCTION BEGINS

Inspect the construction site, on a weekly or other specific schedule, in conjunction with the investor's/owner's request for lender funds. The report should be designed to address the following points:

1. Whether or not the construction is proceeding in accordance with the approved plans and specifications.

2. Whether or not work is being performed in a good and workmanlike manner.

3. The nature and amount of construction in place, along with an estimate of the percent complete relative to the approved trade breakdown schedule.

4. Whether or not the contractor is entitled to receive the amount requested.

5. Review and approval of all building change orders requested by the investor/owner.

6. Whether or not the construction can be completed prior to the original or amended deadline date.

7. Review of all rain delay days requested by the contractor.

8. Review of payment for stored materials. Verification of all stored inventory. Confirm that all stored items are protected from the elements.

9. General comments and/or recommendations regarding slowdowns, labor problems, cost overruns, discrepancies, etc., or any other matters affecting the project.

10. In addition to the above, each report should include general progress photographs (color prints) along with photographs of any problem areas.

Proposed modifications to the plans and specifications, methods of construction or any change orders should be reviewed and reports should address the following points:

1. The description of the change and the overall impact on the project.

2. The reasonableness of the increases or decreases in the cost proposal.

3. The effect on the construction schedule.

4. Whether or not approvals have been or will need to be obtained from governmental authorities.

Inspection may be required at critical stages of construction depending upon the complexity of the job, including the following:

1. Excavation

2. Setting of curbing

3. Staking of buildings

4. Paving

5. Setting of concrete floors

CHECKLIST AT COMPLETION OF CONSTRUCTION

1. Review of final punch-out for property.

2. Drafting of construction completion certificate.

3. Review of twelve-month warranty punch-out.

What Your Attorney and Accountant Should Review

ATTORNEY

During the inspection period, a good real estate attorney should review all the documents: the current mortgage documents, as well as any documents supplied by new lenders; easements; any estoppel letters from both the lenders and tenants; the title work to be completed and, if there are any title objections, work with the seller's attorney to correct them.

The following is a checklist of items to be reviewed by the attorney:

1. Contract for all important dates

2. Zoning letters

3. Utility letters

4. Tenant and estoppel letters

5. Title policy

6. Mortgage documents

7. Easements

8. Development and building permits

9. Search for any mechanic's liens on property

10. Insurance policies

11. Attorney's opinion letters from the seller or lender

12. Service contracts

13. Tenant leases

ACCOUNTANT

The accountant will review the past operating figures and help prepare the future cash flow projections. The accountant might also be called upon to update the investor's financial statement for a loan application.

In summary, these professionals will submit their respective analyses on the proposed transaction. Once the reports are complete, the investor should call a meeting with the team of experts to draw together all the data and recommendations. Based on this input the investor should be able to make an intelligent decision of whether to pass or to proceed.

HOW TO PREPARE A DETAILED INVESTMENT INFORMATION PACKAGE

During this period of time, the investor should be preparing an investor information package including all the information regarding the property. It will detail the terms of the transaction, the financial projections, the mortgage information, and other information needed to raise any additional equity and debt the investor is seeking. Following is an outline for this package.

Investor Information Package Outline

1. Introduction to the property

    a. Brief summary of the property

    b. Brief summary of the transaction

    c. Proposed closing date of the transaction

2. Area Overview

    a. State information

        1. Population

        2. Income

        3. Employment

        4. Industry

        5. Retail buying power

      6. Government

      7. Map

   b. City information

      1. Population demographics

      2. Income

      3. Employment

      4. Industry

      5. Retail buying power

      6. Government

      7. Map

   c. County information

      1. Population demographics

      2. Income

      3. Employment

      4. Industry

      5. Retail buying power

      6. Government

      7. Map

   d. Neighborhood information (by census tract)

      1. Population demographics

      2. Income

      3. Employment

      4. Industry

      5. Retail buying power

      6. Residential housing

         (a) Single family

         (b) Duplex-quadraplex

         (c) Multi-family

         (d) Mobile home

      7. Traffic count

      8. Map

   e. Building permits (Number of properties, dollar value)

      1. Commercial

         (a) State

         (b) City

         (c) County

   2. Residential

      (a) State

      (b) City

      (c) County

3. Property description

   a. Location

      1. State

      2. City

      3. County

      4. Neighborhood

      5. Street address

   b. Property type

      1. Commercial

         (a) Number of buildings

         (b) Number of floors

         (c) Square footage per building (gross/net)

         (d) Square footage per floor (gross/net)

         (e) Number of parking spaces

            (1) Surface

            (2) Covered

      2. Residential

         (a) Number of buildings

         (b) Number of floors

         (c) Number of units

         (d) Unit information

            (1) Unit type

               (a) Flat

               (b) Townhouse

               (c) One level

            (2) Unit mix

            (3) Square footage per unit type (gross/net)

            (4) Number bedrooms, number bathrooms

            (5) Square footage (gross/net)

         (e) Number of parking spaces

            (1) Surface

            (2) Covered

   c. Site description
1. Acreage
2. Zoning
    (a) Current
    (b) Proposed
3. Density
    (a) Commercial
        (1) Square footage per acre
    (b) Residential
        (1) Units per acre
4. Topography description
    (a) Flat
    (b) Rolling
    (c) Wooded
5. Legal description
6. Plat

   d. Construction
1. Type of construction used
    (a) Stick built
    (b) Masonry
    (c) Pre-cast
    (d) Light steel frame
    (e) Concrete
    (f) Steel
2. Type of roof
    (a) Flat
    (b) Pitched
    (c) Built-up
    (d) Seamed
3. Type of exterior facade
    (a) Wood
    (b) Brick
    (c) Stucco
    (d) Stone
    (e) Dry-vit
    (f) Vinyl

       (g) Steel

       (h) Concrete

    4. Utility System

       (a) Electric

       (b) Gas

       (c) Water

       (d) Sewer

       (e) Telephone

       (f) Cable TV

       (g) Steam

       (h) Solar

    5. Insulation factors (R-factors)

       (a) Roof

       (b) Walls

       (c) Ceiling

       (d) Floors

    6. Landscaping

       (a) Ground cover

       (b) Plant material

  e. Unit features

    1. Commercial tenant finish (allowance)

       (a) Partitions

       (b) Ceiling

       (c) Flooring

       (d) Electrical

       (e) Mechanical

       (f) Plumbing

       (g) Telephone

       (h) Doors

       (i) Window coverings

       (j) Wall coverings

       (k) Built-ins

       (l) Signage

       (m) Restrooms

          (1) Plumbing

          (2) Hardware

2. Residential
   (a) Flooring (room location)
       (1) Carpet
       (2) Vinyl
       (3) Tile
       (4) Hardwood
   (b) Kitchen
       (1) Appliances (size, brand name, model number, color, serial number)
           (a) Dishwasher
           (b) Disposal
           (c) Refrigerator
               (1) Ice maker
               (2) Frost free
           (d) Trash compactor
           (e) Oven
               (1) Built-in
               (2) Double oven
               (3) Self-cleaning
               (4) Continuous cleaning
               (5) Electric
               (6) Gas
           (f) Microwave
           (g) Washer
           (h) Dryer
               (1) Electric
               (2) Gas
       (2) Cabinets (manufacturer, model number, color)
       (3) Sink (manufacturer, model number, color)
   (c) Wall coverings (room, brand name, model number)
       (1) Paint
       (2) Wallpaper
   (d) Window coverings (room, brand name, model number, color)
       (1) Drapes
       (2) Blinds
       (3) Rods
   (e) Mechanical (manufacturer, model number, size)
       (1) HVAC

 (f) Bathroom

  (1) Plumbing (manufacturer, model number, color, size)

   (a) Commode

   (b) Bathtub

   (c) Shower

   (d) Bidet

   (e) Sink

  (2) Mirror

  (3) Tile

  (4) Hardware

 (g) Electrical (manufacturer, model number)

  (1) Switches

  (2) Outlets

  (3) Light fixtures

  (4) Telephone outlets

  (5) Cable TV outlets

 (h) Doors (room location, design, manufacturer, model number, color)

 (i) Counter tops (manufacturer, model number, color, type)

  (1) Kitchen

  (2) Bathroom

  (3) Wet bar

 (j) Cabinets (manufacturer, model number, color)

  (1) Kitchen

  (2) Bathroom

  (3) Wet bar

 (k) Closet shelving

  (1) Type shelving

   (a) Wood

   (b) Wire coated

 (l) Laundry room

  (1) Type laundry hook-ups

  (2) Shelving

 (m) Fireplace

  (1) Wood burning

  (2) Gas starter

  (3) Gas logs

            (a) Masonry

            (b) Prefab

        (n) Bar area

            (1) Wet bar

            (2) Dry bar

        (o) Balcony/patio

            (1) Enclosed

            (2) Screen

            (3) Glass

f. Furniture

    1. List inventory (room location, manufacturer, model number, color)

g. Property amenities

    1. Commercial

        (a) Management office

        (b) On-site maintenance staff

        (c) Restaurant

        (d) Mail pick-up

        (e) Parking

        (f) Health club

    2. Residential

        (a) Management office

        (b) On-site maintenance staff

        (c) Clubhouse

            (1) Party room

                (a) Bar

                (b) Fireplace

            (2) Restrooms

            (3) Health facilities

                (a) Steam room

                (b) Sauna

                (c) Exercise room

                (d) Jacuzzi/hot tub

                (e) Jogging track

        (d) Laundry facilities

            (1) Number of washers and dryers

        (e) Pool

  (f) Tennis court

   (1) Lighted

  (g) Racquetball court

  (h) Playground area

  (i) Picnic area

   (1) Barbecue

  (j) Mail pick-up

h. Leasing information

 1. Commercial

  (a) Minimum/maximum floor area

  (b) Rental rate per square foot (gross/net)

   (1) Commercial space

   (2) Parking

   (3) Utilities

    (a) Paid by landlord

    (b) Paid by tenant

  (c) Lease terms

   (1) Option period

  (d) Rent escalations

   (1) Flat rate

   (2) Consumer Price Index (CPI)

    (a) Floor/ceiling

   (3) Operating expense pass through

   (4) Percentage rents

  (e) Common area charges

  (f) Tenant allowances

  (g) Rent concessions

  (h) Security deposit policy

  (i) Real estate commission policy

  (j) Rent schedule

  (k) Occupancy

   (1) History

   (2) Current

  (l) Tenant profile

   (1) Type business

   (2) Length tenancy

(3) Number employees

(4) Years in business

2. Residential

(a) Rental schedule per unit type/location

(1) Utilities

(a) Paid by landlord

(b) Paid by tenant

(2) Parking

(a) Surface

(b) Covered

(b) Lease term

(1) Option period

(c) Rent escalations

(d) Rent concessions

(e) Security deposit policy

(1) Pet deposit

(f) Pet policy

(1) Weight/height

(g) Fees

(1) Application

(2) Cleaning

(3) Pet

(h) Rental profile

(1) All adult

(2) Family

(i) Real estate commission policy

(j) Occupancy

(1) History

(2) Current

(k) Tenant profile

(1) Average age

(2) Length of residency

(3) Marital status

(4) Type employment

(5) Income range

i. Visual descriptions

1. Property photographs
    (a) Entrance
    (b) Building
        (1) Front elevation
        (2) Side elevations
        (3) Rear elevations
    (c) Amenities
    (d) Parking
    (e) Typical landscaping
    (f) Signage
    (g) Aerial
2. Rendering (if to-be-built)
3. Site plans
4. Floor plans

j. Property players (name, address, telephone number, contact)
    1. Current owner
    2. Proposed new ownership
    3. Property management company
    4. Leasing company
    5. Architect
    6. Landscape architect
    7. Engineer
        (a) Civil
        (b) Structural
        (c) Mechanical
        (d) Electrical
        (e) Plumbing
        (f) Surveyor
        (g) Soils test
    8. General contractor
        (a) Bonding company
    9. Construction manager
    10. Attorney
    11. Title company
    12. Accountant
    13. Money raiser

    14. Real estate broker

    15. Mortgage broker

    16. Lenders

        (a) Construction

        (b) Permanent

        (c) Investor Note

            (1) Surety

    17. Appraiser

    18. Tax consultant

    19. Insurance agent

k. Construction dates (if to-be-built)

    1. Date permitted

    2. Date final certificate of occupancy issued

l. Construction information (if to-be-built)

    1. Copy of construction contract

    2. Line-item costs

    3. Critical path

    4. Projected construction draw schedule

    5. Construction penalties

        (a) Date due

m. Investment summary

    1. Purchase price

        (a) Contract price

        (b) Fees paid to seller

        (c) Effective purchase price

    2. Price yardsticks

        (a) Price per unit

        (b) Price per square foot

        (c) Gross rent multiplier

        (d) Capitalization rate

        (e) Internal rate of return

n. Offering summary

    1. Investment unit size (number of investment units)

    2. Projected yearly write-offs

    3. Allocation of benefits

        (a) Cash flow

(1) General partners

(2) Limited partners

(3) Special limited partners

(b) Taxable income (loss)

(1) General partners

(2) Limited partners

(3) Special limited partners

(c) Refinancing/resale

(1) General partners

(2) Limited partners

(3) Special limited partners

4. Proposed closing date

5. Proposed managing/general partners

o. Financial summary

1. Forecast of investment performance

2. Sources and sources of proceeds

3. Forecast of cash flow

4. Forecast of taxable income (loss)

5. Forecast of resale

6. Back-up exhibits

(a) Summary of transaction

(b) Operating expenses

(1) Line-item analysis

(c) Capital expenditure budget

(1) Line-item analysis

(d) Summary of financing

(1) Lender

(2) Original loan closing date

(3) Original loan amount

(4) Current loan balance

(5) Interest rate

(6) Monthly payment

(7) Loan amortization

(8) Loan maturity

(9) Loan extension

(a) Extension fees

(b) Rate increases

    (c) Term

  (10)   Prepayment penalty

    (a) Lock-in period

  (11)   Security for loan

  (12)   Escrows

    (a) Real estate taxes

    (b) Insurance

  (13)   Loan transferability

    (a) Assumption fee

  (14)   Loan points

  (15)   Closing costs

  (16)   Loan buydown

  (17)   Due on sale clause

  (18)   Loan guarantees

  (19)   Lender reporting requirements

(e) Surety bond (if required by note lender)

  (1) Surety company

  (2) Points

  (3) Guarantor

(f) Fees to seller

  (1) Name of fee

  (2) Amount of fee

  (3) Payment date

  (4) Explanation of fee

(g) Fees to general partner

  (1) Name of fee

  (2) Amount of fee

  (3) Payment date

  (4) Explanation of fee

(h) Tax allocation of closing costs and fees

  (1) Items to expense

  (2) Items to add to the basis

  (3) Items to capitalize

  (4) Items to amortize

    (a) Number of years

(i) Depreciation schedule

            (1) Real property

            (2) Personal property

        (j) Debt service amortization schedules

        (k) Construction period interest schedule (if to-be-built)

        (l) Sales tax schedule (if to-be-built)

    p. Inventory

       1. Office

       2. Maintenance shop

       3. Model

       4. Laundry room

       5. Pool equipment

       6. Amenities

    q. Appraisal cover letter

    r. Comparable market study

    s. Seller warranties

    t. Copy of purchase agreement

    u. Copy of development agreement

    v. Copy of management agreement

    w. Resume of the general partner

QUALIFYING POTENTIAL INVESTORS AND MORTGAGE LENDERS

If additional equity will be needed to acquire the proposed property, the inspection period should be used to explore the market and determine whether other investors would be interested in contributing equity dollars to the deal. Further, if the transaction involves any type of new financing, other than the seller's purchase money mortgages, the investors should start to contact and qualify potential lenders.

HOW THE APPRAISAL PROCESS WORKS

Depending on the sophistication of the transaction, a new updated appraisal might be required by the lender or the potential investors. Appraisals can be designed for many needs; in this case it should be commissioned to establish the highest and best use of the property and to determine its market value. The lender will use this appraisal to determine the loan amount, while the investors will want an appraisal to show them that they are not overpaying for the property. Following is an outline for this appraisal process. The appraisal outline is designed to highlight areas the investor feels are necessary.

Appraisal Outline

1. Cover letter with appraised value
2. Certification of appraisal
3. Underlying assumptions and limiting conditions
4. Table of contents
5. Introduction
   a. Identification of the property
   b. Legal description
   c. Purpose of the appraisal
   d. Definition of market value
   e. Property rights appraised
   f. Current ownership
   g. Current zoning/proposed zoning
   h. Date of appraisal
6. Property plat
7. Regional data
   a. Location
   b. Demographics
   c. Climate
   d. Topography
   e. Soil and subsoil
   f. Employment
   g. Economic base
   h. Retail trade
   i. Tourism
   j. Military
   k. Utilities
   l. Municipal services
   m. Transportation
   n. Government
   o. Religious institutions
   p. Recreation
   q. Educational facilities
   r. Regional conclusion
   s. Regional map

8. Neighborhood Data
   a. Location
   b. Demographics
   c. Area development trends
   d. Transportation
   e. Access
   f. Utilities
   g. Neighborhood conclusion
   h. Map

9. Property Description
   a. Location
   b. Site description
   c. Site plan
   d. Site improvement description
   e. Building improvement description
   f. Unit mix
   g. Floor plans
   h. Elevation of buildings
   i. Amenity description
   j. Pictures of property
      1. Entrance
      2. Front elevation
      3. Side elevations
      4. Rear elevation
      5. Aerial
      6. Amenities
      7. Typical neighborhood

10. History of the property

11. Highest and best use of the property
    a. If vacant
    b. If built

12. Area real estate market
    a. Residential
       1. Building permits
          (a) For-sale housing

          (1) Condominium

          (2) Single-family

      (b) Rental

          (1) Multi-family

    2. Area vacancy rates

    3. Absorption history

    4. Pricing averages

  b. Commercial

    1. Building permits

      (a) Office

      (b) Retail

      (c) Lodging

      (d) Industrial

    2. Area vacancy rates

    3. Absorption history

    4. Pricing averages

13. Valuation

  a. Methodology

    1. Cost approach

      (a) Land comparables

          (1) Addresses of land comparables

          (2) Grantor/grantee

          (3) Sale date

          (4) Sales price

          (5) Terms

          (6) Size (acres)

          (7) Dollars per acre

          (8) Adjusted summary versus subject

          (9) Appraised land value

        (10) Land sale map

      (b) Replacement costs

          (1) Direct construction costs

          (2) Indirect costs

          (3) Developer's profit

      (c) Depreciation

    (1) Physical depreciation—curable

    (2) Physical deterioration—incurable

    (3) Functional obsolescence

    (4) External obsolescence

  (d) Cost approach value

2. Market approach

  (a) Improvement sale comparables

    (1) Name/location

    (2) Grantor/grantee

    (3) Sales date

    (4) Sales price

      (a) Cash equivalency

      (b) Financing

    (5) Size of property (number of units, total square feet)

    (6) Total square feet

    (7) Expense ratio

    (8) Dollars per unit

    (9) Dollars per square foot

    (10) Gross income multiplier

    (11) Capitalization rate

    (12) Market approach value

3. Income approach

  (a) Market rental rates

    (1) Name/location

    (2) Number of units

    (3) Year property built

    (4) Occupancy

    (5) Unit type

    (6) Rental rate

    (7) Who pays utilities

    (8) Rent per square foot

    (9) Comments

    (10) Photographs

  (b) Operating expenses

    (1) Breakdown of operating expenses

  (c) Stabilized income and expense statement

(d) Overall capitalization rate technique

    (1) Summary of comparable capitalization rates

(e) Development of interest and capitalization rate through utilizing mortgage equity analysis

    (1) Assumptions of property financing

(f) Rent-up analysis projections

(g) Rent loss analysis valuation

(h) Discounted cash flow analysis

4. Reconciliation

    (a) Final valuation

    (b) Final valuation after construction and absorption

14. Addenda

    a. Accelerated cost recovery system (ACRS)

        1. History of accelerated cost recovery system

        2. Definition of personal property

        3. Class of property

        4. Estimated value of personal property

            (a) Itemized value

            (b) Depreciation schedule

    b. Real estate tax comparables

        1. Millage rate

            (a) Breakdown—2-year history

        2. Comparables

            (a) Name of property

            (b) Location

            (c) Ownership

            (d) Number of units, square footage

            (e) Last tax bill

            (f) Taxes per unit/square foot

            (g) Comments

    c. Market Study

        1. Comparables

            (a) Name of property

            (b) Location

            (c) Total units/square footage

            (d) Unit type

  (e) Unit mix

  (f) Unit size

  (g) Square footage (gross/net)

  (h) Rental rate

   (1) Lease term

  (i) Who pays utilities

  (j) Rent per square foot

  (k) Parking

   (1) Rental rate

  (l) Security deposits/earnest money

  (m) Real estate leasing/sales commissions

  (n) Unit features

  (o) Amenities

  (p) Quality of property

  (q) Condition of property

  (r) Absorption history

  (s) Current occupancy

 2. Summary of comparable pricing

 3. Projected subject pricing schedule

 4. Absorption projection

 5. Comparable map

15. Qualifications of appraiser

WHEN TO DO A FEASIBILITY STUDY

If the property to be acquired is either to-be-built or one bought with a new intended use, the investor may want to have a feasibility study done. This report should be done by an expert in the area of intended use. In order that the report not be biased by the investor, the analyst should review the information supplied by the investor and then make final decisions based on market conditions. Following is a general outline for this feasibility process. It is designed so that the investor can pick out the necessary areas.

Feasibility Study Outline

1. Cover letter (scope of work)

2. Table of contents

3. Conclusions and recommendations

 a. Conclusions

 b. Recommendations

1. Type of property to develop
   (a) Commercial
       (1) Building information
           (a) Total square footage (gross/net)
           (b) Square footage per floor (gross/net)
           (c) Number floors
           (d) Design of building
           (e) Type construction
           (f) Desired zoning
       (2) Parking requirements
       (3) Projected rental/sale rates
           (a) Projected rental/sales concessions
           (b) Lease term
       (4) Tenant interior finish allowances
       (5) Real estate commission policy
       (6) Property amenities
       (7) Projected target market
       (8) Projected absorption period
           (a) Phasing of property
       (9) Projected marketing game plan
      (10) Potential lender sources
   (b) Residential
       (1) Building information
           (a) Total number of units
           (b) Unit mix
           (c) Unit type
           (d) Design of building
           (e) Type construction
           (f) Desired zoning
       (2) Parking requirements
       (3) Projected rental/sales rates
           (a) Projected rental/sales concessions
           (b) Lease term
       (4) Unit features
           (a) Options
       (5) Real estate commission policy

    (6) Property amenities

    (7) Projected target market

    (8) Projected absorption period

      (a) Phasing of property

    (9) Projected marketing game plan

    (10) Projected lender sources

4. Property Description

  a. Identification of the property

  b. Legal description

  c. Neighborhood boundaries

  d. Current zoning

  e. Property plat

  f. Topography

  g. Maps

    1. State

    2. City

    3. County

    4. Neighborhood

5. Overview of the City

  a. *Demographics (census tract)*

    1. Past

    2. Present

    3. Projected

      (a) Population

      (b) Age

      (c) Income

      (d) Sex

  b. Employment trends

    1. Largest employers in the area

      (a) Number of employees

    2. Unemployment statistics

  c. Purchasing power

    1. Past

    2. Present

    3. Projected

      (a) Per person

      (b) Per household

6. Building permits (number, dollar volume)

   a. Past

   b. Present

   c. Projected

      1. Residential

         (a) Single-family

         (b) Condominium/townhome

         (c) Mobile home

         (d) Multi-family

      2. Commercial

         (a) Retail

         (b) Office

         (c) Industrial

         (d) Lodging

7. Supply versus demand

   a. Past

   b. Present

   c. Projected

      1. Residential

         (a) Single-family

         (b) Condominium/townhome

         (c) Mobile home

         (d) Multi-family

            (1) Total number of units

            (2) Total number of properties

            (3) Occupancy

            (4) Absorption

      2. Commercial

         (a) Retail

         (b) Office

         (c) Industrial

         (d) Lodging

            (1) Total square footage

               (a) Class A

               (b) Class B

               (c) Class C

               (d) Class D

           (2) Total number of properties

           (3) Occupancy

           (4) Absorption

8. Overview of subject area

    a. Demographics (census tract)

        1. Population

        2. Age

        3. Income

        4. Sex

    b. Neighborhood analysis

    c. Proximity to

        1. Residential

        2. Commercial

           (a) Retail

           (b) Office

           (c) Industrial

           (d) Lodging

    d. Transportation

    e. Religious institutions

    f. Educational institutions

    g. Municipal services

    h. Recreation

9. Comparables

    a. Residential (rental properties)

        1. Type of property

           (a) Single family

           (b) Duplex-quadraplex

           (c) Multi-family

               (1) Garden

               (2) Townhouse

               (3) Mid-rise

               (4) High-rise

           (d) Mobile home

               (1) Mobile home lot rental

        2. Name of property

        3. Location

4. Year built

5. Ownership

6. Management company

7. Marketing company

8. Acreage

9. Density (units/acre)

10. Building information

    (a) Exterior construction

    (b) Roof

    (c) Utility system

    (d) Number of floors

11. Unit mix

12. Square footage (gross/net)

13. Parking

14. Unit features

15. Amenities

16. Quality of property

17. Condition of property

18. Resident profile

    (a) Age

    (b) Sex

    (c) Marital status

    (d) Length of tenancy

    (e) Income

    (f) Employment

19. Absorption history

20. Occupancy history

21. Rental rate

    (a) Rent concessions

    (b) Furnished rates

    (c) Parking

    (d) Who pays utilities

22. Rent per square foot

23. Lease term

24. Security deposit

    (a) Fees

25. Pet policy

26. Real estate commissions

27. Site plan

28. Floor plans

29. Pictures

30. Brochures

31. Location map

32. Copy of

    (a) Lease

    (b) Application

b. Residential (for-sale)

1. Type of property

    (a) Single-family

    (b) Condominium

    (c) Cooperative

    (d) Townhome

    (e) Mobile home

    (f) Lot sales

2. Name of property

3. Location

4. Year built

5. Developer

6. Marketing company

7. Acreage

8. Density (units/acre)

9. Building information

    (a) Exterior construction

    (b) Roof

    (c) Utility system

    (d) Number of floors

10. Unit mix (number of units)

11. Square footage (gross/net)

12. Parking

13. Unit features

14. Amenities

15. Quality of property

16. Condition of property
17. Resident profile
    (a) Age
    (b) Sex
    (c) Marital status
    (d) Income
    (e) Employment
18. Absorption history
19. Sales price
    (a) Options
20. Sales price per square foot
21. Association fees
    (a) Breakdown
22. Earnest money deposit
23. Financing terms
    (a) Lender
    (b) Interest rate
    (c) Amortization period
    (d) Term
    (e) Buydown
    (f) Closing costs
24. Real estate commissions
25. Site plan
26. Floor plan
27. Pictures
28. Brochure
29. Location map
30. Copy of
    (a) Sales contract
    (b) Condominium/cooperative documents
    (c) By-laws
c. Commercial (rental properties)
    1. Type of property
       (a) Retail
           (1) Strip center
           (2) Neighborhood center

          (3) Community center

          (4) Regional center

          (5) Super regional center

          (6) Theme center

     (b) Office

          (1) Business park

     (c) Industrial

          (1) Light industrial

          (2) Heavy industrial

          (3) Mini-warehouse

2. Name of property

3. Location

4. Year built

5. Ownership

6. Management company

7. Leasing agent

8. Acreage

9. Density

10. Building information

     (a) Exterior construction

     (b) Roof

     (c) Utility system

     (d) Number of floors

     (e) Number of buildings

     (f) Ceiling height

     (g) Bay depth

     (h) Dock loading

11. Total square footage (gross/net)

     (a) Square footage per floor

     (b) Square footage per building

12. Parking

13. Tenant finish allowance

14. Amenities

15. Quality of property

16. Condition of property

17. Tenant profile

       (a) Type of business

       (b) Length of tenancy

  18. Rental rate (per square foot-gross/net)

       (a) Rent concessions

       (b) Who pays utilities

       (c) Common area maintenance

       (d) Lease options

       (e) Escalation

       (f) Participation leases

  19. Lease term

  20. Security deposits

  21. Roster of tenants

  22. Real estate commissions

  23. Absorption history

  24. Occupancy history

  25. Site plan

  26. Floor plan

  27. Picture

  28. Brochure

  29. Location map

  30. Copy of lease

d. Commercial (For Sale)

  1. Type of property

       (a) Retail

       (b) Office

       (c) Industrial

  2. Name of property

  3. Location

  4. Year built

  5. Ownership/developer

  6. Management company

  7. Leasing company

  8. Acreage

  9. Density

  10. Building information

       (a) Exterior construction

       (b) Roof

  (c) Utility system

  (d) Number of floors

  (e) Number of buildings

  (f) Ceiling height

  (g) Bay depth

  (h) Dock loading

11. Total square footage

  (a) Square footage per floor

  (b) Square footage per building

12. Parking

13. Tenant finish allowance

14. Amenities

15. Quality of property

16. Condition of property

17. Buyer profile

18. Sales price (per square foot gross/net)

  (a) Sales price concessions

  (b) Owners association fees

19. Earnest money deposit

20. Financing

  (a) Lender

  (b) Interest rate

  (c) Amortization period

  (d) Term

  (e) Buydown

  (f) Closing costs

21. Roster of buyers

22. Real estate commissions

23. Sales absorption history

24. Site plan

25. Floor plan

26. Picture

27. Brochure

28. Location map

29. Copy of

       (a) Sales contract

       (b) Condominium documents

       (c) By-laws

e. *Lodging*

  1. Type of property

       (a) Motel

       (b) Hotel

       (c) Suites

  2. Name of property

  3. Year built

  4. Ownership

  5. Management company

  6. Acreage

  7. Density

  8. Building information

       (a) Exterior construction

       (b) Roof

       (c) Utility system

       (d) Number of floors

  9. Unit mix (number of units)

10. Square footage (gross/net)

11. Parking

12. Unit features

       (a) Furniture

13. Amenities

14. Quality of property

15. Condition of property

16. Tenant profile

17. Occupancy history

18. Rental rates

       (a) Weekday

       (b) Weekend

       (c) Special discounts

19. Site plan

20. Floor plans

21. Brochure

22. Location map

10. Property Comparison Analysis
    a. Price (rental or sales) per square foot
    b. Features
    c. Amenities
    d. Financing
    e. Correlation of data in relation to subject

11. Surveys
    a. Sample

12. Projected absorption schedule
    a. Unit type
    b. Square footage or number of units per month

13. Qualifications of the analyst
    a. Firm
    b. Principals
    c. Analyst

WHAT TO DO AFTER YOU MAKE YOUR PURCHASING DECISION

If the Purchasing Decision is "No" . . .

If after careful analysis, the investor decides not to acquire the property, she should send a registered letter to her attorney, the seller, the seller's attorney, the broker, and the title company stating that she wishes to terminate the purchase agreement. Instructions should be given as to where the earnest money should be returned.

If the Purchasing Decision is "Yes" . . .

If the investor's decision is to proceed with the acquisition, she should take one last look at all of the facts and figures and then notify the proper parties in writing of her intent to proceed. At this point the investor's money will be "at risk," and the investor should start to prepare to close the transaction.

SUMMARY

The inspection period is the most important stage of the deal. Since time is critical and a lot of money is riding on this decision, the knowledgeable investor will use this time wisely. Since most are not experts in all aspects of real estate transactions, the wise investor should assemble the best team possible to help in the decision making process. The investor should analyze all the data and ask all the right questions. The more questions asked, the easier the decision should be. Even though both time and money have been expended, the investor should not be forced into an uncomfortable deal. With time and experience, the investor should develop a sixth sense about which deals are best.

PROPERTY INSPECTION FORMS

Transaction Summary

These forms are designed to summarize the initial operating pro-forma information.

1. Residential
2. Commercial

Lease Summary

These forms are designed to summarize the rental information for each tenant.

1. Residential
2. Commercial
3. Mini-warehouse

Building Inspection

These forms are to be used when inspecting the interiors and exteriors of various properties.

1. Residential
2. Commercial
   a. Exterior Building Inspection Form
   b. Interior Building Inspection Form

Utility Deposits

This form is designed to keep track of the various utility deposits.

Service Contracts

This form is designed to keep track of the numerous service contracts.

Rent Increase per Month by Lease Expiration

This form is designed to project rent increases on a monthly basis by lease expiration dates.

Staff Analysis

This form is to be used when evaluating each employee on the property.

Market Comparable Study

These forms are to be used when updating the market comparable information.

1. Residential
2. Office

3. Retail

4. Industrial Building

5. Mini-warehouse

6. Hotel/Motel

Comparable Market Summary

These forms are to be used to summarize the data in the market comparable study.

1. Residential

2. Commercial

3. Mini-warehouse

4. Hotel/Motel

Land Sale Comparable Market Study

This form is designed to keep track of various land sales.

Inventory Checklist

This form is designed to keep track of the property inventory.

Insurance Checklist

This form is designed to keep track of the various types of insurance needed.

Property Tax Checklist

This form is to be used to keep track of property taxes on the property.

Professional Services Qualifying Checklists

These forms are to be used to keep track of and to qualify the various types of professionals that will make up the inspection team.

1. Broker

    a. Real Estate Broker

    b. Mortgage Broker

2. Appraiser

3. Professional Services

    a. Architect

    b. Landscape Architect

    c. Construction Management

    d. Engineer

     1. Structural

     2. Mechanical

     3. Electrical

     4. Plumbing

     5. Soils

   e. Surveyor

   f. Interior Decorator

   g. Tax Consultant

4. Management Companies

5. Marketing Companies

6. Attorney

7. Accountant

Deal Rating Sheet

This form is to be used to evaluate the potential transaction.

Demographics Form

This form is to be used to evaluate the demographics of the property.

FORM 5-1
Residential Transaction Summary

PROPERTY NAME _____
ADDRESS _____
_____
SELLER _____
    CONTACT _____
    ADDRESS _____
_____
    TEL. NO. ( ) _____
DATE _____
RATING _____

BROKER _____
    CONTACT _____
    ADDRESS _____
_____
    TEL. NO. ( ) _____
DATE _____

CURRENT OCCUPANCY ____%
SALES PRICE $ _____
GROSS INCOME MULTIPLIER
    (GRM) ____ X
CAPITALIZATION RATE _____
PRICE/SQ.FT. $ _____
PRICE/UNIT $ _____

UNIT INFORMATION

#UNITS	TYPE	SQ.FT.	RENT	RENT/SF
_____	_____	_____	$ _____	$ _____
_____	_____	_____	$ _____	$ _____
_____	_____	_____	$ _____	$ _____
_____	_____	_____	$ _____	$ _____
_____	_____	_____	$ _____	$ _____
_____	_____	_____	$ _____	$ _____
_____	_____	_____	$ _____	$ _____
TOTAL _____	_____	_____	$ _____	$ _____
AVE			$ _____	$ _____
			$ _____	$ _____

TENANT PAYS:
    ELECTRICITY _____
    GAS _____
    WATER _____
    SEWER _____
    CABLE _____
    TRASH _____

12 MONTH OPERATING PROFORMA

YEAR _____

REVENUE:
GROSS POTENTIAL INCOME	$ _____
VACANCY	$ _____
LATE CHARGES	$ _____
NSF CHARGES	$ _____
LAUNDRY	$ _____
APPLICATION FEE	$ _____
FORFEITED DEPOSITS	$ _____
PET FEES	$ _____
VENDING	$ _____
MISC. _____	$ _____
MISC. _____	$ _____

TOTAL REVENUE $ _____

EXPENSES:
SALARIES & WAGES	$ _____
REPAIRS & MAINTENANCE	$ _____
UTILITIES	$ _____
TAXES	$ _____
INSURANCE	$ _____
GENERAL & ADMINISTRATIVE	$ _____
MANAGEMENT FEES	$ _____
PROFESSIONAL FEES	$ _____
MARKETING	$ _____
CONTRACT SERVICES	$ _____
RESERVES & REPLACEMENTS	$ _____

TOTAL EXPENSES $ _____

NET OPERATING INCOME $ _____

DEBT SERVICE:
1ST MTG.	$ _____
2ND MTG.	$ _____
3RD MTG.	$ _____
TOTAL DEBT SERVICE	$ _____

CAPITAL EXPENDITURES $ _____

CASH FLOW $ _____

COMMENTS _____
_____
_____

MORTGAGE TERMS

1ST MTG:
    LENDER _____
    ORIGINAL BAL. $ _____
    CURRENT BAL. (AS OF ____) $ _____
    INTEREST RATE ____% AMORT. _____
    MATURITY DATE _____
    MONTHLY PAYMENT $ _____
COMMENTS _____
_____
_____
_____

MORTGAGE TERMS

2ND MTG:
    LENDER _____
    ORIGINAL BAL. $ _____
    CURRENT BAL. (AS OF ____) $ _____
    INTEREST RATE ____% AMORT. _____
    MATURITY DATE _____
    MONTHLY PAYMENT $ _____
COMMENTS _____
_____
_____

MORTGAGE TERMS

3RD MTG:
    LENDER _____
    ORIGINAL BAL. $ _____
    CURRENT BAL. (AS OF ____) $ _____
    INTEREST RATE ____% AMORT. _____
    MATURITY DATE _____
    MONTHLY PAYMENT $ _____
COMMENTS _____
_____
_____
_____

196

Commercial Transaction Summary

PROPERTY NAME _____
ADDRESS _____
_____
SELLER _____
    CONTACT _____

    ADDRESS _____
_____
TEL. NO. ( ) _____

RATING _____

BROKER _____
    CONTACT _____
    ADDRESS _____
_____
TEL. NO. ( ) _____
DATE _____

CURRENT OCCUPANCY _____%
SALES PRICE $ _____
GROSS INCOME MULTIPLIER
    (GRM) ___ X
CAPITALIZATION RATE _____
PRICE/SQ.FT. $ _____

TYPE PROPERTY	SQ.FT.	RENT/SF
OFFICE _____	_____	_____
RETAIL _____	_____	_____
INDUSTRIAL _____	_____	_____
MINI WAREHOUSE _____	_____	_____
NET/GROSS	_____	_____

TENANT PAYS:
    ELECTRICITY _____   JANITORIAL _____
    GAS _____   MAINTENANCE _____
    WATER _____   TAXES _____
    SEWER _____   INSURANCE _____
    TRASH _____   C.A.M. _____

12 MONTH OPERATING PROFORMA

YEAR _____

REVENUE:
GROSS POTENTIAL INCOME	$ _____
VACANCY	$ _____
LATE CHARGES	$ _____
NSF CHARGES	$ _____
FORFEITED DEPOSITS	$ _____
C.A.M. CHARGES	$ _____
PERCENTAGE RENT	$ _____
VENDING	$ _____
MISC. _____	$ _____
MISC. _____	$ _____
TOTAL REVENUE	$ _____

EXPENSES:
SALARIES & WAGES	$ _____
REPAIRS & MAINTENANCE	$ _____
UTILITIES	$ _____
TAXES	$ _____
INSURANCE	$ _____
GENERAL & ADMINISTRATIVE	$ _____
MANAGEMENT FEES	$ _____
PROFESSIONAL FEES	$ _____
MARKETING	$ _____
CONTRACT SERVICES	$ _____
TENANT IMPROVEMENTS	$ _____
RESERVES & REPLACEMENTS	$ _____
TOTAL EXPENSES	$ _____

NET OPERATING INCOME $ _____

DEBT SERVICE:
1ST MTG.	$ _____
2ND MTG.	$ _____
3RD MTG.	$ _____
TOTAL DEBT SERVICE	$ _____

CAPITAL EXPENDITURES $ _____

CASH FLOW $ _____

COMMENTS _____
_____
_____

MORTGAGE TERMS

1ST MTG:
    LENDER _____
    ORIGINAL BAL. $ _____
    CURRENT BAL. (AS OF _____) $ _____
    INTEREST RATE _____% AMORT. _____
    MATURITY DATE _____
    MONTHLY PAYMENT $ _____
COMMENTS _____
_____
_____
_____

MORTGAGE TERMS

2ND MTG:
    LENDER _____
    ORIGINAL BAL. $ _____
    CURRENT BAL. (AS OF ___) $ _____
    INTEREST RATE _____% AMORT. _____
    MATURITY DATE _____
    MONTHLY PAYMENT $ _____
COMMENTS _____
_____
_____
_____

MORTGAGE TERMS

3RD MTG:
    LENDER _____
    ORIGINAL BAL. $ _____
    CURRENT BAL. (AS OF ___) $ _____
    INTEREST RATE ___% AMORT. _____
    MATURITY DATE _____
    MONTHLY PAYMENT $ _____
COMMENTS _____
_____
_____

FORM 5-3
Residential Lease Summary

PROPERTY NAME _____
ADDRESS _____

TELEPHONE NO. ( ) _____
OWNERSHIP _____
  TEL. NO. ( ) _____
MANAGEMENT _____
  TEL. NO. ( ) _____
LEASING AGENT _____
  TEL. NO. ( ) _____

PAGE ____ OF ____

DATE _____

TENANT PAYS:
  GAS _____
  ELEC _____
  WATER _____
  SEWER _____
  CABLE _____
  UNFURNISHED _____
  FURNISHED _____
  RENT _____
  RENT _____
  RENT _____

FLOOR MEASUREMENT:
  GROSS _____
  NET _____

UNIT MIX:

UNIT TYPE	UNIT MIX	SQ.FT.	STREET RENT	RENT/ S.F.	NO. OCCUPIED	% OCCUPIED
_____	_____	_____	$ _____	_____	_____	____%
_____	_____	_____	$ _____	_____	_____	____%
_____	_____	_____	$ _____	_____	_____	____%
_____	_____	_____	$ _____	_____	_____	____%
_____	_____	_____	$ _____	_____	_____	____%
_____	_____	_____	$ _____	_____	_____	____%
TOTAL _____						
AVERAGE _____			$ _____		_____	____%

DATE OF LAST RENT INCREASE _____

TENANT	ADDRESS	UNIT TYPE	LEASE TERM	BEG. DATE	END DATE	SEC. DEP.	PET DEP.	FURN. DEP.	RENT/ MONTH	FURN. RENT/ MONTH	OPTIONS	COMMENTS
						$	$	$	$	$		
						$	$	$	$	$		
						$	$	$	$	$		
						$	$	$	$	$		
						$	$	$	$	$		
						$	$	$	$	$		
						$	$	$	$	$		
						$	$	$	$	$		
						$	$	$	$	$		
						$	$	$	$	$		
						$	$	$	$	$		
						$	$	$	$	$		
						$	$	$	$	$		
						$	$	$	$	$		

198

FORM 5-4

Commercial Lease Summary

PROPERTY NAME _____
ADDRESS _____

TELEPHONE NO. ( ) _____
OWNERSHIP _____
  TEL. NO. ( ) _____
MANAGEMENT _____
  TEL. NO. ( ) _____
LEASING AGENT _____
  TEL. NO. ( ) _____

PAGE _____ OF _____

DATE _____

TYPE PROPERTY:
  RETAIL _____
  OFFICE _____
  INDUSTRIAL _____

SQ.FT.-RETAIL _____
SQ.FT.-OFFICE _____
SQ.FT.-INDUST. _____
RETAIL OCCUPANCY _____ %
OFFICE OCCUPANCY _____ %
INDUST. OCCUPANCY _____ %

FLOOR MEASUREMENT:
  GROSS _____
  NET _____
  FACTOR _____ %

YEAR BUILT _____
TOTAL SQ. FT. _____
FLOOR SIZE _____
NO. BLDGS. _____
NO. FLOORS _____

STREET RENT $ _____ /S.F.

TENANT PAYS:
  GAS _____
  ELEC _____
  WATER _____
  SEWER _____
  JANITORIAL _____
  R.E. TAXES _____
  INSURANCE _____
  MAINTENANCE _____
  C.A.M. _____

TENANT NAME	SUITE #	SQ. FT.	LEASE TERM	SEC. DEP.	BEG. DATE	END DATE	BASE RATE/SF	RENT/ MONTH	% RENT	RENT ESCAL	CAM	TAX STOP/ YEAR	OPTIONS	COMMENTS
				$			$	$	%					
				$			$	$	%					
				$			$	$	%					
				$			$	$	%					
				$			$	$	%					
				$			$	$	%					
				$			$	$	%					
				$			$	$	%					
				$			$	$	%					
				$			$	$	%					
				$			$	$	%					
				$			$	$	%					
				$			$	$	%					
				$			$	$	%					
				$			$	$	%					
				$			$	$	%					
				$			$	$	%					
				$			$	$	%					

199

FORM 5-5

Mini-Warehouse Lease Summary

PROPERTY NAME _____

ADDRESS _____

TELEPHONE NO. ( ) _____

OWNERSHIP _____

    TEL. NO. ( ) _____

MANAGEMENT _____

    TEL. NO. ( ) _____

LEASING AGENT _____

    TEL. NO. ( ) _____

PAGE _____ OF _____

DATE _____

YEAR BUILT _____

TOTAL SQ. FT. _____

NET SQ. FT. _____

NO. BLDG. _____

NO. FLOORS _____

ELEVATOR _____

OUTSIDE STORAGE _____

UNIT MIX:

LOCATION	SIZE	UNIT MIX	STREET RENT/ MONTH	RENT/ S.F.	% OCCUPIED
			$	$	
			$	$	
			$	$	
			$	$	
			$	$	
			$	$	
TOTAL AVERAGE			$	$	

TENANT NAME	UNIT NO.	SIZE	RENT/ MONTH	SEC. DEP.	LEASE TERM	BEG. DATE	END DATE	OPTIONS	COMMENTS
			$	$					
			$	$					
			$	$					
			$	$					
			$	$					
			$	$					
			$	$					
			$	$					
			$	$					
			$	$					
			$	$					
			$	$					
			$	$					
			$	$					
			$	$					
			$	$					
			$	$					
			$	$					
			$	$					
			$	$					
			$	$					
			$	$					
			$	$					

FORM 5-6
Residential Punch-Out Report

PROPERTY NAME _____
PREPARED BY _____
BLDG. _____ SUITE # _____
DATE _____
PAGE _____ OF _____

DESCRIPTION	EXCEL.	GOOD	POOR	COMMENTS
SITE:				
CURB APPEAL				
SIGNAGE				
LANDSCAPING				
PAVING				
STRIPPING				
SIDEWALKS				
CURBS				
DUMPSTER AREA				
RETAINING WALLS				
FENCING				
RETENSION POND				
CATCH BASINS				
AMENITIES:				
POOL				
POOL EQUIPMENT				
FENCING				
DECKING				
TENNIS COURTS				
LIGHTING				
FENCING				
NET				

DESCRIPTION	EXCEL.	GOOD	POOR	COMMENTS
EXTERIOR BUILDINGS:				
FACADE				
WOOD				
STUCCO				
BRICK				
STONE				
TUCK POINTING				
COPING				
WINDOWS				
CHIMNEYS				
FOUNDATIONS				
MAIL BOXES				
DOOR				
LOCKS				
NAME PLATES				
INTERCOM				
GLASS				

Comments _____

201

FORM 5-6
Residential Punch-Out Report (Cont'd)

PROPERTY NAME _____
PREPARED BY _____ SUITE # _____
BLDG. _____
DATE _____
PAGE _____ OF _____

GRAND TOTAL $ _____

DESCRIPTION	CONDITION	COST ESTIMATE
FOYER:		
FLOOR		$
CEILING		$
WALLS		$
ELECTRICAL		$
LIGHT FIXTURES		$
MECHANICAL DUCTS		$
DOOR		$
WINDOW		$
WINDOW COVERING		$
KITCHEN:		
FLOOR		$
CEILING		$
WALLS		$
ELECTRICAL		$
LIGHT FIXTURES		$
CABINETS		$
HARDWARE		$
APPLIANCES:		$
REFRIGERATOR		$
RANGE		$
DISPOSAL		$
MICROWAVE		$
TRASH COMPACTOR		$
MECHANICAL DUCTS		$
DOOR		$
SHELVING		$
WINDOW		$
WINDOW COVERINGS		$
TOTAL		$

DESCRIPTION	CONDITION	COST ESTIMATE
BATHROOM:		
FLOOR		$
CEILING		$
WALLS		$
ELECTRICAL		$
LIGHT FIXTURES		$
CABINETS		$
HARDWARE		$
MECHANICAL DUCTS		$
DOOR		$
SHELVING		$
WINDOW		$
WINDOW COVERINGS		$
COMMODE		$
TUB		$
SHOWER		$
FIXTURES		$
MIRROR		$
BATHROOM:		
FLOOR		$
CEILING		$
WALLS		$
ELECTRICAL		$
LIGHT FIXTURES		$
CABINETS		$
HARDWARE		$
MECHANICAL DUCTS		$
DOOR		$
SHELVING		$
WINDOW		$
WINDOW COVERINGS		$
COMMODE		$
TUB		$
SHOWER		$
FIXTURES		$
MIRROR		$
TOTAL		$

GRAND TOTAL $ _____

FORM 5-6

Residential Punch-Out Report (Cont'd)

PROPERTY NAME _____
PREPARED BY _____
BLDG. _____ SUITE # _____
DATE _____
PAGE _____ OF _____

DESCRIPTION	CONDITION	COST ESTIMATE
DINING ROOM:		
FLOOR		$
CEILING		$
WALLS		$
ELECTRICAL		$
LIGHT FIXTURES		$
MECHANICAL DUCTS		$
DOOR		$
SHELVING		$
WINDOW		$
WINDOW COVERING		$
DEN:		
FLOOR		$
CEILING		$
WALLS		$
ELECTRICAL		$
LIGHT FIXTURES		$
MECHANICAL DUCTS		$
DOOR		$
SHELVING		$
WINDOW		$
WINDOW COVERING		$
WET BAR		$
MIRROR		$
BEDROOM:		
FLOOR		$
CEILING		$
WALLS		$
ELECTRICAL		$
LIGHT FIXTURES		$
MECHANICAL DUCTS		$
DOOR		$
SHELVING		$
WINDOW		$
WINDOW COVERING		$
CABINETS		$
HARDWARE		$
TOTAL		$

DESCRIPTION	CONDITION	COST ESTIMATE
BEDROOM:		
FLOOR		$
CEILING		$
WALLS		$
ELECTRICAL		$
LIGHT FIXTURES		$
MECHANICAL DUCTS		$
DOOR		$
SHELVING		$
WINDOW		$
WINDOW COVERING		$
CABINETS		$
HARDWARE		$
BEDROOM:		
FLOOR		$
CEILING		$
WALLS		$
ELECTRICAL		$
LIGHT FIXTURES		$
MECHANICAL DUCTS		$
DOOR		$
SHELVING		$
WINDOW		$
WINDOW COVERING		$
CABINETS		$
HARDWARE		$
BEDROOM:		
FLOOR		$
CEILING		$
WALLS		$
ELECTRICAL		$
LIGHT FIXTURES		$
MECHANICAL DUCTS		$
DOOR		$
SHELVING		$
WINDOW		$
WINDOW COVERING		$
CABINETS		$
HARDWARE		$
TOTAL		$

GRAND TOTAL $ _____

Residential Punch-Out Report (Cont'd)

DESCRIPTION	CONDITION	COST ESTIMATE
LAUNDRY ROOM:		
FLOOR		$
CEILING		$
WALLS		$
ELECTRICAL		$
LIGHT FIXTURES		$
MECHANICAL DUCTS		$
PLUMBING CONNECTIONS		$
CABINETS		$
DOOR		$
SHELVING		$
		$
HALLWAY		
FLOOR		$
CEILING		$
WALLS		$
ELECTRICAL		$
LIGHT FIXTURES		$
MECHANICAL DUCTS		$
PLUMBING CONNECTIONS		$
		$
MECHANICAL:		
FLOOR		$
CEILING		$
WALLS		$
ELECTRICAL		$
LIGHT FIXTURES		$
FURNACE		$
AIR CONDITIONER		$
DOOR		$
		$
		$
TOTAL		$

DESCRIPTION	CONDITION	COST ESTIMATE
PATIO/DECK/SUNROOM:		
FLOOR		$
CEILING		$
WALLS		$
ELECTRICAL		$
LIGHT FIXTURES		$
DOOR		$
WINDOW		$
WINDOW COVERING		$
SCREEN		$
RAILING		$
		$
BASEMENT:		
FLOOR		$
CEILING		$
WALLS		$
ELECTRICAL		$
LIGHT FIXTURES		$
DOOR		$
WINDOW		$
WINDOW COVERING		$
		$
GARAGE:		
FLOOR		$
CEILING		$
WALLS		$
ELECTRICAL		$
LIGHT FIXTURES		$
DOOR		$
WINDOW		$
ELECTRIC GARAGE OPENER		$
		$
MISCELLANEOUS:		
CENTRAL VACUUM		$
INTERCOM		$
		$
		$
		$
TOTAL		$
		GRAND TOTAL $

Residential Punch-Out Report (Cont'd)

PROPERTY NAME _____

ADDRESS _____

TEL. NO. ( ) _____

PREPARED BY _____

DATE _____

PAGE ___ OF ___

SUITE # _____

FLOOR # _____

SITE _____

EXTERIOR _____

INTERIOR _____

TYPE PROPERTY _____

BLDG #/ UNIT #	DESCRIPTION	CONDITION	ESTIMATED COST	ACTUAL COST	COMMENTS
			$	$	
			$	$	
			$	$	
			$	$	
			$	$	
			$	$	
			$	$	
			$	$	
			$	$	
			$	$	
			$	$	
			$	$	
			$	$	
			$	$	
			$	$	
			$	$	
			$	$	
			$	$	
			$	$	
			$	$	
			$	$	
			$	$	
			$	$	
			$	$	
			$	$	
			$	$	
			$	$	
TOTAL			$	$	

Form 5-7
Commercial Punch-Out Report

PROPERTY NAME _____
PREPARED BY _____
BLDG. _____ SUITE _____
DATE_____
PAGE _____ OF _____

TYPE PROPERTY:
   RETAIL _____
   OFFICE_____
   INDUSTRIAL _____
   MINI-WAREHOUSE _____
   LODGING_____

DESCRIPTION	CONDITION	COST ESTIMATE	DESCRIPTION	CONDITION	COST ESTIMATE
LOBBY:			PUBLIC RESTROOMS:		
FLOORING	_____	$ _____	FLOORING	_____	$ _____
WALLS	_____	$ _____	WALLS	_____	$ _____
CEILING	_____	$ _____	CEILING	_____	$ _____
WINDOWS	_____	$ _____	MIRRORS	_____	$ _____
DOORS	_____	$ _____	DOORS	_____	$ _____
HVAC	_____	$ _____	HVAC	_____	$ _____
ELECTRICAL	_____	$ _____	ELECTRICAL	_____	$ _____
SIGNAGE	_____	$ _____	HARDWARE	_____	$ _____
DIRECTORY	_____	$ _____	FIXTURES	_____	$ _____
LIGHT FIXTURES	_____	$ _____	SIGNAGE	_____	$ _____
	_____	$ _____	STALL DOORS	_____	$ _____
			LIGHT FIXTURES	_____	$ _____
HALLWAYS:				_____	$ _____
FLOORING	_____	$ _____		_____	$ _____
WALLS	_____	$ _____			
CEILING	_____	$ _____	JANITORIAL AREA:		
ELECTRICAL	_____	$ _____	FLOORING	_____	$ _____
HVAC	_____	$ _____	WALLS	_____	$ _____
DOORS	_____	$ _____	CEILING	_____	$ _____
DOOR HARDWARE	_____	$ _____	DOORS	_____	$ _____
LIGHT FIXTURES	_____	$ _____	HVAC	_____	$ _____
	_____	$ _____	ELECTRICAL	_____	$ _____
			HARDWARE	_____	$ _____
STAIRWAYS:			FIXTURES	_____	$ _____
FLOORING	_____	$ _____	SIGNAGE	_____	$ _____
WALLS	_____	$ _____	LIGHT FIXTURES	_____	$ _____
CEILING	_____	$ _____		_____	$ _____
ELECTRICAL	_____	$ _____		_____	$ _____
HVAC	_____	$ _____			
DOORS	_____	$ _____	TELEPHONE AREA:		
DOOR HARDWARE	_____	$ _____	FLOORING	_____	$ _____
LIGHT FIXTURES	_____	$ _____	WALLS	_____	$ _____
	_____	$ _____	CEILING	_____	$ _____
			MIRRORS	_____	$ _____
ELEVATORS:	_____	$ _____	DOORS	_____	$ _____
SERVICE PERMIT	_____	$ _____	HVAC	_____	$ _____
DOORS	_____	$ _____	ELECTRICAL	_____	$ _____
INTERIOR CAB	_____	$ _____	HARDWARE	_____	$ _____
MOTORS	_____	$ _____	SIGNAGE	_____	$ _____
ELEVATOR SHAFT	_____	$ _____	LIGHT FIXTURES	_____	$ _____
ELECTRICAL	_____	$ _____		_____	$ _____
LIGHT FIXTURES	_____	$ _____		_____	$ _____
	_____	$ _____		_____	$ _____
		$ _____		_____	$ _____
TOTAL		$ _____	TOTAL		$ _____

PROPERTY NAME _____
PREPARED BY _____
BLDG. _____ SUITE _____
DATE _____
PAGE _____ OF _____

TYPE PROPERTY:
  RETAIL _____
  OFFICE _____
  INDUSTRIAL _____
  MINI-WAREHOUSE _____
  LODGING _____

DESCRIPTION	CONDITION	COST ESTIMATE	DESCRIPTION	CONDITION	COST ESTIMATE
MECHANICAL AREA:			BASEMENT AREA:		
FLOORING	_____	$_____	FLOORING	_____	$_____
WALLS	_____	$_____	WALLS	_____	$_____
CEILING	_____	$_____	CEILING	_____	$_____
DOORS	_____	$_____	ELECTRICAL	_____	$_____
HVAC	_____	$_____	HVAC	_____	$_____
ELECTRICAL	_____	$_____	PLUMBING	_____	$_____
HARDWARE	_____	$_____	DRAINS	_____	$_____
SIGNAGE	_____	$_____	PUMPS	_____	$_____
LIGHT FIXTURES	_____	$_____	LIGHT FIXTURES	_____	$_____
_____	_____	$_____	VENTILATION	_____	$_____
_____	_____	$_____	WINDOWS	_____	$_____
_____	_____	$_____	DOORS	_____	$_____
_____	_____	$_____	_____	_____	$_____
_____	_____	$_____	_____	_____	$_____
			_____	_____	$_____
ELECTRICAL AREA:	_____	$_____	_____	_____	$_____
FLOORING	_____	$_____	_____	_____	$_____
WALLS	_____	$_____	LOCKER AREA:	_____	$_____
CEILING	_____	$_____	FLOORING	_____	$_____
DOORS	_____	$_____	WALLS	_____	$_____
HVAC	_____	$_____	CEILING	_____	$_____
ELECTRICAL	_____	$_____	ELECTRICAL	_____	$_____
HARDWARE	_____	$_____	HVAC	_____	$_____
SIGNAGE	_____	$_____	PLUMBING	_____	$_____
LIGHT FIXTURES	_____	$_____	LOCKERS	_____	$_____
_____	_____	$_____	DOORS	_____	$_____
_____	_____	$_____	LIGHT FIXTURES	_____	$_____
_____	_____	$_____	VENTILATION	_____	$_____
_____	_____	$_____	WINDOWS	_____	$_____
			_____	_____	$_____
FIRE SAFETY:			_____	_____	$_____
EXTINGUISHERS	_____	$_____	_____	_____	$_____
_____	_____	$_____	_____	_____	$_____
_____	_____	$_____	_____	_____	$_____
_____	_____	$_____	MISCELLANEOUS:		
_____	_____	$_____	_____	_____	$_____
_____	_____	$_____	_____	_____	$_____
_____	_____	$_____	_____	_____	$_____
_____	_____	$_____	_____	_____	$_____
_____	_____	$_____	_____	_____	$_____
_____	_____	$_____	_____	_____	$_____
_____	_____	$_____	_____	_____	$_____
_____	_____	$_____	_____	_____	$_____
TOTAL		$_____	TOTAL		$_____

PROPERTY NAME _____
PREPARED BY _____
BLDG. _____ SUITE _____
DATE _____
PAGE _____ OF _____

TYPE PROPERTY:
RETAIL _____
OFFICE _____
INDUSTRIAL _____
MINI-WAREHOUSE _____
LODGING _____

GRAND TOTAL $ _____

DESCRIPTION	CONDITION	COST ESTIMATE	DESCRIPTION	CONDITION	COST ESTIMATE
SITE:			EXTERIOR BUILDING:		
PAVING	_____	$ _____	EAST WALLS:		
PAVING STRIPPING	_____	$ _____	EXTERIOR FACADE TYPE	_____	$ _____
CURB & GUTTER	_____	$ _____	TUCK POINTING	_____	$ _____
SIDEWALKS	_____	$ _____	PAINTING	_____	$ _____
LANDSCAPING	_____	$ _____	METAL TRIM	_____	$ _____
SIGNAGE	_____	$ _____	COPING	_____	$ _____
WATER TURN-OFF VALVE	_____	$ _____	_____	_____	$ _____
RETENTION POND	_____	$ _____	_____	_____	$ _____
TRASH AREA	_____	$ _____	_____	_____	$ _____
LIGHTING	_____	$ _____	_____	_____	$ _____
SPRINKLER SYSTEM	_____	$ _____	_____	_____	$ _____
FOUNTAINS	_____	$ _____			
_____	_____	$ _____	WEST WALLS:		
_____	_____	$ _____	EXTERIOR FACADE TYPE	_____	$ _____
_____	_____	$ _____	TUCK POINTING	_____	$ _____
_____	_____	$ _____	PAINTING	_____	$ _____
_____	_____	$ _____	METAL TRIM	_____	$ _____
_____	_____	$ _____	COPING	_____	$ _____
			_____	_____	$ _____
			_____	_____	$ _____
EXTERIOR BUILDING:			_____	_____	$ _____
NORTH WALLS:	_____	$ _____	_____	_____	$ _____
EXTERIOR FACADE TYPE	_____	$ _____	_____	_____	$ _____
TUCK POINTING	_____	$ _____			
PAINTING	_____	$ _____	ROOF:		
METAL TRIM	_____	$ _____	TYPE	_____	$ _____
COPING	_____	$ _____	FLASHING	_____	$ _____
_____	_____	$ _____	VALLEYS	_____	$ _____
_____	_____	$ _____	DRAINS	_____	$ _____
_____	_____	$ _____	_____	_____	$ _____
_____	_____	$ _____	_____	_____	$ _____
_____	_____	$ _____	_____	_____	$ _____
			_____	_____	$ _____
SOUTH WALLS:			_____	_____	$ _____
EXTERIOR FACADE TYPE	_____	$ _____			
TUCK POINTING	_____	$ _____	CHIMNEYS:		
PAINTING	_____	$ _____	TYPE	_____	$ _____
METAL TRIM	_____	$ _____	TUCK POINTING	_____	$ _____
COPING	_____	$ _____	_____	_____	$ _____
_____	_____	$ _____	_____	_____	$ _____
_____	_____	$ _____	_____	_____	$ _____
_____	_____	$ _____	_____	_____	$ _____
_____	_____	$ _____	_____	_____	$ _____
_____	_____	$ _____	_____	_____	$ _____
TOTAL		$ _____	TOTAL		$ _____

Commercial Punch-Out Report (Cont'd)

PROPERTY NAME _____

PREPARED BY _____

BLDG. _____ SUITE _____

DATE _____

PAGE _____ OF _____

TYPE PROPERTY:

RETAIL _____

OFFICE _____

INDUSTRIAL _____

MINI-WAREHOUSE _____

LODGING _____

DESCRIPTION	CONDITION	COST ESTIMATE	DESCRIPTION	CONDITION	COST ESTIMATE
INTERIOR RENTAL SPACE:	_____	$ _____	INTERIOR RENTAL SPACE:	_____	$ _____
SPACE # _____	_____	$ _____	SPACE # _____	_____	$ _____
FLOORING	_____	$ _____	FLOORING	_____	$ _____
WALLS	_____	$ _____	WALLS	_____	$ _____
CEILING	_____	$ _____	CEILING	_____	$ _____
ELECTRICAL	_____	$ _____	ELECTRICAL	_____	$ _____
HVAC	_____	$ _____	HVAC	_____	$ _____
PLUMBING	_____	$ _____	PLUMBING	_____	$ _____
DOORS	_____	$ _____	DOORS	_____	$ _____
DOOR HARDWARE	_____	$ _____	DOOR HARDWARE	_____	$ _____
WINDOWS	_____	$ _____	WINDOWS	_____	$ _____
WINDOW COVERINGS	_____	$ _____	WINDOW COVERINGS	_____	$ _____
BASEBOARDS	_____	$ _____	BASEBOARDS	_____	$ _____
LIGHT FIXTURES	_____	$ _____	LIGHT FIXTURES	_____	$ _____
FIRE EXTINGUISHERS	_____	$ _____	FIRE EXTINGUISHERS	_____	$ _____
CABINETS	_____	$ _____	CABINETS	_____	$ _____
COUNTERTOPS	_____	$ _____	COUNTERTOPS	_____	$ _____
_____	_____	$ _____	_____	_____	$ _____
_____	_____	$ _____	_____	_____	$ _____
_____	_____	$ _____	_____	_____	$ _____
_____	_____	$ _____	_____	_____	$ _____
_____	_____	$ _____	_____	_____	$ _____
		$ _____			$ _____
SPACE # _____	_____	$ _____	SPACE # _____	_____	$ _____
FLOORING	_____	$ _____	FLOORING	_____	$ _____
WALLS	_____	$ _____	WALLS	_____	$ _____
CEILING	_____	$ _____	CEILING	_____	$ _____
ELECTRICAL	_____	$ _____	ELECTRICAL	_____	$ _____
HVAC	_____	$ _____	HVAC	_____	$ _____
PLUMBING	_____	$ _____	PLUMBING	_____	$ _____
DOORS	_____	$ _____	DOORS	_____	$ _____
DOOR HARDWARE	_____	$ _____	DOOR HARDWARE	_____	$ _____
WINDOWS	_____	$ _____	WINDOWS	_____	$ _____
WINDOW COVERINGS	_____	$ _____	WINDOW COVERINGS	_____	$ _____
BASEBOARDS	_____	$ _____	BASEBOARDS	_____	$ _____
LIGHT FIXTURES	_____	$ _____	LIGHT FIXTURES	_____	$ _____
FIRE EXTINGUISHERS	_____	$ _____	FIRE EXTINGUISHERS	_____	$ _____
CABINETS	_____	$ _____	CABINETS	_____	$ _____
COUNTERTOPS	_____	$ _____	COUNTERTOPS	_____	$ _____
_____	_____	$ _____	_____	_____	$ _____
_____	_____	$ _____	_____	_____	$ _____
_____	_____	$ _____	_____	_____	$ _____
_____	_____	$ _____	_____	_____	$ _____
TOTAL		$ _____	TOTAL		$ _____

Commercial Punch-Out Report (Cont'd)

PROPERTY NAME _____
PREPARED BY _____
BLDG. _____ SUITE _____
DATE _____
PAGE _____ OF _____

TYPE PROPERTY:
  RETAIL _____
  OFFICE _____
  INDUSTRIAL _____
  MINI WAREHOUSE _____
  LODGING _____

DESCRIPTION	CONDITION	COST ESTIMATE	DESCRIPTION	CONDITION	COST ESTIMATE
EXTERIOR:			MISCELLANEOUS EXTERIOR:		
WINDOWS:			_____	_____	$_____
TYPE	_____	$_____	_____	_____	$_____
GLAZING	_____	$_____	_____	_____	$_____
WEATHER STRIP	_____	$_____	_____	_____	$_____
FRAME	_____	$_____	_____	_____	$_____
SASH	_____	$_____	_____	_____	$_____
SILL	_____	$_____	_____	_____	$_____
STOPS	_____	$_____	_____	_____	$_____
_____	_____	$_____	_____	_____	$_____
_____	_____	$_____	_____	_____	$_____
_____	_____	$_____	_____	_____	$_____
_____	_____	$_____	_____	_____	$_____
_____	_____	$_____	_____	_____	$_____
			_____	_____	$_____
			_____	_____	$_____
ROOF TOP MECHANICAL:					
_____	_____	$_____	_____	_____	$_____
_____	_____	$_____	_____	_____	$_____
_____	_____	$_____	_____	_____	$_____
_____	_____	$_____	_____	_____	$_____
_____	_____	$_____	_____	_____	$_____
_____	_____	$_____	_____	_____	$_____
_____	_____	$_____	_____	_____	$_____
_____	_____	$_____	_____	_____	$_____
_____	_____	$_____	_____	_____	$_____
			_____	_____	$_____
			_____	_____	$_____
MISCELLANEOUS EXTERIOR:					
_____	_____	$_____	_____	_____	$_____
_____	_____	$_____	_____	_____	$_____
_____	_____	$_____	_____	_____	$_____
_____	_____	$_____	_____	_____	$_____
_____	_____	$_____	_____	_____	$_____
_____	_____	$_____	_____	_____	$_____
_____	_____	$_____	_____	_____	$_____
_____	_____	$_____	_____	_____	$_____
_____	_____	$_____	_____	_____	$_____
_____	_____	$_____	_____	_____	$_____
_____	_____	$_____	_____	_____	$_____
_____	_____	$_____	_____	_____	$_____
_____	_____	$_____	_____	_____	$_____
_____	_____	$_____	_____	_____	$_____
_____	_____	$_____	_____	_____	$_____
_____	_____	$_____			
_____	_____	$_____			
TOTAL		$_____	TOTAL		$_____

FORM 5-8
Utility Deposits

PROPERTY NAME _____
PREPARED BY _____
DATE _____

DESCRIPTION	ADDRESS	TEL. NO.	CONTACT	DEPOSIT AMOUNT	DATE DEPOSITED	COMMENTS
_____	_____	( ) _____	_____	$ _____	_____	_____
_____	_____	( ) _____	_____	$ _____	_____	_____
_____	_____	( ) _____	_____	$ _____	_____	_____
_____	_____	( ) _____	_____	$ _____	_____	_____
_____	_____	( ) _____	_____	$ _____	_____	_____
_____	_____	( ) _____	_____	$ _____	_____	_____
_____	_____	( ) _____	_____	$ _____	_____	_____
_____	_____	( ) _____	_____	$ _____	_____	_____
_____	_____	( ) _____	_____	$ _____	_____	_____
_____	_____	( ) _____	_____	$ _____	_____	_____
_____	_____	( ) _____	_____	$ _____	_____	_____
_____	_____	( ) _____	_____	$ _____	_____	_____
_____	_____	( ) _____	_____	$ _____	_____	_____
_____	_____	( ) _____	_____	$ _____	_____	_____
_____	_____	( ) _____	_____	$ _____	_____	_____
_____	_____	( ) _____	_____	$ _____	_____	_____
_____	_____	( ) _____	_____	$ _____	_____	_____
_____	_____	( ) _____	_____	$ _____	_____	_____
_____	_____	( ) _____	_____	$ _____	_____	_____
_____	_____	( ) _____	_____	$ _____	_____	_____

FORM 5-9
Service Contracts

PROPERTY NAME _____
TYPE PROPERTY _____
PREPARED BY _____
DATE _____
PAGE _____ OF _____

COMPANY NAME	CONTACT	TEL. NO.	TERM	BEG. DATE	END DATE	MONTHLY COST	TERMINATION PENALTY	TERMINATION NOTICE	COMMENTS
		( )				$			
		( )				$			
		( )				$			
		( )				$			
		( )				$			
		( )				$			
		( )				$			
		( )				$			
		( )				$			
		( )				$			
		( )				$			
		( )				$			
		( )				$			
		( )				$			

COMMENTS _____

212

Rent Increase Per Month By
Lease Expiration

PROPERTY NAME _____
PREPARED BY _____
DATE _____
PAGE _____ OF _____

RENT/MONTH INCREASE

SUITE #	TYPE UNIT/ SQ. FT.	LESSEE	LEASE EXPIRATION	RENT	JAN.	FEB.	MAR.	APR.	MAY	JUN.	JUL.	AUG.	SEP.	OCT.	NOV.	DEC.	TOTAL
				$	$	$	$	$	$	$	$	$	$	$	$	$	$
				$	$	$	$	$	$	$	$	$	$	$	$	$	$
				$	$	$	$	$	$	$	$	$	$	$	$	$	$
				$	$	$	$	$	$	$	$	$	$	$	$	$	$
				$	$	$	$	$	$	$	$	$	$	$	$	$	$
				$	$	$	$	$	$	$	$	$	$	$	$	$	$
				$	$	$	$	$	$	$	$	$	$	$	$	$	$
TOTAL				$	$	$	$	$	$	$	$	$	$	$	$	$	$
GR. TOTAL				$	$	$	$	$	$	$	$	$	$	$	$	$	$

213

FORM 5-11
Staff Analysis Form

PROPERTY NAME _____
PREPARED BY _____
DATE _____

JOB DESCRIPTION _____
EMPLOYEE NAME _____
EMPLOYMENT STARTED _____

SALARY HISTORY

YEAR _____	SALARY $_____	BENEFITS _____	JOB DESCRIPTION _____
YEAR _____	SALARY $_____	BENEFITS _____	JOB DESCRIPTION _____
YEAR _____	SALARY $_____	BENEFITS _____	JOB DESCRIPTION _____
YEAR _____	SALARY $_____	BENEFITS _____	JOB DESCRIPTION _____
YEAR _____	SALARY $_____	BENEFITS _____	JOB DESCRIPTION _____
YEAR _____	SALARY $_____	BENEFITS _____	JOB DESCRIPTION _____
YEAR _____	SALARY $_____	BENEFITS _____	JOB DESCRIPTION _____
YEAR _____	SALARY $_____	BENEFITS _____	JOB DESCRIPTION _____
YEAR _____	SALARY $_____	BENEFITS _____	JOB DESCRIPTION _____

COMMENTS _____
_____
_____
_____
_____
_____
_____
_____
_____
_____

Residential Market Comparable Study

PROPERTY NAME _____   CLASS BLDG. _____   TYPE CONSTRUCTION: LEASE INFORMATION:
　　　ADDRESS _____   YEAR BUILT _____   　WOOD _____   　　LEASE TERM _____
_____   GROSS SQ. FT. _____   　CONCRETE _____   　　SEC. DEP. $ _____
OWNERSHIP _____   NET SQ. FT. _____   　STEEL _____   　　APPL. FEE $ _____
　　　ADDRESS _____   NO. BLDGS. _____   　MASONRY _____   　　PET DEP. $ _____
_____   NO. UNITS _____   　　　　　　　　　　　　　　CLEAN FEE $ _____
　　TEL. NO. (   ) _____   NO. FLOORS _____   TYPE BLDG: 　　FURN. DEP. $ _____
MANAGEMENT CO. _____   SQ. FT./FLOOR _____   　LOW RISE _____
　　TEL. NO. (   ) _____   PARKING (NO. SPACES):   　MID RISE _____   SPACE MEASUREMENT:
LEASING AGENT _____   　SURFACE _____   　HIGH RISE _____   　　GROSS _____
　　TEL NO. (   ) _____   　COVERED _____   　ELEVATOR _____   　　NET _____
　　　　　　　　　　　　　　　RATE/MO. _____   　　　　　　　　　　　　　　　FACTOR _____%
　　　　　　　　　　　　　　ACREAGE _____   TENANT PAYS:
MAP NO. _____   DENSITY _____   　GAS _____   UTILITY SYSTEM:
　　　　　　　　　　　　　　　　　　　　　　ELEC _____   　　　　　　　　　　　　HOT
PAGE _____ OF _____   LOCATION: 　WATER _____   　　HEAT   AIR   WATER   DRYER   RANGE
　　　　　　　　　　　　　　EXCELLENT _____   　SEWER _____   ELECTRIC: ____   _____   _____   _____   _____
DATE _____   GOOD _____   　CABLE TV _____   GAS: ____   _____   _____   _____   _____
　　　　　　　　　　　　　AVERAGE _____
　　　　　　　　　　　　　POOR _____

UNIT FEATURES:
　FLOORING: WALLS: APPLIANCES: MICROWAVE _____   FIREPLACE _____   PATIO _____
　　CARPET _____   　PAINT _____   　REFRIG. _____   TRASH COMP. _____   PADDLEFAN _____   BALCONY _____
　　VINYL _____   　WALLPAPER _____   　FROST FREE ___   DISPOSAL _____   CABLE TV _____   SUNROOM _____
　　WOOD _____   WINDOWS: 　ICE MAKER _____   WASHER _____   MASTER ANT. _____   SCR. PORCH _____
　　　　　　　　　　　　　BLINDS _____   　RANGE _____   DRYER _____   　　　　　　　　　GREENHOUSE _____
　　　　　　　　　　　　　DRAPES _____   　SELF CLEAN ____   W/D CONN _____
　　　　　　　　　　　　　SHADES _____   　CONT. CLEAN ___
　　　　　　　　　　　　　RODS _____

AMENITIES:
　LAUNDRY ROOM _____   CLUBHOUSE _____   POOL _____   PLANNED ACTIVITIES _____
　STORAGE AREA _____   PARTY ROOM _____   TENNIS COURT _____
　CAR WASH _____   GAME ROOM _____   JOG TRAIL _____
　DOORMAN _____   EXERCISE ROOM _____   PICNIC AREA _____
　SECURITY _____   BAR _____   BAR B-Q _____
　　　　　　　　　　　　　FIREPLACE _____   PLAYGROUND _____
　　　　　　　　　　　　　SAUNA _____
　　　　　　　　　　　　　STEAM _____

COMMENTS:
_____
_____
_____
_____
_____

UNIT TYPE	SQ. FT.	# UNITS	DATE _____			DATE _____			DATE _____			DATE _____		
			RENT	RENT/SF	OCCUP.	RENT	RENT/SF	OCCUP.	RENT	RENT/SF	OCCUP.	RENT	RENT/SF	OOCUP.
____	____	____	$___	$_____	____%	$___	$_____	____%	$___	$_____	____%	$___	$_____	____%
____	____	____	$___	$_____	____%	$___	$_____	____%	$___	$_____	____%	$___	$_____	____%
____	____	____	$___	$_____	____%	$___	$_____	____%	$___	$_____	____%	$___	$_____	____%
____	____	____	$___	$_____	____%	$___	$_____	____%	$___	$_____	____%	$___	$_____	____%
____	____	____	$___	$_____	____%	$___	$_____	____%	$___	$_____	____%	$___	$_____	____%
____	____	____	$___	$_____	____%	$___	$_____	____%	$___	$_____	____%	$___	$_____	____%
TOTAL	____	____			____%			____%			____%			____%

Office Building Market Comparable Study

PROPERTY NAME _____
ADDRESS _____
_____
OWNERSHIP _____
ADDRESS _____
_____
TEL. NO. (   ) _____
MANAGEMENT CO. _____
TEL. NO. (   ) _____
LEASING AGENT _____
TEL. NO. (   ) _____

MAP NO. _____

PAGE _____ OF _____

DATE _____

CLASS BLDG. _____
YEAR BUILT _____
GROSS SQ. FT. _____
NET SQ. FT. _____
NO. BLDGS. _____
NO. FLOORS _____
SQ. FT./FLOOR _____
PARKING (NO. SPACES):
    SURFACE _____
    COVERED _____
ACREAGE _____
DENSITY _____

LOCATION:
    EXCELLENT _____
    GOOD _____
    AVERAGE _____
    POOR _____

TYPE CONSTRUCTION:
    WOOD _____
    CONCRETE _____
    STEEL _____
    MASONRY _____

TYPE BLDG:
    LOW RISE _____
    MID RISE _____
    HIGH RISE _____

TENANT PAYS:
    GAS _____   JANITORIAL _____
    ELEC _____   NO. DAYS _____
    WATER _____   MAINTENANCE _____
    SEWER _____   R.E. TAXES _____
                    INSURANCE _____

LEASE INFORMATION:
    LEASE TERM _____
    SEC. DEP. $ _____
    R.E. COMM. _____
    TAX STOP YR. _____
    INSUR. STOP YR. _____

BLDG. AMENTIES/FEATURES:
    LOBBY _____
    ELEVATOR _____
    SECR. SERVICE _____
    CONF. ROOM _____
    HEALTH FACIL. _____
    SECURITY _____

RESTAURANT _____
COURIER SERVICE _____
MAIL ROOM _____
DOORMAN _____
VENDING MACHINES _____

LANDSCAPING:
    EXCELLENT _____
    GOOD _____
    AVERAGE _____
    POOR _____

SIGNAGE:
    EXCELLENT _____
    GOOD _____
    AVERAGE _____
    POOR _____

HVAC PROVIDED:
    HVAC/BLDG. _____
    HVAC/FLOOR _____
    HVAC/UNIT _____
    SPRINKLERED _____

COMMENTS:
_____
_____
_____
_____
_____
_____

	DATE _____	DATE _____	DATE _____	DATE _____	DATE _____
RENT RATE/SQ. FT.	$_____	$_____	$_____	$_____	$_____
PARK RATE/SPACE	$_____	$_____	$_____	$_____	$_____
ESCALATIONS	_____	_____	_____	_____	_____
OPTIONS	_____	_____	_____	_____	_____
OCCUPANCY	$_____%	$_____%	$_____%	$_____%	$_____%
SMALLEST SPACE	_____	_____	_____	_____	_____
LARGEST SPACE	_____	_____	_____	_____	_____
TENANT IMPR.					
ALLOWANCES/SQ. FT.	$_____	$_____	$_____	$_____	$_____
RENT CONCESSIONS	_____	_____	_____	_____	_____
LEASING COMMISSION	_____%	_____%	_____%	_____%	_____%

Retail Market Comparable Study

PROPERTY NAME _____
    ADDRESS _____
_____
OWNERSHIP _____
    ADDRESS _____
_____
    TEL. NO. ( ) _____
MANAGEMENT CO. _____
    TEL. NO. ( ) _____
LEASING AGENT _____
TEL. NO. ( ) _____

MAP NO. _____
PAGE _____ OF _____
DATE _____

ANCHOR TENANTS:
_____
_____

CLASS BLDG. _____
YEAR BUILT _____
GROSS SQ. FT. _____
NET SQ. FT. _____
NO. BLDGS. _____
NO. FLOORS _____
SQ. FT./FLOOR _____
PARKING (NO. SPACES):
    SURFACE _____
    COVERED _____
ACREAGE _____
DENSITY _____

LOCATION:
    EXCELLENT _____
    GOOD _____
    AVERAGE _____
    POOR _____

TYPE CONSTRUCTION:
    WOOD _____
    CONCRETE _____
    STEEL _____
    MASONRY _____

TYPICAL BAY:
    FRONTAGE _____
    DEPTH _____

TENANT PAYS:
    GAS _____   JANITORIAL _____
    ELEC _____   NO. DAYS _____
    WATER _____   MAINTENANCE _____
    SEWER _____   R.E. TAXES _____
                         INSURANCE _____

LEASE INFORMATION:
    LEASE TERM _____
    SEC. DEP. $ _____
    R.E. COMM. _____ %
    TAX STOP YR. _____
    INSUR. STOP YR. _____

BLDG. AMENTIES/FEATURES:
    SECURITY _____
    SPRINKLERED _____
    LOADING FAC. _____

LANDSCAPING:
    EXCELLENT _____
    GOOD _____
    AVERAGE _____
    POOR _____

SIGNAGE:
    EXCELLENT _____
    GOOD _____
    AVERAGE _____
    POOR _____

HVAC PROVIDED:
    HVAC/UNIT _____

COMMENTS:
_____
_____
_____
_____
_____

	DATE _____	DATE _____	DATE _____	DATE _____	DATE _____
RENT RATE/SQ. FT.	$ _____	$ _____	$ _____	$ _____	$ _____
ESCALATIONS	_____	_____	_____	_____	_____
OPTIONS	_____	_____	_____	_____	_____
OCCUPANCY	_____	_____	_____	_____	_____
SMALLEST SPACE	_____	_____	_____	_____	_____
LARGEST SPACE	_____	_____	_____	_____	_____
TENANT IMPR. ALLOWANCE/SQ. FT.	$ _____	$ _____	$ _____	$ _____	$ _____
RENT CONCESSIONS	_____	_____	_____	_____	_____
LEASING	_____ %	_____ %	_____ %	_____ %	_____ %

Industrial Building Market Comparable Study

PROPERTY NAME _____   CLASS BLDG. _____   TYPE CONSTRUCTION: LEASE INFORMATION:

ADDRESS _____   YEAR BUILT _____   WOOD _____   LEASE TERM _____

_____   GROSS SQ. FT. _____   CONCRETE _____   SEC. DEP. _____

OWNERSHIP _____   NET SQ. FT. _____   STEEL _____   R.E. COMM. _____%

ADDRESS _____   NO. BLDGS. _____   MASONRY _____   TAX STOP YR. _____

_____   NO. FLOORS _____   TILT UP _____   INSUR. STOP YR. _____

TEL. NO. ( ) _____   SQ. FT./FLOOR _____

MANAGEMENT CO. _____   PARKING (NO. SPACES):

TEL. NO. ( ) _____   SURFACE _____

LEASING AGENT _____   CEILING HT. _____

TEL. NO. ( ) _____   ACREAGE _____

   DENSITY _____

MAP. NO. _____

   LOCATION: TENANT PAYS:

PAGE _____ OF _____   EXCELLENT _____   GAS _____   JANITORIAL _____

   GOOD _____   ELEC _____   NO. DAYS _____

DATE _____   AVERAGE _____   WATER _____   MAINTENANCE _____

   POOR _____   SEWER _____   R.E. TAXES _____

   INSURANCE _____

BLDG. AMENTIES/FEATURES:

SECURITY _____   LANDSCAPING: SIGNAGE: HVAC PROVIDED:

LOADING DOCK _____   EXCELLENT _____   EXCELLENT _____   HVAC/UNIT _____

SPRINKLERED _____   GOOD _____   GOOD _____   HVAC/FLOOR _____

   AVERAGE _____   AVERAGE _____   HVAC/UNIT _____

   POOR_____   POOR _____

COMMENTS:

_____

_____

_____

_____

_____

_____

	DATE _____	DATE _____	DATE _____	DATE _____	DATE _____
RENT RATE/SQ. FT.	$ _____	$ _____	$ _____	$ _____	$ _____
PARK RATE/SPACE	$ _____	$ _____	$ _____	$ _____	$ _____
ESCALATIONS	_____	_____	_____	_____	_____
OPTIONS	_____	_____	_____	_____	_____
OCCUPANCY	_____%	_____%	_____%	_____%	_____%
SMALLEST SPACE	_____	_____	_____	_____	_____
LARGEST SPACE	_____	_____	_____	_____	_____
TENANT IMPR.					
ALLOWANCE/SQ. FT.	$ _____	$ _____	$ _____	$ _____	$ _____
RENT CONCESSIONS	_____	_____	_____	_____	_____
LEASING	_____%	_____%	_____%	_____%	_____%

218

Mini-Warehouse Comparable Study

PROPERTY NAME _____   CLASS BLDG. _____   TYPE CONSTRUCTION: LEASE INFORMATION:
   ADDRESS _____   YEAR BUILT _____   WOOD _____   LEASE TERM _____
_____   GROSS SQ. FT. _____   CONCRETE _____   SEC. DEP. $ _____
OWNERSHIP _____   NET SQ. FT. _____   STEEL _____   APPL. FEE $ _____
   ADDRESS _____   NO. BLDGS. _____   MASONRY _____   CLEAN FEE $ _____
_____   NO. FLOORS _____   R.E. COMM. $ _____
   TEL. NO. ( )_____   SQ. FT./FLOOR _____
MANAGEMENT CO. _____   PARKING (NO. SPACES):
   TEL. NO. ( )_____   SURFACE _____   SPACE MEASUREMENT:
LEASING AGENT _____   ACREAGE _____   GROSS _____
   TEL NO. ( )_____   DENSITY _____   NET _____
                                 CEILING HT. _____   FACTOR _____%

TENANT PAYS:
MAP NO. _____   LOCATION: GAS _____   JANITORIAL _____
   EXCELLENT _____   ELEC _____   NO. DAYS _____
PAGE _____ OF _____   GOOD _____   WATER _____   MAINTENANCE _____
   AVERAGE _____   SEWER _____   R.E. TAXES _____
DATE _____   POOR _____   INSURANCE _____

BLDG. AMENTIES/FEATURES:
   ELEVATOR _____   SEC. GATE _____   LANDSCAPING: SIGNAGE:
   MAIL BOX RENTAL _____   SEC. CAMERA _____   EXCELLENT _____   EXCELLENT _____
   HVAC _____   GOOD _____   GOOD _____
   VENDING MACH. _____   STORAGE SUPPLIES: AVERAGE _____   AVERAGE _____
   SPRINKLERED _____   BOXES _____   POOR _____   POOR _____
                                 LOCKS _____

COMMENTS:
_____
_____
_____
_____
_____
_____

		DATE _____			DATE _____			DATE _____			DATE _____		
SIZE	# UNITS	RENT	RENT/SF	OCCUP.	RENT	RENT/SF	OCCUP.	RENT	RENT/SF	OCCUP.	RENT	RENT/SF	OCCUP.	
_____	_____	$ ____	$ ____	____%	$ ____	$ ____	____%	$ ____	$ ____	____%	$ ____	$ ____	____%	
_____	_____	$ ____	$ ____	____%	$ ____	$ ____	____%	$ ____	$ ____	____%	$ ____	$ ____	____%	
_____	_____	$ ____	$ ____	____%	$ ____	$ ____	____%	$ ____	$ ____	____%	$ ____	$ ____	____%	
_____	_____	$ ____	$ ____	____%	$ ____	$ ____	____%	$ ____	$ ____	____%	$ ____	$ ____	____%	
_____	_____	$ ____	$ ____	____%	$ ____	$ ____	____%	$ ____	$ ____	____%	$ ____	$ ____	____%	
_____	_____	$ ____	$ ____	____%	$ ____	$ ____	____%	$ ____	$ ____	____%	$ ____	$ ____	____%	
_____	_____	$ ____	$ ____	____%	$ ____	$ ____	____%	$ ____	$ ____	____%	$ ____	$ ____	____%	
_____	_____	$ ____	$ ____	____%	$ ____	$ ____	____%	$ ____	$ ____	____%	$ ____	$ ____	____%	
_____	_____	$ ____	$ ____	____%	$ ____	$ ____	____%	$ ____	$ ____	____%	$ ____	$ ____	____%	
_____	_____	$ ____	$ ____	____%	$ ____	$ ____	____%	$ ____	$ ____	____%	$ ____	$ ____	____%	
_____	_____	$ ____	$ ____	____%	$ ____	$ ____	____%	$ ____	$ ____	____%	$ ____	$ ____	____%	
_____	_____	$ ____	$ ____	____%	$ ____	$ ____	____%	$ ____	$ ____	____%	$ ____	$ ____	____%	
_____	_____	$ ____	$ ____	____%	$ ____	$ ____	____%	$ ____	$ ____	____%	$ ____	$ ____	____%	
_____	_____	$ ____	$ ____	____%	$ ____	$ ____	____%	$ ____	$ ____	____%	$ ____	$ ____	____%	
TOTAL	_____	$ ____		____%	$ ____		____%	$ ____		____%	$ ____		____%	

Hotel/Motel Market Comparable Study

PROPERTY NAME _____
    ADDRESS _____
_____
OWNERSHIP _____
    ADDRESS _____
_____
    TEL. NO. ( ) _____
MANAGEMENT CO. _____
    TEL. NO. ( ) _____

TYPE:
    HOTEL _____
    MOTEL _____

MAP NO. _____

PAGE _____ OF _____
DATE _____

CLASS BLDG. _____
YEAR BUILT _____
GROSS SQ. FT. _____
NET SQ. FT. _____
NO. BLDGS. _____
NO. FLOORS _____
SQ. FT./FLOOR _____
PARKING
    (NO. SPACES):
    SURFACE _____
    COVERED _____
ACREAGE _____
DENSITY _____

LOCATION:
    EXCELLENT _____
    GOOD _____
    AVERAGE _____
    POOR _____

TYPE CONSTRUCTION:
    WOOD _____
    CONCRETE _____
    STEEL _____
    MASONRY _____

TYPE BLDG.
    LOW RISE _____
    LOW RISE _____
    MID RISE _____
    HIGH RISE _____

SUITE _____

PRICE RANGE:
    ECONOMY _____
    MID _____
    LUXURY _____

TARGET MARKET:
    CONVENTION _____%
    BUSINESS _____%
    FAMILY _____%
    RESORT _____%

UNIT MIX:

BD/BA	SQ. FT.	# UNITS
_____	_____	_____
_____	_____	_____
_____	_____	_____
_____	_____	_____
_____	_____	_____
_____	_____	_____
_____	_____	_____
TOTAL	_____	_____

UNIT FEATURES:
    COLOR TV _____
    TELEPHONE _____
    BATHTUB _____
    SHOWER _____

    PATIO _____
    BALCONY _____

AMENITIES:
    POOL _____
    KID'S POOL _____
    TENNIS COURT _____
    GOLF COURSE _____
    PLAYGROUND _____

    LAUNDRY ROOM _____
    VENDING MACHINES _____
    ICE MACHINES _____
    BELLBOY _____

    RESTAURANT _____
    HEALTH FACILITIES _____
    MEETING ROOMS _____
    BANQUET ROOMS _____
    CONCIERGE _____
    ROOM SERVICE _____

COMMENTS:
_____
_____
_____
_____
_____
_____
_____

ROOM RATES:	DATE _____	DATE _____	DATE _____	DATE _____	DATE _____
WEEKDAY RATES:	$ _____	$ _____	$ _____	$ _____	$ _____
WEEKEND RATES	$ _____	$ _____	$ _____	$ _____	$ _____
PARK RATE/SPACE	$ _____	$ _____	$ _____	$ _____	$ _____
PHONE CHARGE	$ _____	$ _____	$ _____	$ _____	$ _____
OCCUPANCY	_____%	_____%	_____%	_____%	_____%

FORM 5-18
Residential Comparable Market Summary

PROPERTY NAME _____
PREPARED BY _____
DATE _____
PAGE ____ OF ____

TYPE PROPERTY:
SINGLE FAMILY _____
MULTI-FAMILY _____
ACLF _____
NURSING HOME _____

TYPE BUILDING:
GARDEN _____
TOWNHOUSE _____
MID RISE _____
HIGH RISE _____

MAP REF. NO.	PROPERTY NAME	NO. UNITS	OCCUPANCY	FEATURES	AMENITIES	LESSEE PAYS UTILITIES	TYPE UNIT ____ S.F.	RENT	RENT/S.F.	TYPE UNIT ____ S.F.	RENT	RENT/S.F.	COMMENTS
			%					$	$		$	$	
			%					$	$		$	$	
			%					$	$		$	$	
			%					$	$		$	$	
			%					$	$		$	$	
			%					$	$		$	$	
			%					$	$		$	$	
			%					$	$		$	$	
			%					$	$		$	$	
			%					$	$		$	$	
COMPARABLE AVERAGES			%					$			$		
SUBJECT PROPERTY			%					$	$		$	$	
MAP REF. NO. ____			%					$	$		$	$	
			%					$	$		$	$	

CODE:

TYPE UNIT:
(GD) GARDEN
(TH) TOWNHOUSE
(FU) FURNISHED
(UF) UNFURNISHED

UTILITIES:
(GA) GAS
(EL) ELECTRICITY
(W) WATER
(S) SEWER

FEATURES:
(1) REFRIGERATOR
(2) RANGE
(3) DISHWASHER
(4) DISPOSAL
(5) TRASH COMPACTOR
(6) MICROWAVE
(7) WASHER
(8) DRYER
(9) PATIO/BALCONY
(10) FIREPLACE
(11) SCREENPORCH
(12) SUNROOM
(13) GREENHOUSE
(14) CABLE TV
(15) PADDLEFAN
(16) WALLPAPER
(17) W/D CONNECTIONS

AMENITIES:
(A) LAUNDRY ROOM
(B) STORAGE AREA
(C) CAR WASH
(D) DOORMAN
(E) SECURITY
(F) CLUBHOUSE
(G) POOL
(H) TENNIS COURT
(I) PLAYGROUND
(J) EXERCISE ROOM
(K) SUANA
(L) STEAM ROOM

FORM 5-19

Commercial Comparable Market Summary

PROPERTY NAME _____
PREPARED BY _____
DATE _____
PAGE _____ OF _____

TYPE PROPERTY:
OFFICE _____
SHOPPING CENTER _____
INDUSTRIAL _____

MAP REF. NO.	PROPERTY NAME	OCCUPANCY	GROSS/ NET S.F.	QUOTED RATE/S.F.	LEASE TERM	SERVICES PROVIDED	LESSEE PAYS UTILITIES	RENT CONCESSIONS	TENANT ALLOWANCE	SECURITY DEPOSIT	BROKER COMMISSION	COMMENTS
		___%		$___					$___			
		___%		$___					$___			
		___%		$___					$___			
		___%		$___					$___			
		___%		$___					$___			
		___%		$___					$___			
		___%		$___					$___			
		___%		$___					$___			
		___%		$___					$___			
		___%		$___					$___			
		___%		$___					$___			
COMPARABLE AVERAGES		___%		$___					$___			

SUBJECT PROPERTY
MAP REF. NO. _____   ___% $___ $___

CODE:
SERVICES PROVIDED: UTILITIES:
(J) JANITORIAL   (G) GAS   (W) WATER
(M) MAINTENANCE   (E) ELECTRICITY   (S) SEWER

COMMENTS _____

222

FORM 5-20
Mini-Warehouse Comparable Market Summary

PROPERTY NAME _____

PREPARED BY _____

DATE _____ OF _____

PAGE _____

MAP REF. NO.	PROPERTY NAME	OCCUPANCY	NO. UNITS	SIZE UNIT ___ RENT/NO.	SIZE UNIT ___ RENT/S.F.	SIZE UNIT ___ RENT/MO.	SIZE UNIT ___ RENT/S.F.	SIZE UNIT ___ RENT/NO.	SIZE UNIT ___ RENT/S.F.	COMMENTS
		___ %		$ ___	$ ___	$ ___	$ ___	$ ___	$ ___	
		___ %		$ ___	$ ___	$ ___	$ ___	$ ___	$ ___	
		___ %		$ ___	$ ___	$ ___	$ ___	$ ___	$ ___	
		___ %		$ ___	$ ___	$ ___	$ ___	$ ___	$ ___	
		___ %		$ ___	$ ___	$ ___	$ ___	$ ___	$ ___	
		___ %		$ ___	$ ___	$ ___	$ ___	$ ___	$ ___	
		___ %		$ ___	$ ___	$ ___	$ ___	$ ___	$ ___	
		___ %		$ ___	$ ___	$ ___	$ ___	$ ___	$ ___	
		___ %		$ ___	$ ___	$ ___	$ ___	$ ___	$ ___	
		___ %		$ ___	$ ___	$ ___	$ ___	$ ___	$ ___	
		___ %		$ ___	$ ___	$ ___	$ ___	$ ___	$ ___	
		___ %		$ ___	$ ___	$ ___	$ ___	$ ___	$ ___	
		___ %		$ ___	$ ___	$ ___	$ ___	$ ___	$ ___	
		___ %		$ ___	$ ___	$ ___	$ ___	$ ___	$ ___	
		___ %		$ ___	$ ___	$ ___	$ ___	$ ___	$ ___	
COMPARABLE AVERAGES		___ %		$ ___	$ ___	$ ___	$ ___	$ ___	$ ___	
SUBJECT PROPERTY		___ %		$ ___	$ ___	$ ___	$ ___	$ ___	$ ___	

COMMENTS _____

_____

_____

_____

_____

_____

223

Hotel/Motel Comparable Market Summary

PROPERTY NAME _____

PREPARED BY _____

DATE _____

PAGE _____ OF _____

TYPE:

MOTEL _____

HOTEL _____

LOW RISE _____

MID RISE _____

HIGH RISE _____

SUITES _____

TARGET MARKET:

RESORT _____

TRANSIENT _____

CONVENTION _____

BUSINESS _____

PRICE RANGE:

BUDGET _____

MID-RANGE _____

LUXURY _____

MAP REF. NO.	PROPERTY NAME	AVERAGE OCCUPANCY	NO. ROOMS	ROOM FEATURES	AMENITIES	SINGLE OCCUPANCY		DOUBLE OCCUPANCY		COMMENTS
						RENT/ WEEKNITE	RENT/ WEEKEND	RENT/ WEEKNITE	RENT/ WEEKEND	
___	_____	___ %	___	_____	_____	$___	$___	$___	$___	_____
___	_____	___ %	___	_____	_____	$___	$___	$___	$___	_____
___	_____	___ %	___	_____	_____	$___	$___	$___	$___	_____
___	_____	___ %	___	_____	_____	$___	$___	$___	$___	_____
___	_____	___ %	___	_____	_____	$___	$___	$___	$___	_____
___	_____	___ %	___	_____	_____	$___	$___	$___	$___	_____
___	_____	___ %	___	_____	_____	$___	$___	$___	$___	_____
___	_____	___ %	___	_____	_____	$___	$___	$___	$___	_____
___	_____	___ %	___	_____	_____	$___	$___	$___	$___	_____
___	_____	___ %	___	_____	_____	$___	$___	$___	$___	_____
___	_____	___ %	___	_____	_____	$___	$___	$___	$___	_____

COMPARABLE AVERAGES _____ ___ % $___ $___ $___ _____

SUBJECT PROPERTY _____ ___ % $___ $___ $___ _____

CODE:

ROOM FEATURES:

(1) COLOR TV

(2) CABLE TV

(3) TELEPHONE

(4) PAY MOVIES

AMENITIES:

(5) POOL

(6) TENNIS COURTS

(7) GOLF COURSE

(8) PLAYGROUND

(9) LAUNDRY ROOM

(10) RESTAURANT

(11) HEALTH CLUB

(12) MEETING ROOMS

(13) BANQUET ROOMS

(14) CONCIERGE

(15) ROOM SERVICE

FORM 5-22

Land Sale Comparable Market Summary

SUBJECT PROPERTY_____
ADDRESS_____

SELLER_____
TEL. NO. (   )_____
BROKER_____
TEL. NO. (   )_____
PREPARED BY_____

DATE_____

TYPE SALE:
SOLD_____
FOR SALE_____
UNDER CONTRACT_____

MAP REF. NO.	PROPERTY NAME/ ADDRESS	OWNER	BROKER	TEL. NO.	DATE OF SALE	ASKING/ SALES PRICE	DOWN PAYMENT	TERMS	ACREAGE	ZONING	PRICE/ SQ. FT.	PRICE/ SQ. FT.	COMMENTS
						$	$				$	$	
						$	$				$	$	
						$	$				$	$	
						$	$				$	$	
						$	$				$	$	
						$	$				$	$	
						$	$				$	$	
						$	$				$	$	
						$	$				$	$	
						$	$				$	$	
						$	$				$	$	
						$	$				$	$	

COMMENTS_____

225

FORM 5-23
Inventory Checklist

PROPERTY NAME _____
PREPARED BY _____
DATE _____
PAGE ___ OF _____

ITEM	WARRANTY DATE	SERIAL #	MANUFACTURER	ORIGINAL COST	COPY OF MANUAL	COMMENTS	REVIEW DATE	REVIEW DATE	REVIEW DATE
				$					
				$					
				$					
				$					
				$					
				$					
				$					
				$					
				$					
				$					
				$					
				$					
				$					
				$					
				$					
				$					
				$					
				$					
				$					
				$					
				$					
				$					
				$					
				$					
				$					
				$					
				$					
				$					
				$					
				$					
				$					
				$					
				$					
				$					
				$					
				$					
				$					
				$					
				$					
				$					
				$					
				$					
				$					
				$					
				$					
				$					

Insurance Checklist

BUSINESS NAME _____   SPECIALIZATION   TYPE INSURANCE

CONTACT _____

ADDRESS _____   SPECIALIZATION: PROPERTY _____

_____   RESIDENTIAL: RENT LOSS _____

TEL. NO. (   ) _____   SINGLE FAMILY _____   BOILER/MACHINERY _____

       MULTI-FAMILY _____   FLOOD _____

       CONDOMINIUM/TOWNHOUSE _____   FIDELITY BOND _____

PREPARED BY _____   ADULT CONGREGATE CARE _____   CONTENTS _____

       NURSING HOME _____   ERRORS AND OMISSIONS _____

DATE _____   OFFICE _____   LIFE _____

AREAS WILL INSURE: SHOPPING CENTER _____   HEALTH _____

_____   INDUSTRIAL _____   VEHICLE _____

_____   MINI-WAREHOUSE _____   WORKMAN'S COMPENSATION _____

_____   HOTEL/MOTEL _____   UTILITY BONDS _____

_____   RESORT _____   OTHER: _____

TYPE COVERAGE	TERM	COVERAGE	DEDUCTIBLE	YEARLY PREMIUM	HOW PAID
PROPERTY	_____	$_____	$_____	$_____	_____
RENT LOSS	_____	$_____	$_____	$_____	_____
BOILER/MACHINERY	_____	$_____	$_____	$_____	_____
FLOOD	_____	$_____	$_____	$_____	_____
FIDELITY BOND	_____	$_____	$_____	$_____	_____
CONTENTS	_____	$_____	$_____	$_____	_____
ERRORS AND OMISSIONS	_____	$_____	$_____	$_____	_____
LIFE	_____	$_____	$_____	$_____	_____
WHOLE LIFE	_____	$_____	$_____	$_____	_____
TERM	_____	$_____	$_____	$_____	_____
UNIVERSAL LIFE	_____	$_____	$_____	$_____	_____
HEALTH	_____	$_____	$_____	$_____	_____
VEHICLE	_____	$_____	$_____	$_____	_____
WORKMAN'S COMPENSATION	_____	$_____	$_____	$_____	_____
UTILITY BOND	_____	$_____	$_____	$_____	_____
OTHER:	_____	$_____	$_____	$_____	_____
_____	_____	$_____	$_____	$_____	_____
_____	_____	$_____	$_____	$_____	_____
_____	_____	$_____	$_____	$_____	_____
_____	_____	$_____	$_____	$_____	_____
_____	_____	$_____	$_____	$_____	_____

REFERENCES:

BUSINESS: BUSINESS: BUSINESS:

     DATE _____   DATE _____   DATE _____

     BUSINESS NAME _____   BUSINESS NAME _____   BUSINESS NAME _____

     CONTACT _____   CONTACT _____   CONTACT _____

     ADDRESS _____   ADDRESS _____   ADDRESS _____

     TEL. NO. (   ) _____   TEL. NO. (   ) _____   TEL. NO. (   ) _____

     COMMENTS _____   COMMENTS _____   COMMENTS _____

COMMENTS _____

_____

_____

FORM 5-25
Property Tax Checklist

PROPERTY NAME _____ REAL PROPERTY _____
ADDRESS _____ PERSONAL PROPERTY _____
_____

PREPARED BY _____
DATE _____
TAX DISTRICT _____
PROPERTY TAX NO. _____
   LAND LOT _____
   DISTRICT _____
   SECTION _____

CONTACT _____
TEL. NO. ( ) _____

	ASSESSMENT	MILLAGE RATE	ASSESSMENT RATIO	TAX ASSESSMENT
YEAR _____	_____	$ _____	_____	$ _____
YEAR _____	_____	$ _____	_____	$ _____
YEAR _____	_____	$ _____	_____	$ _____
YEAR _____	_____	$ _____	_____	$ _____
YEAR _____	_____	$ _____	_____	$ _____
YEAR _____	_____	$ _____	_____	$ _____
YEAR _____	_____	$ _____	_____	$ _____
YEAR _____	_____	$ _____	_____	$ _____
YEAR _____	_____	$ _____	_____	$ _____
YEAR _____	_____	$ _____	_____	$ _____

CURRENT MILLAGE RATE _____ YEAR _____ DUE DATE _____
DUE DATE _____

DESCRIPTION	RATE	

                                           LATE DATE _____

_____ $ _____ PENALTY _____
_____ $ _____ _____
_____ $ _____ _____
_____ $ _____ _____
_____ $ _____ _____
_____ $ _____ _____
_____ $ _____ _____
_____ $ _____
_____ $ _____

TOTAL $ _____

COMMENTS _____
_____
_____
_____
_____
_____
_____
_____
_____
_____
_____
_____
_____

FORM 5-26
Broker Checklist

BUSINESS NAME _____

	SPECIALIZATION	FEE STRUCTURE	COMMENTS

CONTACT _____
ADDRESS _____
_____
TEL. NO. ( ) _____

PREPARED BY _____

_____ TYPE BROKER _____

REAL ESTATE _____
MORTGAGE _____

SPECIALIZATION:
  RESIDENTIAL:
    SINGLE FAMILY _____ _____ % _____
    MULTI-FAMILY _____ _____ % _____
    CONDOMINIUM/TOWNHOUSE _____ _____ % _____
    ADULT CONGREGATE CARE _____ _____ % _____
    NURSING HOME _____ _____ % _____
  OFFICE _____ _____ % _____
  SHOPPING CENTER _____ _____ % _____
  INDUSTRIAL _____ _____ % _____
  MINI-WAREHOUSE _____ _____ % _____
  HOTEL/MOTEL _____ _____ % _____
    RESORT _____ _____ % _____

REFERENCES:

BUSINESS:
  DATE _____
  BUSINESS NAME _____
  CONTACT _____
  ADDRESS _____
  _____
  TEL. NO. ( ) _____
  COMMENTS _____
  _____
  _____
  _____
  _____

BUSINESS:
  DATE _____
  BUSINESS NAME _____
  CONTACT _____
  ADDRESS _____
  _____
  TEL. NO. ( ) _____
  COMMENTS _____
  _____
  _____
  _____
  _____

BUSINESS:
  DATE _____
  BUSINESS NAME _____
  CONTACT _____
  ADDRESS _____
  _____
  TEL. NO. ( ) _____
  COMMENTS _____
  _____
  _____
  _____
  _____

COMMENTS _____
_____
_____
_____
_____
_____
_____
_____
_____
_____
_____
_____
_____

FORM 5-27
Appraiser Checklist

BUSINESS NAME _____	SPECIALIZATION	FEE STRUCTURE	COMMENTS
CONTACT _____			
ADDRESS _____	SPECIALIZATION:		
_____	RESIDENTIAL:		
TEL. NO. ( ) _____	SINGLE FAMILY _____	$ _____	_____
	MULTI-FAMILY _____	$ _____	_____
	CONDOMINIUM/TOWNHOUSE _____	$ _____	_____
PREPARED BY _____	ADULT CONGREGATE CARE _____	$ _____	_____
	NURSING HOME _____	$ _____	_____
	OFFICE _____	$ _____	_____
TYPE STUDY	SHOPPING CENTER _____	$ _____	_____
	INDUSTRIAL _____	$ _____	_____
APPRAISAL _____	MINI-WAREHOUSE _____	$ _____	_____
FEASIBILITY STUDY _____	HOTEL/MOTEL _____	$ _____	_____
	RESORT _____	$ _____	_____

REFERENCES:

BUSINESS:	BUSINESS:	BUSINESS:
DATE _____	DATE _____	DATE _____
BUSINESS NAME _____	BUSINESS NAME _____	BUSINESS NAME _____
CONTACT _____	CONTACT _____	CONTACT _____
ADDRESS _____	ADDRESS _____	ADDRESS _____
_____	_____	_____
TEL. NO. ( ) _____	TEL. NO. ( ) _____	TEL. NO. ( ) _____
COMMENTS _____	COMMENTS _____	COMMENTS _____

COMMENTS _____
_____
_____
_____
_____
_____
_____
_____
_____
_____
_____
_____
_____

230

FORM 5-28
Professional Services Checklist

BUSINESS NAME _____

CONTACT _____

ADDRESS _____

_____

TEL. NO. ( ) _____

PREPARED BY _____

_____ TYPE PROFESSIONAL SERVICE _____

ARCHITECTURAL

LANDSCAPE ARCH. _____

CONSTRUCTION MANAGEMENT _____

ENGINEER:

    STRUCTURAL _____

    MECHANICAL _____

    ELECTRICAL _____

    PLUMBING _____

    SOILS _____

SURVEYOR _____

INTERIOR DECORATOR _____

OTHER _____

REFERENCES:

_____ TYPE PROPERTY MARKETED _____

SPECIALIZATION:

    RESIDENTIAL:

        SINGLE FAMILY _____

        MULTI-FAMILY _____

        CONDOMINIUM/TOWNHOUSE _____

        ADULT CONGREGATE CARE _____

        NURSING HOME _____

    OFFICE _____

    SHOPPING CENTER _____

    INDUSTRIAL _____

    MINI-WAREHOUSE _____

    HOTEL/MOTEL _____

    RESORT _____

_____ GENERAL INFORMATION _____

YEARS IN BUSINESS _____

FEE STRUCTURE:

    HOURLY $ _____ BILLED EVERY _____ MINUTES

    BILLED: WEEKLY _____ MONTHLY _____

    OTHER _____

_____

_____

_____

BUSINESS:

    DATE _____

    BUSINESS NAME _____

    CONTACT _____

    ADDRESS _____

    TEL. NO. ( ) _____

    COMMENTS _____

BUSINESS:

    DATE _____

    BUSINESS NAME _____

    CONTACT _____

    ADDRESS _____

    TEL. NO. ( ) _____

    COMMENTS _____

BUSINESS:

    DATE _____

    BUSINESS NAME _____

    CONTACT _____

    ADDRESS _____

    TEL. NO. ( ) _____

    COMMENTS _____

COMMENTS _____

231

Management Companies Checklist

BUSINESS NAME _____

CONTACT _____

ADDRESS _____

_____

TEL. NO. ( ) _____

PREPARED BY _____

GENERAL INFORMATION

YEARS IN BUSINESS _____

NO. PROPERTIES MANAGED _____

NO. SQ. FT. _____ NO. UNITS ___

NO. PROPERTY OWNERS _____

NO. EMPLOYEES _____

OTHER BUSINESS _____

_____

_____

STATEMENTS GENERATED MONTHLY:

MANUAL _____ COMPUTER _____

TYPE PROPERTY MANAGED	FEE STRUCTURE	COMMENTS
SPECIALIZATION:		
RESIDENTIAL _____	_____ %	_____
SINGLE FAMILY _____	_____ %	_____
MULTI-FAMILY _____	_____ %	_____
CONDOMINIUM/TOWNHOUSE _____	_____ %	_____
ADULT CONGREGATE CARE _____	_____ %	_____
NURSING HOME _____	_____ %	_____
OFFICE _____	_____ %	_____
SHOPPING CENTER _____	_____ %	_____
INDUSTRIAL _____	_____ %	_____
MINI-WAREHOUSE _____	_____ %	_____
HOTEL/MOTEL _____	_____ %	_____
RESORT _____	_____ %	_____

REFERENCES:

BUSINESS:

    DATE _____

    BUSINESS NAME _____

    CONTACT _____

    ADDRESS _____

    _____

    TEL. NO. ( ) _____

    COMMENTS _____

    _____

    _____

    _____

    _____

BUSINESS:

    DATE _____

    BUSINESS NAME _____

    CONTACT _____

    ADDRESS _____

    _____

    TEL. NO. ( ) _____

    COMMENTS _____

    _____

    _____

    _____

    _____

BUSINESS:

    DATE _____

    BUSINESS NAME _____

    CONTACT _____

    ADDRESS _____

    _____

    TEL. NO. ( ) _____

    COMMENTS _____

    _____

    _____

    _____

    _____

COMMENTS _____

_____

_____

_____

_____

_____

_____

_____

_____

_____

_____

_____

232

FORM 5-30

Marketing Companies Checklist

BUSINESS NAME _____	TYPE PROPERTY MARKETED	FEE STRUCTURE	COMMENTS
CONTACT _____			
ADDRESS _____	SPECIALIZATION:		
_____	RESIDENTIAL:	____ %	_____
TEL. NO.( ) _____	SINGLE FAMILY _____	____ %	_____
	MULTI-FAMILY _____	____ %	_____
	CONDOMINIUM/TOWNHOUSE ____	____ %	_____
PREPARED BY _____	ADULT CONGREGATE CARE ____	____ %	_____
	NURSING HOME _____	____ %	_____
	OFFICE _____	____ %	_____
	SHOPPING CENTER _____	____ %	_____
	INDUSTRIAL _____	____ %	_____
	MINI-WAREHOUSE _____	____ %	_____
GENERAL INFORMATION	HOTEL/MOTEL _____	____ %	_____
	RESORT _____	____ %	_____

YEARS IN BUSINESS _____
NO. PROPERTIES MARKETED ____
NO. SQ. FT. ____ NO. UNITS __
NO. PROPERTY OWNERS ____
NO. EMPLOYEES _____
OTHER BUSINESS _____
_____
_____

REFERENCES:

BUSINESS:	BUSINESS:	BUSINESS:
DATE ____	DATE ____	DATE ____
BUSINESS NAME _____	BUSINESS NAME _____	BUSINESS NAME _____
CONTACT _____	CONTACT _____	CONTACT _____
ADDRESS _____	ADDRESS _____	ADDRESS _____
TEL. NO. ( ) _____	TEL. NO. ( ) _____	TEL. NO. ( ) _____
COMMENTS _____	COMMENTS _____	COMMENTS _____

COMMENTS _____

233

FORM 5-31
Attorney Checklist

BUSINESS NAME _____   PREPARED BY _____
CONTACT _____
ADDRESS _____
_____

TEL. NO. (   ) _____

FEE STRUCTURE: SPECIALIZATION:
  HOURLY $ _____ BILLED EVERY _____ MINUTES   CORPORATE _____
  BILLED: WEEKLY _____ MONTHLY _____   REAL ESTATE _____
  OTHER _____   TAX _____
  _____   SECURITIES _____
  _____   PARTNERSHIP _____
  _____

REFERENCES:

BUSINESS: BUSINESS: BUSINESS:
  DATE _____   DATE _____   DATE _____
  BUSINESS NAME _____   BUSINESS NAME _____   BUSINESS NAME _____
  CONTACT _____   CONTACT _____   CONTACT _____
  ADDRESS _____   ADDRESS _____   ADDRESS _____

  TEL. NO. (   ) _____   TEL. NO. (   ) _____   TEL. NO. (   ) _____
  COMMENTS _____   COMMENTS _____   COMMENTS _____

PERSONAL: PERSONAL: PERSONAL:
  DATE _____   DATE _____   DATE _____
  BUSINESS NAME _____   BUSINESS NAME _____   BUSINESS NAME _____
  CONTACT _____   CONTACT _____   CONTACT _____
  ADDRESS _____   ADDRESS _____   ADDRESS _____

  TEL. NO. (   ) _____   TEL. NO. (   ) _____   TEL. NO. (   ) _____
  COMMENTS _____   COMMENTS _____   COMMENTS _____

COMMENTS _____

234

Accountant Checklist

BUSINESS NAME _____

CONTACT _____

ADDRESS _____

_____

TEL. NO. ( ) _____

PREPARED BY _____

FEE STRUCTURE:

HOURLY $ _____ BILLED EVERY _____ MINUTES

BILLED: WEEKLY _____ MONTHLY _____

OTHER _____

_____

_____

SPECIALIZATION:

CORPORATE _____

REAL ESTATE _____

TAX _____

SECURITIES _____

PARTNERSHIP _____

REFERENCES:

BUSINESS:

DATE _____

BUSINESS NAME _____

CONTACT _____

ADDRESS _____

_____

TEL. NO. ( ) _____

COMMENTS _____

_____

_____

_____

_____

BUSINESS:

DATE _____

BUSINESS NAME _____

CONTACT _____

ADDRESS _____

_____

TEL. NO. ( ) _____

COMMENTS _____

_____

_____

_____

_____

BUSINESS:

DATE _____

BUSINESS NAME _____

CONTACT _____

ADDRESS _____

_____

TEL. NO. ( ) _____

COMMENTS _____

_____

_____

_____

_____

PERSONAL:

DATE _____

BUSINESS NAME _____

CONTACT _____

ADDRESS _____

_____

TEL. NO. ( ) _____

COMMENTS _____

_____

_____

_____

_____

PERSONAL:

DATE _____

BUSINESS NAME _____

CONTACT _____

ADDRESS _____

_____

TEL. NO. ( ) _____

COMMENTS _____

_____

_____

_____

_____

PERSONAL:

DATE _____

BUSINESS NAME _____

CONTACT _____

ADDRESS _____

_____

TEL. NO. ( ) _____

COMMENTS _____

_____

_____

_____

_____

COMMENTS _____

_____

_____

_____

_____

_____

_____

_____

_____

_____

_____

_____

FORM 5-33
Deal Rating Sheet

PROPERTY NAME _____
PREPARED BY _____
TYPE PROPERTY _____

DATE _____

DESCRIPTION	5	4	3	2	1
PROPERTY:					
LOCATION					
CURB APPEAL					
OCCUPANCY					
RENTAL RATES					
WEEKLY TRAFFIC					
PROSPECTS					
TENANT MIX					
TENANT PROFILE					
CONSTRUCTION					
DESIGN					
FUTURE APPRECIATION					
TRAFFIC COUNT					
ACCESS					
REPUTATION					
TOTAL POINTS	/70				
AVERAGE POINTS					

DESCRIPTION	5	4	3	2	1
DEAL STRUCTURE:					
PRICE/UNIT					
PRICE/SQ. FT.					
CAP RATE					
CRM					
SELLER GUARANTEES					
TERMS					
TOTAL POINTS	/30				
AVERAGE POINTS					
GRAND TOTAL	/100				

COMMENTS _____
_____
_____
_____
_____
_____

236

FORM 5-34
Demographics

PROPERTY NAME _____
ADDRESS _____

PREPARED BY _____
DATE PREPARED _____
DATE OF DATA _____
PAGE _____ OF _____

STATE _____
CITY _____
COUNTY _____
NEIGHBORHOOD _____
CENSUS TRACT _____

YR. _____

POPULATION

TRAFFIC COUNT

DATE _____
DAY _____
EVENING _____

DESCRIPTION	1 MILE	2 MILE	3 MILE	4 MILE	5 MILE
POPULATION					
YR. ___					
YR. ___					
YR. ___					
YR. ___					
GROWTH-% ___	___%	___%	___%	___%	
HOUSEHOLDS					
YR. ___					
YR. ___					
YR. ___					
YR. ___					
GROWTH-% ___	___%	___%	___%	___%	
POPULATION BY RACE:					
WHITE	___%	___%	___%	___%	___%
BLACK	___%	___%	___%	___%	___%
AMERICAN INDIAN	___%	___%	___%	___%	___%
ASIAN	___%	___%	___%	___%	___%
HISPANIC	___%	___%	___%	___%	___%
OTHER	___%	___%	___%	___%	___%
OCCUPIED UNITS					
OWNER OCCUPIED	___%	___%	___%	___%	___%
RENTER OCCUPIED	___%	___%	___%	___%	___%
PERSON PER HOUSEHOLD	___%	___%	___%	___%	___%

DESCRIPTION	1 MILE	2 MILE	3 MILE	4 MILE	5 MILE
INCOME ESTIMATED					
BY HOUSEHOLDS (YEAR ___):					
$75,000 OR GREATER					
$50,000 TO $74,999	$	$	$	$	$
$35,000 TO $49,999	$	$	$	$	$
$25,000 TO $34,999	$	$	$	$	$
$15,000 TO $24,999	$	$	$	$	$
UNDER $7,000					
EST. AVE. HH INC. (YEAR ___)	$	$	$	$	$
EST. MED. HH INC. (YEAR ___)	$	$	$	$	$
EST. PER CAPITA INC. (YEAR ___)	$	$	$	$	$
POPULATION BY SEX:					
MALE	___%	___%	___%	___%	___%
FEMALE	___%	___%	___%	___%	___%
POPULATION-MEDIAN AGE					
POPULATION-AVERAGE AGE					
MALE-MEDIAN AGE					
MALE-AVERAGE AGE					
FEMALE-MEDIAN AGE					
FEMALE-AVERAGE AGE					

237

FORM 5-34
Demographics (Cont'd)

PROPERTY NAME _____
ADDRESS _____

PREPARED BY _____
DATE PREPARED _____
DATE OF DATA _____
PAGE _____ OF _____

DESCRIPTION	1 MILE	2 MILE	3 MILE	4 MILE	5 MILE
HOUSEHOLDS BY TYPE:					
SINGLE MALE					
SINGLE FEMALE					
MARRIED COUPLE					
OTHER FAMILY–MALE HEAD					
OTHER FAMILY–FEMALE HEAD					
NONFAMILY–MALE HEAD					
NONFAMILY–FEMALE HEAD					
OWNER OCCUPIED PROPERTY VALUES:					
UNDER $25,000	$	$	$	$	$
$25,000 TO $39,999	$	$	$	$	$
$40,000 TO $49,999	$	$	$	$	$
$50,000 TO $79,999	$	$	$	$	$
$80,000 TO $99,999	$	$	$	$	$
$100,000 TO $149,999	$	$	$	$	$
$150,000 +	$	$	$	$	$
MEDIAN PROPERTY VALUE	$	$	$	$	$
AVERAGE PROPERTY VALUE	$	$	$	$	$
MARITAL STATUS:					
SINGLE	%	%	%	%	%
MARRIED	%	%	%	%	%
SEPARATED	%	%	%	%	%
WIDOWED	%	%	%	%	%
DIVORCED	%	%	%	%	%
POPULATION 25+ BY EDUCATION LEVEL:					
ELEMENTARY (0–8)	%	%	%	%	%
SOME HIGH SCHOOL (9–11)	%	%	%	%	%
HIGH SCHOOL GRADUATE (12)	%	%	%	%	%
SOME COLLEGE (13–15)	%	%	%	%	%
COLLEGE GRADUATE (16)	%	%	%	%	%
POST GRADUATE	%	%	%	%	%

DESCRIPTION	1 MILE	2 MILE	3 MILE	4 MILE	5 MILE
POPULATION BY TRAVEL TIME TO WORK:					
UNDER 5 MINUTES					
10 TO 14 MINUTES					
15 TO 19 MINUTES					
20 TO 29 MINUTES					
30 TO 44 MINUTES					
45 TO 59 MINUTES					
60+ MINUTES					
AVERAGE TRAVEL TIME IN MINUTES					
POPULATION 16+ BY OCCUPATION:					
EXECUTIVE AND MANAGERIAL	%	%	%	%	%
PROFESSIONAL SPECIALTY	%	%	%	%	%
TECHNICAL SUPPORT	%	%	%	%	%
SALES	%	%	%	%	%
ADMINISTRATIVE SUPPORT	%	%	%	%	%
SERVICE: PRIVATE HOUSEHOLD	%	%	%	%	%
SERVICE: PROTECTIVE	%	%	%	%	%
SERVICE: OTHER	%	%	%	%	%
FARMING: FORESTRY & FISHING	%	%	%	%	%
PRECISION PRODUCTION & CRAFT	%	%	%	%	%
MACHINE OPERATOR					
TRANSPORTATION & MATERIAL MOVING	%	%	%	%	%
LABORERS	%	%	%	%	%
YEAR ROUND UNITS AT ADDRESS:					
SINGLE UNITS	%	%	%	%	%
2 TO 9 UNITS	%	%	%	%	%
10+ UNITS	%	%	%	%	%
MOBILE HOME OR TRAILER	%	%	%	%	%
SINGLE/MULTIPLE UNIT RATIO	%	%	%	%	%

238

ENVIRONMENTAL ISSUES IN REAL ESTATE TRANSACTIONS

Byron Taylor

President
TVG Environmental, Inc.

LEGISLATIVE BACKGROUND

As the nation entered the 1970s, a new issue became the focus of citizen and environmental attention. During this period, the National Environmental Policy Act (NEPA) was enacted, and it in turn triggered the passage of numerous other pieces of legislation which included the Clean Water Act (CWA), the Clean Air Act (CAA), the Solid Waste Disposal Act (SWDA), the Safe Drinking Water Act (SDWA), the Toxic Substances Control Act (TSCA), and of course, the establishment of the U.S. Environmental Protection Agency (EPA). Few, if any, of these acts were anticipated to have any effect on the commercial real estate industry, values or transactions.

However, as with other issues which influence the ease of a real estate transaction or the attractiveness of one property as compared to another, the possibility of an environmental issue negatively influences value. This in turn triggers lender concern for the soundness of its lien on the property. Therefore, properties that are impacted by contamination, whether real or perceived, will likely suffer from reduced marketability from two sources. The first is caused by the cloud that is placed over a contaminated property by the regulatory agencies. The second is the undetermined reduction in value that is driven by the unknown nature of cleanup costs. The regulatory reductions include mandated clean-ups and other remedial activities. Value-driven issues incorporate those matters which may or may not involve regulatory action, but reduce property attractiveness as a result of some perceived problem.

National Environmental Policy Act

In 1969, Congress enacted NEPA to address a growing concern over the environment and the need for its protection. NEPA requires that all federal agencies participate in achieving environmental protection goals. Its most important procedural requirements are those exacting consideration of environmental factors and public participation in federal agency activities. To satisfy NEPA's requirements, federal agencies must prepare environmental assessments for proposed, non-excluded activities. (These environmental assessments are not to be confused with those conducted in today's environment as part of the real estate transaction process.) The findings of the environmental assessment are used to determine if a full Environmental Impact Statement (EIS) is necessary.

NEPA mandates that an EIS be prepared and included in every recommendation or report on proposals for legislation or other major federal action significantly affecting the quality of the human environment. All agencies involved in the decision making process are required to identify issues to be analyzed and to determine the scope and depth of the environmental analysis which, in the EIS, must carefully consider all environmental consequences of the proposed action.

Many states have enacted reflective regulations which incorporate many of the concepts of NEPA and require environmental quality reviews for State agency actions. Like NEPA, the basic purpose of these state regulations is to incorporate consideration of environmental impacts into decisions on permit applications and other discretionary actions taken by state agencies.

Federal Water Pollution Control (Clean Water) Act

GENERALLY

The purpose of the Clean Water Act (CWA) of 1977 is to "restore and maintain the chemical, physical and biological integrity of the nation's waters." The definition of "waters of the United States" is significantly broad to include virtually any continuously running stream, impounded body of water or discharge which enters one of these bodies. The CWA governs discharges of petroleum products and hazardous substances into the waters of the United States.

A principle element is the establishment of the National Pollutant Discharge Elimination System (NPDES) permitting system for all point source discharges to the waters of the United States. Most of the authority for this program has been assigned to the States with Federal oversight.

WETLANDS

Section 404 of the 1972 Federal Water Pollution Control Act Amendments establishes federal authority for protecting the nation's wetlands. Under this section, the Secretary of the Army acting through the U.S. Army Corp of Engineers and the EPA have concurrent jurisdiction over the dredging and filling of the waters of the United States which include wetlands. Although Corps of Engineers Field Personnel are responsible for making the initial decision to grant or deny dredging permits, the EPA is responsible for formulating guidelines used by the Corps to make its decisions. The EPA is empowered to veto or overrule its granting of permits. The permitting process is quite involved and requires detailed information from the entity requesting a permit to change or affect a wetlands. The Secretary of the Army is authorized to issue individual permits for the discharge of dredged or filled material into the waters of the United States which again includes wetlands. In some circumstances, the Corps may issue nationwide permits for certain activities in jurisdictional wetlands that are deemed to have minimal environmental impacts. The application form must describe the purpose, scope and need for the proposed activity, its location and the names and addresses of the adjoining property owners. Prior to issuing the permit, the Corps must invite comments and objections from State agencies affected by the process. The court may decide to issue a permit over the objection of certain federal and State agencies. If the Corps issues such a permit over objections, the applicant may be required to secure additional state and local wetland permits.

Clean Air Act

The Clean Air Act of 1972 (CAA) establishes the federal framework for the control of environmental air pollution. CAA establishes air quality standards for identified primary and secondary contaminant levels in the ambient air. It also establishes standards for certain hazardous air pollutants. 1990 amendments add approximately 190 new substances. Prior to that time, the EPA had identified only eight hazardous air pollutants (asbestos being one).

In May 1993, the EPA issued final regulations applicable to property owners and businesses that own, maintain or repair appliances used for residential or commercial refrigeration or air conditioning. This rule establishes a process for record keeping, control and training of individuals handling fifty pounds or more of chlorofluorocarbons (CFCs) or hydrochlorofluorocarbons (HCFCs).

In addition, the CAA incorporated a mandate for large employers to institute programs for the reduction of mileage by privately-owned vehicles of their employees. The final rule making for this process has not been completed at the time of this writing.

Toxic Substances Control Act

The Toxic Substances Control Act (TSCA) was enacted to regulate chemical substances that pose unreasonable risk of injury to human health and the environment. TSCA is administered primarily by the EPA and incorporates a process whereby new chemicals are added to the list of controlled substances on a regular basis. It imposes specific requirements on the use, storage and disposal of identified chemical components. The handling and disposal of polychlorinated biphenyls (PCBs) is specifically addressed.

Resource Conservation and Recovery Act

The Resource Conservation and Recovery Act (RCRA) was enacted in 1976 as a successor to the Solid Waste Disposal Act (SWDA) of 1965. RCRA establishes a comprehensive regulatory scheme for chemical and hazardous waste management. Its primary focus is on waste minimization and the safe treatment, storage and disposal of wastes. RCRA directs the EPA to promulgate specific practices for generators, transporters, and treatment, storage and disposal facilities (TSDs). Although RCRA only requires TSD facilities to obtain permits, RCRA's record keeping, manifesting, and reporting requirements for generators and transporters are intended to create a framework that will track all hazardous waste from "cradle to grave."

RCRA Subtitle I establishes the federal regulatory base for the underground storage tank program (UST). As a result, UST programs are now established in all fifty states. RCRA identifies two situations when a waste may be considered hazardous. First, if the waste is found on the EPA list of hazardous materials it is thereby considered a "listed hazardous waste." Second, waste may exhibit certain hazardous characteristics which will make it subject to the regulation. This latter category of wastes is commonly referred to as "characteristic hazardous wastes." A chemical waste is considered hazardous if it exhibits any one of four characteristics which include ignitability, corrosivity, reactivity or toxicity.

The 1984 RCRA amendments included directives for the EPA to promulgate restrictions on the disposal of certain highly toxic wastes commonly known as the "Land Ban." Congress also directed the EPA to issue regulations imposing stringent ground water monitoring requirements on all existing land disposal facilities. Finally, Congress added new corrective legislation to RCRA that gives the EPA authority over generators and TSD facilities to perform clean-ups of hazardous waste releases and to undertake investigations and corrective actions at permitted facilities.

The 1984 amendments also included the regulatory scheme for the UST program. Subtitle I mandates the implementation of regulatory programs for all USTs containing petroleum or any one of more than 700 designated hazardous substances. The federal framework requires state programs to cover: (1) the design, construction and operation of USTs from installation to closure, (2) the clean-up of product releases, and (3) record keeping, reporting and financial responsibility of owners and operators of USTs. A UST is defined by the regulation as any tank containing regulated substances that has 10 percent or more of its volume, including piping, underground. The federal regulations list certain tanks by categorical use that are exempt; most prominently, tanks used for petroleum-based heating fuels that are used on the premises, and hydraulic lift tanks in common usage at most automobile service centers.

Solid Waste Management is addressed in Subtitle D of RCRA and establishes the framework for State Solid Waste Management programs. Subtitle D deals mainly with disposal facilities and state plans, whereas Subtitle C deals more directly with the generators of defined hazardous wastes.

Comprehensive Environmental Response, Compensation and Liability Act

The most significant environmental law affecting real estate transactions is the Comprehensive Environmental Response, Compensation and Liability Act (CERCLA) which is also commonly referred to as the "Superfund" law. It is so named because it establishes a fund for the clean-up of properties that have been contaminated by the release of hazardous substances. Its mechanism and functioning will be addressed in greater detail later.

CERCLA was originally enacted in 1980 in order to initiate the clean-up of sites which had been contaminated, such as Love Canal and Times Beach, Missouri. It established a National Priority List (NPL) of the sites that were identified by the government as in need of remediation. Under the original concept of CERCLA, where responsible parties for the cleanup could not be immediately identified or were financially unable to undertake the required cleanup, the funds for the cleanup were to come from the Superfund. As more information on who should be responsible for funding the cleanup was ascertained, action would be taken against the newly identified parties to repay the costs to the Superfund for any expenses for investigation and cleanup. The purpose was to find a financially viable party to pay for the damage. It is a mistaken concept that the Superfund was established singularly as a clean-up mechanism. It was in fact established to provide immediate funds for such clean-ups, but was clearly designed with cost recovery procedures to replenish the fund. CERCLA Section 107(a) (also 42 U.S.C. §9607(a)) identifies four specific classes of PRPs. These are: (1) present owners and operators of the contaminated property; (2) past owners and operators that owned the site at the time that the hazardous substance(s) were released into the environment at the site; (3) generators of the hazardous substance(s) identified at the site; and (4) persons who arranged for the transportation and disposal of the hazardous substance(s) at the site.

The most important feature of this landmark legislation was the establishment of PRP liability as strict, joint and several, and retroactive. Strict liability means that a PRP is responsible (guilty) by definition, as opposed to being held liable based upon proof that such party was responsible for the hazardous condition. Joint and several liability means that each and every PRP is equally responsible for the entire cost of clean-up at a site regardless of the quantity of hazardous substances it actually contributed to the condition. There are conditions for "de minimus" contributors which protect the minor contributor from a major clean-up cost. Retroactivity establishes that if a PRP disposed of some hazardous substance before the enactment of the statute in 1988, the liability would be comparable to a situation where the disposal occurred after the enactment of the law.

The law, 42 U.S.C. ß9607(b), establishes a limited number of defenses to Superfund clean-up liability. These are narrowly defined as: (1) an act of God, (2) an act of war, (3) the act of a third party not associated with a PRP, and (4) a property owner who has established the innocent land owner defense. Since the first two are virtually without precedent, PRPs have relied on third party acts and the innocent land owner defense to avoid liability for clean-up costs. The third party defense was designed to protect owners and operators from the "midnight dumper" (i.e., a party who dumps hazardous substances on a property without the knowledge or concordance of the property owner). This defense is available only when the PRP defendant has exercised due care with respect to protecting the property from the release of hazardous substance(s) and has taken adequate precautionary measures against any foreseeable acts. Under this defense, the defendant carries the burden of proof in demonstrating that a totally unrelated third party is the sole cause of the release. Third parties must be other than one who has a contractual relationship directly or indirectly with the defendant. Courts have clearly established that a lease is a contractual relationship which precludes landlords and tenants from claiming third party defenses with regard to each other's actions. Similarly, courts have established that a generator's business relationship with a waste transporter prevents the assertion of a third party defense when the generator was unaware of the final location of the disposal of the waste. The "adequate due care" of the law requires that the defendant establish by a preponderance of the evidence that it exercised all diligence against foreseeable acts that could have resulted in the deposition of hazardous substances on the site. It has been determined that a property owner who insufficiently controlled its property could not avail itself of the third party defense. Furthermore, certain site preparation contractors have been found to be responsible under CERCLA for cleanups when they engaged in the disturbance of a hazardous substance on a site that resulted in its movement or spread beyond its original point of deposition.

Superfund Amendments and Reauthorization Act

The Superfund Amendments and Reauthorization Act (SARA) of 1986 established the Innocent Landowner Defense. This defense was envisioned to moderate superfund liability by excluding from the group of PRPs those innocent land owners who had fulfilled three basic requirements. These were (1) that the land owner did not know that the property was contaminated at the time of its acquisition, (2) that the land owner acted responsibly when contamination was discovered, and (3) that the land owner made reasonable inquiries into the past uses of the property consistent with customary commercial practice in order to determine if the property was contaminated. Obviously, this defense is available only to the land owner that acquires a property after the disposal or placement of the hazardous substance(s) on the property. To be entitled to this defense, the property owner must establish one of the following three conditions: (1) that the property owner did not know at the time of purchase or had no reason to know that the site was contaminated; (2) that the property owner is a government entity that acquired the contaminated property through condemnation; or (3) that the owner acquired the contaminated property through inheritance. The availability of this defense could be further restricted by (1) whether the landowner had any specialized knowledge or experience regarding the matter; (2) whether the purchase price of the property was significantly less than the value of the property, if uncontaminated; (3) the accessibility of commonly known or reasonably ascertainable information about the property; (4) the obviousness of the presence or likely presence of contamination on the property; and (5) the ability to detect such contamination by appropriate inspection.

INNOCENT LANDOWNER DEFENSE/ENVIRONMENTAL DUE DILIGENCE

Generally

The key element of the Innocent Landowner Defense that has created the greatest change to the real estate industry is the "reasonable inquiry into past uses consistent with customary commercial practices" clause. This has resulted in the emergence of a service which provides buyers, sellers, lenders and brokers with reports of investigations into the past uses and possibilities of environmental contamination. This business grew from early, basic inquiries of past uses to today's highly structured historical reviews and site inspections. The industry standard has been developed by the American Society of Testing and Materials (ASTM) which today serves as the benchmark for environmental due diligence.

Environmental due diligence has significance and benefit to each party in the real estate transaction. Federal legislation and judicial interpretations have created liabilities for buyers, lenders, sellers, lessors, tenants and brokers. The most common environmental due diligence is that which is normally conducted for the interest of the buyer. However, today few lenders will seriously consider a real estate secured loan without having performed complete environmental due diligence.

Federal legislation states clearly and specifically that it is the acquirer's affirmative responsibility to take the necessary actions to avail itself of all information relating to the environmental status of a piece of real estate, prior to acquiring it. However, the clear advantage to the buyer of performing environmental due diligence prior to entering into a real estate transaction is that the buyer significantly reduces the risk of acquiring a site impaired by environmental contamination and the resulting investigation and clean-up that could result. Not only does the buyer position itself to invoke the "innocent land owner defense," but also reduces the risk of an expensive environmental clean-up, if proper due diligence is performed. If a problem is identified by the assessment process, the buyer is then able to negotiate a price reduction or other arrangements for addressing the situation. It is not uncommon for the buyer to extract significant concessions from the seller of a site that is known or suspected to be affected by environmental contamination. In some cases, a knowledgeable buyer will proceed with the acquisition of a known contaminated site at a favorable purchase price with the intent of completing the remediation and improving the property value at greater than the cost to remediate.

Lender Due Diligence

Lenders may also be held liable for environmental clean-ups on properties that they own, operate or manage as a function of the security interest that they hold. This "ownership" can result from foreclosure, as well as outright purchase.

CERCLA does provide a "Secured Creditor Exemption" for lenders who maintain an interest in the property as loan collateral. CERCLA exempts from liability those who "without participating in the management of a vessel or facility, hold an indicia of ownership primarily to protect a security interest." This provision is intended to shield lenders from liability that might otherwise result merely from holding a security interest in a contaminated property, provided they had not participated in the management of the day-to-day activities of the facility.

However, even with the security interest exemption, lenders are faced with significantly reduced asset value on a property that is later determined to be negatively impacted by environmental contamination. Based on the foregoing discussion, few, if any, lending institutions will consider a loan or mortgage on real property unless a complete environmental assessment has been conducted by an approved consultant. Nearly every type of property should be subject to some degree of environmental assessment prior to completing the transaction. The level of detail and investigation necessarily depends upon the inherent characteristics and former uses of the property.

Seller Due Diligence

The benefit to the seller of an assessment is information about any issues that may surface during the processing of the transaction. Advance knowledge of a potential problem allows the seller to carefully define a negotiating position and possibly take corrective action before placing the property on the market. If the property is fully assessed and determined to be "clean" or undergoing approved remedial action, the seller can use this documentation to advantage in negotiating the transaction. Furthermore, another important advantage is that a clean environmental assessment significantly reduces any long term liability resulting from future claims. The environmental assessment report should document the presence and level of any contamination that may be present in order to establish a base line for conditions at the time of the sale. In this manner, future environmental contamination or other environmental problems become the responsibility of the site owner at that time.

Property Manager Due Diligence

While most attention today is focused on minimizing risks in new acquisitions, there has been limited inquiry from the landlord or lessor's perspective with regard to environmental risks posed by tenant property use. Also, questions are being raised by trust officers with regard to environmental risks in existing portfolios. Effective environmental property management is an issue that should be added to those matters of concern to the prudent property owner, trust officer or property manager. The obvious reasons for concern are (1) to avoid an environmental problem or clean-up; (2) to maintain the property in a condition that will not create concerns for subsequent owners/tenants; (3) to maintain asset value in order to meet loan-to-value ratios of many lenders; and (4) to improve the marketability of the property for future resale.

Landowners can be held liable for a toxic release caused by a tenant and they will also suffer a reduction in value which results from such an occurrence. Landlords, property managers and trust officers can avoid many such situations by conducting regular environmental tenant audits. Tenants that use or store chemicals have the potential to cause a release to the environment which can be very expensive to correct. Should such a release occur, in order to recoup any costs expended, the owner usually must demonstrate by a preponderance of the evidence that the problem was caused by the tenant. In the absence of reliable background data, such proof can be virtually impossible.

While an environmental audit of tenant activities cannot change what has occurred in the past, the establishment of such a program can go a long way toward protecting against future problems. The assembling of competent data with regard to the historical chemical practices of multiple tenants can be an arduous and demanding task. However, an accurate record of the detailed uses of the property is necessary for such an audit to be reliable.

Instituting an environmental property management program is something that will be unique to every organization and must be designed with the portfolio and the institution as key elements. Such programs are best designed by qualified environmental consultants, with input from legal counsel and the primary property manager. The three primary functions of the program should be to evaluate new tenants, to audit existing tenants and to conduct audits of spaces being vacated.

Today's property owners are constantly faced with assessing the risk of leasing facilities to tenants who may use hazardous or non-hazardous substances. The situation demands that the lease include language addressing damage deposits, design and installation of tenant improvements and operating rules and regulations, all of which reduce the possibility of environmental contamination. The object of auditing a prospective tenant is to identify potential adverse environmental issues relating to the tenant's hazardous substance management practices. The audit can assist counsel for the property owner in drafting appropriate language to minimize the potential of adverse environmental impacts.

Establishing a baseline through the use of environmental assessments is a process similar to conducting Phase I Environmental Assessments discussed later. The tenant audit is intended to measure or compare current or recent tenant activities with specific requirements or standards such as environmental regulations on materials handling and disposal. Such activity should be compared to the existing lease agreement which, if silent on the subject, would reduce the demands to regulatory compliance only. The ongoing aspect of the program should include periodic audits by the consultant on a predetermined schedule, as well as interim or recorded observations by the property manager.

The vacating of a space by a tenant who has used or handled chemical substances is a normal occurrence in today's market. In some cases, sophisticated tenants will request that the property owner release them from future liability by certifying that the space is free of contamination as of the time they vacate. In either case, an audit of an existing tenant can assist the property owner in evaluating whether there may be a remedial action that the tenant should conduct before leaving the premises.

Tenant Liability

Due to the potential for environmental clean-up liability, sophisticated tenants today are conducting environmental assessments and reviewing environmental issues as part of their site investigation process. Some major companies will completely discount an otherwise acceptable site due solely to the presence of a question about potential environmental liability. Since environmental liability often follows the "deep pocket" theory of responsibility, the more desirable tenants, from a financial responsibility aspect, are often the ones who have the greatest sensitivity to these issues. As a result, property managers are well advised to institute and maintain an environmental management program to reduce uncertainty with respect to the presence of chemical substances, their use and handling at the facility.

Broker Liability

In every transaction, the real estate broker is faced with a unique, and sometimes conflicting, set of environmental issues. The demand for full disclosure of all salient facts can come into direct conflict with the demand that the broker obtain the greatest financial benefit for the seller/client. Therefore, it is advisable that the broker educate the principal to the fullest extent possible about the environmental issues that may affect the transaction. This can often result in a recommendation that the property owner conduct a complete environmental site assessment prior to listing the property for sale or lease. The value of such an undertaking is to identify those issues which will inevitably surface once a transaction reaches its final stages. If environmental problems are identified during this process, they can either be corrected prior to initiating the active marketing program or can be detailed to potential prospects. If the property is determined to be free of any environmental concerns, this fact can be used as a very effective marketing tool. Such a property will be much easier to market than one that may have some question. A realty broker who establishes a policy of conducting such environmental assessments as an integral part of the marketing program will present a professional image and will also be in a position to alleviate the problems that can result from disclosure of environmental information that could be detrimental to seller and/or buyer.

PHASE I ENVIRONMENTAL SITE ASSESSMENTS

Until 1993, there was no "industry standard" for the investigation of property prior to purchasing it or making other financial commitments. However, the statutory phrase "customary commercial practice" has given rise to the use of environmental site assessments for the purpose of establishing the "innocent landowner defense" and general environmental status of a property. Under federal Superfund legislation, this defense can only be established through an appropriate inquiry into the prior and current uses of the property. This process has become known as environmental due diligence or the Phase I Environmental Site Assessment, followed by Phase II and Phase III, if necessary. Although the precise definition of environmental due diligence has not been established by either regulation or legislation, customary commercial practice has resulted in a protocol for such surveys that is generally accepted throughout the marketplace.

Assessments for real property transactions are typically carried out in phases. The initial or Phase I Assessment is performed in an attempt to answer the question: "For the subject property, is there a reasonable basis to suspect the presence of an environmental risk?" Although the extent of a Phase I Site Assessment varies somewhat, depending on the type of property being evaluated, each assessment typically includes investigation into each of the following general categories:

- Records Research
  - Historical
  - Regulatory
- Site Reconnaissance and Inspection
- Evaluation and Reporting

A detailed records search is the first step in a Phase I Environmental Site Assessment. Information is sought concerning land use history and current environmental status from sources such as deed records, tax records, geological records, soil and well surveys, USGS topographic maps, aerial photographs (current and historical) and regulatory agency records.

The next step is a detailed site reconnaissance performed by a registered environmental property assessor, a professional environmental engineer, a registered environmental geologist, or other experienced, technically-educated individual for the purpose of observing any site characteristics that would independently establish the presence of environmental contamination or confirm information developed during the records search. The purpose of the site survey is to identify possible environmental problems such as waste disposal on site, spills of toxic chemicals, PCB-containing equipment, distressed vegetation, underground storage tanks, and other indicators of potential contamination. Surrounding land use and condition are also checked for environmental problems that could affect the site.

While sampling and analysis provide valuable information about contamination on a site, the cost for extensive testing can escalate quickly; and it is for this reason that sampling and analysis are not usually included within the scope of a Phase I Assessment. On the other hand, a buyer may accept considerable risks with some properties if samples are not taken. Limiting the investigation to visual reconnaissance and historical data in an attempt to conclusively determine site contamination is risky at best. It is to balance cost with contingent risk that the phased approach mentioned earlier is used.

Where the results of the Phase I report indicate little likelihood of contamination, many companies opt for no sampling and analysis because the risk of environmental contamination, in their view, is judged so low as not to warrant the expense. Also, in the site selection process, an adverse report from the initial level of inquiry may by itself be adequate justification to seek alternative sites. An effective means of conducting basic soil condition testing is to link the geotechnical soil borings with the environmental consultant's sampling. Since acceptable soil stability is often precedent to an acceptable site, this will also provide a cost effective means of conducting a preliminary environmental screening.

PHASE II ENVIRONMENTAL SITE ASSESSMENTS

Where the results of the Phase I report indicate some likelihood of contamination, there is generally the need for sampling and analysis, two levels of which are common. A Phase II Environmental Site Assessment is the first level of sampling and analysis. The Phase II Assessment program is applied primarily to sites where some questionable prior use gives rise to concern for the possible presence of environmental contamination. The objective of a Phase II Assessment is therefore to confirm or deny, by scientifically and legally accepted methods, the existence of a suspected environmental risk. In the Phase II Assessment, a limited number of shallow samples are taken from those area(s) of the property which are of concern. Groundwater samples should also be taken where surface water runoff from commercial, municipal or industrial settings could possibly contaminate groundwater.

PHASE III ENVIRONMENTAL SITE ASSESSMENTS

The Phase III Assessment is recommended if there have been known activities of concern on the property or in the general area, if there is visible evidence of contamination, or if the results of the Phase II Assessment confirm the existence of a suspected environmental risk. A Phase III Assessment is therefore undertaken to determine the magnitude of the risk, i.e., the vertical and horizontal extent of the contaminant plume, and typically, to develop an appropriate plan of action for reduction or correction of the risk or contamination. The Phase III Assessment provides for soil/sediment samples to be taken at greater densities in areas where problems are confirmed or predicted and the specific contaminants have been ascertained. Samples are also taken at up-gradient and down-gradient boundaries to help evaluate the extent of contamination on the site and the potential for off-site impacts.

ACCELERATED SITE CHARACTERIZATION

As site characterization has become more complex, detailed and comprehensive, the traditional methods for sampling and analysis used in Phase II and III Site Assessments have become prohibitively expensive. Employing separate equipment rigs and crews for the various phases, as well as the preparation, preservation and specialty analyses required, not only lengthens the assessment process, but causes personnel, scheduling and material handling difficulties.

As a result, new methods and procedures have been developed to overcome these problems, and not only have sampling techniques been streamlined, but field analysis methods have also been refined. Site disruption and soil disturbance is minimized by the use of progressive, compact systems which are small truck-mounted and result in no cuttings or removed soil for handling or disposal.

The systems are based on cone penetrometer technology employing direct pressure to hydraulically drive small diameter steel probes to depths exceeding seventy-five feet (75'). Miniaturized rock drilling equipment is also incorporated into some of the systems. By utilizing a variety of sampling attachments, soil vapor, soil and ground water can be readily and efficiently sampled. When combined with mobile laboratory analyses, direct push methods can significantly shorten the time to conduct site assessments; thus *Accelerated Site Characterization.*

The use of direct push methods can also provide a greater density of assessment data points than traditional methods and at a reduced cost. This increases the probability that the vertical and horizontal extent of the contaminant plumes will be accurately and completely defined. Multiple contaminant sources and off-site sources are also more likely to be identified. The information resulting from an *Accelerated Site Characterization* program can be used to better locate and design permanent monitoring wells and remediation systems, should that be necessary.

The direct push system can obtain 20 to 40 soil samples a day from depths of 10 to 15 feet on paved or unpaved sites. The most common use of direct push technology is in the collection of soil gas samples. Soil gas can be collected, analyzed and interpreted to delineate organic contaminant plumes by the use of the advanced, steam-heated sampling probe systems.

Since the systems involve not only drilling equipment operation but also analytical equipment operation, the operating crews are normally comprised of an experienced engineer, geologist or scientist and a technician assistant. The systems can be operated by a single engineer, but normally involve two operators. The reduced equipment size and expense, minimal site disruption and on-site analysis provide the client instantaneous results at a cost of one-half to two-thirds of traditional systems and processes.

AMERICAN SOCIETY FOR TESTING AND MATERIALS STANDARD

In 1993 the American Society for Testing and Materials (ASTM) published its standard for Phase I Environmental Site Assessments, which had been developed over the course of three years. ASTM is a standards development and monitoring group which has developed construction analysis, testing and engineering standards for a variety of construction and technical products and procedures.

The ASTM standard for the Phase I Environmental Site Assessment consists of four components: (1) a review of all applicable public and company records relating to the site; (2) a site reconnaissance conducted by a qualified, technically-trained individual; (3) interviews with current owners and operators; and (4) a report offering an evaluation and conclusions. The standard describes in detail a process for developing the final report. The report should contain (1) all limiting conditions affecting the inquiry; (2) identification of all environmental consultants involved in the project with a qualifications statement for each; and (3) findings and conclusions.

The ASTM standard is rapidly becoming the acceptable level of investigation for environmental due diligence of commercial properties. Although the standard has not received official sanctioning by the EPA or other federal environmental agency, it has become what is defined as "customary commercial practice."

STAFF VS PROFESSIONAL ASSESSMENTS

Not every real estate transaction will require outside consultation. Many of the initial due diligence activities can be undertaken by qualified company personnel. However, the fundamental presumption that underlies today's marketplace is that every commercial real estate transaction of any kind will require at least a minimal environmental review before the transaction closes. If a company retains qualified staff, whose duties include at least the initial phases of an environmental assessment, outside consultation may not be necessary. Without qualified in-house staff, however, consultants must be hired in the early stages of the transaction in order to begin the environmental review and not delay the closing. Real estate brokers should always avoid conducting environmental assessments or making unsubstantiated statements as to the environmental status of a property. Further, brokers are well advised to disclose accurate environmental information in their possession. Failure to adhere to these guidelines could result in broker liability to damaged parties.

Certain common inquiries have developed to determine the appropriateness of a professionally conducted property assessment. Affirmative answers to any of the following questions should be a trigger to initiate an environmental site assessment:

1. Is the property or any contiguous property used for industrial or manufacturing use?

2. Has the property or any contiguous property been used for industrial or manufacturing use in the past?

3. Is there any evidence of storage of quantities of pesticides, batteries, paints or other chemicals?

4. Are there any 55-gallon industrial drums on the property?

5. Has fill dirt been brought onto the site?

6. Is there evidence of unusual pits, ponds, lagoons or sink-holes on the property?

7. Is there any evidence of any seriously stained or abnormally colored soil on the property or adjacent to it?

8. Are there any storage tanks (above or underground) located on the property or adjacent to it?

9. Are there any vent pipes or other indicators of subsurface structures visible on the property?

10. Is there any evidence of stained flooring, drains or walls located in any facility at the property?

11. Is there any knowledge of environmental liens or governmental notifications of violations of environmental laws relating to the property or any facility located near the property?

12. Is there any knowledge of the presence of hazardous materials at the property or any facility located near the property?

13. Have any trash, refuse, construction debris, tires, batteries or other waste materials been dumped on the ground, buried or burned on the site?

Due to the complex nature and the interdisciplinary aspect of the environmental site assessment, it should always be performed by a trained, experienced environmental professional. The effective environmental site assessment requires an understanding of the disciplines of chemistry, biology, engineering, geology, soil mechanics, and toxicology, among others. The process is similar to that of a criminal investigation and often takes on the tone of a process known as "proving a negative."

QUALIFYING ENVIRONMENTAL CONSULTANTS

The completeness and accuracy of an environmental review are directly related to the skill and training of the people involved in the process. Unqualified personnel, whether they are employees or outside consultants, will prepare an incomplete, inaccurate, and, in the worst case, exceptionally misleading environmental report.

An environmental review or assessment team necessarily consists of technical/regulatory compliance personnel, lawyers and real estate professionals. Each team member fulfills a distinct, although sometimes overlapping, function that will complement the objectives of the other team members in completing the investigation.

The scope of the project or phase should be used to determine the complexity and extent of the team. It is not uncommon to see a mismatch between project and consultant. Most often, a consultant with broad capabilities and commensurate overhead is forced to charge for unnecessary services. Also, certain consultants specialize in research or study projects, while others are more project and production oriented.

Environmental projects may require the talents and experience of a multi-disciplinary project team that is not always available from a single firm. The most common way of overcoming this problem is for the client to engage a team consisting of personnel, facilities, and equipment from two or more firms with complementary capabilities. Such teaming agreements may be in the form of consulting agreements, subcontracts or joint ventures. Common groupings include laboratory services, soil boring and geological surveys and remediation experts. The cost savings to the client under such arrangements can be substantial, since only those services necessary for the successful completion of the project are contracted.

If there is one maxim to embrace at the beginning of the environmental review process, it is to recognize that you do not want to be the training ground or guinea pig for an inexperienced consultant. Historically, the three rules of real estate investing were "location, location, location." Today, those rules have evolved into "timing, timing, timing." The three rules for choosing environmental consultants are "experience, experience, experience." An entire industry has grown up around environmental regulation over the last twenty years. Most qualified consultants have experience dating to the early years of the environmental industry. There are, unfortunately, a few that are "re-treads" from other activities and professions.

The discussion of the need for and perceived benefits of errors and omissions insurance covering environmental consultants and assessments is quite controversial and contradictory. Some clients demand unreasonably high levels of liability coverage while others view such insurance as an unnecessary pass-through expense that has no real benefit. Since there have been very few, if any, bona fide attempts to recover real or perceived damages in the area of environmental assessments, there is no historical evidence on which to make a decision. The primary instances of damage recovery have resulted from a clear omission on the part of the consultant resulting principally from inexperience. As a result, some environmental consultants carry high levels of coverage while many others carry little or none. The existence and amount of insurance is often in inverse relationship to the quality of the final work product. The reason for this apparent anomaly is that the larger firms with large coverage policies feel they have adequate protection from direct claims and are therefore comfortable allowing inexperienced technicians to perform critical research and investigations. Smaller, local firms are more likely to produce reports prepared by senior, more experienced professionals.

From the client's point of view, the existence of large liability coverage is small comfort after site decisions have been made and commitments secured. In other words, the attempt to recover damages does little to undo poor quality work.

PROBLEM AREAS

The materials discussed in this section warrant independent treatment for one of two reasons. In some cases, the existing regulatory framework does not clearly apply, while in other cases, these substances are regulated by different, and perhaps conflicting, regulatory schemes.

Asbestos

Although CERCLA defines asbestos as a hazardous material, neither CERCLA nor RCRA specifically regulate asbestos. It is an open issue whether the installation of asbestos-containing building materials (ACBMs) can be a "disposal" under federal regulations. The primary regulatory tools governing asbestos are the Clean-Air Act/National Emissions Standards for Hazardous Air Pollutants (NESHAP), the Occupational Safety and Health Act (OSHA) which sets workplace exposure levels for construction sites, and the Toxic Substances Control Act/Title 3 (TSCA). There are also laws and ordinances adopted by states and local governments that apply to the handling, treatment and removal of asbestos.

Because of its insulating, resistance to abrasion and fire retardant properties, asbestos was once considered to be "the miracle mineral." Earliest recorded uses date to medieval England when it was used for table covering materials that could be burned for cleansing as opposed to washing. It was widely used in building materials from the late 1800s until the mid 1970s. The EPA list of ACBMs includes paper, paint, plaster, curtains, floor tile, roofing, pipe wrap, spray applied ceiling material, as well as others.

The hazardous nature of asbestos results from the inhalation of microscopic fibers which can cause a number of respiratory diseases, cancers and debilitating ailments. Detective epidemiological studies over the past forty years have determined that asbestos fibers have been linked to a number of human maladies. In addition to the danger caused by the fibers themselves, there is also reliable data to suggest that they are a multiplier of carcinogenic effect when found in the presence of other irritants and carcinogens such as tobacco smoke.

The concern with regard to ACBMs when buying, leasing or mortgaging a building are obvious. However, the methods for dealing with these materials is quite controversial. Studies confirming the health hazards associated with "friable" asbestos have resulted in actions to remove ACBMs from many buildings. ("Friable" describes asbestos-containing material that can be reduced to a powder by the crushing motion of the human hand.) It now appears that removal is not automatically the best course of action. Depending on the current condition of the asbestos-containing material, management of ACBM, in place, may be the viable alternative of preference, unless demolition or renovation activities are planned for the space containing the ACBMs.

There is no federal regulation and very few state and local regulations banning the presence of asbestos in private buildings. Certain public buildings, such as public schools, are regulated under the Asbestos Hazard Emergency Response Act of 1987 (HERA). This legislation resulted in a number of cases where materials containing asbestos were removed resulting in a greater problem than existed before removal activities were initiated. Federal regulations establish the standards to be met when asbestos-containing material will be disturbed during renovation or demolition; and such standards are dependent upon the quantity and condition of the materials to be removed. The regulations require notice of such activities to the federal, state or local government. If sufficient quantities of ACBMs are to be disturbed, then routine maintenance activities have the potential to trigger the notice requirements. The methods for dealing with asbestos include removal, encapsulation, encasement and management in place. Removal of ACBMs is precisely stated and is a procedurally bound and very expensive process. Encapsulation or sealing of exposed ACBMs, with various binders, coatings and paints results in sealing the asbestos surface, thus controlling the hazardous fibers from becoming airborne. Encasement is the process of building a rigid airtight wall around the

ACBMs. Costs for encapsulating or remediating asbestos can range from $10 to $30 per square foot, depending on the conditions of the material and the site.

Recently, the EPA has taken the position that management of ACBMs may be preferable to removal. The preparation and implementation of such management plans require the involvement of trained, experienced experts. In addition, management plans place an enormous amount of responsibility on the building owners and managers for record keeping, personnel training, and incident response.

If a real estate transaction involves buildings constructed prior to 1980, the following concerns over ACBMs should be addressed, in addition to the requisite Phase I Environmental Site Assessment: (1) the building should be inspected by a properly trained and certified asbestos-inspector to determine the presence of ACBMs; (2) drawings and building specifications should be made available to the inspector for evaluation in assessing the non-visible ACBMs that may be present; and (3) if ACBMs are determined to be present or suspected, a more in-depth asbestos study may be desirable.

Underground Storage Tanks (USTs)

The use of USTs to store petroleum products and other chemicals dates from the 1930s. Early UST systems were riveted sheet metal and were known to leak a certain amount from their first installation. Later, welding techniques were perfected that allowed the manufacture of USTs that were basically leak-free. However, installation techniques remained somewhat unsophisticated. During the 1960s, tank installation became more of a science. Estimates of leaking USTs in the United States today, range from 300,000 to 500,000. The EPA estimates that for every known leaking UST, there are possibly two to three more that are yet to be discovered.

The matter of USTs, and their potential effect on real estate transactions, is the most common environmental issue with which real estate professionals deal. In addition to the possibility of older, leaking USTs having contaminated the subsurface soil and ground water, there is also the problem of management of existing tank systems and extensive federal and state regulations that must be followed.

The typical UST system consists of the tank, product delivery piping, vent lines, fill ports, and pumps for delivering product to the metering unit. There are two types of pumping and plumbing systems used with USTs. First is the pressurized system that pumps product from the tank to the metering unit. The second system is based on suction where the product is drawn from the tank by a pump at the metering unit.

Pressurized systems are most common for transporting large quantities of product from the tank to the metering pump. However, this system is also most prone to serious product releases in that the system remains under pressure at all times and can pump a considerable amount of product through a relatively small hole. The suction system which is common for lower volume delivery systems, such as most service stations, is less prone to serious leaks; but leaks can still result in a drain of the pumping/sucking volume during the intermittent pumping episodes.

Product releases are more than twice as likely from plumbing systems than from a tank leak itself. Tank leaks are most commonly caused by corrosion and electrolysis, although structural failures from improper installation or tank defects can also occur. The failure rate for an unprotected steel tank, due to corrosion, increases with the age of the tank. EPA records indicate that 80% of USTs will have leaked within 17 years of their original installation. Recently, we have experienced the replacement of steel tanks with higher quality tanks made of fiberglass, fiberglass-coated steel, double-walled tanks and steel tanks that are cathodically protected.

Federal regulation of USTs commenced in 1984 when Congress enacted Subtitle I of RCRA. The purpose of this section was to establish a federal framework for state programs that would follow to address problems with all USTs. The federal regulations cover the design, construction and operation of USTs from installation to closure. They also require the clean-up of leaks and spills and impose record keeping, reporting and financial responsibility requirements on owners and operators of USTs. States were generally given authority to implement their own UST programs, pursuant to the federal guidelines.

At this time, all states have been delegated authority to regulate the USTs within their jurisdiction. Also, most state programs have established UST trust funds to address the financial responsibility requirement of the federal regulations. Without a state underwritten program, it would have been virtually impossible for owners and operators of smaller systems to maintain the necessary insurance, bonding or financial underwriting to meet the federal guidelines.

The primary goal driving the regulation of underground storage tanks is the protection of ground water. Since well over half of the United States depends on ground water for drinking, and even larger areas depend on ground water for irrigation, the protection of this valuable resource from gasoline contamination is critical. Gasoline contains constituents that are extremely toxic and carcinogenic and these substances have been found to be extremely persistent upon reaching ground water. In addition to gasoline, the federal regulations apply to all USTs containing petroleum or one of the more than 700 chemicals designated hazardous under CERCLA.

Federal regulations define underground storage tanks as any vessel including connected piping, holding an accumulation of regulated substances, that has 10% or more of its volume under the surface of the ground. This 10% number can be significant in that some tanks, which most would define as above ground storage tanks, have become redesignated by the simple addition of a few feet of soil around their base.

Federal and state regulations exempt certain tanks from UST regulations and generally control them under other legislation, such as water quality or solid waste. In general terms, exempted tanks are:

- Tanks with a capacity of less than 110 gallons.
- Tanks with a minimal concentration of a regulated substance.
- Emergency spill or overfill containment systems.
- Farm or residential tanks with a capacity of not more than 1100 gallons used to store motor fuel for non-commercial vehicles.
- Tanks used to store heating oil for on-premises consumption.
- Septic tanks.
- Surface impoundments, pits, ponds or lagoons.
- Flow-through process tanks.
- Certain tanks holding hazardous wastes, regulated by Subtitle C of RCRA.
- Waste water treatment tanks, regulated by the CWA.
- Certain regulated pipeline facilities.

- Hydraulic lift tanks and associated equipment.
- Tanks located in basements and mines.

A real estate transaction involving a property that has known or suspected USTs, either currently or in the past, will normally require some level of investigation beyond the basic Phase I Environmental Site Assessment. Tanks that have been properly registered, installed, operated, maintained and tested still raise a red flag for buyers and lenders. Therefore, to prepare for the virtual inevitable question at closing, it is generally advisable to address the UST problem early in the real estate transaction to insure that it is properly answered and not a source of delay for the closing. All USTs installed after May 8, 1985 were previously subject to an interim prohibition against bare steel tanks and should have the required corrosion protection. All other USTs must be retrofitted with corrosion protection, lined with fiberglass, or removed and closed by December 22, 1998. The leak detection compliance guidelines for retrofitting existing tanks became mandatory on December 22, 1989 for tanks installed before 1965 and tanks of an unknown age. For tanks installed between 1965 and 1969, retrofitting was required prior to December 22, 1990. Other UST systems had 1991, 1992 and 1993 deadlines.

UST closure (i.e., taking an active system out of service or bringing an inactive system into regulatory compliance) can fall into either temporary or permanent categories. An owner may temporarily close a UST and leave it in the ground, provided that it is empty and all other applicable tank regulations are observed, with the exception of release detection requirements. If the UST complies with new tank standards or it has been upgraded, it may remain in temporarily closed condition indefinitely. All other tanks must be permanently closed within one year, unless an authorized agency has granted an extension to the owner.

If an owner permanently closes a UST, it must be emptied, cleaned and removed from the ground or filled with an inert material such as sand or concrete. If the owner decides to continue use of the UST for storing non-regulated substances, a change in service procedure must be implemented and all conditions applicable to permanent closure must be followed, with the exception of physically removing the tank from the ground.

Polychlorinated Biphenyls (PCBs)

Polychlorinated biphenyls were manufactured in the United States from 1929 to 1977. Since they exhibited very high dielectric capacity (insulation) and were temperature stable and highly resistant to thermal breakdown and fire, they were commonly used in electrical transformers, capacitors, voltage regulators, and fluorescent light ballasts. Since they also had a stabilizing effect on lubricants and hydraulic fluids, they were often found in large hydraulic systems, including compressors and pumps, hydraulic lifts and railroad operations. Miscellaneous uses included paints, adhesives, caulking compounds and carbonless copy paper. It has also been learned that they were used in road surfacing and sometimes found their way into the environment through the use of PCB-stabilized oils for dust suppression and weed control.

PCBs have been found to be highly toxic in relatively low concentrations and are a carcinogen as well as a mutagen. PCBs are also known to concentrate themselves through the food chain pyramid in that there is no known metabolization of them in animal or plant life. When introduced to partial thermal decomposition, PCBs are converted into an even more toxic chemical known as dioxin. Some references include dioxin as one of the most toxic chemicals identified at this time.

The primary source of PCB contamination results from releases and explosions of electrical equipment. However, other sources of PCB contamination in the environment result from intentional or unintentional disposal of PCB-containing materials. Since virtually all municipal electric companies have surveyed their existing transformers and have replaced the dielectrics with PCB-free mineral oil, existing facilities do not pose a major problem. However, past releases continue to be a point of concern in real estate transactions involving properties that have been associated with any of the potential uses listed above. An effective and complete Phase I Environmental Site Assessment should disclose the possibility that PCB equipment was in use at some time in the past at the subject facility. If there is a determination that this is a possibility, there will most likely be a recommendation that a Phase II Environmental Site Assessment be conducted.

Electromagnetic Fields (EMFs)

Recently, some researchers have raised concerns with regard to the effect on human metabolism of electromagnetic fields, also referred to as EMFs. The sources of these EMFs have been most commonly associated with high tension power lines which are used to transmit electric current, at extremely high voltages, from the generating source, to the principal distribution network. Research has been reported that links such power lines, or the EMFs they create, with certain cancers, including leukemia and brain tumors. Most health professionals continue to stress that the cause and effect relationship is highly theoretical and is based on marginal studies which also contain contradictory findings.

In any event, this public concern has made it an issue of importance to real estate practitioners. Since perception is often more critical than reality in dealing with some real estate issues, the EMF problem is based more on emotions than on sound scientific discovery or fact. Nevertheless, the presence of high tension power lines can have a detrimental effect on a real estate transaction.

In the late 1980s, a device was developed to measure EMF radiation called the Gauss meter. The unit provides a quantitative measure of the Gauss level at any certain point in time. The problem that has arisen is lack of consensus on how to interpret its readings. Detrimental threshold levels vary several orders of magnitude depending on the study being referenced.

Radon

Radon is a colorless, odorless, radioactive gas formed by the decomposition of naturally-occurring pitchblende which is the ore for elemental uranium. It also evolves from other shales and formations which are ubiquitous throughout the earth's crust. Therefore, radon gas is present almost everywhere at relatively low concentrations. In addition, its evolutionary nature makes its high and low concentration levels highly unpredictable. The decaying uranium in the soil or rock formation produces radon gas which rises through the voids in the soil and enters foundation openings where it is trapped within the structure of a building. Radon gas in the open air is not at a hazardous concentration; however, in these trapped environments, it can reach levels which have been determined to be hazardous to human health. Here again, the introduction of radon or radioactive gas into the lungs can induce cancer-causing radioactive particles into the human body. These radioactive particles, when acting in combination with other carcinogens, such as tobacco smoke, create a synergistic effect as a cancer-causing agent.

In buildings where workers may spend many continuous hours, especially in a basement, the question of radon testing may be a consideration. There are no federal or state regulations regarding acceptable radon levels; however, some corporations and institutions require that workers be free from exposure to carcinogens such as radon.

In general, the issue of radon testing should be approached on a case-by-case basis, using the advice of a trained professional for guidance. The test for radon is highly susceptible to variations and should be undertaken with a great deal of consideration for a stabilized environment in which to conduct the test. The testing period should be adequately long to account for natural variations that occur in both the evolution of radon gas and the escape of the gas through openings within the building.

Lead

Human exposure to lead comes primarily from two sources: drinking water and lead-based paint. Another principal source was eliminated when tetraethyl lead was removed from gasoline. Lead exposure can lead to mental retardation, arrested growth, brain and kidney damage and infertility in males. As with many environmental contaminants, children and fetuses are highly susceptible to lead-based maladies.

Human beings can absorb lead through both pulmonary and gastrointestinal routes. The ingestion route is most common through drinking water into which lead is deposited from various sources, including lead pipes, lead solder and lead from various industrial and commercial sources.

Lead-based paint is the principal source of lead-based disease in children. It is ingested when paint flakes, chips or abrades to a fine powder from friction surfaces around windows, drawers and doors. Lead which is washed from the exterior of buildings by normal rains as the paint deteriorates, enters the soil and becomes a source of lead contamination of children and adults.

In 1978, the Consumer Products Safety Commission banned the sale of paint with more than 0.06% lead by weight. Nevertheless, lead-based paint remains a problem in buildings built before 1978. The Lead-Based Paint Poisoning Prevention Act (LPPA) requires the Department of Housing and Urban Development (HUD) to establish procedures to eliminate "as far as practicable" lead-based paint hazards in HUD owned or assisted housing or FHA insured single-family and multi-family dwellings.

Indoor Air Quality

Indoor air quality (IAQ) issues are generally under the purview and responsibility of the building management staff. However, the brokerage of a building which has a history of indoor air quality problems or is a candidate for such problems, can create significant obstacles to the transaction. The earliest instances of IAQ problems were associated with office buildings. However, more recently, properties of general commercial and industrial use have also become vulnerable to the problem.

The indoor air environment in a building is a result of the interaction between the site, local climate, building systems, construction techniques and materials, processes and activities within the building, and the building occupants themselves.

Indoor air contaminants can originate from within the building or enter the building from the outside. Sources outside the building can include a generally contaminated exterior air quality, emission sources located in the proximity of air intakes, soil gases and standing water and moisture promoting microbial growth. Interior sources can be the HVAC system or processes or chemical usage of many mechanical systems. Sources from human activities are most commonly associated with tobacco smoke but can also be the result of personal hygiene.

Should the indoor air quality problems become so significant that the building occupants experience acute health problems or discomfort, the term "sick building syndrome" is commonly applied. When diagnosable illnesses are identified and attributed to environmental contaminants within the building, the next level of the problem is often referred to as "building related illness." Legionnaires' disease is an example of such a situation.

As with most other brokerage situations, a complete knowledge of the problems and pitfalls of a transaction are more easily remedied if addressed early in the transaction, as opposed to the latter phases. Therefore, as with most other environmental issues, indoor air quality situations can often be minimized by availing oneself of all of the factors and perceptions at the onset.

FINANCIAL FORECASTING: HOW TO PROTECT YOUR POTENTIAL RETURN ON INVESTMENT

Since real estate investing is more than just buying brick and sticks, the financial aspects of the property should be thoroughly analyzed. In making financial forecasts, the investor should verify all past and current figures. The investor should also confer with the various experts in the team to help make the best assumptions. This chapter deals with the various methods the investor should use to analyze the financial aspects of the transaction.

An investor who has determined the current cash flow will be able to project the assumptions into the future holding period.

TWELVE WAYS AN ACCOUNTANT CAN MAKE YOUR JOB EASIER

The accountant will play a large part in helping the investor make real estate decisions. Therefore, always use an accountant who is knowledgeable in all phases of real estate.

Making the Ownership Vehicle Decisions

As mentioned in Chapter 1, the investor should carefully analyze the best vehicle for ownership. The accountant should be able to make recommendations to the investor based on knowledge of the investor's or the partnership's financial situation. The accountant will work with the attorney to review the investor's liability as well as the potential tax consequences of the different types of investment vehicles.

Reviewing the Operating Statements

When the investor receives the past operating statements from the seller, these statements should be reviewed for accuracy, and for which items should be exposed and which items are capital expense items. The accountant will interface with the management company in reviewing these statements.

Forecasting Cash Flow

Once the past statements have been reviewed, forecasts should be assembled to project future results. The accountant should work with the investor and the management company to obtain the data necessary to make these forecasts.

Tax Planning

The accountant will help the investor decide the type of accounting method that should be used. The choice is either the cash method or the accrual method. In the cash method, the current income is taxed in the year that it is received and the expenses are deducted in the year that they are paid. Under the accrual method, the income is recognized when all events on which payment is legally conditioned are made, other than by the passage of time. The expenses are deducted in the year they occur, although they might not have been paid yet. Many real estate partnerships use the accrual method.

The accountant will make decisions regarding the preoperating expenses and the depreciation schedule that will be used. The accountant will also make the tax year election. This will depend on the type of ownership vehicle.

If the partners in the deal decide to split up the property, the accountant will be needed to analyze how best to structure this change in ownership.

Reviewing the Deal Structure

The accountant should be called upon to review the structure of the transaction. Since most are complex, the deal should be reviewed for potential tax problems. The best time to correct these problems is before the transaction closes. The investor should not structure a deal that will hurt tax-wise. The accountant who is current on tax law should be able to inform the investor on the best methods of structuring the deal.

Preparing the Investor's Financial Statements

Many times the investor will be called upon to supply a financial statement. This request could be from a seller who is going to take back a purchase money mortgage, from a lender who is going to make a new loan on the property, or from a vendor from whom the investor is going to purchase material. The investor's accountant should always be able to prepare a financial statement that meets generally acceptable accounting practices.

Preparing the Investor's Prior Performance Summary

An investor who is going to form a limited partnership will need an updated prior performance summary, which is a financial history of the partnerships in which the investor has been a general partner. This summary will then be used as a part of the private placement memorandum.

Setting Up the Accounting Systems

The accountant should help review the systems through which the management company will report the profit and loss and the cash flow to the investor. Each management company has a different type of accounting system which the accountant should review to make sure it meets the current needs of the investor.

Preparing the Property and Investor Tax Returns

Every year, the accountant will prepare the tax returns for both the property and the investor. Depending on the type of ownership vehicle used, the accountant might have to prepare tax returns for each individual investor.

Defending Investor and Partnership Audits

If the investor or the ownership vehicle is audited by the Internal Revenue Service, the accountant who originally helped structure the deal and who should be familiar with all financial details will represent the investor. A good accountant will be able to negotiate a good settlement, if one is due.

Reviewing Possible Property Foreclosure or Bankruptcy

If the property runs into financial problems, the accountant should assist the investor in making decisions regarding the financial viability of the investment. The accountant will run forecasts to determine whether putting more money into the property or giving the property back to the lender will be more desirable. In many cases, the accountant might be able to show that the investor would be better off by giving the property back to the lender and facing the tax consequences than by continuing to put good money after bad in order to hold on to the property.

Analyzing Resale Structures

Once the property is ready to resell, the accountant should review each of the proposals. Chances are that each deal will be different. The accountant should analyze these deals and review the tax ramifications to the investor(s) and determine which deal would give the investor the most profit. Even though two deals might have the same offering price, their terms should be analyzed on a present value basis. Depending on the tax position of the investor, the accountant might recommend an installment sale or a tax-free exchange.

HOW TO PREPARE AN OPERATING STATEMENT

An operating statement is a financial statement that lists the income and the expenses for an income property. In preparing the operating statement, the investor should start with a basic outline of the possible line items for which costs need to be obtained.

Examine the Revenue Figures

The first part of an operating statement is to obtain the current revenue items. The investor will need to obtain the current rent collections and make an assumption of the rents that can be obtained for the vacant space. If the property is to-be-built property, the investor will need to review the market study to determine the gross potential income that the property will generate. The investor will then make an assumption regarding the vacancy factor to be used. This is based on current market conditions. Typically, most investors use a 5 percent vacancy factor. Even if the property has historically been 100 percent occupied, the investor should still use a 5 percent factor because even if a property is always filled, some time is needed to get the space refitted for a new tenant. Additionally, the investor should review the payment history of the tenants. If there appears to be a history of uncollectible rents, the investor should take that into consideration and figure a dollar amount for uncollectible income. The next area the investor should review is the miscellaneous income that the property will be able to generate. If the property has a past operating history, the investor should review these numbers as a basis for any forecasts.

Review the Operating Expenses

After a thorough review of all the income that the property can generate, the investor should start to review and forecast the operating expenses, using the past operating history, if available, for any forecasts. To back up each number, the investor should go out into the marketplace and verify as many of these expenses as possible. Once the investor has completed the forecast of expenses, these costs should be confirmed with other management companies in the area to see if they are in line with other similar properties. Additionally, the investor should review the Institute of Real Estate Management's (IREM) book on operating costs.

Following are three methods to be used in analyzing operating expenses. These methods should be used when comparing properties in the market area. The investor should be sure when using these methods to make an "apples to apples" comparison.

1. *Percentage of Effective Gross Income (%EGI).* In using this method, the total Operating Expenses are divided by the effective gross income. The results of this method may be distorted when a property has low rental rates due to an oversupplied rental market. Additionally, new properties tend to have a low percentage rate because there is less maintenance on a new property.

$$\frac{\text{Operating Expenses}}{\text{Effective Gross Income}} = \%EGI$$

2. *Dollars per Unit.* Many apartment properties use this method. The total operating expenses are divided by the total number of units. This method can give distorted results because smaller properties usually have higher dollar per unit costs due to the smaller number of units over which to spread their costs.

$$\frac{\text{Operating Expenses}}{\text{Number of Units}} = \text{Dollars Per Unit}$$

The dollars per unit method can be further divided between fixed and variable expenses.

a. *Fixed Expenses.* These expenses are more predictable, for example:

 1. Utilities-common area

 2. Real estate taxes

 3. Insurance

 4. Contract services.

b. *Variable Expenses.* These are the expenses that vary with the occupancy of the property; for example:

 1. Salaries and wages

 2. Repairs and maintenance

 3. Utilities—if landlord paid

 4. General and administrative

 5. Management fees

 6. Professional fees

    7. Marketing

    8. Supplies

    9. Unit maintenance

  10. Deposits and bonds

  11. Banking

  12. Reserves and replacements

3. *Dollars per Square Foot.* This method divides the total operating expenses by the gross or net square footage in the property.

$$\frac{\text{Operating Expenses}}{\text{Total Square Footage (Gross or Net)}} = \text{Dollars Per Foot (Gross or Net)}$$

Once the operating expenses are determined, the investor can obtain the net operating income for the property. From this figure, the property debt service can then be subtracted. This new figure will give the investor the cash flow for the property.

In preparing the operating forecasts, the investor should also review the capital expenditures for the property. Based on the review of the property by the inspection team, the investor should be prepared to allocate funds to repair or refurbish. Some of this money may have to be spent within a few months of closing, while other funds should be allocated to be spent over the one or two years following closing.

Items Below the Bottom Line

In commercial transactions, such as office or retail, the investor will need to allocate funds for tenant improvements and leasing commissions for both renewed and released space. The investor will need to carefully review each lease and make assumptions as to whether the tenant will release the space or vacate the property. If the tenant releases the space, the investor might still owe a renewal real estate commission and might have to agree to advance the tenant for some space improvements. If the space needs to be re-leased, the investor should review what the competition is offering in the way of real estate commissions or tenant improvements. It should be noted that in some markets, the leasing commissions are cash-out upfront while other markets pay a percentage of the money collections over the term of the lease.

HOW TO SUMMARIZE FINANCIAL TRANSACTIONS FOR AN APARTMENT PROPERTY: A CASE STUDY

The investor should analyze all financial forecasts showing best and worst case scenarios. By using both the conservative and aggressive assumptions for rent increases and expenses, together with the future resale value, the investor can project lowest and potential highest returns.

The following case study is an example of how the financial numbers are prepared for an apartment property syndication. The property used in this example is Oak Terrace Apartments, in Atlanta, Georgia. (Table 7-1) The property has 200 units and is being purchased for $6,670,000, with $1,995,000 in equity being paid to the seller in two payments. At closing the investor is paying $1,000,000. The seller is taking back a purchase money mortgage for $995,000. The terms of this loan are 10.5 percent interest only to accrue and be paid with the principal one year from the closing. The closing date is assumed to be on January 1. The investor is obtaining a new first mortgage of $4,675,000 at 10 percent interest, based on a thirty-year amortization schedule. The loan is due in ten years.

TABLE 7-1

Information Sheet

PROPERTY: OAK TERRACE APARTMENTS						
LOCATION: ATLANTA, GEORGIA						
UNIT INFORMATION						
UNIT TYPE	# UNITS	SQ. FT.*	TOTAL SQ. FT.	RENT/ MONTH	TOTAL RENT/ MONTH	RENT/ MONTH/ SQ. FT.
EFF, 1 BA GDN						
1BR, 1 BA GDN	50	700	35,000	$420.00	$21,000.00	$0.60
1BR, 1 BA LOFT						
2BR, 1 BA GDN						
2BR, 1 1/2 BA GDN						
2BR, 2 BA GDN	100	1,000	100,000	$475.00	$47,500.00	$0.48
2BR, 1 1/2 BA TH						
2BR, 2 BA TH						
2BR, 2 1/2 BA TH						
3BR, 1 BA GDN						
3BR, 2 BA GDN	50	1,200	60,000	$545.00	$27,250.00	$0.45
3BR, 2 BA TH						
3BR, 2 1/2 BA TH						
TOTAL	200		195,000		$95,750.00	
AVERAGE		975		$478.75		$0.49

		YES	NO			
Tenant Pays	Electricity	X				
	Gas	X				
	Water	X				
	Sewer	X				
	Cable	X				
	Trash Pick up		X			

*Net square feet

TABLE 7-2
Oak Terrace Associates, LLC
Investment Summary

	PROPERTY	SYNDICATED MARKUP

VALUE INFORMATION

	PROPERTY	SYNDICATED MARKUP
Sales Price	$6,670,000	$7,249,500
Price per Unit	$44,450	$36,248
Price per Sq. Ft. (Net)	$34.21	$37.18
Gross Rent Multiplier	5.81	6.31
Capitalization Rate	10.02%	9.22%

LOAN INFORMATION

	PROPERTY
Loan	$4,675,000
Debt Coverage	187.52
Interest rate	10.50%
Amortization Period (Years)	30
Loan Maturity (Years)	10
Constant	0.1098
Monthly Debt Service	$42,764.06
Equity 29.91%	$1,995,000

ALLOCATION OF THE PROPERTY BENEFITS

	Limited Partners	General Partners
Cash Flow Distribution Preference:		
Preference 3.00% Years 1-3		
Preference 5.00% Years 4-7		
Preference 8.00% Years 8-10	99.00%	1.00%
Thereafter	75.00%	25.00%
Refinancing or resale:		
Return of original capital contribution	99.00%	1.00%
Thereafter	75.00%	25.00%

ASSUMPTIONS

Closing Date	January 1
Investment Units	35
Operations:	
Vacancy Rate	5.00%
Uncollectibles (% of GPI)	0.27%
Miscellaneous Income (Year 1)	$12,500
Management Fee (% of EGI)	5.00%
Capital Expenditures (% of EGI)	1.50%
Rent & Expense Increase (per Year)	4.00%
Accounting Fee—Year 1	$2,500
Partnership Serving Fee (% of EGI)	1.00%
Working Capital (per Apartment Unit)	$1,000
Financing:	
Financing Costs (% of Loan)	1.00%
Interest on Seller Note	10.00%
Depreciation:	
Realty (% of Depreciable Basis)	90.00%
Personalty (% of Depreciable Basis)	10.00%
Land Value	$500,000
Capital Expenditures (% Depreciated)	100.00%
Resale:	
Resale Date	11th Year
Investor's Tax Rate	28.00%
Resale Sales Commission	3.00%
Resale Costs (% of Sales Price)	0.50%
Holding Period (Years)	10
Resale Cap. Rate (Use 11th Yr-NOI)	9.25%

Notes to Investment Summary (Table 7-2)

Sales Price. The purchase price of the property.

> **Property.** The actual price paid for the property itself.
>
> **Syndicated Markup.** The total purchase price of the property including all syndication costs.

Price per Unit. The price paid based on cost per unit.

Price per Square Foot (Net). The price paid based on square footage. This price could be based on either a gross or net figure.

Gross Rent Multiplier. The figure derived by dividing the sales price by the gross rent collected.

Capitalization Rate. The rate that is calculated by dividing the net operating income by the sales price.

Loan. The amount of debt on the property.

> **Debt Coverage.** The ratio calculated by dividing the net operating income by the annual debt service.
>
> **Interest Rate.** The interest rate charged on the loan.
>
> **Amortization Period.** The time period over which the loan is amortized.
>
> **Loan Maturity.** The date on which the loan is due.
>
> **Constant.** The factor calculated by multiplying the monthly payment by 1,200 and dividing the result by the loan amount.
>
> **Monthly Debt Service.** The debt service payment due on a monthly basis.

Equity. The amount of cash needed in the transaction, calculated by subtracting the loan from the purchase price.

Allocation of the Property Benefits. Allocation of profits and losses to the various partner groups.

> **Cash Flow Distribution Preference.** How the cash flow is split between the partners.
>
> **Preference.** The first cash flow distributed out of the transaction.
>
> **Taxable Income.** The taxable income or tax loss split between the partners.
>
> **Refinancing or Resale.** The refinancing or resale proceeds split between the partners.
>
> **Return of Investor's Original Contribution.** Allocation of the first proceeds prior to a profit split.

Assumptions. The assumptions used in this case study.

Closing Date. The projected date of closing.

Investment Units. The number of investment units that will be allocated in the partnership.

Operations. Operating expense assumptions.

> **Vacancy Rate.** The vacancy rate assumption.
>
> **Uncollectibles.** The uncollectible income from the tenants as a percentage of the effective income.
>
> **Miscellaneous Income.** This is the amount of miscellaneous income projected in the first year. This could also be based on a percentage of gross income or a flat dollar per unit or square foot.
>
> **Management Fee.** The fee charged by the management company based on a percentage of the effective gross income.
>
> **Capital Expenditures.** The money used for capital expense items based on a percentage of the effective gross income or a flat dollar per unit or square foot.
>
> **Rent and Expense Increases.** The percentage increase used on an annual basis to increase the rent and expenses.
>
> **Accounting Fee.** The yearly partnership accounting fee.
>
> **Partnership Servicing Fee.** The fee paid to the managing general partner for handling the partnership affairs, based on a percentage of the effective gross income.
>
> **Working Capital.** The amount of working capital reserves that should be maintained at all times, based on a dollar figure per unit or square foot.

Financing. The financing assumptions.

> **Financing Costs.** The cost to obtain the financing, usually based on a percentage of the loan amount.
>
> **Interest on Seller's Note.** The interest paid to the seller on the split funding down-payment.

Depreciation. The depreciation assumptions.

> **Realty.** The portion of the depreciable basis that is depreciated as realty.
>
> **Personalty.** The portion of the depreciable basis that is allocated to the personalty.
>
> **Land Value.** The portion of the purchase price allocated to land. Land is not depreciable.
>
> **Capital Expenditures.** Capital expenditures are depreciated. Certain items can be expensed.

Resale. The resale assumptions.

> **Resale Date.** The projected resale date.

Investor's Tax Rate. The projected rate of taxation for the investor.

Resale Sales Commission. The commission paid to resell the property, usually based on a percentage of the sales price.

Resale Costs. The cost to resell the property, based on a percentage of the sales price or on projected costs.

Holding Period. The projected holding period.

Resale Cap Rate. The projected resale formula, based on a capitalization rate for the last year or the following year of the holding period. Can also be based on a gross rent multiplier.

PROPERTY OPERATING PROFORMA (TABLE 7-3)

The property operating proforma shows the property income less the operating expenses. The first example is the Property Operating Proforma, which shows revenues and operating expenses. It also shows per unit costs, costs per square foot, and costs as a percentage of the effective gross income (EGI). The second example is the Ten Year Cash Flow Forecast (Table 7-4). This example assumes a ten-year holding period. The assumptions used are increases in the revenue and operating expenses of 4 percent per year. The return on equity (ROI) is based on the net spendable cash flow divided by the down-payment. It should be noted that the first year is based only on the $1,000,000 down-payment, while the last nine years are based on the full $1,995,000 with $95,000 interest paid to the seller on the purchase money mortgage. For simplicity, this example will use the cash method of accounting.

TABLE 7-3
Property Operating Proforma

	Total	Per Unit	Per Sq. Ft. (Yearly)	% EGI	% Equity
REVENUE:					
Gross Potential Income (GPI)	$1,149,000.00		$5,745.00	$5.89	104.36%	
Less: Vacancy	(57,450.00)		(287.25)	(0.29)	−5.22%	
Less: Uncollectibles	(3,102.30)		(15.51)	(0.02)	−0.28%	
Plus: Late Fees	2,500.00		12.50	0.01	0.23%	
Plus: Forfeited deposits	2,800.00		14.00	0.01	0.25%	
Plus: Vending Income	1,200.00		6.00	0.01	0.11%	
Plus: Laundry Income	3,600.00		18.00	0.02	0.33%	
Plus: Miscellaneous Income	2,400.00		12.00	0.01	0.22%	
Effective gross income (EGI)		$1,100,947.70	$5,505	$6	100.00%	
OPERATING EXPENSES:						
Salaries and Wages	40,000		200.00	0.21	3.63%	
Repairs and Maintenance	59,300		296.50	0.30	5.39%	
Utilities	30,000		150.00	0.15	2.72%	
Taxes	70,000		350.00	0.36	6.36%	
Insurance	20,000		100.00	0.10	1.82%	
General and Administrative	65,000		325.00	0.33	5.90%	
Management Fees	55,047		275.24	0.28	5.00%	
Professional Fees	8,000		40.00	0.04	0.73%	
Marketing	30,000		150.00	0.15	2.72%	
Contract Services	30,000		150.00	0.15	2.72%	
Supplies	5,000		25.00	0.03	0.45%	
Unit Maintenance	15,000		75.00	0.08	1.36%	
Deposits and Bonds	500		2.50	0.00	0.05%	
Banking	200		1.00	0.00	0.02%	
Reserves and Replacements	4,655		23.28	0.02	0.42%	
Total operating expenses		432,702.39	$2,163.51	$2.22	39.30%	
NET OPERATING INCOME (NOI)		$668,245.32	$3,341.23	$3.43		
DEBT SERVICE		$513,168.74	$2,565.84	$2.63		
CASH FLOW		$155,076.57	$775.38	$0.80		7.75%
CAPITAL EXPENDITURES		$16,514.22	$82.57	$0.08		
NET SPENDABLE CASH FLOW		$138,562.36	$692.81	$0.71		6.92%

Notes to Property Operating Proforma (Table 7-3)

Revenue. The sum of all revenue generated by the property.

Gross Potential Income (GPI). The total income available to collect, all the current income received plus all the vacant units or space at the current street rent.

Vacancies. The unoccupied units or space receiving no rental.

Uncollectible. Income that is not collectible.

Late Fees. Fees charged to tenants as a penalty for late payment of rent.

Forfeited Deposits. Income obtained from a forfeiture of tenant's original security deposit, resulting from the tenant leaving prior to expiration of the lease or damage caused by the tenant to the leased space.

Vending Income. Income that is generated from vending machines (beverage, candy, or public telephone).

Laundry Income. Income derived from the laundry machines.

Miscellaneous Income. Any income that comes from miscellaneous sources, including the following:

1. Charges to tenants for transfers, insufficient funds (ISF)
2. Charges to tenants for common area maintenance (CAM)
3. Interest earned on security deposits
4. Interest earned on bank accounts
5. Percentage rent paid by tenants
6. Application and processing fees charged to tenants
7. Cleaning fees charged to tenants
8. Pet fees charged to tenants
9. Rent prepaid by tenants

Effective Gross Income (EGI). The income generated by the property after all other income is added to the rental income, and all vacancies and uncollectibles are deducted.

Operating Expenses. All expenses that are charged to the property.

Salaries and Wages. The monies paid to or on behalf of the employees of the property, including:

1. Staff

   a. Resident manager
   b. Assistant manager
   c. Bookkeeper

      d. Office Clerk

      e. Temporary labor

      f. Maintenance

      g. Assistance maintenance

      h. Landscaping

      i. Pool

      j. Housekeeping

      k. Security

      l. Porter

      m. Parking lot attendant

      n. Contract labor

      o. Leasing agent

2. Salary advances
3. Commissions
4. Bonuses
5. Profit sharing
6. Benefits
7. Unemployment tax
8. Payroll tax

Repairs and Maintenance. These expenses are for costs to repair the property, including:

1. HVAC
2. Plumbing
3. Electrical
4. Appliances
5. Lock repairs
6. Exterior repairs
7. Roof repairs
8. Glass repairs
9. Screen repairs
10. Drapes
11. Blinds
12. Rods

13. Wallpaper

14. Paint—exterior

15. Paint—interior

16. Paving

17. Parking lot lighting

18. Directories

19. Signage

20. Landscaping

21. Carpentry

22. Fences

23. Carpet

24. Vinyl

25. Cabinets

26. Mirrors

27. Lighting

28. Brick

29. Stucco

30. Tennis court

31. Playground

32. Clubhouse

Utilities. Costs for the utilities on the property, including:

1. Electric

2. Gas

3. Water

4. Sewer

Taxes. Tax expenses, including the following:

1. Ad valorem property taxes

2. Ad valorem personal property taxes

3. Ad valorem vehicle taxes

Insurance. Expenses associated with insurance coverage, including:

1. Property

2. Liability

3. Contents

4. Fidelity

5. Boiler/machinery

6. Vehicle

7. Flood

8. Rent loss

9. Errors and omissions

10. Health

11. Workman's compensation

12. Life

General and Administrative. Expenses associated with running the office, including:

1. Legal

2. Accounting

3. Dues

4. Subscriptions

5. Donations

6. Travel

7. Entertainment

8. Petty Cash

9. Office supplies

10. Copier lease

11. Postage

12. Business cards

13. Printing

14. Stationery/envelopes

15. Furniture and equipment rental

16. Equipment maintenance

17. Telephone

18. Plant rental/purchase

19. Plant maintenance

20. Office cleaning

21. Office utilities

22. Answering service

23. Pager

24. Credit bureau

25. Courier

26. Business license

27. Uniforms

28. Employment fees

29. Pictures

30. Seminars

31. Training

32. Home office expense

33. Franchise fees

34. Permits

35. Licenses

36. Memberships

37. Data processing fee

Management Fees. Expenses paid to the property management company or to the managing partner as a partnership management fee, usually based on a percentage of the collected income.

Professional Fees. Fees paid for professional services rendered, including:

1. Legal

2. Accounting

3. Architectural

4. Engineering

5. Landscape architectural

6. Appraisal

7. Feasibility studies

8. Consultants

9. Construction management

10. Property management

11. Real estate broker

12. Mortgage broker

13. Tax consultant

Marketing. Expenses associated with the marketing of the property, including:

1. Agency fees
2. Production
3. Business cards
4. Newspaper
5. Magazine
6. Direct mail
7. Postage
8. Photography
9. Signage
10. Frames
11. Renderings
12. Parties
13. Gifts
14. Marketing aids
15. Prospect lists
16. Fliers
17. Radio
18. Television
19. Brochures
20. Billboards
21. Public relations
22. Office displays
23. Model furniture—lease/purchase
24. Tenant relations
25. Promotions
26. Marketing data
27. Printing

Contract Services. Expenses for services that are contracted for, including:

1. Pest control
2. Trash removal
3. Landscaping

   4. Elevator

   5. Janitorial

   6. Maid service

   7. Window washing

   8. Parking lot cleaning

   9. Snow removal

  10. Music

  11. Security

  12. Laundry

  13. HVAC

Supplies. Expenses for supplies needed for maintaining the property, including:

   1. HVAC

   2. Plumbing

   3. Electrical

   4. Appliances

   5. Cleaning

   6. Pool

   7. Painting

   8. Fire safety

Unit Maintenance. Expenses associated with making a space ready for a new tenant, including:

   1. Cleaning

   2. Carpet

   3. Painting

   4. Wallpaper

   5. Sheetrock

   6. Drapery cleaning

   7. Turnkey

Deposits and Bonds. Expenses for deposits or bonds that the property must post, including:

   1. Electric

   2. Gas

   3. Water/sewer

    4. Telephone

    5. Equipment

Banking. Expenses for banking charges, including:

    1. Open bank account

    2. Checks

    3. Returned checks

    4. Wire charges

    5. Service charges

    6. Analysis loss

    7. Loan fees

Reserves and Replacements. Expenses for replacement of items and materials, including:

    1. Flooring

    2. Appliances

    3. Landscaping

    4. Cabinets

    5. Plumbing

    6. Signage

Net Operating Income (NOI). The income received less all operating expenses incurred by the property.

Debt Service. The cost of servicing any loans on the property, including all mortgages.

Cash Flow. The money available after the debt service is paid.

Capital Expenditures. Costs for items that are nonrecurring. These items should be capitalized and not expensed currently. An accountant should make this determination. Examples are:

    1. Commercial tenant improvements

    2. New roof

    3. New parking lot

    4. Appliance purchases

Net Spendable Income Prior to Taxes. The income available after deducting any capital expenditures.

TABLE 7-4
Ten-Year Cash Flow Forecast

ASSUMPTIONS:

Revenue Increases per Year	4.00%
Vacancy	5.00%
Uncollectibles	0.27%
Operating Expenses Increases per Year	4.00%
Management Fees (% of EGI)	5.00%
Capital Expenditures (% of EGI)	1.50%

	YEAR 1	YEAR 2	YEAR 3	YEAR 4	YEAR 5	YEAR 6	YEAR 7	YEAR 8	YEAR 9	YEAR 10
REVENUE:										
Gross Potential Income (GPI)	$1,149,000	$1,194,960	$1,242,758	$1,292,469	$1,344,167	$1,397,934	$1,453,852	$1,512,006	$1,572,486	$1,635,385
Less: Vacancies & Uncollectibles	(60,552)	(59,748)	(62,138)	(64,623)	(67,208)	(69,897)	(72,693)	(75,600)	(78,624)	(81,769)
Plus: Miscellaneous Income	12,500	13,000	13,520	14,061	14,623	15,208	15,816	16,449	17,107	17,791
Effective gross income (EGI)	1,100,948	1,148,212	1,194,140	1,241,906	1,291,582	1,343,246	1,396,975	1,452,854	1,510,969	1,571,407
OPERATING EXPENSES:										
Salaries and Wages	$40,000	$41,600	$43,264	$44,995	$46,794	$48,666	$50,613	$52,637	$54,743	$56,932
Repairs and Maintenance	59,300	61,672	64,139	66,704	69,373	72,148	75,033	78,035	81,156	84,402
Utilities	30,000	31,200	31,668	32,143	32,625	33,115	33,611	34,115	34,627	35,147
Taxes	70,000	72,800	75,712	78,740	81,890	85,166	88,572	92,115	95,800	99,632
Insurance	20,000	20,800	21,632	22,497	23,397	24,333	25,306	26,319	27,371	28,466
General and Administrative	65,000	67,600	70,304	73,116	76,041	79,082	82,246	85,536	88,957	92,515
Management Fees	55,047	57,249	59,539	61,921	64,398	66,974	69,653	72,439	75,336	78,350
Professional Fees	8,000	8,320	8,653	8,999	9,359	9,733	10,123	10,527	10,949	11,386
Marketing	30,000	31,200	32,448	33,746	35,096	36,500	37,960	39,478	41,057	42,699
Contract Services	30,000	31,200	32,448	33,746	35,096	36,500	37,960	39,478	41,057	42,699
Supplies	5,000	5,200	5,408	5,624	5,849	6,083	6,327	6,580	6,843	7,117
Unit Maintenance	15,000	15,600	16,224	16,873	17,548	18,250	18,980	19,739	20,259	21,350
Deposits and Bonds	500	520	541	562	585	608	633	658	684	712
Banking	200	208	216	225	234	243	253	263	274	285
Reserves and Replacements	4,655	4,841	5,035	5,236	5,446	5,664	5,890	6,126	6,371	6,626
Total operating expenses	432,702	450,010	467,231	485,128	503,730	523,064	543,158	564,044	585,753	608,318
NET OPERATING INCOME (NOI)	$668,245	$698,202	$726,910	$756,778	$787,852	$820,182	$853,817	$888,810	$925,215	$963,090
DEBT SERVICE	$513,169	$513,169	$513,169	$513,169	$513,169	$513,169	$513,169	$513,169	$513,169	$513,169
CASH FLOW	$155,077	$185,033	$213,741	$243,609	$274,684	$307,013	$340,648	$375,641	$412,047	$449,921
CAPITAL EXPENDITURES	$16,514	$17,223	$17,912	$18,629	$19,374	$20,149	$20,955	$21,793	$22,665	$23,571
NET SPENDABLE CASH FLOW	$138,562	$167,810	$195,829	$224,980	$255,310	$286,865	$319,694	$353,849	$389,382	$426,350
RETURN ON EQUITY (ROI)	6.92%	8.39%	9.79%	11.24%	12.76%	14.34%	15.98%	17.68%	19.46%	21.31%

SOURCES AND APPLICATIONS OF FUNDS (TABLE 7-5)

The sources and applications of funds are the funds that are put into and the funds that are spent on the transaction. This example assumes that the investors are making their contributions in two installments. The first payment is at closing. The second payment is one year from the closing on the property.

TABLE 7-5
Oak Terrace Associates, LLC
Sources and Applications of Funds

	YEAR 1	YEAR 2	TOTAL
SOURCES:			
Investor Capital Contributions	$1,480,000	$1,094,500	$2,574,500
First Mortgage Proceeds	4,675,000		4,675,000
Total Sources	6,155,000	1,094,500	7,249,500
APPLICATIONS:			
Down Payment to Seller	$1,000,000	$995,000	$1,995,000
Interest to Seller		99,500	99,500
Payoff Old Mortgage Loan	4,675,000		4,675,000
General Partner Fees:			
Initial Partnership Administration Fee	20,000		20,000
Organization Fee	20,000		20,000
Acquisition Services Fee	20,000		20,000
Loan Origination Fee	20,000		20,000
Project Management & Supervision Fee	20,000		20,000
Money Raiser Fees:			
Distribution Commissions	25,000		25,000
Investment Advisory Fee	25,000		25,000
Closing and Financing Costs	130,000		130,000
Working Capital	200,000		200,000
Total Applications	$6,155,000	$1,094,500	$7,249,500
Investor Capital Contributions Per Investment Unit (1/35th)	$42,286	$31,271	$73,557

Notes to Sources and Applications of Funds (Table 7-5)

SOURCES OF FUNDS

Investor Capital Contributions. The contributions that are made by the purchaser or group of investors. These payments can be made all at closing or over a specified time period.

First Mortgage Proceeds. Funds available from securing the property and borrowing additional funds to pay for the property.

APPLICATIONS OF FUNDS

Down-payment to Seller. Cash paid at closing or over a specified time period to the seller.

Interest to Seller. Interest paid to the seller on the purchase money mortgage.

Payoff Old Mortgage Loan. Payoff of the seller's old mortgage loan.

General Partner Fees. Fees that are paid to the general partner at closing or amortized over a specified time period. Examples include the following:

1. *Initial Partnership Administrative Fee.* Fee for setting up the partnership.

2. *Organizational Fee.* Fee for organizing the partnership.

3. *Acquisition Fee.* Fee for acquiring the property.

4. *Loan Origination Fee.* Fee for placing a new loan on the property.

5. *Project Management and Supervision Fee.* Fee for overseeing the management and supervision of property.

Money Raiser Fees. Fees paid to the underwriter or money raiser. These fees can be paid at closing or over a specified time period. Examples include:

1. *Distribution Fees.* Fee paid for raising the equity required to close the transaction.

2. *Investment Advisory Fee.* Fee paid for advising the investors.

Closing and Financing Costs. The costs associated with closing the transaction and any new loans. Examples are:

1. Survey

2. Legal-out-of-pocket

3. Pictures

4. Printing

5. Recording costs

6. Mortgage tax

7. Escrow fees

8. Interest on monies advanced
9. Market study
10. Real estate tax escrow
11. Reserve escrows
12. Courier
13. Telephone
14. Travel
15. Entertainment
16. Maps
17. Title insurance
18. Mortgage insurance
19. Blue sky fees
20. Postage
21. Architectural
22. Engineering
23. Construction management
24. Feasibility study
25. Appraisal
26. Prepaid insurance
27. Pest bond
28. Tax proration
29. Consultant
30. Loan origination fee
31. Loan points
32. Loan transfer fee
33. Lender's legal fee
34. Credit report
35. Loan buydown

Working Capital. These funds should be set aside for a "rainy day," to fund any unforeseen expenditures, for example, funding negative cash flow due to poor property performance or any property improvements that were not originally projected.

FORECAST OF CASH FLOW (TABLE 7-6)

The forecast of cash flow projects the property cash flow over a ten-year period. This cash flow forecast not only takes the property into consideration, but it also forecasts the partnership expenses during this time period.

TABLE 7-6
Oak Terrace Associates, LLC
Forecast of Cash Flow

	YEAR 1	YEAR 2	YEAR 3	YEAR 4	YEAR 5	YEAR 6	YEAR 7	YEAR 8	YEAR 9	YEAR 10
SOURCES:										
Effective Gross Income (EGI)	$1,100,948	$1,148,212	$1,194,140	$1,241,906	$1,291,582	$1,343,246	$1,396,975	$1,452,854	$1,510,969	$1,571,407
Less: Operating Expenses	(432,702)	(450,010)	(467,231)	(485,128)	(503,730)	(523,064)	(543,158)	(564,044)	(585,753)	(608,318)
Plus: Investor Capital Contributions	1,480,000	1,094,500								
Plus: First Mortgage Proceeds	4,675,000									
Total Sources	6,823,245	1,792,702	726,910	756,778	787,852	820,182	853,817	888,810	925,215	963,090
APPLICATIONS:										
Down Payment to Seller	1,000,000	995,000								
Interest to Seller		99,500								
Payoff of Old Mortgage Loan	4,675,000									
General Partner Fees	100,000									
Money Raiser Fees	50,000									
Accounting Fee	2,500	2,600	2,704	2,812	2,925	3,042	3,163	3,290	3,421	3,558
Debt Service	513,169	513,169	513,169	513,169	513,169	513,169	513,169	513,169	513,169	513,169
Closing and Financing Costs	130,000									
Partnership Servicing Fee	11,009	11,450	11,908	12,384	12,880	13,395	13,931	14,488	15,067	15,670
Capital Expenditures	16,514	17,223	17,912	18,629	19,374	20,149	20,955	21,793	22,665	23,571
Increase in Working Capital	200,000									
Total Applications	6,698,192	1,638,942	545,693	546,994	548,347	549,754	551,217	552,739	554,322	555,968
Cash Flow to Partnership	$125,053	$153,760	$181,217	$209,784	$239,506	$270,428	$302,600	$336,071	$370,894	$407,122
Cash Flow to Limited Partners	$123,802	$152,222	$179,405	$207,686	$237,111	$267,724	$299,574	$332,710	$367,185	$403,051
Per Investment Unit (1/35th)	$3,537	$4,349	$5,126	$5,934	$6,775	$7,649	$8,559	$9,506	$10,491	$11,516
Cash Flow Return—%	8.36%	5.91%	6.97%	8.07%	9.21%	10.40%	11.64%	12.92%	14.26%	15.66%

Notes to Forecast of Cash Flow (Table 7-6)

SOURCES OF FUNDS

Effective Gross Income (EGI). The effective gross income of the property on an annual basis.

Operating Expenses. The operating expenses of the property on an annual basis.

Investor Capital Contributions. The contributions made by the investors.

First Mortgage Proceeds. The proceeds of the new first mortgage.

APPLICATION OF FUNDS

Down-Payment to Seller. The down-payment paid to the seller.

Interest to Seller. The interest paid to the seller on the purchase money mortgage.

Payoff of Old Mortgage. The payoff of the seller's old mortgage loan.

General Partner Fees. The fees paid to the general partner.

Money Raiser Fees. The fees paid to the money raiser.

Accounting Fee. The annual accounting fee paid for preparing the partnership and investor tax returns.

Debt Service. The debt service paid on the property.

Closing and Financing Costs. The costs associated with closing the transaction and the new mortgage.

Partnership Servicing Fee. The fee paid to the general partner to administrate the partnership.

Capital Expenditures. The annual costs for capital improvements.

Working Capital. The working capital account.

Cash Flow to Partnership. The total dollar amount that flows to the partnership.

Cash Flow to Limited Partners. The total dollar amount that flows to the limited partners.

Per Investment Unit (1/35th). The total dollar amount per investment unit.

Cash Flow Return—%. The percentage of cash flow as determined by the investor's capital contribution.

FORECAST OF TAXABLE INCOME (LOSS) (TABLE 7-7)

The taxable income (loss) schedule shows the investor the income that will be taxed or sheltered.

Table 7-7
Oak Terrace Associates, KKC
Forecast of Taxable Income (Loss)

	Year 1	Year 2	Year 3	Year 4	Year 5	Year 6	Year 7	Year 8	Year 9	Year 10
INCOME:										
Net Operating Income $963,090	$668,245	$698,202	$726,910	$756,778	$787	852	$820,182	$853,817	$888,810	$925,215
EXPENSES:										
Interest—First Mortgage	489,770	487,192	484,329	481,151	477,622	473,705	469,356	464,527	459,167	453,216
Interest—Seller Loan	99,500									
Amortization—Organization Costs	7,000	7,000	7,000	7,000	7,000					
Amortization—Loan Costs	1,750	1,750	1,750	1,750	1,750	1,750	1,750	1,750	1,750	1,750
Accounting Fee	2,500	2,600	2,704	2,812	2,925	3,042	3,163	3,290	3,421	3,558
Partnership Service Fee	11,009	11,450	11,908	12,384	12,880	13,395	13,931	14,488	15,067	15,670
Depreciation	287,648	365,933	318,931	285,569	262,038	262,701	263,530	233,892	204,353	205,209
Total Expenses	899,177	875,924	826,621	790,666	764,214	754,592	751,730	717,947	683,759	679,403
Taxable Income (Loss) To Partnership	($230,932)	($177,723)	($99,712)	($33,889)	$23,638	$65,590	$102,088	$170,864	$241,457	$283,687
Taxable Income (Loss) To Limited Partners	($228,632)	($175,946)	($98,715)	($33,550)	$23,402	$64,934	$101,067	$169,155	$239,042	$280,850
Taxable Income (Loss) To Ltd. Prt. Per Investment Unit (1/35th)	($6,532)	($5,027)	($2,820)	($959)	$669	$1,855	$2,888	$4,833	$6,830	$8,024
Write-off ratio—%	15.45%	6.83%								

Notes to Taxable Income (Loss) (Table 7-7)

INCOME

Net Operating Income. The income of the property less the operating expenses.

EXPENSES

Interest—First Mortgage. The interest that is paid on the various mortgages on an annual basis.

Interest—Seller Loan. The interest that is paid or accrued on the seller's purchase money mortgage.

Amortization—Organization Costs. The amortization of the organization costs are spread over five years.

Amortization—Loan Costs. The amortization of the loan costs are spread over the ten year term of the loan.

Accounting Fee. If the partnership has an accounting fee, it will be deducted in that year.

Partnership Servicing Fee. Any fees that have been paid over the year period to the managing partner for partnership services will be expensed over that period.

Depreciation. The depreciation of the improvements should be calculated and deducted. (See the Forecasted Depreciation Schedule, Table 7-12.)

Taxable Income (Loss) to Partnership. The sum total of the net operating income less the expenses abovementioned will give the taxable income or the taxable loss. Even though the property can be at a breakeven or a positive cash flow, this schedule will probably show a taxable loss in the early years of ownership. This figure will then be multiplied for each investor in the ownership entity.

Taxable Income (Loss) to Limited Partners. The taxable income or taxable loss that is allocated to the limited partners.

Taxable Income (Loss) to Limited Partners per Investment Unit (1/35th). The taxable income or taxable loss that is allocated to each investment unit.

Write-off Ratio—%. The write-off ratio per investment unit. This ratio is calculated by dividing the annual taxable income (loss) per investment unit by the total investor contribution to date. Since this transaction is based on a two-year contribution, only the first two years have a write-off ratio.

FORECAST OF RESALE (TABLE 7-8)

This schedule is used to show future resale forecasts at a specified future time period. It can show resale assuming foreclosure or at an assumed estimated market value.

TABLE 7-8
Oak Terrace Associates, LLC
Forecast of Resale
January 1—11th Year

	FORECLOSURE	ESTIMATED MARKET VALUE
SOURCES:		
Working Capital	$0	$200,000
Sales Price	4,283,346	10,828,253
Total Sources	4,283,346	11,028,253
APPLICATIONS:		
Sales Commissions @ 3.00%		324,848
Sales Costs @ 0.50%		54,141
Outstanding Indebtedness	4,283,346	4,283,346
Total Applications	4,283,346	4,662,335
Available for Distribution to Partnership	$0	$6,365,918
Distribution to General Partners	$0	$967,358
Distribution to Limited Partners	$0	$5,398,560
Per Investment Unit (1/35th)	$0	$154,245
Taxable Income (Loss) per Unit		
Cash Distribution at Resale	$0	$154,245
Cash Flow during Holding Period	73,442	73,442
Net Taxable Income (Loss) during Holding Period	(9,760)	(9,760)
Less: Investor Contributions	(73,557)	(73,557)
Taxable Gain (Loss) Upon Resale	($9,876)	$144,369
Tax Liability (Savings) @ 28%	($2,765)	$40,423

	LIMITED PARTNERS	GENERAL PARTNERS	TOTAL
RESALE CALCULATIONS:			
Original Contribution	$2,574,500	$26,005	$2,600,505
Resale Proceeds (75%-LP/25%-GP)	2,824,060	941,353	3,765,413
TOTAL	$5,398,560	$967,358	$6,365,918

Notes to Forecast of Resale (Table 7-8)

Foreclosure. This sale assumes that the property is foreclosed upon by the lender. It also assumes that all of the working capital was used and that there will be no return to the investors. This is a worst case example.

Estimated Market Value. This example assumes a resale at the end of the ten-year holding period. Resale value can be determined by the following methods:

- Gross rent multiplier (GRM)
- Capitalization rate
- Dollars per unit
- Dollars per square foot
- Inflation factor

This example takes the forecasted net operating income (NOI) for the eleventh year and uses a predetermined capitalization rate.

Sources

Working Capital Reserve. The total dollars in the property checkbook at the time of closing.

Sales Price. The gross sales price.

Applications

Sales Commissions. The real estate commission paid by the seller at closing.

Sales Costs. Any items that are associated with closing the property, including:

- Legal fees
- Accounting fees
- Sales taxes
- Recording costs
- Courier
- Loan transfer costs

Outstanding Indebtedness. The outstanding balances on all current mortgage loans.

Available for Distribution to Partnership. The cash that is available to distribute to all of the partners in the transaction.

Distribution to General Partners. The cash due the general partners after the profit split.

Distribution to Limited Partners. The cash due the limited partners after the profit split, including distribution of the original contribution of funds.

Per Investment Unit (1/35). Cash paid out to the limited partner per investment unit.

Taxable Income (Loss) Per Unit

Cash Distribution at Resale. The cash distribution per investment unit at the closing of the property.

Cash Flow During Holding Period. The total cash flow per investment unit that was paid out during the holding period.

Net Taxable Income (Loss) During Holding Period. The total net taxable income or taxable loss allocated per investment unit during the holding period.

Less: Investor Contributions. The total investor contribution in the transaction.

Taxable Gain upon Resale. The sum of all the above line items.

Tax Liability. The tax liability (based on 28 percent) of the taxable gain upon resale.

FORECASTED INVESTMENT PERFORMANCE FOR A LIMITED PARTNER (TABLE 7-9)

The forecasted investment performance summarizes all of the foregoing schedules. In one page the investor can see the total benefits of the proposed transaction. By using a sensitivity analysis, the investor will then be able to see the best and worst cases.

TABLE 7-9
Oak Terrace Associates, LLC
Forecasted Investment Performance for a Limited Partner
With an Investment of $73,557 (1/35th of Total Amount)

YEAR	INVESTMENT	ANNUAL TAXABLE INCOME (LOSS)	PASSIVE INCOME (LOSS) AVAILABLE TO SHELTER	(LIABILITY)	ANNUAL TAX CARRYFORWARD	CUMULATIVE DISTRIBUTION	ANNUAL BENEFITS	TOTAL BENEFITS	TOTAL
Year 1	$42,286	($6,532)	($6,532)	$0	$0	($6,532)	$3,537	$3,537	$3,537
Year 2	31,271	(5,027)	(5,027)	0	0	($11,559)	4,349	4,349	$7,886
Year 3		(2,820)	(2,820)	0	0	($14,380)	5,126	5,126	$13,012
Year 4		(959)	(959)	0	0	($15,338)	5,934	5,934	$18,946
Year 5		669	669	0	0	($14,669)	6,775	6,775	$25,721
Year 6		1,855	1,855	0	0	($12,814)	7,649	7,649	$33,370
Year 7		2,888	2,888	0	0	($9,927)	8,559	8,559	$41,929
Year 8		4,833	4,833	0	0	($5,094)	9,506	9,506	$51,435
Year 9		6,830	6,830	1,736	(486)	$1,736	10,491	10,005	$61,440
Year 10		8,024	8,024	8,024	(2,247)	$9,760	11,516	9,269	$70,709
Total	$73,557	$9,760	$9,760	$9,760	($2,733)		$73,442		

FORECASTS OF RESALE ON JANUARY 1—11TH YEAR (PER INVESTMENT UNIT)

ASSUMPTIONS	PRE-TAX RESALE PROCEEDS		RESALE TAX LIABILITY		YEAR OF SALE AFTER-TAX BENEFITS		TOTAL PREVIOUS AFTER-TAX BENEFITS		BENEFITS THROUGH RESALE
FORECLOSURE	$0	—	(2,765)	=	2,765	+	70,709	=	$73,474
RESALE AT ESTIMATED MARKET VALUE	$154,245	—	40,423	=	113,831	+	70,709	=	$184,530

Notes to Forecasted Investment Performance (Table 7-9)

Investment. The total limited partner investment contribution over the pay-in period.

Annual Income (Loss). Summary of the taxable income or losses during the holding period.

Available to Shelter (Loss). The total annual tax losses available to shelter any passive income.

Liability (Loss). The amount of taxable income (loss) after applying the passive loss limitations.

Cumulative Loss Carryforward. The aggregate passive losses available to carry forward until there is passive income to offset the passive losses. This example assumes that the investor has no other passive investment transactions.

Cumulative Distribution. The total annual cash flow paid to the limited partners during the holding period.

Annual Benefits. The total annual benefits derived from the property, calculated by adding the cash distribution and the tax savings or liability.

Total Benefits. The cumulative total of the annual benefits. This column will show the investor when the investment is paid back.

Pre-tax Resale Proceeds. The total cash distribution upon sale per investment unit.

Resale Tax Liability. The tax liability of the taxable gain upon sale per investment unit.

Year of Sale After-Tax Benefits. The after-sale tax benefits are calculated by taking the pre-tax resale proceeds and subtracting the resale tax liability.

Total Previous After-Tax Benefits. The sum of the cash distributions during the holding period.

Benefits Through Resale. The cash benefits received during the holding period and upon the resale of the property.

MORTGAGE AMORTIZATION SCHEDULES (TABLES 7-10, 7-11)

The following is an example of a monthly amortization schedule for a self-amortizing loan.

TABLE 7-10
Amortization Schedule

PROPERTY NAME	OAK TERRACE APARTMENTS
PRINCIPAL	$4,675,00
INTEREST RATE	10.50%
NO. MONTHLY PAYMENTS	360
PAYMENT AMOUNT	$42,764,06

Payment Number	Interest Paid	Principal Paid	Balance Remaining	Total Annual Interest	Total Annual Principal	Total Annual Payments
1	40,906.25	1,857.81	4,673,142.19			
2	40,889.99	1,874.07	4,671,268.12			
3	40,873.60	1,890.47	4,669,377.65			
4	40,857.05	1,907.01	4,667,470.65			
5	40,840.37	1,923.69	4,665,546.95			
6	40,823.54	1,940.53	4,663,606.43			
7	40,806.56	1,957.51	4,661,648.92			
8	40,789.43	1,974.63	4,659,674.29			
9	40,772.15	1,991.91	4,657,682.37			
10	40,754.72	2,009.34	4,655,673.03			
11	40,737.14	2,026.92	4,653,646.11			
12	40,719.40	2,044.66	4,651,601.45	489,770.20	23,398.55	513,168.74
13	40,701.51	2,062.55	4,649,538.90			
14	40,683.47	2,080.60	4,647,458.31			
15	40,665.26	2,098.80	4,645,359.50			
16	40,646.90	2,117.17	4,643,242.34			
17	40,628.37	2,135.69	4,641,106.65			
18	40,609.68	2,154.38	4,638,952.27			
19	40,590.83	2,173.23	4,636,779.04			
20	40,571.82	2,192.25	4,634,586.79			
21	40,552.63	2,211.43	4,632,375.36			
22	40,533.28	2,230.78	4,630,144.59			
23	40,513.77	2,250.30	4,627,894.29			
24	40,494.08	2,269.99	4,625,624.30	487,191.60	25,977.15	513,168.74
25	40,474.21	2,289.85	4,623,334.45			
26	40,454.18	2,309.89	4,621,024.57			
27	40,433.96	2,330.10	4,618,694.47			
28	40,413.58	2,350.49	4,616,343.99			
29	40,393.01	2,371.05	4,613,972.93			
30	40,372.26	2,391.80	4,611,581.14			

Payment Number	Interest Paid	Principal Paid	Balance Remaining	Total Annual Interest	Total Annual Principal	Total Annual Payments
31	40,351.33	2,412.73	4,609,168.41			
32	40,330.22	2,433.84	4,606,734.57			
33	40,308.93	2,455.13	4,604,279.43			
34	40,287.45	2,476.62	4,601,802.82			
35	40,265.77	2,498.29	4,599,304.53			
36	40,243.91	2,520.15	4,596,784.38	484,328.82	28,839.92	513,168.74
37	40,221.86	2,542.20	4,594,242.18			
38	40,199.62	2,564.44	4,591,677.74			
39	40,177.18	2,586.88	4,589,090.86			
40	40,154.55	2,609.52	4,586,481.34			
41	40,131.71	2,632.35	4,583,848.99			
42	40,108.68	2,655.38	4,581,193.61			
43	40,085.44	2,678.62	4,578,514.99			
44	40,062.01	2,702.06	4,575,812.94			
45	40,038.36	2,725.70	4,573,087.24			
46	40,014.51	2,749.55	4,570,337.69			
47	39,990.45	2,773.61	4,567,564.08			
48	39,966.19	2,797.88	4,564,766.20	481,150.57	32,018.18	513,168.74
49	39,941.70	2,822.36	4,561,943.85			
50	39,917.01	2,847.05	4,559,096.79			
51	39,892.10	2,871.97	4,556,224.83			
52	39,866.97	2,897.09	4,553,327.73			
53	39,841.62	2,922.44	4,550,405.29			
54	39,816.05	2,948.02	4,547,457.27			
55	39,790.25	2,973.81	4,544,483.46			
56	39,764.23	2,999.83	4,541,483.63			
57	39,737.98	3,026.08	4,538,457.55			
58	39,711.50	3,052.56	4,535,404.99			
59	39,684.79	3,079.27	4,532,325.72			
60	39,657.85	3,106.21	4,529,219.51	477,622.05	35,546.69	513,168.74
61	39,630.67	3,133.39	4,526,086.12			
62	39,603.25	3,160.81	4,522,925.31			
63	39,575.60	3,188.47	4,519,736.85			
64	39,547.70	3,216.36	4,561,520.48			
65	39,519.55	3,244.51	4,513,275.97			
66	39,491.16	3,272.90	4,510,003.08			
67	39,462.53	3,301.54	4,506,701.54			
68	39,433.64	3,330.42	4,503,371.12			
69	39,404.50	3,359.56	4,500,011.55			

PAYMENT NUMBER	INTEREST PAID	PRINCIPAL PAID	BALANCE REMAINING	TOTAL ANNUAL INTEREST	TOTAL ANNUAL PRINCIPAL	TOTAL ANNUAL PAYMENTS
70	39,375.10	3,388.96	4,496,622.59			
71	39,345.45	3,418.61	4,493,203.98			
72	39,315.53	3,448.53	4,489,755.45	473,704.68	39,464.06	513,168.74
73	39,285.36	3,478.70	4,486,276.75			
74	39,254.92	3,509.14	4,482,767.61			
75	39,224.22	3,539.85	4,479,227.76			
76	39,193.24	3,570.82	4,475,656.94			
77	39,162.00	3,602.06	4,472,054.88			
78	39,130.48	3,633.58	4,468,421.30			
79	39,098.69	3,665.38	4,464,755.92			
80	39,066.61	3,697.45	4,461,058.48			
81	39,034.26	3,729.80	4,457,328.68			
82	39,011.63	3,762.44	4,453,566.24			
83	38,968.70	3,795.36	4,449,770.88			
84	38,935.50	3,828.57	4,445,942.31	469,355.61	43,813.14	513,168.74
85	38,902.00	3,862.07	4,442,080.25			
86	38,868.20	3,895.86	4,438,184.39			
87	38,834.11	3,929.95	4,434,254.44			
88	38,799.73	3,964.34	4,430,290.10			
89	38,765.04	3,999.02	4,426,291.08			
90	38,730.05	4,034.02	4,422,257.07			
91	38,694.75	4,069.31	4,418,187.75			
92	38,659.14	4,104.92	4,414,082.83			
93	38,623.22	4,140.84	4,409,942.00			
94	38,586.99	4,177.07	4,405,764.93			
95	38,550.44	4,213.62	4,401,551.31			
96	38,513.57	4,250.49	4,397,300.82	464,527.25	48,641.50	513,168.74
97	38,476.38	4,287.68	4,393,013.14			
98	38,438.86	4,325.20	4,388,687.94			
99	38,401.02	4,363.04	4,384,324.90			
100	38,362.84	4,401.22	4,379,923.68			
101	38,324.33	4,439.73	4,375,483.95			
102	38,285.48	4,478.58	4,371,005.37			
103	38,246.30	4,517.76	4,366,487.61			
104	38,206.77	4,557.30	4,361,930.31			
105	38,166.89	4,597.17	4,357,333.14			
106	38,126.66	4,637.40	4,352,695.74			
107	38,086.09	4,677.97	4,348,017.77			
108	38,045.16	4,718.91	4,343,298.86	459,166.79	54,001.96	513,168.74

Payment Number	Interest Paid	Principal Paid	Balance Remaining	Total Annual Interest	Total Annual Principal	Total Annual Payments
109	38,003.87	4,760.20	4,338,538.67			
110	37,962.21	4,801.85	4,333,736.82			
111	37,920.20	4,843.86	4,328,892.95			
112	37,877.81	4,886.25	4,324,006.70			
113	37,835.06	4,929.00	4,319,077.70			
114	37,791.93	4,972.13	4,314,105.57			
115	37,748.42	5,015.64	4,309,089.93			
116	37,704.54	5,059.53	4,304,030.41			
117	37,660.27	5,103.80	4,298,926.61			
118	37,615.61	5,148.45	4,293,778.16			
119	37,570.56	5,193.50	4,288,584.65			
120	37,525.12	5,238.95	4,283,345.71	453,215.59	59,953.16	513,168.74

Notes to Mortgage Amortization Schedule (Table 7-10)

Principal. The total loan amount

Interest Rate. The interest rate on the mortgage.

No. Monthly Payments. The total number of months over which the mortgage will be amortized.

Payment Amount. The monthly debt service payment.

Balance Remaining. The remaining balance on the mortgage as the principal balance is paid off.

Total Annual Interest. The total interest paid in the year.

Total Annual Principal. The total principal paid in the year.

Total Annual Payments. The total yearly debt service.

TABLE 7-11
Oak Terrace Associates, LLC
Debt Service Amortizaiton

First Mortgage	Year 1	Year 2	Year 3	Year 4	Year 5	Year 6	Year 7	Year 8	Year 9	Year 10
Beginning Balance	$4,675,000	$4,651,601	$4,625,624	$4,596,784	$4,564,766	$4,529,220	$4,489,755	$4,445,942	$4,397,301	$4,343,299
Interest	489,770	487,192	484,329	481,151	477,622	473,705	469,356	464,527	459,167	453,216
Principal	23,399	25,977	28,840	32,018	35,547	39,464	43,813	48,641	54,002	59,953
Total Debt Service	513,169	513,169	513,169	513,169	513,169	513,169	513,169	513,169	513,169	513,169
Ending Balance	$4,651,601	$4,625,624	$4,596,784	$4,564,766	$4,529,220	$4,489,755	$4,445,942	$4,397,301	$4,343,299	$4,283,346

FORECAST OF DEPRECIATION (TABLE 7-12)

The following is an example of a depreciation schedule for a residential property.

TABLE 7-12
Oak Terrace Associates, LLC
Forecast of Depreciation

Real Property

		TOTAL
Down Payment to Seller		$1,000,000
First Mortgage		4,675,000
Purchase Money Note to Seller		$ 995,000
Purchase Price		6,670,000
Closing Costs (added to basis)		137,500
Total Basis		$6,807,500
Allocation of Basis to Components:		
Land	10%	680,750
Realty	80%	5,446,000
Personal Property	10%	680,750
Total Basis		$6,807,500

Depreciation Percentages

	Realty	Personalty
Year 1	3.485%	14.29%
Year 2	3.636%	24.49%
Year 3	3.636%	17.49%
Year 4	3.636%	12.49%
Year 5	3.636%	8.93%
Year 6	3.636%	8.92%
Year 7	3.636%	8.93%
Year 8	3.636%	4.46%
Year 9	3.636%	
Year 10	3.636%	

DEPRECIATION:

	Basis	YEAR 1	YEAR 2	YEAR 3	YEAR 4	YEAR 5	YEAR 6	YEAR 7	YEAR 8	YEAR 9	YEAR 10	TOTAL
Realty	5,446,000	189,793	198,017	198,017	198,017	198,017	198,017	198,017	198,017	198,017	198,017	1,971,942
Personal Property	680,750	97,279	166,716	119,063	85,026	60,791	60,723	60,791	30,361			680,750
Property Additions:												
Year 1	16,514	576	600	600	600	600	600	600	600	600	600	5,980
Year 2	17,223		600	626	626	626	626	626	626	626	626	5,610
Year 3	17,912			624	651	651	651	651	651	651	651	5,183
Year 4	18,629				649	677	677	677	677	677	677	4,713
Year 5	19,374					675	704	704	704	704	704	4,197
Year 6	20,149						702	733	733	733	733	3,633
Year 7	20,955							730	762	762	762	3,016
Year 8	21,793								759	792	792	2,344
Year 9	22,665									790	824	1,614
Year 10	23,571										821	821
Total	6,325,534	287,648	365,933	318,931	285,569	262,038	262,701	263,530	233,892	204,353	205,209	2,689,804

Notes to Forecast of Depreciation (Table 7-12)

Down Payment to Seller. The total down payment of equity in the deal.

First Mortgage. The total debt on the property.

Purchase Money Note to Seller. The amount of the seller financing.

Purchase Price. The total price paid for the property.

Closing Costs (added to basis). The total dollar amounts of the closing costs added to the basis of the property. (See the Allocation of Legal, Accounting and Closing Costs, Table 7-13.)

Land. The total land cost is deducted from the purchase price, since land is not depreciable.

Realty. The total of the depreciable basis allocated towards the realty. (See the Yearly %—Realty.)

Personal Property. The total of the depreciable basis allocated towards the personalty. Personalty items are as follows:

- Appliances
- Carpet
- Drapes
- Equipment

Total Basis. This is the sum of the land, realty and personal property.

ALLOCATION OF LEGAL, ACCOUNTING AND CLOSING COSTS (TABLE 7-13)

The following is an example of how the closing costs, financing costs and partnership fees are handled for accounting purposes.

TABLE 7-13
Oak Terrace Associates, LLC
Allocation of Legal, Accounting and Closing Costs

ITEM	AMOUNT	AMORT. 5 YR. %	TOTAL	SYNDICATION %	TOTAL	LOAN COSTS	TOTAL	BUILDING BASIS	TOTAL
Closing and Financing Costs	$130,000					25%	$32,500	75%	$97,500
Initial Partnership Administration Fee	$20,000	100%	$20,000						
Organization Fee	$20,000	75%	$15,000	25%	$5,000				
Acquisition Services Fee	$20,000							100%	$20,000
Loan Origination Fee	$20,000					100%	$20,000		
Project Management & Supervision Fee	$20,000							100%	$20,000
Money Raiser Fees:	$50,000		———	100%	$50,000		———		
Total	$280,000		$35,000		$55,000		$52,500		$137,500
A = Amortization—5 Year	$35,000	Annual amortization	7,000				1,750		
C = Capital (Syndication)	$55,000								
L = Loan Costs	$52,500								
B = Basis—Building	$137,500								
Total	$280,000								

302

Notes to Allocation of Legal, Accounting and Closing Costs (Table 7-13)

A = Amortization—5 Year. 100% of the Initial Partnership Administrative Fee and 75% of the Organization Fee are amortized over a 5 year period.

C = Capital (Syndication). 25% of the Organization Fee and 100% of the Money Raiser Fees are capitalized for tax purposes.

L = Loan Costs. 25% of the Closing and Financing Costs and 100% of the Loan Origination Fee are amortized over the 10 year term of the loan.

B = Basis—Building. 75% of the Closing and Financing Costs, 100% of the Acquisition Service Fee and 100% of the Project Management & Supervision Fee are added to the basis of the property and depreciated.

ACCOUNTING AND FORECASTING FORMS

Balance Sheet. Chart of accounts showing the assets and the liabilities of the property.

Statement of Income and Expenses. The line items on this form can be used as a chart of accounts for compiling the monthly operating statements.

Accounting Projection Outline. This form may be used by the investor or the accountant to summarize the financial aspects of the transaction.

Budget Forecasts. Form designed to be used when preparing budget forecasts.

Budget Line Item. Form designed to assist in making the budget forecasts. Each line item is analyzed, with the final data transposed to the main budget forecast form.

Capital Improvement Budget. Form used in preparing the capital improvement budget.

1. Monthly capital improvement budget

2. Yearly capital improvement budget.

Ten Year Operating Forecast. Form used for making ten-year financial forecasts.

FORM 7-1
Balance Sheet

CODE DESCRIPTION

ASSETS:
100 CASH $ _____
101 CHECKING ACCOUNT $ _____
102 MONEY MARKET ACCOUNT $ _____
103 SECURITY DEPOSITS $ _____
104 CASH HELD BY TRUSTEE $ _____
105 TIME DEPOSITS $ _____
106 PETTY CASH ACCOUNTS $ _____
107 CASH IN ESCROW $ _____
108 TRANSFER ACCOUNT $ _____
120 MARKETABLE SECURITIES $ _____
121 SHORT TERM BANK INVESTMENTS $ _____
130 ACCOUNTS RECEIVABLE $ _____
135 LOANS AND NOTES RECEIVABLE $ _____
140 PRE-DEVELOPMENT COSTS $ _____
145 INVESTMENTS $ _____
150 PROPERTY, PLANT, EQUIPMENT $ _____
151 LAND $ _____
152 BUILDINGS $ _____
153 BUILDING IMPROVEMENTS $ _____
154 LEASEHOLD IMPROVEMENTS $ _____
155 FURNITURE AND FIXTURES $ _____
156 AUTOMOTIVE EQUIPMENT $ _____

157 OBJETS D'ART $ _____
165 DEPRECIATION $ _____
166 BUILDINGS $ _____
167 BUILDING IMPROVEMENTS $ _____
168 LEASEHOLD IMPROVEMENTS $ _____
169 FURNITURE AND FIXTURES $ _____
170 AUTOMOTIVE EQUIPMENT $ _____
171 LEASEHOLD $ _____
180 OTHER ASSETS $ _____
181 PREPAID TAXES $ _____
182 PREPAID INTEREST $ _____
183 PREPAID INSURANCE $ _____

184 PREPAID DEBT SERVICE $ _____
185 RENT DEPOSITS $ _____
186 UTILITY DEPOSITS $ _____
187 IMPOUNDS $ _____
188 DEFERRED INTEREST $ _____
189 LOAN FEES $ _____
190 CONSTRUCTION INTEREST $ _____
191 ORGANIZATION EXPENSES $ _____
192 SYNDICATION $ _____
193 TRANSFER FEES $ _____
194 OTHER $ _____ $ _____

CODE DESCRIPTION

LIABILITIES:
200 ACCOUNTS PAYABLE $ _____
201 ACCOUNTS PAYABLE $ _____
202 REFUNDABLE SECURITY DEPOSITS $ _____
203 DUE TO AFFILIATE $ _____
204 ACCRUED PROPERTY TAXES $ _____
205 ACCRUED INTEREST $ _____
206 ACCRUED INSURANCE $ _____
207 ACCRUED PAYROLL $ _____
208 ACCRUED INCOME $ _____
209 DEFERRED INCOME $ _____
210 DEFERRED MAINT. RESERVES $ _____
211 SALES EXPENSE PAYABLE $ _____
212 DEFERRED MANAGEMENT FEES $ _____
213 SALES TAX PAYABLE $ _____
220 TAXES PAYABLE $ _____
221 PAYROLL TAXES $ _____
230 LOANS AND NOTES PAYABLE $ _____
231 TRUST DEED NOTES PAYABLE $ _____
232 LOANS PAYABLE $ _____
233 CONTRACTS PAYABLE $ _____

EQUITY: $ _____

250 PARTNERSHIP CAPITAL ACCOUNTS $ _____
251 PARTNERSHIP ORIGINAL CAPITAL $ _____
252 PARTNERSHIP CONTRIBUTIONS $ _____
253 PARTNERSHIP DRAWS $ _____
254 PARTNERSHIP EARNINGS $ _____
260 STOCKHOLDER EQUITY $ _____
261 COMMON STOCK $ _____
262 RETAINED EARNINGS $ _____
263 DISTRIBUTION TO OWNER $ _____

TOTAL LIABILITIES AND EQUITY $ _____

304

Summary of Income and Expenses

CODE DESCRIPTION

INCOME:

1000 RENTAL
1001 BUILDING BASE RENTAL
1002 RENTAL REFUNDS
1003 DEPOSITS RETAINED INCOME
1004 EMPLOYEES' FREE RENT
1005 ESCALATIONS
1006 PERCENTAGE
1007 CABLE TV
1110 APPLICATION FEES
1120 SECURITY DEPOSITS
1130 FURNITURE RENTAL
1140 VENDING MACHINE INCOME
1141 LAUNDRY
1142 TELEPHONE
1143 VENDING MACHINE
1144 OTHER
1150 PARKING
1160 STORAGE
1170 CONFERENCE ROOM
1180 FINANCE INCOME
1181 TRANSFER, LATE, NSF CHARGES
1182 INTEREST INCOME
1183 GAIN ON SALE OF ASSETS
1184 OTHER
1190 REIMBURSEMENTS
1191 COMMON AREA SERVICES
1192 TAXES
1193 INSURANCE
1194 TENANT IMPROVEMENTS
1195 COMPENSATION
1196 ACCOUNTING
1197 ADMINISTRATIVE
1198 UTILITY
1199 OTHER
1200 ASSOCIATION DUES
1210 FOOD REVENUE
1211 BEVERAGE REVENUE
1220 FEES
1221 BUILDING MANAGEMENT
1222 ASSET MANAGEMENT
1223 DEVELOPMENT

CODE DESCRIPTION

1210 COMMISSIONS
1211 CONSTRUCTION SUPERVISION
1212 CLEANING
1230 CAPITAL CONTRIBUTIONS
1231 INVESTOR CONTRIBUTIONS
1232 G.P. CONTRIBUTIONS
1240 LOANS
1241 MORTGAGE LOANS
1242 G.P. LOANS
1243 L.P. LOANS
1244 NOTE FINANCING LOANS
1260 BUYERS' DEPOSITS
1261 UNIT SALES
1262 LAND SALES

1299 TOTAL INCOME

CODE	DESCRIPTION	CODE	DESCRIPTION	CODE	DESCRIPTION
	OPERATING EXPENSES:		SALARIES & WAGES:	2323	VINYL
				2324	CABINETS
	CLOSING COSTS	2200	RESIDENT MANAGER	2325	MIRROR
		2201	ASSISTANT MANAGER	2326	LIGHTING
2000	CASH TO SELLER	2202	BOOKKEEPER	2327	BRICK
2001	FEES TO SELLER	2203	OFFICE CLERK	2328	STUCCO
2002	PREPAID INTEREST TO SELLER	2204	TEMPORARY LABOR	2329	TENNIS COURT
2003	SURVEY	2205	MAINTENANCE	2330	POOL
2004	LEGAL-OUT OF POCKET	2206	ASSISTANT MAINTENANCE	2331	PLAYGROUND
2005	PICTURES	2207	LANDSCAPING	2332	CLUBHOUSE
2006	PRINTING	2208	POOL		
2007	RECORDING COSTS	2209	HOUSEKEEPING	2399	TOTAL MAINTENANCE & REPAIR
2008	MORTGAGE TAX	2210	SECURITY		
2009	ESCROW FEES	2211	PORTER		
2010	INTEREST ON FRONT MONEY	2212	PARKING LOT ATTENDENT		UTILITIES:
2011	MARKET STUDY	2213	CONTRACT LABOR		
2012	PREPAID INSURANCE	2214	LEASING AGENT	2400	ELECTRIC—COMMON AREA
2013	REAL ESTATE TAX ESCROW	2215	SALARY ADVANCES	2401	ELECTRIC—VACANT AREA
2014	RESERVE ESCROWS	2216	COMMISSIONS	2402	ELECTRIC—LEASED AREA
2015	COURIER	2217	BONUSES	2403	GAS—COMMON AREA
2016	TELEPHONE	2218	PROFIT SHARING	2404	GAS—VACANT AREA
2017	TRAVEL	2219	BENEFITS	2405	GAS—LEASED AREA
2018	ENTERTAINMENT	2220	UNEMPLOYMENT TAX	2406	WATER/SEWER—COMMON AREA
2019	MAPS	2221	PAYROLL TAXES	2407	WATER/SEWER—VACANT AREA
2020	BLUE SKY			2408	WATER/SEWER—LEASED AREA
2021	POSTAGE	2299	TOTAL PAYROLL		
2022	ARCHITECTURAL			2499	TOTAL UTILITIES
2023	ENGINEERING				
2024	CONSTRUCTION MANAGEMENT		REPAIRS & MAINTENANCE		
2025	FEASIBILITY STUDY				TAXES:
2026	APPRAISAL	2300	HVAC		
2027	PREPAID INSURANCE	2301	PLUMBING	2500	REAL ESTATE
2028	PEST BOND	2302	ELECTRICAL	2501	PERSONAL PROPERTY
2029	TAX PRORATION	2303	APPLIANCES	2502	VEHICLE
2030	CONSULTANT	2304	LOCK REPAIRS		
2031	FEES PAID	2305	EXTERIOR REPAIRS	2599	TOTAL TAXES
		2306	ROOF REPAIRS		
2099	TOTAL CLOSING COSTS	2307	GLASS REPAIRS		INSURANCE:
		2308	SCREEN REPAIRS		
	LOAN CLOSING COSTS	2309	DRAPES	2600	PROPERTY
		2310	BLINDS	2601	LIABILITY
2100	LOAN ORIGINATION FEE	2311	RODS	2602	CONTENTS
2101	LOAN POINTS	2312	WALLPAPER	2603	FIDELITY
2102	TITLE INSURANCE	2313	PAINT—EXTERIOR	2604	BOILER/MACHINERY
2103	DEED TAX	2314	PAINT—INTERIOR	2605	VEHICLE
2104	RECORDING COSTS	2315	PAVING	2606	FLOOD
2105	LOAN TRANSFER FEE	2316	PARKING LOT LIGHTING	2607	RENT LOSS
2106	LENDER'S LEGAL	2317	DIRECTORIES	2608	ERRORS AND OMISSIONS
2107	CREDIT REPORT	2318	SIGNAGE	2609	HEALTH
2108	LOAN BUYDOWN	2319	LANDSCAPING	2610	WORKMAN'S COMPENSATION
2109	MORTGAGE INSURANCE	2320	CARPENTRY	2611	LIFE
2110	SURETY COSTS	2321	FENCES		
2150	MISC. LOAN CLOSING COSTS	2322	CARPET	2699	TOTAL INSURANCE
2099	TOTAL LOAN CLOSING COSTS				

FORM 7-2
Summary of Income and Expenses (Cont'd)

CODE	DESCRIPTION	CODE	DESCRIPTION	CODE	DESCRIPTION
	GENERAL & ADMINISTRATIVE:		**PROFESSIONAL FEES:**		**CONTRACT SERVICES:**
2700	LEGAL	2900	LEGAL	3100	PEST CONTROL
2701	ACCOUNTING	2901	ACCOUNTING	3101	TRASH
2702	DUES	2902	ARCHITECTURAL	3102	LANDSCAPING
2703	SUBSCRIPTION	2903	ENGINEERING	3103	ELEVATOR
2704	DONATIONS	2904	LANDSCAPE ARCHITECTURAL	3104	JANITORIAL
2705	TRAVEL	2905	APPRAISAL	3105	MAID SERVICE
2706	ENTERTAINMENT	2906	FEASIBILITY STUDIES	3106	WINDOW WASHING
2707	PETTY CASH	2907	CONSULTANTS	3107	PARKING LOT SWEEPING
2708	OFFICE SUPPLIES	2908	CONSTRUCTION MANAGEMENT	3108	SNOW REMOVAL
2709	COPIER LEASE	2909	PROPERTY MANAGEMENT	3109	MUSIC
2710	POSTAGE	2910	REAL ESTATE BROKER	3110	SECURITY
2711	BUSINESS CARDS	2911	MORTGAGE BROKER	3111	LAUNDRY
2712	PRINTING			3112	HVAC
2713	STATIONERY/ENVELOPES	2999	TOTAL PROFESSIONAL FEES		
2714	FURNITURE & EQUIPMENT RENTAL			3199	TOTAL CONTRACT SERVICES
2715	EQUIPMENT MAINTENANCE				
2716	TELEPHONE		**MARKETING:**		
2717	PLANT RENTAL/PURCHASE				**SUPPLIES:**
2718	PLANT MAINTENANCE	3000	AGENCY FEES		
2719	OFFICE CLEANING	3001	PRODUCTION	3200	HVAC
2720	OFFICE UTILITIES	3002	BUSINESS CARDS	3201	PLUMBING
2721	ANSWER SERVICE	3003	NEWSPAPER	3202	ELECTRICAL
2722	PAGER	3004	MAGAZINE	3203	APPLIANCES
2723	CREDIT BUREAU	3005	DIRECT MAIL	3204	CLEANING
2724	COURIER	3006	POSTAGE	3205	TOOLS
2725	BUSINESS LICENSE	3007	PHOTOS	3206	POOL
2726	UNIFORMS	3008	SIGNAGE	3207	PAINTING
2727	EMPLOYMENT FEES	3009	FRAMES	3208	FIRE SAFETY
2728	PICTURES	3010	RENDERINGS		
2729	SEMINARS	3011	PARTIES	3299	TOTAL SUPPLIES
2730	TRAINING	3012	GIFTS		
2731	HOME OFFICE EXPENSE	3013	MARKETING AIDS		
2732	FRANCHISE FEES	3014	PROMOTIONS		**UNIT MAINTENANCE:**
2733	PERMITS	3015	PROSPECT LISTS		
2734	LICENSES	3016	FLIERS	3300	CLEANING
2735	MEMBERSHIPS	3017	RADIO	3301	CARPET
2736	DATA PROCESSING FEE	3018	TELEVISION	3302	PAINTING
		3019	BROCHURES	3303	WALLPAPER
2799	TOTAL GENERAL & ADMINISTRATIVE	3020	BILLBOARDS	3304	SHEETROCK
		3021	PUBLIC RELATIONS	3305	DRAPERY CLEANING
		3022	OFFICE DISPLAYS	3306	TURNKEY
	MANAGEMENT FEES:	3023	MODEL FURNITURE— LEASE/PURCHASE		
		3024	TENANT RELATIONS	3399	TOTAL UNIT MAINTENANCE
2800	MANAGEMENT FEE	3099	TOTAL MARKETING		
2801	PARTNERSHIP MANAGEMENT FEE				
2899	TOTAL MANAGEMENT FEES				

FORM 7-2
Summary of Income and Expenses (Cont'd)

CODE	DESCRIPTION	CODE	DESCRIPTION	CODE	DESCRIPTION
	BANKING:		**ASSOCIATION:**		**CASH FLOW:**
3600	OPEN BANK ACCOUNT	3900	TRASH	7000	CASH FLOW
3601	CHECKS	3901	WATER/SEWER		
3602	INSUFFICIENT FUNDS	3902	ELECTRIC		**CAPITAL EXPENDITURES:**
3603	WIRE CHARGE	3903	GAS		
3604	SERVICE CHARGES	3904	MANAGEMENT FEE	8000	TENANT IMPROVEMENTS
3605	ANALYSIS LOSS	3905	LANDSCAPING	8001	FLOORING
3606	LOAN FEES	3906	PEST	8002	APPLIANCES
		3907	INSURANCE	8003	CABINETS
3650	TOTAL BANKING	3908	CABLE TV	8004	PLUMBING
		3909	OPERATING EXPENSES	8005	ELECTRICAL
	RESERVES & REPLACEMENTS	3910	JANITORIAL	8006	HVAC
		3911	BUILDING REPAIRS	8007	CEILING
3700	FLOORING	3912	SUPPLIES	8008	CONCRETE
3701	APPLIANCES	3913	COMMON AREA MAINTENANCE	8009	LANDSCAPING
3702	LANDSCAPING	3914	RESERVE FUND	8010	EXTERIOR PAINTING
3703	CABINETS	3915	DEVELOPER'S SUBSIDY	8011	EXTERIOR FACADE
3704	PLUMBING			8012	POOL EQUIPMENT
3705	SIGNAGE	3999	TOTAL ASSOCIATION	8013	TENNIS COURT
				8014	PLAYGROUND
3799	TOTAL RESERVES & REPLACEMENTS			8015	PAVING
				8016	SIGNAGE
			MOTEL EXPENSES:	8017	WINDOWS
	COMMON AREA MAINTENANCE			8018	FENCE
		4000	LINEN EXPENSE	8019	ROOF
3800	ELECTRIC	4001	CREDIT CARD COMMISSIONS	8020	STRUCTURAL
3801	GAS	4002	LAUNDRY SUPPLIES	8021	GUTTERS
3802	WATER/SEWER	4003	GUEST SUPPLIES	8022	ELEVATOR
3803	CLEANING	4004	RESERVATION EXPENSES	8023	PARKING LOT LIGHTING
3804	HVAC	4005	TRAVEL AGENT COMMISSIONS	8024	SECURITY/LOCKS
3805	ELEVATOR	4006	LONG DISTANCE TELEPHONE	8025	SPRINKLER
3806	PLUMBING	4007	PAY STATION COMMISSIONS	8026	FURNITURE
3807	PARKING LOT	4008	TELEPHONE EQUIPMENT LEASE	8027	CONSTRUCTION SUPERVISION
3808	PARKING LOT LIGHTING				
3809	COMMON SIGNS	4099	TOTAL MOTEL EXPENSES	8099	TOTAL CAPITAL EXPENDITURES
3810	VEHICLE				
3811	EQUIPMENT		**NET OPERATING INCOME:**		**EQUIPMENT PURCHASE:**
3812	TRASH				
3813	SWEEPING	5000	NET OPERATING INCOME	8500	OFFICE FURNITURE
3814	SNOW REMOVAL			8501	MODEL FURNITURE
3815	JANITORIAL			8502	OFFICE EQUIPMENT
3816	LANDSCAPING		**DEBT SERVICE:**	8503	MAINTENANCE EQUIPMENT
3817	MISC. MAINTENANCE REPAIR				
3818	SUPPLIES	6000	FIRST MORTGAGE	8599	TOTAL EQUIPMENT PURCHASE
		6001	SECOND MORTGAGE		
3899	TOTAL COMMON AREA MAINTENANCE	6002	THIRD MORTGAGE		**LEASING COMMISSIONS**
		6003	FOURTH MORTGAGE		
		6004	WRAP MORTGAGE	8600	LEASING FEES—INHOUSE
		6005	BANK LOANS	8601	LEASING FEES—OUTSIDE
		6006	NOTE FINANCING LOANS		
		6007	LENDER PARTICIPATION	8699	TOTAL LEASING COMMISSIONS
		6008	GROUND RENTAL		
		6009	MASTER LEASE		
		6099	TOTAL DEBT SERVICE		

308

FORM 7-3

Accounting Projection Outline

PROPERTY _____
PREPARED BY _____
DATE _____
CLOSING DATE: _____   PAGE ___ OF ___

CAPITAL CONTRIBUTIONS: EVERY _____ MONTHS
PAY IN PERIOD OVER _____ MONTHS

CAPITAL CONTRIBUTIONS:

PAY IN PERIOD:	GENERAL PARTNER	LIMITED PARTNERS
DATE: _____	AMOUNT $ _____	AMOUNT $ _____
DATE: _____	AMOUNT $ _____	AMOUNT $ _____
DATE: _____	AMOUNT $ _____	AMOUNT $ _____
DATE: _____	AMOUNT $ _____	AMOUNT $ _____
DATE: _____	AMOUNT $ _____	AMOUNT $ _____
DATE: _____	AMOUNT $ _____	AMOUNT $ _____
DATE: _____	AMOUNT $ _____	AMOUNT $ _____
DATE: _____	AMOUNT $ _____	AMOUNT $ _____
DATE: _____	AMOUNT $ _____	AMOUNT $ _____
DATE: _____	AMOUNT $ _____	AMOUNT $ _____

DOWN-PAYMENT TO SELLER: AMOUNT/DATE

$ _____ AT CLOSING
$ _____ ON _____
$ _____ ON _____
$ _____ ON _____
$ _____ ON _____
$ _____ ON _____
$ _____ ON _____

FEES TO SELLER:	AMOUNT/DATE	FEE NAME	AMOUNT
	$ _____ AT CLOSING	_____	$ _____
	$ _____ ON _____	_____	$ _____
	$ _____ ON _____	_____	$ _____
	$ _____ ON _____	_____	$ _____
	$ _____ ON _____	_____	$ _____
	$ _____ ON _____	_____	$ _____
	$ _____ ON _____	_____	$ _____

FEES TO GENERAL PARTNER:		FEE NAME	DATE PAID
	$ _____ OR ___% OF THE MONEY RAISED	_____	_____
	$ _____ OR ___% OF THE MONEY RAISED	_____	_____
	$ _____ OR ___% OF THE MONEY RAISED	_____	_____
	$ _____ OR ___% OF THE MONEY RAISED	_____	_____
	$ _____ OR ___% OF THE MONEY RAISED	_____	_____
	$ _____ OR ___% OF THE MONEY RAISED	_____	_____
	$ _____ OR ___% OF THE MONEY RAISED	_____	_____
	$ _____ OR ___% OF THE MONEY RAISED	_____	_____

FEES TO BROKER DEALER:		FEE NAME	DATE PAID
	$ _____ OR ___% OF THE MONEY RAISED	_____	_____
	$ _____ OR ___% OF THE MONEY RAISED	_____	_____
	$ _____ OR ___% OF THE MONEY RAISED	_____	_____
	$ _____ OR ___% OF THE MONEY RAISED	_____	_____

Accounting Projection Outline (Cont'd)

PROFORMA YEARS: 19___ TO 19___   PAGE ___ OF ___

MONTH CLOSING: _____

GROSS POTENTIAL INCOME:

YEAR 1 (PARTIAL) $ _____	YEAR 2 _____%	YEAR 7 _____%
YEAR 1 (FULL) $ _____	YEAR 3 _____%	YEAR 8 _____%
	YEAR 4 _____%	YEAR 9 _____%
	YEAR 5 _____%	YEAR 10 _____%
	YEAR 6 _____%	

VACANCY:

YEAR 1 (PARTIAL) $ _____	YEAR 2 _____%	YEAR 7 _____%
YEAR 1 (FULL) $ _____	YEAR 3 _____%	YEAR 8 _____%
	YEAR 4 _____%	YEAR 9 _____%
	YEAR 5 _____%	YEAR 10 _____%
	YEAR 6 _____%	

MISCELLANEOUS INCOME:

YEAR 1 (PARTIAL) $ _____	YEAR 2 _____%	YEAR 7 _____%
YEAR 1 (FULL) $ _____	YEAR 3 _____%	YEAR 8 _____%
	YEAR 4 _____%	YEAR 9 _____%
	YEAR 5 _____%	YEAR 10 _____%
	YEAR 6 _____%	

OPERATING EXPENSES:

YEAR 1 (PARTIAL) $ _____	YEAR 2 _____%	YEAR 7 _____%
YEAR 1 (FULL) $ _____	YEAR 3 _____%	YEAR 8 _____%
	YEAR 4 _____%	YEAR 9 _____%
	YEAR 5 _____%	YEAR 10 _____%
	YEAR 6 _____%	

REPLACEMENT RESERVE:

YEAR 1 (PARTIAL) $ _____	YEAR 2 $ _____	YEAR 7 $ _____
YEAR 1 (FULL) $ _____	YEAR 3 $ _____	YEAR 8 $ _____
	YEAR 4 $ _____	YEAR 9 $ _____
	YEAR 5 $ _____	YEAR 10 $ _____
	YEAR 6 $ _____	

PARTNERSHIP SERVICE FEE:

YEAR 1 (PARTIAL) $ _____	YEAR 2 $ _____	YEAR 7 $ _____
YEAR 1 (FULL) $ _____	YEAR 3 $ _____	YEAR 8 $ _____
	YEAR 4 $ _____	YEAR 9 $ _____
	YEAR 5 $ _____	YEAR 10 $ _____
	YEAR 6 $ _____	

AUDIT FEE:

YEAR 1 (PARTIAL) $ _____	YEAR 2 $ _____	YEAR 7 $ _____
YEAR 1 (FULL) $ _____	YEAR 3 $ _____	YEAR 8 $ _____
	YEAR 4 $ _____	YEAR 9 $ _____
	YEAR 5 $ _____	YEAR 10 $ _____
	YEAR 6 $ _____	

PAGE ___ OF ___

DEBT SERVICE:
FIRST MORTGAGE

ORIGINAL BALANCE: $ _____
CURRENT LOAN BALANCE: $ _____ AS OF: _____
INTEREST RATE: _____% AMORTIZATION PERIOD: _____
MONTHLY P & I: $ _____ MATURITY DATE _____
CLOSING COSTS: $ _____ LOAN POINTS: $ _____
COMMENTS: _____
_____
_____

DEBT SERVICE:
SECOND MORTGAGE

ORIGINAL BALANCE: $ _____
CURRENT LOAN BALANCE: $ _____ AS OF: _____
INTEREST RATE: _____% AMORTIZATION PERIOD: _____
MONTHLY P & I: $ _____ MATURITY DATE _____
CLOSING COSTS: $ _____ LOAN POINTS: $ _____
COMMENTS: _____
_____
_____

DEBT SERVICE:
THIRD MORTGAGE

ORIGINAL BALANCE: $ _____
CURRENT LOAN BALANCE: $ _____ AS OF: _____
INTEREST RATE: _____% AMORTIZATION PERIOD: _____
MONTHLY P & I: $ _____ MATURITY DATE _____
CLOSING COSTS: $ _____ LOAN POINTS: $ _____
COMMENTS: _____
_____
_____

DEBT SERVICE:
FOURTH MORTGAGE

ORIGINAL BALANCE: $ _____
CURRENT LOAN BALANCE: $ _____ AS OF: _____
INTEREST RATE: _____% AMORTIZATION PERIOD: _____
MONTHLY P & I: $ _____ MATURITY DATE _____
CLOSING COSTS: $ _____ LOAN POINTS: $ _____
COMMENTS: _____
_____
_____

DEBT SERVICE:
NOTE FINANCING
MORTGAGE

ORIGINAL BALANCE: $ _____
CURRENT LOAN BALANCE: $ _____ AS OF: _____
INTEREST RATE: _____% AMORTIZATION PERIOD: _____
DEBT SERVICE PAID EVERY: _____ MONTHS
MONTHLY P & I: $ _____ MATURITY DATE _____
CLOSING COSTS: $ _____ LOAN POINTS: $ _____
NOTE COVERAGE: _____%
COMMENTS: _____
_____
_____

311

PAGE ___ OF ___

PARTNERSHIP SPLIT:

GENERAL PARTNER: _____% OF THE CASH FLOW
GENERAL PARTNER: _____% OF THE TAXABLE INCOME (LOSS)

LIMITED PARTNER: _____% OF THE CASH FLOW
LIMITED PARTNER: _____% OF THE TAXABLE INCOME (LOSS)

L.P. CASH FLOW PREFERRED RETURN:
_____% STARTING IN YEAR _____

THEREAFTER CASH FLOW AND TAXABLE INCOME (LOSS) SPLIT:

G.P. _____%
L.P. _____%

REFINANCING PROCEEDS:
L.P. GETS FIRST: $ _____
G.P. GETS FIRST: $ _____

THEREAFTER:
L.P. GETS: _____%
G.P. GETS: _____%

RESALE PROFITS:
L.P. GETS FIRST: $ _____
L.P. GETS MISSING PREFERRED CASH FLOW RETURN OF $ _____
L.P. GETS _____%
G.P. GETS _____%

COMMENTS:
_____
_____
_____
_____
_____
_____
_____
_____
_____
_____
_____

312

Accounting Projection Outline (Cont'd)

PAGE ___ OF ___

CLOSING COSTS:

ITEM	AMOUNT	CODE	COMMENTS
LEGAL	$ _____	_____	_____
LEGAL—OUT OF POCKET	$ _____	_____	_____
BLUE SKY FEES	$ _____	_____	_____
ACCOUNTING	$ _____	_____	_____
APPRAISAL	$ _____	_____	_____
ENGINEERING STUDY	$ _____	_____	_____
MARKET STUDY	$ _____	_____	_____
PHOTOGRAPHS	$ _____	_____	_____
PRINTING	$ _____	_____	_____
LOAN RECORDING	$ _____	_____	_____
PARTNERSHIP RECORDING	$ _____	_____	_____
DEED TAX	$ _____	_____	_____
MORTGAGE TAX	$ _____	_____	_____
TITLE INSURANCE	$ _____	_____	_____
PREPAID INSURANCE	$ _____	_____	_____
MORTGAGE INSURANCE	$ _____	_____	_____
ESCROW FEE	$ _____	_____	_____
CONSTRUCTION MANAGEMENT FEE	$ _____	_____	_____
TRAVEL & ENTERTAINMENT	$ _____	_____	_____
COURIER SERVICE	$ _____	_____	_____
SECRETARIAL COSTS	$ _____	_____	_____
TELEPHONE	$ _____	_____	_____
INTEREST ON FRONT MONEY	$ _____	_____	_____
COPIER COSTS	$ _____	_____	_____
LENDER CLOSING COSTS	$ _____	_____	_____
LENDER BUYDOWN	$ _____	_____	_____
SURVEY	$ _____	_____	_____
PARTNERSHIP FILING FEE	$ _____	_____	_____
UTILITY DEPOSITS	$ _____	_____	_____
PEST BOND/REPORT	$ _____	_____	_____
MISC. _____	$ _____	_____	_____
MISC. _____	$ _____	_____	_____
MISC. _____	$ _____	_____	_____
MISC. _____	$ _____	_____	_____
MISC. _____	$ _____	_____	_____
MISC. _____	$ _____	_____	_____
MISC. _____	$ _____	_____	_____
MISC. _____	$ _____	_____	_____
MISC. _____	$ _____	_____	_____
MISC. _____	$ _____	_____	_____
MISC. _____	$ _____	_____	_____

CODE:
A1–A10 = AMORTIZE OVER ONE TO TEN YEARS
E = EXPENSE
C = CAPITALIZE
B = ADD TO BASIS

FORM 7-3
Accounting Projection Outline (Cont'd)

TAX TREATMENT OF FEES:

FEE NAME	AMOUNT	CODE	COMMENTS
	$ _____		
	$ _____		
	$ _____		
	$ _____		
	$ _____		
	$ _____		
	$ _____		
	$ _____		
	$ _____		
	$ _____		
	$ _____		
	$ _____		
	$ _____		
	$ _____		
	$ _____		
	$ _____		

CODE:
A1–A10 = AMORTIZE OVER ONE TO TEN YEARS
E = EXPENSE
C = CAPITALIZE
B = ADD TO BASIS

314

Accounting Projection Outline (Cont'd)

PAGE ___ OF ___

TAXABLE INCOME (LOSS):

RENOVATIONS: YEAR 1: TOTAL $ _____   EXPENSED _____%   DEPRECIATED _____%
               YEAR 2: TOTAL $ _____   EXPENSED _____%   DEPRECIATED _____%
               YEAR 3: TOTAL $ _____   EXPENSED _____%   DEPRECIATED _____%
               YEAR 4: TOTAL $ _____   EXPENSED _____%   DEPRECIATED _____%
               YEAR 5: TOTAL $ _____   EXPENSED _____%   DEPRECIATED _____%
               YEAR 6: TOTAL $ _____   EXPENSED _____%   DEPRECIATED _____%
               YEAR 7: TOTAL $ _____   EXPENSED _____%   DEPRECIATED _____%
               YEAR 8: TOTAL $ _____   EXPENSED _____%   DEPRECIATED _____%
               YEAR 9: TOTAL $ _____   EXPENSED _____%   DEPRECIATED _____%
               YEAR 10: TOTAL $ _____   EXPENSED _____%   DEPRECIATED _____%

FOR NEW CONSTRUCTION

CONSTRUCTION PERIOD INTEREST: SALES TAX:

		MONTH	SALES TAX
YEAR 1:	$ _____	_____	$ _____
YEAR 2:	$ _____	_____	$ _____
YEAR 3:	$ _____	_____	$ _____
YEAR 4:	$ _____	_____	$ _____
YEAR 5:	$ _____	_____	$ _____
YEAR 6:	$ _____	_____	$ _____
YEAR 7:	$ _____	_____	$ _____
YEAR 8:	$ _____	_____	$ _____
YEAR 9:	$ _____	_____	$ _____
YEAR 10:	$ _____	_____	$ _____
		_____	$ _____
		_____	$ _____
		_____	$ _____
		_____	$ _____
		_____	$ _____
		_____	$ _____
		_____	$ _____
		_____	$ _____
		_____	$ _____
		_____	$ _____

DEPRECIATION SCHEDULE:

CONTRACT PURCHASE PRICE: $ _____
TYPE PROPERTY: _____ NO. YEARS DEPRECIATED: _____ YRS.
LAND COST: $ _____
PERSONALTY: $ _____

COMPLETION OF BUILDINGS: BLDG. 1 VALUE: $ _____ DATE: _____
COMPLETION OF BUILDINGS: BLDG. 2 VALUE: $ _____ DATE: _____
COMPLETION OF BUILDINGS: BLDG. 3 VALUE: $ _____ DATE: _____
COMPLETION OF BUILDINGS: BLDG. 4 VALUE: $ _____ DATE: _____
COMPLETION OF BUILDINGS: BLDG. 5 VALUE: $ _____ DATE: _____
COMPLETION OF BUILDINGS: BLDG. 6 VALUE: $ _____ DATE: _____
COMPLETION OF BUILDINGS: BLDG. 7 VALUE: $ _____ DATE: _____
COMPLETION OF BUILDINGS: BLDG. 8 VALUE: $ _____ DATE: _____
COMPLETION OF BUILDINGS: BLDG. 9 VALUE: $ _____ DATE: _____
COMPLETION OF BUILDINGS: BLDG. 10 VALUE: $ _____ DATE: _____

PAGE ___ OF ___

SELLER GUARANTEES:

NEGATIVE CASH FLOW: FROM (DATE) _____ TO (DATE) _____

WORKING CAPITAL ACCOUNT:

DATE: _____ $ _____
DATE: _____ $ _____
DATE: _____ $ _____
DATE: _____ $ _____
DATE: _____ $ _____
DATE: _____ $ _____
DATE: _____ $ _____

COMMENTS: _____
_____
_____
_____
_____
_____
_____

RESALE:

PROJECTED RESALE DATE: _____
RESALE PROJECTIONS: FORECLOSURE _____ COST _____ MARKET VALUE _____
MARKET VALUE: CAP RATE: _____% OF NET OPERATING INCOME FOR YEAR _____
    APPRECIATION OF _____% STARTING FROM YEAR _____
    GROSS RENT MULTIPLIER OF _____ IN YEAR _____

DESIRED WRITE-OFF RATIOS: DESIRED CASH FLOW PERCENTAGES:

    YEAR 1 _____%   YEAR 1 _____%
    YEAR 2 _____%   YEAR 2 _____%
    YEAR 3 _____%   YEAR 3 _____%
    YEAR 4 _____%   YEAR 4 _____%
    YEAR 5 _____%   YEAR 5 _____%
    YEAR 6 _____%   YEAR 6 _____%
    YEAR 7 _____%   YEAR 7 _____%
    YEAR 8 _____%   YEAR 8 _____%
    YEAR 9 _____%   YEAR 9 _____%
    YEAR 10 _____%   YEAR 10 _____%

COMMENTS: _____
_____
_____
_____
_____
_____

316

FORM 7-4
Budget Forecasts

PROPERTY NAME _____
BUDGET YEAR _____
PREPARED BY _____
DATE _____

PAGE ___ OF ___

CODE	DESCRIPTION	LAST YEAR	JAN	FEB	MAR	APR	MAY	JUN	JUL	AUG	SEP	OCT	NOV	DEC	TOTAL
		$	$	$	$	$	$	$	$	$	$	$	$	$	$
		$	$	$	$	$	$	$	$	$	$	$	$	$	$
		$	$	$	$	$	$	$	$	$	$	$	$	$	$
		$	$	$	$	$	$	$	$	$	$	$	$	$	$
		$	$	$	$	$	$	$	$	$	$	$	$	$	$
		$	$	$	$	$	$	$	$	$	$	$	$	$	$
		$	$	$	$	$	$	$	$	$	$	$	$	$	$
		$	$	$	$	$	$	$	$	$	$	$	$	$	$
		$	$	$	$	$	$	$	$	$	$	$	$	$	$
		$	$	$	$	$	$	$	$	$	$	$	$	$	$
		$	$	$	$	$	$	$	$	$	$	$	$	$	$
		$	$	$	$	$	$	$	$	$	$	$	$	$	$
		$	$	$	$	$	$	$	$	$	$	$	$	$	$
		$	$	$	$	$	$	$	$	$	$	$	$	$	$
		$	$	$	$	$	$	$	$	$	$	$	$	$	$
		$	$	$	$	$	$	$	$	$	$	$	$	$	$
		$	$	$	$	$	$	$	$	$	$	$	$	$	$
		$	$	$	$	$	$	$	$	$	$	$	$	$	$
		$	$	$	$	$	$	$	$	$	$	$	$	$	$
	TOTAL	$	$	$	$	$	$	$	$	$	$	$	$	$	$

COMMENTS _____

317

FORM 7-5
Budget Line Item

PROPERTY NAME _____   DATE _____
LINE ITEM DESCRIPTION _____
CODE _____
BUDGET YEAR _____

PAGE ___ OF ___

MONTHLY BREAKDOWN   EXPLANATION

TOTAL LAST YEAR $ _____   _____
JANUARY $ _____   _____
FEBRUARY $ _____   _____
MARCH $ _____   _____
APRIL $ _____   _____
MAY $ _____   _____
JUNE $ _____   _____
JULY $ _____   _____
AUGUST $ _____   _____
SEPTEMBER $ _____   _____
OCTOBER $ _____   _____
NOVEMBER $ _____   _____
DECEMBER $ _____   _____
  TOTAL YEAR $ _____   _____

COMMENTS

_____
_____
_____
_____
_____
_____
_____
_____

FORM 7-6
Capital Expenditure Monthly Budget

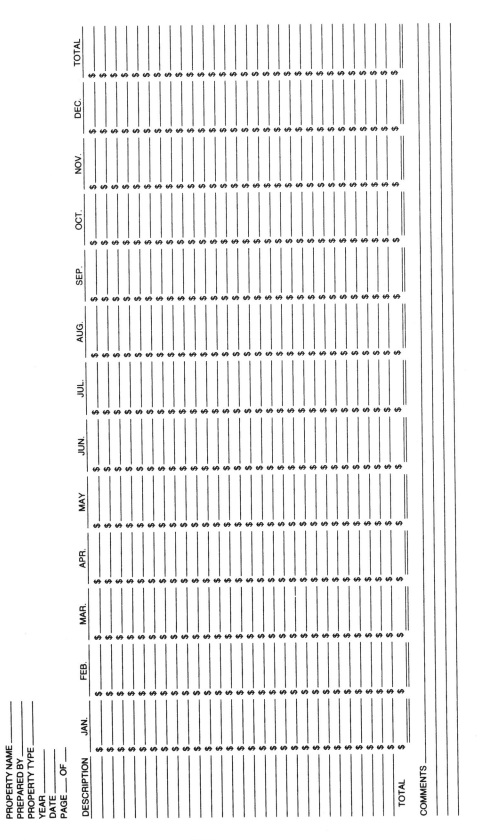

319

FORM 7-7
Capital Expenditure Yearly Budget

PROPERTY NAME _____
PREPARED BY _____
PROPERTY TYPE _____
YEAR _____
DATE _____ OF _____
PAGE _____ OF _____

DESCRIPTION	YR. ___	YR. ___	YR. ___	YR. ___	YR. ___	YR. ___	YR. ___	YR. ___	YR. ___	YR. ___
_____	$	$	$	$	$	$	$	$	$	$
_____	$	$	$	$	$	$	$	$	$	$
_____	$	$	$	$	$	$	$	$	$	$
_____	$	$	$	$	$	$	$	$	$	$
_____	$	$	$	$	$	$	$	$	$	$
_____	$	$	$	$	$	$	$	$	$	$
_____	$	$	$	$	$	$	$	$	$	$
_____	$	$	$	$	$	$	$	$	$	$
_____	$	$	$	$	$	$	$	$	$	$
_____	$	$	$	$	$	$	$	$	$	$
_____	$	$	$	$	$	$	$	$	$	$
_____	$	$	$	$	$	$	$	$	$	$
_____	$	$	$	$	$	$	$	$	$	$
_____	$	$	$	$	$	$	$	$	$	$
_____	$	$	$	$	$	$	$	$	$	$
_____	$	$	$	$	$	$	$	$	$	$
_____	$	$	$	$	$	$	$	$	$	$
_____	$	$	$	$	$	$	$	$	$	$
_____	$	$	$	$	$	$	$	$	$	$
_____	$	$	$	$	$	$	$	$	$	$
_____	$	$	$	$	$	$	$	$	$	$
_____	$	$	$	$	$	$	$	$	$	$
TOTAL	$	$	$	$	$	$	$	$	$	$

COMMENTS _____
_____
_____

320

FORM 7-8

Ten-Year Operating Forecast

PROPERTY NAME _____
PREPARED BY _____
DATE _____

DESCRIPTION	YR. ___	YR. ___	YR. ___	YR. ___	YR. ___	YR. ___	YR. ___	YR. ___
REVENUE:								
GROSS POTENTIAL INCOME (GPI)	$___	$___	$___	$___	$___	$___	$___	$___
LESS: VACANCY	$___	$___	$___	$___	$___	$___	$___	$___
MISCELLANEOUS INCOME	$___	$___	$___	$___	$___	$___	$___	$___
EFFECTIVE GROSS INCOME (EGI)	$___	$___	$___	$___	$___	$___	$___	$___
EXPENSES:								
FIXED OPERATING EXPENSES	$___	$___	$___	$___	$___	$___	$___	$___
VARIABLE EXPENSES	$___	$___	$___	$___	$___	$___	$___	$___
RESERVE REPLACEMENT	$___	$___	$___	$___	$___	$___	$___	$___
TOTAL EXPENSES	$___	$___	$___	$___	$___	$___	$___	$___
NET OPERATING INCOME	$___	$___	$___	$___	$___	$___	$___	$___
DEBT SERVICE	$___	$___	$___	$___	$___	$___	$___	$___
CAPITAL EXPENDITURES	$___	$___	$___	$___	$___	$___	$___	$___
CASH FLOW	$___	$___	$___	$___	$___	$___	$___	$___

COMMENTS _____

321

FINANCING YOUR PURCHASE: HOW TO SECURE A LENDER AND PREPARE A LOAN PACKAGE

Since most real estate investments require a great deal of money, more than many individual investors possess, a successful real estate deal usually requires an outside lending source. Loans are typically made in the form of mortgages, which are instruments of debt secured by real property for a specified time period. Upon repayment of the loan, the debt is then satisfied and the collateral is released.

For example, a lender may provide funds to an investor for the purchase of a rental property in the form of a thirty-year mortgage. The investor will make regular monthly payments to the lender during those thirty years. After making the final mortgage payment, he will obtain clear title to the property.

Of great importance in acquiring real estate is knowing how to find a lender and how to prepare and present a financing proposal. Of equal importance are how to negotiate with lenders, how to set up a closing, and how to close the loan.

The first thing to consider before starting work on a proposal (whether it's new construction or refinancing of an existing deal) is to compile a list of potential lenders.

Sources for finding lenders include the local Yellow Pages, mortgage brokers/bankers, local banking institutions, and industry newsletters, such as the *Crittenden Finance Newsletter* (415-382-2481), which publish the names of various lenders and report on their size and the types of deals that they are currently financing. You will want your list to be large, with twenty to thirty names, because you may need to contact most of them, in addition to contacting any mortgage brokers/bankers. To find out the names of local mortgage brokers/bankers, start with their local association. Realize that if you retain the services of a mortgage banker, you will pay for this service. Remember, in searching for that perfect loan you may have to negotiate with more than one lender at a time. Even though the loan officer tells you that your loan appears to be very favorable, the situation may completely change by the time the final commitment is to be approved by the appropriate loan committee. Since time is generally of the essence, negotiating with more than one lender could prove to be to your advantage.

When preparing your loan proposal, attempt to have a complete submission. This will help to decrease the loan processing timetable.

It is also important to note the sophistication of the lender to whom you plan to submit the proposal. For the more sophisticated lenders, you may want to use all of the items outlined in this chapter. For others, who are relationship-type lenders (those that will only lend funds to existing customers) and are not as sophisticated as you might be, too much information might scare them away from the deal. In this case, you will want

Alvin Arnold, Managing Consultant with BDO Seidman, edited this chapter.

to reduce some of the items in this package and not give it all to them in the initial submission. If they ask for this information later, you will have it and will be able to submit it when required. The last thing you want to do is confuse the loan officer.

HOW TO USE FINANCING TO MAXIMIZE YOUR RETURNS AND MINIMIZE CASH LOSS

Leverage Property for a Higher Yield

Since all investors are looking to maximize their returns, a mortgage can help increase this yield. The higher the amount of debt on a property, the higher the potential yield. This is due to the fact that the greater potential profits will be made on a smaller cash investment. For example: if a property was purchased for $1,000,000 with a $100,000 down payment and sold for $1,200,000 in one year, the investor would have made $200,000 on a $100,000 investment over the one-year period. This is a 200 percent return. If the investor had a $300,000 down payment, he would have made a 66.7 percent return. The investor should make sure that the property is not overleveraged. If a property has too much debt placed on it, it could create "reverse leverage."

Reverse leverage occurs when the net operating income of a property decreases, and due to the high monthly debt service, the property will start to have a reduced or negative cash flow.

EXAMPLE A

Purchase Price	$1,000,000
Down-payment	$100,000
Resale Price—1 Yr	$1,200,000
Profit—1 Yr	$200,000
Return	$200,000 / $100,000 = 200%

EXAMPLE B

Purchase Price	$1,000,000
Down-payment	$300,000
Resale Price—1 Yr	$1,200,000
Return	$200,000 / $300,000 = 66.7%

Borrow to Offset Shortfall of Available Cash

The majority of investors cannot afford to pay all cash for their acquisitions. Even if they could, they would be limited to the number of purchases they could make. By financing property, the investor can structure a loan to fit his needs. Depending on the availability of the investor's cash and the current market rates for loans, the investor can structure his overall investment needs by borrowing more or less.

FOUR REASONS TO CONSIDER FINANCING

Consolidate Total Debt Structure

Many times the existing debt on a property is made up of various loans with different terms and conditions. These loans could have different loan maturity dates that make individual refinancing very difficult. The investor may want to liquidate this assemblage of debt with a new loan, resulting in more advantageous terms.

Improve Cash Flow

The current debt might have been placed on the property at a time of high interest rates. The timing could be that even with new closing costs, a new loan could be arranged with lower interest rates or a longer amortization period, which would increase the annual cash flow.

Generate Tax-free Cash

The existing debt could be an old loan that has been substantially paid down. By refinancing the property, the borrower would be able to increase the loan amount. The excess cash generated could be used to make any needed property improvements required by the investor. Since these new funds were generated by a loan and not from a resale, they are tax free to the investor.

Increase the Salability of the Property

Many times the investor is looking to resell the property, and the existing financing makes it very difficult. The existing mortgage documents might prohibit a resale without the approval of the lender, or a sale without prior written approval of the lender could cause the loan to be accelerated. Rather than waiting for a potential purchaser to arrange for new financing, the investor could refinance the property. This could expedite the sale. Another factor in selling the property is the availability of the down-payment. If the current loan is very small, any new purchaser would have to make a substantial down-payment or the current owner might have to take back a purchase money mortgage. Refinancing, generally, will greatly increase the potential for resale and reduce the time required to sell the property.

FOURTEEN KEY SOURCES OF FINANCING

There are many sources from which the investor can obtain funding. They can be as simple as getting financing from the seller or as complex as borrowing funds from Wall Street.

Depending on the sophistication of the borrower or the complexity of the deal, the investor may seek out the services of a mortgage broker/banker to help determine the most appropriate source of funds and how to structure and obtain this funding.

Mortgage Brokers

Mortgage brokers will charge a fee for their services which usually ranges from one-half to one percent of the mortgage loan amount. Although the borrower will have to pay for this service, a well qualified mortgage broker can assist in obtaining the best possible loan. A good broker can put the initial loan proposal together and has a long list of relationships in the financial community. Additionally, such a broker can help structure the business terms and offer the financial sophistication that the borrower may not possess. Remember, if you decide to use a mortgage broker, seek one who is qualified and has experience in the type of financing you are looking for.

Mortgage Bankers

Mortgage bankers are individuals or companies that originate, close and service mortgage loans in their own name and sell the loans to another investor. Many of these companies put together mortgage pools of either their own funds or funds of other institutions or investors. These funds usually have certain lending restrictions and requirements. Many mortgage bankers act as a correspondent for other institutional lenders.

> **Correspondents:** Many mortgage bankers will act as loan correspondents for large institutional investors, such as pension funds or life insurance companies. The institutions rely on the local knowledge of the mortgage banker to protect their interest.

> The following is a list of the most common sources of financing.

Seller

The seller is probably the best source for financing, whether it be for a first or a second mortgage. Sellers will usually structure a better loan for the purchaser with fewer restrictive terms than a conventional lender. There will usually be no fees, a lower interest rate, and in many cases a longer period of time to repay than with conventional sources. In some cases, the purchaser will not be able to borrow from conventional sources, due to his credit, lack of experience or other market conditions.

Savings and Loans

Local or regional savings and loans are usually good sources of financing. One advantage of dealing with them is that they know the area, and quite often the property you wish to finance. They also tend to have more flexible terms than other lenders.However, S&Ls have suffered a precipitous fall because of the scandals of the early 1990s. Mortgage conduits (see below) have captured much of the S&Ls' smaller commercial loan business. In 1988, S&Ls held nearly 28% of the debt market. By 1996, their share had dropped to under 13%.

Current market and governmental conditions play a large part in the availability of S&L funds to lend. Since they are dependent on a stream of incoming funds from depositors, many savings and loans either run dry of funds or are flush with cash, depending on the current market conditions. (However, this situation is much less serious than formerly because of their ability to securitize loans for sale in the secondary market or to use excess cash to buy mortgage-backed securities.) Savings and loans are regulated by governmental agencies and they are monitored to ensure the institution is following prudent lending procedures.

Commercial Banks

Commercial banks are a good source for both long-term and short-term financing. These institutions will generally be familiar with the area and can act fairly quickly on loan applications. Since their costs of funds are lower than those of savings institutions (because so many of their deposits are in the form of non-interest bearing checking accounts) they can offer more competitive rates. Banks make both construction loans and post-construction (permanent) loans. A recent study showed that commercial banks now dominate the mortgage market with more than a 42% share. One reason is that banks now commonly securitize the loans thay originate for sale in the secondary mortgage market, thus freeing up capital for new loans.

Insurance Companies

Insurance companies are a good source for financing but they have strict loan criteria. Because of the large amount of funds they control, larger insurance companies will only lend on very large transactions. Insurance companies are also a good resource for potential joint venture partners. The cost of their funds is usually much lower than that of banks or savings and loans, and thus they can usually make their loans at lower rates. In many instances, insurance companies will not require personal guarantees and will charge lower front-end fees. For the next few years, a large percentage of their loan capital will be used to refinance maturing loans; an additional percentage will be used to buy securitized loans. Nevertheless, insurance companies remain an important source of mortgage financing.

Pension Funds

Pension funds no longer are a significant source of funds for individual mortgages. Their share of the debt market dropped below 3% in 1996. Instead, the funds are interested in equity investing—either in real estate directly or increasingly in real estate investment trusts (REITs). If a pension fund does wish to invest in mortgages, it is likely to buy mortgage securities rather than whole loans.

Mortgage Real Estate Investment Trusts (REITs)

Mortgage real estate investment trusts (REITs) were a very popular source of financing in the 1970s, but many ran into severe financial problems at that time due to poor lending policies. These troubled REITs have now either been totally liquidated or merged into other sound companies. Today, few REITs invest primarily in mortgages (except for a few that specialize in jumbo home loans).

The one major exception is a class of REITs that loans to nursing homes and other types of health care facilities. Because of the highly specialized nature of these properties, REITs cannot own and operate them directly, but due to their growth potential, some REITs finance them with mortgages that carry a fixed interest rate plus a participation in increasing cash flow and refinancing or resale proceeds.

Wall Street Conduits

Over the last few years, many Wall Street firms and large lending institutions, such as Lehman Brothers, Goldman Sachs, Merrill Lynch, and Nationsbank, have set up lending departments to originate, fund and then resell these large packages of various property loans to other investors on Wall Street. These firms either use their own capital or warehouse lines of credit to fund the loans in their own names or close simultaneously with their correspondents.

Once the lender has a large enough pool of loans to sell, then one of the large national credit rating agencies will review the loan package and rate various pieces or traunches of the package according to the risk associated. This process is similar to how these credit rating agencies rate corporate bonds. In order to review these loans the credit rating agencies take a sampling of the loans and complete a thorough due diligence review. In order to compete effectively in the marketplace, many pools are packaged with those of other lenders to achieve a large enough critical mass to attract the largest number of investors and thus the best pricing.

REAL ESTATE MORTGAGE INVESTMENT CONDUIT (REMIC)

The REMIC, which is a creation of the Tax Reform Act of 1986, provides a new vehicle through which individuals can invest in real estate. In this case, the investments are backed by a pool of mortgages, and are therefore referred to as "mortgage backed securities." Prior to 1986, mortgage-backed securities were available to investors, but were backed only by residential mortgages. Through REMICs, investors for the first time have an option to invest in securities backed by commercial mortgages. This interest is issued to investors in the form of pass-through certificates, bonds, or other legal forms.

The primary effect of a REMIC is to reduce the importance of federal tax considerations in structuring mortgage securities transactions. In order for a pool of mortgages to avoid double taxation and penalty taxes as a REMIC, it must have only three types of assets. They are as follows:

1. Qualified Mortgages. Must be secured by an interest in real property
   a. First mortgages
   b. Second mortgages
   c. Fully amortizing mortgages
   d. Balloon mortgages
   e. Variable rate mortgages
   f. Adjustable rate mortgages
   g. Graduated payment mortgages
   h. Participating mortgages
   i. Residential mortgages
   j. Multifamily mortgages
   k. Commercial mortgages
   l. Industrial mortgages
   m. Farm mortgages
   n. Leasehold mortgages

2. Cash Flow Investment. This is a short-term investment in a passive, interest-bearing asset made solely for the purpose of reinvesting cash flows received from qualified mortgages between regular scheduled payments to investors.

3. Qualified Reserve Fund. This would include long-term investments that are set aside in a reserve to fund the expenses of running the REMIC pool or to insure the investors against a default in a qualified mortgage.

MORTGAGE-BACKED SECURITIES (MBS)

Mortgage-backed securities were created in the 1970s. Since they were introduced, they have been well received by the marketplace as an alternative source of real estate financing. There are two types:

- A certificate that evidences ownership of an interest in a mortgage loan or pool of mortgage loans

- An obligation that is secured by a mortgage loan or a pool of mortgage loans

Mortgage-backed securities can be issued and purchased by:

- Government National Mortgage Association (GNMA)

- Federal National Mortgage Association (FNMA)

- Federal Home Loan Mortgage Corporation (FHLMC)

- Homebuilders

- Multi-builder Issuers

- Investment bankers

- Banks

- Savings and loans

- Private mortgage insurance companies

- Arbitragers

COLLATERALIZED MORTGAGE OBLIGATIONS (CMOs)

Collateralized mortgage obligations (CMOs) were developed in 1983 as another type of mortgage security. CMOs divide the cash flow from a pool of mortgages into two or more classes. They use the cash flow from the various types of underlying securities to repay the bond classes in the order of their priority. Because each bond class has a different maturity date, the cash flow can be structured to pay out at the stated maturity date of that particular bond class.

Credit Companies

Credit companies, such as Heller Real Estate Financial Services, General Electric or General Motors Acceptance Corporation (GMAC), are an excellent source of mortgage financing. These lenders are usually short-term lenders. They will make construction loans or short-term permanent loans. Because they have large sums of money to lend, they usually have a higher minimum loan limit.

Local Development and Housing Agencies

Local development and housing agencies issue both taxable and tax-exempt financing to help stimulate new development activity in a local market area. These loans usually have very restrictive lending criteria.

The development agency will issue an inducement letter to the borrower who will, in turn, obtain a credit enhancement, such as an insurance policy or a letter of credit, to guarantee the bonds. Because they are tax-exempt bonds, a potential lender can offer the borrower a reduced interest rate and still be able to meet its yield requirements.

Charitable Foundations

Many large corporations and wealthy families have established foundations for charitable purposes. While these large sums of money are waiting to be permanently allocated, these foundations will invest funds in high-grade, quality investments. If the real estate is of special interest to the foundation (for example, a medical research facility might interest a cancer foundation), it will make a mortgage loan.

Religious and Fraternal Associations

Associations such as religious or fraternal organizations have sums of money that they are looking to invest. These sources might make loans to members at below-market rates. To find out if such loans are available, the investor should contact the head of the association.

Individual Investors

In the early days of lending, all lenders were wealthy individuals. Since individual investors are not governed by any governmental lending requirements, they are free to negotiate creative mortgage loans. Their motives are for profit as well as to help a family member or friend in need of some money.

MORTGAGE LOANS AVAILABLE FROM GOVERNMENTAL AND QUASI-GOVERNMENTAL AGENCIES

Federal Housing Administration (FHA)

The Federal Housing Administration was formed in 1934 to encourage an increase in home ownership, improve the standard of housing, and to create a better method of financing mortgage loans. These loans are made by local lenders and must comply with a long set of restrictions in order to be guaranteed by the credit of the government. The following are various programs offered by the Federal Housing Administration:

- **Multifamily Rental Housing (Section 207):** Federal mortgage insurance to finance construction or rehabilitation of a broad cross section of rental housing.

- **Manufactured Home Parks (Section 207):** Federal mortgage insurance to finance construction or rehabilitation of manufactured home parks.

- **Cooperative Housing (Section 213):** Federal mortgage insurance to finance cooperative housing projects.

- **Mortgage and Major Home Improvement Loan Insurance for Urban Renewal Areas (Section 220):** Federally insured loans used to finance mortgages for housing in urban renewal areas in which concentrated revitalization activities have been undertaken by local government, or to alter, repair, or improve housing in those areas.

- **Multifamily Rental Housing for Moderate-Income Families (Section 221(d)(3) and (4)):** Mortgage insurance to finance rental or cooperative multifamily housing for moderate-income households, including projects designated for the elderly. Single Room Occupancy (SRO) projects are also eligible for mortgage insurance.

- **Existing Multifamily Rental Housing (Section 223(f)):** Federal mortgage insurance under Section 207 pursuant to Section 223(f) for the purchase or refinance of existing apartment projects; to refinance an existing cooperative housing project; or for the purchase and conversion of an existing rental project to cooperative housing.

- **Mortgage Insurance for Single Room Occupancy Projects (Section 221(d) pursuant to Section 223(g)):** Mortgage insurance for the new construction and substantial rehabilitation of single room occupancy (SRO) facilities.

- **Mortgage Insurance for Housing for the Elderly (Section 231):** Federal mortgage insurance to finance the construction or rehabilitation of rental housing for the elderly or handicapped.

- **Nursing Homes, Intermediate Care Facilities, and Board and Care Homes (Section 232):** Federal mortgage insurance to finance or rehabilitate nursing, intermediate care, or board and care facilities.

- **Supplemental Loans for Multifamily Projects (Section 241):** Federal loan insurance to finance improvements, additions, and equipment to multifamily rental housing and health care facilities. It provides owners of eligible low-income housing with an adequate return on their investment and the ability to finance the acquisition of eligible low-income housing.

Veterans Administration (VA)

In 1944 Congress passed the G.I. Bill of Rights to give returning veterans of World War II a chance for a better life than their fathers had after returning from World War I. This law gave various benefits to the veterans, including loan guarantees for home ownership. The major benefit of this type of loan is that the borrower can get up to 100 percent financing. Over the years the loan limit has increased due to inflation.

Small Business Administration (SBA)

The Small Business Administration is a governmental agency that will insure a percentage of the loan that is made by a local lender. These loans can be made on real property for business use, for example, when a business owner wants to purchase the building that he is currently renting. These loans have many restrictions and take a long time to process, but the interest rate is usually lower than the current market because the government is guaranteeing a portion of the loan.

Farmers' Home Administration (FmHA)

Founded in 1934, the Farmers' Home Administration was established to revitalize the economy from the depths of the Depression. The purpose of this agency was to lend farmers money for the purchase of land and housing.

Federal National Mortgage Association (FNMA)

The Federal National Mortgage Association, or "Fannie Mae," was created in 1938 as a subsidiary of the Reconstruction Finance Corporation (RFC) to Title III of the National Housing Act. The principal function of FNMA is to purchase FHA-insured mortgages from private lenders in the secondary mortgage market. By purchasing large packages of these residential loans, FNMA helps to replenish the residential housing market with a new supply of mortgage capital.

Since 1970, FNMA has been listed on the New York Stock Exchange. Although it is a private corporation, it is considered a quasi-governmental agency due to its long established ties to the government.

Federal Housing Loan Mortgage Corporation (FHLMC)

The Federal Housing Loan Mortgage Corporation, or "Freddie Mac," was formed during the 1969 credit crunch by the Federal Home Loan Bank Board (FHLBB). Freddie Mac was established to sell bonds on the open market to provide additional funds with which to purchase mortgages from savings institutions. Similar to Fannie Mae, Freddie Mac has certain lending restrictions.

Government National Mortgage Association (GNMA)

The Government National Mortgage Association, or "Ginnie Mae," was established as a new corporation by the Housing Act of 1968. Its main purpose is to carry on the FNMA functions which were left with the Department of Housing and Urban Development

MULTIFAMILY FINANCE PROGRAMS

For those investors in multifamily properties there is a wide variety of loans offered by the Federal Housing Administration, the Federal National Mortgage Association, the Federal Housing Loan Mortgage Corporation and the Farmers' Home Administration. The following is a summary of the current loan programs available today.

TABLE 8-1

Multifamily Finance Programs

NAME OF PROGRAM	HUD 232	HUD 232 PURSUANT TO 223(f)	HUD 223 (a)(7)
Description	Offers mortgage insurance for new construction or rehab of assisted living facilities, board & carehomes and nursing facilities. (Substantial rehab is when work exceeds 15% of value or two or more major building components replaced.)	Program offers mortgage insurance for the refinance, acquisition or moderate upgrading of existing residential care facilities.	Program provides refinance of mortgages on multifamily projects already insured under the National Housing Act. It results in prepayment of existing insured mortgages and endorsement of new insured mortgage.
Loan Amount	No minimum or maximum.	No minimum or maximum.	Maximum mortgage amount cannot exceed the lower of: the original principal amount of the existing insured mortgage, or the unpaid principal amount of the existing insured mortgage plus eligible transaction costs.
Terms	Up to 40 years.	Up to 35 years.	
Rates	Fixed rate for term of loan; based upon current market conditions.	Fixed rate for term of loan; based upon current market conditions.	
Prepayment	Negotiable.	Negotiable.	Negotiable.
Assumability	Full, must go through HUD transfer of Physical Assets process.	Full, with approval. Must go through HUD Transfer of Physical Assets process.	Full, with approval. Must go through HUD Transfer of Physical Assets process.
Max. LVR	Up to 95% of value for non-profit borrowers. Up to 90% of value for profit-motivated borrowers.	Up to 85% of value or acquisition cost for profit-motivated. 90% for non-profits.	None.
Fees	Application, financing & placement. Annual mortgage insurance premium and inspection fee.	Application, financing & placement. Annual mortgage insurance premium and inspection fee.	Application, financing & placement. Annual mortgage insurance premium and inspection fee.
Timing	Typically 8-18 months, depending on number of stages. "Fast track" available in many offices.	Typically 8-18 months, depending on number of stages. "Fast track" available in many offices.	Typically 8-18 months, depending on number of stages. "Fast track" available in many offices.
Eligible Properties	New construction or substantial rehab required.	Existing skilled nursing or assisted living facilities. Facility must be at least 3 years old. Boarding care and assisted living facilities must be licensed.	Projects with loans that are fully insured at time of application.
Restrictions	None.	None.	No HUD-held loans are eligible.

Table 8-1
Multifamily Finance Programs (Cont'd)

Name of Program	HUD 232	HUD 232 Pursuant to 223(f)	HUD 223 (a)(7)
Escrows	2% of working capital escrow, initial operating deficit, 4% GNMA escrow, if required during construction.	50% of required repairs & potential operating deficit escrow.	10% of repairs escrow.
Reserves	Deposited monthly commencing with amortization and based on percentage of structured costs.	Established at closing and paid monthly commencing with amortization.	Established with original mortgage. Annual deposits continue under (a)(7). Additional deposits may be required.
Advantages	1.00-1.1 DSCR, long term, fixed rate, full amortization, non recourse, competitive rates.	1.00-1.17 DSCR, long term, fixed rate, full amortization, non recourse, competitive rates.	Expedited processing. Minimal application requirements.
Disadvantages	Processing time in some offices, prevailing wage rates. Skilled nursing facilities must be underwritten assuming 70% Medicaid residency.	Processing time in some offices. Skilled nursing facilities must be underwritten assuming 70% Medicaid residency.	Cannot exceed original mortgage.

Name of Program	Farmers' Home Adm (FmHA) Section 515	Freddie Mac (FHLMC) Conventional Cash Program	HUD 221 (d)(4)
Description	Povides insured loans to finance the construction, acquisition and/or rehab of rental & cooperative housing in rural areas.	Freddie Mac purchases qualified rental or cooperative multifamily mortgages. The program provides financing for acquistions, refinances and moderate rehab.	The program provides mortgage insurance for new construction or substantial rehab of rental or cooperative multifamily housing. (Substantial rehab when cost exceeds $6,500 per unit adjusted by area high cost percentage, 15% of value or when two or more major building components must be replaced.
Loan Amount	Varies state to state.	Small loan program: $300,000-$999,000. Large loan program: $1,000,000-$50,000,000.	No minimum or maximum
Terms	40 to 50 years, fully amortized.	5, 7, 10, 15, 25, 30 years, or others by request; 25-30 year amortization, or less, by request; 5+5 rate resets also available.	Up to 40 years.

TABLE 8-1
Multifamily Finance Programs (Cont'd)

NAME OF PROGRAM	FARMERS' HOME ADM (FMHA) SECTION 515	FREDDIE MAC (FHLMC) CONVENTIONAL CASH PROGRAM	HUD 221 (d)(4)
Rates	Range from 1% to market value.	Fixed for term of loan. Competitive rates based on risk-based pricing for loan's quality; Wall Street access for PC One Program. Rate reset mortgages fixed for 5-year term. Interest only option available for certain loans.	Fixed for term of loan; based upon current market conditions.
Prepayment	Restricted. No prepayment in the first 20 years.	Yield maintenance or fixed fee schedule.	Negotiable.
Assumability	Loans are assumable.	Yes, per the terms of the loan documents.	Full, with approval. Must go through HUD Transfer of Physical Assets.
Max. LVR	97-100% of appraisal development costs.	80%, based upon Freddie Mac value.	Up to 90% of eligible replacement costs, which includes a 10% allowance for developer profit and risk.
Fees	N/A	.10% application fee.	Application, financing and placement, annual mortgage insurance premium and inspection fees.
Timing	Varies from state to state. Can take up to one year.	Typically 20-30 days between receipt of full application and commitment issuance.	Typically 8-18 months, depending on number of stages. "Fast track" available in many offices.
Eligible Properties	Properties of modest design for very low-, low & moderate-income families, the elderly and disabled.	5+ units, garden, mid-rise, high-rise and cooperative properties in good condition.	Multifamily properties. Units must have kitchens and baths and comply with local building codes.
Restrictions	Restrictions on return.	N/A	Minimum 30 day leases, no transient services, single asset entity borrower.
Escrows	2% escrow required at closing.	Tax and insurance escrows required.	Initial operating deficit escrow, if any. 2% working capital escrow, 4% GNMA escrow if required during construction.
Reserves	Required.	Replacement reserve escrows typically required.	Deposited monthly commencing with amortization and based on percentage of structured costs.
Advantages	N/A	Competitive terms, conditions process and rates. Early rate lock delivery option locks interest rate at preliminary package stage.	1.00-1.11 DSCR. Long term, fixed rate, full amortization, non recourse, competitive interest rate. Construction and permanent financing.
Disadvantages	Program may have rules and regulations.	DSCR is high compared with other conduit programs. Small loans have a 35% recourse.	Processing time in some offices, prevailing wage rates.

TABLE 8-1
Multifamily Finance Programs (Cont'd)

NAME OF PROGRAM	HUD 223(f)	FANNIE MAE DELEGATED UNDERWRITING AND SERVICING (DUS)	FANNIE MAE PRIOR APPROVAL PRODUCT LINE
Description	Provides mortgage insurance for the refinance, acquisition or moderate renovation of existing apartments and housing cooperatives. Projects meeting definition of substantial rehab (left) are not eligible for 223(f).	Under DUS, Fannie Mae purchases qualified multifamily mortgages from specially designated lenders. These DUS lenders have been delegated responsibilities for originating, underwriting, closing and servicing Fannie Mae multifamily mortgages without prior review by Fannie Mae.	Individual transactions are submitted by approved Prior Approval lenders to Fannie Mae regional offices, where they receive full review prior to commitment. Underwriting standards are the same as DUS. Current priority is given to special affordable housing transactions.
Loan Amount	No minimum or maximum.	$1,000,000-$50,000,000. Average $5,000,000.	$1,000,000-$50,000,000.
Terms	Up to 35 but not less than 10 years.	5, 7, 10, 15, 18, 25 years, or others by request; 25-30 year amortization. ARMs available also.	5, 7, 10, 15, 18, 25 years, or others by request; 25-30 year amortization, or less by request. ARMs available also.
Rates	Fixed for term of loan. Based on current market conditions.	Priced daily. Best prices to most conservative transactions on a four-tier basis. Special pricing available for special affordable housing transactions. Wall Street access.	Priced daily. Best prices to most conservative transactions on a four-tier basis. Special pricing available for special affordable housing transactions. Wall Street access.
Prepayment	Negotiable.	Numerous yield maintenance options depending upon execution chosen.	Numerous yield maintenance options depending upon execution chosen.
Assumability	Full, with approval. Must go through HUD Transfer of Physical Assets.	Yes, under the conditions of the mortgage documents.	Yes, under the conditions of the mortgage documents.
Max. LVR	Up to 85%.	80%. Special underwriting, up to 90% for special affordable housing transactions.	80%. Special underwriting, up to 90% for special affordable housing transactions.
Fees	Application, financing and placement. HUD inspection and annual mortgage insurance premium.	Origination fee varies with DUS lender. 2% Fannie Mae commitment fee refunded at closing (except $10,000, which is refunded when legal documents are cleared).	Vary with transaction size.
Timing	Typically 4-8 months, depending on number of stages. "Fast track" available in many offices.	Varies with DUS lender workload. No Fannie Mae review required.	Depends on complexity of transaction and regional workload.

TABLE 8-1

Multifamily Finance Programs (Cont'd)

NAME OF PROGRAM	HUD 223(f)	FANNIE MAE DELEGATED UNDERWRITING AND SERVICING (DUS)	FANNIE MAE PRIOR APPROVAL PRODUCT LINE
Eligible Properties	Multifamily units. All units must have kitchens and baths.	5+ units, garden, mid-rise, high-rise and cooperative properties in good condition.	Wide range, with priority to special affordable housing. Rental and cooperatives, new to moderate rehab.
Restrictions	Property must be minimum of 3 years old. Lease terms must be for at least month. No transient services on the property.	N/A	N/A
Escrows	50% of required repairs and potential operating deficit escrow.	May need escrow for repairs if not completed by closing.	May need escrow for repairs if not completed by closing.
Reserves	Established at closing and paid monthly commencing with amortization.	Depends on structure, but not automatically required; may be waived for certain transactions with over 1.35 DSCR.	Depends on structure, but not automatically required for under 10 year transactions, may be waived for certain transactions with over 1.35 DSCR.
Advantages	1.00-1.17 DSCR. Long term, fixed rate, full amortization, nonrecourse, competitive interest rates.	Cash-out, 80% LVR, up to 30 year amortization, MBS/DUS provides access to Wall Street pricing.	Because of direct review by Fannie Mae's Prior Approval, can handle a greater range of complexities than other product lines.
Disadvantages	Processing time. Properties must be at least 3 years old.	N/A	N/A

Source: Multi-Housing News Magazine (August 1997).

HOW TO PREPARE A LOAN PROPOSAL

When requesting a loan from an institution, the borrower should prepare a loan proposal with all the necessary personal and property information that will enable a lender to make a loan submission. The following outline is a sample format to use for this purpose. Depending on the sophistication of the lender, all or part of this outline may be used.

Loan Proposal Outline

Cover Page
    Picture of Building
    Table of Contents
I. Investment Merits
    The Improvements
    The Location
    The Site Description
    The Market
    The Mitigating Factors
    The Investment
    The Summary
II. Summary of Salient Facts
    Loan Request
      Loan Amount
      Index
      Spread
      Rate
      Term
      Amortization Period
      Annual Debt Service
      Debt Service Coverage Ratio (DSCR)
      Loan to Value Ratio (LVR)
      Loan Per Square Foot (Gross)
      Loan Per Square Foot (Rentable)
      Loan Per Unit
      Loan Per Bed
    Property Information
      Number of Buildings
      Number of Units (If Residential)
      Unit Mix
      Square Footage (Gross)
      Square Footage (Rentable)
      Efficiency %
      Year Built
      Number of Elevators
        Passenger
        Service
      Parking
        Surface

        Covered
      Land Area (Acres)
      Average Rent Per Square Foot
      Number of Tenants
      Average Lease Terms
        Rent Per Square Foot
        Utilities Paid By
        Janitorial Paid By
      Proforma Expenses Per Square Foot
      Borrower
      Loan Guarantor (If Applicable)
      Management & Leasing Firm
III. The Property
    Locational Narrative
    Locational Maps
    Subject Photographs
    Neighborhood Photographs
    Aerials/Legend
    Site Plan
    Floor Plans
    Elevations
IV. The Economics
    Proforma
    Rent Roll
    Operating History
V. City Economy
VI. Property Type Market Summary
VII. Rent Comparables
    Photographs & Summaries
    Locational Map
VIII. Sales Comparables
    Photographs & Summaries
    Locational Map
IX. Neighborhood Analysis
    1, 3, 5 Mile Demographics
X. Articles
XI. Borrower Resume
XII. Management/Leasing Resume

EIGHT POINTS TO REMEMBER FOR OBTAINING A LOAN

Keep Your Loan Proposal Complete and Up-to-Date

If any of the information regarding the property changes during the time you are searching for the loan, make sure that this new information is reflected in a revised loan proposal. A complete loan proposal will help the lender make a timely and positive lending decision.

Learn to Use the Loan Proposal

A working knowledge of the material in the loan proposal will impress the lender. This knowledge will also help in the loan presentation. How the loan proposal is presented is crucial to a favorable outcome.

Qualify the Most Qualified Mortgage Broker/banker and Potential Lenders

If you decide to use a mortgage broker/banker, make sure that this individual is the person best qualified to handle the contemplated loan. Since time is extremely critical at this stage, the borrower must have a well-rounded and knowledgeable individual to assist in obtaining the most favorable loan terms available. The investor should ask to see the mortgage broker's/banker's resume showing some recent transactions. This will help establish credibility and ability to obtain loans for investors.

When your list of potential lenders has been compiled, start the process of identifying the most qualified lenders. Once this list has been narrowed down, you will be in a position to negotiate successfully. (See lender's qualification questions later in this chapter.)

Review the Important Issues

Each borrower will have different "hot buttons" when it comes to borrowing money. The issues that the borrowers are concerned about are as follows:

1. The maximum amount that they can borrow

2. The term of the loan

3. The rate of the loan

4. The monthly debt service payment on the loan

5. Can they prepay the loan without a heavy prepayment penalty?

6. The costs to close the loan, i.e., legal and other closing costs

7. How soon the loan can be closed

8. The personal guarantees on the loan

9. The carve-out guarantees required by the lender

10. Will the lender charge interest based on a 365-day-year or a 360-day-year?

When negotiating for a loan, the borrower should have his list of important issues and try to get as many of them "his way" as possible.

Know Your Lender's Likes and Dislikes

Be sure to identify your lender's product likes and dislikes. Develop a sense of whether your lender is lending on the property or the experience and integrity of the borrower. The key to obtaining a loan is to develop a lasting relationship with the lender. They are conservative individuals and must have the utmost confidence in the borrower's ability to pay back the loan.

Be Creative About Structuring Your Financial Needs

Since there are many ways to "skin a cat," the borrower must fine tune the loan to meet her needs. Each party has its own needs and wants, and with good, creative thinking each party can obtain its goals. This is where using a knowledgeable mortgage broker/banker and your accountant and attorney can help you obtain the best possible financing package.

The basic tenet of creativity is that nothing is carved in stone. Just because 75 percent financing is the norm, this does not mean that 100 percent financing is not possible. Lenders are in the business of lending money, and they really do want to make loans. If one structure on their "menu" does not work, another might. Remember: if you don't ask, you don't get. If one proposal doesn't work, probe other possibilities with the lender, until you hit upon one that will match the needs of both parties.

Plan to "Unwind" Your Loan

Always remember to plan how to unwind the loan. It is easier to plan this strategy in advance than down the road. If the loan lock-in provisions, the prepayment penalty, subordinate financing, and the due-on-sale clause are determined at the start, the borrower can better control the flexibility of the loan when it needs to be assumed, or the property resold. Without these favorable provisions, the borrower will have a difficult time maneuvering within the loan. It is easier to negotiate these points at the beginning of the transaction than down the road when time is critical. You may be on good terms with your lender today who might not be there tomorrow, or the policy of the lending institution might change.

Lockout and Prepayment Penalties

The majority of loans today with fixed rates will have a period of time that the lock is locked out from a prepayment. Thereafter the loan can be paid off prior to the maturity but there will be a cost or penalty paid to the lender. There are two types of prepayment penalties. See box on the next page.

STEPPED DOWN PENALTIES: These penalties are typically where the loan might be locked for the first four years, then a 3% penalty of the outstanding balance in the fifth year, followed by a 2% penalty in the sixth year, a 1% penalty in the seventh year, with no penalty in the eighth year.

YIELD MAINTENANCE: For lenders who allow an early repayment of the loan to achieve their required returns, they will charge the borrower a fee upon prepayment that is calculated to make their yield whole. The prepayment premium is calculated as follows:

Yield Maintenance Provision—Make Whole

The product is determined by multiplying the outstanding principal amount being prepaid times the Net Interest Rate Differential Percentage times the number of years (whole or partial) remaining under the contract. The "Net Interest Rate Differential Percentage" shall be the difference between the then applicable contract interest rate on the Note and the Applicable Treasury Rate plus some percentage. The "Applicable Treasury Rate" shall mean the per-annum interest rate adjusted to a constant maturity for a term equal to the remaining term of the contract interest rate on the Note (the "Applicable Term"), as published in the Federal Reserve Statistical Release H-15(519), under the heading "U.S. Government Securities Treasury Constant for the Applicable Term" for the last full week prior to prepayment. If the product is a negative amount, then the prepayment premium shall be zero.

Example:

Outstanding Principal Balance of Loan:
$1,000,000
Contract Interest Rate on the Note:
8.25%
48 months remaining until maturity of the Note (therefore, the "Applicable Treasury Rate" is the 4 year U.S. Treasury Rate + 2.0% (6.00 + 2.00% = 8.00%):
8.00%

Therefore:

Contract Interest Rate:
8.25%
- Applicable Treasury Rate + 2.0%:
(8.00%)
=Net Interest Rate Differential Percentage:
.25%

Thus, the Net Interest Rate Differential Percentage times the Principal Amount to be Prepaid times the number of years (whole or partial) remaining under the contract = Prepayment Premium Calculation:

.25% x $1,000,000 x 4 years = 10,000 Prepayment Premium

Yield Maintenance Provision—Sum of Lost Yield

The product is determined by multiplying the outstanding principal amount being prepaid times the Net Interest Rate Differential Percentage times the number of years (whole or partial) remaining under the contract. The "Net Interest Rate Differential Percentage" shall be the difference between the then applicable contract interest rate on the Note and the Applicable Treasury Rate. The "Applicable Treasury Rate" shall mean the per annum interest rate adjusted to a constant maturity for a term equal to the remaining term of the contract interest rate on the Note (the "Applicable Term"), as published in the Federal Reserve Statistical Release H-15(519), under the heading "U.S. Government Securities Treasury Constant for the Applicable Term" for the last full week prior to prepayment. If the product is a

negative amount, then the prepayment premium shall be zero.

Example:

Outstanding Principal Balance of Loan:
$1,000,000
Contract Interest Rate on the Note:
8.25%
48 months remaining until maturity of the Note (therefore, the "Applicable Treasury Rate" is the 4 year U.S. Treasury Rate:
6.00%

Therefore:

Contract Interest Rate:
8.25%
- Applicable Treasury Rate:
(6.00%)
=Net Interest Rate Differential Percentage:
2.25%

Thus, the Net Interest Rate Differential Percentage times the Principal Amount to be Prepaid times the number of years (whole or partial) remaining under the contract = Prepayment Premium Calculation:

2.25% × $1,000,000 × 4 years = 90,000 Prepayment Premium

Yield Maintenance Provision—Discounted:

If a prepayment is made on the Note, the Borrower shall pay the Lender, together with the payment, an amount equal to the sum of the present values of the differences (if a positive amount) of:

(i) the aggregate amount of the interest that would have otherwise been payable, in the case of the Note, from the date of the prepayment to the date of the maturity of such loan or scheduled payments (for purposed of mathematical simplicity, all monthly or quarterly principal payments are assumed to mature at the mid-point of each 12 month period following the date of the prepayment), minus

(ii) the aggregate amount of the interest that the Lender would earn if the prepaid amount were reinvested for the period from the date of prepayment to the scheduled maturity [as determined in (i) above at the Treasury Rate (as defined below)].

The difference shall be discounted to present value at a discount rate equivalent to the Treasury Rate for the applicable term to maturity as determined in (i) above. For purposed of the subsection, the "Treasury Rate" shall mean a rate per annum (computed on the basis of actual days elapsed and a year of 365 days), equal to the rate determined by the Lender in its sold discretion on the date two (2) business days prior to the date of prepayment (or such later date when the Lender shall not have had knowledge of such prepayment), to be the yield expressed as a rate in the secondary market in United States Treasury securities having substantially the same term to maturity [as determined in (i) above] and the prepaid amount, such determination to be based upon quotes obtained by the Lender from established dealers in such market. Each prepayment hereunder shall be accompanied by the payment of the interest accrued on the amount of such prepayment to the date hereof. Any prepayment of the Note shall be applied against the installments of principal due on the Note in inverse order of maturity. Each notice of prepayment given under this section shall irrevocably commit the Borrower to prepay the loans referred to in such notice on the date and in the amount set forth therein.

Have a Qualified Attorney Review All Mortgage Documents

A well qualified real estate attorney should review the mortgage commitment letter and the actual mortgage documents, since they are long and complicated.

MORTGAGE FINANCING: HOW TO CHOOSE THE RIGHT LOAN FOR YOUR INVESTMENT

Mortgage financing comes in many different forms. Listed below are several of the most common types.

Land Acquisition Loan

A land acquisition loan is used to secure the purchase of raw land. Such a loan can be negotiated for up to 100 percent of the purchase price or a certain percentage of the appraised value. Some lenders will also commit additional dollars for future interest carry.

Construction Loan

A construction loan is used to finance erection of buildings. The loan can be structured as individual loans for condominiums or as a large blanket loan on a large building. These loans are usually for a short period of time (nine to thirty-six months) depending on the type of property. Most require interest-only payments based on a fixed or a floating interest rate. Most lenders will require that the borrower have a source of permanent financing to pay off the construction loan at the end of the designated period. Some lenders may give a borrower an open-ended construction loan, which does not require a takeout loan, if the borrower has sufficient financial strength, or if the borrower can show strong preleasing activity at the property.

Standby Loan

A standby loan is usually made when a construction lender requires a permanent loan to pay off the construction loan. This loan is obtained by the borrower with the intention of using it if a better loan is not available when the construction loan matures. Most standby lenders charge fees for issuing their loan commitment.

Forward Commitment

In a loan with a forward commitment a borrower will pay a fee in advance to insure that funds will be available at a predetermined rate at a predetermined date in the future. Many times developers of housing projects will purchase this type of permanent mortgage funds to ensure that when completed, the buyers will have adequate mortgage funds to finance their homes.

Gap Loan

A gap loan is used when a lender will not lend the borrower all the funds that are needed to complete the construction of a property. For example, a lender will commit to a loan of $1,000,000 on a proposed construction project. However, in many instances, there will be a specific amount held back by the lender until the borrower has achieved a specified occupancy level. Typically this is the break-even point; upon the achievement of this level, the construction lender will advance the funds. During this holdback period the borrower must obtain a gap loan as an alternative lending source to make up this temporary lack of dollars.

Bridge Loan

A bridge loan is a mortgage that is used between the termination of one loan and the beginning of another loan. In short, it is used to "buy time." For example, if someone has contracted to buy a new home, but has not yet sold the current home, he or she may obtain a bridge loan to help make the double mortgage payments until the original home is sold.

Or an investor may have to pay off an existing loan, but has not yet finalized any long-term financing. In this case a short-term bridge loan can be obtained to pay off the existing loan. The bridge loan will then be paid off when the long-term financing is obtained.

Take-out Mortgage

A take-out mortgage pays off (takes out) the construction loan at a specified time period. This may either be a permanent loan or a gap loan.

Chattel Mortgage

Chattel mortgages are those placed on personal property, that is, property that is movable. An example is a loan to finance the purchase of furniture in an apartment or a hotel property.

Piggyback Mortgage

A piggyback mortgage is a combination construction loan and permanent loan. This type of loan is typically structured so that on a predetermined date or event the construction loan will automatically convert into a permanent loan.

Permanent First Mortgage

A permanent first mortgage loan is made with the intention of being placed on the property for a long period of time. Most savings institutions make these loans for five to thirty years. Frequently savings institutions make the loans and then sell them in the secondary market to long-term investors. Life insurance companies will make permanent loans at a lower rate (their cost of funds is usually lower) and for a longer period of time.

These loans can be made at a fixed rate of interest, or the interest rate may be adjustable, tied to a specific index. Some lenders will lend more than others, depending on how aggressive they are and how much cash is available to them. Some lenders will lend more funds if they are able to negotiate a participation of cash flow. This participation plus the fees paid in advance will help increase their overall yield.

The following are various types of permanent first mortgages that are available:

SELF-AMORTIZING OR LEVEL PAYMENT MORTGAGE

Self-amortizing mortgages require level monthly payments each month over the amortization period. Each month's interest is charged on the outstanding balance.

ADJUSTABLE RATE OR RENEGOTIATED RATE MORTGAGE

Adjustable rate mortgages were authorized in 1981 by the Comptroller of the Currency. The interest rate in this type of mortgage is adjusted on a periodic basis and is based on a specified point spread over a specified rate index. These loans typically will have a yearly and a lifetime ceiling on the rate adjustment. Some of these indices are as follows:

- Interest rate on three, six, or twelve-month Treasury bills

- The yield on a one, two, three, five, or ten-year Treasury securities

- The average cost of funds to the lending institution

- Prime rate

- Labor

For example, a loan rate could be set at 2 percent over the current six-month Treasury bill rate and would be adjusted every six months. Many of these loans have a "floor" and a "ceiling," that is, interest rates below which or above which the rate on the loan cannot go.

NEGATIVE OR ACCELERATED AMORTIZATION MORTGAGE

Negative or accelerated amortization mortgages are based on a predetermined index. Depending on how this index fluctuates over the time period, the loan balance will either amortize more quickly or will accrue interest which will be added to the original loan balance. In some extreme cases, the borrower could even end up owing more than was originally borrowed. This is called negative amortization. Usually, the lender will place a cap on the amount of negative loan amortization; a borrower who hits this cap will usually be required to pay any of this accrual on a current basis with the usual monthly mortgage payment.

ACCRUAL MORTGAGE WITH A FIXED PAYMENT RATE

This type of mortgage is originally set up with a fixed payment rate but with a higher accrual rate. The payment rate is determined by what the borrower or property can afford to pay, and the accrual rate is the rate currently charged in the marketplace. This type of loan is used during periods of high interest rates. The accrued interest on the principal balance plus the accrued interest due on the accrued interest is all due at a specified date in the future.

INTEREST-ONLY MORTGAGE

Interest-only mortgage loans will have a monthly payment based on interest only for a short period of time. This loan will be due in a short period of time, or else after a specified date it will start amortizing over a scheduled term. Since the borrower is not re-paying principal during this time period, the monthly mortgage payments will be lower than those loans that amortize the principal as well.

For example, a borrower might negotiate a loan for $1,000,000 at 10 percent interest for five years and then will amortize this loan balance over a twenty-five year period at the same 10 percent interest rate. During the interest only period the borrower will pay $100,000 per year in interest versus the $110,168.07 in principal reduction and interest payments that will be due during that last twenty-five years of the loan.

GRADUATED PAYMENT MORTGAGE (GPM)

A graduated payment mortgage is designed to start at a specified interest rate and then graduate to a higher specified interest rate over a defined time period.

BUYDOWN MORTGAGE

Buydown mortgages are those in which the borrower advances money to the lender to reduce a portion of the current interest rate. In residential lending this is a common practice by a builder to help the purchaser qualify for a loan. In commercial property this advance payment may be added to the initial funding of a transaction and will reduce the current mortgage rate in order to produce a positive cash flow. Buydowns are more common during periods of high interest rates.

For example, a builder may prepay the lender to reduce the interest rate from 11 percent to 9 percent for a specified number of years. The lender will calculate the interest rate spread during this time period and then discount the amount to be paid in cash at the loan closing.

SHARED EQUITY MORTGAGE (SEM)

Shared equity mortgages are typically used for residential properties to help a borrower afford the purchase. A purchaser is brought together with a qualified investor who will co-sign with the purchaser on the mortgage and provide all or part of the down-payment and monthly debt service payment. The investor will then negotiate with the purchaser to share in the tax benefits and the resale appreciation of the property.

SHARED APPRECIATION MORTGAGE (SAM) OR PARTICIPATING MORTGAGE

A shared appreciation or participating mortgage is one in which the lender will reduce the interest rate to a below-market rate in return for a specified share of future cash flow and resale profits.

GROWING EQUITY MORTGAGE (GEM)

In a growing equity mortgage there is a set interest rate, but the monthly debt service payment is increased over a specific time period. This increased payment can be predetermined or it can be based on a spread over a specified index. This increased funding is then applied toward the principal loan balance and will help amortize the loan at a much faster pace.

PLEDGED ACCOUNT MORTGAGE (PAM)

A pledged account mortgage is typically found in residential lending. In this type the lender requires that the borrower pledge a specific amount of money into an escrow account. These funds will then be used in the initial years to supplement the periodic monthly mortgage payments.

REVERSE ANNUITY MORTGAGE (RAM)

A reverse annuity mortgage is typically designed for elderly homeowners who have substantial equity in their home. The lender will periodically pay an amount of money back to the homeowner for bills that need to be paid. Because of these payments the loan can increase over time and thus create negative amortization.

ZERO INTEREST MORTGAGE

Zero interest mortgages were used in the high interest rate environment of the early 1980s by homebuilders. These loans are similar to the low interest rate offers by automobile dealers. The borrower must make a large down-payment, and then the loan will be for a relatively short period of time. However, the builder will generally increase the sales price of the house in order to provide this incentive.

Blanket Mortgage

A blanket mortgage is a single mortgage that covers more than one piece of property. Many times an owner will get a loan on a number of smaller properties under one mortgage.

Second Mortgage

A second mortgage loan is subordinate to any first mortgage loan. In many cases, the debt on the property has been substantially reduced and the borrower desires to increase the leverage or wishes to pull out some cash from the property. This type of loan usually has a higher interest rate than a first mortgage. Also, these loans are junior to the first mortgage upon foreclosure.

Purchase Money Mortgage

A purchase money mortgage is one taken by a seller from a buyer in lieu of purchase money, i.e., the seller helps finance the purchase. A PM mortgage can be either a first or second mortgage. As a first mortgage, the PM substitutes for a bank or other third-party loan, either because the buyer is unable to qualify for a loan or because the PM is more favorable to the buyer with respect to the interest rate, term or other loan provisions. In addition, the PM will avoid loan costs, including appraisal fees, charged by a third party. The seller will offer the loan if this is the only way to make the sale or because the seller regards it as a secure investment with a good return.

As a second mortgage, the PM enables a buyer to acquire the property with less cash. In addition, a second PM will increase the buyer's return (upside leverage) if the annual debt service on the PM is below the free and clear return from the property.

Prior to the 1986 Tax Reform Act, purchase money mortgages sometimes were used to inflate the purchase price in order to give the buyer high depreciation write-offs. This rarely happens today because annual depreciation deductions are far smaller as a result of the longer recovery periods created by the 1986 law. Nevertheless, professional counsel should be sought if a PM mortgage is for an unusually high amount or has unusual provisions.

Mini-Permanent (Bullet or Balloon) Mortgage

A mini-permanent mortgage is a permanent loan with a long amortization period but a short maturity due date. This type of loan could be interest only. Careful planning should be used when obtaining this type of loan. Due to its short term, the borrower will have to refinance within a three- to five-year period. In many cases, the financing market can take a ride upwards and this will reduce the chances of refinancing the loan; new market conditions might even reduce the chances of obtaining a loan for the same dollar amount.

Wraparound Mortgage (All-Inclusive Trust Deed)

A wraparound mortgage is subordinate (junior) to the existing first or second mortgages. This type of loan will "wraparound" the current debt and will include all new funds advanced.

For example, the owner of a property with an existing loan of $900,000 at 10 percent might make a new wraparound mortgage for $1 million at 11 percent. In this example, the new lender is only lending $100,000 of "new" funds, but is also receiving the interest rate "point spread" (the difference between 10 percent and 11 percent) on the original $900,000.

This kind of loan can be obtained from three possible sources—the existing seller, a new institutional lender, or the existing lender. The seller will "wrap" the existing debt plus take back any new secondary financing required by the purchaser. She will then get the benefits of any principal reduction of the original existing debt. Many times, due to the low interest rate of the existing debt, the seller can make what appears to be a below-market rate loan to the new purchaser.

Another source for this type of loan is lenders who specialize in wrap mortgages. These lenders will wrap the existing debt and advance any new funds required for which they will charge points and closing costs. These lenders will then benefit from any reduction in principal paid down on the underlying mortgages and from picking up an interest spread on the underlying mortgage. This helps increase their overall yield.

Still another potential wrap lender could be the existing lender who, due to the reduction in principal from the original loan balance, might agree to advance the new funds required and thus increase their original yield. Rather than making a new first mortgage the lender might just wraparound the old loan.

Investor Note Loan

Investor note loans are those made by a lender to finance the down-payment of a property acquisition. Many sellers want to be paid all cash over the existing debt at closing. Depending on personal desires, the purchaser might want to borrow the down-payment and then repay the note lender over a predetermined time period. Many tax structured real estate partnerships in the early 1980s used this kind of loan to increase the leverage deal. These loans are typically made at prime plus a margin with from one to five points and are amortized over two to seven years.

Many lenders also require a surety company to insure the repayment of the notes that are pledged as collateral for the loan. By using the surety the lender will offer a lower rate. The surety will then charge additional points to sell the policy.

Leasehold Mortgage

A leasehold mortgage is one with a lease that acts as the primary security rather than the real estate itself. This loan is based on the income that is generated from the property via the lease. The lender usually requires that the rental income cover the debt service as well as the other expenses. The lender looks at the creditworthiness of the tenant and will require an assignment of this lease and possibly an insurance policy that will guarantee the payment of the lease. It might further be required that the lender has a right to approve any cancellation or changes in the lease.

Great care should be taken by the lender in such a transaction. The lender does not want the loan to appear as a lease as opposed to a financing transaction. This type of loan should be structured as a loan, and not as giving the lender an economic interest in the property.

Cash Flow Mortgage

Cash flow mortgages are those that are negotiated by the borrower with the lender or lender/owner when the property is in a distressed situation. Since the property cannot afford to pay a monthly debt service based on current market rates, the monthly debt service is based on the availability of cash flow after the expenses are paid. The time period for this type of mortgage is a function of how quickly the property can be turned around to generate additional cash flow to service a current market rate of interest.

Bifurcated Loans

A bifurcated loan is one that is made in more than one piece. Piece A might be a 50% loan to value loan priced at 135 basis points over a ten year Treasury with a four year lock-out and yield maintenance prepayment. The B piece might have spread and have no lockout provision. At the time the B piece is paid down the A piece's spread might lower, due to the higher debt service coverage ratio the property will then have. This type of loan would be ideal for a Class A property in which the borrower wants a full loan but might sell the property in a few years to a buyer would not need but 50% leverage on the property.

Earnouts

In many situations, the lender may not fund all that the borrower is looking for. Based on certain performance requirements, the lender may be willing to fund additional dollars at a later date.

Participating Loans

Participating loans are those in which the lender will usually loan an amount greater than 75-80% of the value of the property. Because of this the lender will require either a higher rate of interest, either with a set pay rate and an accrual or will require a set pay rate with a percent of the cash flow and future refinance or resale proceeds.

MEZZANINE LOANS

Mezzanine loans are typically debt disguised as equity. The funds are usually for the portion above the typical 75% loan up to 100% of the equity requirement. Since most first mortgage lenders will prohibit any junior financing, the mezzanine lender will take a pledge of the borrower's ownership entity as collateral, thus avoiding the senior lender's requirement. Mezzanine loans can either be higher rate loans with a participation feature with a shorter amortization period or can have a term that matches the senior debt. Many mezzanine lenders are looking to achieve a target return and may require a "look-back" at the end of the loan period to make them whole if they are still short their required return when the deal unwinds.

HOW LENDERS DETERMINE IF THEY WILL LEND TO YOU

Since lenders are conservative by nature, they normally have conservative and rigid lending policies. Most will have a loan policy committee that determines their loan parameters which determine what types of properties they will lend on, what areas they will lend in, and what the minimum and maximum loan amounts are. This committee will usually meet at least once a week to discuss its loan policy, review any problem loans, and to approve or disapprove any new loan applications.

Prior to submitting a proposal to the loan committee's agenda, the loan officer of the institution will carefully screen out the potential borrowers and review the structure of the deals.

Screening of the Potential Borrower

In reviewing the potential borrower, the lender will want to verify the borrower's credit history, personal and business references, real estate track record, and will look very carefully at the borrower's record of loan repayments. The lender wants to make sure that there will be a high probability of getting the loan repaid on time. No lender wants to take back the property and then have to go after the borrower for the loan deficiency. Lenders want to make sure that the borrower's financial character is impeccable.

Evaluating the Potential Deal: Four Formulas Used to Review the Transaction

In evaluating the potential deal, the lender will review all of the market conditions in the area local to the subject property. The lender whose monies are based upon a future income stream wants to make sure that the property will be able to support these monthly payments today and in the future.

The borrower will have to pay for and complete an updated appraisal of the property. With this appraisal and past experiences, the lender should be able to analyze the current cash flow and the cash flow forecasts. Once the lender has determined what the net operating income should be, then how much money the borrower will get will be determined.

The lender will base the loan amount decision either on a formula based on the debt coverage and the current loan constant, or upon a specific loan to value ratio.

DEBT SERVICE COVERAGE RATIO (DSCR)

The debt service coverage ratio is a formula that shows the lender how much coverage there is after all the expenses and the debt service is paid. The formula is as follows:

$$\frac{\text{Net Operating Income (NOI)}}{\text{Annual Debt Service}} = \text{Debt Coverage Ratio}$$

Example: If the property has a net operating income of $100,000, and its annual debt service payment is $80,000, the debt coverage ratio is 1.25. This means that there is 25 percent coverage over and above the total expenses of the property.

As shown above, the Debt Service Coverage Ratio is based on how the lenders calculate the Net Operating Income (NOI). The Net Operating Income depends on how the Revenue and Operating Expenses are underwritten. The Revenue can be determined by the current month's collections multiplied by 12 months or the last trailing 3 months multiplied by 4, or the projected 12 months. The vacancy rate can be determined by the actual rate of the property or by the average vacancy of the market. The operating expenses can be based on the last 12 months with an inflation factor, the last month multiplied by 12 months, the last 3 months multiplied by 4 or based on the borrower's projected operating budget. Another factor that lenders vary on when underwriting is how they handle reserve placements, tenant improvements and leasing commissions. Some lenders will project a cost for these items and underwrite for them above the bottom line of the Net Operating Income, while others will put them below the Net Operating Income bottom line. How the lenders underwrite these costs will cause a variance in the amount they will loan to a borrower.

ANNUAL LOAN CONSTANT

By using a loan constant table (See Appendix D), the lender can look up the loan constant for the current loan terms offered. This loan constant is then multiplied by the loan amount and divided by 1200 to get the monthly debt service payment.

$$\text{Annual Loan Constant} = \frac{1200 \times \text{Monthly Payment}}{\text{Loan Amount}}$$

POTENTIAL LOAN AMOUNT

The lender will divide the net operating income by the debt coverage ratio and then divide that number by the annual loan constant to get the loan amount to be loaned.

Net Operating Income (NOI) ÷ Debt Coverage Ratio ÷ Annual Loan Constant = Loan Amount

Example: A property has a net operating income of $1,000,000, and the lender is currently using a 1.2 debt coverage ratio. Current loans are made at 10 percent for thirty years.

$$\frac{\$1,000,000 \text{ (NOI)}}{1.2 \text{ (Debt Coverage Ratio)}} = \$833,333.33$$

$$\frac{\$833,333.33}{.1053 \text{ (Loan Constant)}} = \$7,913,896.80$$

$$\$7,914,000 = \text{Potential Loan Amount}$$

TABLE 8-2

Loan Underwriting

HIGHRISE TOWER
Atlanta, Georgia

PROFORMA			
Preliminary Underwriting			$/SF
INCOME:			
(1) Gross Scheduled Rent		$8,020,000	$17,822
Laundry Income		$162,000	$360
Interest Income		$0	$0
Other		$162,000	$360
Total Gross Potential Income		$8,344,000	$18,542
(2) Less Vacancies/Collection	@ 7.5%	$625,800	$1,391
EFFECTIVE GROSS INCOME		**$7,718,200**	**$17,152**
OPERATING EXPENSES:			
Operating Expenses		$1,425,000	$3,167
Insurance		$110,000	$244
(3) Management Fee		$385,910	$858
Property Tax		$735,000	$1,633
TOTAL EXPENSES		**$2,655,910**	**$5,902**
Expense Ratio *(% EGI)*		$0	$0
NET OPERATING INCOME		**$5,062,290**	**$11,250**
(4) Replacement Reserve	@ $150 per unit	$67,500	$150
UNDERWRITING CASH FLOW		**$4,994,790**	**$11,100**
Capital Improvements		$0	$0
Other Non-Operating Expenses		$0	$0
NET CASH FLOW		**$4,994,790**	**$11,100**
Annual Debt Service		**$3,184,934**	**$7,078**
NET CASH FLOW AFTER DS	**$1,809,856**	**$4,022**	

COMMENTS: Unless otherwise noted, income and expense represent YTD (6/97) annualized.

(1) Gross scheduled income represents actual income as shown on current rent roll plus market rent for vacant units.

(2) Actual vacancy.

(3) Management fee of 5%.

(4) Reserves at $150/unit.

Holliday Fenoglio, Inc.
an AMRESCO subsidiary

TABLE 8-2
Loan Underwriting (Cont'd)

HIGHRISE TOWER
Atlanta, Georgia

PROPERTY INFORMATION				
Number of Units		450	**Year Built**	1994
			Year Renovated	N/A
Number of Buildings		1	**Construction Type**	Concrete Block
Number of Floors		15		
Land Area	Acres	4.00	**Project Amenities**	Pool
	Square Feet	174,240		Workout Facility
Parking Spaces	Covered	750	**Unit Amenities**	Decks
	Uncovered	0		Furnished Kitchen
Parking Ratio *(Spaces/1000 SF)*		1666.67	**Unit HVAC**	Chiller
			Unit Appliances	Yes
COMMENTS:				

BORROWER INFORMATION					
Borrower Name		Richard T. Jordan	**Address**		3340 Peachtree Street
Contact		Same	**City/State**		Atlanta, GA
Ownership Structure		Limited Partnership	**Phone Number**		303/231-2100

List Partners with >20% Interest:					
NAME	**GP/LP**	**% INTEREST**	**NET WORTH**	**LIQUID ASSETS**	**AS OF DATE**
Richard Jordan	GP	65.0%	$25,000,000	$4,000,000	Sep-97
Scott Jordan	LP	20.0%	$10,000,000	$1,000,000	Sep-97
Brandy Sibley	GP	15.0%	$5,000,000	$500,000	Sep-97

COMMENTS *(ownership, financial capabilities, negative references, deeds in lieu, etc.)*:
Owns similar properties in 10 markets. Clear track record.

MANAGEMENT			
Management Firm	Happy Management, Inc.	**Address**	1234 Sun Lane
Contact	Happy Herman	**City/State**	Atlanta, Ga
Relation to Borrower	3rd Party	**Phone Number**	404/555-1212

COMMENTS *(management experience, properties managed, etc.)*:
Manages 15 highrise residential properties in the Southeast.

Holliday Fenoglio, Inc.
an AMRESCO subsidiary

TABLE 8-2
Loan Underwriting (Cont'd)

HIGHRISE TOWER
Atlanta, Georgia

LEASING INFORMATION

RENT ROLL SUMMARY	#	%		RENTAL RANGE	Actual	Market
Total Units	450	100.0%	1 Bedroom/1 Bath		$1,100-$1,300	$1,200
Vacant Units	23	5.1%	2 Bedroom/1 Bath		$1,300-$1,500	$1,400
			2 Bedroom/2 Bath		$1,500-$1,700	$1,650
			3 Bedroom/2 Bath		$1,800-$2,200	$2,000
Month-to-Month Units	15	3.3%				
Employee Units	2	0.4%		**OCCUPANCY**		
Subsidized Units	0	0.0%	Current		94.9%	
Down Units	0	0.0%	Stabilized		95.0%	
			Market		95.0%	

COMMENTS:
Market is currently operating at 7.5 vacancy rate.

UNIT MIX AND RENTAL RATES

Rent Roll Date | April 97

UNIT TYPE	#	%	UNIT SF	TOTAL SF	CURRENT RENT	AVERAGE RENT/SF	TOTAL ANNUAL RENT
1 Bedroom/1 Bath	150	33.3%	985	147,750	$1,200	$1.22	$2,160,000
2 Bedroom/1 Bath	125	27.8%	1,200	150,000	$1,400	$1.17	$2,100,000
2 Bedroom/2 Bath	100	22.2%	1,500	150,000	$1,650	$1.10	$1,980,000
3 Bedroom/2 Bath	75	16.7%	1,750	131,250	$2,000	$1.14	$1,800,000
TOTAL	**450**	**100.0%**		**579,000**			**$8,040,000**

COMMENTS:

RESERVES

OPERATING RESERVES	Total	$/Unit	CAPITAL IMPROVEMENT RESERVES	Total	$/Unit
Annual Deposit	$0.00	$0.00	Roof	$0.00	$0.00
Proposed Floor Amount	$0.00	$0.00	Parking Lot	$0.00	$0.00
Proposed Ceiling Amount	$0.00	$0.00	Unit Rehab	$0.00	$0.00
			HVAC/Appliances	$0.00	$0.00
			Other	$0.00	$0.00
			Total	$0.00	$0.00

COMMENTS:
Information is not available.

Holliday Fenoglio, Inc.
an AMRESCO subsidiary

TABLE 8-2
Loan Underwriting (Cont'd)

HIGHRISE TOWER
Atlanta, Georgia

THIRD PARTY REPORTS			
ENVIRONMENTAL REPORT			
Firm: Environmental Advisors, Inc. **Address:** 1234 Sunny Lane **City/State:** Atlanta, Ga **Phone:** 404/555-1212		**Type of Report:** **Date of Inspection:** **Estimated Cost to Cure:**	Phase I 8/25/97 0
Recommended Follow Up/Comments: No known environmental issues.			
SEISMIC (PML) REPORT			
Firm: NAP **Address:** — **City/State:** — **Phone:** —		**Type of Report:** **Date of Inspection:**	
Comments: N/A Not required in Georgia			
APPRAISAL REPORT			
Firm: Appraisal, Inc. **Address:** 1234 Tree Lane **City/State:** Atlanta, Ga **Phone:** 404/555-1212		**Date of Value:** **Reconciled Appraised Value:**	8/25/97 $45,000,000
Comments: N/A			

INVESTMENT MERITS
(1) Subject property is located in top multifamily market in Atlanta.   **(2)** Offers unique amentities to tenants that are unique to market.   **(3)** High debt cover.   **(4)** The most respected owner in the Southeast, many successful projects.
UNDERWRITING ISSUES (WITH MITIGATING FACTORS)
(1) Highrise projects scheduled for delivery in 1998; subject is located in superior location to new developments.   **(2)**   **(3)**   **(4)**

Holliday Fenoglio, Inc.
an AMRESCO subsidiary

LOAN TO VALUE RATIO

Many lenders use the loan to value ratio to arrive at their lending decisions. This method involves lending funds based upon a maximum predetermined percentage of the appraised value of the property. Different percentages determined by the various types of property and the creditworthiness of the borrower are often used.

For example, a lender might make an 80 percent loan to value loan on an apartment property. If the property is appraised at $1,000,000, the lender will then lend a maximum of $800,000 on the property.

$$\text{Appraised Value} \times \text{Loan to Value Ratio (LVR)} = \text{Loan Amount}$$

$$\$1,000,000 \times 80\% = \$800,000 \text{ (Loan Amount)}$$

HOW A LENDER PRICES A LOAN

A lender who has reviewed the credit history of the borrower, the tenant(s) and the financial information on the proposed property, and is comfortable with them, is ready to price out the loan terms and conditions. In pricing the loan, the lender takes into consideration the pricing currently being offered by other competing institutions in the marketplace.

Interest Rate

Since money has a cost, the lender will review the costs of funds and figure out the desired profit margin to receive on the funds. This profit margin is based on the risk taken, the length of time that the funds will be outstanding, and the repayment schedule. Also calculated into the formula is a reduction in this profit margin if the borrower is a good customer and has substantial compensating bank balances in the institution.

INDEX

The index used by lenders today is:

- Prime
- Treasury bills (5, 7, 10 years)

SPREAD

Each lender prices the spread based on basis points over a given index. Lenders today compile a matrix of spreads that are based on property types, loan to value ratios and debt service coverage ratios, the class of property, the age of the property and how competitive the market is in making loans. The riskier the loan, the higher its cost.

FIXED VS. FLOATING RATES

Lenders will either fix the rate for a specified period based on the spread over the index or will float the loan over a specified index, such as the prime rate or libor. A borrower who thinks the indexes will go down and stay there in the near term might be more inclined to take a floating rate versus fixing at a higher rate.

INTEREST CALCULATION

Another aspect of financing that merits careful consideration is how the interest is calculated or, more specifically, how the mortgage servicing company allocates every debt service payment between the interest and principal reduction. All lenders must disclose the specific methodology for how interest is calculated. Even so, few borrowers realize that the specific methodology can often be negotiated to one's advantage.

A lender will usually quote the interest calculation based on the total days per month, and a certain number of days per year, typically 360 or actual. The interest cost is calculated as the annual interest rate divided by the number of days per either (actual or stipulated) times the number of days in the month (actual or stipulated) times the prior month's ending principal. Deducting the interest cost from the monthly debt service payment will yield the amount that is available for principal reduction. The monthly debt service is usually the same no matter which interest calculation is used.

Under the 360/360 day scenario, every month is stipulated to have 30 days (12 months × 30 days = 360 days) and every year is stipulated to have 360 days; therefore, the allocation between the principal and interest is relatively uniform over the term of the loan. The calculation that favors the lender is the 365/360 day scenario. The daily interest factor reflects a 360 day year, but interest is charged for every day of the month. Over the loan term, the slightly higher interest cost results in a significant loss in principal reduction.

The example below shows the impact on the balloon payment due to the interest calculation. The example assumes a loan amount of $10,000,000 with a 30-year amortization, an 8.0% interest rate and a 10-year term. The balloon payment shown below does not include the monthly debt service payment that would also be due at the end of the loan term.

A borrower cannot fairly compare the two financing offers without considering the

SCENARIO	360/360	365/360	DIFFERENCE
Interest Rate	8.0%	8.0%	
Daily Interest Factor	.000222	.000222	
Days per Month	30	Actual	
Monthly Payment	$73,376	$73,376	
Balloon Payment	$8,787,264	$8,954,065	$166,801

method used to calculate the interest. In the example above, the borrower will end up paying an extra $166,801 in interest cost over the term of the loan due to the 365/360 method of calculating the interest.

RATE LOCK-IN

Due to fluctuations in the various indexes, many lenders will lock in a rate for the borrower prior to closing. The lender who does this will charge the borrower a fee upfront that is typically refundable at closing. If the borrower does not close the loan, the lender will keep the fee as a penalty for not closing and will use this fee to offset the cost incurred to lock in the funds.

Loan Fees

In addition to the interest rate charged, the lender will most likely charge the borrower an origination fee or points on the loan. This fee will range from 1 percent to 4 percent of the loan amount. The higher the risk, the higher the fees charged. In a competitive marketplace, lenders might loan at par or will not charge a fee to the borrower.

DUE DILIGENCE FEES

Many lenders will charge the borrower an upfront due diligence fee to review the transaction and visit the site.

Amortization Period

Since every loan has to be repaid, the lender will determine the amount of time allowed to the borrower to repay the loan. The time period will be based on the type of property. Certain properties, such as mini-warehouses, will have shorter loan amortization periods than Class A office buildings.

Maturity Period

Many times the lender will give the borrower a longer amortization period but will require the loan to mature at an earlier date. This will benefit the borrower who will have a lower monthly mortgage payment and thus more potential cash flow. On the other hand, the lender will get the funds back at an earlier date and will be able to lend them out once again. An example would be a thirty-year loan with a ten-year maturity date.

Recourse (Personal Loan) Guarantees

Depending on the type of loan being sought, the borrower may be required to personally guarantee the loan for the total term of the loan, or a portion of the loan for a specified time period. Many borrowers may negotiate a "burn off" of the guarantee based on specified net operating income achievements.

Carve-Out Provisions

Lenders today, having been burned during the last real estate depression, are now requiring borrowers to personally guarantee a series of acts that will convert a non-recourse loan into a recourse loan. Following are a number of acts by the borrower that will create this recourse:

- Transferring the property without the consent of the lender
- Placing junior financing on the property without the consent of the lender
- Acquiring another property within the same borrowing entity without the consent of the lender
- Fraud or misrepresentation by the borrower
- Misapplication of insurance proceeds, condemnation proceeds or security deposits
- Misapplied rents (not using rents first to pay the operating expenses and the debt service)

- Failure to pay transfer fees on an approved transfer

- After a default, turning over the rents, security deposits, books and records to the lender

In addition, lenders today are also requiring the borrower to be personally liable for any environmental problems of the property.

The guarantee for these acts can either be guarantees by a "warm body" individual or by the borrower's corporation.

Conditions Stipulated in the Loan Agreement

The conditions of every loan are different. The lender is going to add extra stipulations into the loan documents that will require the borrower to collateralize the loan, either through securing the property with a mortgage or even by adding the borrower's personal guarantee of the loan repayment. The lender might also require the borrower to contribute to an escrow account to fund projected negative cash flow during a rent-up period. Each lender will usually base these conditions on items that have caused problems in the past. This is where the borrower should negotiate as hard as possible in order to gain the most favorable loan terms.

THIRD PARTY REPORTS

Prior to making the final commitment on the loan, the lender will require borrowers at their expense to have third party reports for:

- **Environmental:** This is a Phase I study to assess any environmental problems that might affect the property.

- **Architectural and Engineering:** This study reviews the structural integrity of the improvements and what type of reserves should be allocated for future spending.

- **Appraisal:** This study determines the current market value for the property. The value might be lower or higher than what was originally thought by the borrower.

- **Feasibility Study:** For new construction or change in the property use, the lender might require a study that reviews the economic and market feasibility of this change.

HOW TO SECURE THE BEST LOAN AVAILABLE: LENDER QUALIFICATION QUESTIONS

Once the lender's proposal is complete, it is time to seek out the best loan available. The first step in choosing the most qualified lender from your list of potential lenders is to ask the following questions:

1. Will the lender lend on the type of property you need financing on?

2. Will the lender lend in the location of your property?

3. Can the lender lend the approximate amount needed?

4. Will the lender lend the funds at your desired interest rate?

If the answer to these four questions is "yes," then proceed to the following questions:

Permanent Loan Questions

1. Will the lender lend on a percentage of the appraised value or on a certain debt service coverage ratio?

2. What debt coverage ratio will be used?

3. Will the lender project out the rents?

4. What is the current loan rate charge?

5. What methodology will be used to calculate the interest?

6. Will the lender make accrual loans with lower pay rates?

7. Are the rates fixed or tied to an index? What indexes are used?

8. Will the lender lend interest only?

9. What is the loan term?

10. What loan amortization period is used?

11. Can the loan be extended?

12. If so, for what period of time and at what cost?

13. How many points are charged at the commitment stage?

14. How many points are charged at loan closing?

15. Who pays for the closing costs?

16. What are the closing costs?

17. Whose attorney will close the loan?

18. Is an appraisal needed?

19. Will the appraisal be used?

20. Which appraisers are approved to do the appraisal?

21. When will the loan be funded?

22. Can the loan be funded with an earn-out based on a higher net operating income?

23. Can the loan be prepaid?

24. Is there a loan lock-in period?

25. Is there a prepayment penalty for early payoff?

26. Are any personal guarantees required for this loan?

27. Can these guarantees be for less than the total amount of the loan, and can they be released based on the property performance?

28. Are any escrows for taxes and insurance required?

29. Can the borrower receive interest on the escrow funds?

30. Is there a dragnet clause in the loan documents?

31. Is the loan assignable upon resale?

32. Is there a transfer fee upon assumption by a new borrower?

33. Will the loan rate or terms change upon resale?

34. Will the new borrower have to qualify for the loan?

35. What items will the new borrower have to submit to the lender?

36. Can the interest rate be brought down?

37. What will the cost be to buy-down the rate?

38. Does the loan require any cash flow or future resale profit participation by the lender?

39. What items does the borrower need to supply to the lender prior to underwriting?

40. What is the response time for a firm commitment?

41. Can the commitment be extended, if need be? If so, for how long? What will the cost be?

42. Can the borrower obtain a copy of the loan documents prior to closing?

43. Does the lender require any monthly, quarterly, or yearly operating statements?

KEY MORTGAGE CLAUSES

As you start to select your lenders, you should start ranking each loan offering. At this point, you should narrow down the field to the best two or three loans. Each loan will be somewhat different and needs to be analyzed carefully. Once you have decided on the best offering, you should get a written commitment from the lender. The lender will most likely request a nonrefundable binder to be paid upon acceptance of this commitment. At this point you should request that your attorney be given copies of all the loan closing documents.

Probably one of the most important things to remember when structuring your loan is to consider how you will unwind it. This may include language regarding nonrecourse liability, loan extensions upon maturity, or transferability of the loan in case of resale. Remember, without this language you may be at the mercy of the lender if you run into problems or unique situations. It is always easier to negotiate solutions to potential problems in advance when everyone is friendly rather than down the road in a crisis situation. Your lender might be your friend today, but five years from now a new loan officer may be involved.

When reviewing the mortgage documents presented by the lender, the borrower should take special care to analyze the obligations being made. An attorney who specializes in this area of the law will be of great assistance. Typically, most lenders slant these documents to their benefit. Many of these clauses will not be subject to negotiation, while others can be reworded for the benefit of the borrower. In many cases some clauses can be totally removed from the documents.

It is more common to negotiate these clauses in commercial transactions than in residential home loans. As in any negotiation, if you find a clause that you cannot live with, ask that it be removed. It must be remembered and understood that when borrowing money the "Golden Rule" applies—"He who has the gold rules."

- **Due-on-Sale Clause.** This is a clause in the mortgage documents that states that the loan is due upon any sale or transfer of the property. Since low interest rate financing is attractive upon resale, the borrower should not want to have this clause in the documents.

- **Right-to-Transfer Clause.** A right-to-transfer clause in the mortgage documents will give the right to the borrower to transfer the property to another party. Usually if the borrower is able to have a right-to-transfer clause in the documents, the lender will have the right to approve the new purchaser. This right to approve should have the language "not to be unreasonably withheld."

- **Acceleration Clause.** The acceleration clause in the mortgage documents gives the lender the right to accelerate the total unpaid principal balance in case of a default. The borrower should negotiate a grace period in which to try to cure any default, whether it be monetary or nonmonetary.

- **Lock-in Clause.** Many mortgages have a lock-in clause providing that the loan cannot be prepaid for a specified period of time for any reason. The investor should try to negotiate to take it out.

- **Prepayment Clause.** Many lenders require a specified prepayment penalty for early loan payoff. A borrower who takes out a mortgage during a period of high interest rates might want to refinance this mortgage when rates come down. The borrower will have to evaluate the cost of this penalty and the closing costs on a new loan as opposed to the savings in the interest rate under a new loan.

- **Escrow Clause.** Many lenders will require the borrower to escrow funds monthly for the real estate taxes and the insurance policy. If this is a requirement of the lender, the borrower should make sure that any interest earned on these funds shall accrue to him or her, since it is a major source of revenue for most lenders.

- **Foreclosure and Right of Redemption Clause.** Foreclosure is the last option for a lender to recover payment on a property that is in default. The borrower should know the foreclosure regulations in the state that the property is in as well as any redemption laws.

- **Defeasance Clause.** A defeasance clause gives the borrower the right to redeem the property after a default if the borrower pays off the total indebtedness to the lender.

- **Subordination Clause.** Many lenders insist that no secondary financing be allowed on the property, or they may require the right to approve any junior financing. Lenders want to make sure that the property is not burdened with too much monthly debt. If there is a total prohibition of any junior debt, this could preclude the borrower from reselling the property and providing any seller financing.

- **Release Clause.** A release clause in a mortgage stipulates that upon paying a specified amount of money, the borrower can release a portion of the property that the lender has been holding as collateral for the loan.

- **Recourse Liability Clause.** A recourse liability clause pertains to the personal liability of the borrower in case of default. If possible the borrower should negotiate all of the personal liability out of the mortgage or at least liability for only a small portion of the loan amount.

- **Dragnet Clause.** A dragnet clause is an open-ended clause in which the property stands as security for all of the obligations that the borrower has to the lender—the note contemplated in the deed to secure debt, as well as any other indebtedness to the lender.

- **Cross-default Clause.** A cross-default clause is a provision in a mortgage that pledges several pieces of properties to the lender as collateral. If one of these loans is in default it will trigger a default in the other properties as well.

CLOSING THE LOAN

After the investor has submitted the loan package and has narrowed down the choice of lender, the lender will issue either a loan application or loan commitment that will outline all of the basic business points of the loan. The following is a sample Loan Application Letter:

Loan Application Letter

_____, 19__

RE: (Property Name)
        (Property Location)

Dear (Borrower):

The following terms and conditions outline in proposal form how _____ ("Lender") will provide a loan (the "Loan") to _____ ("Borrower") for the above referenced property. This proposal is subject to the Lender's due diligence and other conditions.

Loan Amount:	$_____
Loan Term:	____ years
Loan Maturity:	____ years
Loan Amortization Period:	____ years
Interest Rate:	____ basis points over the ____ year U.S. Treasury at the time of rate lock. The interest calculation will be based on a ____ day year.
Monthly Debt Service Payment:	The monthly debt service payment will be $_____.
Commitment Fee:	____% of the Loan Amount, paid with the Loan Commitment Agreement
Rate Lock:	A ____% deposit fee of the loan amount for a rate lock 60 days prior to closing or ____% deposit fee of the loan amount for a rate lock 30 days prior to closing. There shall be no deposit fee for a rate lock ____ days prior to closing. If the borrower does not close once the commitment fee is paid, then the rate lock deposit fee will be kept by the lender as damages. If the loan is closed, the deposit fee will be credited back to the borrower.
Commitment Letter:	If the Commitment Letter is issued, it will be effective for ____ days from the issue date (the "Commitment Period"). This Letter will set forth the final remaining issues to be addressed and will be subject to the completion of the final legal documentation.
Minimum DSCR:	____% of the Lender's underwriting

Maximum LTV: ____% of the Lender's underwriting

Minimum Occupancy Requirement: ____%

Third Party Reports: All third party reports are to be paid by the borrower. The borrower is to deposit with the lender $_____ for these reports.

Appraisal: An appraisal that conforms with USPAP and FIRREA guidelines and that is acceptable to the Lender.

Environmental: A Phase I Environmental Report that is prepared by a qualified firm that is approved by the lender.

Architectural & Engineering: An Architectural and Engineering Report that is prepared by a qualified firm that is approved by the lender.

Survey: A current as-built ALTA survey that is dated or recertified by the surveyor that is approved by the lender.

Recourse: This loan will be non-recourse to the Borrower, with the exception of the customary "carve-outs." The Borrower and key principals will be required to execute a standard environmental indemnification.

Collateral: The collateral for this loan will be a perfected first fee mortgage (or deed of trust). The first priority perfected security interest will include all furniture, fixtures, and equipment and an assignment of leases, rents, profits, permits, licenses, contracts, and a pledge of all escrow and reserve accounts.

Borrower: The Borrower will be _____.

Escrows and Reserves:
Capital Improvement: If Capital Improvements are identified by the Architectural and Engineering Report, the Lender will require the Borrower to escrow ____% of this deferred maintenance amount. All required Capital Improvements must be completed within ____ months of the closing of the Loan.

Replacement Reserve: The Borrower will be required to fund $_____ per unit or $_____ per rentable square foot as a Replacement Reserve. A monthly escrow deposit equal to 1/12 of the annual replacement reserve amount will be required and is subject to change based on the Lender's review of the third party due diligence reports and the Borrower's capital improvement plan. The replacement reserve will be available to the Borrower for qualified capital expenditures. All interest earned on this account will accrue to the Borrower.

Operating Escrows:	A monthly escrow for real estate taxes and insurance will be required. All interest earned on this account will accrue to the Borrower.
Tenant Improvement and Leasing Commissions:	A monthly escrow for tenant improvements and leasing commissions may be required based upon expected turnover of the property.
Prepayment Penalty:	There will be a five-year lockout, then the greater of standard Treasury yield maintenance or 1%. The Lender will retain the right to require the substitution of U.S. Treasuries as collateral rather than the repayment in cash of the mortgage loan. No prepayment penalty will apply for the last six months of the loan.
Loan Assumability:	Subject to the prior approval of the Lender, the Borrower may transfer the property one time for a ____% assumption fee based on the then current outstanding loan balance.
Additional Encumbrances:	None permitted during the term of the loan without the prior approval of the Lender.
Additional Loan Expenses:	A $_____ Due Diligence fee is to be paid to the Lender upon execution of the Loan Commitment. The Borrower will pay all customary closing costs associated with this loan, to include: title insurance, mortgage tax, recording fees, surveys, appraisals, the Lender legal fees (approximately $_____.00), and all cost of the Third Party Reports.

This letter is not a commitment to lend, either expressed or implied, and does not impose any obligation on the Lender. The general terms and conditions outlined above are not all inclusive, fully exhaustive or final and are subject to change at the Lender's option. Any loan commitment that may be issued by the Lender will include other conditions which may result from the Lender's due diligence.

Sincerely,

_____

(Lender)

Accepted By:

_____   _____

(Borrower)   (Date)

Loan Commitment Letter

Once the Loan Application is signed, the Lender will prepare the Loan Commitment Letter. As discussed in the Loan Application Letter, this agreement will be a binding document that will include all the terms and conditions of the proposed loan.

Rate Lock Agreement

This agreement will outline the terms and conditions of locking in the final rate on the proposed loan.

The Lender Closing Checklist for Due Diligence

In order for the Lender to complete a thorough due diligence on the property, it will require the Borrower to submit a number of items for review. Since some of these items come from various sources, the borrower should allow adequate time to compile and review these items.

The following are typically required by the lender for review:

I. General Information

Borrower

Guarantor(s)

Loan Purpose

Loan Amount

Proposed Closing Date

Lender's Attorney

Borrower's Attorney

II. Property Information

1. Property Brochure

2. Property Description

3. Legal Description

4. Site Map

5. Color Photographs of the Property

6. Site Plan

7. Floor Plans

III. Property Financial Information

1. Current Rent Roll showing:

Tenant name

Rent rates

Square footage

Lease start/end dates

        CAM

        Tax and insurance stops

        Options

  2. Operating Statements

        Past 3 years

        Current year-to-date

  3. Current Budget

  4. Tenant Sales Reports and Percentage Rent Paid (if Retail)

  5. Tenant Delinquency Report

  6. Prior 12-month bank statements

  7. Historical occupancy for last 3 years (monthly if multifamily)

  8. Schedule of security deposits

  9. Current and last 3 years real estate tax bills

 10. Copies of all service contracts

 11. Copy of management/marketing agreements

 12. List of all on-site employees with salary and benefits history

 13. Schedule of capital expenditures for past 2 years and current budget

 14. Schedule of tenant improvement and leasing commissions due for property

 15. Letter from Borrower showing:

        Current lender and loan balance

        Equity to be in deal

        Sources and applications of funds

IV. Market Analysis

  1. Market Study of all Comparables

        Property name

        Address

        Total number of units/square footage

        Property age

        Unit mix

        Rental rates

  2. Map showing location of comparables

  3. Demographics (1, 3, 5-mile radius)

V. Title

  1. Copy of current as-built survey

  2. Current ALTA policy

    3. Copy of all encumbrances and encroachments on property

VI. Borrower Information

    1. Letter authorizing credit check of Borrower and each key principal, including tax ID and Social Security number

    2. Resumes of Borrower and key principals

    3. Description of borrowing entity

    4. Signed and dated financial statements for the borrowing entity and key principals

    5. Tax returns for the borrowing entity and key principals for the last 3 years

VII. Third Party Reports

    1. Appraisal: Copy of a current appraisal

    2. Architectural and Engineering Study: Copy of a current architectural and engineering study

    3. Environmental Study: Copy of a current Phase I or Phase II report

    4. Feasibility Study: Copy of a current feasibility study

Items for the Borrower to Bring to the Closing

I. Organization Documents

If Corporate Borrower:

1. Certificate of Incorporation and all amendments

2. By-laws, certified by Borrower

3. Certificate of Good Standing issued by the Secretary of State where incorporated

4. Certificate of Good Standing issued by the Secretary of State where the property is located.

5. Certificate of Corporate Resolutions

6. Affidavit of Corporate Borrower regarding ownership of stock in corporation

If Borrower is a Limited Partnership:

1. Certificate of partner or officer of corporate general partner

2. Certificate of Limited Partnership and all amendments thereto, certified as filed by the appropriate office in the state where organized

3. Limited Partnership Agreement and all amendments thereto, certified by the Borrower

4. Fictitious Name Affidavit or Certificate of Limited Partnership as filed by appropriate office in state where the property is located

5. Evidence of publication

If Borrower is a Limited Liability Company:

1. Articles of Organization and all amendments thereto, certified as filed by the Secretary of State where formed

2. Operating Agreement and all amendments thereto, certified by the Borrower

3. Certificate of Good Standing issued by the Secretary of State where incorporated
4. Certificate of Good Standing issued by the Secretary of State where the property is located
5. Fictitious Name Certificate or evidence of authority to do business in state where property is located

II. Estoppel Letters

1. Tenant estoppel letters (commercial only)

III. Subordination Agreements

1. Subordination Agreements (commercial only)
2. Subordination, Non-disturbance and Attornment Agreements

IV. Zoning, Use and Occupancy

1. Certificates of Occupancy
2. Zoning letter from local municipality

V. Management Agreements

1. Copy of Management Agreement

VI. Insurance Policies

1. All risk policy
2. Boiler damage and liability policy
3. Business and rent loss policy
4. Public liability policy
5. Umbrella policy
6. Flood insurance policy or evidence that property is not located in a flood zone

VII. Title Insurance

1. Title insurance commitment
2. Copies of recorded easements, rights of way, restrictive covenants, leases and other instruments of record
3. Approval of title company, co-insuring title companies and/or re-insuring title companies (if any) and amounts taken
4. Evidence that required co-insurance title policies will be issued by companies and in amounts satisfactory to Lender
5. UCC-1 financing statement search, tax lien search and judgement search
6. Real estate tax search and most recent tax bills
7. Municipal departmental violation searches, including environmental lien searches
8. Title insurance policy
9. Evidence of required affirmative insurance and special endorsements required by Lender
10. Insuring closing letter from the title insurance company

VIII. Surveys

    1. Copies of survey

IX. Opinion Letters

    1. Counsel for Borrower with respect to the due execution and enforceability of the loan documents and other matters

    2. Local counsel opinion

    3. Substantive non-consolidation opinion

X. Ground Leases

    1. Copy of ground lease, including all amendments and modifications

    2. Estoppel letter from ground lessor

    3. Notice from lender of ground lessor

    4. Subordination of existing fee mortgages to current leasehold mortgage

XI. Existing Mortgages to Be Assigned

    1. Copies of recorded existing mortgages to be assigned

    2. Copies of all notes secured by the existing mortgages being assigned to Lender

    3. Assignment of the existing mortgages and the notes secured thereby to Lender

    4. Borrower's Statement Under Oath for Assignment of Mortgage

    5. Estoppel Certificate or pay-out letter from the holder of the existing mortgages being assigned to Lender

    6. Instructions from the holders of the existing mortgages as to the method of payment

XII. Miscellaneous Items to Bring to Closing

    1. Corporate seal

    2. Certified funds for closing

        Payment of interest due for month

        Lender's attorney fees

        Borrower's attorney fees

        Payment of required escrows

        Payment of tax and insurance escrow deposit

        Payment of title insurance premiums

        Payment of attorney disbursements

        Payment of Lender fees and expenses

    3. Wiring instructions

Closing Documents to Review and Sign

Just prior to the closing the Lender's attorney will prepare and send to the Borrower's attorney a package of closing documents to review. The following is a list of the typical loan closing documents:

1. Closing statement

2. Promissory Note

3. Mortgage and Security Agreement/Deed of Trust and Security Agreement

4. Assignment of Leases and Rents

5. Conditional Assignment of Management Agreement (and Subordination of Management Fees)

6. UCC-1 Financing Statements

7. Assignment of Agreements, Permits and Contracts

8. Asbestos Operations and Maintenance Agreement

9. Lead-Based Paint Acknowledgement and Indemnification Agreement

10. Reserve Letter

11. Borrower's Certificate

12. Borrower's Financial Certificate

13. Guaranty of Recourse Obligations

14. Guarantor's Certificate

15. Environmental Indemnity

16. Completion/Repair and Security Agreement

17. Assignment of Mortgages, Deeds and Trust and Assignments of Leases and Rights

18. Borrower's Certificate—No Adverse Change

19. Escrow Instructions

Post Closing Items

After the closing of the loan, the Borrower should request a loan amortization schedule from the Lender.

FINANCING FORMS

- **Mortgage Lender Prospect Sheet.** This form helps keep track of potential lenders.

- **Mortgage Lender.** This form can be used to categorize and rate lenders for the various types of loans that are available.

FORM 8-1
Mortgage Lender Prospect Sheet

PROPERTY NAME _____
PREPARED BY _____
TYPE PROPERTY _____
DATE _____
PAGE _____ OF _____

LENDER	CONTACT	ADDRESS	TEL. NO.	LOAN FLOOR	DEBT COVERAGE	CONSTANT	LOAN TO VALUE RATIO	COMMENTS
			( )	$			%	
			( )	$			%	
			( )	$			%	
			( )	$			%	
			( )	$			%	
			( )	$			%	
			( )	$			%	
			( )	$			%	
			( )	$			%	
			( )	$			%	
			( )	$			%	
			( )	$			%	
			( )	$			%	
			( )	$			%	
			( )	$			%	
			( )	$			%	
			( )	$			%	
			( )	$			%	
			( )	$			%	

COMMENTS _____

372

Mortgage Lender

BUSINESS NAME _____
CONTACT _____
ADDRESS _____
_____
TEL. NO. (   ) _____

PREPARED BY _____

AREAS WILL LEND:
_____
_____
_____
_____

SPECIALIZATION _____	DEAL SIZE _____	TYPE LOANS:
		LAND ACQUISITION _____
RESIDENTIAL:		DEVELOPMENT _____
SINGLE FAMILY _____	$_____	CONSTRUCTION _____
MULTI-FAMILY _____	$_____	STANDBY _____
CONDOMINIUM/TOWNHOME ____	$_____	PERMANENT _____
ADULT CONGREGATE CARE ____	$_____	
NURSING HOME _____	$_____	
OFFICE _____	$_____	
SHOPPING CENTER _____	$_____	
INDUSTRIAL _____	$_____	
MINI-WAREHOUSE _____	$_____	
HOTEL/MOTEL _____	$_____	
RESORT _____	$_____	

TYPICAL DEAL _____

CONSTRUCTION
LOAN AMOUNT $ _____
LOAN TO VALUE RATIO ___%
LOAN RATE _____
LOAN TERM _____
POINTS _____
CLOSING COSTS $ _____
FREQUENCY OF DRAWS _____
DRAW HOLDBACK _____
LIABILITY _____
COMMENTS _____
_____
_____
_____
_____
_____
_____
_____
_____
_____
_____
_____
_____

PERMANENT LOAN:
TYPE LOAN _____
LOAN TO VALUE RATIO _____
LOAN AMORTIZATION _____
LONG TERM _____
LOAN PAYMENT RATE ___%
LOAN ACCRUAL RATE ___%
INDEX RATE _____
_____
LOAN BUYDOWN COST ___%
   FOR A ___% BUYDOWN FOR ___ YEARS
CLOSING COSTS ___% OF THE LOAN
_____
_____
_____
_____

ESCROWS: TAXES ___ INSURANCE _____
INTEREST PAID ON ESCROWS:
   YES ___ RATE ___% NO ___

LIABILITY _____
DUE ON SALE CLAUSE _____
JUNIOR FINANCING PROHIBITION _____
DATE LOAN DELINQUENT _____
   LATE CHARGE _____
   GRACE PERIOD _____
ASSIGNABILITY _____
TRANSFER FEE _____
NEW INTEREST RATE ___%
PREPAYMENT:
   LOCK IN _____
   PENALTY _____
   COMMENTS _____
_____
_____
_____
_____
_____

BUSINESS:	BUSINESS:	BUSINESS:
DATE _____	DATE _____	DATE _____
BUSINESS NAME _____	BUSINESS NAME _____	BUSINESS NAME _____
CONTACT _____	CONTACT _____	CONTACT _____
ADDRESS _____	ADDRESS _____	ADDRESS _____
TEL. NO. ( ) _____	TEL. NO. ( ) _____	TEL. NO. ( ) _____
COMMENTS _____	COMMENTS _____	COMMENTS _____
_____	_____	_____
_____	_____	_____
_____	_____	_____
_____	_____	_____

COMMENTS _____
_____
_____
_____

Chapter 9

RAISING THE EQUITY: HOW TO FIND PARTNERS TO HELP FUND THE DEAL

In almost every type of real estate transaction, there is some type of equity required. This equity typically represents a cash down-payment as well as closing cost fees, repair expenses and working capital or other reserves.

Depending on cash position, the investor might contribute the equity personally, borrow funds, or have other individuals contribute the equity needed to close.

Assuming that the investor decides not to put in all the equity personally, the necessary capital must be raised from other sources. This chapter provides an outline for the investor to follow for this alternative. It should further be noted that the investor who is seeking out new partners in the deal will now be called the "managing partner," while the new partners will either be general partners or limited partners.

HOW TO DETERMINE THE EQUITY YOU NEED

To determine the amount of equity needed for the acquisition, the investor should review all the areas in which funds will be needed including the following:

1. Down-payment to seller
2. Fees paid to seller
3. Fees paid to real estate broker (usually paid by seller)
4. Fees paid to general partner
5. Fees paid to money raiser
6. Legal fees and other closing costs
7. Loan closing costs and buydown costs
8. Fees paid to mortgage broker
9. Property repairs and capital improvements
10. Interest on deferred down-payment
11. Interest carry on investor note loan financing
12. Negative cash flow funding
13. Working capital reserves

375

Working Capital Reserves: Key to the Whole Transaction

Working capital is one of the most important aspects of the whole transaction. Since real estate is normally held for a relatively long period of time, it will go through many economic cycles. Financial problems occur in real estate deals when there is a cash flow problem due to loss of potential rents and increased costs of operating expenses plus unforeseen repairs.

The amount of working capital raised should be determined by the purchaser assuming a worst case scenario, that is, how much money should be raised to carry the property in the poorest of times. There are no hard and fast rules on the exact amount needed, either on a per-unit or percent of income basis. This amount of money will be a function of the length of time you will be holding the property and how conservative you are.

Most deals get into trouble when they run out of working capital. Many limited partnerships have an initial funding of this working capital account and then are reluctant to ask the investment partners for additional funding to replenish this account. If a property is funded with a conservative working capital account it should have the staying power to ride out the tough times.

WHERE TO LOOK FOR EQUITY INVESTORS

Once the amount of equity is determined, the investor should start making a list of potential equity investors. Examples include:

1. Friends

2. Business associates

3. Money raisers

    a. Broker/dealers who specialize in real estate

    b. Financial planners who specialize in real estate

    c. Wholesalers who have contacts with money raisers

4. Accountants who have clients who want to invest in real estate

5. Attorneys who have clients who want to invest in real estate

6. Real estate brokers who know of potential investors

7. Bankers who have clients who might be potential investors

8. Insurance agents who have clients who might be potential investors

9. Real estate investment firms

10. Institutional joint venture partners

    a. Banks

    b. Savings and loan

    c. Insurance companies

    d. Pension funds

HOW TO SELECT A MONEY RAISER

The investor who is not going to raise the equity personally should contact a wholesaler or an underwriter to coordinate the raising of this equity. As in selecting any professional in the acquisition process, the investor should interview potential money raisers and check on their qualifications. Since most money raisers work on a "best efforts" basis, making no guarantee that they can raise all the funds, the investor should make sure to have a plan to fall back on in case the money raiser does not complete the job.

A wholesaler is an individual who for a fee will coordinate the fund raising. The wholesaler will either market the deal to an individual money raiser or to a group of money raisers who have the retail clients.

An underwriter is an individual or corporation that has clients who are looking for real estate investments.

HOW TO SELECT POTENTIAL INVESTORS

Once the list of potential investors is completed, the Managing Partner should ask the investors of their representatives the following questions:

Thirteen Questions to Ask Potential Investors

1. Will the investor invest in this type of property?

2. Will the investor purchase property in this location?

If the answer to the first two questions is yes, the managing partner should then ask the following questions to narrow down the potential list.

3. Will the investor be passive or active?

4. What is the investor's typical holding period?

5. What is the reason for investing?
   a. Capital appreciation
   b. Cash flow
   c. Tax benefits

6. What rates of return do the potential investors want to achieve?
   a. Cash flow
   b. Tax losses
   c. Internal rate of return

7. How should the profits and tax benefits be split?
   a. Cash flow
   b. Tax losses
   c. Refinancing proceeds
   d. Resale proceeds

8. Who gets the first proceeds, and how are they allocated among the partners?

9. Does the managing partner receive any fees?

   a. Fees paid in advance for putting the deal together

   b. Property management fees

   c. Partnership management fees

   d. Leasing fees

   e. Refinancing fees

   f. Resale brokerage fees

10. What fees are due the money raiser?

11. Will the money raiser take any ownership in the deal?

    a. If the money raiser will stay in the deal, will it be an active or passive role?

12. What form of investment vehicle will the new investors use?

    a. Corporation

    b. Subchapter S

    c. General partnership

    d. Limited partnership

    e. Joint venture

    f. Tenants in common

    g. Joint tenancy with right of survivorship

13. Will the investment group pay cash at closing or will it want to finance its equity?

    a. If the group finances the equity, over what period of time will it pay off this loan?

Determine Whether Passive or Active Investors Are Needed

In many types of real estate transactions, the managing partner is in need not only of equity but expertise in certain deficient areas. In many cases, the managing partner (the individual or individuals who will oversee the daily operations of the property) will seek an active joint venture partner who will not only infuse the deal with the necessary equity but will also be able to play an active part in the development, management, or leasing of the property.

The managing partner who is capable of handling all the facets of the transaction is probably going to look for a passive money partner, typically a limited partner.

The managing partner who is capable of handling the deal but wants a partner to share the financial risks over and above the partners' contribution can look for this type of partner and structure the deal accordingly.

Checking References

In any type of business transaction, it is a good idea to know who you are dealing with. The investor should submit a complete set of references to the potential investment group. These references should include a track record in this type of transaction, past educational and business background, net worth and both personal and business references. The potential investor should receive a complete package, including the following.

1. References, track record, and resume of the managing partner

2. Investment information package

3. Property appraisal

4. Feasibility study

5. Engineering studies

6. Sample partnership documents

The managing partner should also obtain information on the potential investment group.

This package should include the investor's investment experience, net worth, yearly salary history, and banking references. The managing partner does not want to discover inexperienced investors or investors who are not capable of the financial requirements. The managing partner has enough problems to deal with, without having to "baby sit" any investors.

HOW TO STRUCTURE THE DEAL WITH A LIMITED PARTNERSHIP

Just as no two real estate transactions are exactly alike, there are many ways to structure a deal with the equity investors. The main points in doing this are to determine what type of ownership vehicle is most advantageous as well as what fees, if any, will be paid to the investor, who in this case will be acting as the managing partner in the new ownership entity.

As discussed in Chapter 1, there are many types of ownership vehicles. The investor should consult both an attorney and accountant at this point to assist in weighing the alternatives and deciding which of these vehicles is most appropriate for the new investment group.

One of the most common ownership vehicles when raising funds from passive investors is the limited partnership. A real estate limited partnership is a partnership formed between two or more individuals or corporations. One party is the managing general partner, and the other party or parties are the limited partners. Unless the partnership agreement states otherwise, the limited partners are only liable for their contribution.

Limited partnerships have become very popular over the past fifteen years because they enable investors to pool their funds to purchase larger and more sophisticated properties than they could have acquired individually.

Types of Limited Partnerships

PRIVATE PLACEMENT LIMITED PARTNERSHIP

Private placement limited partnerships are partnerships that are designed to have a limited number of investors who meet certain knowledge, net worth, and liquidity requirements.

INTERSTATE OFFERING

Interstate offerings are deals that may be sold to investors in any of the fifty states. It does not matter what state the property is located in or where the managing general partner is based. Each investor has to meet certain suitability requirements to invest.

INTRASTATE OFFERING

Intrastate offerings are deals that are only sold to a specified number of investors who reside in the same state in which the managing general partner and the property are located.

PUBLIC LIMITED PARTNERSHIP

Public limited partnerships are those that are offered to the public. These deals are usually sold to a large number of investors in small investment units. They typically are sold on the basis of cash flow. Restrictions include no staged payments, that is, all equity is paid in at the beginning of the partnership.

BLIND POOL FUND

Blind pool funds are public offerings in which no properties have been contracted for prior to the public offering. The offering will describe the types of properties to be purchased as well as the potential investment criteria sought. Once the equity is raised, the partnership will then acquire properties at the managing general partner's discretion, within the partnership parameters.

SPECIFIED POOL FUND

Specified pool funds are public offerings in which specified properties are contracted prior to the raising of the offering. Once the offering is fully subscribed, the properties are closed.

A Seven-step Checklist for Establishing Limited Partnership

STEP 1: PREPARE THE MEMORANDUM

In preparing the memorandum, the managing partner should hire a law firm that specializes in not only real estate law but in securities law as well. This is due to the fact that in raising the cash for the transaction, the managing partner is not selling real estate but is in fact selling a security. Because a security is being sold, a whole new group of rules and regulations must be followed.

OUTLINE OF A LIMITED PARTNERSHIP MEMORANDUM

1. Cover page
   a. Name of the Partnership
   b. Size of the offering
   c. Number of units to be sold
   d. Footnotes

2. Suitability requirements of the investor

3. Summary of the offering

4. Risk factors

5. Capitalization

6. Use of proceeds

7. Plan of offering

8. Profits and cash flow distribution to partners

9. Description of the property

10. Acquisition of the property

11. Compensation of the general partners and their affiliates

12. General partners' biography fact sheet and net worth statements

13. Prior offerings of the general partners

14. Fiduciary responsibilities of the general partners

15. Conflicts of interest of the general partners

16. Purchase agreement

17. Development agreement (if to-be-built)

18. Property management agreement

19. Federal tax consequences

20. State and local taxes

21. Restriction on transfer of partnership interest

22. Summary of the limited partnership agreement

23. Current litigation of the general partner

24. Glossary of terms

25. Balance sheet of the partnership

26. Accounting forecasts

    a. Cash flow forecasts

    b. Taxable income (loss) forecasts

    c. Resale forecasts

27. Exhibits

    a. Amended and restricted certificate and agreement of limited partnership

    b. Prior performance of the general partner

    c. Draft of the tax opinion from the law firm

OUTLINE OF A SUBSCRIPTION BOOKLET

1. Subscription instructions

2. Investor questionnaire

3. Representative questionnaire

4. Copy of the amendment and restated certificate and agreement of limited partnership

5. Subscription agreement

6. Promissory note

7. Financial statement

8. Banking references

9. Indemnity agreement

STEP 2: REVIEW THE SELLING AGREEMENT

The selling agreement is the agreement between the managing general partner and the underwriter that defines the duties of the parties as well as the fee structure to be paid to the selling group.

STEP 3: PREPARE THE OFFERING CIRCULAR

To help expedite the marketing program, the managing partner should prepare a simple, one to four page brochure that includes the facts on the proposed offering. This circular should include the following information:

1. Picture or rendering of the property

2. Purchase price and terms of the deal

3. Financing

4. Use of proceeds

5. Description of the property

6. Location map

7. Rental schedule and unit mix

8. Financial schedules

    a. Cash flow projections

    b. Taxable income (loss) projections

    c. Resale projections

9. The unique advantages of this investment

10. Marketing contact/telephone number

STEP 4: APPLY FOR BLUE SKY CLEARANCE

Each of the fifty states has different rules and regulations governing the sale of real estate securities. Once all of the home states of the potential investors have been determined, the securities attorney should then apply to these states for blue sky clearance. Each state has different requirements and a different fee structure. An official offer cannot be made to any investor until blue sky clearance has been obtained in the appropriate state.

STEP 5: MARKET THE SECURITIES

Since the selling of a limited partnership is a security, it is highly regulated by governmental agencies. Care should be taken that all rules and regulations are followed to the letter. Noncompliance with these regulations can cause future problems, potential litigation with investors, and other serious consequences, such as fines or jail sentences.

You should be certain that you are not misrepresenting or omitting any material facts in the transaction.

To market these securities, do the following:

1. Identify the potential investors

2. Confirm that investors meet deal suitability requirements

3. Acquaint the investors with this type of ownership vehicle

4. Inform the investors of the benefits of the deal

5. Review the track record of the general partner with the potential investor

6. Close the deal

The following are methods that could be used to identify potential investors:

1. Seminars on the benefits of real estate ownership

2. Advertising

3. Researching the state records for investors who have invested in other partnerships.

4. Contacting attorneys, accountants, bankers, or insurance agents who have clients looking for real estate investments.

5. Contact broker/dealers or financial planners.

STEP 6: REVIEW THE INVESTOR SUBSCRIPTION PACKAGE

As the units are sold, each investor should send in the copy of the subscription booklet and a check for the unit purchased. The managing general partner should carefully review the subscription booklet to make sure that all the information requested is completed and that the investor meets the suitability requirements of the transaction. If any of this information is not correct, the managing general partner should notify the investor to correct the information or notify the investor that the suitability requirements have not been met. After a careful review of this package, the managing general partner should sign off on the various documents in this package.

STEP 7: SET UP AN ESCROW ACCOUNT FOR THE INITIAL CONTRIBUTIONS

Prior to any investor contributions being collected, the managing general partner should establish an escrow account with a local bank. The bank should have a set of instructions as to how and when to break escrow and to distribute these collected funds.

As these funds are collected the managing general partner should compile a list with the names of the investors and the monies collected. Once this transaction is completely subscribed and closed, the managing general partner should contact the bank to disburse the collected funds.

WHAT THE GENERAL AND LIMITED PARTNERS ARE RESPONSIBLE FOR

Managing General Partner

The managing general partner (managing partner) is the individual or entity who controls and oversees the daily operations of the property, as well as the partnership affairs. If there are a number of general partners, one individual might be appointed managing partner.

General Partner

The general partner is an individual or entity that has general partnership liability. This liability includes a fiduciary responsibility to the investors, as well as unlimited liability for the partnership obligations.

Special Limited Partner

The special limited partner is an individual or entity that is considered a limited partner but may have a profit split different from the other limited partners.

Limited Partner

Limited partners are those individuals or entities whose liabilities are limited only to their original contribution. An accredited investor is a limited partner who does not count as one of the thirty-five investors in an interstate offering. To qualify, this investor must have a net worth of at least $1,000,000, or an annual income of at least $200,000, or must invest at least $150,000 in the offering. This investment should not be more than 20 percent of the investor's total net worth.

FIGURE 9-1
Partnership Organizational Chart

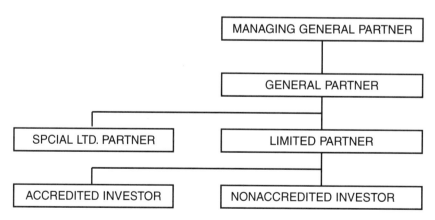

WHAT FEES ARE PAID TO THE MANAGING PARTNER FOR SERVICES

The investor or managing partner who will be performing various services for the new investment group will be entitled to compensation for these services. The following paragraphs explain many of the sources of fee revenue.

Syndication Fee

Some fees are paid to the managing partner either at closing or over a specified time period. These fees are for services rendered for the new partnership. The services performed to the partnership are: the negotiating of the transaction, the placement of the financing, the guaranteeing of any leases or loans, and the setting up of the property and management accounting systems. Some managing partners take a small fee and a larger share of the deal. These fees are usually negotiated prior to the investor's decision to invest. There may be a flat fee or a fee based on a percentage of the equity raised, usually ranging from 1 percent to 15 percent of the equity raised.

Property Markup Fee

A fee may be taken when the managing general partner marks up the purchase price of the property and then resells the property to the new investment group. Typically, this involves a wraparound mortgage.

Property Management Fee

A management fee is paid to the property management company. In many cases, the managing partner has his own management company and will charge a fee that is competitive with other management firms in the area. This fee is usually based on a percentage of the rental income of the property and ranges between 3 percent and 6 percent of the effective gross income.

Partnership Management Fee

The managing partner will usually charge the partnership a fee to service the partnership. The duties include the partnership accounting, tax preparation, and investor correspondence. This fee is usually a flat monthly fee or based on a percentage of the collections from the property, and ranges between 1/2 to 2 percent of the effective gross income.

Leasing Commission

If the transaction is a new residential property that is under rent-up or a commercial property, the managing partner will usually charge a leasing commission for renting up the property. This fee is usually based on a flat rate per tenant or a percentage of the total volume of the lease. In some cases, the managing partner might have to share this fee with outside real estate agents, particularly for commercial properties. This fee is usually competitive with the local market and ranges between 4 percent to 5 percent of the total lease value.

Refinancing Fee

If the existing debt on the property is refinanced during the ownership period, the managing partner may take a fee for this service. The managing partner would search for and negotiate a new loan when the current financing becomes due or when the timing is right to obtain a new loan with better terms and conditions. This fee could either be based on a flat rate or on a percentage of the new loan. Similar to the leasing commission, all or a portion of this fee may be paid to an outside mortgage broker, and usually will range between one-half to one percent of the new loan amount.

Resale Brokerage Fee

Upon resale, the managing partner can take a fee for handling the resale. The services provided by the managing partner are: the search for the new buyer, structuring of the transaction, working with the attorneys and the accountants, communicating with the investment group, and closing the transaction. Again, an outside broker may be involved in the resale, and this could result in either an additional brokerage fee or in splitting of the managing partner's resale brokerage fee. The fee usually charged for this service ranges from one percent to five percent of the sales price or can be based on a flat fee.

Mortgage Servicing Fee

If the resale includes any financing that is taken back by the partnership, the managing partner will have to service this loan for the remaining time period. When these payments are received, the managing partner will have to deposit these funds in a bank and then disburse these funds to the investment group as they are received. A fee may be charged to the partnership for this service which could be either a set monthly fee with an escalation over time or a percentage of the dollars collected.

PROFIT: HOW TO STRUCTURE THESE BENEFITS

Since all investors are making an economic decision when they invest in real estate, they will carefully analyze how much money they will invest and how they will get their original investment back with profits. In terms of priority, the money partner will typically have her investment returned first, including a preferred return. Subsequent funds will be split between the managing partner and the investment group. The money may be split equally between the parties, or the split may range to 75 percent to the investors and 25 percent to the managing partner. Many deals are also structured on a sliding scale based on predetermined benchmarks.

Cash Flow

The cash flow that the property generates after servicing the debt will be available to distribute to the investors. There are many ways that the cash flow can be split among the partners. One way is to split this cash equally between the investors and the managing partner; another is to allocate to the investors 99 percent of the cash flow until they receive a preferred return, typically in a range of 8 percent to 12 percent on the funds invested. Any cash available over that amount can then be split. A common arrangement at this point splits this available cash flow by allocating 75 percent to the investment partners and 25 percent to the managing partner.

Refinancing Proceeds

Upon the refinancing of the property, new funds could be generated either by increased cash flow or from tax-free dollars from the difference between the old and the new mortgages. These funds could then be available to fund any renovation work, to fund the working capital account, or to distribute to the partners. If the decision is made to distribute this cash, the deal could be structured to give these proceeds back to the investors as a return of their initial capital, or they could be split between the investors and the managing partner.

Resale Proceeds

When the resale occurs, the deal is coming to a close. Typically, the deal is structured one of two ways. In the first, the investors receive the remaining dollars due from their original investment, plus any dollars due from their preferred cash flow agreement. The remaining cash would then be split between the investors and the managing partner. This split can be equal or 75 percent to 25 percent with increases to the managing partner based upon certain predetermined formulas. The second method used could be to split the profits 90 percent to 10 percent with increases to the managing partner based upon a specific formula.

In determining these splits, the managing partner and the investment group or joint venture partner should negotiate a deal that meets the needs and wants of each party. The equity side of the deal should remember that the managing partner typically makes her living from real estate and that she should always have a vested interest in the deal, as well as a future incentive for good management.

HOW TO TERMINATE A PARTNERSHIP OR CORPORATION

Since people have different needs and desires and cannot foresee the future, each ownership entity should have a method of terminating the relationship. This termination could be based upon a formula or an agreement to have an appraiser determine the property value. Another method could be a "Chinese Option," in which one party offers to buy the other party's interest for a certain price. The other party can then either accept this offer or can turn around and pay that price and buy out the other partner.

The agreement should also contain language regarding the death, bankruptcy, or incompetence of the managing partner.

EQUITY RAISING FORMS

Equity Raiser. This form will assist in selecting the equity raiser.

Investor Information. This form will list each investor in the deal as well as all the pertinent information needed.

Blue Sky Clearance. This form lists each state and can be used to update the blue sky application dates and approval dates.

Private Placement Memorandum Tracking Report. This form tracks each memorandum that was logged out.

FORM 9-1

Equity Raiser

BUSINESS NAME _____
CONTACT _____
ADDRESS _____
_____
TEL. NO. (   ) _____

PREPARED BY _____

TYPE EQUITY RAISER:
  WHOLESALER _____
  FINANCIAL PLANNER _____
  BROKER DEALER _____
  ACCOUNTANT _____
  ATTORNEY _____
  OTHER _____

SPECIALIZATION:
  RESIDENTIAL:
    SINGLE FAMILY _____
    MULTI-FAMILY _____
    ADULT CONGREGATE CARE _____
    NURSING HOME _____
  OFFICE _____
  SHOPPING CENTER _____
  INDUSTRIAL _____
  MINI-WAREHOUSE _____
  HOTEL/MOTEL _____
  RESORT _____

FEE STRUCTURE:

GENERAL PARTNER FEES ___% OF THE EQUITY RAISED
  FEES PAID OVER _____
  COMMENTS _____
_____
_____

MONEY RAISER FEES ___% OF THE EQUITY RAISED
  FEES PAID OVER _____
  COMMENTS _____
_____
_____

MONEY RAISER:
  CO-GENERAL PARTNER _____
  SPECIAL LIMITED PARTNER _____
  NO OWNERSHIP _____

OBJECTIVES:
  CASH FLOW: YR 1 ___% YR 2 ___% YR 3 ___% YR 4 ___% YR 5 ___%
  TAX LOSS RATIO: YR 1 ___% YR 2 ___% YR 3 ___% YR 4 ___% YR 5 ___%
  HOLDING PERIOD ___ YRS.
  INTERNAL RATE OF RETURN ___%

DEAL SPLIT:
  CASH FLOW:
_____
_____
_____
_____

TAXABLE INCOME (LOSS):
_____
_____
_____
_____

REFINANCING:
_____
_____
_____
_____

RESALE:
_____
_____
_____
_____

BUSINESS:
  DATE _____
  BUSINESS NAME _____
  CONTACT _____
  ADDRESS _____
_____
  TEL. NO. (   ) _____
  COMMENTS _____
_____
_____
_____
_____

BUSINESS:
  DATE _____
  BUSINESS NAME _____
  CONTACT _____
  ADDRESS _____
_____
  TEL. NO. (   ) _____
  COMMENTS _____
_____
_____
_____
_____

BUSINESS:
  DATE _____
  BUSINESS NAME _____
  CONTACT _____
  ADDRESS _____
_____
  TEL. NO. (   ) _____
  COMMENTS _____
_____
_____
_____
_____

COMMENTS _____
_____
_____
_____
_____
_____

FORM 9-2
Investor Information

PARTNERSHIP NAME _____
GENERAL PARTNER (S) _____
CO-GEN. PARTNER(S) _____
SPECIAL LIMITED PARTNER _____

PREPARED BY _____
DATE _____

NO. UNITS _____
UNIT SIZE $ _____
TOTAL EQUITY RAISED $ _____

PAGE ___ OF ___

PPM #	INVESTOR NAME	ADDRESS	TEL. NO.	SOC. SEC. #	UNDER-WRITER	SALESMAN	BLUE SKY STATE	DATE RECEIVED CHECK	AMOUNT CHECK	# UNITS	COMMENTS
									$		
									$		
									$		
									$		
									$		
									$		
									$		
									$		
									$		
									$		
									$		
									$		
									$		
									$		
									$		
									$		
									$		
									$		
									$		
									$		
									$		

390

FORM 9-3
Blue Sky Clearance

PARTNERSHIP NAME _____   PAGE ___ OF ___
GENERAL PARTNER(S) _____
_____

CO-GEN. PARTNER(S) _____

SPECIAL LIMITED PARTNER _____

DATE _____

NAME OF STATE	FEE	DATE APPLIED	DATE CLEARED	COMMENTS

391

Private Placement Memorandum Tracking Report

PARTNERSHIP NAME _____

GENERAL PARTNER(S) _____

PAGE ___ OF ___

CO-GEN. PARTNER(S) _____

SPECIAL LIMITED PARTNER _____

DATE _____

PPM #	ISSUED TO	ISSUE DATE	RETURN DATE	COMMENTS

392

A COMPLETE GUIDE TO CLOSING THE TRANSACTION

HOW TO SET UP AN EFFICIENT PROPERTY FILE SYSTEM TO KEEP TRACK OF THE TRANSACTION

Once it is clear that the deal is going forward to the closing table, a file system for the transaction should be established to make retrieving documents easier. During the period prior to closing and after the closing, numerous aspects of the transaction will require constant review. The following is a sample format in designing a property file system.

Property File System Outline

1. Pre-acquisition facts
   - *a.* Property facts
   - *b.* Seller's proforma
   - *c.* Rent roll/security deposit
   - *d.* Past operating statements
   - *e.* Demographic information
   - *f.* Chamber of commerce information
   - *g.* Local residential/office guide
   - *h.* Local residential/commercial classified advertisements
   - *i.* Local newspaper articles on area
2. Seller/real estate broker
   - *a.* Seller correspondence
   - *b.* Real estate broker correspondence
3. Financial analysis
   - *a.* Investment information package
   - *b.* Proforma worksheets
4. Property studies
   - *a.* Market studies
   - *b.* Engineering studies

      c. Appraisal

      d. Land comparables

      e. Property management inspection report

      f. Correspondence

5. Photos, maps, brochures, floor plans, site plan

      a. Photos—subject property

      b. Photos—comparables

      c. Photos—neighborhood

      d. Maps—city

      e. Maps—neighborhood

      f. Brochures—subject

      g. Brochures—comparables

      h. Floor plans—subject

      i. Floor plans—comparables

      j. Site plan—subject

6. Contracts/agreements

      a. Letter of intent

      b. Purchase agreement

      c. Development agreement

      d. Management agreement

      e. Earnest money escrow letter

      f. Correspondence

7. Closing documents

      a. Property closing statement

      b. Title insurance

      c. Property survey

      d. Termite bond/report

      e. Utility letters

      f. Tenant estoppel letters

      g. Rent roll/security deposit

      h. Service contracts

      i. Flood plain letters

      j. Fire code letters

      k. Property deed

      l. Seller fee agreements

      m. Zoning letter

      n. Building permit

      o. Correspondence

  8. Partnership agreements

      a. Partnership agreements

      b. Partnership amendments

      c. Subscription booklets

      d. Memorandum

      e. Blue sky

      f. Partnership correspondence

  9. Financing

      a. Potential lenders

      b. Loan package

      c. Lender commitment

      d. Mortgage documents

      e. Loan amortization schedules

      f. Loan closing statement

      g. Lender estoppel letters

      h. Loan broker agreements

      i. Loan broker correspondence

      j. Lender correspondence

10. Management

      a. Budget

      b. Sample copy of management company reports

      c. Weekly traffic reports

      d. Monthly financial statements/variance reports

      e. Property inspection reports

      f. Management contract

      g. Management correspondence

11. Marketing

      a. Budget

      b. Marketing report

      c. Marketing fee agreement

      d. Advertising agency agreement

      e. Marketing company correspondence

      f. Advertising agency correspondence

12. Partnership administration
    a. Quarterly partnership reports
    b. Monthly tracking reports

13. Banking
    a. Bank account—operating
    b. Bank account—partnership
    c. Bank account—security deposit
    d. Bank correspondence

14. Investors
    a. Broker/dealer fee agreements
    b. List of investors
    c. Investor promissory notes
    d. Sample investor letters
    e. Broker/dealer correspondence
    f. Investor correspondence
    g. Blue sky correspondence

15. Accounting
    a. Monthly accounting statements
    b. Property tax returns
    c. Investor tax returns
    d. IRS audit
    e. Accountant fee agreement
    f. Accountant correspondence
    g. IRS correspondence

16. Legal
    a. Litigation
    b. Lawyer fee agreement
    c. Lawyer correspondence

17. Real estate/personal property taxes
    a. Tax assessments
    b. Tax consultant fee agreement
    c. Tax correspondence
    d. Tax consultant correspondence

18. Insurance
    a. Insurance policies
    b. Insurance claims
    c. Insurance agent correspondence

19. Service contracts
    a. Pest
    b. Laundry
    c. Elevator
    d. Landscaping
    e. Mechanical
    f. Vending
    g. Trash
    h. Janitorial
    i. Music
    j. Security
    k. Snow removal
    l. Parking lot sweeping
    m. Maid service
    n. Window washing

20. Inventory
    a. List of inventory/serial numbers
    b. Equipment warranties
    c. Operational manuals

21. Capital improvement
    a. Budget/schedule

22. Architectural, engineering, construction management
    a. Architect fee agreement
    b. Landscape architect fee agreement
    c. Engineer fee agreement
    d. Construction manager fee agreement
    e. Plans and specifications
    f. Soils/seismic tests
    g. Topography survey
    h. Property survey
    i. Color/material selection board
    j. Material brochures
    k. Landscape plans and specifications
    l. Architect correspondence
    m. Engineer correspondence
    n. Landscape architect correspondence
    o. Construction manager correspondence

23. Construction

    a. General contractor resume/financials/references

    b. General contractor contract

    c. Construction budget

    d. Construction draw forms

    e. Construction management reports

    f. Development/building permits

    g. Construction critical path

    h. Construction progress reports

    i. Builder's risk policy

    j. Contractor bond/letter of credit

    k. Change orders

    l. Construction penalty

    m. Lien waivers

    n. Contractor's affidavit

    o. Certificate of occupancies

    p. Lender completion certificate

    q. Punch-out reports

    r. Warranties

    s. List of material/subcontractors

    t. General contractor correspondence

    u. City building department correspondence

24. Resale

    a. List of potential purchasers

    b. Real estate broker fee agreement

    c. Offers

    d. Resale projections

    e. Purchase contract

    f. Closing documents

    g. Closing statement

    h. Lender estoppel letter

    i. Tenant estoppel letter

    j. Pest bond/report

    k. As-built survey

    l. Title insurance

    m. Investor ballot

     n. Inventory

     o. Rent roll/security deposit

     p. Earnest money escrow

     q. Purchase money mortgage

     r. Purchase money mortgage loan schedule

     s. Real estate broker correspondence

     t. Potential purchaser correspondence

     u. Final purchaser correspondence

25. Miscellaneous

     a. Correspondence

SETTING UP THE CLOSING: A CHECKLIST OF "TO DO'S" FOR THE PRINCIPALS INVOLVED

At this point in the deal, the clock is ticking away. The investor or managing partner should be coordinating all of the players to complete their work in order to meet at the closing table.

The investor or managing partner will be extremely busy at this point, constantly checking the progress of each of the team players. This is a period of time in which he will have to be organized and able to keep his team members organized. As the team leader, he alone will have the total picture while each team member will be responsible for one or a few of the pieces of this complex puzzle. By using an organized and systematic approach, he will be able to expedite this progress as well as to avoid potential problems and pitfalls. Since a good team leader should know how to delegate responsibility, he should give each member his assignment, complete with a timetable and then follow up on a daily basis to assure the assignments are being carried out correctly and completely.

The following is a list of activities that each team member should be responsible for during this period.

Investor/Managing Partner/Asset Manager

Some of these functions can be delegated to the asset manager if the purchaser's firm is large enough to require a separate individual to fill that position.

1. Work with each team member to coordinate preclosing activities.

2. Order a tax identification number for the ownership entity.

3. Set up bank accounts for the ownership entity.

4. Review the closing statement and the prorations with the seller.

5. Order the insurance binder for the closing.

6. Make sure the management contract is signed.

7. Make sure the marketing agreement is signed.

8. Make sure that all investors or partners are aware of when the closing will take place.

9. If property is to be syndicated, prepare the following:

   a. Get states to blue sky.

   b. Write "Property Description" section in the Memorandum.

   c. Order maps, pictures, site plan, renderings and floor plan for the memorandum.

   d. Set up investor escrow account at local bank.

   e. Review for investor suitability and sign-off on each Investor Subscription Package.

   f. Order memoranda from local partner.

   g. Log in each investor package and initial contribution on the investor log form.

   h. Endorse and deposit investor checks into the escrow account.

   i. If partnership is using investor note financing, do the following:

      (1) Review all investor note documentation.

      (2) Send original investor promissory note to the note lender.

      (3) Set up investor note payment schedule form.

   j. If partnership is using a surety company to insure the investor note payments, do the following:

      (1) Review all surety company documents.

      (2) Send copy of the investor promissory notes to the surety company.

      (3) Send surety company a copy of the investor note payment schedule form.

Management Company

1. Set up the accounting systems for the property.

2. Set up the bank accounts for the operating account and the security deposit account.

3. Make sure there are no changes in the physical and structural aspects of the property prior to closing.

4. Verify the rent roll and security deposit as of the date of the closing.

5. Review the prorating of all income and expenses as of the date of closing.

6. Review any new leases or service contracts made prior to the closing.

7. Review the rentability of the vacant units or space immediately prior to closing.

8. Review the inventory of the property the day of the closing and check against the inventory in the contract.

9. Make sure all existing tenants are occupying their space.

10. Notify the investor/managing partner of any changes in any of the above items.

Marketing Company

1. Prepare list of potential tenants.

2. Prepare list of potential co-brokers.

3. Finalize marketing plan and budget.

4. Prepare to contract for media placement.

5. Prepare print advertisements and public relations articles.

6. Prepare contracts for advertising, signage, etc.

Money Raiser

1. Coordinate the sale of the investment units.

2. Collect investor subscription agreements and investor contributions.

3. Review investor subscription agreements.

4. Send investor funds to the managing partner for deposit into the escrow account.

Accountant

1. Review accounting forecasts for the property.

2. If the ownership vehicle is a limited partnership, prepare accounting section for the memorandum.

Attorney

1. Prepare to close the real estate.

   a. Review the purchase agreement.

   b. Prepare the closing documents.

   c. Review the closing statement with the management company.

   d. Review all seller fee agreements.

   e. Review the lender and tenant estoppel letters.

   f. Review all property easements.

   g. Review the land survey or the as-built survey.

   h. Review the zoning letter.

   i. Review the utility letters.

   j. Review the escrow agreement.

   k. Review owner's title insurance policy.

   l. Check the final title checkdown.

   m. Review all insurance policies relating to basic liability, automobile, workman's compensation, employer's liability, and umbrella policies.

   n. Review U.C.C. financing statements.

   o. Review property management agreements.

   p. Review satisfaction of existing loans to be paid off.

   q. Review all deeds.

   r. Review commercial leases.

   s. Review service contracts.

2. If the property requires new financing, do the following:

    a. Review closing documents.

    b. Review closing statements.

    c. Review borrower guarantees.

    d. Review assignment of rents to lender.

    e. Review right to have subordinate financing letter.

    f. Review lender's title insurance policy and endorsements.

    g. Review security agreement from borrower to lender.

    h. Review disbursing agreement between borrower, lender, and the escrow agent.

    i. Review letter authorizing purchaser to do business in state.

    j. Review articles of incorporation.

3. If the property requires investor note financing, do the following:

    a. Review the closing documents.

    b. Review the closing statements.

    c. Review borrower guarantees.

4. If the property requires a surety bond by the investor note lender, review the surety bond documents.

5. If the ownership vehicle is going to be a limited partnership, do the following:

    a. Prepare the partnership agreement.

    b. Prepare the broker/dealer agreement.

    c. Prepare the purchaser representative affidavit/purchaser representative letter.

    d. Prepare Form D.

    e. Submit blue sky and amended Form D.

    f. Review qualification of partnership to do business in state.

    g. Review investor subscription package.

    h. Draft general partner letter giving partnership authorization to close.

    i. Review consent of general partner.

    j. Review consent of limited partners.

    k. Draft the memorandum.

    l. Finalize the memorandum with the managing partner and the broker/dealer.

    m. Draft the opinion letter for the memorandum.

6. If the ownership vehicle is going to be a joint venture, do the following:

    a. Prepare the joint venture documents.

    b. Finalize the documents with the venture partner's attorney.

7. If the property is to-be-built, do the following:

> *a.* Review the general contractor's agreement.
>
> *b.* Review the general contractor's bond or letter of credit.
>
> *c.* Review development and building permits.
>
> *d.* Review builder's risk policy.
>
> *e.* Review subcontractor contracts.
>
> *f.* Review architect's certificate letter.
>
> *g.* Review engineer's certificate letter.
>
> *h.* Review waiver and subordination of lien letter.

Architect/Engineer/Construction Manager

1. Review the property inspection report.
2. If the property is to-be-built, review the following:
   - *a.* General contractor's agreement
   - *b.* Builder's risk policy
   - *c.* Subcontractor agreements
   - *d.* Critical path
   - *e.* Construction budget
   - *f.* Architect and engineer agreements
   - *g.* Working drawings and the specifications

HOW TO PREPARE FOR THE CLOSING

The Preclosing Period

A well organized investor or managing partner will have his attorney meet with the seller's attorney and the lender's attorney (if the property requires any new financing) prior to the actual closing. During this period the attorneys will iron out any wrinkles in the transaction. By going through this process, the investor should be able to come to the closing table confident that all should go smoothly.

What to Include in the Closing Statement

The day prior to the actual closing, the purchaser, together with her attorney, should start putting the closing statement together, which is a financial worksheet showing what monies the seller and purchaser are spending for the property. This statement will also reflect any operating prorations that are owed between the buyer and the seller.

Since all of the revenue and expenses might not have been received as of the date of closing, the purchaser and seller should agree to meet in thirty days to re-prorate any new items.

The following is an example of a closing statement for an income property. In this example, the purchaser is paying $1,000,000 for an apartment property. The purchaser has already deposited $10,000 with the title insurance company. The purchaser is getting a new $800,000 first mortgage at 10 percent for thirty years. Since the purchaser is closing this transaction on the twenty-sixth day of the month, the lender will receive $936 for the last four days of the month as interest. The seller is paying off a $750,000 first mortgage at 12 percent and a $50,000 mortgage at 14 percent. The property operating prorations show that the purchaser owes the seller $5,000. The closing statement shows that the purchaser owes $205,586 at the closing while the seller will receive $177,500.

TABLE 10-1

Sample Closing Statement

Gross Amount Due from Borrower (Purchaser)	
Sales Price	$1,000,000
CLosing Costs	$ 14,086
Real Estate Taxes Due	$ 1,500
Gross Amount Due from Borrower	$1,015,586
Earnest Money	$ 10,000
New First Mortgage	$ 800,000
Total	$ 810,000
Cash Due from Purchaser	$ 205,586
Gross Amount Due to Seller	
Sales Price	$1,000,000
Gross Amount Due to Seller	$1,000,000
Closing Costs	$ 22,000
Payoff First Mortgage	$ 750,000
Payoff Second Mortgage	$ 50,000
Real Estate Taxes Due	$ 500
Total Reduction Due from Seller	$ 822,500
Cash Due to Seller	$ 177,500
Closing Costs (Paid by Seller)	
Deed Tax	$ 2,000
Real Estate Commission	$ 15,000
Prorated Property Expenses	$ 5,000
Total Closing Costs—Seller	$ 22,000
Closing Costs (Paid by Purchaser)	
Mortgage Tax	$ 1,500
Recording Tax	$ 500
Loan Points	% 8,000
Lender's Legal	$ 2,000
Title Insurance	$ 1,000
Interest Adjustment (4 days)	$ 936
Survey	$ 150
Total Closing Costs—Purchaser	$ 14,096

At the Closing Table

The day of the closing, the purchaser should arrive an hour early with his attorney to review any last minute changes or problems in the deal. Once the seller and his legal counsel arrive, the closing can take place. If all the parties have properly prepared for the closing, it should proceed smoothly; otherwise, problems may arise. The closing should be the culmination of a lot of hard work by many individuals and should be a pleasant experience.

THE POSTCLOSING CHECKLIST FOR COORDINATING FOLLOW-UP ACTIVITIES

Once all the documents have been signed, there is still much to be done. The investor or managing partner will have to coordinate the postclosing activities with the team players and constantly follow up on those activities. An asset manager, if there is one involved, will oversee these activities. The following is an outline of the postclosing activities.

Investor/Managing Partner/Asset Manager

Some of these functions can be delegated to the asset manager if the purchaser's firm is large enough to require a separate individual to fill that position.

1. Coordinate all the postclosing activities with the team members.

2. Prepare and distribute the postclosing memorandum.

3. File all closing documents in the property file system.

4. Send out investor confirmation letters (see Chapter 12).

5. Make sure that the first month's debt service is paid.

6. Set up property tickler file system.

7. Reimburse seed money advanced to investor or managing general partner.

8. Pay down any lines of credit that were used to secure the property.

9. Pay all fees and bills from the closing proceeds.

10. Send list of investors to accountant.

Management Company

1. Notify existing tenants of the new management company and where to send rent.

2. Notify all utility companies to set up all security deposits and billing information.

3. Notify all existing vendors and establish new accounts in the new owner's name.

4. Prorate any new invoices with seller within thirty to forty-five days of the closing.

5. Set up insurance program for property employees.

6. Start any property improvements that are to be made.

7. If to-be-built property, review the following:
   a. Review the build-out and punch-out of units or tenant space.
   b. Review with the construction manager the twelve-month warranty list.

Marketing Company

Use this checklist if the marketing company is separate from the management company. If not, these responsibilities will be undertaken by the management company.

1. Start advertising program.
2. Send out public relations articles.
3. Send out fliers to area real estate brokers.
4. Start contacting prospective tenants.

Money Raiser

1. Complete review of any remaining investor documentation.
2. Send out letters informing investors that the transaction is completed.

Accountant

1. Reconcile the closing expenses.

Attorney

1. Record all notes, deeds and U.C.C. financing statements.
2. Contact escrow agent to disburse all funds.
3. Bind all documents for the investor or managing partner.
4. Tie up any loose ends from the closing.

Architect/Engineer/Construction Manager

1. Coordinate any property improvements to be made.
2. If property is to-be-built, review the following:
   a. Weekly construction progress
   b. All the construction draws
   c. All the lien waivers
   d. The final punch-out
   e. General contractor's completion letter
   f. The lender's completion certificate
   g. The twelve-month warranty with the management company

POSTCLOSING MEMORANDUM: A COMPLETE RECORD FOR SUCCESSFULLY MANAGING THE PROPERTY

The postclosing memorandum is a document to be used by various members of the team. It will not only include all the information contained in the investor information package, but it will also contain all information needed to manage the property or the partnership in the future. The following is an outline to be used for this memorandum:

Postclosing Memorandum Outline

1. Overview of deal
    a. Summary of the players (name, address, telephone number, contact)
        (1) Seller
        (2) Ownership entity
            (a) General partners
            (b) Special limited partners
            (c) Joint venture partner
        (3) Seller's attorney
        (4) Purchaser's attorney
        (5) Lender
        (6) Lender's attorney
        (7) Note lender
        (8) Note lender's attorney
        (9) Note surety company
        (10) Note surety attorney
        (11) Property management company
        (12) Leasing company
        (13) Architect
        (14) Landscape architect
        (15) Engineer
            (a) Civil
            (b) Structural
            (c) Mechanical
            (d) Electrical
            (e) Plumbing
            (f) Surveyor
            (g) Soils test

       (16) General contractor

          (a) Bonding company

       (17) Construction manager

       (18) Title company

       (19) Accountant

       (20) Money raiser

       (21) Real estate broker

       (22) Mortgage banker/broker

       (23) Appraiser

       (24) Tax consultant

       (25) Insurance company

   b. Summary of Investors

       (1) Name

       (2) Address

       (3) Telephone number

       (4) Social security number

       (5) Number of investment units purchased

       (6) Total dollars invested

       (7) Sales representative

2. Banking information

   a. Property operating account

       (1) Checking account

          (a) Bank name, telephone number, contact

          (b) Account number

          (c) Signatures

          (d) Interest earned

       (2) Money market account

          (a) Bank name, telephone number, contact

          (b) Account number

          (c) Signatures

          (d) Interest earned

   b. Partnership operating account

       (1) Checking account

          (a) Bank name, address, telephone number, contact

          (b) Account number

          (c) Signatures

          (d) Interest earned

        (2) Money market account

            (a) Bank name, address, telephone number, contact

            (b) Account number

            (c) Signatures

            (d) Interest earned

    c. Security deposit escrow account

        (1) Checking account

            (a) Bank name, address, telephone number, contact

            (b) Account number

            (c) Signatures

            (d) Interest earned

        (2) Money market account

            (a) Bank name, address, telephone number, contact

            (b) Account number

            (c) Signatures

            (d) Interest earned

3. Tax identification number

4. Investor call for funds

    a. Dates due

    b. Amount due

    c. Letters to investors due date

        (1) Where to send payments

5. Debt service payment instructions (for each mortgage)

    a. Lender

        (1) Address

        (2) Telephone

        (3) Contact

    b. Surety

        (1) Address

        (2) Telephone

        (3) Contact

    c. Account number

    d. Account debt service paid from

    e. Payment responsibility

        (1) Address

        (2) Telephone number

        (3) Contact

    f. Mortgage payment due date—first payment

    g. Mortgage payment due date

    h. Mortgage payment late date

    i. Monthly payment—amount due

       (1) Payment increase date

          (a) New payment amount

    j. Loan maturity date

    k. Balloon payment amount

    l. Debt service amortization schedule

    m. Lender reporting requirements

       (1) Monthly statements

       (2) Quarterly statements

       (3) Yearly statements

          (a) Audit statements

          (b) Borrower financials

    n. Escrows

       (1) Real estate taxes

       (2) Insurance

6. Real estate tax escrows

    a. Bank

       (1) Type of account

          (a) Checking

          (b) Money market

       (2) Address

       (3) Telephone number

       (4) Contact

    b. Account number

    c. Payment responsibility

    d. Due date

    e. Monthly payment

    f. Interest earned

    g. Tax consultant

       (1) Yearly fee

    h. Local tax department

       (1) Address

       (2) Telephone number

       (3) Contact

    i. Tax account number

    j. Most recent tax statement

    k. Most recent millage rate

    l. Date tax bill due

7. Insurance

    a. Insurance company

        (1) Agent

        (2) Address

        (3) Telephone number

        (4) Contact

    b. Effective date of coverage

    c. Name of insured

    d. Yearly premium

    e. Is premium paid in advance?

    f. Monthly escrow

        (1) Bank

            (a) Address

            (b) Telephone number

            (c) Contact

        (2) Due date

        (3) Interest earned

    g. Policy coverage (dollar amount)

        (1) Liability

        (2) Content

        (3) Rent loss

        (4) Fidelity bond

    h. Renewal date

    i. Copy of policy

8. Reporting requirements (sent by managing partner)

    a. Investors

        (1) Quarterly reports

        (2) Yearly summary

        (3) Tax returns

        (4) Call for funds

    b. Lender

        (1) Monthly cash flow

        (2) Yearly statements

        (3) General partner financials

   c. Money raiser

    (1) Weekly traffic reports

    (2) Monthly cash flow statements

    (3) Quarterly reports

    (4) Yearly summary

9. Reporting requirements (sent by management company)

  a. Weekly traffic reports

  b. Monthly cash flow statements

    (1) Monthly variance reports

  c. Monthly profit and loss statements

  d. Quarterly comparable report

  e. Quarterly property report

  f. Yearly property report

  g. Yearly budget

    (1) Line item summary

    (2) Capital budget summary

10. Partnership service fees

  a. Paid to

  b. Payment due date

  c. Fee amount

  d. Responsibility to send out

11. Deposits

  a. Insurance

  b. Utilities

    (1) Gas

    (2) Electricity

    (3) Water

    (4) Sewer

    (5) Cable TV

    (6) Telephone

    (7) Equipment

    (8) Furniture

12. Service contracts

  a. Landscaping

  b. Janitorial

  c. Laundry

     d. Vending

     e. Tax consulting

     f. Pool

     g. Mechanical

     h. Pest

     i. Trash

     j. Window cleaning

     k. Sprinkler system—landscaping

     l. Sprinkler system—building

     m. Elevator

     n. Parking lot sweeping

     o. Sign maintenance

     p. Vehicle maintenance

     q. Equipment maintenance

     r. Plant maintenance

     s. Security system

     t. Security personnel

13. Inventory (item description, location, serial number, dollar value)

     a. Office

     b. Model

     c. Maintenance shop

     d. Pool area

     e. Units

        (1) Appliances

        (2) Mechanical

14. Builder warranties (if new construction)

     a. Copy of warranty

        (1) Roof

        (2) Plumbing

        (3) Mechanical

        (4) Electrical

        (5) Pool

        (6) Paving

        (7) Landscaping

        (8) Flooring

        (9) Elevator

(10) Sprinkler systems—landscaping

(11) Sprinkler systems—building

(12) Equipment

(13) Appliances

15. Subcontractors (name, address, telephone number, contact)

    a. Mechanical

    b. Electrical

    c. Plumbing

    d. Landscaping

    e. Paving

    f. Drywall

    g. Painting

    h. Wallpaper

    i. Flooring

    j. Cabinets

    k. Pool

    l. Windows

    m. Appliances

    n. Signage

    o. Security system

16. Material identification (manufacturers, model number, color)

    a. Appliances

    b. Cabinets

    c. Flooring

    d. Paint

    e. Wallpaper

    f. Lighting

    g. Landscaping

    h. Signage

    i. Bathroom fixtures

    j. Security system

17. Operating manuals (copies)

    a. Appliances

    b. HVAC

    c. Hot water heater

    d. Pool

    e. Sprinkler—landscaping

    f. Sprinkler—building

    g. Elevator

    h. Security system

18.　Seller warranties (copies)

    a. Rent-up guarantee

    b. Negative cash flow

    c. Construction completion

19.　Rent roll/security deposit schedule (from closing statement)

20.　Closing statement

    a. Property closing

    b. Mortgage closings

21.　Reconciliation of purchaser closing costs

    a. Payee

    b. Amount

    c. Check number

    d. Date

    e. Explanation

22.　Completion certification letter from lender (if new construction)

23.　Lien waiver release at closing (if new construction)

24.　Construction penalty computation (if new construction)

25.　Copies of all certificates of occupancy (if new construction)

26.　Date tickler file (date, amount, responsibility, comments)

    a. Property information

    b. Investor call for funds

    c. Payments to sellers

    d. Note financing payments

    e. Cash flow distributions

    f. Debt service extension payments

    g. Loan maturities

    h. Seller guarantees

    i. Lender reporting

    j. Partnership reporting

      k. Tax returns

      l. Insurance renewals

     m. Real estate taxes

     n. Fees receivable

     o. Miscellaneous

27. Copy of investor information package

How ASSET MANAGEMENT WORKS: PRACTICAL TIPS FOR NEW AND EXPERIENCED INVESTORS

The intent of this chapter is to describe the asset management process and its duties. This chapter will not deal with how to manage the property per se, but rather will discuss how to oversee the management company that has been hired for that purpose. A small investor, basically a one-man operation, will have to handle the asset management function personally. As the responsibility becomes greater, the investor will probably hire an individual in either a full-time or part-time capacity.

The owner who decides to hire an asset manager should seek an individual who possesses experience and skills in the types of properties that are to be managed. This individual should have strong interpersonal communication skills, analytical and accounting skills, and hands-on practical management skills. The investor should advertise and interview various individuals and contact local management companies in the area to find out who might be looking for this type of position. Since this individual is really the eyes and the ears of the owner, the investor should have great confidence in this person.

Since the asset manager might have a large number of properties to oversee, he should standardize his reporting system and have the various property management firms report to him with his set of forms. This will make his job easier and will help in comparing and analyzing the properties that he oversees. It must be remembered that he is the one who is paying the management firms and that if they want to manage for him they should conform to his systems.

EIGHT KEY FUNCTIONS OF THE ASSET MANAGER

1. Oversee Management Company

The asset management function is to be the owner's representative and to oversee all aspects of property ownership. The asset manager should design a set of policy procedures and paperwork to be used to handle the flow of data that will need to be analyzed. The following is a list of items that the asset manager will review and report to the owner:

1. Weekly traffic reports

2. Monthly financial statements

3. Quarterly reports

4. Annual budget

5. Proposed capital expenditures

6. Quarterly comparable studies

7. Property tax assessments

8. Management policies and procedures

   a. Rent rates

   b. Lease terms

   c. Security deposits

   d. Pet policy and deposit/fee

   e. Application fee

   f. Cleaning fee

   g. Late fee

   h. Lease options and terms

   i. Credit approval policy

   j. Office hours

   k. Real estate commissions

   l. Job descriptions

   m. Dress code

   n. Employee salary and benefits

2. Oversee Marketing Company

This includes review of the following:

1. Marketing plans

2. Marketing budgets

3. New leases and their terms

3. Oversee Construction Manager

This includes review of the following:

1. Property improvements with the construction manager

2. Commercial tenant budget and construction schedules

4. Review All Investor Correspondence

This involves handling all the correspondence with the investment partners.

5. Conduct Property Inspections

The property should be inspected on a regular basis.

6. Handle All Lender Correspondence

7. Review All Insurance Requirements

This includes the following:

1. Annual review of the insurance coverage for the property with the management company

2. Annual review of the insurance needs of the ownership entity

8. Review Partnership Business

You should:

1. Correspond with investor partners.

2. Pay managing partner monthly partnership servicing fees.

3. Pay all note financing debt servicing.

4. Send out all investor returns.

HOW CAREFUL MANAGEMENT HELPS INCREASE YOUR PROPERTY'S VALUE

The main point of the asset management process is to help create an increased value for the property; this comes from careful management, tight controls, creative thinking, inflation, and a bit of luck. It must be remembered that since value is determined by the income stream, every additional dollar that falls to the bottom line helps to increase the value of the property. The following methods are used to create an increase in value.

Renovation

A property that is in need of renovation work, either structural or cosmetic, can be refurbished. The dollars spent for this work will then be returned by increased rental rates to the existing tenants or from prospective new tenants.

Change in Use

Many times properties, due to their age or poor initial planning, will have to be readapted to other uses. A creative asset manager should be able to analyze the current use of a property and to see other uses that will increase its value.

Tightening Management Controls

As rental rates rise and expenses fall, the net operating income will increase. Since property is valued as a function of this income, the asset manager must find ways to increase the revenues while decreasing or eliminating any unnecessary expenditures.

Finding a Higher Caliber of Tenants

Once the quality of a property has been raised through renovation, a more favorable environment exists for potential tenants, tenants whose standards would not have been met by the property in its original condition. Thus, the asset manager should now be able to find a higher caliber of tenant for the existing space. Due to the property improvements, these tenants should be willing to pay more rent. This increase in rents will help increase the property's value.

Offering New Tenant Services

Additional rental income could be obtained by adding new services. For example, an office building could add valet parking or a health club to the property which will entice a higher caliber of tenant who is willing to pay a higher monthly rental rate to obtain those services.

Adding Rental Space to the Property

If the property has additional undeveloped land, building additional rental space will help increase the value due to increased revenues. This additional space should not increase proportionately the expense ratio, since the expenses will be spread over a larger base and there will be some economies of scale for these expenses.

Adding New Profit Centers

A creative asset manager can increase revenues by adding new profit centers. This revenue can be generated through a laundry room, vending machines, or charging for parking. The asset manager should analyze the needs of the current tenants and check out the competition to determine what new profit centers can be added to the property.

Refinancing

Due to the increase in the net operating income or a reduction in the current mortgage rates, the property might be in a position to refinance the current debt with a new mortgage at better rates and terms. This refinancing can help increase the cash flow and also put some tax-free cash into the owner's pocket.

Resale

While any or all of the above methods can increase revenues and thereby cash flow to the investor, their greatest value is through the final resale of the property. This is when investors reap the rewards for their labors—their profits. The asset manager should be knowledgeable about current property values to assist the owner in determining the best time to sell the property and maximize the overall return.

ASSET MANAGEMENT FORMS

Weekly Summary of Operations Form

This is a three page form that will show the asset manager at a glance what is happening on the property on a weekly basis. This information will help the asset manager to spot trends as they are happening. It includes information on the following subjects:

f. Capital improvement budget

g. General ledger

h. Rent roll reconciliation

i. Rent roll development—recap

j. Delinquency detail listing

k. Schedule of rent and policy

l. Property tracking report

4. Receipt of partnership servicing fees

5. Quarterly comparable study

6. Quarterly partnership letters

7. Property inspection visits

8. Property tickler system

9. Annual inventory

10. Annual financial comparison analysis

11. Annual budget

12. Annual tax returns

13. Tax return audit report

14. Investor call for funds

15. Monthly Seller Financing Tracking Report

Investor Payment Schedule

This form tracks the collection of the investor contributions.

Partnership Information

This form helps keep track of the partners in the deal.

Fee Payment Schedule

This form helps keep track of the fees due the managing partner and the money raiser.

FORM 11-1
Weekly Summary of Operations

PROPERTY NAME _____ OPERATING MONTH _____ YEAR _____ PREPARED BY _____

DATE _____

PAGE _____ OF _____

OCCUPANCY:

	UNITS/SQ. FT.	%
BEGINNING OF MONTH	_____	_____%
ADD: MOVE-INS	_____	_____%
DEDUCT: MOVE-OUTS	_____	_____%
END OF MONTH	_____	_____%
CHANGE	_____	_____%

RENTALS:

OCCUPIED	_____	_____%
OCCUPIED—FREE RENT	_____	_____%
OCCUPIED—NONREVENUE	_____	_____%
VACANT—LEASED	_____	_____%
VACANT—AVAILABLE	_____	_____%
TOTAL	_____	100%

UNIT MIX:

CODE	# UNITS	TYPE	BD/BA	SQ. FT.	STREET RENT	LAST RENT INCREASE	# VACANT
1	_____	_____	_____	_____	$_____	_____	_____
2	_____	_____	_____	_____	$_____	_____	_____
3	_____	_____	_____	_____	$_____	_____	_____
4	_____	_____	_____	_____	$_____	_____	_____
5	_____	_____	_____	_____	$_____	_____	_____
6	_____	_____	_____	_____	$_____	_____	_____
7	_____	_____	_____	_____	$_____	_____	_____
8	_____	_____	_____	_____	$_____	_____	_____
9	_____	_____	_____	_____	$_____	_____	_____
TOTAL	_____				$_____		_____

SOURCE OF TRAFFIC:

	TRAFFIC	CALLS	LEASED
DRIVE BY	_____	_____	_____
NEWSPAPER	_____	_____	_____
MAGAZINE	_____	_____	_____
RADIO	_____	_____	_____
TELEVISION	_____	_____	_____
BILLBOARD	_____	_____	_____
YELLOW PAGES	_____	_____	_____
REAL ESTATE BROKER	_____	_____	_____
DIRECT MAIL	_____	_____	_____
APT. LOCATORS	_____	_____	_____
COLD CALL	_____	_____	_____
OTHER _____	_____	_____	_____
TOTAL	_____	_____	_____

ADVERTISING:

DAY	WALK-IN	CALLS	WEATHER
SUN	_____	_____	_____
MON	_____	_____	_____
TUE	_____	_____	_____
WED	_____	_____	_____
THUR	_____	_____	_____
FRI	_____	_____	_____
SAT	_____	_____	_____
TOTAL	_____	_____	

REASONS FOR MOVE-OUTS:

CODE	DESCRIPTION	NUMBER TENANTS	SQ. FT.
A	NEED MORE SPACE	_____	_____
B	NEED LESS SPACE	_____	_____
C	SKIPPED	_____	_____
D	DID NOT LIKE UNIT	_____	_____
E	BUSINESS TRANSFER	_____	_____
F	PROPERTY TRANSFER	_____	_____
G	GETTING MARRIED	_____	_____
H	PURCHASED HOME/CONDO	_____	_____
I	CLOSER TO WORK	_____	_____
J	RENT INCREASE	_____	_____
K	EVICTION	_____	_____
L	GOING OUT OF BUSINESS	_____	_____
M	OTHER _____	_____	_____
N		_____	_____
O		_____	_____
P		_____	_____

NONREVENUE UNITS:

# SUITE	CODE	SQ. FT.	STREET RENT/MO.	COMMENTS
_____	_____	_____	$_____	_____
_____	_____	_____	$_____	_____
_____	_____	_____	$_____	_____
_____	_____	_____	$_____	_____
_____	_____	_____	$_____	_____
TOTAL		_____	$_____	

Weekly Summary of Operations (Cont'd)

PROPERTY NAME _____

PAGE _____ OF _____

OPERATING MONTH _____

PREPARED BY _____

YEAR _____

DATE _____

NO.	SUITE #	UNIT MIX CODE	SQ. FT.	STREET RENT	DATE VACATED	DATE READY	SUITE #	UNIT MIX CODE	DATE RENTED	MOVE-IN DATE	RENT/ MONTH	SQ. FT.	SUITE #	REASON CODE	UNIT MIX CODE	MOVE-OUT DATE
		VACANCIES							PRELEASED					MOVE-OUT NOTICES		
1				$							$					
2				$							$					
3				$							$					
4				$							$					
5				$							$					
6				$							$					
7				$							$					
8				$							$					
9				$							$					
10				$							$					
11				$							$					
12				$							$					
13				$							$					
14				$							$					
15				$							$					
16				$							$					
17				$							$					
18				$							$					
19				$							$					
20				$							$					
21				$							$					
22				$							$					
23				$							$					
24				$							$					
25				$							$					
26				$							$					
27				$							$					
28				$							$					
29				$							$					
30				$							$					
31				$							$					
32				$							$					
33				$							$					
34				$							$					
35				$							$					
TOTAL				$			TOTAL				$		TOTAL			

Form 11-1
Weekly Summary of Operations (Cont'd)

PROPERTY NAME _____ OPERATING MONTH _____ YEAR _____ PREPARED BY _____

PAGE _____ OF _____ DATE _____

RECEIVABLES

DESCRIPTION	WEEK	MONTH
CURRENT RENT	$	$
DELINQ. RENT	$	$
ADVANCE RENT	$	$
PERCENTAGE RENT	$	$
LATE CHARGES	$	$
NSF CHARGES	$	$
OTHER:	$	$
	$	$
	$	$
	$	$
TOTAL	$	$

DELINQUENCY REPORT: STARTS ON THE 5TH OF THE MONTH:

NO.	SUITE #	AMOUNT DUE	DATE PROMISED	COMMENTS
1		$		
2		$		
3		$		
4		$		
5		$		
6		$		
7		$		
8		$		
9		$		
10		$		
11		$		
12		$		
13		$		
14		$		
15		$		
16		$		
17		$		
18		$		
19		$		
20		$		
21		$		
22		$		
23		$		
24		$		
TOTAL		$		

DAILY BANK DEPOSITS

DATE	TOTAL AMOUNT	RENT	MISC.
1	$	$	
2	$	$	
3	$	$	
4	$	$	
5	$	$	
6	$	$	
7	$	$	
8	$	$	
9	$	$	
10	$	$	
11	$	$	
12	$	$	
13	$	$	
14	$	$	
15	$	$	
16	$	$	
17	$	$	
18	$	$	
19	$	$	
20	$	$	
21	$	$	
22	$	$	
23	$	$	
24	$	$	
25	$	$	
26	$	$	
27	$	$	
28	$	$	
29	$	$	
30	$	$	
31	$	$	
TOTAL	$	$	

FORM 11-2(A)
Residential Prospect Report

PROPERTY NAME _____
WEEK OF _____
PREPARED BY _____

PAGE _____ OF _____

NAME	ADDRESS	TEL. NO.	DATE	PRESENT UNIT SIZE	LEASE EXPIRES	TYPE UNIT NEEDED	UNIT (S) SHOWN	MARKETING SOURCE	DATE NEEDED	RATE QUOTED	TERM QUOTED	RENT CONCESSIONS	COMMENTS
										$			
										$			
										$			
										$			
										$			
										$			
										$			
										$			
										$			
										$			
										$			
										$			
										$			
										$			
										$			
										$			
										$			
										$			

427

FORM 11-2(B)
Commercial Prospect Report

PROPERTY NAME _____

WEEK OF _____

PREPARED BY _____

PAGE _____ OF _____

CODE: TENANT PAYS FOR:

1 GAS	4 SEWER
2 ELECTRICITY	5 INSURANCE
3 WATER	6 R.E. TAXES

| 7 MAINTENANCE |
| 8 JANITORIAL |
| 9 CAM |

TYPE PROPERTY:

RETAIL _____

OFFICE _____

INDUSTRIAL _____

COMPANY NAME/CONTACT ADDRESS/TEL. NO.	DATE	PRESENT SQ. FT.	SPACE SHOWN	MARKETING SOURCE	DATE NEEDED	RATE QUOTED	PERCENT RENT	TERM QUOTED	OPTIONS	RENT ESCAL.	TENANT ALLOWANCE	TENANT PAYS FOR	OPERATING PASSTHROUGH	CAM CHARGES	SECURITY DEPOSIT	RENT CONCESSION	BROKER/ COMMISSION
						$	%				$		$	$			%
						$	%				$		$	$			%
						$	%				$		$	$			%
						$	%				$		$	$			%
						$	%				$		$	$			%
						$	%				$		$	$			%
						$	%				$		$	$			%
						$	%				$		$	$			%
						$	%				$		$	$			%
						$	%				$		$	$			%
						$	%				$		$	$			%
						$	%				$		$	$			%
						$	%				$		$	$			%
						$	%				$		$	$			%
						$	%				$		$	$			%
						$	%				$		$	$			%
						$	%				$		$	$			%
						$	%				$		$	$			%
						$	%				$		$	$			%
						$	%				$		$	$			%
						$	%				$		$	$			%
						$	%				$		$	$			%
						$	%				$		$	$			%

428

FORM 11-3(A)
Property Monthly Financial Tracking Report

PROPERTY: _____
GENERAL PARTNER: _____
ASSET MANAGER: _____
PREPARED BY: _____

NUMBER OF UNITS: _____ SQ. FT.: _____
MANAGEMENT CO: _____
ADDRESS: _____

TELEPHONE NO:( ) _____
PROPERTY MGR: _____
PROPERTY TEL. NO:( ) _____

YEAR: _____
PAGE _____ OF _____

PROPERTY OPERATING ACCOUNT:

DESCRIPTION	LAST YEAR	JAN	FEB	MAR	APR	MAY	JUN	JUL	AUG	SEP	OCT	NOV	DEC	TOTAL
LEASED ACTUAL	%	%	%	%	%	%	%	%	%	%	%	%	%	%
OCCUPANCY ACTUAL	%	%	%	%	%	%	%	%	%	%	%	%	%	%
BUDGETED OCCUPANCY	%	%	%	%	%	%	%	%	%	%	%	%	%	%
PPM	%	%	%	%	%	%	%	%	%	%	%	%	%	%
REVENUE														
ACTUAL	$	$	$	$	$	$	$	$	$	$	$	$	$	$
BUDGETED	$	$	$	$	$	$	$	$	$	$	$	$	$	$
VARIANCE	$	$	$	$	$	$	$	$	$	$	$	$	$	$
OPERATING EXPENSES														
ACTUAL	$	$	$	$	$	$	$	$	$	$	$	$	$	$
BUDGETED	$	$	$	$	$	$	$	$	$	$	$	$	$	$
VARIANCE	$	$	$	$	$	$	$	$	$	$	$	$	$	$
NET OPERATING INCOME														
ACTUAL	$	$	$	$	$	$	$	$	$	$	$	$	$	$
BUDGETED	$	$	$	$	$	$	$	$	$	$	$	$	$	$
VARIANCE	$	$	$	$	$	$	$	$	$	$	$	$	$	$
NOI CUMULATIVE														
ACTUAL	$	$	$	$	$	$	$	$	$	$	$	$	$	$
BUDGETED	$	$	$	$	$	$	$	$	$	$	$	$	$	$
VARIANCE	$	$	$	$	$	$	$	$	$	$	$	$	$	$
PPM	$	$	$	$	$	$	$	$	$	$	$	$	$	$

429

FORM 11-3(A)

Property Monthly Financial Tracking Report (Cont'd)

DESCRIPTION	LAST YEAR	JAN	FEB	MAR	APR	MAY	JUN	JUL	AUG	SEP	OCT	NOV	DEC	TOTAL
DEBT SERVICE														
ACTUAL	$	$	$	$	$	$	$	$	$	$	$	$	$	$
BUDGETED	$	$	$	$	$	$	$	$	$	$	$	$	$	$
VARIANCE	$	$	$	$	$	$	$	$	$	$	$	$	$	$
PPM	$	$												$
CASH FLOW TO WORKING CAPITAL														
ACTUAL	$	$	$	$	$	$	$	$	$	$	$	$	$	$
BUDGETED	$	$	$	$	$	$	$	$	$	$	$	$	$	$
VARIANCE	$	$	$	$	$	$	$	$	$	$	$	$	$	$
CUMULATIVE CASH FLOW TO WORKING CAPITAL														
ACTUAL	$	$	$	$	$	$	$	$	$	$	$	$	$	$
BUDGETED	$	$	$	$	$	$	$	$	$	$	$	$	$	$
VARIANCE	$	$	$	$	$	$	$	$	$	$	$	$	$	$
PPM	$	$												$
ACTUAL/PPM VAR.	$	$												$
CAPITAL EXPENDITURES														
ACTUAL	$	$	$	$	$	$	$	$	$	$	$	$	$	$
BUDGETED	$	$	$	$	$	$	$	$	$	$	$	$	$	$
VARIANCE	$	$	$	$	$	$	$	$	$	$	$	$	$	$
PPM	$	$												$
ACTUAL/PPM VAR.	$	$												$
TOTAL NET CASH FLOW														
ACTUAL	$	$	$	$	$	$	$	$	$	$	$	$	$	$
BUDGETED	$	$	$	$	$	$	$	$	$	$	$	$	$	$
VARIANCE	$	$	$	$	$	$	$	$	$	$	$	$	$	$
PPM	$	$												$
ACTUAL/PPM VAR.	$	$												$
ENDING BANK BALANCE	$	$	$	$	$	$	$	$	$	$	$	$	$	$

430

FORM 11-3(B)

Sources and Applications of Funds

PAGE OF _____ OF _____

DESCRIPTION	LAST YEAR	JAN	FEB	MAR	APR	MAY	JUN	JUL	AUG	SEP	OCT	NOV	DEC	TOTAL
SOURCES OF FUNDS:														
RENTAL	$	$	$	$	$	$	$	$	$	$	$	$	$	$
MISC. RENTAL INCOME	$	$	$	$	$	$	$	$	$	$	$	$	$	$
FEES	$	$	$	$	$	$	$	$	$	$	$	$	$	$
CAPITAL CONTRIBUTIONS	$	$	$	$	$	$	$	$	$	$	$	$	$	$
LOANS	$	$	$	$	$	$	$	$	$	$	$	$	$	$
BUYER DEPOSITS	$	$	$	$	$	$	$	$	$	$	$	$	$	$
SALES	$	$	$	$	$	$	$	$	$	$	$	$	$	$
	$	$	$	$	$	$	$	$	$	$	$	$	$	$
	$	$	$	$	$	$	$	$	$	$	$	$	$	$
TOTAL SOURCES OF FUNDS	$	$	$	$	$	$	$	$	$	$	$	$	$	$
APPLICATIONS OF FUNDS:														
CLOSING COSTS	$	$	$	$	$	$	$	$	$	$	$	$	$	$
LOAN CLOSING COSTS	$	$	$	$	$	$	$	$	$	$	$	$	$	$
OPERATING EXPENSES	$	$	$	$	$	$	$	$	$	$	$	$	$	$
RESALE COSTS	$	$	$	$	$	$	$	$	$	$	$	$	$	$
PARTNERSHIP COSTS	$	$	$	$	$	$	$	$	$	$	$	$	$	$
DEBT SERVICE	$	$	$	$	$	$	$	$	$	$	$	$	$	$
	$	$	$	$	$	$	$	$	$	$	$	$	$	$
	$	$	$	$	$	$	$	$	$	$	$	$	$	$
TOTAL APPLICATIONS OF FUNDS	$	$	$	$	$	$	$	$	$	$	$	$	$	$
ENDING BALANCE	$	$	$	$	$	$	$	$	$	$	$	$	$	$
SECURITY DEPOSITS	$	$	$	$	$	$	$	$	$	$	$	$	$	$
BANK BALANCES:														
PROPERTY—CHECKING	$	$	$	$	$	$	$	$	$	$	$	$	$	$
PROPERTY—SAVINGS	$	$	$	$	$	$	$	$	$	$	$	$	$	$
PARTNERSHIP—CHECKING	$	$	$	$	$	$	$	$	$	$	$	$	$	$
PARTNERSHIP—SAVINGS	$	$	$	$	$	$	$	$	$	$	$	$	$	$
	$	$	$	$	$	$	$	$	$	$	$	$	$	$
TOTAL BANK BALANCES	$	$	$	$	$	$	$	$	$	$	$	$	$	$

431

FORM 11-3(c)
Investment Summary

PAGE OF _____ OF _____

DESCRIPTION	LAST YEAR	JAN	FEB	MAR	APR	MAY	JUN	JUL	AUG	SEP	OCT	NOV	DEC	TOTAL
SOURCES OF FUNDS:														
RENTAL														
MISC. RENTAL INCOME														
FEES														
CAPITAL CONTRIBUTIONS														
LOANS														
BUYER DEPOSITS														
SALES														
TOTAL SOURCES OF FUNDS														
APPLICATIONS OF FUNDS:														
CLOSING COSTS														
LOAN CLOSING COSTS														
OPERATING EXPENSES														
RESALE COSTS														
PARTNERSHIP COSTS														
DEBT SERVICE														
TOTAL APPLICATIONS OF FUNDS														
ENDING BALANCE														
SECURITY DEPOSITS														
BANK BALANCES:														
PROPERTY—CHECKING														
PROPERTY—SAVINGS														
PARTNERSHIP—CHECKING														
PARTNERSHIP—SAVINGS														
TOTAL BANK BALANCES														

432

FORM 11-3(D)
Rent Schedule

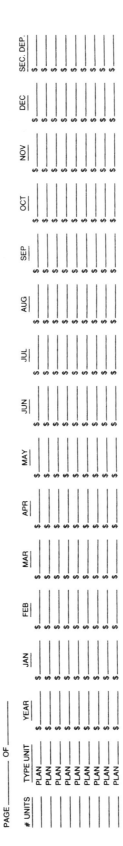

PAGE _____ OF _____

# UNITS	TYPE UNIT	YEAR	JAN	FEB	MAR	APR	MAY	JUN	JUL	AUG	SEP	OCT	NOV	DEC	SEC. DEP.
_____	PLAN _____	$ _____	$ _____	$ _____	$ _____	$ _____	$ _____	$ _____	$ _____	$ _____	$ _____	$ _____	$ _____	$ _____	$ _____
_____	PLAN _____	$ _____	$ _____	$ _____	$ _____	$ _____	$ _____	$ _____	$ _____	$ _____	$ _____	$ _____	$ _____	$ _____	$ _____
_____	PLAN _____	$ _____	$ _____	$ _____	$ _____	$ _____	$ _____	$ _____	$ _____	$ _____	$ _____	$ _____	$ _____	$ _____	$ _____
_____	PLAN _____	$ _____	$ _____	$ _____	$ _____	$ _____	$ _____	$ _____	$ _____	$ _____	$ _____	$ _____	$ _____	$ _____	$ _____
_____	PLAN _____	$ _____	$ _____	$ _____	$ _____	$ _____	$ _____	$ _____	$ _____	$ _____	$ _____	$ _____	$ _____	$ _____	$ _____
_____	PLAN _____	$ _____	$ _____	$ _____	$ _____	$ _____	$ _____	$ _____	$ _____	$ _____	$ _____	$ _____	$ _____	$ _____	$ _____
_____	PLAN _____	$ _____	$ _____	$ _____	$ _____	$ _____	$ _____	$ _____	$ _____	$ _____	$ _____	$ _____	$ _____	$ _____	$ _____
_____	PLAN _____	$ _____	$ _____	$ _____	$ _____	$ _____	$ _____	$ _____	$ _____	$ _____	$ _____	$ _____	$ _____	$ _____	$ _____

433

Date Tickler System

PAGE _____ OF _____

DATE/ACTIVITY:	CALL FOR FUNDS	PAYMENTS TO SELLERS	INF PAYMENTS	L.P. CASH DISTRIB	G.P. FEES RECEIVABLE	MONEY RAISER FEES RECEIVABLE	WORKING CAPITAL CONTRIBUTION
JANUARY	$	$	$	$	$	$	$
FEBRUARY	$	$	$	$	$	$	$
MARCH	$	$	$	$	$	$	$
APRIL	$	$	$	$	$	$	$
MAY	$	$	$	$	$	$	$
JUNE	$	$	$	$	$	$	$
JULY	$	$	$	$	$	$	$
AUGUST	$	$	$	$	$	$	$
SEPTEMBER	$	$	$	$	$	$	$
OCTOBER	$	$	$	$	$	$	$
NOVEMBER	$	$	$	$	$	$	$
DECEMBER	$	$	$	$	$	$	$
TOTAL	$	$	$	$	$	$	$

DATE/ACTIVITY:	DEBT SVC. EXT. DATE	LOAN MATURITIES	NEGATIVE CASH FLOW GUARANTEES	LENDER REPORTING	QUARTERLY PARTNERSHIP REPORTING	TAX RETURNS	NEW BUDGET	QUARTERLY COMPARABLES	REVIEW INSURANCE	REVIEW R.E. TAXES	COLLECT ADM. SVC. G.P. FEES
JANUARY											
FEBRUARY											
MARCH											
APRIL											
MAY											
JUNE											
JULY											
AUGUST											
SEPTEMBER											
OCTOBER											
NOVEMBER											
DECEMBER											

PAGE _____ OF _____

NOTES: (INCLUDE INFORMATION ON MARKETING, PUNCH-OUT, LEGAL, ETC.)

JANUARY:

FEBRUARY:

MARCH:

APRIL:

MAY:

JUNE:

JULY:

AUGUST:

SEPTEMBER:

OCTOBER:

NOVEMBER:

DECEMBER:

NEXT YEAR:

435

Statement of Income and Expenses—Summary

PROPERTY NAME _____   MONTH _____   PREPARED BY _____

ADDRESS _____   YEAR _____

_____

MANAGEMENT _____   PAGE _____ OF _____

TEL. NO.( ) _____   DATE PREPARED _____

DESCRIPTION	CURRENT MONTH			YEAR TO DATE		
	ACTUAL	BUDGET	VARIANCE	ACTUAL	BUDGET	VARIANCE
REVENUE:						
GROSS POTENTIAL INCOME (GPI)	$_____	$_____	$_____	$_____	$_____	$_____
VACANCY	$_____	$_____	$_____	$_____	$_____	$_____
UNCOLLECTIBLES	$_____	$_____	$_____	$_____	$_____	$_____
MISC. INCOME _____	$_____	$_____	$_____	$_____	$_____	$_____
MISC. INCOME _____	$_____	$_____	$_____	$_____	$_____	$_____
MISC. INCOME _____	$_____	$_____	$_____	$_____	$_____	$_____
MISC. INCOME _____	$_____	$_____	$_____	$_____	$_____	$_____
EFFECTIVE GROSS INCOME (EGI)	$_____	$_____	$_____	$_____	$_____	$_____
OPERATING EXPENSES:						
SALARIES & WAGES	$_____	$_____	$_____	$_____	$_____	$_____
REPAIRS & MAINTENANCE	$_____	$_____	$_____	$_____	$_____	$_____
TAXES	$_____	$_____	$_____	$_____	$_____	$_____
INSURANCE	$_____	$_____	$_____	$_____	$_____	$_____
GENERAL & ADMINISTRATIVE	$_____	$_____	$_____	$_____	$_____	$_____
MANAGEMENT FEES	$_____	$_____	$_____	$_____	$_____	$_____
PROFESSIONAL FEES	$_____	$_____	$_____	$_____	$_____	$_____
MARKETING	$_____	$_____	$_____	$_____	$_____	$_____
CONTRACT SERVICES	$_____	$_____	$_____	$_____	$_____	$_____
SUPPLIES	$_____	$_____	$_____	$_____	$_____	$_____
UNIT MAINTENANCE	$_____	$_____	$_____	$_____	$_____	$_____
DEPOSITS & BONDS	$_____	$_____	$_____	$_____	$_____	$_____
BANKING	$_____	$_____	$_____	$_____	$_____	$_____
RESERVES & REPLACEMENTS	$_____	$_____	$_____	$_____	$_____	$_____
TOTAL OPERATING EXPENSES	$_____	$_____	$_____	$_____	$_____	$_____
NET OPERATING INCOME (NOI)	$_____	$_____	$_____	$_____	$_____	$_____
DEBT SERVICE:						
FIRST MORTGAGE	$_____	$_____	$_____	$_____	$_____	$_____
SECOND MORTGAGE	$_____	$_____	$_____	$_____	$_____	$_____
MISC. MORTGAGE	$_____	$_____	$_____	$_____	$_____	$_____
MISC. MORTGAGE	$_____	$_____	$_____	$_____	$_____	$_____
TOTAL DEBT SERVICE	$_____	$_____	$_____	$_____	$_____	$_____
CASH FLOW	$_____	$_____	$_____	$_____	$_____	$_____
CAPITAL EXPENDITURES	$_____	$_____	$_____	$_____	$_____	$_____
CASH FLOW AFTER CAP. EXP.	$_____	$_____	$_____	$_____	$_____	$_____

FORM 11-5
Property Visit Report

PROPERTY NAME _____   GRADING SYSTEM:
PREPARED BY _____   1. EXCELLENT   4. POOR   TOTAL POINTS _____
DATE OF VISIT _____   2. VERY GOOD   5. VERY POOR   AVERAGE _____
PAGE _____ OF _____   3. GOOD

DESCRIPTION	CONDITION	APPEARANCE	FUNCTION	DESCRIPTION	CONDITION	APPEARANCE	FUNCTION
SITE:				INTERIOR:			
CURB APPEAL				LOBBY			
SIGNAGE				HALLWAYS			
LANDSCAPING				STAIRWELLS			
RETENTION PONDS				JANITORIAL AREAS			
PAVING				TRASH AREA			
SIDEWALKS				LIGHTING			
TRASH AREAS				CLEANLINESS			
STRIPPING				GENERAL APPEARANCE			
FENCING							
POOL AREAS							
TENNIS COURTS							
GENERAL APPEARANCE							
				INTERIOR SPACE:			
				WALLS			
				FLOORING			
				DOORS			
				CEILING			
EXTERIOR:				WINDOW COVERINGS			
EXTERIOR FACADE				APPLIANCES			
PAINT				CLEANLINESS			
GUTTERS							
ROOFS							
STEPS							
RAILINGS							
DOORS				MANAGEMENT STAFF & FACILITIES:			
PARKING FACILITIES				STAFF—APPEARANCE			
GENERAL APPEARANCE				STAFF—ATTITUDE			
				LEASING OFFICE			
				MODEL			
				CLUBHOUSE			
				MAINTENANCE AREA			
TOTAL							

COMMENTS:

_____
_____
_____
_____
_____
_____
_____

437

FORM 11-6

Commercial Lease Summary

PROPERTY NAME _____ BUSINESS _____ ADDRESS _____ TEL. NO. ( ) _____
LESSEE _____ CONTACT _____ TAX I.D. NO. _____

LEASE INFORMATION:
LEASED REVIEWED BY _____ LEASE TERM _____ END LEASE DATE _____ RENT INCREASES:
LEASED APPROVED BY _____ MOVE-IN DATE _____ ESCALATION DATE _____ ESCALATION/YR. _____
DATE LEASE SIGNED _____ BEG. LEASE DATE _____ ESCALATION/YR _____
SUITE # _____

SQUARE FOOTAGE: RENTAL RATE: PERCENTAGE RENTS:
GROSS SQ. FT. _____ BASE RENT/SQ. FT. $ _____ END DATE _____
NET SQ. FT. _____ BASE RENT/MONTH $ _____ BREAKPOINT $ _____

OPERATING EXPENSES
PARKING: PASSTHROUGH: RENEWAL/EXPANSION OPTIONS: TERMINATION CLAUSE:
PARKING RATE/MONTH $ _____ BASE YEAR _____ NOTIFICATION DATE _____ DATE _____
NO. PARKING SPACES: FREE _____ TAXES _____ NO. OPTIONS _____ PENALTY _____
NO. PARKING SPACES: PAID _____ INSURANCE _____ TERM: _____
RATE: _____
EXPANSION SQ. FT. _____

SECURITY DEPOSIT: UTILITIES PAID BY LESSEE: SERVICES PAID BY LESSOR:
SECURITY DEPOSIT $ _____ GAS _____ JANITORIAL _____
DATE RECEIVED _____ ELECTRICITY _____ NO. DAYS/WEEK _____
SEC. DEP. HELD BY _____ WATER _____ MAINTENANCE _____
INTEREST EARNED: YES __ NO __ SEWER _____
RATE EARNED ___ %

R.E. COMMISSION:
BROKER _____ ADDRESS _____ COMMISSION _____

AGENT _____ TEL. NO. ( ) _____

LESSEE CREDIT CHECK:
BANK REFERENCE: BANK REFERENCE: BUSINESS REFERENCE: BUSINESS REFERENCE:
BANK _____ BANK _____ BANK _____ BANK _____
CONTACT _____ CONTACT _____ CONTACT _____ CONTACT _____
TEL. NO. ( ) _____ TEL. NO. ( ) _____ TEL. NO. ( ) _____ TEL. NO. ( ) _____
CREDIT RATING _____ CREDIT RATING _____ CREDIT RATING _____ CREDIT RATING _____

DUN & BRADSTREET _____ LOCAL CREDIT _____ CREDIT APPROVED BY _____

ESTIMATED CONSTRUCTION COSTS:
ALLOWANCE $ _____ COST/SQ. FT. $ _____ LESSEE TO PAY EXTRA COST OF $ _____
TOTAL COST $ _____ COST/SQ. FT. $ _____ BY CASH $ _____
DIFFERENCE $ _____ COST/SQ. FT. $ _____ AMORTIZATION $ _____
TERM _____ RATE _____ %

MOVE-IN INFORMATION:
RENT COMMENCEMENT DATE _____ DIRECTORY LISTING _____ INSPECTION REPORT _____
SUITE # _____ SIGN INSTALLED _____ APPROVED BY _____
TENANT INFO PACKAGE ISSUED _____ PARKING PERMITS _____ KEYS ISSUED _____ NO. _____

438

Financial Comparison Analysis

PREPARED BY _____

PROPERTY NAME _____ PAGE _____ OF _____   REVIEWED BY _____

NO. UNITS _____ DATE _____   APPROVED BY _____

UNIT SIZE _____

G.P. SPLIT _____

SPECIAL L.P. SPLIT _____ %

L.P. SPLIT _____ %

YEAR _____

	ORIGINALLY PROJECTED	BUDGET	ACTUAL	VARIANCE PROJ.- BUDG.	VARIANCE PROJ. ACTUAL.	VARIANCE BUDG. ACT.	COMMENTS
RENTAL INCOME	$_____	$_____	$_____	$_____	$_____	$_____	_____
MISC. INCOME	$_____	$_____	$_____	$_____	$_____	$_____	_____
INTEREST INCOME	$_____	$_____	$_____	$_____	$_____	$_____	_____
EFFECTIVE GROSS INCOME	$_____	$_____	$_____	$_____	$_____	$_____	
OPERATING EXPENSES	$_____	$_____	$_____	$_____	$_____	$_____	_____
NET OPERATING INCOME	$_____	$_____	$_____	$_____	$_____	$_____	
DEBT SERVICE: (DESCRIBE)							
_____	$_____	$_____	$_____	$_____	$_____	$_____	_____
_____	$_____	$_____	$_____	$_____	$_____	$_____	_____
_____	$_____	$_____	$_____	$_____	$_____	$_____	_____
_____	$_____	$_____	$_____	$_____	$_____	$_____	_____
_____	$_____	$_____	$_____	$_____	$_____	$_____	_____
CASH FLOW	$_____	$_____	$_____	$_____	$_____	$_____	_____
CAPITAL EXPENDITURES	$_____	$_____	$_____	$_____	$_____	$_____	_____
NET PROPERTY CASH FLOW	$_____	$_____	$_____	$_____	$_____	$_____	_____
PARTNERSHIP EXPENSES: (DESCRIBE)							
_____	$_____	$_____	$_____	$_____	$_____	$_____	_____
_____	$_____	$_____	$_____	$_____	$_____	$_____	_____
_____	$_____	$_____	$_____	$_____	$_____	$_____	_____
_____	$_____	$_____	$_____	$_____	$_____	$_____	_____
_____	$_____	$_____	$_____	$_____	$_____	$_____	_____
TOTAL NET SPENDABLE CASH FLOW	$_____	$_____	$_____	$_____	$_____	$_____	_____
PARTNERSHIP CASH FLOW DISTRIBUTION	$_____	$_____	$_____	$_____	$_____	$_____	_____
GENERAL PARTNER C.F. DISTRIBUTION	$_____	$_____	$_____	$_____	$_____	$_____	_____
LIMITED PARTNER C.F. DISTRIBUTION	$_____	$_____	$_____	$_____	$_____	$_____	_____
L.P. CASH FLOW DISTRIB. PER UNIT	$_____	$_____	$_____	$_____	$_____	$_____	_____
PARTNER CONTRIBUTIONS	$_____	$_____	$_____	$_____	$_____	$_____	_____

Investor Call for Funds

PREPARED BY _____
YEAR _____

PROPERTY	JAN	FEB	MAR	APR	MAY	JUN	JUL	AUG	SEP	OCT	NOV	DEC	TOTAL	COMMENTS
	$	$	$	$	$	$	$	$	$	$	$	$	$	
	$	$	$	$	$	$	$	$	$	$	$	$	$	
	$	$	$	$	$	$	$	$	$	$	$	$	$	
	$	$	$	$	$	$	$	$	$	$	$	$	$	
	$	$	$	$	$	$	$	$	$	$	$	$	$	
	$	$	$	$	$	$	$	$	$	$	$	$	$	
	$	$	$	$	$	$	$	$	$	$	$	$	$	
	$	$	$	$	$	$	$	$	$	$	$	$	$	
	$	$	$	$	$	$	$	$	$	$	$	$	$	
	$	$	$	$	$	$	$	$	$	$	$	$	$	
	$	$	$	$	$	$	$	$	$	$	$	$	$	
	$	$	$	$	$	$	$	$	$	$	$	$	$	
	$	$	$	$	$	$	$	$	$	$	$	$	$	
	$	$	$	$	$	$	$	$	$	$	$	$	$	
	$	$	$	$	$	$	$	$	$	$	$	$	$	
	$	$	$	$	$	$	$	$	$	$	$	$	$	
	$	$	$	$	$	$	$	$	$	$	$	$	$	
	$	$	$	$	$	$	$	$	$	$	$	$	$	
	$	$	$	$	$	$	$	$	$	$	$	$	$	
	$	$	$	$	$	$	$	$	$	$	$	$	$	
	$	$	$	$	$	$	$	$	$	$	$	$	$	
	$	$	$	$	$	$	$	$	$	$	$	$	$	
	$	$	$	$	$	$	$	$	$	$	$	$	$	
	$	$	$	$	$	$	$	$	$	$	$	$	$	
	$	$	$	$	$	$	$	$	$	$	$	$	$	
	$	$	$	$	$	$	$	$	$	$	$	$	$	
	$	$	$	$	$	$	$	$	$	$	$	$	$	
	$	$	$	$	$	$	$	$	$	$	$	$	$	
	$	$	$	$	$	$	$	$	$	$	$	$	$	
	$	$	$	$	$	$	$	$	$	$	$	$	$	
	$	$	$	$	$	$	$	$	$	$	$	$	$	
	$	$	$	$	$	$	$	$	$	$	$	$	$	

Internal Revenue Service Tax Audit

PROPERTY NAME _____

PARTNERSHIP NAME _____   IRS AUDIT _____

MANAGING PARTNER _____   DATE NOTIFIED _____

CPA FIRM _____   YEAR _____

_____   AGENT _____

ADDRESS _____   ADDRESS _____

_____

TEL. NO. (   ) _____   TEL. NO. (   ) _____

SUMMMARY OF AUDIT _____

_____

_____

_____

_____

_____

_____

DATE CPA NOTIFIED _____

DATE ENGAGEMENT LETTER RECEIVED _____

COST ESTIMATE $ _____

BILLING: WEEKLY _____ MONTHLY _____

ACTUAL COST $ _____

IRS CORRESPONDENCE

    DATE   COMMENTS

_____   _____

_____   _____

_____   _____

_____   _____

_____   _____

_____   _____

_____   _____

_____   _____

_____   _____

_____   _____

_____   _____

_____   _____

_____   _____

FINAL OUTCOME: DATE _____   AMOUNT TAXES TO BE PAID $ _____   TAXABLE INCOME (LOSS) $ _____

_____

_____

_____

_____

_____

_____

Seller Financing Tracking Report

PREPARED BY _____

PROPERTY NAME _____

MORTGAGEE _____
CONTACT _____
ADDRESS _____

TEL. NO. ( ) _____

ORIGINAL MORTGAGE BALANCE $ _____
INTEREST RATE _____ %
AMORTIZATION PERIOD _____
MATURITY DATE _____
LOAN BALANCE DUE $ _____

YEAR _____

	PAYMENT	OPERATING STATEMENT
JAN	$	
FEB	$	
MAR	$	
APR	$	
MAY	$	
JUN	$	
JUL	$	
AUG	$	
SEP	$	
OCT	$	
NOV	$	
DEC	$	
TOTAL	$	

YEAR _____

	PAYMENT	OPERATING STATEMENT
JAN	$	
FEB	$	
MAR	$	
APR	$	
MAY	$	
JUN	$	
JUL	$	
AUG	$	
SEP	$	
OCT	$	
NOV	$	
DEC	$	
TOTAL	$	

YEAR _____

	PAYMENT	OPERATING STATEMENT
JAN	$	
FEB	$	
MAR	$	
APR	$	
MAY	$	
JUN	$	
JUL	$	
AUG	$	
SEP	$	
OCT	$	
NOV	$	
DEC	$	
TOTAL	$	

YEAR _____

	PAYMENT	OPERATING STATEMENT
JAN	$	
FEB	$	
MAR	$	
APR	$	
MAY	$	
JUN	$	
JUL	$	
AUG	$	
SEP	$	
OCT	$	
NOV	$	
DEC	$	
TOTAL	$	

YEAR _____

	PAYMENT	OPERATING STATEMENT
JAN	$	
FEB	$	
MAR	$	
APR	$	
MAY	$	
JUN	$	
JUL	$	
AUG	$	
SEP	$	
OCT	$	
NOV	$	
DEC	$	
TOTAL	$	

YEAR _____

	PAYMENT	OPERATING STATEMENT
JAN	$	
FEB	$	
MAR	$	
APR	$	
MAY	$	
JUN	$	
JUL	$	
AUG	$	
SEP	$	
OCT	$	
NOV	$	
DEC	$	
TOTAL	$	

Accounting of All Asset Management Reports

PROPERTY NAME _____ PREPARED BY _____ YEAR _____

PROPERTY REPORTS:

1 WEEKLY SUMMARY OF OPERATIONS	6 QUARTERLY PARTNERSHIP LETTERS	11 YEARLY BUDGET
2 WEEKLY PROSPECT REPORT	7 PROPERTY INSPECTION VISITS	12 YEARLY TAX RETURN
3 MONTHLY PROPERTY TRACKING REPORT	8 PROPERTY TICKLER SYSTEM	13 TAX RETURN AUDIT REPORT
4 RECEIPT OF PARTNERSHIP SERVICING FEES	9 YEARLY INVENTORY	14 INVESTOR CALL FOR FUNDS
5 QUARTERLY COMPARABLE STUDY	10 YEARLY FINANCIAL COMPARISON ANALYSIS	15 MONTHLY SELLER FINANCING TRACKING REPORT

WEEK OF/PROPERTY _____

SUMMARY OF OPERATIONS:

WEEK OF _____
WEEK OF _____
WEEK OF _____
WEEK OF _____
WEEK OF _____
WEEK OF _____
WEEK OF _____
WEEK OF _____
WEEK OF _____
WEEK OF _____
WEEK OF _____
WEEK OF _____
WEEK OF _____
WEEK OF _____
WEEK OF _____
WEEK OF _____
WEEK OF _____
WEEK OF _____
WEEK OF _____
WEEK OF _____
WEEK OF _____
WEEK OF _____
WEEK OF _____
WEEK OF _____
WEEK OF _____
WEEK OF _____
WEEK OF _____
WEEK OF _____
WEEK OF _____
WEEK OF _____
WEEK OF _____
WEEK OF _____
WEEK OF _____
WEEK OF _____
WEEK OF _____
WEEK OF _____
WEEK OF _____
WEEK OF _____
WEEK OF _____
WEEK OF _____
WEEK OF _____
WEEK OF _____
WEEK OF _____
WEEK OF _____
WEEK OF _____
WEEK OF _____
WEEK OF _____
WEEK OF _____

Accounting of All Asset Management Reports (Cont'd)

YEAR _____ PAGE ____ OF ____

WEEK OF/PROPERTY   ____ ____ ____ ____ ____ ____ ____ ____ ____ ____ ____

PROSPECT REPORTS:
WEEK OF _____   ____ ____ ____ ____ ____ ____ ____ ____ ____ ____ ____
WEEK OF _____   ____ ____ ____ ____ ____ ____ ____ ____ ____ ____ ____
WEEK OF _____   ____ ____ ____ ____ ____ ____ ____ ____ ____ ____ ____
WEEK OF _____   ____ ____ ____ ____ ____ ____ ____ ____ ____ ____ ____
WEEK OF _____   ____ ____ ____ ____ ____ ____ ____ ____ ____ ____ ____
WEEK OF _____   ____ ____ ____ ____ ____ ____ ____ ____ ____ ____ ____
WEEK OF _____   ____ ____ ____ ____ ____ ____ ____ ____ ____ ____ ____
WEEK OF _____   ____ ____ ____ ____ ____ ____ ____ ____ ____ ____ ____
WEEK OF _____   ____ ____ ____ ____ ____ ____ ____ ____ ____ ____ ____
WEEK OF _____   ____ ____ ____ ____ ____ ____ ____ ____ ____ ____ ____
WEEK OF _____   ____ ____ ____ ____ ____ ____ ____ ____ ____ ____ ____
WEEK OF _____   ____ ____ ____ ____ ____ ____ ____ ____ ____ ____ ____
WEEK OF _____   ____ ____ ____ ____ ____ ____ ____ ____ ____ ____ ____
WEEK OF _____   ____ ____ ____ ____ ____ ____ ____ ____ ____ ____ ____
WEEK OF _____   ____ ____ ____ ____ ____ ____ ____ ____ ____ ____ ____
WEEK OF _____   ____ ____ ____ ____ ____ ____ ____ ____ ____ ____ ____
WEEK OF _____   ____ ____ ____ ____ ____ ____ ____ ____ ____ ____ ____
WEEK OF _____   ____ ____ ____ ____ ____ ____ ____ ____ ____ ____ ____
WEEK OF _____   ____ ____ ____ ____ ____ ____ ____ ____ ____ ____ ____
WEEK OF _____   ____ ____ ____ ____ ____ ____ ____ ____ ____ ____ ____
WEEK OF _____   ____ ____ ____ ____ ____ ____ ____ ____ ____ ____ ____
WEEK OF _____   ____ ____ ____ ____ ____ ____ ____ ____ ____ ____ ____
WEEK OF _____   ____ ____ ____ ____ ____ ____ ____ ____ ____ ____ ____
WEEK OF _____   ____ ____ ____ ____ ____ ____ ____ ____ ____ ____ ____
WEEK OF _____   ____ ____ ____ ____ ____ ____ ____ ____ ____ ____ ____
WEEK OF _____   ____ ____ ____ ____ ____ ____ ____ ____ ____ ____ ____
WEEK OF _____   ____ ____ ____ ____ ____ ____ ____ ____ ____ ____ ____
WEEK OF _____   ____ ____ ____ ____ ____ ____ ____ ____ ____ ____ ____
WEEK OF _____   ____ ____ ____ ____ ____ ____ ____ ____ ____ ____ ____
WEEK OF _____   ____ ____ ____ ____ ____ ____ ____ ____ ____ ____ ____
WEEK OF _____   ____ ____ ____ ____ ____ ____ ____ ____ ____ ____ ____
WEEK OF _____   ____ ____ ____ ____ ____ ____ ____ ____ ____ ____ ____
WEEK OF _____   ____ ____ ____ ____ ____ ____ ____ ____ ____ ____ ____
WEEK OF _____   ____ ____ ____ ____ ____ ____ ____ ____ ____ ____ ____
WEEK OF _____   ____ ____ ____ ____ ____ ____ ____ ____ ____ ____ ____
WEEK OF _____   ____ ____ ____ ____ ____ ____ ____ ____ ____ ____ ____
WEEK OF _____   ____ ____ ____ ____ ____ ____ ____ ____ ____ ____ ____
WEEK OF _____   ____ ____ ____ ____ ____ ____ ____ ____ ____ ____ ____
WEEK OF _____   ____ ____ ____ ____ ____ ____ ____ ____ ____ ____ ____
WEEK OF _____   ____ ____ ____ ____ ____ ____ ____ ____ ____ ____ ____
WEEK OF _____   ____ ____ ____ ____ ____ ____ ____ ____ ____ ____ ____
WEEK OF _____   ____ ____ ____ ____ ____ ____ ____ ____ ____ ____ ____
WEEK OF _____   ____ ____ ____ ____ ____ ____ ____ ____ ____ ____ ____
WEEK OF _____   ____ ____ ____ ____ ____ ____ ____ ____ ____ ____ ____
WEEK OF _____   ____ ____ ____ ____ ____ ____ ____ ____ ____ ____ ____
WEEK OF _____   ____ ____ ____ ____ ____ ____ ____ ____ ____ ____ ____
WEEK OF _____   ____ ____ ____ ____ ____ ____ ____ ____ ____ ____ ____

Accounting of All Asset Management Reports (Cont'd)

YEAR _____ PAGE ____ OF ____

REPORT/PROPERTY

OPERATING STATEMENTS:

JANUARY

FEBRUARY

MARCH

APRIL

MAY

JUNE

JULY

AUGUST

SEPTEMBER

OCTOBER

NOVEMBER

DECEMBER

PARTNERSHIP SERVICE FEES:

JANUARY

FEBRUARY

MARCH

APRIL

MAY

JUNE

JULY

AUGUST

SEPTEMBER

OCTOBER

NOVEMBER

DECEMBER

1ST QTR. COMPS.

2ND QTR. COMPS.

3RD QTR. COMPS.

4TH QTR. COMPS.

1ST QTR. PARTNERSHIP
LETTER

2ND QTR. PARTNERSHIP
LETTER

3RD QTR. PARTNERSHIP
LETTER

4TH QTR. PARTNERSHIP
LETTER

PROPERTY INSPECTION VISITS: (DATES)

JANUARY

FEBRUARY

MARCH

APRIL

MAY

JUNE

JULY

AUGUST

SEPTEMBER

OCTOBER

NOVEMBER

DECEMBER

445

FORM 11-11

Accounting of All Asset Management Reports (Cont'd)

YEAR_____ PAGE ____ OF _____

REPORT/PROPERTY _____ _____ _____ _____ _____ _____ _____ _____ _____ _____ _____
PROPERTY TICKLER
SYSTEM:
   JANUARY _____ _____ _____ _____ _____ _____ _____ _____ _____ _____ _____
   FEBRUARY _____ _____ _____ _____ _____ _____ _____ _____ _____ _____ _____
   MARCH _____ _____ _____ _____ _____ _____ _____ _____ _____ _____ _____
   APRIL _____ _____ _____ _____ _____ _____ _____ _____ _____ _____ _____
   MAY _____ _____ _____ _____ _____ _____ _____ _____ _____ _____ _____
   JUNE _____ _____ _____ _____ _____ _____ _____ _____ _____ _____ _____
   JULY _____ _____ _____ _____ _____ _____ _____ _____ _____ _____ _____
   AUGUST _____ _____ _____ _____ _____ _____ _____ _____ _____ _____ _____
   SEPTEMBER _____ _____ _____ _____ _____ _____ _____ _____ _____ _____ _____
   OCTOBER _____ _____ _____ _____ _____ _____ _____ _____ _____ _____ _____
   NOVEMBER _____ _____ _____ _____ _____ _____ _____ _____ _____ _____ _____
   DECEMBER _____ _____ _____ _____ _____ _____ _____ _____ _____ _____ _____

INVENTORY _____ _____ _____ _____ _____ _____ _____ _____ _____ _____ _____

FINANCIAL COMPARISON _____ _____ _____ _____ _____ _____ _____ _____ _____ _____ _____
ANALYSIS

YEARLY BUDGET _____ _____ _____ _____ _____ _____ _____ _____ _____ _____ _____

YEARLY TAX RETURNS _____ _____ _____ _____ _____ _____ _____ _____ _____ _____ _____

TAX RETURN AUDIT _____ _____ _____ _____ _____ _____ _____ _____ _____ _____ _____
REPORT
INVESTOR CALL FOR _____ _____ _____ _____ _____ _____ _____ _____ _____ _____ _____
FUNDS
MONTHLY SELLER FINANC-
   ING TRACKING REPORTS _____ _____ _____ _____ _____ _____ _____ _____ _____ _____ _____

FORM 11-12
Investor Payment Schedule

PROPERTY NAME
PREPARED BY
UNITS____ UNIT SIZE____
PAGE____ OF____

NAME OF INVESTOR	# UNITS	TOTAL INVESTMENT	DATE	DATE	DATE	DATE	DATE	DATE	DATE	DATE	DATE	DATE	DATE
		$	$	$	$	$	$	$	$	$	$	$	$
		$	$	$	$	$	$	$	$	$	$	$	$
		$	$	$	$	$	$	$	$	$	$	$	$
		$	$	$	$	$	$	$	$	$	$	$	$
		$	$	$	$	$	$	$	$	$	$	$	$
		$	$	$	$	$	$	$	$	$	$	$	$
		$	$	$	$	$	$	$	$	$	$	$	$
		$	$	$	$	$	$	$	$	$	$	$	$
		$	$	$	$	$	$	$	$	$	$	$	$
		$	$	$	$	$	$	$	$	$	$	$	$
		$	$	$	$	$	$	$	$	$	$	$	$
		$	$	$	$	$	$	$	$	$	$	$	$
		$	$	$	$	$	$	$	$	$	$	$	$
		$	$	$	$	$	$	$	$	$	$	$	$
TOTAL		$	$	$	$	$	$	$	$	$	$	$	$

447

FORM 11-13
Partnership Information

PROPERTY NAME _____
ENTITY NAME _____
PREPARED BY _____
DATE _____
PAGE _____ OF _____

PARTNERS	NAME	ADDRESS	TEL. NO.	COMMENTS
GENERAL PARTNER (S)	_____	_____	( ) _____	_____
	_____	_____	( ) _____	_____
	_____	_____	( ) _____	_____
	_____	_____	( ) _____	_____
CO-GEN. PARTNER (S)	_____	_____	( ) _____	_____
	_____	_____	( ) _____	_____
	_____	_____	( ) _____	_____
SPEC. LTD. PARTNER (S)	_____	_____	( ) _____	_____
	_____	_____	( ) _____	_____
	_____	_____	( ) _____	_____
EQUITY RAISER (S)	_____	_____	( ) _____	_____
	_____	_____	( ) _____	_____
	_____	_____	( ) _____	_____
	_____	_____	( ) _____	_____
	_____	_____	( ) _____	_____
INVESTOR (S)	_____	_____	( ) _____	_____
	_____	_____	( ) _____	_____
	_____	_____	( ) _____	_____
	_____	_____	( ) _____	_____
	_____	_____	( ) _____	_____
	_____	_____	( ) _____	_____
	_____	_____	( ) _____	_____
	_____	_____	( ) _____	_____
	_____	_____	( ) _____	_____
	_____	_____	( ) _____	_____
	_____	_____	( ) _____	_____
	_____	_____	( ) _____	_____
	_____	_____	( ) _____	_____
	_____	_____	( ) _____	_____
	_____	_____	( ) _____	_____
	_____	_____	( ) _____	_____
	_____	_____	( ) _____	_____
	_____	_____	( ) _____	_____
	_____	_____	( ) _____	_____
	_____	_____	( ) _____	_____
	_____	_____	( ) _____	_____

Fee Payment Schedule

PROPERTY NAME _____
ENTITY NAME _____
PREPARED BY _____
DATE _____

PAGE ____ OF _____

DATE:
DESCRIPTION/FEE

GENERAL PARTNER FEES	AMOUNT	AMOUNT	AMOUNT	AMOUNT	AMOUNT	AMOUNT	AMOUNT	AMOUNT	AMOUNT	AMOUNT	AMOUNT	AMOUNT
_____	$____	$____	$____	$____	$____	$____	$____	$____	$____	$____	$____	$____
_____	$____	$____	$____	$____	$____	$____	$____	$____	$____	$____	$____	$____
_____	$____	$____	$____	$____	$____	$____	$____	$____	$____	$____	$____	$____
_____	$____	$____	$____	$____	$____	$____	$____	$____	$____	$____	$____	$____
_____	$____	$____	$____	$____	$____	$____	$____	$____	$____	$____	$____	$____
_____	$____	$____	$____	$____	$____	$____	$____	$____	$____	$____	$____	$____
_____	$____	$____	$____	$____	$____	$____	$____	$____	$____	$____	$____	$____
_____	$____	$____	$____	$____	$____	$____	$____	$____	$____	$____	$____	$____
_____	$____	$____	$____	$____	$____	$____	$____	$____	$____	$____	$____	$____
_____	$____	$____	$____	$____	$____	$____	$____	$____	$____	$____	$____	$____
TOTAL	$____	$____	$____	$____	$____	$____	$____	$____	$____	$____	$____	$____

EQUITY RAISER FEES

	AMOUNT	AMOUNT	AMOUNT	AMOUNT	AMOUNT	AMOUNT	AMOUNT	AMOUNT	AMOUNT	AMOUNT	AMOUNT	AMOUNT
_____	$____	$____	$____	$____	$____	$____	$____	$____	$____	$____	$____	$____
_____	$____	$____	$____	$____	$____	$____	$____	$____	$____	$____	$____	$____
_____	$____	$____	$____	$____	$____	$____	$____	$____	$____	$____	$____	$____
_____	$____	$____	$____	$____	$____	$____	$____	$____	$____	$____	$____	$____
_____	$____	$____	$____	$____	$____	$____	$____	$____	$____	$____	$____	$____
_____	$____	$____	$____	$____	$____	$____	$____	$____	$____	$____	$____	$____
_____	$____	$____	$____	$____	$____	$____	$____	$____	$____	$____	$____	$____
TOTAL	$____	$____	$____	$____	$____	$____	$____	$____	$____	$____	$____	$____

PARTNERSHIP ADMINISTRATIVE SERVICE FEE:
_____ % OF THE COLLECTED INCOME/MONTH
$ _____ FLAT FEE/MONTH
DUE ON THE _____DAY OF THE MONTH

SEND ALL FEES TO:
_____
_____
_____
_____
_____
_____

449

Chapter 12

INVESTOR CORRESPONDENCE: SAMPLE LETTERS AND FORMS

If the decision is made to bring in outside investors, whether they be passive or active partners, the managing partner should have a set program for corresponding to these investors at specific times.

The following are sample letters that could be used to keep each investor informed of the activities of the property and the partnership. Please bear in mind that these are intended to provide general guidelines, and must be adapted to the particular needs of each investor or partnership.

- **Partnership Confirmation Letter.** This letter will inform the investor whose subscription package and check have been received and reviewed.

- **Partnership Investor Note Financing Loan Letter.** This letter is sent to the investor note lender.

- **Bank Escrow Letter.** This letter should be sent with the investor checks to the bank that will escrow these funds prior to closing.

- **Limited Partner Call for Funds Letter.** This letter should be used to notify the investors of the upcoming investor funding.

- **Limited Partner Call for Funds—Follow-up Letter.** This letter should be used if the investor has not responded to the original call for funds letter.

- **Cash Distribution Letter.** This letter should be used to accompany the investor distribution check.

- **Quarterly Property and Partnership Status Letter.** This letter should be used as a guide in reporting to the investors on the property progress in the previous quarter.

- **K-1 Tax Return Letter.** This letter should be used to accompany the yearly partnership K-1 tax return.

- **IRS Audit Letter.** This letter should be used to notify the investors of a pending IRS tax audit. It will also include instructions on how to respond to the IRS questionnaire.

- **IRS Protest Letter.** This letter should be sent by the investor or accountant to the IRS to protest the audit.

- **Instructions for IRS Questionnaire.** This exhibit contains instructions for the IRS questionnaire.

- **IRS Questionnaire.** This questionnaire should be completed by the investor and sent to the managing general partner.

- **IRS Follow-up Letter.** This letter should be used as a follow up to the original IRS audit letter.

- **Resale Ballot Letter.** This letter should be used to notify the investors of a proposed resale offer. A ballot on which the investor accepts or rejects the offer will be included.

- **Exhibit A—Estimated Sources and Applications of Funds at Closing.** This exhibit shows the investor the estimated cash distribution schedule at the closing.

- **Exhibit B—Summary of Cash Flow and Taxable Income per Investment Unit.** This exhibit shows the investor a summary of the overall investment during the total investment period.

- **Ballot.** This exhibit is a sample resale ballot to be used to poll the investment partners in a resale.

- **Certificate.** This exhibit should be sent to the managing partner with the resale ballot.

PARTNERSHIP CONFIRMATION LETTER

DATE

NAME
ADDRESS
CITY, STATE, ZIP CODE

RE: PARTNERSHIP NAME

Dear Partner:

This letter is to confirm that your subscription package and initial contribution to the above mentioned partnership have been received and accepted. We are pleased to inform you that the acquisition of the (property name) was completed on (date) as scheduled. Enclosed for your files is a copy of the recorded admission amendment with the signature page which evidences your ownership in the partnership. Also, we are enclosing a list of all the limited partners in this investment.

Your total investment will be $_____$. Your initial subscription payment of $_____$ has been received along with the following promissory notes:

Due on _____ in the amount of $_____$
Due on _____ in the amount of $_____$

As described in the private placement memorandum, the promissory note you signed to the partnership has been assigned to (name of note lender) as collateral for the investor note financing loan. Enclosed is a letter acknowledging this obligation and assignment. Will you please sign the letter at the circled red "X" and return it in the enclosed envelope. We will then present these letters in one package to the lender for their records. *The return of these letters is a requirement of the lender, so we ask that you mail your letter back to us right away.* Your General Partner will contact you thirty days prior to any investor contributions to be made regarding the procedure for making these payments to the partnership.

Your General Partner will be reporting a property and partnership status report on a quarterly basis starting on (date). The tax accounting for the partnership should be completed near the end of February each year, and we anticipate having the Schedule 1065 K-1 forms in your hands shortly thereafter to help you prepare your individual tax returns.

Your name and address given on your subscription package have been entered into our records. Should you wish to receive your correspondence at another address, should you move, or should you have any other changes or additions you would like made in connection with the partnership's mailing list, please write or telephone (contact name) of our office.

Thank you for your participation in (partnership name). Should you have any questions, please do not hesitate to call.

Sincerely,

General Partner

Enc.

PARTNERSHIP INVESTOR NOTE FINANCING LETTER

DATE

BANK NOTE
ADDRESS
CITY, STATE, ZIP CODE

RE: PARTNERSHIP INVESTOR NOTE FINANCING LOAN
    PARTNERSHIP NAME

Gentlemen:

In this transaction, I acknowledge that you ("the Bank") are acting solely as a lender to the Partnership and not as an investment advisor; that the Bank has made no representations to me concerning my intended investment or persons involved; and that the Bank has given me no opinion or advice whether or not it is prudent for me to invest funds as intended. In making this intended investment, I am not relying in any way upon the Bank's role as a lender to me or to other investors or upon any knowledge the Bank may have with respect to my intended investment or the Partnership in which I am investing. I understand and acknowledge that I will be personally liable for the repayment of the promissory note in the amount of $_____ (representing a total of $_____ per unit of partnership interest) delivered to the Partnership, out of my earnings or other assets, in accordance with the terms of such promissory note, whether or not there is any return on my intended investment and regardless of whether my intended investment results in a gain or a loss.

Sincerely,

Signature

Name:
(Please type or print)

BANK ESCROW LETTER

DATE

BANK NAME
ADDRESS
CITY, STATE, ZIP CODE

RE: PARTNERSHIP NAME

Dear _____:

Enclosed please find (number of checks) checks to be deposited in the above referenced partnership escrow account. These checks represent the following:

INVESTOR NAME   # UNITS   AMOUNT OF CHECK

The beginning balance prior to this deposit was $_____. With these checks totaling $_____, the new balance should be $_____.

As other checks come in they will be forwarded to you.

Please sign below to indicate that you have received the above funds and return this letter to me for our records.

Sincerely,

RECEIVED THIS _____ DAY OF _____ 19 ____

BY:

General Partner

Enc.

LIMITED PARTNER CALL FOR FUNDS LETTER

DATE

NAME
ADDRESS
CITY, STATE, ZIP CODE

RE: PROMISSORY NOTE OF $_____
    PARTNERSHIP NAME

Dear Partner:

This letter is to remind you that the above mentioned promissory note in the amount of $_____ executed by you in connection with the purchase of your limited partnership interest in (partnership name) is due no later than (date).

Please make your check payable to (partnership name) and return your payment in the enclosed envelope.

The notes were assigned to (name of note lender) to obtain additional financing as outlined in the private placement memorandum.

Thank you for your participation in (partnership name).

Sincerely,

General Partner

Enc.

LIMITED PARTNER CALL FOR FUNDS: FOLLOW-UP LETTER

DATE

NAME
ADDRESS
CITY, STATE, ZIP CODE

RE: PROMISSORY NOTE OF $_____
    PARTNERSHIP NAME

Dear Partner:

This letter is to notify you that your payment on the promissory note you executed to (partnership name), dated (date), in the amount of $_____, is now past due.

Please make your check payable to (partnership name) and return your payment in the enclosed envelope.

Time is of the essence for the payment of this note. Your general partner wishes to advise you that the terms of this note give for the holder the right to accrue interest on overdue principal. Further, the terms of this note provide for appropriate legal action to be taken, if needed, at your expense. These features are designed into the partnership agreement and each promissory note in the best interest of the partnership and for the protection of each investor.

Your general partner, of course, prefers not to exercise these options. However, in our fiduciary capacity your general partner must take action to protect the partnership if your payment is not received immediately.

If your records indicate that you have made this payment, please contact our office at (_____). Again, your general partner stresses the importance of immediate payment.

Sincerely,

General Partner

Enc.

CASH DISTRIBUTION LETTER

DATE

NAME
ADDRESS
CITY, STATE, ZIP CODE

RE: PARTNERSHIP NAME

Dear Partner:

Operations for (partnership name) performed well during the _____ quarter of this year. Accordingly, enclosed is a check in the amount of $_____ ($_____ per limited partnership investment unit) representing your cash distribution. A summary of the total distribution to the partnership is enclosed.

Thank you for your participation in (partnership name). If you have any questions, please feel free to contact us.

Sincerely,

General Partner

Enc.

QUARTERLY PROPERTY AND PARTNERSHIP STATUS LETTER

DATE

NAME
ADDRESS
CITY, STATE, ZIP CODE

RE: PARTNERSHIP NAME

Dear Partner:

The following is an overview for (partnership name) for the past quarter of (year).

Occupancy

Month _____   Average Occupancy _____%
Month _____   Average Occupancy _____%
Month _____   Average Occupancy _____%

The current market area is _____% occupancy. Last quarter's occupancy was _____%. It appears that the market is (softening, tightening, stable). The reasons for this change are (state reasons).

Operations (Unaudited)

	Actual Operations	Private Placement Memorandum	Variance
Effective Gross Income	$_____	$_____	$_____
Less: Operating Expenses	$_____	$_____	$_____
Net Operating Income	$_____	$_____	$_____
Less: Debt Service	$_____	$_____	$_____
Less: Capital Expenditures	$_____	$_____	$_____
Cash Flow	$_____	$_____	$_____
Working Capital Balance	$_____	$_____	$_____

The year to date variance is $_____ (better/worse) than the original projections. The reasons for this variance are (state reasons).

Market Strategy

The market strategy for the upcoming quarter will be (state market strategy).

Summary

Your general partner is (optimistic/pessimistic) for the remainder of the year. (State reasons.)

Sincerely,

General Partner

K-I TAX RETURN LETTER

DATE

NAME
ADDRESS
CITY, STATE, ZIP CODE

RE: PARTNERSHIP NAME

Dear Partner:

Enclosed is your schedule K-1 tax return to be used in conjunction with the preparation of your (year) personal income tax return.

The year-end property status report and financial statements for (year) will be forthcoming. Should you have any questions, please feel free to contact us.

Sincerely,

General Partner

Enc.

IRS AUDIT LETTER

DATE

NAME
ADDRESS
CITY, STATE, ZIP CODE

RE: PARTNERSHIP NAME

Dear Partner:

Several of the limited partners have recently received a "thirty-day letter" from the Internal Revenue Service as part of the agency's examination of the partnership's tax return for (year).

In the event that you receive such a letter from the IRS, we recommend that your accountant or tax advisor file a protest letter in your tax district. We further recommend that in the event you receive a form (number) requesting an extension, you promptly execute and return it to the IRS.

You are advised that the partnership will have its accountants review the IRS claim and prepare an answer to the IRS.

We are enclosing a questionnaire for you or your accountant to fill out that will assist the partnership's accountant. Please complete this questionnaire and mail it back in the enclosed envelope.

If you have any questions, please feel free to contact us or contact the partnership's accountant (name, address, telephone number).

Sincerely,

General Partner

Enc.

IRS PROTEST LETTER

DATE

NAME
ADDRESS
CITY, STATE, ZIP CODE

RE: PARTNERSHIP NAME

Gentlemen:

On (date), I received a notification letter from the Internal Revenue Service regarding an audit on (partnership name) for the year (year). This letter will serve as my formal protest of this audit. The accounting firm of (name partnership's accounting firm) will handle any correspondence regarding this matter. Please send copies of any correspondence to (investor's accounting firm) at the following address:

CONTACT NAME
FIRM NAME
ADDRESS
CITY, STATE, ZIP CODE

TELEPHONE NUMBER

Sincerely,

Investor Name

INSTRUCTIONS FOR THE IRS QUESTIONNAIRE

1. If you have filed your income tax return after April 15 of the specified year, the statute of limitations on assessments begins on the date you filed your return with the IRS. If your return was filed after April 15 of the specified year, indicate the approximate date the return was filed in the appropriate space for each year. If your return was filed on April 15 or before, designate April 15 in the space for each year.

2. Indicate whether or not the IRS has contacted you for each year by writing YES or NO.

3. The IRS may request that you consent to the extension for the statute of limitations on your individual income tax return until the partnership issues are resolved. The IRS may request that you sign either a Form 872 or 872A. A Form 872 extends the statute of limitations until a specified date. Form 872A extends the statute of limitations until the partnership issues are resolved. Indicate whether you have signed either a Form 872 or 872A for each year. If you have signed a Form 872, indicate the date on which the extension will expire.

4. The IRS may send you a letter outlining the proposed adjustments to your individual income tax return and giving you thirty days to object to the proposed adjustments. Such a letter is known as a "thirty-day letter." Indicate by writing YES or NO whether or not you have received a thirty-day letter for each year.

5. If you have received a thirty-day letter, indicate by writing YES or NO whether or not you have filed a protest for each year. A form protest was included in our letter of (date).

6. If you have received a thirty-day letter and have submitted a protest to the IRS, indicate YES or NO for each year whether or not you have had a conference with the Appellate Division of the IRS.

7. If the IRS has contacted you and (1) you have refused to consent to the extension of the statute of limitations or (2) you have received a thirty-day letter and we have not responded to the IRS, the IRS may send you a letter notifying you of the proposed assessment stating that you have ninety days to petition the United States Tax Court. Such a letter is known as a ninety-day letter. Indicate YES or NO for each year whether or not you have received a ninety-day letter.

8. If you have received a ninety-day letter, indicate YES or NO for each year whether or not you have petitioned the United States Tax Court.

9. If you have paid or have agreed to pay the amount of the proposed adjustment, indicate the years for which you have paid or have agreed to pay.

10. If you have paid the proposed adjustment, you may request the IRS to refund the taxes you previously paid. Indicate by writing YES or NO whether or not you have filed a claim for a refund for that year.

11. If you are represented by an accountant or attorney in this matter, indicate the name, address and telephone number for your representative.

12. It is not necessary to inform us of the nature of these unrelated adjustments at this time. However, it will be helpful for us to know of their existence so that we can know whether the resolution of the partnership issues will completely resolve your return.

IRS QUESTIONNAIRE

Partnership Name: _____

Partner's Name: _____

Partner's Address: _____

	FOR 19__	FOR 19__
1. Date income tax was filed: April 15 or later	_____	_____
2. Have you been contacted by the IRS?	_____	_____
3. Have you extended the statute of limitations by signing Form 872 or 872A?		
872: indicate extension date	_____	_____
4. Have you received a "thirty-day letter" from the IRS?	_____	_____
5. Have you submitted a protest to the IRS?	_____	_____
6. Have you had a conference with the Appellate Office of the IRS?	_____	_____
7. Have you received a "ninety-day letter" from the IRS?	_____	_____
8. Have you filed a petition in the United States Tax Court?	_____	_____
9. Have you paid the additional tax proposed by the IRS?	_____	_____
10. Have you filed a claim for a refund for the additional tax paid to the IRS?	_____	
11. Name, address and telephone number of the accountant or attorney, if any, representing you in this matter.	_____	
	_____	
	_____	
12. For the years in which the partnership adjustments are proposed, has the IRS proposed adjustments to your returns other than those arising out of your interest in the partnership?	_____	_____

IRS FOLLOW-UP LETTER

DATE

NAME
ADDRESS
CITY, STATE, ZIP CODE

RE: PARTNERSHIP NAME

Dear Partner:

This letter follows up on our correspondence dated (date), which requested that you complete a questionnaire. According to our records, your response has not yet reached our office.

The partnership's detailed objection to the IRS's argument against your tax deductions will be strengthened if you or your accountant will take a few moments to respond to the enclosed questionnaire. If you have already mailed this questionnaire, please disregard this second request.

Sincerely,

General Partner

Enc.

RESALE BALLOT LETTER

DATE

NAME
ADDRESS
CITY, STATE, ZIP CODE

RE: PARTNERSHIP NAME
    RESALE BALLOT

Dear Partner:

This letter is to inform you that we have executed a contract to sell the (property name), subject to our obtaining approval of those limited partners who own _____% of the limited partnership units. Your general partner recommends this resale and, accordingly, would appreciate your immediate response by returning the enclosed ballot by (date).

Resale Highlights

The contract sales price is $_____. The purchaser will pay $_____ in cash at closing. (State the basic terms of the transaction.) The anticipated closing date is (date).

The Purchaser

The purchaser is (name of individual/company). (State background on the Purchaser.)

Reasons for the Sale

Your general partner recommends the resale of (property name) at this time for the above stated price and terms for the following reasons: (State reasons.)

Detailed Outline of the Resale Price and Terms

(Detail summary of the resale price and terms.)

****

Since the partnership is taking back secondary financing, your general partner will continue to monitor all activities on the property, including review of all management reports. Further, your general partner will process all future debt service payments and will continue to provide annual reports and necessary income tax information to all limited partners.

An Administrative Service fee of $_____ per year will be paid on a monthly basis by the Partnership to your general partner.

Attached Schedule

Exhibit A is attached to provide you with the details of the sources and applications of funds at the time of closing, including closing costs, legal and accounting fees, and other expenses of the partnership. Also shown on this exhibit is a breakdown of total funds that will be distributed in the years subsequent to the closing. Exhibit B is a summary pro-forma statement for each limited partner investment unit that projects on a calendar year basis the pre-tax and after-tax consequences of this sale. The allocations and distributions shown in these Exhibits are described on pages _____ of the Private Placement Memorandum.

Tax Considerations

(Explain tax considerations.)

Your general partner recommends approval and consent to the resale transaction described herein. However, each limited partner's individual situation may differ from others, and each must exercise independent judgment. No appraisal or other investigation has been made to determine that the purchase price, as set forth in the contract with this purchaser, is equal to or more than its fair market value.

Attached is a ballot on which you should indicate your decision. Please mark this ballot and return it in the enclosed envelope. We would appreciate your doing so immediately so that we may meet the projected closing date.

Sincerely,

General Partner

Enc.

EXHIBIT A
ESTIMATED SOURCES AND APPLICATIONS OF FUNDS AT CLOSING

Sources of Funds	
Cash down-payment	$_____
Working capital account	$_____
Total source of funds	$_____
Application of Funds	
Legal fees	$_____
Accounting fees	$_____
Brokerage commissions	$_____
Prorated expenses	$_____
Debt service	$_____
Resale closing costs	$_____
Total application of funds	$_____
Funds available for distribution	$_____
Limited partner distribution—return of initial contribution per investment unit	$_____
Limited partner distribution—return of preferred cash flow per investment unit	$_____
Limited partner distribution—resale profit per investment unit	$_____
General partner distribution	$_____

Note: These figures are estimates, subject to final verification. Deviations from these numbers would cause adjustment to the distributable funds. The distribution will be made within thirty days following the closing.

Distribution in Subsequent Years

End of Year	Limited Partners	General Partners
_____	$_____	$_____
_____	$_____	$_____
_____	$_____	$_____
_____	$_____	$_____

EXHIBIT B
SUMMARY OF CASH FLOW AND TAXABLE INCOME PER INVESTMENT UNIT

Year	Investment	Cash Flow	Ordinary Income (Loss)	Gain	Tax Benefit (Liability)	After Tax Cash Flow
_____	$_____	$_____	$_____	$_____	$_____	$_____
_____	$_____	$_____	$_____	$_____	$_____	$_____
_____	$_____	$_____	$_____	$_____	$_____	$_____
_____	$_____	$_____	$_____	$_____	$_____	$_____
_____	$_____	$_____	$_____	$_____	$_____	$_____
_____	$_____	$_____	$_____	$_____	$_____	$_____
_____	$_____	$_____	$_____	$_____	$_____	$_____
_____	$_____	$_____	$_____	$_____	$_____	$_____
_____	$_____	$_____	$_____	$_____	$_____	$_____
_____	$_____	$_____	$_____	$_____	$_____	$_____
Total	$_____	$_____	$_____	$_____	$_____	$_____

BALLOT

Sale of (Property Name)
by ((Partnership Name)

The undersigned, a limited partner of (partnership name), a (state) limited partnership (the "Partnership") does hereby (check one):

_____ APPROVE of the sale of the (property name) located in (city, state) to (purchaser's name) for $_____ and substantially in accordance with the terms and conditions as described in that certain letter dated (date). The approval of the foregoing sale shall constitute the approval and consent of the undersigned to the execution and delivery by the general partner of any and all documents and other items required to consummate such transaction.

_____ DISAPPROVE of the sale

_____

Signature

Name: _____

Number of limited partnership units owned: _____

Date: _____

CERTIFICATE

Under section _____ of the Internal Revenue Code, a corporation, trust, or estate must withhold tax with respect to certain transfers of property if a holder of an interest in the entity is a foreign person. To inform (partnership name) that no withholding is required with respect to my interest in it I, _____, hereby certify the following:

1. I am not a nonresident alien for purposes of U.S. income taxation (as defined in Code _____ and regulations thereunder);
2. My U.S. taxpayer identification number (Social Security Number) is _____; and
3. My home address is _____.

I understand that this certification may be disclosed to the Internal Revenue Service by (partnership name), and that any false statement I have made herein could be punishable by fine, imprisonment, or both.

Under penalties of perjury, I declare that I have examined this certificate, and to the best of my knowledge and belief it is true, correct, and complete.

_____

Signature

_____

Date

THE RESALE PROCESS: WHEN TO SELL, HOW TO PROFIT

WHY INVESTORS CHOOSE TO SELL THEIR PROPERTY

There are many reasons for selling property, including the following:

1. Need cash quickly
2. Disagreement with partners
3. Running out of working capital
4. Tax benefits quickly running out
5. Receive offer that cannot be refused
6. Investors want to see profit
7. Major tenant's lease will soon expire
8. Neighborhood area deteriorating
9. The loan is coming due

The above are all valid reasons for selling, although economic theory tells us that all properties should be sold when the profit yield peaks.

HOW TO DECIDE ON THE INITIAL ASKING PRICE AND TERMS

The owner who has decided to sell the property should outline the acceptable price and terms. Many times this initial asking price is based on emotion and will be higher than the market will accept. Since most purchasers want to negotiate from the initial asking price, this initial sales price should be somewhat higher to leave room for negotiations. However, the price should not be set so high that prospective buyers will back off and not make any offers.

The terms that a property sells for are also very important. Many buyers are "terms" buyers and will pay a higher price for a property if they can get their terms which might include a lower or staged down-payment, seller financing, or deductible fees paid to the seller in lieu of a hard dollar down-payment. Still other buyers might want the seller to make certain cash flow guarantees.

In making the final decision on the price and terms, the owner should analyze the current market conditions and should review the resales of competing properties in the market area. If, after reviewing the most recent resales, the owner finds out that all the properties recently sold were sold only after a long period of time and at much lower prices than they were originally put on the market for, the owner would have to readjust the pricing strategy or possibly decide to defer the resale until the market conditions change.

EIGHT KEY TYPES OF RESALE METHODS

1. Installment Sales Contract

Sellers of a property will use an installment sale either when they want to split their gain over a period of years or when the market dictates that they must split the down-payment into a number of payments over a few years. The recognized gain is spread over the life of the debt in the same proportion that the payments are received.

2. Exchanges

A "tax-free" exchange is a method used to sell a property and to avoid paying any taxes upon resale. Tax-free exchanges are covered in Section 1031 of the Internal Revenue Code. This transaction is handled by exchanging the property for another property of "like kind," that is, a property that has the same use or character but does not have to be the same grade or quality. For example, an office building could be exchanged for an apartment building because both are income-producing properties.

Exchanges may also involve cash or nonqualifying property. This nonqualifying property is commonly referred to as "boot." The gain on the sale is recognized to the extent of any boot received. To prevent the seller from converting a nonrecognizable loss by the transfer of boot, the IRS disallows the recognition of any loss, notwithstanding the receipt of boot. The transfer of boot in the form of nonqualifying property whose fair market value exceeds its adjusted basis will cause a taxable gain to be recognized.

Many times exchanges will take place with more than one property involved. Party A might want to purchase a property from Party B. Because Party B does not want to be taxed on this sale, he writes into the contract with Party A that he wants thirty days to find a suitable property to purchase. Party B then finds a property he would like to purchase. He then contracts with Party C to purchase this property and to close simultaneously with his sale to Party A.

3. Sale of the Partnership Interest

In many cases, the lender will have a "due on sale clause" in the mortgage documents. This will prohibit a resale without paying off the debt or a restructuring of the debt in the lender's favor. The sale of the partnership interest might be a resale method used to avoid this problem. Many lenders will not include any language prohibiting a sale of the partnership interest.

In order to use this resale technique, the new purchaser must be totally satisfied that there are no current liens or other obligations attached to the existing partnership. The purchaser's attorney should verify that the partnership is free of any obligations and will make the partnership indemnify the new owner against any obligations that arise after a closing.

4. Donating the Real Estate

For tax purposes, the seller might choose to donate the property. However, if the property is highly leveraged it might trigger recognition of the same amount of gain and depreciation recapture as a sale. This would be especially true if the property were held in a partnership and the partnership interest was donated.

　　Another method is to give the property to a family member who is in a lower tax bracket. This gift may be subject to a gift tax, but this can be offset by donating the property subject to indebtedness. This indebtedness can later be forgiven on an annual basis.

5. Incorporating the Real Estate Interest

The IRS will permit a tax-free transfer of an interest in real estate to a corporation. To use this method the individual making the transfer must own at least 80 percent of the value of all issued and outstanding stock immediately after the transfer.

6. Foreclosure

In many instances, due to a variety of reasons the property owner may not be able to carry the property's debt service. If the owner is not able to work out a viable solution with the lender, the lender may choose to foreclose on the property.

　　Although the sale is an involuntary one, the tax treatment to the mortgagor is the same as a voluntary sale of the property. The amount of gain or loss is a function of whether the foreclosure left the mortgagor liable for any deficiency and whether the mortgagor retained a right of redemption.

　　If a foreclosure takes place, the mortgagor realizes a gain or loss equal to the difference between his basis in the property and the amount realized on the sale. The mortgagor usually realizes a loss upon foreclosure. The tax consequences may be quite severe, since there could be substantial gain generated with no cash flow to help pay this tax burden.

7. Deed-in-Lieu of Foreclosure

Many times the lender will not want to foreclose upon the borrower. The reasons may include the facts that the borrower is going bankrupt or that the lender does not want to go through a long protracted period of trying to foreclose on the property. In this case the borrower can deed over the title to the property to the lender in lieu of any foreclosure.

8. Sale Leaseback

A sale leaseback is a sale in which the seller sells his property to an investor and simultaneously leases the property back from the investor. Many larger corporations execute this type of transaction to free up their capital for other purposes.

HOW TO PREPARE A PROFESSIONAL—AND SUCCESSFUL—RESALE PACKAGE

The owner who has decided upon an initial asking price and terms should prepare a package with all the pertinent information that will be needed to entice a prospective purchaser to make an offer. This sales package could be designed as one or two different packages. The first package could contain just basic information on the property. A potential purchaser who is interested would then contact the owner for a more complete package of information. By using this method, the owner would be able to distinguish the serious prospects. The following is an outline of the information that should be in this package.

Detailed Sales Package Outline

1. Name of property
2. Address of property
3. Description of the improvements
   - *a.* Year built
   - *b.* Type of construction
   - *c.* Acreage
   - *d.* Type utility system
   - *e.* Unit features
   - *f.* Property amenities
4. Property information
   - *a.* Unit mix
   - *b.* Square footage (gross/net)
   - *c.* Rent per month
     - (1) Common area maintenance charges
     - (2) Lease options
       - *(a)* Terms
   - *d.* Who pays utilities
   - *e.* Lease terms
   - *f.* Security deposit
   - *g.* Pet policy
5. Tenant information/profile
   - *a.* Tenant name
   - *b.* Tenant profile
6. Description of the area
   - *a.* Demographics
7. Seller's proforma
8. Description of the existing financing
   - *a.* Lender
   - *b.* Loan balance

     c. Interest rate

     d. Amortization period

     e. Maturity date

     f. Monthly payment

     g. Loan extension

        (1) Extension fees

        (2) Interest rate

        (3) Loan term

     h. Prepayment penalty

        (1) Prepayment fee

     i. Escrows

     j. Loan transferability

        (1) Assumption fee

     k. Due on sale clause

     l. Loan guarantees

9. Floor plans

10. Site plan

11. Location map

12. Pictures (rendering if to-be-built)

13. Comparables

     a. Name/address

     b. Number units/Total square footage

     c. Type units

        (1) Residential

           (a) Number of units

           (b) Square footage

           (c) Rent/month

           (d) Rent/square foot/month

           (e) Who pays utilities

        (2) Commercial

           (a) Number of floors

           (b) Square footage/floor

           (c) Rent/square foot

           (d) Percentage rents

           (e) Who pays utilities

    (f) Rent escalations

    (g) Common area maintenance charges

14. Asking price and terms

15. Seller/broker name and telephone number

EIGHT STEPS TO A PROFITABLE RESALE

Step 1: Determine If Services of a Real Estate Broker Are Needed

When the decision is made to sell the property, the owner should also decide if the services of a real estate broker are needed. If the owners are active in the real estate business or have accumulated a list of prospective purchasers over the years, they might decide that they can sell the property by themselves. If owners decides that they want to use a real estate broker, they should select a few local brokers who specialize in the type of property to be sold and interview these brokers to decide who would be the best person to coordinate this sale. The best qualified broker should have the following characteristics.

1. Knowledge of the product

2. Knowledge of the market area

3. Contacts with other brokers in the market area

4. Knowledge of current financing techniques

5. Contacts with local lenders

6. Contacts with potential purchasers for product type

7. Honesty and integrity

8. Diligence

    Once the broker has been selected, the owner should negotiate the real estate commission to be paid which will either come out of the current asking price or will be added to the sales price. The owner should remember that if this commission is added to the asking price, the new price might be higher than the market will bear. A good broker should be able to facilitate a quicker sale and bring a higher sales price.

Step 2: Prepare a List of Potential Purchasers

Prior to sending out the sales package, a list of potential purchasers should be assembled. This list should include the following:

1. Property owners in the immediate area

2. Current property owners in the city who own similar properties

3. Individuals who have already contacted the owner

4. Regional or national purchasers who have advertised the desire to buy this type of property

Step 3: Collect and Review Offers

Once the list of potential purchasers has been assembled, the owner or broker should then send out the sales package. The owner should collect as many offers as he can. Each offer will most likely be different; many buyers may not be real buyers, that is, they may not be capable of closing on the transaction, or may be looking to steal a property.

Once all the offers have been assembled, the owner should have his accountant review these offers. Since the present value of the sales price is the important factor, the accountant will help analyze all the offers. The following are other important items when deciding on the best offers:

1. Sales price

2. Cash paid at closing

3. Date of closing

4. Guarantees of seller required by buyer

    a. Rental achievements

    b. Occupancy achievements

    c. Negative cash flow

5. Seller financing required by buyer

    a. Dollar amount

    b. Interest rate paid or accrued

    c. Loan maturity

6. Qualifications and financial capability of the prospective buyer

Step 4: Negotiate Counteroffers

The seller narrows down the field and should then either accept the best offer or negotiate with the best three offers. The seller should send out a letter with a counteroffer to these buyers and through this negotiation period reduce the field to the best offer.

Step 5: Finalize the Deal with an Accountant

Once the seller has finalized the negotiation on the business aspects of the transaction, he should sign a letter of intent with the purchaser, outlining the proposed transaction.

The letter of intent should then be analyzed by the seller's accountant to determine the tax ramifications. In reviewing the potential tax impact to the investor, the accountant will look at the realized and the recognized gain from the sales transaction. If the accountant finds that the seller negotiated a deal that would hurt him or the investment group tax wise, now is the time to make any modifications. If there are any changes, the seller should notify the purchaser of such changes.

Realized Gain

The realized gain in a sales transaction is sales price less all of the selling expenses.

Sales Price – Real Estate Commission – Adjusted Basis

RECOGNIZED GAIN

Recognized gain is the dollar amount that is subject to either ordinary income or capital gains taxes.

$$\text{Realized Gain} \times \frac{\text{Cash Received}}{\text{Gross Cash Proceeds}} = \text{Recognized Gain}$$

The following example is a simplified version of how recognized gain is calculated. This example does not take into consideration any first year depreciation recapture, nor that the seller has any other indebtedness.

PROPERTY SALE COMPUTATION

ASSUMPTIONS

Sales price	$1,000,000
Real estate commission	50.000
Adjusted basis	800,000
First mortgage balance	600,000
Second mortgage balance	50,000
Down-payment at closing	250,000
Equity to seller at closing	200,000
Purchase money mortgage—due twelve months	100,000
Sales price	$1,000,000
Real estate commission	($ 50,000)
Net sales price	950,000
Adjusted basis	($ 800,000)
Realized gain	150,000
Sale price	$1,000,000
Mortgages assumed—first and second	($ 650,000)
Gross cash proceeds	350,000
Real estate commission	($ 50,000)
Net cash proceeds	300,000

Recognized gain:

First year $\dfrac{\$250,000}{\$350,000} \times \$150,000 = \$107,142.86$

Second year $\dfrac{\$100,000}{\$350,000} \times \$150,000 = \$42,857.14$

Step 6: Prepare the Purchase Contract

A copy of the purchaser's letter of intent should go to the attorney who is preparing the purchase agreement. The first draft should be reviewed by the seller and his attorney and then should be sent to the purchaser and his attorney. Most likely there will still need to be some negotiations over the legal language in the contract. To expedite this process, the seller, purchaser, and their respective attorneys should meet and finalize any changes to the contract.

Each party should then sign this contract and the purchaser should deposit the required earnest money.

BALLOT INVESTORS

If there is an investment partnership that must approve this resale, the managing partner should prepare an investor letter and ballot outlining the following facts.

1. Resale highlights

2. Information on the purchaser

3. Reason for the resale
   a. Price and terms
   b. Diminished tax benefits
   c. Market conditions
   d. Financing

4. Detailed outline of the resale price and terms

5. Exhibits
   a. Estimated sources and applications of funds at closing
   b. Distribution of cash in subsequent years
   c. Summary of cash flow and tax benefits per investment unit

6. Resale ballot

7. Investor certificate

Step 7: Close the Deal

During the purchaser's inspection period, the seller should be supplying the purchaser with any information required. The seller should make certain that during this time period and up until the closing, the purchaser does not disrupt the operations of the property. All employees should be notified that a sale is pending.

The day of the closing, all income and expenses should be prorated and a closing statement prepared. The attorney should then start the process of signing all the necessary documents.

Step 8: Distribute the Profits and Administrate the Mortgage Proceeds

Once all the documents have been signed, the seller's attorney should distribute the sales proceeds to the seller and pay any closing expenses. The seller will then distribute any proceeds to the other partners or investors in the deal.

If there was any seller financing taken back in the transaction, the managing partner will have to coordinate receiving these payments and handling the distribution split with the other partners as well as the distribution split of the final balloon payment when received.

RESALE FORMS

Resale Prospects. This form is used to keep track of potential purchasers.

Sales Comparable Market Study. This form is designed to keep track of sale comparables.

Resale Offering Summary Sheet. This form will help keep track of offers made.

FORM 13-1
Resale Prospects

PROPERTY NAME _____
PREPARED BY _____
PAGE _____ OF _____

COMPANY NAME	CONTACT	ADDRESS	TEL. NO.	DATE CONTACTED	TYPE PROPERTIES	CAP. RATES	COMMENTS

COMMENTS _____

FORM 13-2
Sale Comparable Market Study

SUBJECT PROPERTY _____
ADDRESS _____

SELLER _____
  TEL. NO. ( ) _____
BROKER _____
  TEL. NO. ( ) _____

DATE _____

TYPE PROPERTY:
  RESIDENTIAL:
    SINGLE FAMILY _____
    MULTI-FAMILY _____

TYPE SALE:
  SOLD _____
  FOR SALE _____

CONDOMINIUM/TH _____
ADULT CONGREGATE CARE _____
NURSING HOME _____

OFFICE _____
SHOPPING CENTER _____
INDUSTRIAL _____

MINI-WAREHOUSE _____
HOTEL/MOTEL _____

PREPARED BY _____

MAP REF. NO.	PROPERTY NAME/ ADDRESS	OWNER	BROKER	TEL. NO.	DATE OF SALE	ASKING/ SALES PRICE	DOWN-PAYMENT	TERMS	# UNITS/ SQ. FT.	CRM	CAP RATE	PRICE/ SQ. FT.	COMMENTS
				( )		$	$					$	
				( )		$	$					$	
				( )		$	$					$	
				( )		$	$					$	
				( )		$	$					$	
				( )		$	$					$	
				( )		$	$					$	
				( )		$	$					$	
				( )		$	$					$	
				( )		$	$					$	
				( )		$	$					$	
				( )		$	$					$	
				( )		$	$					$	

COMMENTS _____

FORM 13-3

Resale Offering Summary Sheet

PROPERTY NAME _____
PREPARED BY _____

COMPANY NAME	ADDRESS	TEL. NO.	CONTACT/BROKER	TEL. NO.	OFFER DATE	OFFER PRICE	DOWN PAYMENT	CLOSING DATE	TERMS
						$	$		
						$	$		
						$	$		
						$	$		
						$	$		
						$	$		
						$	$		
						$	$		
						$	$		
						$	$		
						$	$		
						$	$		
						$	$		
						$	$		
						$	$		
						$	$		
						$	$		
						$	$		

COMMENTS _____

INFORMATION TECHNOLOGY USED BY THE REAL ESTATE INVESTOR

Thomas E. Hanszen

Director, Real Estate Information Technology
and Process Improvement
KPMG Peat Marwick LLP

INTRODUCTION

The best real estate investment practitioners are generally extroverted people with a high level of social skill. As such, they tend to be much more comfortable with people than with machines and technology. In most instances they have trailed behind their corporate clients in the integration of technology into their day-to-day business activities. While the people involved with running and supporting some commercial real estate offices have been using computers for many years, such capabilities are foreign to many individual real estate professionals.

The successful methodologies and processes of many real estate practitioners and investors were developed when desk top computers were still in their infancy; finding the benefit to a real estate professional of this infant technology was a stretch. Some progressive real estate firms did, however, see the future potential and made the jump, or perhaps the leap of faith is a better way to describe their embrace of technology. They moved from a pure paper environment to a partially electronic one in the early 1980s with the use of the Commodore computer, then with the first IBM personal computers (PCs), and have continued to follow the technology advancements in hardware and software. Early adopters of technology can share experiences with programs such as Visicalc, Supercalc and early releases of Lotus. Today they are probably using the most current versions of a Lotus or Excel spreadsheet, a word processing software and a database software combined with a communications application to link with remote offices and even clients. Some are today marketing on the Internet or, better yet, using the free information on the Internet as a source of research data.

For a long while during the "spool up" of real estate technology, the only people in commercial real estate who focused on computers were the younger analysts or researchers and the "techies" who may not have been among the more productive members in terms of sales or transaction dollars.

But the times are changing. While there are a few high producers in the market that have resisted the technology, most of the heavy hitters have made the jump. Although

479

some in the market believe they are fully computerized, they have in fact simply created a high-priced address book.

Stephen Covey, in his book *The Seven Habits of Highly Effective People,* devotes a chapter to the concept of "sharpening the saw." The essence of this concept is that by taking the time to learn to use the computer and its capabilities we lessen our effort and make ourselves far more productive.

This chapter is aimed at the individual in the small to medium investment firm and how he or she can become more productive. This overview will look at the primary areas of computer application software: contact/personal information management, word processing, presentation, spreadsheet, project management, data base, valuation applications and communications. In each area there will be discussion of benefits to the commercial real estate investor. As with other chapters in this textbook, the uses will be coordinated with the six major processes in the life cycle of a typical real estate transaction: Prospecting for Deals, Contracting for the Deal, Packaging for Investors or Lenders, Due Diligence and Number Crunching, Valuation and Financing, and Asset Management. I do not intend to suggest that only one software could or should be used in any one given step of the life cycle, only that limiting the examples would provide a more concise discussion. Obviously there are potentials for many other application software packages that one could employ depending on the exact nature of your business. Also, other equally functional products will be listed, if appropriate, which you may want to consider.

PROSPECTING FOR DEALS

Contact Management/Personal Information Management (PIM)

Our first category of software has become very popular over the last few years. Just about everyone, regardless of profession, has to keep track of names, addresses, phone numbers, appointments, phone calls and other bits of miscellaneous information. But in the commercial real estate business it's absolutely critical for a professional, who may be juggling a dozen different deals, to stay on top of this data. A lost phone number or missed appointment can be, at best, a major hassle and at worst, a disaster. And yet, while walking past offices in commercial real estate firms, how often do we see desks littered with Post-it notes, business cards, and other assorted scraps of paper. Using a good PIM (not just buying and installing one on your computer) can totally change this situation by keeping you organized and thus increasing your productivity.

FEATURES AND BENEFITS

At its simplest level, a PIM functions as an address book or rolodex allowing you to store and quickly access information on a large number of people and companies (your contacts). A PIM lets you tag your contacts with labels and/or keywords to facilitate categorization and searching. All PIMs let you enter the usual contact address and telephone information. In addition, a good system should also have fields in which you can store background information such as birthdays, anniversaries, names of spouse and children, interests and hobbies. (See Harvey Mackay's book *Swimming with the Sharks* for his suggestions on contact background data.)

There are many generic PIMs available which are useful in just about any profession. But while most allow varying degrees of customization, they cannot be totally adapted to some of the specialized tasks required by a commercial real estate professional. For example, a generic PIM is difficult, if not impossible, to use for generating property surveys and fliers. However, commercial real estate software is a very narrow market and, as such, there are very few PIMs written specifically for its use. RE•View InfoMgr is one such product that has been highly adapted for the real estate environment. (See Figure 14-1.) It was developed with the needs of the real estate investor specifically in mind. The application has most, if not all, of the contact management functionality contained in a product such as ACT, but also allows the real estate practitioner to collect property-specific data.

RE•View InfoMgr allows the user to store a comprehensive amount of information on each contact, including all the background data mentioned above. It is also one of a few PIMs which allow each contact to have an unlimited number of phone numbers. This is useful because of the proliferation of car and portable phones and pagers. Contacts can be assigned a category, a business type, and an unlimited number of keywords.

FIGURE 14-1

RE•View InfoMgr screen capture with real estate contact. RE•View InfoMgr stores information in a convenient layout; it includes user-defined fields and is completely tailored to the needs of the real estate environment.

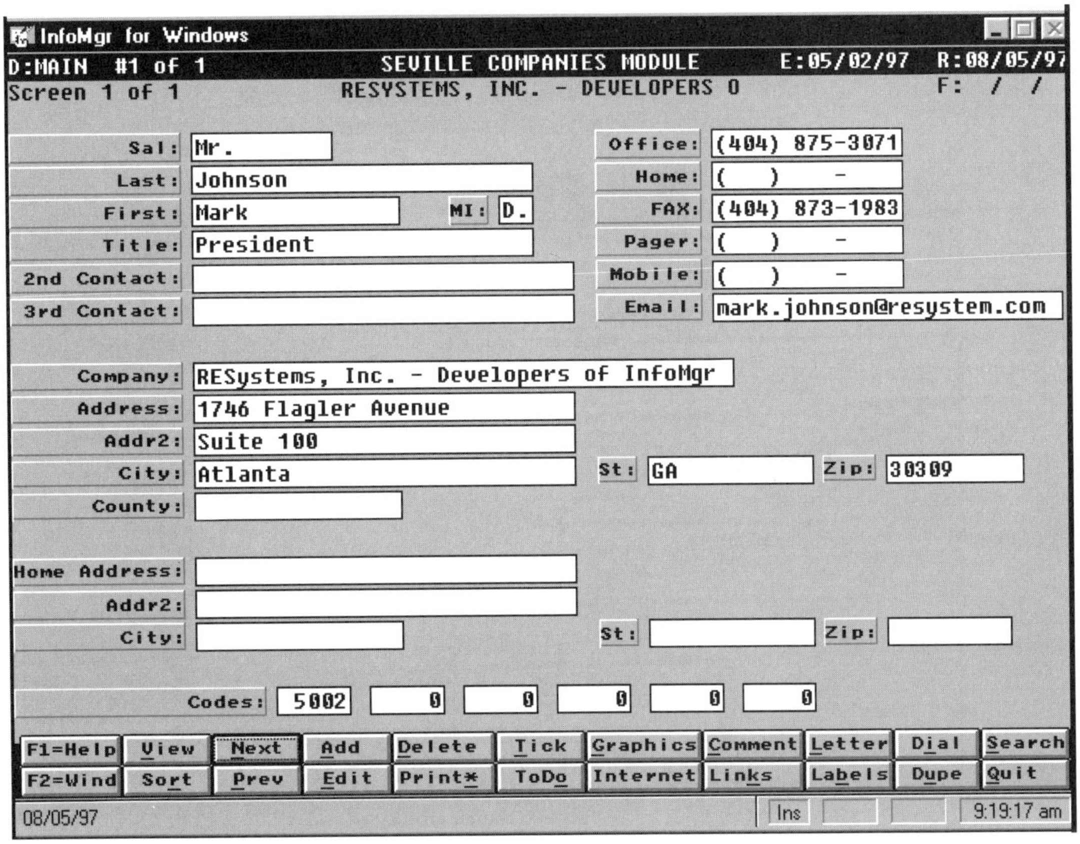

This PIM also helps you keep on track and, more important, allows you to schedule or reminds you of all the activities you have with your contacts such as phone calls, letters, faxes, meetings, etc. Maintaining such information enables you to both generate status reports for clients, showing actions taken on their behalf, and allows you as the user to see the progression of a deal.

Also included are modules for the capture of information and data that are specific to various product types, such as apartment, office and retail. The information can include property owners, property managers, property contacts and a multitude of other specifics regarding the properties. (See Figure 14-2.)

Using the "export and mail merge" feature of a PIM facilitates the generation of a large volume of standard mailouts without having to re-key names and addresses. RE•View InfoMgr has pre-defined address merge formats that were designed for MS-Word or WordPerfect that allow you to combine the power of a contact manager with the flexibility of a state-of-the-art word processor.

In addition to the usual address, phone and activity information, RE•View InfoMgr allows the user to enter some user-defined fields. Another nice feature that has begun appearing in PIMs is the ability to link records in a PIM to files on the computer's hard drive which allows the user to link records in its database. This means that any disk file—such as a word processing document, spreadsheet, drawing—can be linked to a contact, property, activity or other record.

FIGURE 14-2

RE•View InfoMgr screen capture with real estate property data. The application can capture and track most of the property-specific information needed, and can link the owner and other property contacts.

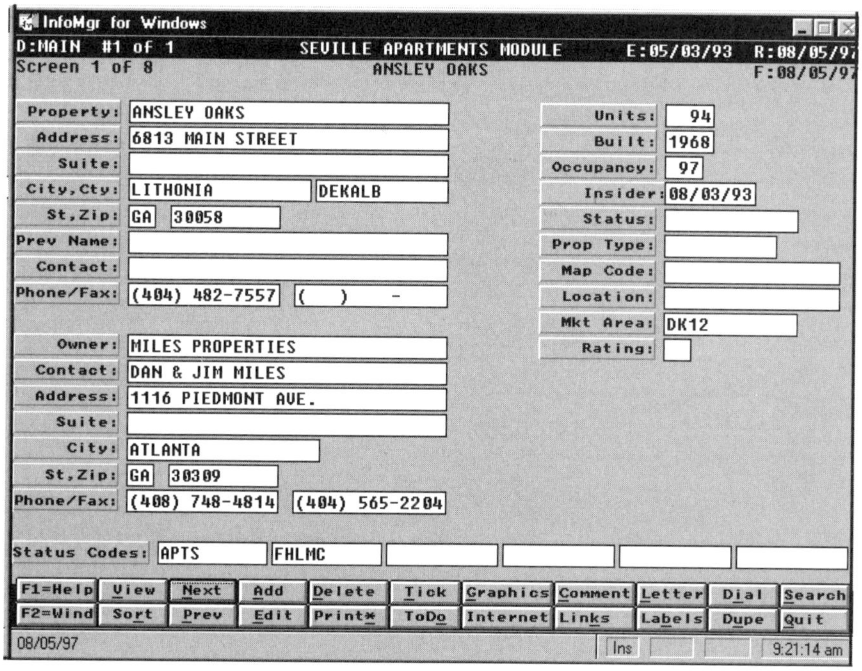

FIGURE 14-2 (CONT'D)

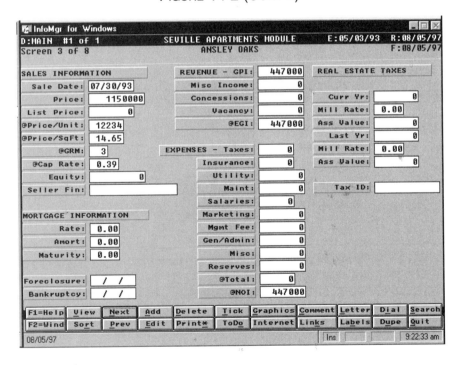

FIGURE 14-2 (CONT'D)

FIGURE 14-2 (CONT'D)

CONTACTS

Mgmt Co:	MILES PROPERTIES	Broker: GRUBB & ELLIS
Contact:		Contact: FRANK ABRAHAMSON
Address:		Address:
Suite:		Suite:
City:		City:
St,Zip:		St,Zip:
Ph/Fax:	( ) - ( ) -	Ph/Fax: (404) 522-5477 ( ) -

Lender: FEDERAL HOME LOAN/FREDDIE MAC/
Contact: ERNIE EDEN,TIM SOLOMON,ETAL
Address:
Suite:
City:
St,Zip:
Ph/Fax: (404) 438-3800 ( )   -

F1=Help	View	Next	Add	Delete	Tick	Graphics	Comment	Letter	Dial	Search
F2=Wind	Sort	Prev	Edit	Print*	ToDo	Internet	Links	Labels	Dupe	Quit

08/05/97   Ins   9:23:01 am

FIGURE 14-2 (CONT'D)

PROPERTY DESCRIPTION

CONSTRUCTION   PARKING

Gross SqFt: 78520   Type Parking:
Net SqFt: 0   Total Spaces: 0
#Bldgs: 0   #Covered: 0
Stories: Carport: 0
Construction: Garage: 0
Finish: Assigned/Unit: 0
Roof: Rent/Mo: 0

                              UTILITIES   TENANT PAYS

SITE   Master Meter: Elec:
Total Acres: 4.60   Heating: Gas:
Units/Acre: 0.00   Cooling: Water:
Zoning: Hot Water: Sewer:
                              Range: Cable:
                              Dryer:

F1=Help	View	Next	Add	Delete	Tick	Graphics	Comment	Letter	Dial	Search
F2=Wind	Sort	Prev	Edit	Print*	ToDo	Internet	Links	Labels	Dupe	Quit

08/05/97   Ins   9:24:31 am

FIGURE 14-2 (CONT'D)

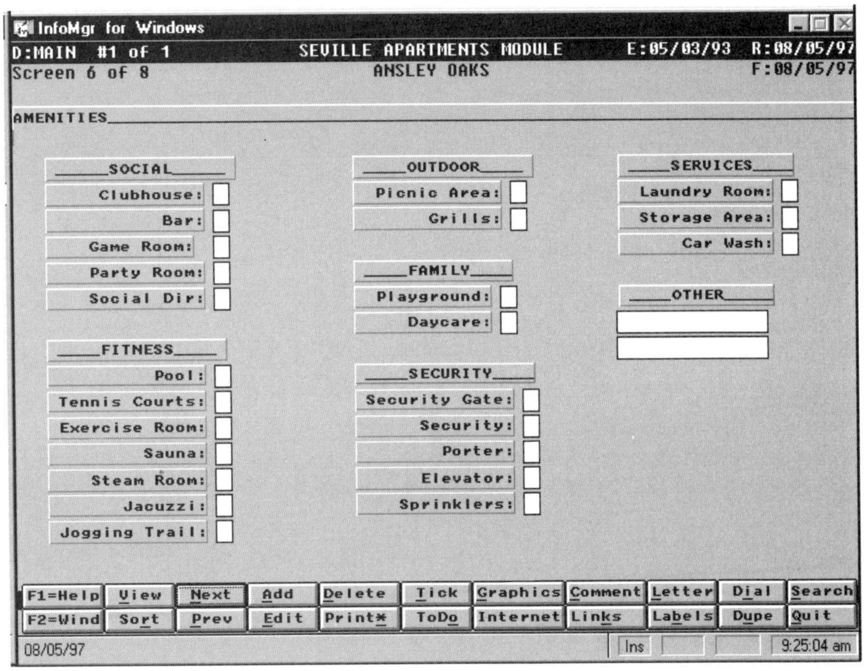

FIGURE 14-2 (CONT'D)

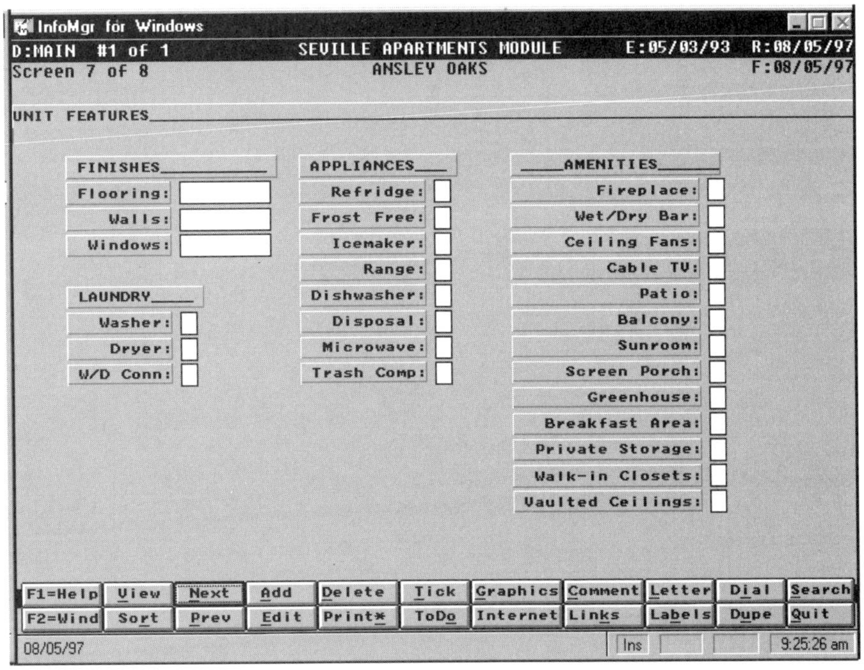

FIGURE 14-2 (CONT'D)

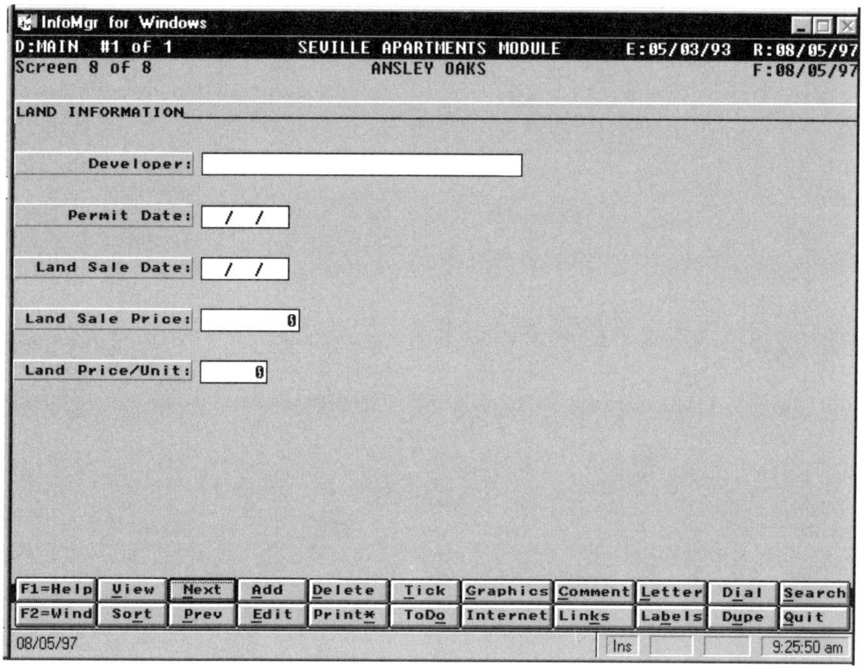

Other well-known PIMs include ACT, MS-Scheduler, Lotus Organizer and ECCO, several of which may come pre-loaded on a new computer for no additional cost.

BOTTOM LINE

A PIM has the potential to dramatically improve your organization and productivity. However, in order for any such software to be effective it must be used religiously. Lots of people dislike reading computer manuals, but if you do manage to sit down and read just one, make it the manual for your PIM.

CONTRACTING FOR THE DEAL

Word Processing

The single most commonly used computer application in business is word processing, which allows you to do things you could never do with a typewriter. In most offices computer word processing has relegated the typewriter to such specialized tasks as filling out forms and typing envelopes (though sometimes even these jobs can be performed better on a computer).

Word processing skills will help users communicate more effectively and be less dependent on clerical help (though, of course, it will not turn someone with poor written communication skills into a great writer). They also allow for a significant degree of flexibility and self-sufficiency when working the odd hours that are often required in the commercial real estate business. When using a word processing program, you will be able to write your letters, faxes and reports more efficiently, reducing or eliminating the time-consuming drafting and redrafting cycle. Also, standard forms such as letters of intent, purchase and sale agreements, and property inspection forms can be set in a template format with the company's logo included for everyone in the office to use.

FEATURES AND BENEFITS

A word processing application or program gives the user tremendous flexibility in the writing, revising, manipulating and formatting of documents. It allows you to add, delete, move, or copy text within a document and between documents. Word processing documents can be formatted or reformatted at any point during or after the text of a document has been entered. Once completed, the document can be checked for spelling and grammar (though this capability does not in any way eliminate the necessity for a good proofreading) before it is printed.

Formatting of letters, memos, reports and other documents can be simplified and made more consistent through the use of saved style formats. For example, Microsoft Word (available for Macintosh and IBM-compatible computers) uses style sheets and templates to record the formatting of paragraphs. These can be applied automatically as you type. By using these you can speed the formatting of documents and maintain consistent formats within an office.

Another common feature of word processing programs is the glossary catalog which stores frequently used text and graphics, such as your logo or your customer's logo. These glossary entries can be quickly inserted into a document, saving the user from retyping them. For example, a common glossary item is the complimentary close for a letter which can then be inserted with just a few key strokes.

Tables have also become common in word processing software. They allow tabular data to be entered easily into a document and presented in an attractive format. One of the best features of using a table is that text will automatically wrap to the next line within each cell, which cannot be done using tabs. In addition, Excel spreadsheets and PowerPoint pages can be easily copied and pasted into a letter for special purpose areas.

Once a word processing document has been completed and printed, it can be stored either on a floppy diskette, local hard disk, or on a central file server. It can then be retrieved in the future in case another copy is needed, or to use the information in another document. By storing documents in computer archives, an office can reduce substantially the need for storing hard copies of letters and other documents that already exist electronically.

I should discuss quickly the field of desktop publishing and how it relates to word processing. It is, let's say, the next level above word processing. Desktop publishing software typically takes a word processing text file and completes a complex page layout for a magazine or brochure. Given the vast capabilities of any well-known word processing software in this area, a real estate firm should not need any additional software unless you are doing your own page layout for something like a monthly magazine. Moreover, today most printers will accept a well-formatted word processing document with graph and pictures included and complete the page layout for little or no additional cost. They may even prefer this as they want a file that is compatible with their printers.

Bottom Line

Word processing software is an essential part of any professional's computer tool box. It can be the single most time-saving technology in the office, saving hundreds of hours in duplicating a similar format, editing, re-editing and sharing drafts around an office. The capabilities of current word processors will allow all but the most complex printing and duplicating to be done on the user's desktop. Once a word processing document has been completed and printed, it can be stored either on a floppy diskette, local hard disk, or on a central file server. It can then be retrieved in the future in case another copy is needed, or to use the information in another document. And a copy of a computer document archive can be backed-up onto a tape and stored off-site to safeguard in case of fire. Try doing that with a file cabinet of paper documents!

Project Management

Beyond creating the myriad of documents that encompass the process of contracting for the deal, one may want to consider using a project management software to schedule and track all the necessary tasks, events and benchmarks. This type of software application could be especially useful in a large and complex transaction with many parties involved. One of the most outstanding applications on the market is Microsoft's. It has been well received by the construction industry and land developers.

Features and Benefits

Many of these applications are relatively easy to use and have significant flexibility built into them. They allow the user to input all required tasks, assign beginning and end dates to each, as well as the responsible parties. Another valuable feature is their ability to develop a critical path scenario. In other words they can establish dependencies between tasks and indicate the order in which the tasks must be completed.

The ability of a package such as Project to present, at varying levels of detail, a subject that is otherwise difficult to visualize is a major benefit. Project will allow the user to select tasks or a group of tasks and display or print all the pertinent information. One way that it allows the user to print the schedule is in a Gantt Chart format which allows a multi-level view of a selected timeline in a graphical and easy-to-understand view.

You can establish a standard template from a checklist of tasks that you would typically need to complete during the course of a transaction. The template can then be modified for the specifics of the current deal and estimated dates applied to each task. You can use this as a planning tool to set a realistic and achievable closing date.

BOTTOM LINE

Though these types of applications do take some effort to master effectively, they can be a very valuable tool in a complex transaction. The more complex, the more people involved, and the longer the duration, the more value these packages can provide, to the point that they may be the only way to schedule and track a transaction that is extremely large. More important they may provide the only way to ensure that a critical step is not missed.

PACKAGING FOR INVESTORS OR LENDERS

Presentations

Creating a quality presentation takes many of the same skills used for desktop publishing since both contain original aspects. The presentation needs to be attractive and the information well organized. However, creating a presentation is somewhat more difficult in one aspect: because you are working with far fewer words, each one needs to be carefully chosen and each sentence carefully constructed. The good news—programs like Microsoft PowerPoint have made presentation development one of the easiest computer skills that will be required of the typical computer neophyte.

FEATURES AND BENEFITS

One of the most important features to look for in a presentation program is a built-in outliner. Using one to develop your presentation forces you to focus on content. Microsoft PowerPoint (Macintosh and PC-compatible computers) lets you work in an outline view. (See Figure 14-3.) It shows the titles and body text of each slide and, if there are any other objects on the slide, PowerPoint displays an icon to the left of the slide title. The outline can be collapsed to show only the titles, which makes it easy to rearrange the outline. You can also switch between showing formatted and un-formatted text in the outline view. Looking at the outline in plain or un-formatted text is generally easier to read on-screen.

It's important to add graphic elements to keep a presentation interesting. Presentation software allows you to create these graphics within the program, or to import them from other programs. For example, you will frequently want to include a chart or graph. Some presentation programs have the ability to create them within the program; some will let you import a chart from your spreadsheet application, and some will do both. If you use a spreadsheet program regularly, you will probably be already familiar with its charting features. A spreadsheet program will likely have more pow-

FIGURE 14-3

PowerPoint chart with NOI graphed. With a presentation tool like PowerPoint, data and information can be easily presented in a graphical format.

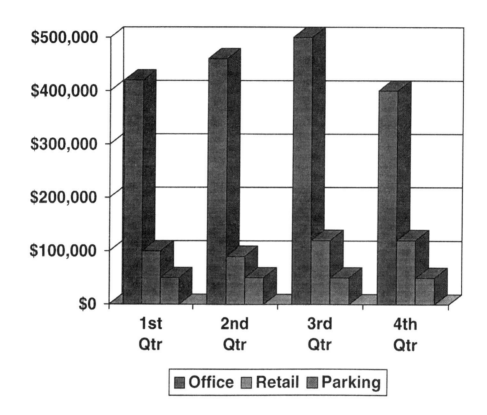

1996 NOI: *Sterling Office Tower*

erful graphing abilities. In that case you will want to create your charts there and import them into the presentation.

Most presentation programs come with pre-designed templates that you can use as you create your presentation, or you can apply one to it after completion. A template contains all the design elements and color schemes for a presentation. PowerPoint comes with 160 artist-created templates which are grouped into families for different types of presentations—35 mm slides, on-screen slide shows, color overheads, and black-and-white overheads. You can switch between them until you find one that gives your presentation the look you want.

Most programs also let you add transitions for your presentation. A transition is the way you move from one slide to the next; there are a variety available in PowerPoint which you can use depending on the type of presentation you are giving. For example, if you are doing on-screen presentations there are "wipes," where the current slide is wiped off and the next slide is gradually displayed. It can occur at a slow, medium, or fast speed. If you are doing an on-screen, 35 mm or overhead slide presentation you can use "builds." With this type, only the slide sub-topic you are currently discussing is highlighted; the others are grayed-out.

Once your presentation is completed PowerPoint can print out your slides, speaker's notes, the outline, and audience handouts. When printing to a black-and-white printer there is an option to turn color slides into black and white, which makes for more readable handouts.

Many offices do not have color printers and/or a file recorder to create 35 mm slides. However, there are many printers and copy shops in most medium to large cities which can produce these materials from your presentation file. These services will work with your PowerPoint file. Check with the copy shop you wish to use ahead of time to see if it produces slides from the program you are using. If you cannot find one in your area, or if it is not convenient to take your presentation there on a disk, you can usually transfer the file via modem. The shop will produce your materials and send them to you via overnight. To find a printer or copy shop check your phone book's Yellow Pages or the back pages of most computer magazines.

Bottom Line

In creating a presentation it's important to be conservative. Do not substitute flash for content. Do not try to get too fancy with either type or colors. Your presentation will end up looking very busy or will come back with the wrong typeface and garish colors. At all costs, keep the text down to the minimum necessary to make your point. The audience should not be reading your presentation off the slide; they should be paying attention to you with the slide providing reinforcement.

Due Diligence and Number Crunching

It would be difficult to cover all the possible information technology platforms and applications that support due diligence and number crunching. This is partly because there are many facets and the seemingly similar processes that anyone may employ can be vastly different. Due diligence can take many different forms based upon the asset class and property type. Nonetheless, this section will cover spreadsheets to address the number crunching and communications, including the Internet, to share information with various parties involved. Other than as a public communications vehicle, the Internet can support the research that may be required with a wealth of market data.

Spreadsheets

Another common computer software tool that will be important to the commercial real estate practitioner is the spreadsheet which allows the user to organize, manipulate, analyze and chart data. The spreadsheet was designed primarily for financial data and analysis. However, charts and tables created in a spreadsheet can be used in presentations and reports, and information from databases, title companies, contact managers, etc. can be imported and manipulated.

Features and Benefits

The center of any spreadsheet program is the grid of rows, columns and cells, sometimes referred to as the worksheet. This is where you enter, store, manipulate, calculate and analyze data. Spreadsheets can manipulate both numbers and text.

Calculations are performed by using formulas including scientific, statistical, financial and mathematical functions. These formulas can easily be applied to the numbers in the spreadsheet by use of menus, templates and examples in the application.

A wide variety of charts can be easily created from worksheet data. Two- and 3-D chart types include column, bar, pie, line, area, and others. They can be created directly on a worksheet or as a separate document in its own window. When worksheet data are changed, the chart is immediately updated to reflect the alteration.

A spreadsheet can also be used as a simple database. Using Excel, the user can create a database on a worksheet and thereby easily store and manipulate small amounts of data. Excel can search or query to find specific data, sort data alphabetically and numerically, and perform calculations on the data for analysis.

Most useful to a commercial real estate analyst are the many spreadsheet templates which perform such things as: cash flow analysis, project cost analysis, mortgage-equity capitalization, rent versus buy comparisons, lease analysis and much more. These templates come ready for you to enter the variables. After you do so, typically you can press a button or select a menu command which runs a spreadsheet macro. This automates a series of actions taken by the program such as performing the calculations and formatting the results into an attractive report.

BOTTOM LINE

The spreadsheet application will be very useful, if not mandatory, for most commercial real estate due diligence. Real estate professionals have an advantage in learning to use a spreadsheet due to their experience working with numbers and financial calculations. However, by spending a little extra time to learn to use a spreadsheet program the user will discover what a powerful and flexible tool it can be. Moreover, in today's environment the spreadsheet is a completely necessary tool to utilize in the due diligence phase and is mandatory to be competitive.

Communications

The methods of communication in business are changing and those in commercial real estate who do not want to be left behind need to start thinking about adapting to these changes. While they currently may not have as much impact on the commercial real estate business as they have on many other businesses, they will, nonetheless, have some effect. Every business needs to communicate well with its customers or suffer the consequence.

FAX MODEM

The fax machine has for years been an indispensable tool for sending information. However, in most offices, fax cover pages are messy, hand-scrawled affairs. Even when they are computer generated, they are still printed out and placed in a fax machine, which is a wasteful and time-consuming procedure.

Using a fax modem is a much better way to send a document that has been created on a computer. Not only does the user save time and paper, but the fax arrives at its destination looking much sharper and, just as important, it can be sent from anywhere a phone connection can be made.

ELECTRONIC MAIL

More and more communications are occurring via electronic mail. E-mail has become an important and efficient way to communicate with people within an office and around the world. To quote an article in the November 14, 1994 issue of *BusinessWeek*: "For business people on the go, E-mail is the best thing to come along since frequent-flyer miles." Although there may not currently be many clients with whom a user can communicate via E-mail, that is changing at a dramatic pace, as E-mail rapidly becomes more widely accepted.

When used in an office, E-mail has many benefits over paper and voice-mail messages and interoffice memos. Paper phone messages become lost, are difficult to file, and require you to decipher someone's handwriting. On the other hand, an E-mail message is easily filed electronically, can be retrieved and printed as needed. Most E-mail systems allow the user to set up multiple folders or mail boxes in which to file messages. These can be searched and information within a message can be copied or exported to other programs.

An E-mail message is much easier to send to a group of people than a paper memorandum. E-mail software generally allows the user to set a priority for a message such as urgent, ASAP, etc. The software can also allow you to set up address groups such as for select clients and administrative staff. Moreover, many programs allow the user or administrator to create specialized forms to tell people, for example, about a new property becoming available. The form would have fields for lease rates, footage, sale price, and other specialized information.

An E-mail system does not have to be limited to exchanging messages within an office. Using a modem, many E-mail packages allow messages to be exchanged with other offices, or with commercial on-line services such as CompuServe, or with the Internet. Since all these systems have gateways to each other, it is now possible to reach anyone in the world on any system, as long as that person has an E-mail address.

Another valuable feature of E-mail is the ability to attach and include a file from another program. This alternate delivery is almost instantaneous and is incredibly cheaper. The monthly cost of Internet access with unlimited use can be less than the cost of one overnight hard copy delivery.

REMOTE ACCESS

Another form of communication is remote access which allows someone with a computer and a modem to connect with his or her office's network and access any available resource. For example, you are in your hotel room in New York working on your laptop computer, making some last minute changes to a presentation you are giving the next morning. Suddenly you realize that you forgot some critical information which is on your office computer in Los Angeles. It's late and the office is closed. No need to panic. You simply use your laptop's internal modem (you made sure to book a room that has a modem port) to dial into the office. Once the modem connection is established you connect to your computer using File Sharing and simply copy the file to your laptop.

With remote access, once you are connected you can access a network resource such as a file, E-mail, or database server, any networked printer, or anything else on your network.

ON-LINE SERVICES

Use of on-line services has grown dramatically over the past few years. With an account on one of these systems (and a computer and modem) you can access a wide variety of services. Typically offered are forums where users with similar interests can post and read messages, download files, and engage in real-time "chat" sessions. Also available are services such as shopping, booking airline flights, and news, weather and sports reports. Most on-line services also give the user some degree of access to the Internet.

One of the largest and fastest growing on-line services is America On-line (AOL). In the news department, AOL has ABC News, *New York Times, Chicago Tribune,* Time Magazine and other periodicals. There are forums for people interested in real estate, business strategies and finance, bicycling, politics, astronomy, military and veteran affairs, Star Trek fans, trivia, and many more. Another consumer-oriented service is CompuServe.

There are also now many real estate-oriented services available. Unlike those that are consumer-oriented, like CompuServe, these business-focused services offer news, information and data targeted to the real estate practitioner. They are also somewhat more costly, but nonetheless do provide a mechanism for collecting data and information to support the due diligence process that otherwise might have taken weeks to collect, if the sources were known at all. These services can provide commercial real estate news, market data, listings and comparables, just to name a few.

Teleres is one of the most comprehensive services; however, there are many others with a more regional or local focus that may be able to provide more specific market information. (See Figure 14-4.) A few of the names of these services are REIS Reports, COMPS, MPF, CREOL, Dorhing On-Line, Jameson Research and Amrex.

Another example of how beneficial and how much more effective a product can be when in an electronic format is COMPS which can be delivered on diskette or accessed on-line. (See Figure 14-5.) COMPS provides detailed commercial property comparables. With on-line delivery the information and data can be quickly re-formatted, combined with other information and copied into a document or presentation.

Many vendors of demographic and economic data make their product and services available on-line. Some of these can be provided either through direct dial-up or on the Internet. The data can be extremely detailed, even down to the block level. This information is becoming more widely accepted as a standard component of due diligence. On-line delivery format allows the data to be integrated much more effectively.

In addition, many local commercial real estate associations are establishing broker networks for their members which will provide complete commercial listing services and local market data.

THE INTERNET

The Internet originated in 1969 as an experimental network by the U.S. Department of Defense. Today, it combines the networks and almost 2 million computers of academic, military, government, and commercial entities from the United States and over 40 countries. And it is growing at an incredible rate.

Using the Internet you can send E-mail to people throughout the world. Using the Internet as a gateway, you can also send E-mail to people who have accounts on commercial information services such as CompuServe, America On-line, GEnie, Prodigy, and a host of other on-line services or Internet sites. High performance access can also be provided by services known as local Internet service providers which make available a fixed low-cost service.

FIGURE 14-4

Teleres showing office market data for Atlanta. Teleres and other on-line services can provide a wealth of market data to support the due diligence process.

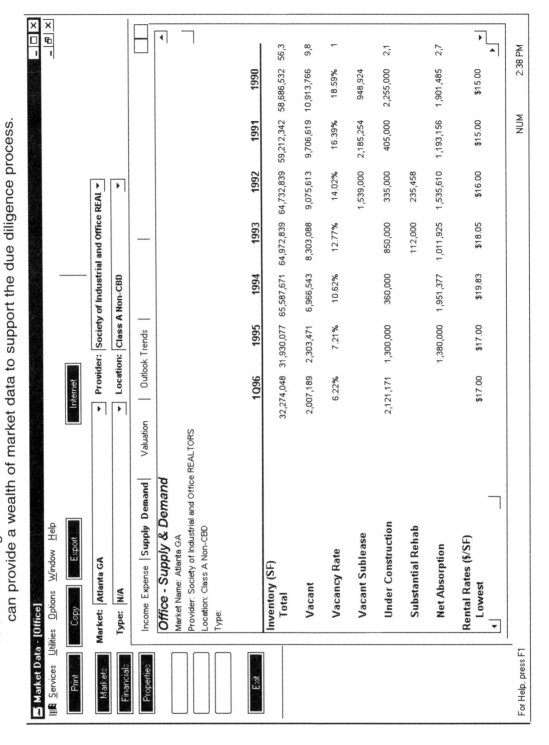

Office - Supply & Demand

Market Name: Atlanta GA
Provider: Society of Industrial and Office REALTORS
Location: Class A Non-CBD
Type:

	1Q96	1995	1994	1993	1992	1991	1990
Inventory (SF)							
Total	32,274,048	31,930,077	65,587,671	64,972,839	64,732,839	59,212,342	58,686,532	56,3
Vacant	2,007,189	2,303,471	6,966,543	8,303,088	9,075,613	9,706,619	10,913,766	9,8
Vacancy Rate	6.22%	7.21%	10.62%	12.77%	14.02%	16.39%	18.59%	1
Vacant Sublease					1,539,000	2,185,254	948,924	
Under Construction	2,121,171	1,300,000	360,000	850,000	335,000	405,000	2,255,000	2,1
Substantial Rehab				112,000	235,458			
Net Absorption		1,380,000	1,951,377	1,011,925	1,535,610	1,193,156	1,901,485	2,7
Rental Rates ($/SF)							
Lowest	$17.00	$17.00	$19.83	$18.05	$16.00	$15.00	$15.00	

495

FIGURE 14-5

COMP's Quick COMP Report. Having this type of information in your computer can be extremely valuable and reduce significantly the production time of reports and presentations.

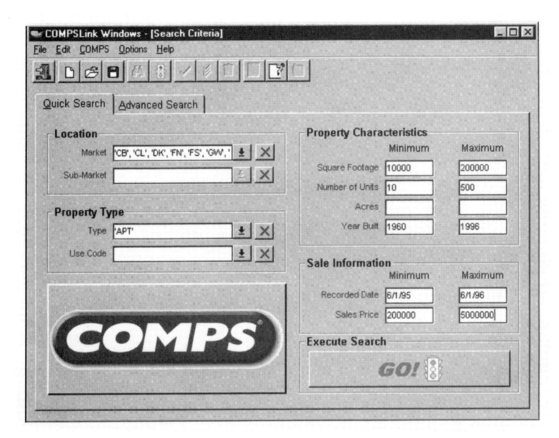

COMPSLink® Windows™ from COMPS® InfoSystems, Inc. is powerful database management software specifically designed to access COMPS' information quickly and effectively. Using an intuitive Windows interface, subscribers have access to high-quality data with the added flexibility of setting their own parameters to let the computer do the tedious sorting and searching. This is an example of COMPSLink's Quick Search Screen.

Like commercial on-line services, the Internet offers forums for users with similar interests to exchange messages through what are called Newsgroups. As of January 1994 there were over 6000 Newsgroups in existence covering just about every imaginable topic. The Internet also allow users to download files to their computers through the use of File Transfer Protocol (FTP).

One of the most popular parts of the Internet is the World Wide Web (WWW or Web). There are literally many thousands of "real estate" sites on the Web. These range from free sites through which an individual is marketing his or her individual house, to commercial listings from leading brokerage firms, to market data, to public and private

FIGURE 14-5 (CONT'D)

COMPSLink® Windows™ gives a summary view and color thumbnail photograph of the properties matching each query. Tabs make the information easy to read.

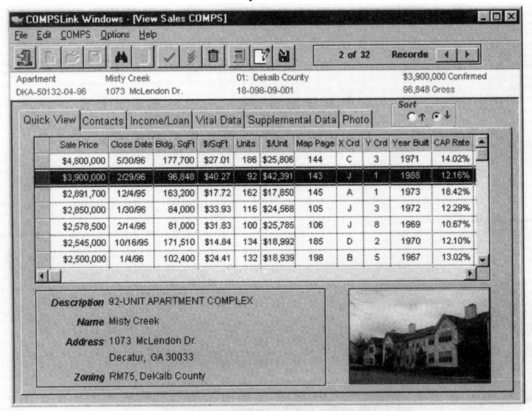

market data. Many chambers of commerce and economic development councils provide a wealth of real estate, economic, demographic, financial and even political information via the World Wide Web.

The Internet now also has many real-estate oriented search listings where someone can find web sites that contain desired information. PIKE-NET, REVIEW ON-LINE and those sponsored by organizations like ULI and NAREIT contain hundreds of links to other web sites containing useful information. (See Figure 14-6.) In many cases the content of the linked sites is reviewed and a synopsis provided.

BOTTOM LINE

The Internet is an incredibly vast and fast-growing network of information. More and more business organizations are discovering at an increasingly rapid rate how important it is to be connected within an office and with the outside world. Electronic communications in whatever form you choose should be an integral part of your information technology tools set.

FIGURE 14-6

PikeNet showing Atlanta market area toolkit. This is just one source from literally thousands that an investor can review to see what the market activity is and even prospect for deals.

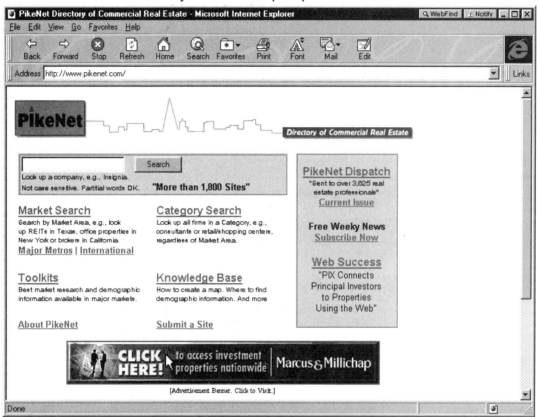

VALUATION AND FINANCING

Cash flow modeling tools also known as discounted cash flow tools ("DCF") have become the standard for analyzing a property's cash flow down to the lease level. These applications can handle all the variations and complexities involved in all but the most complicated leases. Another reason for their acceptance as a standard is that any model completed will employ the same methodology. The significance is that other parties that may review the model do not have to review the methodology or mathematics involved, rather only the assumptions made.

BENEFITS AND FEATURES

The DCF allows a user basically to answer questions regarding property, tenant, lease, and market variables and then make some assumptions about rent and expense growth. The application then provides detailed cash flows at the property and lease level, computes a present value of the cash flows for each period, and calculates a value for the asset. This is done without the user spending what could be hundreds of hours developing computer code that performs the mathematical equations and algorithms necessary.

FIGURE 14-6

REVIEW ON-LINE is another example of the wealth of information available to the real estate investor within easy reach on the Internet.

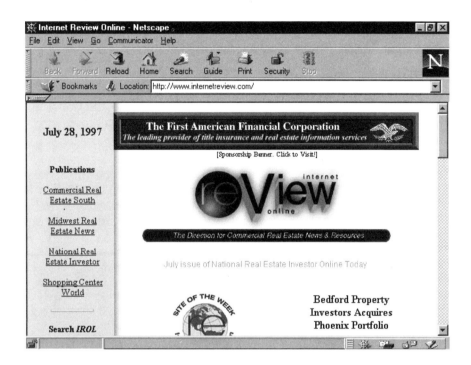

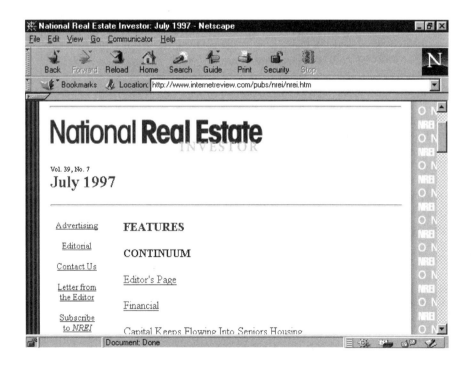

The leading programs also include a variety of standard reports that have been developed over the years with input from the market place. These are generally in the format and contain the information that investors, rating agencies and lenders want to review.

The file for an individual property can be provided electronically to others within the firm or to third parties to review; the assumptions can even be adjusted without starting from scratch. Many appraisers and asset managers that need to complete annual evaluations simply pull up the file from last year and then update the tenant and lease information, adjust the rent and expense escalations as necessary, and re-run the program.

The leading applications include ARGUS, Dyna and ProJect. (See Figure 14-7.) Each of these is a mature product, well recognized in the market and widely used. There are a few others that are perhaps more specialized and several that include additional features, but are not the industry standards and will not be as well received by a broad range of users.

BOTTOM LINE

These applications are a very strong tool to effectively and definitively analyze cash flows and establish values. The fact that many real estate finance practitioners utilize and even require a DCF tool to be used to underwrite an investment cannot be overlooked. They also allow an evaluation to be repeatable with minimum effort once the original model is completed.

ASSET MANAGEMENT

Databases

Today, the words "asset management" and "databases" seem to be synonymous. Perhaps this is as they should be, since one requires the capture, retention and analysis of large amounts of data, and the other was designed for the capture, retention and analysis of large amounts. A database management program is a tool for designing and constructing, storing, organizing, managing and retrieving information. It allows the user to custom design the database structures to suit the users' needs. This includes specifying and designing the fields, entry forms, reports and other aspects of database design.

Nearly all database development is now done in what is known as relational database applications. They are called "relational" because the technology was constructed around the concept of relating data types and groups of data to one another in a logical and physical organization. The programs allow the user to view the data in this relational organization which is much more logical to the typical user. Relational databases' speed, versatility, and degree of control have made this type prominent in businesses.

However, these advantages come at the price of dramatically increased complexity. Hence, creating such a relational database is most often a job best left to a database consultant. It consists of one or more files (sometimes referred to as tables). A file or table usually stores one type of data. For example, a table could hold a list of clients which would include the name, company, address and phone number. Another related table could hold the data pertaining to the client's properties. Each file in a database is made up of one or more records, while each record consists of one or more "fields." A single record might contain separate fields for a person's first and last name, company, address and phone number. Since a good database will let you sort or search by name, company, address, etc., it is necessary to put these different types of data that make up this single record into separate fields.

FIGURE 14-7

ARGUS showing rent roll or cash flow summary page. ARGUS can quickly provide a detailed cash flow for analysis.

Property Description

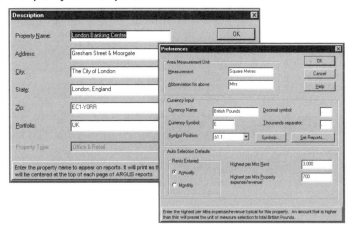

Area Measures

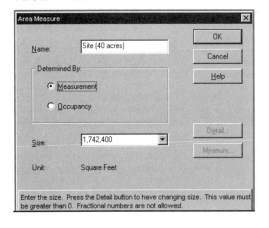

Inflation Rates

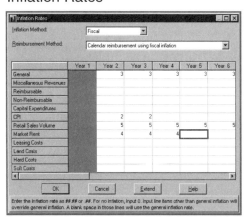

FIGURE 14-7 (CONT'D)

Expenses, Revenues & Expenditures

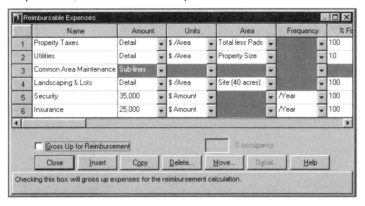

Rent Roll

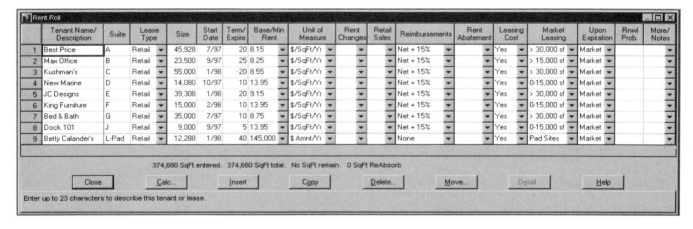

Detailed Reimbursement Methods

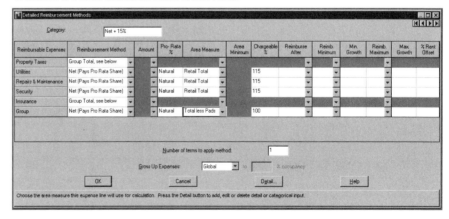

FIGURE 14-7 (CONT'D)

Market Leasing Assumptions

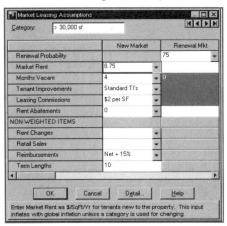

Property Purchase and Resale

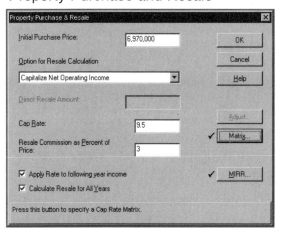

Debt Financing

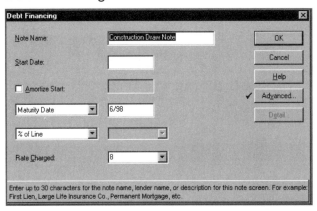

FIGURE 14-7 (CONT'D)

Property Level Reports

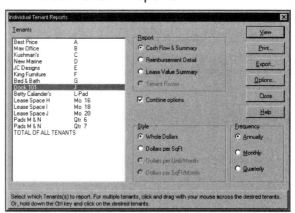

SCHEDULE OF PROSPECTIVE CASH FLOW In Inflated Dollars for the Fiscal Year beginning 1/1/1997					
For the Years Ending	Year 1 Dec-1997	Year 2 Dec-1998	Year 3 Dec-1999	Year 4 Dec-2000	Year 5 Dec-2001
POTENTIAL GROSS REVENUE					
Base Rental Revenue	$594,699	$3,620,341	$3,637,779	$3,637,779	$3,637,779
Expense Reimbursement Revenue	83,325	834,863	984,398	1,013,934	1,044,348
TOTAL POTENTIAL GROSS REVENUE	678,024	4,455,204	4,622,177	4,651,713	4,682,127
REVENUE ADJUSTMENTS					
Absorption & Turnover Vacancy	98,838	550,950			
General Vacancy			231,109	232,586	234,106
TOTAL REVENUE ADJUSTMENTS	98,838	550,950	231,109	232,586	234,106
EFFECTIVE GROSS REVENUE	579,186	3,904,254	4,391,068	4,419,127	4,448,021
OPERATING EXPENSES					
Property Taxes	287,144	591,516	609,261	627,539	646,365
Utilities	15,356	75,473	89,597	92,295	95,054
Repairs & Maintenance	58,022	89,734	92,426	95,198	98,054
Security	36,000	37,080	38,192	39,338	40,518
Insurance	25,000	25,750	26,523	27,318	28,138
Management Fee	23,167	156,170	175,643	176,765	177,921
TOTAL OPERATING EXPENSES	444,689	975,723	1,031,642	1,058,443	1,086,050
NET OPERATING INCOME	134,497	2,928,531	3,359,426	3,360,684	3,361,971
LEASING & CAPITAL COSTS					

Close   Cancel   ClipBrd   Graph

Individual Tenant Reports

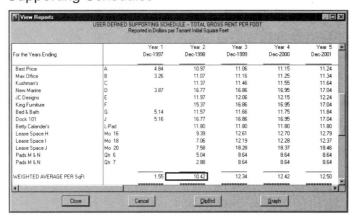

Supporting Schedules

USER DEFINED SUPPORTING SCHEDULE – TOTAL GROSS RENT PER FOOT Reported in Dollars per Tenant Initial Square Feet						
For the Years Ending		Year 1 Dec-1997	Year 2 Dec-1998	Year 3 Dec-1999	Year 4 Dec-2000	Year 5 Dec-2001
Best Price	A	4.84	10.97	11.06	11.15	11.24
Max Office	B	3.26	11.07	11.16	11.25	11.34
Kushman's	C		11.37	11.46	11.55	11.64
New Marine	D	3.87	16.77	16.86	16.95	17.04
JC Designs	E		11.97	12.06	12.15	12.24
King Furniture	F		15.37	16.86	16.95	17.04
Bed & Bath	G	5.14	11.57	11.66	11.75	11.84
Dock 101	J	5.16	16.77	16.86	16.95	17.04
Betty Calander's	L-Pad		11.80	11.80	11.80	11.80
Lease Space H	Mo 16		9.39	12.61	12.70	12.79
Lease Space I	Mo 18		7.06	12.19	12.28	12.37
Lease Space J	Mo 20		7.58	18.28	18.37	18.46
Pads M & N	Qtr 6		5.04	8.64	8.64	8.64
Pads M & N	Qtr 7		2.88	8.64	8.64	8.64
WEIGHTED AVERAGE PER SqFt		1.55	10.42	12.34	12.42	12.50

Close   Cancel   ClipBrd   Graph

FIGURE 14-7 (CONT'D)

Graphs and "Fast Graphs"

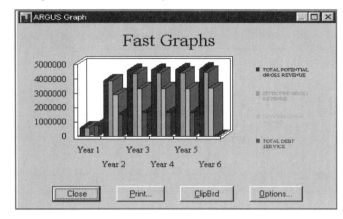

Portfolios and Scenarios

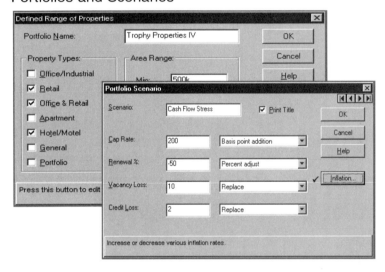

Development

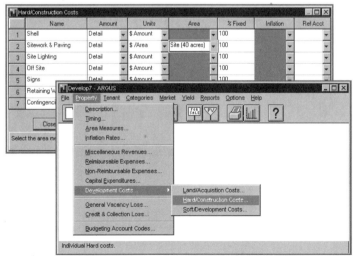

FIGURE 14-7 (CONT'D)

Property Level Reports

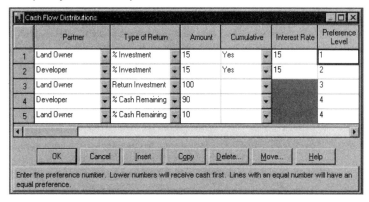

Individual Tenant Reports

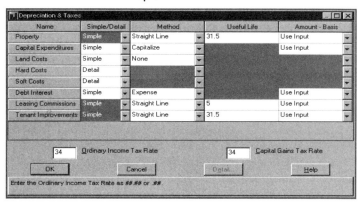

Supporting Schedules

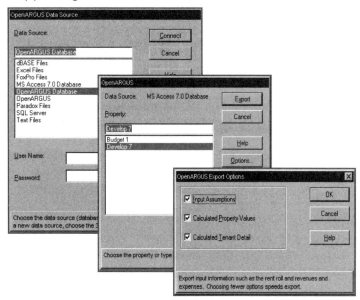

BENEFITS AND FEATURES

The relational database can store large of amounts of related data in logical groupings and allow almost unlimited retrieval, analysis and reporting. The database is designed so that any desktop computer can handle virtually thousands of records. This is a feat that Lotus or Excel cannot do as they require too much memory to process large number of records.

BOTTOM LINE

Just as the word processing application can be the most time-saving tool in the office, an asset management database system can be the most powerful and, with a bit of work, the most flexible.

A simple relational database can be very easy for anyone to set up and use. However, as needs become more sophisticated and the project more complex, one can soon find oneself frustrated and spending too much time trying to get things to work right. At that point, consider hiring a professional, especially if the database is going to play an important role in the operations of a business.

COMPUTING BOTTOM LINE

Getting set up with a computer and software requires many different decisions, each of which forces you to choose between many pros and cons. Here are a few very general guidelines:

Don't be penny wise and pound foolish—a mistake many people make when it comes to computers. Stated another way, do not cost yourself hundreds of hours of work and lost productivity because you wanted to save some money. Remember that you can always make more money, but time lost is gone forever. Too often people try to make do and plod along with the wrong computer and/or the wrong application software. While you also do not want to go overboard, make sure you do not handicap yourself and your business for the sake of saving a few bucks. If you get the wrong program, or you buy something that does not work for you, be willing to admit that it is the wrong tool and go and get the right one. But do not toss something away until you have given it a good try and made an effort to evaluate it properly.

Get the right tool for the job. If you are going to be running a major database, get a computer with the processing power, memory and disk space to handle it. When it comes to contact managers and PIMs, the simple ones can run with adequate performance on just about any computer. But the heavy-duty PIMs usually require more horsepower. Word processing and spreadsheet software generally do not require much in the way of computing power. However, there are some exceptions to this rule. If you are working on very long and/or complex word processing documents, or if you are using a very feature-rich word processing program (such as Microsoft Word) then you will need a computer with processing power and more RAM memory. The same applies if you are manipulating large sets of data in a spreadsheet program.

When considering an application, evaluate all necessary criteria and priorities. At a high level, these should include functionality, ease of use, technology platform compatibility, vendor support, vendor's reputation and vendor's market share. If you are not certain or do not know how to establish your requirements and criteria to make a selection, do not hesitate to solicit advice and consultation support.

Howto successfully acquire a real estate investment from start to finish: two case studies

To give the reader a better understanding of the acquisition process, two case studies have been developed. These case studies show how an investor finds and analyzes a real estate transaction. Although this book mentions many types of real estate investments, these case studies will use an apartment property and an office building as their subjects. The same due diligence process and analytical tools used here can be easily applied to other types of real estate. Since the acquisition process is rather lengthy and requires much hard work backed up by experience, these case studies were designed to give the reader an overview of the process. No single study can completely give the reader the total picture of the acquisition process; for that you must go through the experience yourself. And it may take several "false starts" before you become comfortable with the process. However, with this book, combined with the experience of the real world, the reader should start to develop the skills needed to complete a successful transaction.

CASE STUDY: HOW TO BUY AN APARTMENT BUILDING

Background Information About the Purchaser

Mr. Hal Burton, a thirty-five year old businessman from Atlanta, Georgia, has recently inherited $4,000,000 from his great uncle's estate. Hal has decided, after sitting down with his advisors, that after the taxes on his income, he will invest $1,000,000 in real estate and put the balance in a liquid portfolio of stocks and bonds.

Deciding on the Investment Strategy

Because Hal had had some experience in real estate investing and actually managed a small twenty-unit apartment property while he was in college, he decided that he would like to buy an apartment property somewhere in the Atlanta area. Prior to beginning his search for this investment, Hal started to enumerate his investment criteria. Since his past experiences with partners had not been fully satisfactory, he thought he would feel more comfortable investing in this property by himself. Due to his limited time schedule, he also decided that he should find himself a capable local management company that specializes in managing apartment properties. After many hours of talking to local real estate brokers, bankers and management companies, Hal drafted his investment strategy.

Type of Property:	Apartment complex
Location:	Atlanta, Georgia
Age of Property:	Five to ten years old
Size of Investment:	$3 million-$5 million
Investment Quality:	Class B
Tenant Profile:	Middle income
Construction:	Two-story walk-up, stick built, brick exterior, pitched roof, individual utility meters
Holding Period:	5-7 years
Return on Investment:	Minimum 5 percent cash on cash—year 1

Choosing the Investment Ownership Vehicle

Although Hal had decided that he did not want any outside partners, he chose to purchase this future property in partnership with his wife. This way, he could use the partnership vehicle while sharing the transaction with someone close to him. Why he chose this vehicle was to shelter whatever income the property generated with whatever tax benefits were derived from this ownership.

Finding the Right Property

Once Hal completed his shopping list for this purchase, he set about sending this list to local real estate brokers, management companies, bankers, and local appraisers. Since finding a suitable investment was hard work, he wanted to spread the word to as many people as possible. Hal also put a small advertisement in a local Atlanta newspaper. This ad read as follows:

APARTMENT PROPERTY WANTED

$1,000,000 EQUITY

5-10 YEARS OLD

BRICK CONSTRUCTION, INDIVIDUAL METERS, PITCHED ROOF

SEND COMPLETE PACKAGE TO

HAL BARTON

P.O. BOX 4444

ATLANTA, GEORGIA 30067

Narrowing Down the Selection

Over the next thirty days, Hal received over 100 packages on various properties for sale. He was amazed that even with his ad and the letters he sent out, many of the properties did not even come close to what he was looking for. After another month of sorting through the responses, Hal started putting these packages in three categories: Category 1, for properties that did not match his criteria; Category 2. for those that met at least 50 percent of his buying criteria; Category 3, for those that met at least 80 percent. Out of more than 100 packages, Hal had only five that were in Category 3.

With these five properties in hand, Hal set up appointments with the property owners or their brokers. Since he was relatively new to buying property, he decided to take someone knowledgeable along with him. During his search for this investment, Hal had met John Martin, owner of a local management company that managed over 3,000 apartment units, and who was also president of the local apartment association. Hal spent many hours with him discussing real estate, as well as the philosophy of managing property. He felt very comfortable with Mr. Martin and decided that when he found his ideal investment, he would use him to manage the property. However, just for reassurance, he told his new acquaintance that he would still like to get a second opinion regarding the property.

Negotiating a Successful Deal

After meeting with the five property owners, Hal made offers to three. It seemed that out of the two other properties, one was misrepresented in the package and the other property was not really for sale. Hal's three offers were very similar. He knew that the capitalization rates for these types of properties were in the 10 percent range and that he was looking for at least 5 percent cash flow the first year. With the help of Mr. Martin, Hal prepared a cash flow statement and noticed that in all three cases his statements were somewhat different from the figures given in the packages.

After sending out the three letters of intent, he started to negotiate with each seller. The first seller held firmly to a price that equated to a 9 percent cap rate. Hal decided that although the property met all his buying criteria, the price was too high. The second property was in his range of acceptable price, but due to problems that the seller had with his partners, it had to be taken off the market. That left the third property, Spanish Oaks Apartments.

After many hours of negotiating with the owners of this property, Hal was able to structure a deal that was acceptable to both parties. He had the seller sign the letter of intent, and then sent it to his attorney to prepare the purchase contract. When the contracting was completed, he reviewed it, made some minor changes, and sent it to the seller and his attorney. Over the next week, Hal was able to finalize the negotiations of the contract; both parties signed it and he deposited $10,000 earnest money with a local title company. He then had thirty days to complete his inspection of the property. Within minutes of signing the contract, he contacted John Martin and asked him to help assemble his inspection team.

Finalizing the Agreement During the Inspection Period

The next day, Hal met at John Martin's office with Bob Morgan, a local engineer who specialized in reviewing the structural aspects of apartment properties, and Gary Polster, Hal's attorney. He instructed Martin to complete a thorough inspection of the property with Bob Morgan to determine what structural problems the property had, as well as what the costs would be to correct any deferred maintenance items. Hal also asked John to complete a total analysis of the past operating history of the property for the last year and then to make a realistic forecast of the next twelve months' cash flow position. This report was also to include a complete market analysis of all the competition in the area. He then told his attorney to review the existing mortgage documents on the property, to review and update the title policy, to review any current easements on the property, and to order a new as built survey for the property.

As this information started to come in, Hal set up meetings with these individuals to discuss their findings. Due to this intensive investigation process, Hal uncovered some interesting information. For example, he found out from Bob Morgan that the property was in excellent shape overall, but there was one building that had some termite damage that would require $10,000 to correct. On the other hand, John Martin's market study showed that the current rates were actually 5 percent under current market rates. It appeared that the seller's management company was not very aggressive in raising the rents. With this information, Hal concluded that he might have a better deal than he originally thought. He decided that even though the rents could be raised, he would still go back to the seller and ask him to pay the $10,000 for the termite damage. After two days of haggling back and forth, Hal finally negotiated a settlement and split the $10,000 down the middle.

During this thirty-day period, the seller came back and told Hal that the first mortgage lender was giving him problems in having the loan assumed. In response, Hal asked for a meeting with the lender, which was represented by Phil Johnson, the vice president of First Bank of Atlanta. Mr. Johnson said that they were unhappy with the seller's record of monthly debt service payment. He also wanted to know what expertise Hal had in owning properties of this type. Hal told him of his association with John Martin and his philosophy of managing his investments. In addition, it came up in the conversation that he had just received a rather large inheritance. Mr. Johnson then stated that it would make a big difference in their future lending relationship if Hal would make a deposit into the bank. Although Hal had a banking relationship with another local institution, he felt that in order to expedite matters and to build another banking relationship, he would deposit $250,000 in the bank. Mr. Johnson was happy with this arrangement, but told Hal that there still would be a $20,000 fee to transfer the loan into his name. Hal asked the banker to hold on while he got the seller on the phone and told him the situation. Hal then negotiated that he would pay 25% of this fee and the seller would pay the balance. He then went back and told the lender that he felt that $20,000 was too high and that with his new balance in the bank he should only pay $15,000. Mr. Johnson thought about it for a minute and agreed.

With all of the deal negotiations completed, Hal told his team that he would like one more meeting before the thirty-day inspection period was over, to review the deal one more time. At this meeting, Hal once again had everyone review their area of expertise. He then had everyone complete his deal rating sheet. Although this deal got high marks from all parties, Hal still had some reservations. His fears were that even though the market was 95 percent occupied and this property was 96 percent occupied with rents below the market, someone could come in and build some more new units down the street. John Martin told him that this was true, but due to the high cost of apartment land in the area and the fact that the local zoning department just lowered the number of apartment units that could be built per acre, any new apartment development would have rents at least 10 percent higher than his property. With this information in hand, Hal took a deep breath and told his attorney to write the seller and tell him that he was prepared to close the transaction. Hal then told everyone that he would like to meet again the following Monday to plan the closing strategy.

The Closing Process

PRECLOSING

At the preclosing meeting, Hal told John Martin to prepare to take over the management of the property. He asked him to do some specific assignments: to meet with the current management, to compile an updated rent roll and list of all deposits, to be prepared to notify all the tenants after the closing as well as the property vendors, and to personally walk through all the vacant units the morning of the closing to make sure that they were in rent-ready condition. He also requested that John prepare the operating prorations for the closing statement. He asked Bob Morgan to oversee the repair work on the building with the termite damage once the property was closed. Hal then asked his attorney to prepare all the closing documents and to make sure that he met with the lender's attorney and the seller's attorney prior to the closing to work out any last minute problems.

THE CLOSING DAY

The morning of the closing, Hal got a call from John Martin. John told him that not only were three units not in rent-ready condition, but that there were now ten units vacant. It appeared that the current resident manager was bitter over the fact that the property was going to be sold and that the new management company was going to replace her. Because of this situation, she quit the week before the closing and told a number of the tenants that the property was going to be purchased. These residents, fearing that the new owners were going to be worse than the current owner, decided to leave within the month. Luckily, Hal had a clause in the contract stating that if the property was not 95 percent rented with a minimum of six-month leases the day of the closing, the seller would have to guarantee the units at the current rent levels until those units were rented. In addition, the contract stated that any units not in rent-ready condition would cost the seller $200 per unit. With this information in hand, Hal contacted the seller and got him to reconfirm his guarantee as well as to readjust the sales price due to the moneys needed to prepare these three units.

AT THE CLOSING TABLE

Due to the fact that he had done his homework and kept after his team, Hal was able to go to the closing and in one hour sign all of the documents necessary to complete his intended acquisition.

POSTCLOSING ACTIVITIES

The day after the closing, Hal noticed that he felt different. The last few weeks had been extremely hectic. This morning he felt somewhat depressed. He realized that his first large real estate deal was now completed and that all of the excitement of the chase was now over. With this in mind, he realized that now was the time to reap the benefits of his time and efforts through efficient property management.

He then contacted his team members once again and told them to start the next phase of their duties.

Throughout this process, Hal used many forms, such as the following, to aid the search for his ideal investment.

Investment Criteria Checklist

PREPARED BY <u>Hal Barton</u>
DATE PREPARED <u>July 18, 19XX</u>

TYPE PROPERTY:

RESIDENTIAL:		WAREHOUSE BUILDINGS:		LODGING:		
SINGLE FAMILY	_____	LIGHT INDUSTRIAL	_____	MOTEL		_____
DUPLEX-QUADRAPLEX	_____	HEAVY INDUSTRIAL	_____	HOTEL		_____
MULTI-FAMILY	X	MINI-WAREHOUSE:	_____	SINGLE PURPOSE BUILDINGS:		
MOBILE HOME	_____	LODGING:		_____		_____
CONDOMINIUM	_____	MOTEL	_____	_____		_____
COOPERATIVE	_____	HOTEL	_____	_____		_____
CONVERSION	_____	MULTI-USE PROPERTIES:		_____		_____
RETIREMENT HOUSING	_____	RESIDENTIAL/RETAIL	_____	_____		_____
REHABILITATION	_____	RESIDENTIAL/OFFICE	_____	RAW LAND:		
NURSING HOME	_____	OFFICE/HOTEL	_____	RESIDENTIAL		_____
COMMERCIAL:		OFFICE/RETAIL	_____	RETAIL		_____
RETAIL:		RES/OFF/RETAIL/HOTEL	_____	OFFICE		_____
STRIP CENTER	_____	CONDOMINIUM:		INDUSTRIAL		_____
NEIGHBORHOOD CENTER	_____	RESIDENTIAL	_____	AGRICULTURAL		_____
COMMUNITY CENTER	_____	OFFICE	_____	DISTRESSED PROPERTY:		
REGIONAL CENTER	_____	RETAIL	_____	RESIDENTIAL		_____
SUPER REGIONAL CENTER	_____	INDUSTRIAL	_____	RETAIL		_____
THEME CENTER:		RECYCLING:		OFFICE		_____
OFF-PRICE CENTER	_____	RESIDENTIAL	_____	INDUSTRIAL		_____
FACTORY OUTLET	_____	OFFICE	_____	LODGING		_____
FASHION CENTER	_____	RETAIL	_____	LAND PLAY		_____
CAR CARE CENTER	_____	INDUSTRIAL	_____			
OFFICE BUILDING:	_____					
BUSINESS PARKS:	_____					

LOCATION: <u>Atlanta, Georgia</u>   AGE OF PROPERTY: <u>5–10</u>   HOLDING PERIOD: <u>5–7</u>

INVESTMENT VEHICLE:

				SIZE OF INVESTMENT:		INVESTMENT QUALITY:	
SOLE OWNERSHIP	_____	JT. TENANCY	_____	NUMBER UNITS	80–150	CLASS A	
LTD. PARTN'P	_____	CORPORATION	_____	SQUARE FOOTAGE	_____	CLASS B	X
GEN. PARTN'P	X	SUBCHAPTER S	_____	EQUITY	$1M	CLASS C	_____
TENANTS-COMMON	_____	REIT	_____	MAX. PRICE	$3–5M	CLASS D	_____
						TRIPLE NET PROPERTIES	_____

TENANT PROFILE:

RESIDENTIAL:		OFFICE:		RETAIL:		INDUSTRIAL:		LODGING:	
WHITE COLLAR	X	FORTUNE 500	_____	ANCHORED:	_____	FORTUNE 500:	_____	BUSINESS:	_____
BLUE COLLAR	_____	FORTUNE 1000	_____	LOCALS	_____	FORTUNE 1000	_____	CONVENTION:	_____
ALL ADULT	X	REGIONAL	_____			REGIONAL	_____	FAMILY:	_____
FAMILY	_____	LOCAL	_____			LOCAL	_____	RESORT:	_____

TYPE CONSTRUCTION:

RESIDENTIAL:				COMMERCIAL:			
STICK BUILT	X	UTILITY SYSTEM:		STICK BUILT	_____	UTILITY SYSTEM:	
MASONRY	X	2 PIPE	_____	MASONRY	_____	2 PIPE	_____
ONE LEVEL	_____	4 PIPE	_____	TILT UP	_____	4 PIPE	_____
2–3 STORY WALK UP	X	MASTER METER	_____	LIGHT STEEL	_____	MASTER METER	_____
MID RISE	_____	INDIVIDUAL METER	X	CONCRETE	_____	INDIVIDUAL METER	_____
HIGH RISE	_____	ROOF SYSTEM:		STEEL	_____	ROOF SYSTEM:	
		FLAT	_____	LOW RISE	_____	FLAT	_____
		PITCHED	X	MID RISE	_____	PITCHED	_____
				HIGH RISE	_____		

RETURN ON INVESTMENT:

				BUYING PRICE RANGE:	
CASH FLOW	5 %	RESALE YIELD ON PURCH. PRICE	_____ %	GROSS RENT MULTIPLIER	6.5–7.5
TAX LOSSES	_____ %	INTERNAL RATE OF RETURN	_____ %	CAP RATE	9–10
RESALE YIELD ON CAPITAL	_____ %			PRICE/SQ.FT.	$50's
				PRICE/UNIT	$38–45,000

Property Log In Report

PREPARED BY: Hal Barton
TYPE PROPERTY: Apartment

DATE	PROPERTY NAME	ADDRESS	RECEIVED FROM	TEL. NO.	ASKING PRICE	GRM	PRICE/ SQ.FT.	PRICE/ UNIT	CAP. RATE	COMMENTS
7-1	Oak Leaf	123 Spring St.	Adams Realty	(404) 555-1111	$ 4M	7.8	$ 54.00	$ 40,000	8.3	Poor Access
7-4	Spanish Oaks	510 River Rd.	Bill Thomas-owner	(404) 555-1236	$ 4.2M	7.37	$ 52.50	$ 42,000	8.92	Good Possibilities
7-8	Knob Hill	81 Temple Ave.	Jim Best	(404) 555-6871	$ 5.1M	7.9	$ 58.00	$ 44,000	8.6	Poor Construction
				( )	$		$	$		
				( )	$		$	$		
				( )	$		$	$		
				( )	$		$	$		
				( )	$		$	$		
				( )	$		$	$		
				( )	$		$	$		
				( )	$		$	$		
				( )	$		$	$		
				( )	$		$	$		
				( )	$		$	$		
				( )	$		$	$		
				( )	$		$	$		
				( )	$		$	$		
				( )	$		$	$		
				( )	$		$	$		

515

Residential Transaction Summary

PROPERTY NAME Spanish Oaks
ADDRESS 510 River Rd.
Atlanta Ga
SELLER Bill Thomas
    CONTACT
    ADDRESS

TEL. NO. (404) 555-1236

DATE Aug. 1, 19XX

RATING 85/100

12 MONTH OPERATING PROFORMA

BROKER
    CONTACT
    ADDRESS

TEL. NO. ( )
DATE

CURRENT OCCUPANCY 96%
SALES PRICE $ 4,200,000
GROSS RENTAL MULTIPLIER
  (GRM) 7.37 X
CAPITALIZATION RATE 8.92
PRICE/SQ.FT. $ 52.50
PRICE/UNIT $ 42,000

UNIT INFORMATION

#UNITS	TYPE	SQ.FT.	RENT	RENT/SF
50	1,1 Gdn	600	$ 450	$ .75
50	2, 2 Gdn	1,000	$ 500	$ .50
			$	$
			$	$
			$	$
			$	$
TOTAL 100		80,000	$ 47,500	$
AVE		800	$ 475	$ .59

YEAR 19XX

REVENUE:

GROSS POTENTIAL INCOME	$ 570,000
VACANCY	$ 28,500
LATE CHARGES	$
NSF CHARGES	$
LAUNDRY	$
APPLICATION FEE	$
FORFEITED DEPOSITS	$
PET FEES	$
VENDING	$ 5,500
MISC.	$
MISC.	$
TOTAL REVENUE	$ 547,000

EXPENSES:

SALARIES & WAGES	$ 20,000
REPAIRS & MAINTENANCE	$ 10,000
UTILITIES	$ 10,000
TAXES	$ 25,000
INSURANCE	$ 10,000
GENERAL & ADMINISTRATIVE	$ 20,000
MANAGEMENT FEES	$ 27,350
PROFESSIONAL FEES	$ 4,000
MARKETING	$ 15,000
CONTRACT SERVICES	$ 25,700
RESERVES & REPLACEMENTS	$ 5,500
TOTAL EXPENSES	$ 172,550

NET OPERATING INCOME — $ 374,450

DEBT SERVICE:

1ST MTG.	$ 315,925
2ND MTG.	$
3RD MTG.	$
TOTAL DEBT SERVICE	$ 315,925

CAPITAL EXPENDITURES — $ 8,205
CASH FLOW — $ 50,320

MORTGAGE TERMS

1ST MTG:
  LENDER 1st Bankers
  ORIGINAL BAL. $ 3M
  CURRENT BAL. (AS OF ___) $
  INTEREST RATE 10 %   AMORT. 30
  MATURITY DATE 19XX
  MONTHLY PAYMENT $ 26,327.15
  COMMENTS Tax & Insurance Escrow

TENANT PAYS:
  ELECTRICITY ___ X
  GAS ___ NA
  WATER
  SEWER
  CABLE
  TRASH

MORTGAGE TERMS

2ND MTG:
  LENDER
  ORIGINAL BAL. $
  CURRENT BAL. (AS OF ___) $
  INTEREST RATE ___%   AMORT.
  MATURITY DATE
  MONTHLY PAYMENT $
  COMMENTS

MORTGAGE TERMS

3RD MTG:
  LENDER
  ORIGINAL BAL. $
  CURRENT BAL. (AS OF ___) $
  INTEREST RATE ___%   AMORT.
  MATURITY DATE
  MONTHLY PAYMENT $
  COMMENTS

COMMENTS

516

FORM 15-3

Residential Lease Summary

PROPERTY NAME Spanish Oaks
ADDRESS 510 River Rd.
Atlanta, GA

TELEPHONE NO. (404) 555-6100
OWNERSHIP Bill Thomas
TEL. NO. (404) 555-1236

MANAGEMENT Bill Thomas
TEL. NO. ( )
LEASING AGENT
TEL. NO. ( )

PAGE ___ OF ___

DATE Aug 1, 19XX

TENANT PAYS:
GAS ___
ELEC X
WATER ___
SEWER ___
CABLE ___

UNFURNISHED X
FURNISHED ___
RENT ___
RENT ___
RENT ___

FLOOR MEASUREMENT:
GROSS ___
NET 80,000

UNIT MIX:

UNIT TYPE	UNIT MIX	SQ.FT.	STREET RENT	RENT/ S.F.	NO. OCCUPIED	% OCCUPIED
1,1 Gdn	50	600	$ 450	$ .75	48	96 %
2,2 Gdn	50	1000	$ 500	$ .50	48	96 %
			$	$		%
			$	$		%
			$	$		%
			$	$		%
			$	$		%
TOTAL	100	80,000			96	96 %
AVERAGE		800	$ 475	$ .59		

DATE OF LAST RENT INCREASE Jan 1, 19xx

TENANT	ADDRESS	UNIT TYPE	LEASE TERM	BEG. DATE	END DATE	SEC. DEP.	PET DEP.	FURN. DEP.	RENT/ MONTH	FURN. RENT/ MONTH	OPTIONS	COMMENTS
Jones, B	1-A	1, 1	12 mo	Feb 1	Jan 31	$ 450	$	$	$ 450	$		
Smith, C	2-A	1, 1	12 mo	March 1	Feb 28	$ 450	$	$	$ 450	$		
Martin, D	3-A	1, 1	12 mo	April 11	Mar 31	$ 450	$	$	$ 450	$		
Howell, B	4-A	1, 1	12 mo	Nov 1	Oct 31	$ 430	$	$	$ 430	$		
						$	$	$	$	$		
						$	$	$	$	$		
						$	$	$	$	$		
						$	$	$	$	$		
						$	$	$	$	$		
						$	$	$	$	$		
						$	$	$	$	$		
						$	$	$	$	$		
						$	$	$	$	$		
						$	$	$	$	$		
						$	$	$	$	$		
						$	$	$	$	$		
						$	$	$	$	$		

517

FORM 15-4

Budget Forecasts

PROPERTY NAME Spanish Oaks
BUDGET YEAR 19XX
PREPARED BY John Martin
DATE Aug 15, 19XX

PAGE ___ OF ___

CODE	DESCRIPTION	LAST YEAR	JAN	FEB	MAR	APR	MAY	JUN	JUL	AUG	SEP	OCT	NOV	DEC	TOTAL
	Salaries	$	$ 1,667	$ 1,667	$ 1,667	$ 1,667	$ 1,667	$ 1,667	$ 1,667	$ 1,667	$ 1,667	$ 1,667	$ 1,667	$ 1,667	$ 20,000
	Repairs & Maint	$	$ 800	$ 800	$ 800	$ 900	$ 1,000	$ 1,000	$ 1,000	$ 740	$ 740	$ 740	$ 740	$ 740	$ 10,000
	Utilities	$	$ 900	$ 900	$ 850	$ 783	$ 783	$ 783	$ 783	$ 783	$ 730	$ 850	$ 900	$ 900	$ 10,000
	Taxes	$	$ 2,083	$ 2,083	$ 2,083	$ 2,083	$ 2,083	$ 2,083	$ 2,083	$ 2,083	$ 2,083	$ 2,083	$ 2,083	$ 2,083	$ 25,000
	Insurance	$	$ 833	$ 833	$ 833	$ 833	$ 833	$ 833	$ 833	$ 833	$ 833	$ 833	$ 833	$ 833	$ 10,000
	Gen. & Adm.	$	$ 1,667	$ 1,667	$ 1,667	$ 1,667	$ 1,667	$ 1,667	$ 1,667	$ 1,667	$ 1,667	$ 1,667	$ 1,667	$ 1,667	$ 20,000
	Mgmt. Fee	$	$ 2,279	$ 2,279	$ 2,279	$ 2,279	$ 2,279	$ 2,279	$ 2,279	$ 2,279	$ 2,279	$ 2,279	$ 2,279	$ 2,279	$ 27,350
	Prof. Fee	$	$ 333	$ 333	$ 333	$ 333	$ 333	$ 333	$ 333	$ 333	$ 333	$ 333	$ 333	$ 333	$ 4,000
	Marketing	$	$ 1,250	$ 1,250	$ 1,250	$ 1,250	$ 1,250	$ 1,250	$ 1,250	$ 1,250	$ 1,250	$ 1,250	$ 1,250	$ 1,250	$ 15,000
	Contract Svc.	$	$ 2,142	$ 2,142	$ 2,142	$ 2,142	$ 2,142	$ 2,142	$ 2,142	$ 2,142	$ 2,142	$ 2,142	$ 2,142	$ 2,142	$ 25,700
	Res. & Replace	$	$ 458	$ 458	$ 458	$ 458	$ 458	$ 458	$ 458	$ 458	$ 458	$ 458	$ 458	$ 458	$ 5,500
	TOTAL	$	$ 14,413	$ 14,413	$ 14,363	$ 14,396	$ 14,396	$ 14,396	$ 14,396	$ 14,236	$ 14,236	$ 14,303	$ 14,353	$ 14,353	$ 172,550

COMMENTS

518

FORM 15-5
Budget Line Item

PROPERTY NAME Spanish Oaks   DATE Aug 15, 19XX
LINE ITEM DESCRIPTION Taxes
CODE _____
BUDGET YEAR 19XX

PAGE ___ OF ___

MONTHLY BREAKDOWN   EXPLANATION
TOTAL LAST YEAR $ 20,776
JANUARY $ 2083.33
FEBRUARY $ 2083.33
MARCH $ 2083.33
APRIL $ 2083.33
MAY $ 2083.33
JUNE $ 2083.33
JULY $ 2083.33
AUGUST $ 2083.33
SEPTEMBER $ 2083.33
OCTOBER $ 2083.33
NOVEMBER $ 2083.33
DECEMBER $ 2083.33
   TOTAL YEAR $ 25,000

COMMENTS
Taxes escrowed with mortgage payment. Assumed
increased to $25,000 per year.

FORM 15-6(A)
Residential Punch-Out Report

PROPERTY NAME Spanish Oaks
PREPARED BY John Martin
BLDG. _____ SUITE # _____
DATE Sept 1, 19XX
PAGE 1 OF 500

DESCRIPTION	EXCEL.	GOOD	POOR	COMMENTS
SITE:				
CURB APPEAL		X		
SIGNAGE		X		
LANDSCAPING		X		
PAVING		X		
STRIPPING			X	
SIDEWALKS		X		
CURBS		X		
DUMPSTER AREA		X		
RETAINING WALLS		NA		
FENCING		NA		
RETENTION POND		X		
CATCH BASINS		X		
AMENITIES:				
POOL		X		
POOL EQUIPMENT		X		
FENCING		X		
DECKING		X		
TENNIS COURTS		NA		
LIGHTING		NA		
FENCING		NA		
NET		NA		

DESCRIPTION	EXCEL.	GOOD	POOR	COMMENTS
EXTERIOR BUILDINGS:				
FACADE				
WOOD				
STUCCO				
BRICK		X		
STONE				
TUCK POINTING		X		
COPING		X		
WINDOWS		X		
CHIMNEYS		NA		
FOUNDATIONS		X		
MAIL BOXES				
DOOR		X		
LOCKS		X		
NAME PLATES		NA		
INTERCOM		NA		
GLASS		NA		

Comments _____

520

Form 15-6(B)
Residential Punch-Out Report (Cont'd)

PROPERTY NAME Spanish Oaks
PREPARED BY John Martin
BLDG. 1 SUITE # A
DATE Sept 1, 19XX
PAGE 2 OF 500

GRAND TOTAL $ 100

DESCRIPTION	CONDITION	COST ESTIMATE
FOYER:		
FLOOR		$
CEILING		$
WALLS		$
ELECTRICAL		$
LIGHT FIXTURES		$
MECHANICAL DUCTS		$
DOOR		$
WINDOW		$
WINDOW COVERING		$
		$
		$
		$
		$
KITCHEN:		
FLOOR		$
CEILING		$
WALLS		$
ELECTRICAL		$
LIGHT FIXTURES		$
CABINETS		$
HARDWARE		$
APPLIANCES:		$
REFRIGERATOR		$
RANGE		$
DISPOSAL		$
MICROWAVE		$
TRASH COMPACTOR	Needs Replacement	$ 100
MECHANICAL DUCTS		$
DOOR		$
SHELVING		$
WINDOW		$
WINDOW COVERINGS		$
		$
		$
		$
TOTAL		$ 100

DESCRIPTION	CONDITION	COST ESTIMATE
BATHROOM:		
FLOOR		$
CEILING		$
WALLS		$
ELECTRICAL		$
LIGHT FIXTURES		$
CABINETS		$
HARDWARE		$
MECHANICAL DUCTS		$
DOOR		$
SHELVING		$
WINDOW		$
WINDOW COVERINGS		$
COMMODE		$
TUB		$
SHOWER		$
FIXTURES		$
MIRROR		$
BATHROOM:		
FLOOR		$
CEILING		$
WALLS		$
ELECTRICAL		$
LIGHT FIXTURES		$
CABINETS		$
HARDWARE		$
MECHANICAL DUCTS		$
DOOR		$
SHELVING		$
WINDOW		$
WINDOW COVERINGS		$
COMMODE		$
TUB		$
SHOWER		$
FIXTURES		$
MIRROR		$
TOTAL		$ 100

GRAND TOTAL

FORM 15-6(c)

Capital Expenditure Monthly Budget

PROPERTY NAME Spanish Oaks
PREPARED BY John Martin
PROPERTY TYPE Apartment
YEAR 19XX
DATE Aug 1, 19XX
PAGE 1 OF 1

DESCRIPTION	JAN.	FEB.	MAR.	APR.	MAY	JUN.	JUL.	AUG.	SEP.	OCT.	NOV.	DEC.	TOTAL
Prof Bldg C	$	$	$	$	$ 3,505	$	$	$	$	$	$	$	$ 3,505
Paving	$	$	$	$	$ 2,700	$	$	$	$	$	$	$	$ 2,700
Landscaping	$	$	$	$	$ 1,000	$ 1,000	$	$	$	$	$	$	$ 2,000
	$	$	$	$	$	$	$	$	$	$	$	$	$
	$	$	$	$	$	$	$	$	$	$	$	$	$
	$	$	$	$	$	$	$	$	$	$	$	$	$
	$	$	$	$	$	$	$	$	$	$	$	$	$
	$	$	$	$	$	$	$	$	$	$	$	$	$
	$	$	$	$	$	$	$	$	$	$	$	$	$
	$	$	$	$	$	$	$	$	$	$	$	$	$
	$	$	$	$	$	$	$	$	$	$	$	$	$
	$	$	$	$	$	$	$	$	$	$	$	$	$
	$	$	$	$	$	$	$	$	$	$	$	$	$
	$	$	$	$	$	$	$	$	$	$	$	$	$
	$	$	$	$	$	$	$	$	$	$	$	$	$
	$	$	$	$	$	$	$	$	$	$	$	$	$
	$	$	$	$	$	$	$	$	$	$	$	$	$
	$	$	$	$	$	$	$	$	$	$	$	$	$
	$	$	$	$	$	$	$	$	$	$	$	$	$
	$	$	$	$	$	$	$	$	$	$	$	$	$
	$	$	$	$	$	$	$	$	$	$	$	$	$
TOTAL	$ 0	$ 0	$ 0	$ 0	$ 7,205	$ 1,000	$ 0	$ 0	$ 0	$ 0	$ 0	$ 0	$ 8,205

COMMENTS

FORM 15-7

Capital Expenditure Yearly Budget

PROPERTY NAME Spanish Oaks
PREPARED BY John Martin
PROPERTY TYPE Apartment
YEAR 19XX–19XX
DATE Aug 15, 19XX
PAGE 1 OF 1

DESCRIPTION	YR. 19XX	YR. 19XX	YR. 19XX	YR. 19XX	YR. 19XX	YR. 19XX	YR. 19XX	YR. 19XX	YR. 19XX	YR. 19XX
Roof	$ 3,505	$	$	$	$	$	$	$	$	$
Paving	$ 2,700	$	$	$	$	$	$	$	$	$
Landscaping	$ 2,000	$	$	$	$	$	$	$	$	$
Appliances	$	$ 10,000	$ 10,600	$ 11,236	$ 11,310	$ 12,623	$ 13,362	$ 14,183	$ 13,066	$ 13,938
Misc.	$	$	$	$	$	$	$	$	$	$
TOTAL	$ 8,205	$ 10,000	$ 10,600	$ 11,236	$ 11,310	$ 12,623	$ 14,183	$ 14,183	$ 13,066	$ 13,938

COMMENTS $100 per unit—2nd year, thereafter 6% increase

523

FORM 15-8

Ten-Year Operating Forecast

PROPERTY NAME Spanish Oaks
PREPARED BY John Martin
DATE Aug 1, 19XX

DESCRIPTION	YR. 19XX	YR. 19XX	YR. 19XX	YR. 19XX	YR. 19XX	YR. 19XX	YR. 19XX	YR. 19XX	YR. 19XX	YR. 19XX
REVENUE:										
GROSS POTENTIAL INCOME (GPI)	$ 570,000	$ 592,000	$ 616,512	$ 641,172	$ 666,819	$ 693,492	$ 721,232	$ 750,081	$ 780,084	$ 811,288
LESS: VACANCY	$ (28,500)	$ (29,640)	$ (30,826)	$ (32,059)	$ (33,341)	$ (34,675)	$ (36,062)	$ (37,504)	$ (39,004)	$ (40,564)
MISCELLANEOUS INCOME	$ 5,500	$ 5,720	$ 5,949	$ 6,187	$ 6,434	$ 6,692	$ 6,599	$ 7,238	$ 7,527	$ 7,828
EFFECTIVE GROSS INCOME (EGI)	$ 547,000	$ 568,000	$ 591,635	$ 615,301	$ 639,913	$ 665,509	$ 692,130	$ 719,815	$ 748,607	$ 778,552
EXPENSES:										
FIXED OPERATING EXPENSES	$ 66,700	$ 70,702	$ 74,944	$ 79,441	$ 84,207	$ 89,260	$ 94,615	$ 100,292	$ 106,310	$ 112,688
VARIABLE EXPENSES	$ 100,350	$ 106,371	$ 112,753	$ 119,518	$ 126,690	$ 134,291	$ 142,348	$ 150,889	$ 159,943	$ 169,539
RESERVE REPLACEMENT	$ 5,500	$ 5,830	$ 6,180	$ 6,551	$ 6,944	$ 7,360	$ 7,802	$ 6,270	$ 8,766	$ 9,292
TOTAL EXPENSES	$ 172,550	$ 182,903	$ 193,877	$ 205,510	$ 217,840	$ 230,911	$ 244,765	$ 259,451	$ 275,018	$ 291,520
NET OPERATING INCOME	$ 347,450	$ 385,977	$ 397,750	$ 409,791	$ 422,072	$ 434,538	$ 447,364	$ 460,363	$ 473,589	$ 487,032
DEBT SERVICE	$ 319,925	$ 319,925	$ 319,925	$ 319,925	$ 319,925	$ 319,925	$ 319,925	$ 319,925	$ 319,925	$ 319,925
CAPITAL EXPENDITURES	$ 8,205	$ 10,000	$ 10,006	$ 11,236	$ 11,310	$ 12,625	$ 13,382	$ 14,185	$ 15,036	$ 15,938
CASH FLOW	$ 50,320	$ 60,052	$ 71,233	$ 82,630	$ 94,237	$ 106,049	$ 110,037	$ 130,253	$ 142,627	$ 153,168

COMMENTS 4% increase in revenue and expenses after 1st year. Capital expenditures are $100 per unit in second year increasing at 6% per year.

524

FORM 15-9
Utility Deposits

PROPERTY NAME <u>Spanish Oaks</u>
PREPARED BY <u>John Martin</u>
DATE <u>Sept 1, 19XX</u>

DESCRIPTION	ADDRESS	TEL. NO.	CONTACT	DEPOSIT AMOUNT	DATE DEPOSITED	COMMENTS
Gas		(404) 555-6789	Atlanta Gas	$ 1,000	July 19xx	
Electric		(404) 555-4321	Atlanta Power	$ 500	July 19xx	
Water		(404) 555-9999	Atlanta Water	$ 500	July 19xx	
		( )		$		
		( )		$		
		( )		$		
		( )		$		
		( )		$		
		( )		$		
		( )		$		
		( )		$		
		( )		$		
		( )		$		
		( )		$		
		( )		$		
		( )		$		
		( )		$		
		( )		$		
		( )		$		

Form 15-10
Rent Increase per Month by Lease Expiration

PROPERTY NAME Spanish Oaks
PREPARED BY John Martin
DATE Sept 1, 19XX
PAGE _____ OF _____

RENT/MONTH INCREASE

SUITE #	TYPE UNIT/ SQ. FT.	LESSEE	LEASE EXPIRATION	RENT	JAN.	FEB.	MAR.	APR.	MAY	JUN.	JUL.	AUG.	SEP.	OCT.	NOV.	DEC.	TOTAL
1-A	1,1 Gdn	Jones, B	Jan 31	$450	$	$450	$450	$450	$450	$450	$450	$450	$450	$450	$450	$450	$4950
2-B	1,1 Gdn	Smith C	Feb 28	$450	$	$	$450	$450	$450	$450	$450	$450	$450	$450	$450	$450	$4500
3-A	1,1 Gdn	Martin, D	March 31	$450	$450	$430	$430	$450	$450	$450	$450	$450	$450	$450	$450	$450	$4050
4-A	1,1 Gdn	Howell, B	Oct 31	$430	$450	$430	$430	$430	$430	$430	$430	$430	$430	$430	$450	$450	$5200
				$	$	$	$	$	$	$	$	$	$	$	$	$	$

TOTAL $ =====

GR. TOTAL $ =====

FORM 15-18

Residential Comparable Market Summary

PROPERTY NAME Spanish Oaks
PREPARED BY John Martin
DATE Sept 1 19XX
PAGE ___ OF ___

TYPE PROPERTY:
SINGLE FAMILY ____
MULTI-FAMILY __X__
ACLF ____
NURSING HOME ____

TYPE BUILDING:
GARDEN __X__
TOWNHOUSE ____
MID RISE ____
HIGH RISE ____

MAP REF. NO.	PROPERTY NAME	NO. UNITS	OCCUPANCY	FEATURES	AMENITIES	LESSEE PAYS UTILITIES	TYPE UNIT 1,1 Gdn S.F.	RENT	RENT/S.F.	TYPE UNIT 2,2 Gdn S.F.	RENT	RENT/S.F.	COMMENTS
1	Long Tree	150	92 %	1,2,3,4,9	G	EL	600	$ 460	$ .77	980	$ 510	$ .52	
2	The Woods	200	93 %	1,2,3,4,9	G,H	EL	550	$ 440	$ .80	1000	$ 510	$ .51	
			%					$	$		$	$	
			%					$	$		$	$	
			%					$	$		$	$	
			%					$	$		$	$	
			%					$	$		$	$	
			%					$	$		$	$	
			%					$	$		$	$	
			%					$	$		$	$	
			%					$	$		$	$	
COMPARABLE AVERAGES		175	92.67 %				575	$ 450	$ .78	990	$ 510	$ .52	
SUBJECT PROPERTY		100	96 %	1,2,3,4,9	G	EL	600	$ 450	$ .75	1000	$ 500	$ .50	
MAP REF. NO. 3			%					$	$		$	$	
			%					$	$		$	$	

CODE:

TYPE UNIT:
(GD) GARDEN
(TH) TOWNHOUSE
(FU) FURNISHED
(UF) UNFURNISHED

UTILITIES:
(GA) GAS
(EL) ELECTRICITY
(W) WATER
(S) SEWER

FEATURES:
(1) REFRIGERATOR
(2) RANGE
(3) DISHWASHER
(4) DISPOSAL
(5) TRASH COMPACTOR
(6) MICROWAVE
(7) WASHER
(8) DRYER
(9) PATIO/BALCONY
(10) FIREPLACE
(11) SCREENPORCH
(12) SUNROOM
(13) GREENHOUSE
(14) CABLE TV
(15) PADDLEFAN
(16) WALLPAPER
(17) W/D CONNECTIONS

AMENITIES:
(A) LAUNDRY ROOM
(B) STORAGE AREA
(C) CAR WASH
(D) DOORMAN
(E) SECURITY
(F) CLUBHOUSE
(G) POOL
(H) TENNIS COURT
(I) PLAYGROUND
(J) EXERCISE ROOM
(K) SAUNA
(L) STEAM ROOM

527

FORM 15-24
Insurance Checklist

BUSINESS NAME __ABC Insurance Co.__
CONTACT __Bill Moyer__
ADDRESS _____
_____
TEL. NO. (404) 555-6810 _____

PREPARED BY __John Martin__
DATE __Sept 1, 19XX__
DATE __Sept 1, 19XX__
AREAS WILL INSURE:
_____
_____
_____
_____

SPECIALIZATION

SPECIALIZATION:
  RESIDENTIAL:
    SINGLE FAMILY _____
    MULTI-FAMILY _____X_____
    CONDOMINIUM/TOWNHOUSE _____
    ADULT CONGREGATE CARE _____
    NURSING HOME _____
  OFFICE _____
  SHOPPING CENTER _____
  INDUSTRIAL _____
  MINI-WAREHOUSE _____
  HOTEL/MOTEL _____
  RESORT _____

TYPE INSURANCE

PROPERTY _____X_____
RENT LOSS _____X_____
BOILER/MACHINERY _____
FLOOD _____
FIDELITY BOND _____
CONTENTS _____X_____
ERRORS AND OMISSIONS _____
LIFE _____
HEALTH _____
VEHICLE _____
WORKMAN'S COMPENSATION _____
UTILITY BONDS _____
OTHER: _____

TYPE COVERAGE	TERM	COVERAGE	DEDUCTIBLE	YEARLY PREMIUM	HOW PAID
PROPERTY	12 Mo	$ 3.5 M*	$ 1,000	$ 10,000	Monthly
RENT LOSS		$	$	$ INC	Monthly
BOILER/MACHINERY		$	$	$	
FLOOD		$	$	$	
FIDELITY BOND		$	$	$	
CONTENTS		$	$	$ INC	Monthly
ERRORS AND OMISSIONS		$	$	$	
LIFE		$	$	$	
WHOLE LIFE		$	$	$	
TERM		$	$	$	
UNIVERSAL LIFE		$	$	$	
HEALTH		$	$	$	
VEHICLE		$	$	$	
WORKMAN'S COMPENSATION		$	$	$	
UTILITY BOND		$	$	$	
OTHER:		$	$	$	
		$	$	$	
		$	$	$	
		$	$	$	
		$	$	$	
		$	$	$	

REFERENCES:

BUSINESS:
  DATE __Sept 1, 19XX__
  BUSINESS NAME __Phil Randall Co.__
  CONTACT __Phil Randall__
  ADDRESS _____

  TEL. NO. (404) 555-6661 _____
  COMMENTS __Says they have good__
  __rates and excellent service__
  _____
  _____
  _____
  _____

BUSINESS:
  DATE _____
  BUSINESS NAME _____
  CONTACT _____
  ADDRESS _____

  TEL. NO. (   ) _____
  COMMENTS _____
  _____
  _____
  _____
  _____

BUSINESS:
  DATE _____
  BUSINESS NAME _____
  CONTACT _____
  ADDRESS _____

  TEL. NO. (   ) _____
  COMMENTS _____
  _____
  _____
  _____
  _____

COMMENTS _____
_____
_____

* Less land value and foundations ($700,000)

FORM 15-25
Property Tax Checklist

PROPERTY NAME Spanish Oaks

ADDRESS 510 River Road

     Atlanta, GA

PREPARED BY John Martin

DATE Sept 1, 19XX

TAX DISTRICT Oakwood

PROPERTY TAX NO. 567-B-10

  LAND LOT 580

  DISTRICT 17th

  SECTION 6th

CONTACT Fred Meir

TEL. NO. (404) 555-7560

REAL PROPERTY   X

PERSONAL PROPERTY Included

	ASSESSMENT	MILLAGE RATE	ASSESSMENT RATIO	TAX ASSESSMENT
YEAR 19XX	$ 2,800,000	$ $18.55/$1000	40%	$ 20,776
YEAR	$	$		$
YEAR	$	$		$
YEAR	$	$		$
YEAR	$	$		$
YEAR	$	$		$
YEAR	$	$		$
YEAR	$	$		$
YEAR	$	$		$
YEAR	$	$		$

CURRENT MILLAGE RATE 18.55   YEAR 19XX

DUE DATE Sept 15

DUE DATE

DESCRIPTION	RATE
County	$ 10.30
State	$ 6.00
School	$ 1.30
Roads	$ .75
	$
	$
	$
	$
	$
TOTAL	$ 18.55/$1000

LATE DATE Nov 15

PENALTY 1% per month

COMMENTS Assessment should go up upon resale

529

FORM 15-28
Professional Services Checklist

BUSINESS NAME Morgan Engineering
CONTACT Bob Morgan
ADDRESS _____
_____
TEL. NO. (404) 555-6874

PREPARED BY Martin France

TYPE PROFESSIONAL SERVICE

ARCHITECTURAL
LANDSCAPE ARCH. _____
CONSTRUCTION MANAGEMENT _____
ENGINEER:
   STRUCTURAL _____ X _____
   MECHANICAL _____ X _____
   ELECTRICAL _____ X _____
   PLUMBING _____ X _____
   SOILS _____
SURVEYOR _____
INTERIOR DECORATOR _____
OTHER _____

REFERENCES:

BUSINESS:
   DATE Aug 15, 19XX
   BUSINESS NAME Bankers First
   CONTACT Martin France
   ADDRESS _____
   _____
   TEL. NO. (404) 555-3408
   COMMENTS _____
   Very knowledgable
   in construction

TYPE PROPERTY MARKETED

SPECIALIZATION:
  RESIDENTIAL:
    SINGLE FAMILY _____
    MULTI-FAMILY _____ X _____
    CONDOMINIUM/TOWNHOUSE _____
    ADULT CONGREGATE CARE _____
    NURSING HOME _____
  OFFICE _____
  SHOPPING CENTER _____
  INDUSTRIAL _____
  MINI-WAREHOUSE _____
  HOTEL/MOTEL _____
  RESORT _____

BUSINESS:
   DATE _____
   BUSINESS NAME _____
   CONTACT _____
   ADDRESS _____
   _____
   TEL. NO. ( ) _____
   COMMENTS _____

GENERAL INFORMATION

YEARS IN BUSINESS 16

FEE STRUCTURE:
  HOURLY $ 50 BILLED EVERY 15 MINUTES
  BILLED: WEEKLY ____ MONTHLY X
  OTHER _____
  _____
  _____

BUSINESS:
   DATE _____
   BUSINESS NAME _____
   CONTACT _____
   ADDRESS _____
   _____
   TEL. NO. ( ) _____
   COMMENTS _____

COMMENTS _____
_____
_____
_____
_____
_____
_____
_____
_____
_____
_____

530

FORM 15-29
Management Company's Checklist

BUSINESS NAME Martin Management
CONTACT John Martin
ADDRESS _____

TEL. NO. (404) 555-3874

PREPARED BY Martin France

GENERAL INFORMATION

YEARS IN BUSINESS 8
NO. PROPERTIES MANAGED 14
  NO. SQ. FT. ____ NO. UNITS 1509
  NO. PROPERTY OWNERS 11
  NO. EMPLOYEES 26
OTHER BUSINESS _____
_____
_____

STATEMENTS GENERATED MONTHLY:
  MANUAL _____ COMPUTER X

REFERENCES:

TYPE PROPERTY MANAGED	FEE STRUCTURE	COMMENTS
SPECIALIZATION:		
RESIDENTIAL _____	____ %	_____
SINGLE FAMILY _____	____ %	_____
MULTI-FAMILY ____X____	5 %	_____
CONDOMINIUM/TOWNHOUSE ____	____ %	_____
ADULT CONGREGATE CARE ____	____ %	_____
NURSING HOME _____	____ %	_____
OFFICE _____	____ %	_____
SHOPPING CENTER _____	____ %	_____
INDUSTRIAL _____	____ %	_____
MINI-WAREHOUSE _____	____ %	_____
HOTEL/MOTEL _____	____ %	_____
RESORT _____	____ %	_____

BUSINESS:
  DATE July 5, 19XX
  BUSINESS NAME Bankers First
  CONTACT Martin France
  ADDRESS _____
  TEL. NO. (404) 555-3408
  COMMENTS Very quality and
  cost conscious
_____
_____
_____
_____

BUSINESS:
  DATE _____
  BUSINESS NAME _____
  CONTACT _____
  ADDRESS _____
  TEL. NO. ( ) _____
  COMMENTS _____

BUSINESS:
  DATE _____
  BUSINESS NAME _____
  CONTACT _____
  ADDRESS _____
  TEL. NO. ( ) _____
  COMMENTS _____

COMMENTS _____

531

BUSINESS NAME Polster and Perelman

CONTACT Gary Polster

ADDRESS _____

TEL. NO. (404) 555-7508

PREPARED BY Roger Stanton

FEE STRUCTURE:
HOURLY $ 100 BILLED EVERY 20 MINUTES
BILLED: WEEKLY _____ MONTHLY _____ X
OTHER _____

SPECIALIZATION:
CORPORATE _____
REAL ESTATE _____ X
TAX _____
SECURITIES _____
PARTNERSHIP _____ X

REFERENCES:

BUSINESS:
DATE July 1, 19XX
BUSINESS NAME Stanton Co.
CONTACT Roger Stanton
ADDRESS _____
TEL. NO. (404) 555-1941
COMMENTS _____
Very knowledgable
and reliable

BUSINESS:
DATE _____
BUSINESS NAME _____
CONTACT _____
ADDRESS _____
TEL. NO. ( ) _____
COMMENTS _____

BUSINESS:
DATE _____
BUSINESS NAME _____
CONTACT _____
ADDRESS _____
TEL. NO. ( ) _____
COMMENTS _____

PERSONAL:
DATE _____
BUSINESS NAME _____
CONTACT _____
ADDRESS _____
TEL. NO. ( ) _____
COMMENTS _____

PERSONAL:
DATE _____
BUSINESS NAME _____
CONTACT _____
ADDRESS _____
TEL. NO. ( ) _____
COMMENTS _____

PERSONAL:
DATE _____
BUSINESS NAME _____
CONTACT _____
ADDRESS _____
TEL. NO. ( ) _____
COMMENTS _____

COMMENTS _____

PROPERTY NAME Spanish Oaks
PREPARED BY Hal Barton
TYPE PROPERTY Apartment

DATE Aug 1, 19XX

DESCRIPTION	5	4	3	2	1
PROPERTY:					
LOCATION	5				
CURB APPEAL	5				
OCCUPANCY	5				
RENTAL RATES		4			
WEEKLY TRAFFIC		4			
PROSPECTS		4			
TENANT MIX		4			
TENANT PROFILE		4			
CONSTRUCTION		4			
DESIGN					
FUTURE APPRECIATION	5				
TRAFFIC COUNT	5				
ACCESS	5				
REPUTATION		4			
TOTAL POINTS	6/70				
AVERAGE POINTS	4.357				

COMMENTS Looks like possible deal could be structured

DESCRIPTION	5	4	3	2	1
DEAL STRUCTURE:					
PRICE/UNIT		4			
PRICE/SQ. FT.		4			
CAP RATE		4			
CRM		4			
SELLER GUARANTEES		4			
TERMS		4			
TOTAL POINTS	24/30				
AVERAGE POINTS	4				
GRAND TOTAL	85/100				

533

CASE STUDY: HOW TO BUY AN OFFICE BUILDING

Background Information About the Purchaser

Jane Taylor, a commercial real estate agent in Atlanta, Georgia, had just cleared a $100,000 commission on a real estate transaction that she brokered for a group of physicians. Having been in the real estate business for ten years, she had sold and leased many commercial properties to her clients. After her deal closed, Jane sat down and decided that she was tired of helping to make money for her clients and that it was time for her to use her time and talents to make more money for herself. She decided that with her experience and contacts, she would try to acquire some commercial property for her own account. Since Jane was used to selling properties of approximately $5,000,000, she thought she would pursue an acquisition in this price range. Although her own resources were fairly limited, she made the decision to find other partners to put up the bulk of the equity. At this point, Jane sat down in her office to determine the parameters of this investment.

Deciding on the Investment Strategy

Over the last ten years, Jane had made over thirty deals in various types of commercial properties. In the last two years, she had started to specialize in office properties in the 50,000 to 100,000 square foot range on the north side of Atlanta and, using her experience, had also started to build up a rather complete set of files for this type of office building. They included the following information on each building over 50,000 square feet:

1. Name, address, ownership, leasing and management firms

2. Total square footage, current vacancy

3. Rental rate information

4. Absorption history over the last five years

5. Building brochures and floor plans

In addition, Jane also had access to information on over 80 percent of the tenant leases in this market area because she was trying to sell these properties.

On the basis of this information she decided that she would rather purchase an undervalued property. She knew from her experiences that she must have a prime location, but she could settle for a property that had a vacancy problem and some deferred maintenance. She reasoned that with her tenant contacts and her knowledge of when tenants' leases were due to expire, she would be able to fill up the vacancies with aggressive marketing.

The day after Jane closed an important deal, Dr. Bart Kurtz called her to tell her how he appreciated the good job that she had done to get all of the parties together to complete the deal. He also told her that he and five other doctors in his practice would like to invest between $1,500,000 and $2,000,000 in a piece of property that had some good upside potential. Jane told him of her desire to start having an equity position in her future deals. She then told him that she would like to meet with him and his group the following week to discuss how she could set up a partnership to invest these funds. She asked him to prepare a shopping list of their investment criteria; for her part, she would prepare a presentation for the doctors on the market and the past history for office properties in the Atlanta area.

The following week, Jane prepared a thorough presentation for the doctors. She was able to show a list of every office property in Atlanta by market area. Her information also included current rental rates, occupancy, and absorption for the last five years. An appraisal contact gave Jane a copy of all the office building sales over the last three years. Jane also had a map of the city that showed where all the buildings were located. Due to her thorough working knowledge of the city and her professional presentation, Jane was able to persuade the doctors that, even though she had never set up a partnership before, she would be able to handle the responsibility required for this large investment.

Dr. Kurtz, spokesman for the group, said that the doctors had met the previous day to set up a list of their investment desires. They were as follows:

Type of Property:	Office building
Location:	North side of Atlanta, Georgia
Age of Property:	New-7 years old
Size of Investment:	$5 million-$10 million
Square Footage:	50,000-100,000 square feet
Investment Quality:	Class B
Tenant Profile:	Regional and local tenants
	No one tenant over 20 percent of the total space
Construction:	Low-rise to mid-rise, concrete or brick
Holding Period:	7-10 years
Return on Investment:	0 percent to 5 percent cash flow in the first year
	9 percent to 10.25 percent capitalization rate

The doctors told Jane that they would like to find a property that they could go into, clean up the tenancy and any deferred maintenance, and then start to increase the rents to increase the value.

Choosing the Investment Ownership Vehicle

The doctors had decided that after their last experience in trying to let one of their fellow physicians manage their partnership, they would never make the same mistake again. Dr. Kurtz said they wanted an experienced person acting as the managing partner. He also stated that each of the doctors had decided to invest his funds through each of his pension funds. Their business manager, who was also their accountant, suggested they set up a partnership in which they would be limited partners.

At the end of the meeting, Dr. Kurtz told Jane he would discuss her proposal with the other doctors and would contact her in the next few days regarding their decision. The following week, Jane received his call in which he said that both he and the doctors were so impressed with Jane's presentation that not only did they want to invest but they were able to add five other doctors to the group. Jane told him how much she appreciated their vote of confidence and that she would get to work to start the search process. Dr. Kurtz said that to show their good faith in the proposed venture, the business manager for the group would help Jane set up a $100,000 line of credit at the doctors' bank to be used for any seed money needed.

Finding the Right Property

The following morning, Jane started what would be an extensive search for the ideal property. She decided that since she needed an ongoing income, she would spend at least 75 percent of her time in brokerage and leasing and 25 percent looking for a property to buy. Because she knew the real estate business, she started to compose a letter to real estate agents, appraisers, and bankers listing the basic criteria she was looking for. Additionally, she had a complete listing of all the property owners for office buildings in the city to whom she drafted and mailed another letter. Over the next six weeks Jane started receiving replies to her inquiries.

Narrowing Down the Selection

As Jane received her responses, she recorded each property on a Property Log In Form to systematize her search. Since she was in the real estate brokerage business as well, she also used this list to keep track of potential product to sell to other investors.

To distinguish potential good deals from the bad deals, she used some basic rules of thumb to see what properties were either overpriced or underpriced. She knew that office buildings in the 50,000 to 100,000 square foot range were selling in the $85 to $125 per square foot range, and she also knew that other investors were buying at 9 percent to 10.5 percent capitalization rates. Expenses for these types of properties were running in the $5.50 to $6.50 per square foot range. Jane also realized that occupancies were in the 89 percent range with over ten new buildings with 1,550,000 square feet coming on line within the next eighteen months.

Although Jane had looked at thousands of properties during her real estate career, she was amazed at just how incomplete most of these offering packages were. During this six-week period, over 150 properties were submitted to her. From these, Jane narrowed down her search to four that appeared to meet her criteria.

> *Property #1:* An 80,000 square foot building that was 96 percent occupied.

> *Property #2:* A 66,000 square foot building that was 93 percent occupied.

> *Property #3:* A 105,000 square foot building that was currently under rent-up.

> *Property #4:* A 55,000 square foot building that was 86 percent occupied.

With these four properties in hand, Jane set up meetings with the owners to feel them out.

Property #1

This property was brought to Jane's attention by Bart Cranshaw, a local accountant whom Jane had known for years. It was owned by Bart's client. Jane asked Bart to set up a meeting with his client and to make sure that he brought all the information on the property.

As this meeting Jane's approach was to get the seller comfortable with her by discussing their interests and how he came to own the property. Jane had found that this tactic would more than likely get the other party to trust her and would put him at ease. She found out that Bart's client has owned the property for the last six years and was selling because he was retiring to California and did not feel comfortable owning property that would be over 2,500 miles away. He also stated that since he was quite wealthy, he was going to wait to make his move when he "got" his price for the property. Jane knew that his price was based on a 9 percent capitalization rate, the lowest in her range of buying parameters. She also knew from doing her homework prior to the meeting that this price was based on an unrealistic expense factor. When she plugged in her own figures, this price went to an 8.5 percent capitalization rate. She figured that if the seller would readjust his price downward by 10 percent, the deal might make sense. When she told the seller of her concern for the low capitalization rate and the fact that his expenses appeared to be out of line, the seller stated that this might be true but that he already had a legitimate offer on his desk for his asking price.

PROPERTY #2

This property was a real beauty. Located about four miles from her office, Jane came across this property listed in the local newspaper for sale by the owner. She called the number in the paper and requested a package be sent to her. The package was a one-page flier with only the basic information; a buyer who was interested could contact the owner directly to receive a more complete package. Jane did have an interest and contacted Ken Myers from Cleveland, Ohio. After receiving the second package, Jane called Mr. Myers to request a meeting. He told Jane he would be glad to meet her, but he had just had surgery and was told by his doctors not to travel. Although Jane had an expense account from the doctor investors, she knew better than to fly off and spend money without more knowledge of the seller and his intentions for selling, and his flexibility in negotiating a deal.

Jane told Mr. Myers that she was going to prepare a letter of intent outlining how she'd like to purchase his property and would mail it to him that afternoon. Her deal structure was to base her price on a 10.25 percent capitalization rate, using the rent roll provided to her and an expense ratio of 45 percent. Since Jane had access to up to $2 million to use as equity, she was not as concerned about leverage as she was about cash flow. She structured her offer to reflect a projected 6 percent cash flow based on a split down-payment over thirty-six months. She also requested that Mr. Myers take back a purchase money mortgage at 10 percent interest for only five years. Her projections showed that if she was able to only get a 2 percent increase in the net operating income over the next five years, she would still be able to refinance a new second mortgage at 15 percent interest with a twenty-year amortization period and still pay up to four points on this new mortgage.

PROPERTY #3

This property had just been completed twelve months ago. Jane contacted Steve Komppa, the broker who had sent her the deal. He told her that this deal would not last long on the market. He said that the owner, a man from Canada, was having financial problems back home and needed to direct his time, financial resources, and efforts to his situation there. Steve said that someone who was able to react quickly could get a very good deal. He said that he had an exclusive on the property and that she was only the second person to hear about the deal.

Jane knew the property location and asked Steve to met her that afternoon at her office, suggesting that they go out and visit the site and look at the market. Since Jane had a file on the city, she was able to have her secretary compile a package on the area and the market comparables for her meeting.

At the property, Jane was impressed with the quality of the building and especially with the quality of the tenants who had already moved in. At the meeting, Jane also met Steve Robins, the young leasing agent for the owner who had been with the property since it opened. He was extremely knowledgeable about both the property and the market. Jane thought to herself that if she were able to acquire this property, she would like to have Steve continue the marketing program. Steve told Jane that he was actually four months ahead of the original absorption schedule and was also able to lease the space at market rates. He also said his only concessions were that he had to increase the tenant's allowance by $1.50 per square foot to induce the tenants, but on his last two leases this allowance was only $.50 over his budget.

With this information, Jane went back to her office and started to draft a letter of intent to the owner. The broker told her that he was more concerned with getting quick cash than with what the sales price would be. She did some calculations regarding what it would cost to complete the rent-up. To be conservative, Jane figured to cash out any brokerage commissions at closing at 5 percent of the gross rental. She also thought that with all of the new buildings coming onto the market over the next eighteen months, she would factor in at least six months' free rent on any of the future leases. Moreover, even though the leasing agent told her that they would be 95 percent occupied in the next six months, she would figure at least fifteen months. Over the years, Jane had seen many developers get into trouble by being too optimistic in their projections. Since this was her first deal, she did not want to ruin her opportunity with her new investment partners.

Property #4

This property came to Jane from her local banker who told her that the bank was about to foreclose on this seven-year-old property which was located about fifteen miles from her office. The original owner had passed away the year before, and a nephew had taken over the management for the estate. Due to tax problems in the estate, the nephew was unable to get the funds necessary to keep the property in top condition and to retain its current tenants. The current occupancy was 86 percent, but two tenants had just given notice. Within the next sixty days the occupancy would drop to 79 percent. The banker told Jane that since the nephew did not want to have the property foreclosed on or have the property put into bankruptcy, a good deal could be worked out for the right buyer. Jane decided that she would go over to the building and investigate the tenant profile. Once there, Jane decided to meet the managing partner of Reisenfeld & Felman, a law firm in the building that occupied 24 percent of the total space. She was able to walk into their office and meet Jeff Felman who told her that he was very happy in the building, but that his firm was merging with a much larger firm in the city and was going to be moving within six months. He told Jane that his firm would continue to pay rent for its space, but the new firm was willing to cut the rental rate in half to sublease the space. Jane had figured that since this particular market had a 15 percent vacancy factor, it would hurt her marketing efforts for this building if she were competing with her own tenants to lease space. Based on these facts, Jane called her banker, thanked him for the lead, but told him that due to market conditions, she felt that her chances of success were limited unless she could steal the property. The banker told her that the nephew had been unreasonable in his expectations in selling the property, and he felt that he would put the property in bankruptcy rather than face foreclosure.

Negotiating a Successful Deal

After careful thought, Jane decided to pass on Property #1 and Property #4. Jane contacted Mr. Myers in Ohio and was told that he had taken a turn for the worse and that it was not known when he would be able to meet with her regarding the purchase of his property. Jane then turned her attentions to Property #3. She contacted Steve Komppa and asked him if he had heard from the Canadian seller. He said that he had just received a call from the seller who was going to be in town in two days and would very much like to meet with Jane.

She then started to prepare for the meeting. She contacted her banker and asked him if he had any contacts in Canada. He said that he would make a few calls. Jane knew from past dealings with her other clients that those clients who were the best prepared always got the good deals. She wanted to discover more information regarding the seller's financial problems. She felt that with this knowledge she could strike a better deal for herself. The next day her banker called and told Jane to contact Mike Walker, a banker in Toronto. Mr. Walker told Jane that there were rumors on the street that the seller was in serious trouble with a gold mine that he had invested in and that he was short of cash. Jane also contacted two friends who were in the office leasing business and confidentially asked them of their thoughts on the building. Their comments were very favorable. One of them said that he was working a deal for 10,000 square feet and that the building was one of two his client was interested in. The other broker told Jane that if she was able to purchase the property he might be interested in investing some money with her investment group.

At the meeting Jane noticed that the seller appeared rather nervous. He told Jane that if they struck a deal she would have to do her inspection period within ten days and would have to close within thirty days. She was not really prepared to act that quickly and told the seller that she needed to call her investment partners before she could commit to that time frame. Jane went into another office and called Dr. Kurtz. The doctor told Jane that he had already looked at the preliminary information that she had supplied him, and that he and the four other doctors had already visited the property in anticipation of a quickly needed answer. He told Jane that, based on her negotiations, they were prepared to meet the time constraints.

Jane then went back into the meeting and told the seller that she was prepared to meet his time schedule if they could come to terms and if he was able to provide her with all of the necessary documents that she would need to review. The seller said that in his briefcase were all the documents she would need, including a letter from his lender stating it would approve a qualified borrower, and a copy of an updated appraisal.

Prior to the meeting, Jane had contacted Alan Gerber, the contractor of the building. She had told him that she was thinking about buying the building and that she would be interested in having him complete the tenant improvements. She was also able to get a complete cost breakdown from him on what it would take to complete the improvements. She also was told what the original cost of the contract was.

During the meeting, the seller told Jane that her offer was $250,000 low, but that if she paid another $100,000 cash at closing he would take back the $150,000. Jane told the seller that $250,000 was too steep; moreover, if she paid a higher price for the property, she would want the seller to guarantee the rent-up of the remaining space and to pay any leasing commissions and overages in the tenant allowances. Due to the fact that the seller had a cash flow problem, she demanded that he escrow $500,000 with the lender until the property was 95 percent occupied. Jane did not want the seller taking his money back to Canada and then defaulting on his guarantee. The seller, knowing that the property was 65 percent leased and confident that he could rent up the property in six months, decided to agree to the rental guarantee for a higher price. At this point she showed a copy of a letter from her banker indicating that the doctors' investment account had $2 million currently on deposit; she noticed that the seller became very anxious. He countered with a $150,000 increase in price, with only $75,000 extra at closing. Jane knew that using her assumptions and what the original cost of the building was she was still able to purchase the property at 8 percent under market value.

She then told the seller that she would accept his deal, but that, since the investment group had the funds available and was willing to close within thirty days, she wanted fifteen days to inspect the property and she was willing to put up only $25,000 as earnest money instead of the $100,000 that the seller wanted. Because time was of the essence and the seller felt comfortable with Jane and her investment group, he agreed to this offer.

Jane then shook hands with the seller and agreed to meet him with her attorney that afternoon to finalize the contract. She then contacted her attorney, briefed him on the basic terms of the deal, and told him of the urgent need for a finalization meeting. That afternoon, all parties met to review and negotiate the language. By 11:30 that night all the parties were exhausted but were able to finally sign the purchase agreement. Jane had figured that since the seller was very anxious to sign, she would be able to negotiate language that was more in her favor than in his.

Finalizing the Agreement During the Inspection Period

The following morning, Jane contacted Les Dolan who was with Jane's real estate company. He was the head of the property management company and was currently managing over 1 million square feet of commercial properties in the city. Jane asked him to assist her in setting up an inspection team to evaluate the property. Because of the fifteen-day time period, she told him that everyone must act very quickly. Les told Jane that he would contact his engineer and that they would inspect the property together. Jane then contacted the current leasing agent and told him that she might be interested in retaining him if the deal went through. She asked him to compile all the marketing information and projections as well as a list of his current prospects.

Over the next week, Jane completely dropped any other work that she was involved in and immersed herself in learning everything about the property and its market. She reviewed the leases and even met with the tenants to confirm all the facts. She shopped all of her competition and got a total handle on the market. She also contacted all of the local leasing agents to get their thoughts on the area.

Jane then set up a meeting with her attorney to go over the mortgage documents. Her attorney told her that the documents seemed in order. The current market for interest rates had dropped since the original mortgage was negotiated, so Jane contacted the lender and asked about the possibility of reducing the interest rate. Since the lender was still holding the loan in his portfolio but was looking to sell off the mortgage, he told Jane that if she paid a 1 percent fee on the outstanding balance of the loan, he would approve a reduction in the loan of 0.5 percent as well as reamortize the loan over thirty years instead of twenty-five years. Jane did some quick calculations and discovered that her pay back was a little over one year, but her cash would increase by $57,000. She then told the banker that this would be agreeable, but she would like to finance the $75,000 that the seller was taking back as a second mortgage. Her reasoning was that she was going to have to pay the seller 10 percent on the $75,000 and then refinance this amount in five years. She thought that it would be easier to just add that into the original $7 million mortgage and amortize the full amount now rather than find a lender for that amount in five years.

FINANCIAL CALCULATIONS

Jane performed some simple calculations to review her deal.

	ORIGINAL DEAL	REVISED DEAL	REFINANCED DEAL
GPI	$1,680,000	$1,680,000	$1,680,000
Vacancy—5%	($ 84,000)	($ 84,000)	($ 84,000)
EGI	$1,596,000	$1,596,000	$1,596,000
Expenses—45% EGI	$ 638,400	$ 638,400	$ 638,400
NOI	$ 957,600	$ 957,600	$ 957,400
Debt Svc.—1st Mtg.	$ 763,309	$ 763,309	$ 713,885
Debt Svc.—2nd Mtg.		$ 7,500	
Cash Flow	$ 194,291	$ 186,791	$ 243,715
Sales Price	$9,000,000	$9,150,000	$9,150,000
Mortgage—1st	$7,000,000	$7,000,000	$7,075,000
Mortgage—2nd		$ 75,000	
Equity	$2,000,000	$2,075,000	$2,075,000
ROI	9.71%	9.00%	11.75%
Capitalization Rate	10.64	10.47	10.47
Price/sq.ft.	$85.71	$85.71	$85.71
GRM	5.36	5.45	5.45

Jane's figures showed a pretty good deal. Her original task was to find an office property with a 9 percent to a 10.25 percent cap rate with between zero and 3 percent cash flow. She was able to negotiate a price that was better than her expectations, and although she was not able to get any current cash flow, once the property was 95 percent occupied it would cash flow at an 11.75 percent return. Jane also noticed that with her reduction in the debt service payment, she was able to not only pay off the seller the $75,000 at closing but was able to save him on negative cash flow during the rent-up period due to the reduction in debt service payments. Even though she had signed the contract with the seller, she contacted him and told him she could prepay him the $75,000 and reduce his negative cash flow at the same time. She told him that to do this for him, she would like him to pay half of the 1 percent fee the lender wanted her to pay to renegotiate the loan. The seller did not have to think long to realize that this was a fair deal.

On the tenth day of the inspection period, Jane assembled her inspection team and reviewed everyone's reports. Les Dolan, the property manager, reported that he felt that the expense of 45 percent of the effective gross income, or $6.08 per square foot, was in line with buildings of this type in the market area. He had reviewed the property with an engineer and had seen no deferred maintenance or any problems. He did tell Jane to make sure to review the insurance for the property and make sure that it was adequate for the lender. He also gave her a copy of the real estate tax comparables and showed Jane that even though the taxes were low now, she should take into account the sale of the property and a rumored real estate tax increase. He also mentioned that even though all of the leases were brand new, she should have an adequate reserve starting in two and a half years to fund the re-leasing of any tenant spaces and to pay for any new leasing commissions. Jane made note of this and readjusted her cash flow projections. Steve Robins, the leasing agent, gave her his projections for lease-up as well as an update on two new leases that he was working on.

She also met with the appraiser who originally did the seller's appraisal. He said that he originally appraised the property at $10 million, based on a 9.5 capitalization rate and felt that, based on the terms of her deal, she was getting a super deal.

Jane's attorney updated her on the title work, pointing out some minor problems that appeared on the title. It appeared that two subcontractors had liens on the property for work that was disputed with the contractor. The attorney said that the seller was able to get the contractor to bond off on these two liens until the problem could be worked out.

With all of the inspection team reporting good feelings on the property, Jane decided to spend the next five days double-checking all the information before contacting the seller and telling him that she was willing to go ahead and close the deal. The next day Jane started to complete her final investor package for the group of doctors. The day before the inspection period was over she arranged to meet Dr. Kurtz who was going to make the final decision for the group. At the meeting with the doctor, Jane went over all the facts and figures. She discussed the downside of the deal as well as the upside. Before giving Jane his final decision, the doctor contacted his business manager to discuss the deal. The business manager gave his blessing, and the doctor told Jane that he would prepare a letter that afternoon confirming his investment group's intent to invest with Jane.

The Closing Process

PRECLOSING

That evening, Jane received the doctors' letter. She contacted her attorney and told him to fax a letter to the seller and the escrow agent telling them that they were prepared to close within fifteen days.

The next fifteen days were very hectic for Jane. She once again met with her attorney to go over the new mortgage documents. During the fifteen-day period her attorney had had great difficulty meeting with the lender's attorney who, it seemed, was busy on more pressing matters. Jane's attorney knew the senior partner in the lender's law firm and asked him to push the attorney or else get a new attorney to work on the documents. The call worked. The following morning a senior partner called to say that he would finalize the documents that afternoon.

Jane also reviewed the partnership documents with her attorney and then told him to send a copy to the doctors' business manager and their attorney to review. Over the next two days that part of the deal was finalized.

Jane also met with Les Dolan to finalize all property management matters. She told Les to prepare to take over the property the day of the closing. The morning of the closing she wanted Les to meet with the seller's management company to review the closing prorations as well as to verify the security deposit account and to confirm that all the existing tenants were still in the space.

Jane contacted Les's insurance agent and told him to prepare an insurance binder for the property and to deliver it to the closing.

As part of the refinancing of the property, the lender required an updated appraisal so Jane contacted the appraiser. Since the original appraisal had been completed within the last year, Jane was able to negotiate a lower price. Jane told the appraiser that she had to have it no later than the day before the closing.

THE CLOSING DAY

The day of the closing, Jane once again contacted all the parties and made sure that everyone would be at the closing with all the necessary documents. She also contacted the bank to verify that the business manager did fund the escrow account. She told the banker that when her attorney finished the closing, he would contact him with instructions to wire the funds to the seller's Canadian bank.

AT THE CLOSING TABLE

At 1:00 that afternoon the closing proceeded. The attorney took out his closing agenda and everyone proceeded to sign the documents. About half way through the signing, the seller's attorney noticed that he had not brought copies of the tenant's estoppel letters. He quickly contacted his office, and within the hour the documents were delivered to the closing.

Since the closing entailed the refinancing of the loan, there were additional documents that needed to be signed. While reviewing these documents one last time, Jane noticed that the documents reflected that the loan was to be fully guaranteed. This was contrary to the loan commitment that Jane had signed with the lender three weeks prior to the closing. Her attorney told the lender's attorney to contact the banker to confirm the fact that there would not be any recourse to the borrowers. Within an hour the lender's attorney was able to track down the banker and confirm that Jane was correct.

At 6:00 that evening, Jane and the seller finally signed the last of the documents. Since it was too late to wire the funds out that day, the attorneys agreed that the funds could be wired out the next morning, but any interest earned on these funds overnight would accrue to the seller.

POSTCLOSING ACTIVITIES

The next morning, Jane made sure that the banker had wired the funds to Canada. She then contacted Dr. Kurtz to tell him that the deal was completed and that she would draft a letter informing the investors.

She then contacted Les Dolan to have him send out notices to the tenants and all vendors notifying them of the sale and of the fact that he would be handling the management of the property.

Thirty days following the closing, she met with Les to review any expenses that should be reimbursed by the seller. She then drafted a letter to the seller informing him that he owed the partnership $4,506.60.

Over the next eight months Jane was able to lease the property up to 96 percent occupancy. As soon as the last tenant moved in, she notified the lender, who then released the $500,000 escrow to the seller.

Following are some of the forms Jane used in completing her investigations of her property acquisition.

FORM 15-1(A)
Investment Criteria Checklist

Prepared by <u>Jane Taylor</u>
Date Prepared <u>Feb 1, 19XX</u>

TYPE PROPERTY:

RESIDENTIAL:		**WAREHOUSE BUILDINGS:**		**LODGING:**	
SINGLE FAMILY	___	LIGHT INDUSTRIAL	___	MOTEL	___
DUPLEX-QUADRAPLEX	___	HEAVY INDUSTRIAL	___	HOTEL	___
MULTI-FAMILY	___	MINI-WAREHOUSE:	___	SINGLE PURPOSE BUILDINGS:	
MOBILE HOME	___	**LODGING:**		_____	___
CONDOMINIUM	___	MOTEL	___	_____	___
COOPERATIVE	___	HOTEL	___	_____	___
CONVERSION	___	**MULTI-USE PROPERTIES:**		_____	___
RETIREMENT HOUSING	___	RESIDENTIAL/RETAIL	___	_____	___
REHABILITATION	___	RESIDENTIAL/OFFICE	___	**RAW LAND:**	
NURSING HOME	___	OFFICE/HOTEL	___	RESIDENTIAL	___
COMMERCIAL:		OFFICE/RETAIL	___	RETAIL	___
RETAIL:		RES/OFF/RETAIL/HOTEL	___	OFFICE	___
STRIP CENTER	___	**CONDOMINIUM:**		INDUSTRIAL	___
NEIGHBORHOOD CENTER	___	RESIDENTIAL	___	AGRICULTURAL	___
COMMUNITY CENTER	___	OFFICE	___	**DISTRESSED PROPERTY:**	
REGIONAL CENTER	___	RETAIL	___	RESIDENTIAL	___
SUPER REGIONAL CENTER	___	INDUSTRIAL	___	RETAIL	___
THEME CENTER:		**RECYCLING:**		OFFICE	___
OFF-PRICE CENTER	___	RESIDENTIAL	___	INDUSTRIAL	___
FACTORY OUTLET	___	OFFICE	___	LODGING	___
FASHION CENTER	___	RETAIL	___	LAND PLAY	___
CAR CARE CENTER	___	INDUSTRIAL	___		
OFFICE BUILDING:	X				
BUSINESS PARKS:	___				

LOCATION: <u>North side—Atlanta</u> AGE OF PROPERTY: <u>0–7</u> HOLDING PERIOD: <u>7–10</u>

INVESTMENT VEHICLE:

				SIZE OF INVESTMENT:		**INVESTMENT QUALITY:**	
SOLE OWNERSHIP	___	JT. TENANCY	___	NUMBER UNITS	___	CLASS A	___
LTD. PARTN'P	___	CORPORATION	___	SQUARE FOOTAGE	___	CLASS B	X
GEN. PARTN'P	___	SUBCHAPTER S	___	EQUITY	$2M	CLASS C	___
TENANTS-COMMON	___	REIT	___	MAX. PRICE	___	CLASS D	___
						TRIPLE NET PROPERTIES	___

TENANT PROFILE:

RESIDENTIAL:		**OFFICE:**		**RETAIL:**		**INDUSTRIAL:**		**LODGING:**	___
WHITE COLLAR	___	FORTUNE 500	___	ANCHORED:	___	FORTUNE 500:	___	BUSINESS:	___
BLUE COLLAR	___	FORTUNE 1000	___	LOCALS	___	FORTUNE 1000	___	CONVENTION:	___
ALL ADULT	___	REGIONAL	X			REGIONAL	___	FAMILY:	___
FAMILY	___	LOCAL	___			LOCAL	___	RESORT:	___

TYPE CONSTRUCTION:

RESIDENTIAL:				**COMMERCIAL:**			
STICK BUILT	___	**UTILITY SYSTEM:**		STICK BUILT	___	**UTILITY SYSTEM:**	
MASONRY	___	2 PIPE	___	MASONRY	X	2 PIPE	___
ONE LEVEL	___	4 PIPE	___	TILT UP	___	4 PIPE	___
2–3 STORY WALK UP	___	MASTER METER	___	LIGHT STEEL	___	MASTER METER	X
MID RISE	___	INDIVIDUAL METER	___	CONCRETE	___	INDIVIDUAL METER	___
HIGH RISE	___	**ROOF SYSTEM:**		STEEL	X	**ROOF SYSTEM:**	
		FLAT	___	LOW RISE	___	FLAT	___
		PITCHED	___	MID RISE	X	PITCHED	___
				HIGH RISE	___		

RETURN ON INVESTMENT:

				BUYING PRICE RANGE:	
CASH FLOW	<u>5–10</u> %	RESALE YIELD ON PURCH. PRICE ___ %		GROSS RENT MULTIPLIER	<u>5–6.2</u>
TAX LOSSES	___ %	INTERNAL RATE OF RETURN ___ %		CAP RATE	<u>9–10.25</u>
RESALE YIELD ON CAPITAL ___ %				PRICE/SQ.FT.	<u>$90–100</u>
				PRICE/UNIT	___

545

Property Log In Report

PREPARED BY: Jane Taylor
TYPE PROPERTY: Office

DATE	PROPERTY NAME	ADDRESS	RECEIVED FROM	TEL. NO.	ASKING PRICE	GRM	PRICE/ SQ.FT.	PRICE/ UNIT	CAP. RATE	COMMENTS
3-1	Mill Creek	8751 9th St.	Arnie Mikes	(404) 555-1968	$ 8.5M	5.7	$ 99.00	$	9.3	Needs repair
3-1	Oak Leaf Plaza	123 4th St	Steve Komppa	(404) 555-7787	$ 9.2M	5.98	$ 87.62	$	9.7	Motivated seller
				( )	$		$	$		
				( )	$		$	$		
				( )	$		$	$		
				( )	$		$	$		
				( )	$		$	$		
				( )	$		$	$		
				( )	$		$	$		
				( )	$		$	$		
				( )	$		$	$		
				( )	$		$	$		
				( )	$		$	$		
				( )	$		$	$		
				( )	$		$	$		
				( )	$		$	$		
				( )	$		$	$		
				( )	$		$	$		
				( )	$		$	$		
				( )	$		$	$		
				( )	$		$	$		
				( )	$		$	$		
				( )	$		$	$		
				( )	$		$	$		
				( )	$		$	$		
				( )	$		$	$		
				( )	$		$	$		
				( )	$		$	$		

Commercial Transaction Summary

PROPERTY NAME Oak Leaf Plaza
ADDRESS 123 4th St
    Atlanta, GA
SELLER Frank Case
  CONTACT _____

ADDRESS _____

TEL. NO. ( ) _____

RATING _____

BROKER Komppa Reany
  CONTACT Steve Komppa
  ADDRESS _____
  _____
TEL. NO. (404) 555-7787

DATE March 5, 19XX

CURRENT OCCUPANCY 65 %
SALES PRICE $ 9,150,000
GROSS INCOME MULTIPLIER
  (GRM) 5.45 X
CAPITALIZATION RATE 10.47
PRICE/SQ.FT. $ 87.14

TYPE PROPERTY	SQ.FT.	RENT/SF
OFFICE X	105,000	$16.00
RETAIL ____	____	____
INDUSTRIAL ____	____	____
MINI WAREHOUSE ____	____	____

TENANT PAYS:

ELECTRICITY ____	JANITORIAL ____
GAS ____	MAINTENANCE ____
WATER ____	TAXES ____
SEWER ____	INSURANCE ____
TRASH ____	C.A.M. ____

12 MONTH OPERATING PROFORMA

YEAR 19XX

REVENUE:	
GROSS POTENTIAL INCOME	$ 1,680,000
VACANCY	$ 84,000
LATE CHARGES	$ ____
NSF CHARGES	$ ____
FORFEITED DEPOSITS	$ ____
C.A.M. CHARGES	$ ____
PERCENTAGE RENT	$ ____
VENDING	$ ____
MISC. ____	$ ____
MISC. ____	$ ____
TOTAL REVENUE	$ 1,596,000

EXPENSES:	
SALARIES & WAGES	$ 27,000
REPAIRS & MAINTENANCE	$ 28,800
UTILITIES	$ 175,560
TAXES	$ 127,680
INSURANCE	$ 24,000
GENERAL & ADMINISTRATIVE	$ 9,600
MANAGEMENT FEES	$ 71,820
PROFESSIONAL FEES	$ 6,000
MARKETING	$ 36,000
CONTRACT SERVICES	$ 63,840
TENANT IMPROVEMENTS	$ 48,000
RESERVES & REPLACEMENTS	$ 20,100
TOTAL EXPENSES	$ 638,400
NET OPERATING INCOME	$ 957,600

DEBT SERVICE:	
1ST MTG.	$ 713,885
2ND MTG.	$ ____
3RD MTG.	$ ____
TOTAL DEBT SERVICE	$ 713,885
CAPITAL EXPENDITURES	$ -0-
CASH FLOW	$ 243,715

MORTGAGE TERMS

1ST MTG:
  LENDER Atlanta First Bank
  ORIGINAL BAL. $ 7,075,000
  CURRENT BAL. (AS OF ____) $ ____
  INTEREST RATE 9.5 % AMORT. 30
  MATURITY DATE 10
  MONTHLY PAYMENT $ 59,490.44
COMMENTS ____
Renegotiated from $7M 10%, 25 Yr ____
____
____

MORTGAGE TERMS

2ND MTG:
  LENDER ____
  ORIGINAL BAL. $ ____
  CURRENT BAL. (AS OF ___) $ ____
  INTEREST RATE ____% AMORT. ____
  MATURITY DATE ____
  MONTHLY PAYMENT $ ____
COMMENTS ____
____
____
____

MORTGAGE TERMS

3RD MTG:
  LENDER ____
  ORIGINAL BAL. $ ____
  CURRENT BAL. (AS OF ___) $ ____
  INTEREST RATE ___% AMORT. ____
  MATURITY DATE ____
  MONTHLY PAYMENT $ ____
COMMENTS ____
____
____
____

COMMENTS ____
____
____

Form 15-4(A)
Commercial Lease Summary

PROPERTY NAME Oak Leaf Plaza
ADDRESS _____

TELEPHONE NO. ( ) _____
OWNERSHIP _____
  TEL. NO. ( ) _____
MANAGEMENT _____
  TEL. NO. ( ) _____
LEASING AGENT _____
  TEL. NO. ( ) _____

PAGE ____ OF ____

DATE March 6, 19XX

TYPE PROPERTY:
  RETAIL _____
  OFFICE X _____
  INDUSTRIAL _____

YEAR BUILT 19XX
TOTAL SQ. FT. 105,000
FLOOR SIZE 21,000
NO. BLDGS. 1
NO. FLOORS 5

SQ.FT.-RETAIL _____
SQ.FT.-OFFICE 105,000
SQ.FT.-INDUST. _____
RETAIL OCCUPANCY ____ %
OFFICE OCCUPANCY ____ %
INDUST. OCCUPANCY ____ %

FLOOR MEASUREMENT:
  GROSS 120,000
  NET 105,000
  FACTOR ____ %

STREET RENT $ 16.00 ____ /S.F.

TENANT PAYS:
  GAS _____
  ELEC _____
  WATER _____
  SEWER _____
  JANITORIAL _____
  R.E. TAXES Tax stop
  INSURANCE _____
  MAINTENANCE _____
  C.A.M. _____

TENANT NAME	SUITE #	SQ. FT.	LEASE TERM	SEC. DEP.	BEG. DATE	END DATE	BASE RATE/SF	RENT/ MONTH	% RENT	RENT ESCAL	CAM	TAX STOP/ YEAR	OPTIONS	COMMENTS
ABC Corp	100	20,000	5 yr	$ -0-	Apr 19xx	Mar 19xx	$ 16.00	$ 26,667	%	C.P.I.		19XX	1-5 yr	2 mo free
				$			$	$	%					
				$			$	$	%					
				$			$	$	%					
				$			$	$	%					
				$			$	$	%					
				$			$	$	%					
				$			$	$	%					
				$			$	$	%					
				$			$	$	%					
				$			$	$	%					
				$			$	$	%					
				$			$	$	%					
				$			$	$	%					
				$			$	$	%					
				$			$	$	%					
				$			$	$	%					

FORM 15-4(B)
Budget Forecasts

PROPERTY NAME Oak Leaf Plaza
BUDGET YEAR 19XX
PREPARED BY Les Dolan

PAGE ____ OF ____

CODE	DESCRIPTION	LAST YEAR	JAN	FEB	MAR	APR	MAY	JUN	JUL	AUG	SEP	OCT	NOV	DEC	TOTAL
	Salaries	$	$ 2,250	2,250	2,250	2,250	2,250	2,250	2,250	2,250	2,250	2,250	2,250	2,250	$ 27,000
	Reprs. & Maint.	$	$ 2,400	2,400	2,400	2,400	2,400	2,400	2,400	2,400	2,400	2,400	2,400	2,400	$ 28,800
	Utilities	$	$ 14,630	14,630	14,630	14,630	14,630	14,630	14,630	14,630	14,630	14,630	14,630	14,630	$ 175,560
	Taxes	$	$ 10,640	10,640	10,640	10,640	10,640	10,640	10,640	10,640	10,640	10,640	10,640	10,640	$ 127,680
	Insurance	$	$ 2,000	2,000	2,000	2,000	2,000	2,000	2,000	2,000	2,000	2,000	2,000	2,000	$ 24,000
	Gen. & Adm.	$	800	800	800	800	800	800	800	800	800	800	800	800	$ 9,600
	Mgmt. Fee	$	5,963	3,963	3,963	3,963	3,963	3,963	3,963	3,963	3,963	3,963	3,963	3,963	$ 71,820
	Prof. Fee	$	500	300	300	300	300	300	300	300	300	300	300	300	$ 6,000
	Marketing	$	3,000	3,000	3,000	3,000	3,000	3,000	3,000	3,000	3,000	3,000	3,000	3,000	$ 36,000
	Contract Svc.	$	5,320	3,320	3,320	3,320	3,320	3,320	3,320	3,320	3,320	3,320	3,320	3,320	$ 63,840
	Tenant Improv.	$	4,000	4,000	4,000	4,000	4,000	4,000	4,000	4,000	4,000	4,000	4,000	4,000	$ 48,000
	Res. & Replace.	$	1,673	1,873	1,873	1,873	1,873	1,873	1,873	1,873	1,873	1,873	1,873	1,873	$ 20,100
		$													$
		$													$
		$													$
		$													$
		$													$
		$													$
		$													$
	TOTAL	$	$ 53,200	53,200	53,200	53,200	53,200	53,200	53,200	53,200	53,200	53,200	53,200	53,200	$ 638,400

COMMENTS

FORM 15-7

Capital Expenditure Yearly Budget

PROPERTY NAME Oak Leaf Plaza
PREPARED BY Les Dolan
PROPERTY TYPE Office
DATE March 6, 19XX
PAGE ___ OF ___

DESCRIPTION	YR. 19XX	YR. 19XX	YR. 19XX	YR. 19XX	YR. 19XX	YR. 19XX	YR. 19XX	YR. 19XX	YR. 19XX
Roof	$	$	$	$	$	$	$	$	$
Paving	$	$	$	$	$	$	$	$	$
Landscaping	$ 20,000	$ 21,200	$ 22,472	$ 23,820	$ 25,250	$ 26,760	$ 28,370	$ 30,073	$ 31,877
Misc.	$	$	$	$	$	$	$	$	$
	$	$	$	$	$	$	$	$	$
	$	$	$	$	$	$	$	$	$
	$	$	$	$	$	$	$	$	$
	$	$	$	$	$	$	$	$	$
	$	$	$	$	$	$	$	$	$
	$	$	$	$	$	$	$	$	$
	$	$	$	$	$	$	$	$	$
	$	$	$	$	$	$	$	$	$
	$	$	$	$	$	$	$	$	$
	$	$	$	$	$	$	$	$	$
	$	$	$	$	$	$	$	$	$
	$	$	$	$	$	$	$	$	$
TOTAL	$ 0	$ 20,000	$ 21,200	$ 22,472	$ 23,820	$ 25,250	$ 26,760	$ 28,370	$ 30,073	$ 31,877

COMMENTS

550

Ten-Year Operating Forecast

PROPERTY NAME Oak Leaf Plaza
PREPARED BY Lee Dolan
DATE March 6, 19XX

DESCRIPTION	YR. 19XX	YR. 19XX	YR. 19XX	YR. 19XX	YR. 19XX	YR. 19XX	YR. 19XX	YR. 19XX	YR. 19XX	YR. 19XX
REVENUE:										
GROSS POTENTIAL INCOME (GPI)	$ 1,680,000	$ 1,747,200	$ 1,817,088	$ 1,889,772	$ 1,966,362	$ 2,043,977	$ 2,125,736	$ 2,210,765	$ 2,299,196	$ 2,391,164
LESS: VACANCY	$ (84,000)	$ (87,360)	$ (90,854)	$ (151,182)	$ (157,229)	$ (163,518)	$ (170,059)	$ (176,861)	$ (183,936)	$ (191,293)
MISCELLANEOUS INCOME	$	$	$	$	$	$	$	$	$	$
EFFECTIVE GROSS INCOME (EGI)	$ 1,596,000	$ 1,659,840	$ 1,726,234	$ 1,738,590	$ 1,808,133	$ 1,880,459	$ 1,955,677	$ 2,033,904	$ 2,115,260	$ 2,199,871
EXPENSES:										
FIXED OPERATING EXPENSES	$ 391,080	$ 414,545	$ 439,417	$ 465,783	$ 493,729	$ 523,353	$ 554,754	$ 588,040	$ 623,322	$ 660,721
VARIABLE EXPENSES	$ 227,220	$ 240,853	$ 255,304	$ 270,623	$ 286,860	$ 304,072	$ 322,316	$ 341,655	$ 362,154	$ 383,883
RESERVE REPLACEMENT	$ 20,100	$ 21,306	$ 22,584	$ 23,939	$ 25,376	$ 26,898	$ 28,512	$ 30,223	$ 32,036	$ 33,959
TOTAL EXPENSES	$ 638,400	$ 676,704	$ 717,306	$ 760,345	$ 805,965	$ 854,323	$ 905,583	$ 959,918	$ 1,017,513	$ 1,078,563
NET OPERATING INCOME	$ 957,600	$ 983,136	$ 1,008,927	$ 978,245	$ 1,002,168	$ 1,026,136	$ 1,050,094	$ 1,073,987	$ 1,097,748	$ 1,121,307
DEBT SERVICE	$ 763,309	$ 763,309	$ 763,309	$ 763,309	$ 763,309	$ 763,309	$ 763,309	$ 763,309	$ 763,309	$ 763,309
CAPITAL EXPENDITURES	$	$ 20,000	$ 21,200	$ 22,472	$ 23,820	$ 25,250	$ 26,760	$ 28,370	$ 30,073	$ 31,877
CASH FLOW	$ 194,291	$ 199,827	$ 224,418	$ 192,464	$ 215,039	$ 237,577	$ 260,021	$ 282,307	$ 304,366	$ 326,121

COMMENTS Vacancy—5% first three years, thereafter 8% per year. Expenses—6% increase per year.
Capital expenditures, year 1—0; year 2—$20,000; thereafter 6% increase.
Rent 4% increase per year.

FORM 15-13
Office Building Market Comparable Study

PROPERTY NAME Overlook
ADDRESS 891 10th St.
Atlanta GA
OWNERSHIP Overlook Corp.
ADDRESS _____
_____
TEL. NO. (   ) _____
MANAGEMENT CO. _____
TEL. NO. (   ) _____
LEASING AGENT _____
TEL. NO. (   ) _____

MAP NO. _____

PAGE _____ OF _____

DATE March 6, 19XX

CLASS BLDG. B
YEAR BUILT 19XX
GROSS SQ. FT. 90,000
NET SQ. FT. 77,000
NO. BLDGS. 1
NO. FLOORS 4
SQ. FT./FLOOR 22,500
PARKING (NO. SPACES):
SURFACE 385
COVERED _____
ACREAGE 4 Ac
DENSITY _____

LOCATION:
EXCELLENT _____
GOOD ___ X ___
AVERAGE _____
POOR _____

TYPE CONSTRUCTION:
WOOD _____
CONCRETE _____
STEEL ___ X ___
MASONRY _____

TYPE BLDG:
LOW RISE _____
MID RISE ___ X ___
HIGH RISE _____

TENANT PAYS:
GAS _____   JANITORIAL _____
ELEC _____   NO. DAYS _____
WATER _____   MAINTENANCE _____
SEWER _____   R.E. TAXES _____
INSURANCE _____

LEASE INFORMATION:
LEASE TERM 5 Yr
SEC. DEP. $ _____
R.E. COMM. 5%
TAX STOP YR. _____
INSUR. STOP YR. _____

BLDG. AMENTIES/FEATURES:
LOBBY ___ X ___
ELEVATOR ___ X ___
SECR. SERVICE _____
CONF. ROOM _____
HEALTH FACIL. _____
SECURITY ___ X ___

RESTAURANT _____
COURIER SERVICE _____
MAIL ROOM ___ X ___
DOORMAN _____
VENDING MACHINES _____

LANDSCAPING:
EXCELLENT _____
GOOD ___ X ___
AVERAGE _____
POOR _____

SIGNAGE:
EXCELLENT _____
GOOD ___ X ___
AVERAGE _____
POOR _____

HVAC PROVIDED:
HVAC/BLDG. _____
HVAC/FLOOR _____
HVAC/UNIT _____
SPRINKLERED ___ X ___

COMMENTS:
1 mile from subject, leasing very well

	DATE Mar 19XX	DATE _____	DATE _____	DATE _____	DATE _____
RENT RATE/SQ. FT.	$ 16	$ _____	$ _____	$ _____	$ _____
PARK RATE/SPACE	$ Free	$ _____	$ _____	$ _____	$ _____
ESCALATIONS	C.P.I.	_____	_____	_____	_____
OPTIONS	5 Yr	_____	_____	_____	_____
OCCUPANCY	$ 85 %	$ _____%	$ _____%	$ _____%	$ _____%
SMALLEST SPACE	1,000	_____	_____	_____	_____
LARGEST SPACE	8,000	_____	_____	_____	_____
TENANT IMPR.					
ALLOWANCES/SQ. FT.	$ 15	$ _____	$ _____	$ _____	$ _____
RENT CONCESSIONS	2 Mo	_____	_____	_____	_____
LEASING COMMISSION	5 %	_____%	_____%	_____%	_____%

552

Commercial Comparable Market Summary

PROPERTY NAME Oak Leaf Plaza

DATE March 6, 19XX

PAGE _____ OF _____

TYPE PROPERTY:
OFFICE X
SHOPPING CENTER _____
INDUSTRIAL _____

MAP REF. NO.	PROPERTY NAME	OCCUPANCY	GROSS/ NET S.F.	QUOTED RATE/S.F.	LEASE TERM	SERVICES PROVIDED	LESSEE PAYS UTILITIES	RENT CONCESSIONS	TENANT ALLOWANCE	SECURITY DEPOSIT	BROKER COMMISSION	COMMENTS
1	Overlook	85 %	77,000	$ 16.00	5	J, M	None	2 mo	$ 15	1 mo	5%	Leasing well
2	The Towers	93 %	110,000	$ 16.50	5	J, M	None	3 mo	$ 16	1 mo	5%	Poor location
		%		$					$			
		%		$					$			
		%		$					$			
		%		$					$			
		%		$					$			
		%		$					$			
		%		$					$			
		%		$					$			
		%		$					$			
		%		$					$			
		%		$					$			
COMPARABLE AVERAGES		%		$					$			

| SUBJECT PROPERTY MAP REF. NO. 3 | 65 % | 106,000 Net | $ 16 | 5 | J, M | None | 2 mo | $ 18 | 1 mo | 5% | Rent up |

CODE:
SERVICES PROVIDED:
(J) JANITORIAL
(M) MAINTENANCE

UTILITIES:
(G) GAS
(E) ELECTRICITY

(W) WATER
(S) SEWER

COMMENTS _____

Chapter 16

ARGUS FINANCIAL SOFTWARE CASE STUDY

The pages which follow present a detailed case study which has been prepared and analyzed using one of the most widely used commercial property analysis software programs on the market today: ARGUS Lease By Lease for Windows (Version 7). ARGUS is a powerful Cash Flow and Investment Modeling software application that provides the ultimate in flexibility and user-friendly features. Through a group of intuitively designed, easy-to-follow input screens, users detail existing lease and property information, proposed lease-up of vacant space, current and future market leasing assumptions for rollovers and renewals of leases, matrices of cap rates and discount rates, purchaser and sale parameters, debt structuring, development, partnership and portfolio consolidations. Any analysis can be quickly and easily modified to reflect changes in assumptions or "what if" scenarios. ARGUS enables total data integration with other applications through Open ARGUS, calculates projected cash flows in numerous formats, derives present values plus a variety of yield and return factors while producing over 200 presentation quality reports and unlimited line item color graphics.

CASE STUDY—SMALL OFFICE BUILDING

The property under consideration is a 101,500-square-foot multi-tenant office building. The analysis spans a 10-year holding period from January 1997 to December 2007. ARGUS calculates the internal rate of return based on an initial purchase price of $2,750,000, annual cash flows after capital expenditures over the 10-year holding period, plus the net property reversion. The property reversion is calculated by capitalizing the Year 11 net operating income and deducting sales costs. The model indicates an unleveraged internal rate of return of 23.43%, and a leveraged internal rate of return of 45.86%, assuming an acquisition loan equal to 75% of the purchase price.

Input Assumptions

Pages 560 to 573 show a comprehensive listing of the input assumptions. These cover every aspect of the property economics from growth rates applied to rent and expense estimates to the methodology applied to calculate the property reversion.

Pages 574 to 599 contain some of the detail and summary reports available with ARGUS. Within the program, the user can select the display options for monthly, quarterly, semi-annual, or annual reporting, for both the property level and the individual tenant reports.

Property Summary Report

This exhibit on page 574 restates the most important assumptions: Timing & Inflation; Property Size & Occupancy; Space Absorption; General Vacancy; Credit & Collection Loss; Debt Financing; Property Purchase & Resale; and Present Value Discounting.

Presentation Rent Roll and Current Term Tenant Summary

The entire tenant Rent Roll for both existing tenants and vacant spaces to be leased-up can be found on pages 575 to 578. This schedule shows, for each lease, all the relevant details of the rent roll: Tenant Name; Area; Base Rent; Rent Adjustments; Abatements; Reimbursements; Leasing Costs; Retail Sales; Breakpoint; and Expiration Assumptions.

Schedule of Prospective Cash Flow

Pages 579 to 582 detail the monthly and annual operating cash flow projections for the property. In this case, the monthly schedule allows the user to track the cash outlays associated with achieving stabilized occupancy and completing the renovations and repairs. Note that the property cannot meet debt service (after capital expenditures) for five months during Year 1, so additional draws on the partnership may be required.

Detailed Lease Expiration Schedule

The table on page 599 groups the tenant roster by lease expiration dates during the first lease term. The annual totals are shown as a percentage of the total building. Rollover exposure can be a critical factor in the measure of ownership risk.

Individual Loan & Debt Service Summary

This schedule on page 583 highlights all the debt financing information and calculates both coverage and loan-to-value ratios. In addition, this schedule shows the lender's yield inclusive of any origination fees and all earned interest.

Schedule of Sources and Uses of Capital

Refer to page 584 for the best summary of the property's capital structure. This report gives the cash-on-cash returns for every year of the holding period. Initial outlays of equity and debt capital are itemized at the beginning of the holding period and are followed by operating cash flows over the term. At disposition, this schedule shows the net proceeds from the property sale.

Most important, this schedule presents the leveraged and unleveraged internal rate of return and the modified internal rate of return. ARGUS allows the user to select the methodology for calculating the property reversion and to select a range in values for use as the capitalization rate and discount rate.

Cash Flow Distribution Tracking—General Partners and Limited Partners

Pages 585 to 588 show the initial investment outlays and the annual participation in cash flows for the general and limited partners. These schedules illustrate the returns to the owners in real dollars and calculate the internal rates of return for each partnership interest.

Prospective Present Value—General Partners and Limited Partners

Pages 589 to 590 continue the detailed reporting for the partnership interests. Each interest shares in a percentage of the annual cash flows after capital items and the net property reversion. That participation is reduced to a present value indication using a range of discount rates.

Prospective Present Value

ARGUS calculates the total property present value on a Before Debt Service basis (page 591) and on an After Debt Service basis (page 592).

Resale—Cap Rate Matrix

The tables on pages 593 and 594 show the various present values that can be calculated using a range of capitalization rates and discount rates. This type of schedule is particularly useful in initial discussions.

Supporting Schedules

Pages 595 to 599 are examples of some of the tenant reports that ARGUS can generate. These tables show supporting details for: Base Rent per Square Foot; Base Rental Revenue; Tenant Improvements, and Leasing Commissions.

Conclusion

ARGUS is an extremely powerful tool for modeling property economics. Complex lease structures and changing assumptions can be handled with ease and the resulting information can be presented in a variety of formats.

ARGUS FINANCIAL SOFTWARE CASE STUDY

Small Office Building

INPUT ASSUMPTIONS

1. Property Description
2. Property Timing
3. Area Measures
4. General Inflation
5. Overall Inflation Rates
6. Reimbursable Expenses
7. Detail of Utilities
8. Detail of Real Estate Taxes
9. Non-Reimbursable Expenses
10. Percent of Line Detail

11. Capital Expenditures

12. Detail of Lobby Renovation

13. Detail of Roof Repairs

14. General Vacancy

15. Credit & Collection Loss

16. Rent Roll

17. Space Absorption

18. Rent Abatements

19. Detailed Reimbursement Methods

20. Leasing Assumptions

21. Renewal Probability

22. Market Rent

23. Tenant Improvements

24. Intelligent Renewals

25. Property Resale

26. Modified Internal Rate of Return

27. Cap Rate Range

28. Debt Financing

29. Present Value Discounting

30. Equity Contributions

31. Percent of Line Detail for Limited Partners

32. Detail of General Partner/Developer

33. Cash Flow Distribution

34. Resale Distribution

REPORTS

1. Property Summary Report

2. Presentation Rent Roll & Current Term Tenant Summary

3. Schedule of Prospective Cash Flow-12 Months

4. Schedule of Prospective Cash Flow-11 Years

5. Individual Loan & Debt Service Summary

6. Schedule of Sources & Uses of Capital

7. Cash Flow Distribution Tracking—General Partner/Developer

8. Partner Return Summary—General Partner/Developer

9. Cash Flow Distribution Tracking—Limited Partners

10. Partner Return Summary—Limited Partners

11. Prospective Present Value—General Partner/Developer

12. Prospective Present Value—Limited Partners

13. Prospective Present Value—CFBDS + Property Resale

14. Prospective Present Value—CFADS + Property Resale

15. Cash Flow Before Debt Service + Property Resale

16. Cash Flow After Debt Service + Property Resale

17. Supporting Schedule—Detailed Lease Expiration Schedule (First Term Only)

18. Supporting Schedule—Scheduled Base Rent Per SQFT

19. Supporting Schedule—Scheduled Base Rental Revenue

20. Supporting Schedule—Tenant Improvements

21. Supporting Schedule—Leasing Commissions

SAMPLE SMALL OFFICE BUILDING

Input Assumptions

PROPERTY DESCRIPTION

Name:	SAMPLE SMALL OFFICE BUILDING
Address:	
City:	
State:	
Zip:	
Portfolio:	ARGUS Sample Properties
Property Type:	Office & Retail

PROPERTY TIMING

Analysis Start Date:	Jan-97
First Year Ends:	Dec-97
Years of Analysis:	10

AREA MEASURES

	Label	Area
	Property Size	101,500 SqFt
	Alt. Prop. Size	101,500 SqFt

GENERAL INFLATION

Inflation Method: Fiscal
Reimbursement Method: Calendar reimbursement using fiscal inflation

	Year 1	Year 2	Year 3	Year 4	Year 5	Year 6	Year 7	Year 8	Year 9	Year 10	Year 11
Rate:	0	3	3	4	4	4	4	4	4	4	4

OVERALL INFLATION RATES

Market Rent Inflation

	Year 1	Year 2	Year 3	Year 4	Year 5	Year 6	Year 7	Year 8	Year 9	Year 10	Year 11
Rate:	0	0	3	5	7	10	7	5	4	4	4

REIMBURSABLE EXPENSES

Name	Acct Code	Amount	Units	Area	Frequency	% Fixed	Inflation	Ref Acct
Common Area Maintenance		Sub-lines						
Real Estate Taxes		Detail	$Amount			100		
Administrative & General		25,000	$Amount		/Year	100		
Insurance		0.38	$/Area	Property Size	/Year	100		

Gross Up for Reimbursement: Yes, 95% Occupancy

REIMBURSABLE EXPENSES - Sublines for Common Area Maintenance

Name	Acct Code	Amount	Units	Area	Frequency	% Fixed	Inflation	Ref Acct
Utilities		Detail	$Amount			50		
Repairs & Mtce.		97,000	$Amount		/Year	100		
Janitorial		0.86	$/Area	Property Size	/Year	15		
Security		1,250	$Amount		/Month	100		

SAMPLE SMALL OFFICE BUILDING

Input Assumptions

DETAIL OF Utilities

Monthly pattern - before inflation. Inflation rate reported below Annual Total; Inflated Total is calculated result.

	Year 1	Year 2	Year 3	Year 4	Year 5	Year 6	Year 7	Year 8	Year 9	Year 10	Year 11
January	12,000	12,000	12,000	12,000	12,000	12,000	12,000	12,000	12,000	12,000	12,000
February	12,000	12,000	12,000	12,000	12,000	12,000	12,000	12,000	12,000	12,000	12,000
March	13,500	13,500	13,500	13,500	13,500	13,500	13,500	13,500	13,500	13,500	13,500
April	13,500	13,500	13,500	13,500	13,500	13,500	13,500	13,500	13,500	13,500	13,500
May	13,000	13,000	13,000	13,000	13,000	13,000	13,000	13,000	13,000	13,000	13,000
June	13,000	13,000	13,000	13,000	13,000	13,000	13,000	13,000	13,000	13,000	13,000
July	12,500	12,500	12,500	12,500	12,500	12,500	12,500	12,500	12,500	12,500	12,500
August	12,500	12,500	12,500	12,500	12,500	12,500	12,500	12,500	12,500	12,500	12,500
September	12,000	12,000	12,000	12,000	12,000	12,000	12,000	12,000	12,000	12,000	12,000
October	12,000	12,000	12,000	12,000	12,000	12,000	12,000	12,000	12,000	12,000	12,000
November	12,000	12,000	12,000	12,000	12,000	12,000	12,000	12,000	12,000	12,000	12,000
December	12,000	12,000	12,000	12,000	12,000	12,000	12,000	12,000	12,000	12,000	12,000
Annual Total	150,000	150,000	150,000	150,000	150,000	150,000	150,000	150,000	150,000	150,000	150,000
Inflation		0	0	0	0	0	0	0	0	0	0
Inflated Total	150,000	156,000	162,240	168,730	175,479	182,498	189,798	197,390	205,285	213,497	222,037

DETAIL OF Real Estate Taxes

Monthly pattern - before inflation. Inflation rate reported below Annual Total; Inflated Total is calculated result.

	Year 1	Year 2	Year 3	Year 4	Year 5	Year 6	Year 7	Year 8	Year 9	Year 10	Year 11
January											
February											
March											
April	22,500	22,500	22,500	22,500	22,500	22,500	22,500	22,500	22,500	22,500	22,500
May											
June											
July											
August											
September											
October	22,500	22,500	22,500	22,500	22,500	22,500	22,500	22,500	22,500	22,500	22,500
November											
December											
Annual Total	45,000	45,000	45,000	45,000	45,000	45,000	45,000	45,000	45,000	45,000	45,000
Inflation		2	2	2	2	2	2	2	2	2	2
Inflated Total	45,000	45,900	46,818	47,754	48,709	49,684	50,677	51,691	52,725	53,779	54,855

561

SAMPLE SMALL OFFICE BUILDING

Input Assumptions

NON-REIMBURSABLE EXPENSES

Name	Acct Code	Amount	Units	Area	Frequency	% Fixed	Inflation	Ref Acct
Property Management Fees			% of Line					

PERCENT OF LINE DETAIL for Property Management Fees

Percent	Report Line Label
3	EFFECTIVE GROSS REVENUE

Range:
Start Date:
End Date:
Monthly Minimum:
Inflation:
Monthly Maximum:
Inflation:

2,000

CAPITAL EXPENDITURES

Name	Acct Code	Amount	Units	Area	Frequency	% Fixed	Inflation	Ref Acct
Structural Reserves		0.05	$/Area	Property Size	/Year	100		
Lobby Renovation		Detail	$Amount			100		
Roof Repairs		Detail	$Amount			100		

DETAIL OF Lobby Renovation   Monthly pattern - before inflation.   Inflation rate reported below Annual Total; Inflated Total is calculated result.

	Year 1	Year 2	Year 3	Year 4	Year 5	Year 6	Year 7	Year 8	Year 9	Year 10	Year 11
January											
February											
March	50,000										
April	25,000										
May											
June											
July											
August											
September											
October											
November											
December											
Annual Total	75,000										
Inflation											
Inflated Total	75,000										

562

SAMPLE SMALL OFFICE BUILDING

Input Assumptions

DETAIL OF Roof Repairs Monthly pattern - before inflation. Inflation rate reported below Annual Total; Inflated Total is calculated result.

	Year 1	Year 2	Year 3	Year 4	Year 5	Year 6	Year 7	Year 8	Year 9	Year 10	Year 11
January											
February											
March											
April											
May											
June											
July											
August	35,000										
September											
October											
November											
December											
Annual Total	35,000										
Inflation											
Inflated Total	35,000										

GENERAL VACANCY

Option:	Percent of Potential Gross Revenue
Percent Based on Revenue Minus Absorption and Turnover Vacancy:	No
Reduce General Vacancy Result by Absorption & Turnover Vacancy:	Yes
Rate:	5

CREDIT & COLLECTION LOSS

Option:	Percent of Potential Gross Revenue
Rate:	1

563

SAMPLE SMALL OFFICE BUILDING

Input Assumptions

RENT ROLL

Tenant Name/ Description	Suite	Lease Type	Total Area	Start Date	Term/ Expir	Base/Min Rent	Unit of Measure	Rent Chng	Rtl Sls	Reimbur- sements	Rent Abatemnt	Leasing Cost	Market Leasing	Upon Expiration	Rnwl Prob
Systems Inc.	200	Office	7,834	1/93	12/98	9.75	$/SqFt/Yr			4.75			3 Yr Mkt	Market	90
Smith Leasing Co.	225	Office	1,675	Oct-94	9/99	9.50	$/SqFt/Yr			4.50			3 Yr Mkt	Vacate	
The Home Group	240	Office	2,901	3/93	2/00	9.00	$/SqFt/Yr	Yes		4.25			3 Yr Mkt	Renew	
BBB Travel	250	Office	4,110	6/95	5/00	9.25	$/SqFt/Yr			4.50			3 Yr Mkt	Vacate	
Proposed - Vacant Sui	280	Office	1,550	7	5	10.00	$/SqFt/Yr	Yes		Base Stop		Yes	5 Yr Mkt	Market	
Taylor & Murphy	3/4/05	Office	35,579	3/93	2/03	Detail		Yes		Modified Gross	2		10 Yr Mkt	Renew	
USA Brokerage	Full 6	Office	11,875	9/93	8/98	Detail				4.25			5 Yr Mkt	Option	
USA Brokerage	Full 6	Option	11,875			Detail		Yes		Base Stop		Yes	5 Yr Mkt	Market	
China Hut	Lobby	Retail	3,000	7/94	6/04	Detail			Yes	CAM+15% Admin	1 Mo/Yr		Retail Mkt	> Mkt or Curr $	
Italian Pizza Parlor	Lobby	Retail	2,750	Dec-94	11/97	18.00	$/SqFt/Yr		Yes	CAM+15% Admin			Retail Mkt	Market	
Storage - China Hut	A-1	Office	500	7/94	6/04	5.00	$/SqFt/Yr			None			Storage	Market	
Storage - U.S. Broker	A-2	Office	1,000	9/93	8/98	5.00	$/SqFt/Yr			None			Storage	Market	

Rent Changes: The Home Group
Step: $ .50/Ft/Yr
Porters' Wage:
Miscellaneous:
CPI Rent
Category:
Current Amount:
Parking
Spaces:
Amount:

Rent Changes: Proposed - Vacant Suite
Step: $ .50/Ft/Yr
Porters' Wage:
Miscellaneous:
CPI Rent
Category:
Current Amount:
Parking
Spaces:
Amount:

Leasing Cost
Proposed - Vacant Suite
Tenant Improvements: 6
Leasing Commissions: 0.05

Detail Base Rent
Taylor & Murphy

Date	Amount	Unit
3/85	6.00	$/SqFt/Yr
3/87	7.00	$/SqFt/Yr
3/89	8.00	$/SqFt/Yr
3/91	9.00	$/SqFt/Yr
3/93	10.00	$/SqFt/Yr

Detail Base Rent
USA brokerage

Date	Amount	Unit
9/90	8.50	$/SqFt/Yr
9/92	9.25	$/SqFt/Yr
9/94	10.00	$/SqFt/Yr
9/96	10.75	$/SqFt/Yr

Detail Base Rent
USA brokerage

Date	Amount	Unit
1	0.9	% Market

SAMPLE SMALL OFFICE BUILDING

Input Assumptions

Rent Changes: USA Brokerage
Step:
Porters' Wage:
Miscellaneous:
CPI Rent
  Category: Lease Year
  Current Amount:
Parking
  Spaces:
  Amount:

Leasing Cost
USA Brokerage
Tenant Improvements: 5.00
Leasing Commissions: 0.02

Detail Base Rent
China Hut

Date	Amount	Unit
1	15.00	$/SqFt/Yr
13	16.00	$/SqFt/Yr
25	17.00	$/SqFt/Yr
37	18.00	$/SqFt/Yr
49	19.00	$/SqFt/Yr
61	20.00	$/SqFt/Yr
73	21.00	$/SqFt/Yr
85	22.00	$/SqFt/Yr
97	23.00	$/SqFt/Yr
109	24.00	$/SqFt/Yr

SPACE ABSORPTION

No.	Space Description	Lease Type	Total Area	Date Avail	Begin Lsng	#/Size Leases	Crte Lses	Term/ Expir	Base/Min Rent	Unit of Measure	Rent Chng	Rtl Sls	Reimbursements	Rent Abatemnt	Lsg Cst	Market Leasing	Upon Expiration
1	Currently Vacant	Office	28,726		2	6	Qrt	5		%Market	Yes		Base Stop	25% 1st Yr	Yes	5 Yr Mkt	Market

Rent Changes: Currently Vacant
Step: $1.00/Ft/Yr
Porters' Wage:
Miscellaneous:
CPI Rent
  Category:
  Current Amount:
Parking
  Spaces:
  Amount:

Leasing Cost
Currently Vacant
Tenant Improvements: 5
Leasing Commissions: 0.05

SAMPLE SMALL OFFICE BUILDING

Input Assumptions

RENT ABATEMENTS

Rent Abatement Category:
25% 1st Yr
Modifier: Standard

Date	Pct	Mos
1	25.00	12

Rent Abatement Category:
1 Mo/Yr
Modifier: Standard

Date	Pct	Mos
1	100	1.00
13	100	1.00
25	100	1.00

DETAILED REIMBURSEMENT METHODS

Reimbursement Category: Modified Gross

Reimbursable Expenses	Reimbursement Method	Amount	Pro-rata	Area Measure	Area Minimum	Reimburse After	Charg-able %	Reimb. Minimum	Min. Growth	Reimb. Max	Max Growth	% Rent Offset
Common Area Maintenance	Net (Pays Pro Rata Share)		Natural	Occupied Total	100		100					
Real Estate Taxes	Group Total, see below											
Administrative & General	Group Total, see below											
Insurance	Group Total, see below											
Group	Increases over $/SqFt Stop	3	Natural	Property Size			100				5	

Number of terms to apply method: 1
Gross up Expenses: Yes to 95% occupancy

Reimbursement Category: CAM-15% Admin

Reimbursable Expenses	Reimbursement Method	Amount	Pro-rata	Area Measure	Area Minimum	Reimburse After	Charg-able %	Reimb. Minimum	Min. Growth	Reimb. Max	Max Growth	% Rent Offset
Common Area Maintenance	Net (Pays Pro Rata Share)		Natural	Property Size			115					100
Real Estate Taxes	Group Total, see below											
Administrative & General	Group Total, see below											
Insurance	Group Total, see below											
Group	Increases over $ Amount:	440,000	Natural	Property Size			100					

Number of terms to apply method: 9
Gross up Expenses: Yes to 95% occupancy

SAMPLE SMALL OFFICE BUILDING

Input Assumptions

MARKET LEASING ASSUMPTIONS

Leasing Assumptions Category: 3 Yr Mkt

	New Market	Renewal Mkt	Term 2	Term 3	Term 4
Renewal Probability		50-70% Changing			
Market Rent	3 Yr Mkt				
Months Vacant	4	0			
Tenant Improvements	2.40	1.20			
Leasing Commissions	5	2.5			
Rent Abatements	0				
NON-WEIGHTED ITEMS					
Rent Changes	Yes				
Retail Sales	No				
Reimbursements	Base Stop				
Term Lengths	3				

Rent Changes: 3 Yr Mkt, current term
Changing Base:
Step:
Porters' Wage:
Miscellaneous:
CPI Rent
Category: 50% CPI

Leasing Assumptions Category: 5 Yr Mkt

	New Market	Renewal Mkt	Term 2	Term 3	Term 4
Renewal Probability		50-70% Changing			
Market Rent	5 Yr Mkt				
Months Vacant	4	0			
Tenant Improvements	4.00	2.00			
Leasing Commissions	5	2.5			
Rent Abatements	0				
NON-WEIGHTED ITEMS					
Rent Changes	Yes				
Retail Sales	No				
Reimbursements	Base Stop				
Term Lengths	5				

Rent Changes: 5 Yr Mkt, current term
Changing Bas
Step:
Porters' Wage:
Miscellaneous:
CPI Rent
Category: 50% CPI

SAMPLE SMALL OFFICE BUILDING

Input Assumptions

Leasing Assumptions Category: Retail Mkt

	New Market	Renewal Mkt	Term 2	Term 3	Term 4
Renewal Probability		75			
Market Rent	Retail Mkt	0			
Months Vacant	4	1.00			
Tenant Improvements	2.00	2.5			
Leasing Commissions	5				
Rent Abatements	0				
NON-WEIGHTED ITEMS					
Rent Changes	Yes				
Retail Sales	No				
Reimbursements	Net				
Term Lengths	5				

Rent Changes: Retail Mkt, current term
Changing B
Step: $1.00/Ft/Yr
Porters' Wage:
Miscellaneous:
CPI Rent
Category:

Leasing Assumptions Category: Storage

	New Market	Renewal Mkt	Term 2	Term 3	Term 4
Renewal Probability	5.00	100			
Market Rent	0	0			
Months Vacant	0				
Tenant Improvements	0				
Leasing Commissions	0				
Rent Abatements					
NON-WEIGHTED ITEMS					
Rent Changes	No				
Retail Sales	No				
Reimbursements	None				
Term Lengths	5				

Leasing Assumptions Category: 10 Yr Mkt

	New Market	Renewal Mkt	Term 2	Term 3	Term 4
Renewal Probability	9	50-70% Changing			
Market Rent	4	0			
Months Vacant	5	3			
Tenant Improvements	5	2.5			
Leasing Commissions	0				
Rent Abatements					
NON-WEIGHTED ITEMS					
Rent Changes	Yes				
Retail Sales	No				
Reimbursements	Base Stop				
Term Lengths	10				

Rent Changes: 10 Yr Mkt, current term
Changing Base:
Step:
Porters' Wage:
Miscellaneous:
CPI Rent
Category: 50% CPI

SAMPLE SMALL OFFICE BUILDING

Input Assumptions

RENEWAL PROBABILITY

Renewal Probability Category: 50-70% Changing

	Year 1	Year 2	Year 3	Year 4	Year 5	Year 6	Year 7	Year 8	Year 9	Year 10	Year 11
% to Renew	50	55	60	65	70	70	70	70	70	70	70

MARKET RENT

Market Rent Category: 3 Yr Mkt

	Year 1	Year 2	Year 3	Year 4	Year 5	Year 6	Year 7	Year 8	Year 9	Year 10	Year 11
New	10.00	10.00	10.50	10.50	10.00	10.00	10.00	10.50	10.50	10.50	10.50
Renew	9.50	9.50	10.00	10.00	9.50	9.50	9.50	10.00	10.00	10.00	10.00
Inflation		0	0	3	3	3	3	3	3	3	3

Market Rent Category: 5 Yr Mkt

	Year 1	Year 2	Year 3	Year 4	Year 5	Year 6	Year 7	Year 8	Year 9	Year 10	Year 11
New	9.50	9.50	10.00	10.00	10.00	10.00	10.00	10.00	10.00	10.00	10.00
Renew	9.00	9.00	9.50	9.50	9.50	9.50	9.50	9.50	9.50	9.50	9.50
Inflation		0	0	3	3	3	3	3	3	3	3

TENANT IMPROVEMENTS

Tenant Improvements Category: Slab

	Year 1	Year 2	Year 3	Year 4	Year 5	Year 6	Year 7	Year 8	Year 9	Year 10	Year 11
New	15.00	15.00	15.00	15.00	15.00	15.00	15.00	15.00	15.00	15.00	15.00
Renew											
Inflation											

SAMPLE SMALL OFFICE BUILDING

Input Assumptions

INTELLIGENT RENEWALS

Renewal Category: > Mkt or Curr $

New Rent Based on the Greater of Last Rent or
90% of Market Leasing Assumptions Rent.
Last Rent is based on Base Rent
Sales Percent Revenue.

MODIFIED INTERNAL RATE OF RETURN

Reinvestment Rate: 11
Safe Rate: 7

DEBT FINANCING

Name: First Mortgage
Start Date: 1
Term Length: 25
Percent of Value: 75
Rate Charged: 9

PROPERTY RESALE

Initial Purchase Price:	2,750,000
Option:	Capitalize Net Operating Income
Cap Rate:	9
Resale Commission (%):	4
Apply Rate to following ye	Yes
Calculate Resale for All Y	Yes

CAP RATE RANGE

Low Rate:	7
High Rate:	10
Increment:	0.5

First Mortgage - Advanced

Rate Paid:	
Rate on Accrual:	
Payments/Year:	12
Payments Delaye	Yes
Interest Calculati	USA <end>
% CF Pays Accru	0
Other Payments:	No
Points Fees:	1
Prepay Penalty:	0
Call or Balloon:	0

PRESENT VALUE DISCOUNTING

Unleveraged Discount Range
Low Discount Rate:	9
High Discount Rate:	12
Increment:	0.5

Leveraged Discount Range
Low Discount Rate:	10
High Discount Rate:	14
Increment:	0.5
Discount Method:	Annually (Endpoint on Cash Flow & Resale)
Secondary Discount Timing	
Start Date:	37
End Date:	12/09
Length:	10

570

SAMPLE SMALL OFFICE BUILDING

Input Assumptions

EQUITY CONTRIBUTIONS

Name	Acct Code	Amount	Units	Area	Frequency	% Fixed	Inflation	Non-Cash
Limited Partners			% of Line					
General Partner/Developer	Detail		$Amount			100		Yes

PERCENT OF LINE DETAIL for Limited Partners

Percent	Report Line Label
-100	AVAILABLE CASH FLOW
	(Funds all Negative Cash Flow as Equity Contribution)

Range:
Start Date:
End Date:
Monthly Minimum   0
Inflation:
Monthly Maximum
Inflation:

DETAIL OF General Partner/Developer

	Year 1	Year 2	Year 3	Year 4	Year 5	Year 6	Year 7	Year 8	Year 9	Year 10	Year 11
January	100,000.00										
February											
March											
April											
May											
June											
July											
August											
September											
October											
November											
December											
Annual Total	100,000.00										
Inflation											
Inflated Total	100,000.00										

571

SAMPLE SMALL OFFICE BUILDING

Input Assumptions

CASH FLOW DISTRIBUTION

Partner	Type of Return	Amount	Cumulative	Interest Rate	Preference Level	Begin Date/Amount	After Distribution to	End Date/Amount	After Distribution t	Reduce Equity
Limited Partners	% Investment	20	Yes	15	1					
General Partner/Developer	% Investment	10	Yes	15	2					
Limited Partners	Return Investment	100			3					
General Partner/Developer	% Cash Remaining	90			4					
Limited Partners	% Cash Remaining	10			4					

RESALE DISTRIBUTION

Partner	Type of Return	Amount	Preference Level	Begin Date/Amount	After Distribution to	End Date/Amount	After Distribution to
Limited Partners	Unpaid Preference	100	1				
Limited Partners	IRR rate	25	2				
General Partner/Developer	Unpaid Preference	100	3				
General Partner/Developer	IRR rate	15	4				
General Partner/Developer	% Cash Remaining	50	5				
Limited Partners	% Cash Remaining	50	5				

SAMPLE SMALL OFFICE BUILDING

Input Assumptions

CASH FLOW DISTRIBUTION

Partner	Type of Return	Amount	Cumulative	Interest Rate	Preference Level	Begin Date/Amount	After Distribution to	End Date/Amount	After Distribution t	Reduce Equity
Limited Partners	% Investment	20	Yes	15	1					
General Partner/Developer	% Investment	10	Yes	15	2					
Limited Partners	Return Investment	100			3					
General Partner/Developer	% Cash Remaining	90			4					
Limited Partners	% Cash Remaining	10			4					

RESALE DISTRIBUTION

Partner	Type of Return	Amount	Preference Level	Begin Date/Amount	After Distribution to	End Date/Amount	After Distribution to
Limited Partners	Unpaid Preference	100	1				
Limited Partners	IRR rate	25	2				
General Partner/Developer	Unpaid Preference	100	3				
General Partner/Developer	IRR rate	15	4				
Limited Partners	% Cash Remaining	50	5				
General Partner/Developer	% Cash Remaining	50	5				

573

SAMPLE SMALL OFFICE BUILDING
PROPERTY SUMMARY REPORT

TIMING & INFLATION

Analysis Period: January 1, 1997 to December 31, 2006, 10 years
Inflation Method: Fiscal
General Inflation Rate: 3.00% for 2 years
4.00% thereafter

PROPERTY SIZE & OCCUPANCY

Property Size: 101,500 Square Feet
Number of rent roll tenants: 11
Total Occupied Area: 71,224 Square Feet, 70.17% during first month of analysis

SPACE ABSORPTION

Currently Vacant 28,726 Square Feet, leasing from 2/97 to 5/98
1 lease per quarter 4,788 SqFt per lease

GENERAL VACANCY

Method: Percent of Potential Gross Revenue
Amount: 5.00%

CREDIT & COLLECTION LOSS

Method: Percent of Potential Gross Revenue
Amount: 1.00%

DEBT FINANCING

Number of Notes: 1
Beginning Principal Balance: $2,062,500
Average Year 1 Interest Rate: 9.00%

PROPERTY PURCHASE & RESALE

Purchase Price: $2,750,000
Resale Method: Capitalize Net Operating Income
Cap Rate: 9.00%
Cap Year: Year 11
Commission/Closing Cost: 4.00%
Net Cash Flow from Sale: $5,324,952

PRESENT VALUE DISCOUNTING

Discount Method: Annually (Endpoint on Cash Flow & Resale)
Unleveraged Discount Rate: 9.00% to 12.00%, 0.50% increments
Unleveraged Present Value: $5,204,450 at 12.00%
Unleveraged Annual IRR: 23.43%

Leveraged Discount Rate: 10.00% to 14.00%, 0.50% increments
Value of Equity Interest: $3,050,165 at 14.00%
Leveraged Annual IRR: 45.86%

574

SAMPLE SMALL OFFICE BUILDING
PRESENTATION RENT ROLL & CURRENT TERM TENANT SUMMARY
As of Jan-1997 for 101,500 Square Feet

DESCRIPTION (Tenant Name, Type & Suite Number, Lease Dates & Term)	AREA (Floor SqFt, Bldg Share)	BASE RENT (Rate & Amount per Year, per Month)	RENT ADJ. & CATEGORIES (Changes on)	ABATEMENTS (Changes to)	REIMBURSEMENT (CPI & Current Porters' Wage Miscellaneous)	LEASING COSTS (Months to Abate)	RETAIL (Pcnt to Abate)	UPON EXPIRATION (Description of Operating Expense Reimbursements)	Imprvmnts Rate / Amount	Commssns Rate / Amount	Sales Breakpoint Overage %	Assumption about subsequent terms for this tenant
Systems Inc. / Office Suite 200 / Jan-1993 to Dec-1998 / 72 Months	7,834 / 7.72%	9.75 / 76,382 / 0.81 / 6,365						Gross. Pays the increases over an expense stop of 4.75				Market @90% / See assumption: / 3 Yr Mkt
Smith Leasing Co / Office Suite 225 / Oct-1994 to Sep-1999 / 60 Months	1,675 / 1.65%	9.50 / 15,913 / 0.79 / 1,326						Gross. Pays the increases over an expense stop of 4.5				Vacate / See assumption: / 3 Yr Mkt
The Home Group / Office Suite 240 / Mar-1993 to Feb-2000 / 84 Months	2,901 / 2.86%	9.00 / 26,109 / 0.75 / 2,176	Mar-1994 / Mar-1995 / Mar-1996 / Mar-1997	9.50 / 10.00 / 10.50 / 11.00				Gross. Pays the increases over an expense stop of 4.25				Renew / See assumption: / 3 Yr Mkt
BBB Travel / Office Suite 250 / Jun-1995 to May-2000 / 60 Months	4,110 / 4.05%	9.25 / 38,018 / 0.77 / 3,168						Gross. Pays the increases over an expense stop of 4.5				Vacate / See assumption: / 3 Yr Mkt
Proposed - Vacant Suite / Office Suite 280 / Jul-1997 to Jun-2002 / 60 Months	1,550 / 1.53%	10.00 / 15,500 / 0.83 / 1,292	Jul-1998 / Jul-1999 / Jul-2000 / Jul-2001	10.50 / 11.00 / 11.50 / 12.00		1-2	100%	Gross. Pays the increases over a base year ending Dec-1997: 4.44	6.00 / 9,300	2.67 / 5.00% / 4,133		Market / See assumption: / 5 Yr Mkt
Taylor & Murphy / Office Suite 3-4-5 / Mar-1993 to Feb-2003 / 120 Months	35,579 / 35.05%	10.00 / 355,790 / 0.83 / 29,649						See method: Modified Gross reimbursement.				Renew / See assumption: / 10 Yr Mkt

575

SAMPLE SMALL OFFICE BUILDING

PRESENTATION RENT ROLL & CURRENT TERM TENANT SUMMARY

As of Jan-1997 for 101,500 Square Feet

DESCRIPTION — Tenant Name / Type & Suite Number / Lease Dates & Term	AREA — Floor SqFt / Bldg Share	BASE RENT — Rate & Amount per Year / per Month	RENT ADJ. & CATEGORIES — Changes on	ABATEMENTS — Changes to	REIMBURSEMENT — CPI & Current Porters' Wage / Miscellaneous	LEASING COSTS — Months to Abate	RETAIL — Pcnt to Abate	UPON EXPIRATION — Description of Operating Expense Reimbursements	Imprvmnts Rate / Amount	Commssns Rate / Amount	Sales Breakpoint / Overage %	Assumption about subsequent terms for this tenant
USA Brokerage / Office Suite Full 6 / Sep-1993 to Aug-1998 / 60 Months	11,875 / 11.70%	9.25 / 109,844 / 0.77 / 9,154	Sep-1994 / Sep-1996	10.00 / 10.75				Gross: Pays the increases over an expense stop of 4.25				Option / See assumption: / 5 Yr Mkt
USA Brokerage / Option Suite Full 6 / Sep-1998 to Aug-2003 / 60 Months	11,875 / 11.70%	8.10 / 96,188 / 0.68 / 8,016			Lease Year			Gross: Pays the increases over a base year ending Dec-1998. 4.63	5.00 / 59,375	0.81 / 2.00% / 9,619		Market / See assumption: / 5 Yr Mkt
China Hut / Retail Suite Lobby / Jul-1994 to Jun-2004 / 120 Months	3,000 / 2.96%	15.00 / 45,000 / 1.25 / 3,750	Jul-1995 / Jul-1996 / Jul-1997 / Jul-1998 / Jul-1999 / Jul-2000 / Jul-2001 / Jul-2002 / Jul-2003	16.00 / 17.00 / 18.00 / 19.00 / 20.00 / 21.00 / 22.00 / 23.00 / 24.00		1 / 13 / 25 / 37 / 49 / 61 / 73 / 85 / 97 / 109	100% / 100% / 100% / 100% / 100% / 100% / 100% / 100% / 100% / 100%	See method: CAM+15% Admin reimbursement.			See category: Retail 1	Market / See assumption: / Retail Mkt
Italian Pizza Parlor / Retail Suite Lobby / Dec-1994 to Nov-2004 / 120 Months	2,750 / 2.71%	18.00 / 49,500 / 1.50 / 4,125						See method: CAM+15% Admin reimbursement			300 / Natural / 5.00%	> Mkt or Curr $ / See assumption: / Retail Mkt
Storage - China Hut / Office Suite A-1 / Jul-1994 to Jun-2004 / 120 Months	500 / 0.49%	5.00 / 2,500 / 0.42 / 208						Full Service: Pays no expense reimbursement				Market / See assumption: / Storage

576

SAMPLE SMALL OFFICE BUILDING
PRESENTATION RENT ROLL & CURRENT TERM TENANT SUMMARY

As of Jan-1997 for 101,500 Square Feet

DESCRIPTION — Tenant Name / Type & Suite Number / Lease Dates & Term	AREA — Floor SqFt / Bldg Share	BASE RENT — Rate & Amount per Year / per Month	RENT ADJ. & CATEGORIES — Changes on	ABATEMENTS — Changes to	REIMBURSEMENT — CPI & Current Porters' Wage / Miscellaneous	LEASING COSTS — Months to Abate	RETAIL — Pcnt to Abate	UPON EXPIRATION — Description of Operating Expense Reimbursements	Imprvmnts Rate / Amount	Commssns Rate / Amount	Sales Breakpoint Overage %	Assumption about subsequent terms for this tenant
Storage - U.S. Brokerage; Office Suite: A-2; Sep-1993 to Aug-1998; 60 Months	1.000; 0.99%	5.00; 5,000; 0.42; 417						Full Service. Pays no expense reimbursement.				Market; See assumption:; Storage
Currently Vacant; Office Suite: Qtr 1; Feb-1997 to Jan-2002; 60 Months	4,787; 4.72%	9.50; 45,477; 0.79; 3,790 @ 100% of Mkt	Feb-1998; Feb-1999; Feb-2000; Feb-2001	10.50; 11.50; 12.50; 13.50		1-12	25%	Gross: Pays the increases over a base year ending Dec-1997. 4.44	5.00; 23,935	2.76 / 5.00%; 13,194		Market; See assumption:; 5 Yr Mkt
Currently Vacant; Office Suite: Qtr 2; May-1997 to Apr-2002; 60 Months	4,788; 4.72%	9.50; 45,486; 0.79; 3,791 @ 100% of Mkt	May-1998; May-1999; May-2000; May-2001	10.50; 11.50; 12.50; 13.50		1-12	25%	Gross: Pays the increases over a base year ending Dec-1997. 4.44	5.00; 23,940	2.76 / 5.00%; 13,197		Market; See assumption:; 5 Yr Mkt
Currently Vacant; Office Suite: Qtr 3; Aug-1997 to Jul-2002; 60 Months	4,788; 4.72%	9.50; 45,486; 0.79; 3,791 @ 100% of Mkt	Aug-1998; Aug-1999; Aug-2000; Aug-2001	10.50; 11.50; 12.50; 13.50		1-12	25%	Gross: Pays the increases over a base year ending Dec-1997. 4.44	5.00; 23,940	2.76 / 5.00%; 13,197		Market; See assumption:; 5 Yr Mkt
Currently Vacant; Office Suite: Qtr 4; Nov-1997 to Oct-2002; 60 Months	4,787; 4.72%	9.50; 45,477; 0.79; 3,790 @ 100% of Mkt	Nov-1998; Nov-1999; Nov-2000; Nov-2001	10.50; 11.50; 12.50; 13.50		1-12	25%	Gross: Pays the increases over a base year ending Dec-1997. 4.44	5.00; 23,935	2.76 / 5.00%; 13,194		Market; See assumption:; 5 Yr Mkt

577

SAMPLE SMALL OFFICE BUILDING
PRESENTATION RENT ROLL & CURRENT TERM TENANT SUMMARY

As of Jan-1997 for 101,500 Square Feet

DESCRIPTION	AREA	BASE RENT	RENT ADJ. & CATEGORIES		ABATEMENTS	REIMBURSEMENT	LEASING COSTS	RETAIL	UPON EXPIRATION				
Tenant Name Type & Suite Number Lease Dates & Term	Floor SqFt Bldg Share	Rate & Amount per Year per Month	Changes on		Changes to	CPI & Current Porters' Wage Miscellaneous	Months to Abate	Pcnt to Abate	Description of Operating Expense Reimbursements	Imprvmnts Rate Amount	Commssns Rate Amount	Sales Breakpoint Overage %	Assumption about subsequent terms for this tenant
Currently Vacant		9.50		Feb-1999	10.50		1-12	25%	Gross: Pays the	5.00	2.76		Market
Office Suite Qtr 5	4,788	45,486		Feb-2000	11.50				increases over a		5.00%		See assumption:
Feb-1998 to Jan-2003	4.72%	0.79		Feb-2001	12.50				base year ending	23,940	13,197		5 Yr Mkt
60 Months		3,791		Feb-2002	13.50				Dec-1998: 4.63				
	@ 100% of Mkt												
Currently Vacant		9.50		May-1999	10.50		1-12	25%	Gross: Pays the	5.00	2.76		Market
Office Suite Qtr 6	4,788	45,486		May-2000	11.50				increases over a		5.00%		See assumption
May-1998 to Apr-2003	4.72%	0.79		May-2001	12.50				base year ending	23,940	13,197		5 Yr Mkt
60 Months		3,791		May-2002	13.50				Dec-1998: 4.63				
	@ 100% of Mkt												

578

SAMPLE SMALL OFFICE BUILDING
SCHEDULE OF PROSPECTIVE CASH FLOW
In Inflated Dollars for the Fiscal Year beginning 1/1/1997

For the Analysis Months	Month 1	Month 2	Month 3	Month 4	Month 5	Month 6	Month 7	Month 8	Month 9	Month 10	Month 11	Month 12	Total
POTENTIAL GROSS REVENUE													
Base Rental Revenue	85,661	85,760	85,761	85,755	85,860	85,863	86,204	86,305	86,310	86,304	86,407	86,405	1,032,595
Absorption & Turnover Vacancy	(23,339)	(19,649)	(19,649)	(19,645)	(15,957)	(15,958)	(14,762)	(11,070)	(11,072)	(11,072)	(7,382)	(7,380)	(176,935)
Base Rent Abatements	0	(947)	(947)	(948)	(1,895)	(1,896)	(7,686)	(4,134)	(2,844)	(2,841)	(3,791)	(3,790)	(31,719)
Scheduled Base Rental Revenue	62,322	65,164	65,165	65,162	68,008	68,009	63,756	71,101	72,394	72,391	75,234	75,235	823,941
Base Rental Step Revenue	363	363	483	484	483	484	483	484	483	484	483	483	5,560
CPI & Other Adjustment Revenue	0	0	0	0	0	0	0	0	0	0	0	0	0
Expense Reimbursement Revenue													
Common Area Maintenance	14,335	14,335	14,335	14,335	14,334	14,336	14,334	14,336	14,334	14,335	14,336	14,334	172,019
Real Estate Taxes	24	24	22	24	22	24	22	24	22	24	22	22	276
Administrative & General	13	13	12	14	12	13	13	13	12	13	13	13	154
Insurance	20	20	20	20	20	20	20	20	18	20	20	20	238
Total Reimbursement Revenue	14,392	14,392	14,389	14,393	14,388	14,393	14,389	14,393	14,386	14,392	14,391	14,389	172,687
Overtime HVAC	1,418	1,457	1,457	1,458	1,497	1,497	1,509	1,549	1,549	1,549	1,588	1,587	18,115
Vending Machines	585	624	624	624	663	663	676	716	715	716	755	754	8,115
TOTAL POTENTIAL GROSS REVENUE	79,080	82,000	82,118	82,121	85,039	85,046	80,813	88,243	89,527	89,532	92,451	92,448	1,028,418
Collection Loss	(857)	(857)	(857)	(857)	(857)	(857)	(857)	(857)	(857)	(857)	(857)	(857)	(10,284)
EFFECTIVE GROSS REVENUE	78,223	81,143	81,261	81,264	84,182	84,189	79,956	87,386	88,670	88,675	91,594	91,591	1,018,134
OPERATING EXPENSES													
Common Area Maintenance													
Utilities	10,210	10,493	11,805	11,805	11,674	11,675	11,321	11,616	11,151	11,151	11,434	11,433	135,768
Repairs & Mtce.	8,083	8,083	8,083	8,084	8,083	8,083	8,084	8,083	8,083	8,084	8,083	8,084	97,000
Janitorial	5,430	5,721	5,721	5,722	6,013	6,013	6,108	6,399	6,399	6,399	6,691	6,691	73,307
Security	1,250	1,250	1,250	1,250	1,250	1,250	1,250	1,250	1,250	1,250	1,250	1,250	15,000
Total	24,973	25,547	26,859	26,861	27,020	27,021	26,763	27,348	26,883	26,884	27,458	27,458	321,075
Real Estate Taxes	0	0	0	22,500	0	0	0	0	0	22,500	0	0	45,000
Administrative & General	2,083	2,083	2,084	2,083	2,083	2,084	2,083	2,083	2,084	2,083	2,083	2,084	25,000
Insurance	3,214	3,214	3,214	3,214	3,214	3,215	3,214	3,214	3,214	3,214	3,214	3,215	38,570
Property Management Fees	2,347	2,434	2,438	2,438	2,525	2,526	2,399	2,622	2,660	2,660	2,748	2,747	30,544
TOTAL OPERATING EXPENSES	32,617	33,278	34,595	57,096	34,842	34,846	34,459	35,267	34,841	57,341	35,503	35,504	460,189
NET OPERATING INCOME	45,606	47,865	46,666	24,168	49,340	49,343	45,497	52,119	53,829	31,334	56,091	56,087	557,945

SAMPLE SMALL OFFICE BUILDING
SCHEDULE OF PROSPECTIVE CASH FLOW
In Inflated Dollars for the Fiscal Year beginning 1/1/1997

For the Analysis Months	Month 1	Month 2	Month 3	Month 4	Month 5	Month 6	Month 7	Month 8	Month 9	Month 10	Month 11	Month 12	Total
LEASING & CAPITAL COSTS													
Tenant Improvements	0	23,935	0	0	23,940	0	9,300	23,940	0	0	23,935	0	105,050
Leasing Commissions	0	13,194	0	0	13,197	0	4,133	13,197	0	0	13,194	0	56,915
Structural Reserves	423	423	423	423	423	423	423	423	423	423	423	422	5,075
Lobby Renovation	0	0	50,000	25,000	0	0	0	0	0	0	0	0	75,000
Roof Repairs	0	0	0	0	0	0	0	35,000	0	0	0	0	35,000
TOTAL LEASING & CAPITAL COSTS	423	37,552	50,423	25,423	37,560	423	13,856	72,560	423	423	37,552	422	277,040
CASH FLOW BEFORE DEBT SERVICE	45,183	10,313	(3,757)	(1,255)	11,780	48,920	31,641	(20,441)	53,406	30,911	18,539	55,665	280,905
DEBT SERVICE													
Interest Payments	0	15,469	15,455	15,441	15,427	15,413	15,399	15,384	15,370	15,355	15,341	15,326	169,380
Principal Payments	0	1,840	1,853	1,867	1,881	1,896	1,910	1,924	1,938	1,953	1,968	1,983	21,013
Origination Points & Fees	20,625	0	0	0	0	0	0	0	0	0	0	0	20,625
TOTAL DEBT SERVICE	20,625	17,309	17,308	17,308	17,308	17,309	17,309	17,308	17,308	17,308	17,309	17,309	211,018
CASH FLOW AFTER DEBT SERVICE BUT BEFORE INCOME TAX	24,558	(6,996)	(21,065)	(18,563)	(5,528)	31,611	14,332	(37,749)	36,098	13,603	1,230	38,356	69,887

580

SAMPLE SMALL OFFICE BUILDING
SCHEDULE OF PROSPECTIVE CASH FLOW
In Inflated Dollars for the Fiscal Year beginning 1/1/1997

For the Analysis Years	Year 1	Year 2	Year 3	Year 4	Year 5	Year 6	Year 7	Year 8	Year 9	Year 10	Year 11
POTENTIAL GROSS REVENUE											
Base Rental Revenue	1,032,595	1,029,726	1,014,938	1,026,237	1,033,050	1,055,469	1,161,148	1,194,483	1,192,394	1,197,574	1,218,092
Absorption & Turnover Vacancy	(176,935)	(18,404)	(4,271)	(15,821)	0	(25,431)	(27,686)	(8,243)	(7,912)	(9,036)	(21,087)
Base Rent Abatements	(31,719)	(43,600)	(9,739)	(5,250)	(5,500)	(5,750)	(6,000)	0	0	0	0
Scheduled Base Rental Revenue	823,941	967,722	1,000,928	1,005,166	1,027,550	1,024,288	1,127,462	1,186,240	1,184,482	1,188,538	1,197,005
Base Rental Step Revenue	5,560	16,562	44,068	68,734	97,268	72,968	7,980	0	1,250	7,000	12,750
CPI & Other Adjustment Revenue	0	0	1,175	6,430	13,130	16,023	15,840	20,117	37,114	55,895	65,117
Expense Reimbursement Revenue	172,687	160,587	169,953	183,094	199,975	203,745	71,484	55,453	75,266	94,181	102,324
Overtime HVAC	18,115	20,398	21,174	21,903	22,949	23,588	24,515	25,754	26,761	27,822	28,792
Vending Machines	8,115	10,098	10,565	10,869	11,475	11,654	12,104	12,847	13,337	13,861	14,272
TOTAL POTENTIAL GROSS REVENUE	1,028,418	1,175,367	1,247,863	1,296,196	1,372,347	1,352,266	1,259,385	1,300,411	1,338,210	1,387,297	1,420,260
General Vacancy	0	(41,285)	(58,336)	(49,780)	(68,617)	(43,454)	(36,668)	(57,190)	(59,394)	(60,781)	(50,980)
Collection Loss	(10,284)	(11,754)	(12,479)	(12,962)	(13,723)	(13,523)	(12,594)	(13,004)	(13,382)	(13,873)	(14,203)
EFFECTIVE GROSS REVENUE	1,018,134	1,122,328	1,177,048	1,233,454	1,290,007	1,295,289	1,210,123	1,230,217	1,265,434	1,312,643	1,355,077
OPERATING EXPENSES											
Common Area Maintenance	321,075	358,222	373,021	386,147	404,159	416,151	432,548	453,713	471,534	490,202	507,654
Real Estate Taxes	45,000	45,900	46,818	47,754	48,709	49,684	50,677	51,691	52,725	53,779	54,855
Administrative & General	25,000	25,750	26,523	27,583	28,687	29,834	31,028	32,269	33,559	34,902	36,298
Insurance	38,570	39,727	40,919	42,556	44,258	46,028	47,869	49,784	51,775	53,846	56,000
Property Management Fees	30,544	33,670	35,311	37,004	38,700	38,859	36,304	36,907	37,963	39,379	40,652
TOTAL OPERATING EXPENSES	460,189	503,269	522,592	541,044	564,513	580,556	598,426	624,364	647,556	672,108	695,459
NET OPERATING INCOME	557,945	619,059	654,456	692,410	725,494	714,733	611,697	605,853	617,878	640,535	659,618

581

SAMPLE SMALL OFFICE BUILDING
SCHEDULE OF PROSPECTIVE CASH FLOW
In Inflated Dollars for the Fiscal Year beginning 1/1/1997

For the Analysis Years	Year 1	Year 2	Year 3	Year 4	Year 5	Year 6	Year 7	Year 8	Year 9	Year 10	Year 11
LEASING & CAPITAL COSTS											
Tenant Improvements	105,050	107,255	10,971	19,159	0	78,811	218,508	4,840	21,019	18,917	60,072
Leasing Commissions	56,915	36,013	6,495	11,625	0	43,942	156,570	9,002	17,851	10,572	31,610
Structural Reserves	5,075	5,227	5,384	5,599	5,823	6,056	6,299	6,551	6,813	7,085	7,368
Lobby Renovation	75,000	0	0	0	0	0	0	0	0	0	0
Roof Repairs	35,000	0	0	0	0	0	0	0	0	0	0
TOTAL LEASING & CAPITAL COSTS	277,040	148,495	22,850	36,383	5,823	128,809	381,377	20,393	45,683	36,574	99,050
CASH FLOW BEFORE DEBT SERVICE	280,905	470,564	631,606	656,027	719,671	585,924	230,320	585,460	572,195	603,961	560,568
DEBT SERVICE											
Interest Payments	169,380	182,720	180,377	177,813	175,010	171,943	168,589	164,920	160,907	156,517	0
Principal Payments	21,013	24,981	27,324	29,888	32,691	35,758	39,112	42,781	46,795	51,184	0
Origination Points & Fees	20,625	0	0	0	0	0	0	0	0	0	0
TOTAL DEBT SERVICE	211,018	207,701	207,701	207,701	207,701	207,701	207,701	207,701	207,702	207,701	0
CASH FLOW AFTER DEBT SERVICE	69,887	262,863	423,905	448,326	511,970	378,223	22,619	377,759	364,493	396,260	560,568
SOURCES & USES OF CAPITAL											
Property Purchase Price	(2,750,000)	0	0	0	0	0	0	0	0	0	0
Debt Funding Proceeds	2,062,500	0	0	0	0	0	0	0	0	0	0
Limited Partners	752,843	30,772	0	0	0	0	283,394	0	0	0	0
CASH AVAILABLE FOR DISTRIBUTION	135,230	293,635	423,905	448,326	511,970	378,223	306,013	377,759	364,493	396,260	0
PARTNER DISTRIBUTIONS											
Limited Partners	135,230	272,581	388,287	184,967	191,248	177,873	209,276	228,971	227,782	230,891	0
General Partner/Developer	0	21,054	35,618	263,359	320,722	200,350	96,737	148,789	136,711	165,370	0
CASH UNDISTRIBUTED	0	0	0	0	0	0	0	0	0	0	0

SAMPLE SMALL OFFICE BUILDING
INDIVIDUAL LOAN & DEBT SERVICE SUMMARY

Loan number 1 - First Mortgage

For the Analysis Years	Year 1	Year 2	Year 3	Year 4	Year 5	Year 6	Year 7	Year 8	Year 9	Year 10
MINIMUM DEBT SERVICE										
Interest Payments	169,380	182,720	180,377	177,813	175,010	171,943	168,589	164,920	160,907	156,517
Principal Payments	21,013	24,981	27,324	29,888	32,691	35,758	39,112	42,781	46,795	51,184
TOTAL MINIMUM DEBT SERVICE	190,393	207,701	207,701	207,701	207,701	207,701	207,701	207,701	207,702	207,701
FEES & CONTINGENCIES										
Origination Points & Fees	20,625									
TOTAL FEES & CONTINGENCIES	20,625									
REDUCTIONS & RETIREMENT										
Principal Balloon or Call										1,710,973
TOTAL REDUCTIONS & RETIREMENT										1,710,973
TOTAL CASH FLOW PAID TO LENDER	211,018	207,701	207,701	207,701	207,701	207,701	207,701	207,701	207,702	1,918,674
PRINCIPAL BALANCE SUMMARY										
Beginning Principal Balance	2,062,501	2,041,487	2,016,505	1,989,182	1,959,294	1,926,603	1,890,845	1,851,733	1,808,952	1,762,157
Periodic Principal Reductions	(21,013)	(24,981)	(27,324)	(29,888)	(32,691)	(35,758)	(39,112)	(42,781)	(46,795)	(51,184)
Principal Balloon Payments	0	0	0	0	0	0	0	0	0	(1,710,973)
Ending Principal Balance	2,041,488	2,016,506	1,989,181	1,959,294	1,926,603	1,890,845	1,851,733	1,808,952	1,762,157	0
INTEREST RATES										
Interest Rate on Principal	9.00%	9.00%	9.00%	9.00%	9.00%	9.00%	9.00%	9.00%	9.00%	9.00%
CASH FLOW COVERAGE RATIOS										
Cash to Total Interest Charged	329.40%	338.80%	362.83%	389.40%	414.54%	415.68%	362.83%	367.36%	384.00%	409.24%
Cash to Minimum Debt Service	293.05%	298.05%	315.10%	333.37%	349.30%	344.12%	294.51%	291.69%	297.48%	308.39%
LOAN TO VALUE RATIOS										
Loan to Purchase Price	75.00%	74.24%	73.33%	72.33%	71.25%	70.06%	68.76%	67.34%	65.78%	64.08%
Loan to Capitalized Value	33.27%	29.68%	27.73%	25.86%	24.31%	24.26%	27.82%	27.51%	26.35%	24.76%
Loan to Lowest Present Value	39.63%	39.23%	38.75%	38.22%	37.65%	37.02%	36.33%	35.58%	34.76%	33.86%
Loan to Highest Present Value	32.56%	32.23%	31.84%	31.41%	30.93%	30.42%	29.85%	29.24%	28.56%	27.82%
LENDERS YIELDS (IRR)										
Base Yield to Maturity										8.88%
Including Fees & Penalties										9.04%

583

SAMPLE SMALL OFFICE BUILDING
SCHEDULE OF SOURCES & USES OF CAPITAL
Equity is Based on Property Value, Leverage and Operating Requirements

For the Analysis Years	Year 1	Year 2	Year 3	Year 4	Year 5	Year 6	Year 7	Year 8	Year 9	Year 10
SOURCES OF CAPITAL										
Net Operating Gains	557,945	619,059	654,456	692,410	725,494	714,733	611,697	605,853	617,878	640,535
Debt Funding Proceeds	2,062,500	0	0	0	0	0	0	0	0	0
Equity Contributions	752,843	30,772	0	0	0	0	0	0	0	0
Net Proceeds from Sale							283,394			7,035,925
TOTAL SOURCES OF CAPITAL	3,373,288	649,831	654,456	692,410	725,494	714,733	895,091	605,853	617,878	7,676,460
USES OF CAPITAL										
Property Purchase Price	2,750,000									
Total Debt Service	211,018	207,701	207,701	207,701	207,701	207,701	207,701	207,701	207,702	207,701
Tenant Improvements	105,050	107,255	10,971	19,159	0	78,811	218,508	4,840	21,019	18,917
Leasing Commissions	56,915	36,013	6,495	11,625	0	43,942	156,570	9,002	17,851	10,572
Capital Costs & Reserves	115,075	5,227	5,384	5,599	5,823	6,056	6,299	6,551	6,813	7,085
Retirement & Penalties										1,710,973
DEFINED USES OF CAPITAL	3,238,058	356,196	230,551	244,084	213,524	336,510	589,078	228,094	253,385	1,955,248
AVAILABLE CASH FLOW	135,230	293,635	423,905	448,326	511,970	378,223	306,013	377,759	364,493	5,721,212
TOTAL USES OF CAPITAL	3,373,288	649,831	654,456	692,410	725,494	714,733	895,091	605,853	617,878	7,676,460
UNLEVERAGED CASH ON CASH RETURN										
Cash to Purchase Price	10.21%	17.11%	22.97%	23.86%	26.17%	21.31%	8.38%	21.29%	20.81%	21.96%
NOI to Book Value	18.43%	19.49%	20.46%	21.41%	22.39%	21.21%	16.31%	16.07%	16.19%	16.62%
LEVERAGED CASH ON CASH RETURN										
Cash to Initial Equity	19.67%	42.71%	61.66%	65.21%	74.47%	55.01%	44.51%	54.95%	53.02%	57.64%
UNLEVERAGED ANNUAL IRR										23.43%
UNLEVERAGED ANNUAL MIRR										19.07%
LEVERAGED ANNUAL IRR										45.86%
LEVERAGED ANNUAL MIRR										31.42%

584

SAMPLE SMALL OFFICE BUILDING
CASH FLOW DISTRIBUTION TRACKING

General Partner/Developer

For the Analysis Years	Year 1	Year 2	Year 3	Year 4	Year 5	Year 6	Year 7	Year 8	Year 9	Year 10
Equity Contribution	100,000									
Cumulative Equity	100,000	100,000	100,000	100,000	100,000	100,000	100,000	100,000	100,000	100,000
Adjusted Equity	100,000	100,000	100,000	100,000	100,000	100,000	100,000	100,000	100,000	100,000
Level 2										
Distributions		21,054	10,000	10,010	10,000	10,000	10,190	10,021	10,042	10,042
Cumulative Distributions		21,054	31,054	41,064	51,064	61,064	71,254	81,275	91,317	101,359
Unpaid Distributions	10,716									
Interest	851	203		10			190	21	42	42
Level 4										
Distributions			25,618	253,349	310,722	190,350	86,547	138,768	126,669	155,328
Cumulative Distributions			25,618	278,967	589,689	780,039	866,586	1,005,354	1,132,023	1,287,351
Unpaid Distributions										
Interest										
Cash Flow Total										
Distributions		21,054	35,618	263,359	320,722	200,350	96,737	148,789	136,711	165,370
Cumulative Distributions		21,054	56,672	320,031	640,753	841,103	937,840	1,086,629	1,223,340	1,388,710
Unpaid Distributions	10,716									
Interest	851	203		10			190	21	42	42
Resale Distributions										
Level 5										2,616,731
Total Resale Distribution										2,616,731

585

SAMPLE SMALL OFFICE BUILDING
PARTNER RETURN SUMMARY

General Partner/Developer

For the Analysis Period	For the Year Ending	Equity Investment	Cumulative Investment	Taxes	Cash Distributed	Net Inflow	Cumulative Inflows	Annual Return	Cumulative Return
Year 1	Dec-97		100,000			(100,000)	(100,000)		
Year 2	Dec-98		100,000	8,950	21,054	12,104	(87,896)	12.10%	12.10%
Year 3	Dec-99		100,000	15,047	35,618	20,571	(67,325)	20.57%	32.67%
Year 4	Dec-00		100,000	110,698	263,359	152,661	85,336	152.66%	185.34%
Year 5	Dec-01		100,000	129,910	320,722	190,812	276,148	190.81%	376.15%
Year 6	Dec-02		100,000	102,887	200,350	97,463	373,611	97.46%	473.61%
Year 7	Dec-03		100,000	39,176	96,737	57,561	431,172	57.56%	531.17%
Year 8	Dec-04		100,000	61,471	148,789	87,318	518,490	87.32%	618.49%
Year 9	Dec-05		100,000	56,213	136,711	80,498	598,988	80.50%	698.99%
Year 10	Dec-06		100,000	67,564	165,370	97,806	696,794	97.81%	796.79%
Total		100,000		591,916	1,388,710	696,794			
Property Resale			100,000	644,328	2,616,731	1,972,403	2,669,196		2769.20%
Total		100,000		1,236,245	4,005,441	2,669,196			
ANNUAL IRR		54.51%							

586

SAMPLE SMALL OFFICE BUILDING
CASH FLOW DISTRIBUTION TRACKING

Limited Partners

For the Analysis Years	Year 1	Year 2	Year 3	Year 4	Year 5	Year 6	Year 7	Year 8	Year 9	Year 10
Equity Contribution	752,843	30,772					283,394			
Cumulative Equity	752,843	783,615	783,615	783,615	783,615	783,615	1,067,009	1,067,009	1,067,009	1,067,009
Adjusted Equity	752,843	783,615	783,615	783,615	783,615	783,615	1,067,009	1,067,009	1,067,009	1,067,009
Level 1										
Distributions	135,230	167,232	156,723	156,817	156,723	156,723	199,660	213,552	213,708	213,632
Cumulative Distributions	135,230	302,462	459,185	616,002	772,725	929,448	1,129,108	1,342,660	1,556,368	1,770,000
Unpaid Distributions	13,775									
Interest	5,129	596		94			1,365	150	306	230
Level 3										
Distributions		105,349	228,718							
Cumulative Distributions		105,349	334,067	334,067	334,067	334,067	334,067	334,067	334,067	334,067
Unpaid Distributions										
Interest										
Level 4										
Distributions			2,846	28,150	34,525	21,150	9,616	15,419	14,074	17,259
Cumulative Distributions			2,846	30,996	65,521	86,671	96,287	111,706	125,780	143,039
Unpaid Distributions										
Interest										
Cash Flow Total										
Distributions	135,230	272,581	388,287	184,967	191,248	177,873	209,276	228,971	227,782	230,891
Cumulative Distributions	135,230	407,811	796,098	981,065	1,172,313	1,350,186	1,559,462	1,788,433	2,016,215	2,247,106
Unpaid Distributions	13,775									
Interest	5,129	596		94			1,365	150	306	230
Resale Distributions										
Level 2										91,491
Level 5										2,616,731
Total Resale Distribution										2,708,222

587

SAMPLE SMALL OFFICE BUILDING
PARTNER RETURN SUMMARY

Limited Partners

For the Analysis Period	For the Year Ending	Equity Investment	Cumulative Investment	Taxes	Cash Distributed	Net Inflow	Cumulative Inflows	Annual Return	Cumulative Return
Year 1	Dec-97	*****	752,843	82,101	135,230	(699,714)	(699,714)	7.06%	7.06%
Year 2	Dec-98		783,615	133,587	272,581	108,222	(591,492)	17.74%	24.52%
Year 3	Dec-99		783,615	170,113	388,287	218,174	(373,318)	27.84%	52.36%
Year 4	Dec-00		783,615	87,005	184,967	97,962	(275,356)	12.50%	64.86%
Year 5	Dec-01		783,615	78,687	191,248	112,561	(162,795)	14.36%	79.23%
Year 6	Dec-02		783,615	101,129	177,873	76,744	(86,051)	9.79%	89.02%
Year 7	Dec-03		1,067,009	105,456	209,276	(179,574)	(265,625)	9.73%	75.11%
Year 8	Dec-04		1,067,009	100,379	228,971	128,592	(137,033)	12.05%	87.16%
Year 9	Dec-05		1,067,009	108,894	227,782	118,888	(18,145)	11.14%	98.30%
Year 10	Dec-06		1,067,009	104,833	230,891	126,058	107,913	11.81%	110.11%
Total		1,067,009		1,072,184	2,247,106	107,913			
Property Resale			1,067,009	666,856	2,708,222	2,041,366	2,149,279		301.43%
Total		1,067,009		1,739,040	4,955,328	2,149,279			
ANNUAL IRR	19.47%								

***** Limited Partners Equity Investment is 100% of Negative Cash Flow

SAMPLE SMALL OFFICE BUILDING

PROSPECTIVE PRESENT VALUE - General Partner/Developer

Discounted Annually (Endpoint on Cash Flow & Resale) over a 10-Year Period

Analysis Period	For the Year Ending	Annual Cash Flow	P.V. of Cash Flow @ 9.00%	P.V. of Cash Flow @ 9.50%	P.V. of Cash Flow @ 10.00%	P.V. of Cash Flow @ 10.50%	P.V. of Cash Flow @ 11.00%	P.V. of Cash Flow @ 11.50%	P.V. of Cash Flow @ 12.00%
Year 1	Dec-1997	(100,000)	(91,743)	(91,324)	(90,909)	(90,498)	(90,090)	(89,686)	(89,286)
Year 2	Dec-1998	12,104	10,188	10,095	10,004	9,913	9,824	9,736	9,649
Year 3	Dec-1999	20,571	15,884	15,668	15,455	15,246	15,041	14,840	14,642
Year 4	Dec-2000	152,661	108,149	106,187	104,270	102,395	100,563	98,771	97,019
Year 5	Dec-2001	190,812	124,015	121,209	118,479	115,823	113,238	110,721	108,272
Year 6	Dec-2002	97,463	58,114	56,540	55,015	53,538	52,108	50,721	49,378
Year 7	Dec-2003	57,561	31,488	30,495	29,538	28,615	27,725	26,866	26,037
Year 8	Dec-2004	87,318	43,822	42,247	40,735	39,283	37,890	36,552	35,266
Year 9	Dec-2005	80,498	37,064	35,568	34,139	32,774	31,469	30,221	29,028
Year 10	Dec-2006	97,806	41,314	39,466	37,708	36,036	34,446	32,932	31,491
Total Cash Flow		696,794	378,294	366,150	354,433	343,126	332,212	321,674	311,497
Property Resale @ 9% Cap Rate		1,972,403	833,164	795,892	760,447	726,730	694,650	664,121	635,061
Total Present Value			$1,211,459	$1,162,043	$1,114,880	$1,069,856	$1,026,861	$985,794	$946,558
Rounded to Thousands			$1,211,000	$1,162,000	$1,115,000	$1,070,000	$1,027,000	$986,000	$947,000

589

SAMPLE SMALL OFFICE BUILDING
PROSPECTIVE PRESENT VALUE - Limited Partners
Discounted Annually (Endpoint on Cash Flow & Resale) over a 10-Year Period

Analysis Period	For the Year Ending	Annual Cash Flow	P.V. of Cash Flow @ 9.00%	P.V. of Cash Flow @ 9.50%	P.V. of Cash Flow @ 10.00%	P.V. of Cash Flow @ 10.50%	P.V. of Cash Flow @ 11.00%	P.V. of Cash Flow @ 11.50%	P.V. of Cash Flow @ 12.00%
Year 1	Dec-1997	(699,714)	(641,939)	(639,008)	(636,104)	(633,225)	(630,373)	(627,546)	(624,745)
Year 2	Dec-1998	108,222	91,088	90,258	89,439	88,632	87,835	87,049	86,274
Year 3	Dec-1999	218,174	168,471	166,173	163,918	161,703	159,527	157,391	155,292
Year 4	Dec-2000	97,962	69,398	68,140	66,909	65,706	64,530	63,381	62,256
Year 5	Dec-2001	112,561	73,157	71,502	69,892	68,325	66,800	65,315	63,870
Year 6	Dec-2002	76,744	45,760	44,521	43,320	42,157	41,031	39,939	38,881
Year 7	Dec-2003	(179,574)	(98,233)	(95,136)	(92,150)	(89,270)	(86,493)	(83,814)	(81,230)
Year 8	Dec-2004	128,592	64,536	62,216	59,989	57,852	55,799	53,829	51,936
Year 9	Dec-2005	118,888	54,739	52,530	50,420	48,403	46,476	44,634	42,872
Year 10	Dec-2006	126,058	53,248	50,866	48,601	46,446	44,396	42,445	40,587
Total Cash Flow		107,913	(119,775)	(127,938)	(135,765)	(143,272)	(150,472)	(157,379)	(164,006)
Property Resale @ 9% Cap Rate		2,041,366	862,295	823,720	787,035	752,139	718,937	687,341	657,265
Total Present Value			$742,520	$695,782	$651,269	$608,867	$568,465	$529,962	$493,260
Rounded to Thousands			$743,000	$696,000	$651,000	$609,000	$568,000	$530,000	$493,000

SAMPLE SMALL OFFICE BUILDING
PROSPECTIVE PRESENT VALUE

Cash Flow Before Debt Service plus Property Resale
Discounted Annually (Endpoint on Cash Flow & Resale) over a 10-Year Period

Analysis Period	For the Year Ending	Annual Cash Flow	P.V. of Cash Flow @ 9.00%	P.V. of Cash Flow @ 9.50%	P.V. of Cash Flow @ 10.00%	P.V. of Cash Flow @ 10.50%	P.V. of Cash Flow @ 11.00%	P.V. of Cash Flow @ 11.50%	P.V. of Cash Flow @ 12.00%
Year 1	Dec-1997	280,905	257,711	256,534	255,368	254,213	253,068	251,933	250,808
Year 2	Dec-1998	470,564	396,064	392,456	388,896	385,384	381,920	378,502	375,131
Year 3	Dec-1999	631,606	487,716	481,065	474,535	468,122	461,825	455,640	449,564
Year 4	Dec-2000	656,027	464,746	456,315	448,075	440,021	432,145	424,446	416,917
Year 5	Dec-2001	719,671	467,737	457,155	446,859	436,840	427,090	417,599	408,361
Year 6	Dec-2002	585,924	349,367	339,905	330,739	321,860	313,259	304,925	296,847
Year 7	Dec-2003	230,320	125,993	122,020	118,191	114,498	110,935	107,499	104,186
Year 8	Dec-2004	585,460	293,823	283,259	273,121	263,390	254,047	245,075	236,457
Year 9	Dec-2005	572,195	263,454	252,824	242,667	232,961	223,685	214,818	206,339
Year 10	Dec-2006	603,961	255,120	243,707	232,853	222,529	212,706	203,357	194,460
Total Cash Flow		5,336,633	3,361,731	3,285,240	3,211,304	3,139,818	3,070,680	3,003,794	2,939,070
Property Resale @ 9% Cap Rate		7,035,925	2,972,051	2,839,096	2,712,654	2,592,379	2,477,944	2,369,041	2,265,380
Total Property Present Value			$6,333,782	$6,124,336	$5,923,958	$5,732,197	$5,548,624	$5,372,835	$5,204,450
Rounded to Thousands			$6,334,000	$6,124,000	$5,924,000	$5,732,000	$5,549,000	$5,373,000	$5,204,000
Per SqFt			$62.40	$60.34	$58.36	$56.47	$54.67	$52.93	$51.28

PERCENTAGE VALUE DISTRIBUTION

			P.V. @ 9.00%	P.V. @ 9.50%	P.V. @ 10.00%	P.V. @ 10.50%	P.V. @ 11.00%	P.V. @ 11.50%	P.V. @ 12.00%
Assured Income			34.44	35.12	35.81	36.50	37.20	37.90	38.61
Prospective Income			18.64	18.52	18.40	18.28	18.14	18.01	17.86
Prospective Property Resale			46.92	46.36	45.79	45.22	44.66	44.09	43.53
			100.00	100.00	100.00	100.00	100.00	100.00	100.00

SAMPLE SMALL OFFICE BUILDING
PROSPECTIVE PRESENT VALUE

Cash Flow After Debt Service plus Property Resale
Discounted Annually (Endpoint on Cash Flow & Resale) over a 10-Year Period

Analysis Period	For the Year Ending	Annual Cash Flow	P.V. of Cash Flow @ 10.00%	P.V. of Cash Flow @ 10.50%	P.V. of Cash Flow @ 11.00%	P.V. of Cash Flow @ 11.50%	P.V. of Cash Flow @ 12.00%	P.V. of Cash Flow @ 12.50%	P.V. of Cash Flow @ 13.00%	P.V. of Cash Flow @ 13.50%	P.V. of Cash Flow @ 14.00%
Year 1	Dec-1997	69,887	63,534	63,246	62,961	62,679	62,399	62,122	61,847	61,574	61,304
Year 2	Dec-1998	262,863	217,242	215,281	213,346	211,436	209,553	207,694	205,860	204,051	202,265
Year 3	Dec-1999	423,905	318,486	314,182	309,955	305,805	301,727	297,722	293,788	289,922	286,124
Year 4	Dec-2000	448,326	306,213	300,708	295,327	290,064	284,919	279,888	274,966	270,153	265,445
Year 5	Dec-2001	511,970	317,893	310,766	303,829	297,078	290,506	284,107	277,877	271,810	265,901
Year 6	Dec-2002	378,223	213,497	207,766	202,213	196,833	191,619	186,566	181,668	176,918	172,313
Year 7	Dec-2003	22,619	11,607	11,244	10,895	10,558	10,232	9,917	9,614	9,322	9,040
Year 8	Dec-2004	377,759	176,227	169,948	163,920	158,130	152,571	147,230	142,098	137,167	132,426
Year 9	Dec-2005	364,493	154,581	148,398	142,489	136,841	131,439	126,275	121,334	116,607	112,085
Year 10	Dec-2006	396,260	152,775	146,002	139,557	133,423	127,586	122,026	116,734	111,692	106,889
Total Cash Flow		3,256,305	1,932,055	1,887,541	1,844,492	1,802,847	1,762,551	1,723,547	1,685,786	1,649,216	1,613,792
Property Resale @ 9% Cap Rate		5,324,952	2,053,000	1,961,973	1,875,365	1,792,945	1,714,492	1,639,798	1,568,669	1,500,918	1,436,373
Value of Equity Interest			$3,985,055	$3,849,514	$3,719,857	$3,595,792	$3,477,043	$3,363,345	$3,254,455	$3,150,134	$3,050,165
Rounded to Thousands			$3,985,000	$3,850,000	$3,720,000	$3,596,000	$3,477,000	$3,363,000	$3,254,000	$3,150,000	$3,050,000
Per SqFt			$39.26	$37.93	$36.65	$35.43	$34.26	$33.14	$32.06	$31.04	$30.05
Value of Equity Interest			3,985,055	3,849,514	3,719,857	3,595,792	3,477,043	3,363,345	3,254,455	3,150,134	3,050,165
Debt Balance as of Jan-1997		2,062,500	2,062,500	2,062,500	2,062,500	2,062,500	2,062,500	2,062,500	2,062,500	2,062,500	2,062,500
Total Leveraged Present Value			$6,047,555	$5,912,014	$5,782,357	$5,658,292	$5,539,543	$5,425,845	$5,316,955	$5,212,634	$5,112,665
Rounded to Thousands			$6,048,000	$5,912,000	$5,782,000	$5,658,000	$5,540,000	$5,426,000	$5,317,000	$5,213,000	$5,113,000
Per SqFt			$59.58	$58.25	$56.97	$55.75	$54.58	$53.46	$52.38	$51.36	$50.37

SAMPLE SMALL OFFICE BUILDING
RESALE - CAP RATE MATRIX
Cash Flow Before Debt Service plus Property Resale in Year 10, Dec-2006
Discounted Annually (Endpoint on Cash Flow & Resale)

For the Cap Rates	Net Proceeds From Sale	P.V. of Property @ 9.00%	P.V. of Property @ 9.50%	P.V. of Property @ 10.00%	P.V. of Property @ 10.50%	P.V. of Property @ 11.00%	P.V. of Property @ 11.50%	P.V. of Property @ 12.00%
7.00%	9,046,189	7,182,939	6,935,506	6,699,002	6,472,876	6,256,607	6,049,704	5,851,701
7.50%	8,443,110	6,928,192	6,692,155	6,466,488	6,250,672	6,044,212	5,846,643	5,657,525
8.00%	7,915,416	6,705,288	6,479,222	6,263,039	6,056,244	5,858,367	5,668,965	5,487,622
8.50%	7,449,803	6,508,608	6,291,341	6,083,526	5,884,689	5,694,385	5,512,190	5,337,707
9.00%	7,035,925	6,333,782	6,124,336	5,923,958	5,732,197	5,548,624	5,372,835	5,204,450
9.50%	6,665,613	6,177,358	5,974,909	5,781,186	5,595,756	5,418,205	5,248,148	5,085,219
10.00%	6,332,333	6,036,577	5,840,426	5,652,692	5,472,959	5,300,829	5,135,931	4,977,912

SAMPLE SMALL OFFICE BUILDING
RESALE - CAP RATE MATRIX
Cash Flow After Debt Service plus Property Resale in Year 10, Dec-2006
Discounted Annually (Endpoint on Cash Flow & Resale)

For the Cap Rates	Net Proceeds From Sale	P.V. of Property @ 10.00%	P.V. of Property @ 10.50%	P.V. of Property @ 11.00%	P.V. of Property @ 11.50%	P.V. of Property @ 12.00%	P.V. of Property @ 12.50%	P.V. of Property @ 13.00%	P.V. of Property @ 13.50%	P.V. of Property @ 14.00%
7.00%	7,335,216	4,760,098	4,590,193	4,427,841	4,272,661	4,124,294	3,982,399	3,846,655	3,716,758	3,592,421
7.50%	6,732,137	4,527,585	4,367,989	4,215,446	4,069,600	3,930,119	3,796,683	3,668,995	3,546,771	3,429,744
8.00%	6,204,443	4,324,136	4,173,561	4,029,600	3,891,922	3,760,215	3,634,181	3,513,543	3,398,032	3,287,402
8.50%	5,738,830	4,144,622	4,002,006	3,865,619	3,735,148	3,610,301	3,490,798	3,376,378	3,266,792	3,161,806
9.00%	5,324,952	3,985,055	3,849,514	3,719,857	3,595,792	3,477,043	3,363,345	3,254,455	3,150,134	3,050,165
9.50%	4,954,640	3,842,283	3,713,073	3,589,439	3,471,106	3,357,813	3,249,309	3,145,365	3,045,756	2,950,276
10.00%	4,621,360	3,713,789	3,590,276	3,472,063	3,358,888	3,250,505	3,146,677	3,047,185	2,951,816	2,860,375

594

SAMPLE SMALL OFFICE BUILDING
SUPPORTING SCHEDULE -- DETAILED LEASE EXPIRATION SCHEDULE (FIRST TERM ONLY)

No.	Tenant	Suite	Market Leasing	Base Rent/ SqFt/Yr	Expiration Date	Square Feet	Percent of Total
7	USA Brokerage	Full 6	5 Yr Mkt	7.17	8/98	11,875	11.70
12	Storage - U.S. Brokerag	A-2	Storage	5.00	8/98	1,000	1.00
1	Systems, Inc.	200	3 Yr Mkt	9.75	12/98	7,834	7.70
2	Smith Leasing Co.	225	3 Yr Mkt	7.13	9/99	1,675	1.70
3	The Home Group	240	3 Yr Mkt	10.08	2/00	2,901	2.90
4	BBB Travel	250	3 Yr Mkt	6.56	5/00	4,110	4.00
13	Currently Vacant	Qtr 1	5 Yr Mkt	9.58	1/02	4,787	4.70
14	Currently Vacant	Qtr 2	5 Yr Mkt	9.32	4/02	4,788	4.70
5	Proposed - Vacant Suite	280	5 Yr Mkt	9.39	6/02	1,550	1.50
15	Currently Vacant	Qtr 3	5 Yr Mkt	9.06	7/02	4,788	4.70
16	Currently Vacant	Qtr 4	5 Yr Mkt	8.80	10/02	4,787	4.70
17	Currently Vacant	Qtr 5	5 Yr Mkt	9.84	1/03	4,788	4.70
6	Taylor & Murphy	3-4-5	10 Yr Mkt	11.88	2/03	35,579	35.10
18	Currently Vacant	Qtr 6	5 Yr Mkt	9.50	4/03	4,788	4.70
9	China Hut	Lobby	Retail Mkt	19.17	6/04	3,000	3.00
11	Storage - China Hut	A-1	Storage	6.08	6/04	500	0.50
10	Italian Pizza Parlor	Lobby	Retail Mkt	16.50	11/04	2,750	2.70

595

SAMPLE SMALL OFFICE BUILDING
SUPPORTING SCHEDULE -- SCHEDULED BASE RENT PER SQFT

For the Analysis Years	SUITE	Year 1	Year 2	Year 3	Year 4	Year 5	Year 6	Year 7	Year 8	Year 9	Year 10	Year 11
TENANT												
Smith Leasing Co.	200	9.50	9.50	7.13	9.91	10.81	10.81	10.42	11.42	11.42	11.27	12.48
The Home Group	225	9.00	9.00	9.00	10.08	10.30	10.30	10.28	11.42	11.42	11.18	12.48
BBB Travel	240	9.25	9.25	9.25	6.56	10.81	10.81	10.02	11.42	11.42	10.56	12.48
Proposed - Vacant Suite	250	3.33	10.00	10.00	10.00	10.00	9.39	10.54	10.54	10.54	10.54	10.23
Taylor & Murphy	280	10.00	10.00	10.00	10.00	10.00	10.00	11.88	12.26	12.26	12.26	12.26
USA Brokerage	3/4/5	10.75	7.17	0.00	0.00	0.00	0.00	0.00	0.00	0.00	0.00	0.00
USA Brokerage	Full 6	0.00	2.70	8.10	8.10	8.10	8.10	8.12	10.86	10.86	10.86	10.86
China Hut	Full 6	16.00	16.92	17.83	18.75	19.67	20.58	21.50	19.17	17.20	17.20	17.20
Italian Pizza Parlor	Lobby	18.00	18.00	18.00	18.00	18.00	18.00	18.00	16.50	18.00	18.00	18.00
Storage - China Hut	Lobby	5.00	5.00	5.00	5.00	5.00	5.00	5.00	6.08	7.15	7.15	7.15
Storage - U.S. Brokerag	A-1	5.00	5.00	5.00	5.00	5.00	5.00	5.60	6.81	6.81	6.81	6.81
Currently Vacant	A-2	6.53	9.30	9.50	9.50	9.50	9.58	10.54	10.54	10.54	10.54	10.93
Currently Vacant	Qtr 1	4.75	8.71	9.50	9.50	9.50	9.32	10.54	10.54	10.54	10.54	10.51
Currently Vacant	Qtr 2	2.97	8.11	9.50	9.50	9.50	9.06	10.54	10.54	10.54	10.54	10.09
Currently Vacant	Qtr 3	1.19	7.52	9.50	9.50	9.50	8.80	10.54	10.54	10.54	10.54	9.67
Currently Vacant	Qtr 4	0.00	6.53	9.30	9.50	9.50	9.50	9.84	10.86	10.86	10.86	10.86
Currently Vacant	Qtr 5	0.00	4.75	8.71	9.50	9.50	9.50	9.50	10.86	10.86	10.86	10.86
Currently Vacant	Qtr 6	0.00	4.75	8.71	9.50	9.50	9.50	9.50	10.86	10.86	10.86	10.86
WEIGHTED AVERAGE PER SqFt		8.12	9.53	9.86	9.90	10.12	10.09	11.11	11.69	11.67	11.71	11.79

SAMPLE SMALL OFFICE BUILDING
SUPPORTING SCHEDULE -- SCHEDULED BASE RENTAL REVENUE

For the Analysis Years	SUITE	Year 1	Year 2	Year 3	Year 4	Year 5	Year 6	Year 7	Year 8	Year 9	Year 10	Year 11
TENANT												
Systems, Inc.	200	76,382	76,382	78,732	78,732	78,732	79,648	86,888	86,888	86,362	94,945	94,945
Smith Leasing Co.	225	15,912	15,912	11,934	16,606	18,115	18,115	17,455	19,135	19,135	18,871	20,909
The Home Group	240	26,109	26,109	26,109	29,252	29,880	29,880	29,836	33,141	33,141	32,428	36,214
BBB Travel	250	38,018	38,018	38,018	26,953	44,450	44,450	41,163	46,952	46,952	43,402	51,306
Proposed - Vacant Suite	280	5,167	15,500	15,500	15,500	15,500	14,560	16,344	16,344	16,344	16,344	15,850
Taylor & Murphy	3/4/5	355,790	355,790	355,790	355,790	355,790	355,790	422,746	436,137	436,137	436,137	436,137
USA Brokerage	Full 6	127,656	85,104	0	0	0	0	0	0	0	0	0
USA Brokerage	Full 6	0	32,062	96,187	96,187	96,187	96,187	96,369	128,976	128,976	128,976	128,976
China Hut	Lobby	48,000	50,750	53,500	56,250	59,000	61,750	64,500	57,504	51,610	51,610	51,610
Italian Pizza Parlor	Lobby	49,500	49,500	49,500	49,500	49,500	49,500	49,500	45,375	49,500	49,500	49,500
Storage - China Hut	A-1	2,500	2,500	2,500	2,500	2,500	2,500	2,500	3,038	3,575	3,575	3,575
Storage - U.S. Brokerag	A-2	5,000	5,000	5,000	5,000	5,000	5,000	5,603	6,810	6,810	6,810	6,810
Currently Vacant	Qtr 1	31,265	44,529	45,476	45,476	45,476	45,855	50,478	50,478	50,478	50,478	52,301
Currently Vacant	Qtr 2	22,743	41,696	45,486	45,486	45,486	44,614	50,489	50,489	50,489	50,489	50,302
Currently Vacant	Qtr 3	14,214	38,853	45,486	45,486	45,486	43,363	50,489	50,489	50,489	50,489	48,292
Currently Vacant	Qtr 4	5,685	36,002	45,476	45,476	45,476	42,104	50,478	50,478	50,478	50,478	46,272
Currently Vacant	Qtr 5	0	31,272	44,538	45,486	45,486	45,486	47,127	52,003	52,003	52,003	52,003
Currently Vacant	Qtr 6	0	22,743	41,696	45,486	45,486	45,486	45,497	52,003	52,003	52,003	52,003
TOTAL AMOUNT PER YEAR		823,941	967,722	1,000,928	1,005,166	1,027,550	1,024,288	1,127,462	1,186,240	1,184,482	1,188,538	1,197,005
WEIGHTED AVERAGE PER SqFt		8.12	9.53	9.86	9.9	10.12	10.09	11.11	11.69	11.67	11.71	11.79

597

SAMPLE SMALL OFFICE BUILDING
SUPPORTING SCHEDULE -- TENANT IMPROVEMENTS

For the Analysis Years	SUITE	Year 1	Year 2	Year 3	Year 4	Year 5	Year 6	Year 7	Year 8	Year 9	Year 10	Year 11
TENANT												
Systems, Inc.	200	0	0	10,971	0	0	14,584	0	0	0	0	0
Smith Leasing Co.	225	0	0	0	4,435	0	0	3,243	0	0	3,648	0
The Home Group	240	0	0	0	3,841	0	0	5,617	0	0	6,318	0
BBB Travel	250	0	0	0	10,883	0	0	7,957	0	0	8,951	0
Proposed - Vacant Suite	280	9,300	0	0	0	0	4,809	0	0	0	0	5,851
Taylor & Murphy	3/4/5	0	0	0	0	0	0	132,472	0	0	0	0
USA Brokerage	Full 6	0	0	0	0	0	0	0	0	0	0	0
USA Brokerage	Full 6	0	59,375	0	0	0	0	38,319	0	0	0	0
China Hut	Lobby	0	0	0	0	0	0	0	4,840	0	0	0
Italian Pizza Parlor	Lobby	0	0	0	0	0	0	0	0	4,614	0	0
Storage - China Hut	A-1	0	0	0	0	0	0	0	0	0	0	0
Storage - U.S. Brokerag	A-2	0	0	0	0	0	0	0	0	0	0	0
Currently Vacant	Qtr 1	23,935	0	0	0	0	14,853	0	0	0	0	18,071
Currently Vacant	Qtr 2	23,940	0	0	0	0	14,856	0	0	0	0	18,075
Currently Vacant	Qtr 3	23,940	0	0	0	0	14,856	0	0	0	0	18,075
Currently Vacant	Qtr 4	23,935	0	0	0	0	14,853	0	0	0	0	0
Currently Vacant	Qtr 5	0	23,940	0	0	0	0	15,450	0	0	0	0
Currently Vacant	Qtr 6	0	23,940	0	0	0	0	15,450	0	0	0	0
TOTAL AMOUNT PER YEAR		105,050	107,255	10,971	19,159	0	78,811	218,508	4,840	21,019	18,917	60,072
WEIGHTED AVERAGE PER SqFt		1.03	1.06	0.11	0.19	0	0.78	2.15	0.05	0.21	0.19	0.59

598

SAMPLE SMALL OFFICE BUILDING
SUPPORTING SCHEDULE -- LEASING COMMISSIONS

For the Analysis Years	SUITE	Year 1	Year 2	Year 3	Year 4	Year 5	Year 6	Year 7	Year 8	Year 9	Year 10	Year 11
TENANT												
Systems, Inc.	200	0	0	6,495	0	0	8,472	0	0	9,257	0	0
Smith Leasing Co.	225	0	0	0	2,717	0	0	1,866	0	0	2,039	0
The Home Group	240	0	0	0	2,241	0	0	3,231	0	0	3,531	0
BBB Travel	250	0	0	0	6,667	0	0	4,578	0	0	5,002	0
Proposed - Vacant Suite	280	4,133	0	0	0	0	2,656	0	0	0	0	3,079
Taylor & Murphy	3/4/5	0	0	0	0	0	0	109,034	0	0	0	0
USA Brokerage	Full 6	0	0	0	0	0	0	0	0	0	0	0
USA Brokerage	Full 6	0	9,619	0	0	0	0	20,959	0	0	0	0
China Hut	Lobby	0	0	0	0	0	0	0	9,002	0	0	0
Italian Pizza Parlor	Lobby	0	0	0	0	0	0	0	0	8,594	0	0
Storage - China Hut	A-1	0	0	0	0	0	0	0	0	0	0	0
Storage - U.S. Brokerag	A-2	0	0	0	0	0	0	0	0	0	0	0
Currently Vacant	Qtr 1	13,194	0	0	0	0	8,203	0	0	0	0	9,509
Currently Vacant	Qtr 2	13,197	0	0	0	0	8,204	0	0	0	0	9,511
Currently Vacant	Qtr 3	13,197	0	0	0	0	8,204	0	0	0	0	9,511
Currently Vacant	Qtr 4	13,194	0	0	0	0	8,203	0	0	0	0	0
Currently Vacant	Qtr 5	0	13,197	0	0	0	0	8,451	0	0	0	0
Currently Vacant	Qtr 6	0	13,197	0	0	0	0	8,451	0	0	0	0
TOTAL AMOUNT PER YEAR		56,915	36,013	6,495	11,625	0	43,942	156,570	9,002	17,851	10,572	31,610
WEIGHTED AVERAGE PER SqFt		0.56	0.35	0.06	0.11	0.00	0.43	1.54	0.09	0.18	0.10	0.31

599

GLOSSARY

Abandonment A voluntary surrender of owned or leased property without naming a successor as an owner or a tenant.

Absentee Owner A property owner who does not personally manage or reside at the property.

Absorption Rate An estimated time period in which the property will be leased.

Abstract of Title A historical summary of all the recorded instruments and legal proceedings that affect title to a property.

Accelerated Cost Recovery System (ACRS) A method of depreciation introduced by the Economic Recovery Act of 1981 which determines the useful life of various types of property.

Accelerated Depreciation A method of depreciation in which the asset is written off more quickly than under the Straight Line Method.

Acceleration Clause A clause in a mortgage document which gives the mortgagee the right to accelerate full repayment of the debt if the mortgagor defaults on any of the obligations.

Acceptance The act of agreeing to accept an offer.

Access Right The right of ingress and egress to a property.

Accredited Investor Under the Securities and Exchange Commission Regulation D, a wealthy investor who does not count as one of the thirty-five investors allowed to invest in a private limited partnership. To qualify the investor must have a net worth of at least $1,000,000 or an annual income of at least $200,000 or must have invested at least $150,000 into the deal, and the investment must not be more than 20 percent of the investor's net worth.

Accrual Basis An accounting method in which income and expenses are recognized as they are earned or incurred, even though they might not have been received or paid.

Accrued Interest Interest that is owed but has not been currently paid.

Accumulated Depreciation The sum total of all depreciation taken to date.

Acknowledgment A declaration by an individual stating that he or she has signed a document voluntarily.

Acquisition The process of acquiring property.

Acquisition Cost The total cost of acquiring a purchase of a piece of property including all fees, closing costs, and expense of renovation.

Acquisition Fee A fee paid to a syndicator for services in acquiring a property.

Acre A measurement of land that contains 43,560 square feet, 160 square rods, 10 square chains, or 4,840 square yards.

Adjustable Rate Mortgage (ARM) A mortgage in which the rate of interest is tied to a floating index. The interest rate is adjusted at specified time periods.

Adjusted Tax Basis The price on which a capital gain or loss is based, the sales price less closing costs and commissions.

Administrator An individual appointed by a court to administer the estate of a person who died intestate.

Administrator's Deed A deed that conveys property of an individual who died without a will.

Ad Valorem Tax (Latin) A tax on property based on the current value of the property.

Adverse Possession Acquisition of title to property in which an occupant has been in actual, open, notorious and continuous use of such property for a period specified by state law.

After Tax Cash Flow Amount of money that is available after all expenses, including taxes, are paid.

After Tax Real Rate of Return Amount of money the investor can keep after paying any taxes from a sale, adjusted for inflation.

Agency Legal relationship between a principal and the agent arising from a contract in which the principal engages the agent to perform certain acts on the principal's behalf.

Agent Individual who is authorized by another person (principal) to act in the latter's behalf in a transaction involving a third party.

Agreement of Sale Written agreement between a buyer and a seller of a piece of property.

Air Rights The right to use, occupy, or control the space above a designated property. These rights can be sold, leased, or donated to another party.

Alternative Minimum Tax Flat rate tax that applies to individual taxpayers at certain income levels.

Amenities Attractive improvement features of a piece of property.

Amortization The gradual repayment of debt through systematic payment of the principal over a specified period of time. The loan will be fully amortized when the loan balance is zero.

Amortization Schedule Table that shows the periodic principal and interest payments on a mortgage loan. This schedule will also show the remaining balance due on this loan as the loan is being paid off.

Anchor Tenant Key tenant in a shopping center that will attract other businesses and shoppers.

Annual Debt Service The sum total of the monthly debt service payments required by a lender.

Annual Percentage Rate (APR) The actual cost of borrowing on an annual basis.

Apartment A dwelling unit within a multifamily structure.

Appraisal The value of a piece of property estimated by a qualified person.

Appraiser A qualified individual who conducts appraisals.

Appreciation The increase in the value of a property, resulting from an increase in the performance of the property through management or inflation.

Appurtenance Something that is outside the property lines but is considered a part of the property and adds to its greater enjoyment.

Arm's Length Transaction A transaction that takes place between unrelated parties.

Arrears Denotes a payment at the end of a term. Most mortgage interest payments are made in arrears.

Articles of Partnership A document describing the terms and conditions of a partnership, including the nature of its business and the rights and responsibilities of the partners.

As Is A condition of property without guarantees.

Asking Price The amount of value a property owner sets as the selling price.

Assemblage The combination of two or more properties to sell as one.

Assessed Value The value placed on a property by the local taxing authority.

Assessment A special payment or tax on a property by a local taxing authority.

Assessment Ratio The ratio of assessed value to market value.

Assessor An official who determines property taxes for a local government.

Assets Everything owned by a person or other entity that can be used to make payments on a debt.

Assignee One to whom a transfer of interest in property is made.

Assignment of Contract or Lease The transfer of all title, rights and interest that a lease possesses in certain real property.

Assignor One who makes an assignment of interest in a property

Assumable Loan Loan that can be taken over by a new borrower when property is resold. The new borrower will assume all the liabilities of the original borrower.

Assumption Fee A fee charged by a lender to permit the transfer of a mortgage.

At Risk Those dollars that are exposed to the danger of loss. Investors in a limited partnership can claim tax deductions only if they can prove to the IRS that there is a chance that they will never realize a profit and that they can lose their investment.

At Risk Rules The tax law that limits tax losses to the amount of money that an investor can lose.

Attachment A legal taking of a property to force payment of a debt.

Attornment A tenant's formal agreement to be a tenant of a new landlord.

Auction A public sale of a property to the highest bidder.

Automatic Renewal Clause A lease clause that automatically renews the lease unless both tenant and landlord notify each other of a desire to terminate.

Backup Contract A contract to buy property that becomes effective if a prior contract fails to perform.

Balance Sheet A financial statement that lists all assets, liabilities, and equity, where the assets must be equal to the liabilities and equity.

Balloon Loan A debt repayment in which the outstanding principal balance is due at a specified time.

Band of Investment An appraisal technique in which the overall interest rate is derived from weighing mortgage and equity rates.

Bank A financial institution that is authorized to provide a variety of financial services.

Bankruptcy A condition one seeks through the courts when one cannot pay one's debts.

Base Rent The minimum rent due under a lease that has a participation requirement.

Basis In determining taxes, that point from which gains, losses, and depreciation are computed.

Basis Point One hundredth of one percent.

Bay Depth The distance from the corridor wall to the real window or wall.

Before Tax Cash Flow The cash flow available prior to paying income taxes.

Beneficiary An individual who receives or is to receive the benefits resulting from certain acts.

Best Efforts The effort made by an underwriter of a limited partnership in raising the equity for a transaction.

Bid The amount an individual offers to pay.

Bilateral Contract A contract in which each party must perform.

Bill of Sale A written instrument used to pass title of personal property from a seller to a buyer.

Binder The earnest money deposit made to secure a piece of property at agreed-upon terms.

Blanket Mortgage A mortgage that covers more than one piece of real property.

Blended Rate Mortgage An interest rate that applies to a refinanced loan where the new interest rate is the average of the old and new rates.

Blind Pool An investment by a partnership in which the property is not designated in advance, but is acquired after the funds are raised.

Blue Sky Laws State laws that protect the public against securities fraud.

BOMA Building Owners and Managers Association

BOMA Standard Methods A standard method of measuring office space developed by BOMA.

Book Value The owner's original cost plus the cost of any improvements less the depreciation taken for tax purposes. This is the value that is carried on the owner's accounting records.

Boot In a property exchange, the unlike property that is included to balance the value in the transaction.

Breach of Contract A violation of terms of a contract that causes a default.

Break-Even Point The income required to cover all operating expenses and the debt service.

Bridge Loan A mortgage loan used between the termination of one loan and the beginning of another loan.

Broker An individual who acts as an intermediary between two parties. This individual receives a commission for the services rendered.

Broker-Dealer One who is licensed by the Commissioner of Corporations to sell securities.

Budget A prediction of the income and expenses for a property over a specified time period.

Building Codes Standards established by local governmental agencies to enforce minimum safety requirements.

Buy-Back Sales Agreement A provision in a sales agreement in which the seller agrees to repurchase the property in the future.

Buydown The payment of additional moneys to reduce the rate of interest charged on a loan.

Buyer's Market A real estate marketplace in which there are more sellers than buyers, giving the buyer an opportunity to negotiate a better purchase price and terms.

Buy-Sell Agreement An agreement between parties in which either party can purchase the other party's interest.

Bylaws A set of regulations according to which an organization conducts its business or activities.

Call Provision A clause in a mortgage document giving the lender the right to accelerate the debt upon the occurrence of a specified event prior to the original maturity date.

Cancellation Clause A clause in a contract giving the right to terminate the agreement upon a specified event.

Capital Expenditure A property improvement that will last longer than a repair. This item is added to the basis of the property rather than being expensed.

Capital Gains The gains or profit realized from the sale of property and taxed at a rate lower than earned income.

Capital Loss A loss from the sale of a capital asset.

Capitalization The conversion of an income stream into a property valuation.

Capitalization Rate The current rate of return derived by dividing the net operating income by the estimated value or resale price.

Carrying Costs Those costs associated with holding a property.

Cash Basis An accounting method that recognizes revenue when cash is received and recognizes expenses when cash is paid out.

Cash on Cash Return The rate of return of an investment. Calculated by dividing the cash flow by the down payment.

Cash Flow The positive difference between the revenue generated from the property and the expenses paid out. This cash flow is the owner's net spendable income.

Caveat Emptor (Latin) "Let the buyer beware." The purchaser must examine the property prior to closing and is buying at his or her own risk.

Central Business District (CBD) The center of the downtown in a city, the main commercial area.

Certificate of Insurance A document issued by an insurance company verifying the property insurance coverage.

Certificate of Occupancy A document issued by a local government permitting occupancy of a property.

Certificate of Title An opinion given by an attorney of the status of the title to a property.

Chain A measurement of land used in surveying equal to 66 feet in length. Each chain contains 100 links.

Chain of Title A history of ownership of a piece of property from the date the original patent was granted until the present.

Chattel Personal property that can be moved.

Chattel Mortgage A mortgage secured by personal property.

Clear Title A title that is not encumbered by or burdened with any defects.

Client An individual who engages another individual to perform a service.

Closed-End Fund An offering by a partnership which, after the sale of a maximum number of units, is closed unless there is an amendment to the partnership.

Closing The consummation of the real estate transaction in which the ownership rights are transferred to the buyer in exchange for consideration paid to the seller.

Closing Costs The expenses associated with the closing.

Closing Date The date on which the transaction is closed.

Closing Statement A document used to account for all of the funds from a real estate sale, listing all of the buyer's and seller's costs.

Cloud on Title An outstanding claim or encumbrance against a property that impairs the title to property.

Coinsurance A clause in an insurance policy stating the minimum percentage of value that is insured in order to collect the full amount of a loss.

Collateral Marketable real or personal property that a borrower pledges as security for a loan.

Commercial Property Real property that is intended to be used for commerce, such as offices, motels, hotels, and retail outlets.

Commingle The act of mixing funds, as in mixing personal and business funds together in one checking account.

Commission The fee paid to the real estate broker or mortgage broker for services rendered, usually based on a percentage of the purchase price.

Commitment The act of promising to complete an obligation.

Commitment Fee The fee paid to a lender for a loan.

Common Area The space not used or occupied by tenants, for example, hallways, lobbies, restrooms, or stairways.

Common Area Maintenance Charge (CAM) A provision in a shopping center lease requiring the tenant to pay a share of the common area operating expenses.

Community Shopping Center A medium-sized shopping center with a small department store or supermarket as the anchor tenant and usually about fifty smaller retail stores. The typical size is 150,000 square feet.

Co-Mortgagor An individual who co-signs a mortgage.

Comparables Properties with similar economic characteristics.

Comparative Market Approach An appraisal method basing its value estimate on the recent sale prices of comparable properties.

Completion Bond A legal document guaranteeing completion of the construction of a property.

Compound Interest Interest paid on the original principal and also on the unpaid accumulated interest.

Concessions Discounts in a lease or sales contract used to induce a party to sign an agreement.

Condemnation A government act of taking property for public use with compensation to the owner of the property.

Conditions Certain provisions in an agreement on which the fulfillment of the agreement depends.

Condominium A type of ownership in which each individual has fee-simple title to a specific unit in a multi-tenant building. Each unit owner has an individual mortgage and contributes a share of the common area maintenance and operating expenses of the property.

Condominium Association The nonprofit governing body of a condominium property. Each condominium owner automatically belongs to the association upon purchase of a unit.

Condominium Conversion The subdivision of an existing rental property into condominium ownership, either in a residential or commercial property.

Consideration The cash or services given in exchange for property.

Constant Payment Loan A loan in which the payments made are equal during the term of the repayment.

Construction Draw Periodic advances on a construction loan.

Construction Loan A loan that is made for the purpose of constructing a property, usually for a term of under three years. It is usually based on prime rate and interest only paid with a balloon payment due at maturity of the loan.

Constructive Notice The legal presumption that all individuals have knowledge of a fact when that fact is a matter of public record.

Consumer Price Index (CPI) An index that is published monthly by the U.S. Department of Labor, Bureau of Labor Statistics, showing the cost of a cross-section of consumer goods and services.

Contiguous Adjacent and touching properties.

Contingency Fund A fund set aside for unforeseen expenses.

Contingent Liability The liability assumed by a third party. If the original obligor defaults, the third party will be responsible for the obligation.

Contract An agreement between two or more parties that creates or modifies a legal relationship, generally based upon an offer and acceptance.

Contract for Deed An agreement in which the seller will deliver title to the purchaser after all payments have been made.

Contract Price The price at which a property is contracted for.

Contractor An individual who agrees legally to supply goods or services.

Conventional Mortgage Loan A loan made by a source other than by a federal agency.

Conveyance An instrument by which title to property is transferred.

Co-op An arrangement between two individuals to split a real estate commission.

Cooperative Ownership A corporate ownership in which each individual owns shares of stock. Each shareholder then gets a proprietary lease to occupy a unit.

Core Space The space in a building that includes the square footage used for the public corridors, elevators, restrooms, stairways, electrical and telephone rooms, and the janitorial closet.

Corporation A legal entity registered by the secretary of state, limiting the individual liability of the individuals comprising it.

Cost Approach An appraisal method that estimates the value of the property based on the cost to reconstruct the property plus the land cost.

Cost Basis The original price of an asset used in determining a capital gain, usually the purchase price.

Counteroffer An offer, instead of an acceptance, made in response to an offer.

Covenant Promise written into a deed or other instrument by which a party agrees to perform or not to perform certain acts.

Covenant Not to Compete A contract restricting one party from competing with another party.

Creative Financing Any financing arrangement other than a conventional level-paid amortizing loan.

Credit The capacity to obtain financing.

Creditor An individual to whom money is owed.

Curable Depreciation Deterioration of a property that can be corrected.

Curb Appeal The aesthetic image and appearance projected by a property on a first impression.

Current Yield Current income divided by the investment cost.

Dealer An individual who buys and sells property.

Debt An obligation to be repaid by a borrower to a lender.

Debt Coverage Ratio A ratio used by a lender which expresses the loan amount in relationship to the net operating income, usually between 1.05 and 1.25.

Debt Service The monthly cost of repaying a mortgage loan, including interest on the outstanding balance and, in many cases, a reduction in the loan principal.

Declining Balance Depreciation A method of depreciation in which a rate is applied to the remaining balance to derive the depreciation deduction.

Dedication The gift of property by its owner for public use.

Deed A written document signed by the seller transferring title in a piece of real estate.

Deed in Lieu of Foreclosure A deed that is given by an owner to the lender instead of foreclosure.

Deed Restrictions A clause in the deed that limits the use of the conveyed property.

Deed of Trust A mortgage that conveys real property to a third party by holding in trust the deed until the loan is repaid.

Default The failure to perform on an obligation as agreed in a contract.

Defeasance Clause A clause giving the mortgagor the right to redeem the property on payment of any obligation to the mortgage.

Defect in Title Any recorded instrument that prevents the seller from giving clear title to a property.

Deferred Maintenance The ordinary maintenance that is not performed and will negatively affect the property's use and value.

Deferred Payment The taking of a promissory note for payment of a debt to be repaid over time.

Deficiency Judgment A court order stating that the debtor still owes money on a debt that is in default.

Delinquency The failure to make a payment on an obligation when due.

Delivery The transfer of a property from one party to another.

Demographics Statistical information on the population of an area.

Density The average number of individuals in a given space.

Deposit Money taken in good faith to assure performance of a contract.

Depreciable Life For tax purposes, the number of years in which to depreciate an asset.

Depreciation An expense reflecting the loss in value of the improvements in real estate.

Depreciation Recapture The excess of the sales proceeds on a property over the initial cost, limited to the amount of accumulated depreciation taken on the property up until the resale period.

Descent The act of acquiring property when an heir is deceased and leaves no will.

Description A formal depiction of the dimensions and location of a property.

Deteriorating Neighborhood An area in which the properties have been neglected and are in disrepair.

Developer An individual who transforms raw land into improved property.

Developing Neighborhood An area that is growing with recently constructed property.

Development Contract An agreement between a developer and a purchaser in which the developer will construct a particular type of property and the purchaser will buy the property within a specified time period.

Development Loan A loan to construct improvements on real property.

Devise A gift of property by will.

Devisee An individual who inherits property through a will.

Direct Participation Program (DPP) A program that lets investors participate directly in the cash flow and tax benefits of an investment.

Disclosure The release of all important information, both positive and negative, needed to make an investment decision.

Discount Points The amount of money a borrower must pay a lender to obtain a mortgage with a stated interest rate.

Discount Rate A percentage rate used to compute the present value of a future cash flow.

Discounted Cash Flow The present value of an expected future cash flow, reduced by an estimated discount rate reflecting the difference in the value of the money now and the value of the money received at a later time period.

Distraint The legal right of a landlord to seize a tenant's personal property to satisfy payment of back rent.

Distressed Property Property that is about to be foreclosed on or has been foreclosed on due to insufficient cash flow.

Diversification Investing in different areas so that the average results will not threaten the success of the overall investment program.

Donee The recipient of a gift.

Donor The giver of a gift.

Double-Declining-Balance Depreciation Method A method of accelerated depreciation in which twice the annual straight line depreciation is taken.

Down-Payment The initial equity paid on a piece of property at closing.

Down Zoning The act of rezoning a property for a less intensive use.

Dragnet Clause A mortgage clause that extends a lien of the mortgage to any and all indebtedness of the mortgagor to the mortgagee, whether or not the debt is specifically referred to in the mortgage itself. The indebtedness may have originated in the past, or it may be in the future.

Dry Mortgage A nonrecourse mortgage.

Dual Contract The illegal practice of providing two contracts for the same transaction.

Due Diligence The investigation of all the important facts regarding a potential investment.

Due-on Sale Clause A mortgage clause requiring the mortgage to be paid in full at the time of resale. This type of loan cannot be assumed by a new purchaser.

Duplex Two dwelling units under one roof.

Dwelling A place of residence.

Earnest Money The deposit that is made by the purchaser when a purchase contract is made, evidencing the purchaser's serious intent.

Easement A right, privilege, or interest that entitles the holder to a specific limited use.

Economic Base The industry within a geographic market area that provides employment opportunities needed to support a community.

Economic Benefits The total benefits of an investment exclusive of the tax benefits, such as the equity buildup, cash flow, and the resale profits.

Economic Depreciation The loss of value of a property due to outside forces.

Economic Feasibility Study An in-depth analysis of the potential real estate investment detailing the economic and financial factors.

Economic Life The period of time over which a building can be used to produce a service or asset.

Effective Age The age of a property based on wear and tear, not its chronological age.

Effective Rate The true rate of return taking into consideration all of the costs and discounts.

Egress Access from a property to an exit or public road.

Eminent Domain The right of the government or a public utility to acquire property needed for public use.

Encroachment A building or part of a building that physically intrudes upon the property of another.

Encumbrance A lien or liability that affects the fee-simple title to property.

End Loan A permanent mortgage.

Equalization Board A governmental agency that determines the fairness of any taxes levied against a property.

Equitable Title The interest held by a party who has agreed to purchase a property but has not closed on the transaction.

Equity The ownership interest in a property after all debt is subtracted.

Equity Kicker The participation in the cash flow or resale proceeds that a lender can receive for making a loan.

Equity REIT A Real Estate Investment Trust that invests in the ownership of income producing property.

Escalation Clause A contract clause requiring an upward adjustment in price.

Escheat The reversion of a property to the state in the event the owner dies without a will or any heirs.

Escrow Property or other consideration held by a third party in accordance with an agreement.

Escrow Agent An individual who holds an escrow payment.

Established Neighborhood A sound, stable, healthy area in which all the land has been developed.

Estate The degree of interest an individual has in real property.

Estate at Sufferance The wrongful occupancy by a tenant when a lease has expired.

Estate at Will The occupation of a property by a tenant for an indefinite period. It can be terminated by either party.

Estate for Life An interest in a property that terminates upon the death of a specified individual.

Estate for Years An interest in land that allows possession for a specified and limited time period.

Estate in Reversion An estate left by a grantor that begins after the termination of estate granted by that individual.

Estate Tax The tax based on the value of a property left by a decedent.

Estoppel A doctrine of law prohibiting a party from denying facts which that person once acknowledged were true and others accepted in good faith.

Estoppel Certificate A document signed by tenants or underlying lender stating any and all claims they may have against the property owner. These certificates protect the buyer from any claims made at a later date by any of these parties.

Et al. (Latin) Abbreviation for *et alii*, "and others."

Eviction, Actual The removal of a party from a property either by force or by process of law.

Eviction, Constructive The termination of a lease by lessor when the property is unfit for the purposes it was leased for.

Eviction Notice A notice given to a tenant when a tenant is in default of the rental obligations.

Evidence of Title A document demonstrating ownership of property.

Exchange A tax-free exchange of like properties under Section 1031 of the Internal Revenue Code.

Exclusive Agency Listing An agreement between a seller and a broker in which the broker has the exclusive right to sell a property during a specified time period. This agreement also gives the seller the right to sell the property personally without paying the broker a commission.

Exclusive Right to Sell Listing An agreement between a seller and a broker giving the broker the exclusive right to sell a property during a specified time period. The broker can collect a commission no matter who sells the property.

Exculpatory Clause A mortgage provision stating that the borrower shall not be personally liable in case of default.

Execute To sign a contract.

Executed Contract A contract whose terms have been satisfied.

Executory Contract A contract in which one or more parties have not yet performed.

Expense Ratio The relationship between the total expenses, exclusive of the debt service, and the gross income.

Expenses The costs incurred in the process of operating, acquiring, or organizing an investment entity.

Expenses of the Syndicator The expenses incurred by a syndicator who intends to pay personally without reimbursement.

Extension An agreement between two parties lengthening the term of a contract.

Facade The exterior front of a building.

Face Interest Rate The rate of interest that appears on a mortgage document.

Face Value The dollar amount shown on a document.

Factory Outlet A shopping center comprised of manufacturers' retail outlet facilities where the goods are sold directly to the public in stores that are owned and operated by the manufacturer.

Fact Sheet The data presented on a property for sale.

Fair Market Rent If available, the amount of rent a property could demand at a given time.

Fair Market Value The value of a property at a given time.

Fannie Mae The nickname for the Federal National Mortgage Association (FNMA).

Farmers Home Administration (FMHA) A governmental agency, under the U.S. Department of Agriculture, that administrates assistance to buyers of homes and farms in rural areas.

Fashion Oriented Center A shopping center that consists of a concentration of apparel shops, boutiques and handcraft shops that carry selected merchandise that is usually of a high quality and a high price. It may include a small specialty department store. Usually located in a high income area.

Feasibility Study A report that takes into consideration many factors that relate to an investment and gives an opinion as to the probability of success of the same.

Federal Deposit Insurance Corporation A public corporation that was established in 1933. It insures up to $100,000 in most commercial banks.

Federal Home Loan Mortgage Corporation (FHLMC) An organization that buys mortgage loans.

Federal Housing Administration (FHA) An agency of the U.S. Department of Housing and Urban Development (HUD) that administers many loan programs, loan guarantee programs and loan insurance programs. It is designed to create more housing.

Federal National Mortgage Association (FNMA) A corporation that specializes in purchasing mortgage loans.

Federal Savings and Loan Insurance Corporation (FSLIC) An agency of the government that insures deposits of savings and loan associations against loss of principal.

Fee Simple A term denoting title to property without any encumbrance.

Fenestration The design and placement of windows in a building.

Fidelity Bond A bond on an employee insuring against theft of funds or valuables.

Fiduciary A person, company, or association holding assets in trust for a beneficiary and charged with investing the money wisely for the beneficiary's benefit.

Financial Management Rate of Return (FMRR) A variation of the internal rate of return measurement in which two after-tax reinvestment rates are used.

Financial Risk The risk due to the use of borrowed money and the difficulty that will result if the investor is unable to meet the necessary debt service.

Financial Statement A statement showing income and expenses for an accounting period or assets, liabilities, and equity as of a certain date.

Financing The borrowing of money to acquire property.

Finder's Fee A fee to someone other than a broker who performs a service.

First Mortgage A first lien against a property.

First Right of Refusal The right of one party to have the first right to purchase or lease a property.

Fiscal Year A twelve-month time period used for financial reporting that may or may not coincide with the calendar year.

Fixtures Improvements or personal property attached to the land that becomes part of the real estate.

Flood Insurance Insurance that covers property damage due to natural flooding.

Floodplain An area of land that is subject to periodic flooding, usually designated by a local government.

Floor Area Ratio (FAR) Total floor area of a building (gross or net) divided by the total square footage of the land.

Floor Loan The minimum amount a lender is willing to lend.

Floor Plan The arrangement of the rooms in a building.

Force Majeure Clause A clause in a construction contract that allows additional construction time to complete a building due to an unavoidable cause of delay, such as weather, labor disputes, or accidents.

Foreclosure A legal process whereby the rights of the owner who is in default on a loan payment are lost.

Forfeiture The loss of money or other valuables due to a failure to perform under a contract.

Freddie Mac The nickname for the Federal Home Loan Mortgage Corporation (FHMLC).

Free and Clear Title Real property against which there are no liens.

Freehold An interest in a property for an unspecified time period.

Frontage A linear distance a property has along a road, lake, river, or ocean.

Front-end Load The total compensation that is received by the syndicator on the sale of property to a partnership, including commissions on the sale of the units, loans or acquisition fees, or a resale markup of the property to be sold to the partnership.

Front Foot A measurement of land based on its frontage.

Front Money The sum of money used to initiate a transaction prior to its closing.

Full Disclosure The requirement to disclose any and all material relevant to a financial transaction.

Functional Depreciation A loss of value of a property determined from within the property and not due to physical deterioration. Examples: poor floor plan or outdated plumbing fixtures.

Functional Obsolescence The same as functional depreciation.

Future Interest A property right or interest available in the future.

Gain An increase in money or value of property.

Gap Loan A mortgage that fills a spread in mortgage financing.

Garden Apartment A low-rise apartment property, usually in a suburban area.

General Contractor An individual or firm who constructs a building for another party for a fee.

General Partner An individual or corporation acting as the managing partner in a limited partnership and responsible for the debts of the partnership.

General Partnership An entity in which all partners are jointly and severally liable for the debts and obligations of the partnership.

General Warranty Deed A deed in which a seller agrees to protect the purchaser against any claims to the title of the property.

Gift Deed A deed for which the consideration is not money but love and affection.

Ginnie Mae The nickname for the Government National Mortgage Association (GNMA).

Good Faith An act that is done honestly between two parties.

Government National Mortgage Association (GNMA) A government agency that assists in financing housing.

Grace Period A period of time allowed before a party is considered in default.

Graduated Lease Payment A lease payment that increases by a specific dollar amount over the term.

Graduated Payment Mortgage (GPM) A mortgage featuring lower payments in the early years and increasing payments over a specified time period.

Grandfather Clause A clause allowing activities that were legal under an old law to continue under a superseding law.

Grantee A person who acquires an interest in a property by deed or grant.

Grantor A person who transfers an interest in a property to a grantee by deed or grant.

Gross Floor Area The total floor area including all common areas.

Gross Income The total rental income received from an income property.

Gross Leasable Area (GLA) The total floor area designed for tenant occupancy and exclusive use, and on which rent is paid, including any basement, mezzanines, or upper floors, measured in square feet from the centerline of joining partitions and from outside wall faces.

Gross Lease A lease under which the landlord pays all the expenses normally associated with the ownership of the property.

Gross Profit Ratio (GPR) In an installment sale, the gross profit divided by the contract price.

Gross Rent Multiplier (GRM) The ratio of the sales price of a property to the gross rents collected.

Ground Lease An agreement in which for a fee a lessor can lease a piece of land for a specified term.

Growing Equity Mortgage (GEM) A mortgage in which the payment is increased by a predetermined amount each year. The additional payments are used to pay off the principal balance. Due to this repayment of principal, the mortgage will be paid off over a shorter time period.

Guaranty A pledge by a borrower to repay a debt or creditor.

Hard Dollars Money given in exchange for an improved equity or ownership position in a transaction, for example the down payment.

Hazard Insurance Insurance that protects against fires or certain weather conditions.

Hectare A measurement of land equal to 2,471 acres or about 107,637 square feet.

Heir An individual who inherits property.

Highest and Best Use The use that is most likely to produce the greatest return at a specific time on a piece of land or a piece of property.

High-Rise A building that is over 6 stories.

Historic Structure A building that is officially recognized by a governmental agency for its historic significance, usually receiving special tax treatment to encourage rehabilitation.

Hold Harmless Clause A contract clause in which one party agrees to indemnify another party against any claims.

Holdback Funds retained until certain events occur.

Holder in Due Course An individual who acquires a bearer instrument in good faith and is eligible to keep it even though it may have been stolen.

Holding Costs Carrying costs.

Holding Period That time period during which one owns a property.

Holdover Tenant A tenant who remains in possession of leased property after the lease has expired.

Homeowner's Association An association that is formed by a subdivision or condominium property to enforce deed restrictions and manage common elements.

Homestead Exemption In certain jurisdictions, a reduction in assessed property value allowed on one's principal residence.

Horizontal Property Law A statute that enables condominium ownership of property.

Housing and Urban Development (HUD) A government department set up in 1965 to assist in stimulating housing development in the United States.

Housing Codes Codes set up by local governments setting certain minimum safety and sanitation standards for housing.

Housing Starts The number of housing permits issued in an area during a certain time period.

Hybrid REIT A real estate investment trust that invests in both property and mortgages.

Illiquid Not easily converted into cash.

Implied Contract A contract created by actions but not necessarily written or spoken.

Implied Warranty A warranty that is not written but exists under the law.

Impound Account An escrow account.

Improved Land Land on which there are improvements.

Improvements Additions to raw land that tend to increase its value, such as buildings, streets, and utilities.

Income The revenue that is generated by an investment in property.

Income Approach An appraisal method used to calculate value based on the income generated, when the income is capitalized at the current market rate for the particular type of property.

Income Property Real estate capable of producing an income stream.

Income Stream The regular flow of money generated by an investment.

Incurable Depreciation A defect that cannot be corrected or is not financially practical to correct.

Indemnify To protect another against damage or loss.

Independent Contractor A contractor who is self employed.

Index A benchmark indicating a current economic or financial condition.

Indexed Lease A lease in which the lease rate can increase or decrease at specified times based upon a specified index.

Indexed Loan A loan in which the interest rate can increase or decrease at specified times based upon a specified index.

Individual Metering Utility System A metering system in which each tenant has its own utility meter.

Industrial Development Bond (IDB) A bond that is issued by a local or state government to help finance an industrial plant or facility to be leased to a private business.

Industrial Park An area that is zoned for industrial use.

Industrial Property Real property that is intended to be used for industry, such as manufacturing or warehousing.

Inflation A general increase in prices, resulting in a decrease in purchasing power.

Inner City An older area in a city adjacent to the central business district.

Inspection A review of documents or of the physical aspects of a property.

Inspection Period A time period during which a purchaser reviews the property and the documents relating to a transaction.

Installment Contract A land contract.

Installment Sale A sale in which the proceeds are paid in installments over a fixed period of time, allowing the capital gains to take place over a number of years.

Installments The periodic payments on a debt.

Instrument A written legal document that creates the rights and obligations of the parties to it.

Insurable Title A title that can be insured by a title company.

Insurance An agreement in which one party agrees to pay a sum of money to another if the latter suffers a particular loss, in exchange for a premium paid by the insured.

Insurance Coverage The amount of money and type of insurance that a property carries.

Interest A payment for the use of money.

Interest-Only Loan A loan in which only interest is paid during the term of the loan.

Interest Rate A percentage of a sum of money charged for its use.

Interim Financing A loan made prior to permanent financing.

Internal Rate of Return (IRR) The discounted rate that produces a zero value for the net present value. The internal rate of return can be interpreted as the rate of return on the investment.

Internal Revenue Code The law specifying how and what income is taxed and what expenses can be deducted.

Internal Revenue Service (IRS) The governmental agency that administers the collection of federal income taxes.

Interstate Offering An offering to residents of one or more states.

Intestate A person who dies having no valid will.

Intrastate Offering An offering in which all the investors reside in the state that the property is located in.

Inventory Property held for sale or use.

Investment Life Cycle The time span of property ownership.

Investment Property Property that is acquired for its current income and capital appreciation.

Investment Tax Credit A reduction in income tax based on the cost and life of certain assets purchased.

Investor An individual or company that invests in a financial transaction.

Investor Note Financing The financing of investor promissory notes.

Involuntary Lien A lien placed on property without the consent of the owner.

Joint and Several Liability When two or more parties guarantee repayment of debt, all or any one of the parties are obligated to pay the debt.

Joint Tenancy Joint property ownership, in which two or more persons take title jointly for life. Upon death, the survivors acquire the decedent's interest in the property.

Joint Venture An agreement by two or more parties to work on a project together.

Judgment A decree by a court evidencing the amount of and the parties to an indebtedness.

Judgment Foreclosure The sale of a defaulted debtor's property according to court-approved terms.

Judgment Lien A claim upon a property of a debtor that results in a judgment.

Junior Mortgage A mortgage that is subordinate to a first mortgage lien.

Kicker Additional payment of interest or rent required in a contract.

Land The surface of the earth that is not water.

Land Banking The purchase of land to hold for future need.

Land Contract A sale of property wherein the seller retains the title of the property; the purchaser is given possession and obtains title upon a predetermined loan paydown.

Land Lease Ground lease.

Landlocked A condition of a property having no access to a public street.

Landlord The entity that owns a property which is leased to a tenant.

Land Packaging The assembly of several tracts of land into a larger tract for a specific use.

Land Sale Leaseback The sale of land and the simultaneous leasing back of the land by the seller, who becomes the tenant of the landowner.

Latent Defects Defects that are hidden but will appear in the future.

Lease A contract for the use of rental property.

Lease with Option to Purchase A lease giving the lessee the right to purchase property at an agreed-upon price and terms at a specific date.

Leasehold An interest or estate on which a tenant has a lease.

Leasehold Mortgage A lien on the tenant's interest in property.

Leasing Agent A person responsible for the leasing of space in a building.

Legal Description A description of a piece of property that enables it to be located on government surveys or recorded maps.

Legal Name The name used for official purposes.

Legal Notice A notification of other parties using the method required by law.

Legatee An individual who receives property by will.

Lender An individual or firm who lends money to a borrower for a fee with the expectation of being repaid in the future.

Lessee The tenant under a lease.

Lessor The owner who gives the lease to a lessee

Letter of Intent A nonbinding expression of intent conditioned upon the approval and further documentation of a second party.

Level Payment Mortgage A mortgage having the same payment due each month during its amortization period.

Leverage The use of borrowed capital to make an investment.

Liability A general term encompassing all types of debt and obligations.

Liability Insurance Insurance protection for a property that covers any claims from injuries or damage to another's property.

License Permission.

License Laws The laws of a state governing the activities of real estate salespersons.

Lien A claim against a property for a debt.

Life Estate A freehold interest in property that will expire upon the death of the owner or some other specified person.

Life Tenant An individual who is allowed use of property for life or the lifetime of another specified person.

Like-Kind Property In an exchange, property that has the same nature.

Limited Liability Liability limited to the amount invested.

Limited Partners Passive investors in a limited partnership who have no personal liability beyond their investment.

Limited Partnership A partnership in which some partners' contributions and liabilities are limited.

Liquidated Damages An agreed-upon amount that one party will reimburse the other party in the event of a breach of contract.

Liquidity Assets that are readily converted to cash.

Lis Pendens (Latin) "Suit pending."

List To obtain a listing.

Listing A contract authorizing an agent to sell property for an owner.

Loan A granting of the use of money for a specified time.

Loan Application A written application giving all information required by a lender prior to issuing a loan commitment.

Loan Commitment A written document drafted by a lender outlining the terms and conditions of a mortgage loan.

Loan Constant A factor or multiplier used to compute the monthly mortgage payments that amortize a loan.

Loan to Value Ratio (LVR) The percentage that a lender will lend a borrower against the appraised value of the property.

Location A reference to the comparative advantages of one site in consideration of factors such as convenience, transportation and social benefits.

Lock-In Period A specified period of time during which a loan may not be prepaid.

Long-Term Capital Gains For income tax purposes, the gain on a capital asset that is held for a specified time period.

Lot and Block A method of identification of a parcel of land.

Maintenance Activities required to correct normal wear and tear on a property.

Maintenance Fee A fee that is charged by an owners' association to cover the costs of operating the property.

Mall An enclosed public area connecting individual retail stores in a shopping center.

Management Contract The contract between an owner of property and a management company, stipulating the duties, term, and fees to be paid to the management company.

Managing Partner In a limited partnership, that partner who makes the decisions and bears the largest part of the risk.

Marginal Property Property that is barely profitable to use.

Market Approach An appraisal method that values property based on the market value of similar buildings sold in a recent time period in a comparable market area.

Market Research The research done to review market conditions in a specified area.

Market Value The price a qualified buyer is willing to pay for a property.

Marketable Title A title free of any defects.

Master Lease A controlling lease.

Maturity The date on which a loan is due.

Mechanic's Lien A lien filed for nonpayment of a labor or material debt.

Meeting of the Minds An agreement of all parties to a contract.

Merchants' Association An association set up by the merchants in a shopping center to promote the tenants' businesses.

Metes and Bounds A land description giving the boundary lines of a parcel of land, together with its terminal points and angles.

Millage A rate used by local taxing authorities, equal to one-tenth of a cent.

Mini-Warehouse A warehouse providing small storage areas for commercial and residential users.

Mixed Use Project A planned development in which there are at least two different types of real estate projects involved.

Mobile Home A factory manufactured dwelling without a permanent foundation, located on a fixed lot and connected to local utilities.

Mobile Home Park A subdivision of land used for mobile homes.

Model Unit A representative unit in a property used to demonstrate the future appearance of the space.

Month-to-Month Tenancy A lease agreement cancelable each month.

Mortgage A legal instrument used to secure the payment of a debt or an obligation.

Mortgage Banker An individual who originates, sells and services mortgage loans.

Mortgage Broker An individual who specializes in bringing a borrower and a lender together for a commission.

Mortgage Commitment An agreement between a borrower and a lender, whereby the lender agrees to lend the borrower money at a future date, subject to the conditions of the commitment.

Mortgage Correspondent An individual who will originate and service a loan for a fee.

Mortgage Insurance Insurance that is used to protect a lender against any financial loss resulting from a mortgagor defaulting on a loan.

Mortgage Lien An encumbrance on a property that is used to secure a mortgage loan.

Mortgage Note A description of the debt and the promise by the mortgagor to repay.

Mortgage REIT A Real Estate Investment Trust that lends money on property.

Mortgage Release A disclaimer of any further liability on the mortgage note issued by the mortgagee.

Mortgagee One who holds a lien on a property as security for a loan.

Mortgagor One who pledges property as security for a loan.

Multi-Family Housing A residential structure with more than one dwelling unit in the same building.

Negative Amortization A loan in which the loan balance increases rather than decreases over time.

Negative Cash Flow When expenses exceed income.

Negative Leverage Reverse leverage.

Negotiation The dealings between two or more parties to reach an agreement on terms and conditions of a transaction.

Neighborhood An area in which there are common characteristics of population and land use.

Neighborhood Shopping Center A small shopping center with a supermarket or drug store as the anchor tenant and usually around another twenty retail stores. The typical size is 50,000 square feet.

Net Leasable Area (NLA) The floor space that is leased to a tenant.

Net Lease An agreement in which the tenant pays the rent and also certain expenses connected with the operations of the property.

Net Listing A listing in which the real estate commission is not added in.

Net Net Lease An agreement in which the tenant pays all maintenance and operating expenses, plus the property taxes.

Net Net Net Lease An agreement in which the tenant pays all maintenance and operating expenses, plus the property taxes and insurance.

Net Operating Income The income available after all expenses are paid out of the income received.

Net Present Value (NVP) The present value of the cash inflow from an investment less the present value of the cash outflow.

Nondisturbance Clause A mortgage clause providing for a continuation of any leases in the event of a loan foreclosure.

Non Recourse No personal liability.

Normal Wear and Tear The physical depreciation that arises through ordinary use of a property.

Note A written promise to repay a specified amount to an entity on a specified date.

Notice of Default A letter sent to a defaulting party as a reminder of the default.

Notice to Quit A notice sent by a tenant to vacate the rental property.

Notorious Possession Generally acknowledged possession of real property.

Null and Void A contract that is not enforceable.

Obligee An individual in whose favor an obligation is entered into.

Obligor An individual who makes an obligation to another party.

Obsolescence A loss in property value brought about by changes in design, technology, taste, or demand.

Occupancy Level A percentage of space that is currently rented.

Offer to Purchase A buyer's purchase offer, which if accepted becomes a binding document.

Off-Price Shopping Center A shopping center that consists of retail stores offering brand name merchandise usually found in specialty shops and department stores for 20 to 70 percent below the manufacturer's suggested price.

One Hundred Percent Location A location where a retail establishment will achieve the highest sales volume compared to other locations in a market area.

Open-Ended Mortgage A mortgage written to secure the advancement of additional funds over and above the original amount disbursed.

Open Mortgage A mortgage that has matured or is overdue and is therefore subject to foreclosure at any time.

Operating Expenses The expenses essential to operating a property.

Operating Lease A lease between a lessee and a sublessee who actually occupies and uses the property.

Operating Statement The financial statement that lists the income and expenses for an income property.

Opinion Letter A written opinion of an attorney relating to the tax and legal consequences of certain aspects of a syndication.

Opinion of Title A certificate, usually by an attorney, confirming the validity of the title to property being sold.

Option The right to purchase or lease a property at an agreed-upon price within a specified time period.

Option Fee The consideration paid by the optionee to obtain an option.

Option Price The negotiated price the optionee is willing to pay to obtain the option.

Oral Contract A verbal agreement.

Ordinary Income As defined by the Internal Revenue Service, any income that is taxed at regular tax rates, such as fees, commissions, and interest.

Ordinary Loss For tax purposes, loss that is deductible against ordinary income.

Organizational Fee A fee that a general partner receives for services in organizing a syndicate.

Origination Fee A fee charged by a mortgage loan company for services rendered in connection with processing a loan application.

Other Income The income that is derived from an income property, but not from the rental of the tenant space.

Other People's Money (OPM) The use of borrowed funds for investment purposes.

Outstanding Loan Balance The amount currently outstanding on a loan.

Overage Lease Additional rental charged in some retail leases based on a percentage of sales over a predetermined sales base.

Overall Rate of Return (OAR) The percentage of net operating income divided by the purchase price of a property, the capitalization rate.

Overimprovement A land or building use that is considered too intense.

Parcel A piece of property that is under one ownership.

Partial Release The removal of a general mortgage lien from a specific portion of the property pledged.

Partial Taking In a condemnation, the taking of only a part of the property or property rights.

Participation Loan A loan whereby the lender will participate in the future cash flow and resale profits of a property.

Partition The division of property between those who own the property with undivided interest.

Partnership An association of two or more individuals as co-owners for the purpose of carrying on a business for profit.

Partnership Agreement An agreement between partners describing the duties and rights of each party.

Passive Income Income derived from rents, royalties, dividends, interest, and gains from the sale of securities.

Passive Investor An individual who invests money in an investment but does not take an active part in management.

Penalty A fee charged for breaking the law or violating the terms of a contract.

Percentage Lease A lease in which the rental is based on a percentage of the gross business conducted by the lessee.

Percolation Test A test designed to measure the drainage characteristics of soil.

Performance Bond A bond issued by an insurance company to guarantee completion of a construction contract.

Permanent Financing A long-term mortgage on a piece of real property.

Personal Guarantee A guarantee given by an individual to endorse a note or obligation.

Personal Property A possession or item that is not real property, personalty.

Phantom Income Income that is taxed but that might not have been received.

Physical Depreciation The loss in value of property from all causes of age and action of the elements.

Physical Life The length of time that a building is a sound structure, dependent on the quality of maintenance.

Piggyback Loan A combination construction and permanent loan.

Planned Unit Development (PUD) A zoning classification that allows flexibility in the design of a subdivision.

Plat A plan or map of a specific land area.

Plat Book A public record that contains the maps of land and the division of streets.

Pledged Account Mortgage (PAM) A mortgage in which the mortgagor must pledge a sum of money at loan closing to be set aside to be used to supplement periodic mortgage payments.

Plot Plan A diagram showing the proposed or existing use of a specified parcel of land.

Points A charge made by a lender equal to one percentage point of the principal loan amount.

Power of Attorney An instrument granting another person the right to act as an agent of the grantor.

Power of Sale A mortgage clause giving the lender the right to sell the property upon default.

Preclosing A rehearsal of the closing.

Prelease To obtain a lease commitment prior to the certificate of occupancy.

Premium The cost of an insurance policy.

Prepaid Expenses Expenses paid prior to the period that they cover.

Prepayment Clause A mortgage clause defining the terms of early prepayment of the mortgage loan.

Prepayment Penalty A penalty charged by a lender for early retirement of a loan.

Presale The sale of a property prior to its completion.

Prescription The acquisition rights to a property through adverse possession.

Present Value A sum of money which, if invested today at a specified interest rate, would be equivalent to a specified amount of money in the future.

Preventive Maintenance A program designed to regularly inspect the various physical aspects of a property.

Primary Lease A lease between the owner and a tenant whose interest, all or part, has been sublet.

Prime Rate The rate of interest charged by a lender to its most creditworthy borrowers.

Prime Tenant An anchor tenant in a commercial property.

Principal The major party in a transaction.

Principal Amount The amount of the mortgage loan.

Principal and Interest Payment (P & I) The periodic loan payment, usually paid monthly, of both the principal reduction and the interest due.

Private Limited Partnership A limited partnership in which the shares are not offered to the general public and having a relatively small number of investors.

Private Mortgage Insurance (PMI) Insurance coverage on a mortgage that pays off in case of default.

Profit and Loss Statement A statement showing the operating results of a property.

Pro Forma A projection of future income and expenses.

Project A proposed development plan for a property.

Projection The estimate of the future performance of a property.

Promoter A syndicator.

Property The rights that an individual has in lands or goods to the exclusion of all others.

Property Line The recorded boundary of a parcel of land.

Property Management The operation of property as a business.

Property Management Fee A fee that is received by a management company for services rendered, usually based on a percentage of the income collected.

Property Residual Technique In appraisal, a method for estimating the value of a property based on the estimated future income and the reversionary value of the improvements and land.

Property Taxes A tax levied by a local government on the assessed value of a piece of property.

Proprietary Lease A document giving a shareholder in a cooperative the right to occupy a unit under certain terms and conditions.

Prorations The prepaid or accrued expenses that are due at the time of sale and are split between the buyer and seller.

Prospectus A document that describes the details of an investment offering.

Public Limited Partnership A limited partnership in which the shares are offered to the general public, thus having a large number of investors.

Public Sale An auction sale of property with notice to the general public.

Punch List A list of items that need to be finished or corrected prior to a sale.

Purchase Contract A formal agreement in which the seller agrees to sell and the buyer agrees to buy a property.

Purchase Money Mortgage A mortgage that the purchaser gives the seller simultaneously with the purchase of real estate to secure the unpaid balance of the purchase price.

Quadraplex Four dwelling units that are connected or under one roof.

Quitclaim Deed A deed in which the grantor conveys whatever interest he or she may have in the property without even implying that any interest exists.

Rate of Return The percentage return on an investment.

Raw Land Unimproved land.

Ready, Willing, and Able An individual capable of either buying or selling a piece of property.

Real Estate Land and the attached improvements, including any minerals and resources inherent to the land.

Real Estate Commission A fee paid to a real estate broker or agent when a transaction is consummated.

Real Estate Cycle A period of time during which real property goes through predevelopment to maturity to decline, and then renovation or demolition.

Real Estate Investment Trust (REIT) A trust that invests in real estate. By law, 95 percent of the profits must be distributed to the investors.

Real Estate Security A form of personal property that is secured by real property and which is evidence of real estate ownership or indebtedness.

Realized Gain In an exchange, a gain that has occurred financially, but is not necessarily taxed.

Realty Real estate.

Recapture The amount of gain charged by the IRS on the sale of depreciable property taken by the excess depreciation taken over the straight line depreciation.

Recapture Clause A contract clause permitting the party who grants an interest or right to take it back under certain conditions.

Recognized Gain In an exchange, the portion of gain that is taxable.

Recording Filing a legal document in the public records of a county.

Recourse Loan A loan in which the borrower is personally liable for the debt in the event of a default.

Recreational Property Homesites with recreational amenities, including campgrounds and recreational vehicle parks, or properties that offer fishing, boating, skiing, hunting, or other such activities.

Recycling The process of reclaiming an old building for an adaptive re-use.

Red Herring A proposed prospectus that has not been approved by the Securities and Exchange Commission (SEC) or the state securities commission.

Redemption Period A period in which a former owner can reclaim foreclosed property.

Refinancing The process of paying off an old loan with a new loan.

Regional Shopping Center The largest type of shopping center with two to five major department stores as anchors and 100 to 150 smaller retail stores. Usually the centers are called "malls" and are enclosed. These centers range from 400,000 to more than 1,000,000 square feet.

Regulation D A regulation of the Securities and Exchange Commission (SEC) that sets forth the conditions necessary for a private placement exemption.

Rehabilitation Renovating property for use or for resale.

Release Clause A mortgage clause allowing the release of pledged property after full payment of the debt.

Relocation Clause A clause in a lease that gives the landlord the right to relocate a tenant.

Renegotiate To legally revise the terms of a contract.

Renegotiated Rate Mortgage (RRM) A mortgage in which the mortgage interest rate is adjusted over the term of the loan.

Renewal Option An option to renew a lease at a specified term and rent.

Rent The consideration received from a lessee for the use of the occupied space.

Rent Control Regulation by a local governing board restricting the amount of rent a lessee can charge to tenants.

Rent Roll A balance sheet for the account of each tenant, listing the name, unit number, lease term, and rent.

Rent Schedule A listing of rent levels for the various types of units in a property.

Rental Area Net rentable area.

Rental Concessions Concessions given by the lessor to the lessees to induce the lessee to sign a lease.

Rent-Up Period The period of time it takes for a property to become fully rented up following the completion of construction.

Repairs Work performed to return property to a former condition without exceeding its useful life.

Replacement Cost Approach An appraisal method in which the value is based on the estimated cost to replace the improvements less any depreciation plus the appraised value of the land.

Replacement Reserve A cash reserve for the future replacement of fixed assets.

Reproduction Cost The cost to duplicate a property as of a certain date.

Resale Proceeds The profit an individual receives after selling a property and deducting all sales expenses.

Rescind To withdraw a contract.

Rescission A cancellation of a contract.

Reserve Fund An account set aside for funding upcoming capital expenditures or negative cash flow.

Resident Manager An individual who supervises the care of an apartment property while residing in one of the apartment units.

Residential Property Real estate that is intended for the owner's living quarters.

Restriction A limitation that is placed on the use of a property.

Resyndication A partnership that has been resold to new investors.

Retainage An amount of money that is held back in a construction contract until the contractor has completed all contractual obligations.

Retire a Mortgage To pay off a mortgage.

Return of Capital The return of the original investor's capital contribution, not directly taxable.

Return on Equity The amount that is returned to the investor on the original contribution, expressed by a percentage.

Revenue Sharing The profit and tax benefits split between the general partners and the limited partners.

Reverse Annuity Mortgage A mortgage that is designed for the elderly with substantial equity, in which the lender periodically pays an amount to the borrower, creating negative amortization.

Reverse Leverage A situation in which the financial benefits from ownership accrue at a lower rate than the mortgage interest rate.

Reversion The right of a landlord to possess leased property upon the termination of a lease.

Rider An attachment to a contract.

Right of Redemption The right to recover property that has been transferred by a mortgage or lien by paying off the debt prior to or after a foreclosure.

Right of Survivorship A right that entitles one owner of a property that is held jointly to take title to it when the other owner dies.

Risk The possibility that the financial return of an investment will not be as expected.

Risk Return Relationship The financial principle that recognizes that in order to obtain a chance at a high rate of return, the investor will have to take a high risk.

Rod A linear unit of measurement equal to $16\frac{1}{2}$ feet.

Rollover Mortgage A mortgage loan amortized over a long-term with the interest rate adjusted periodically.

Rollover Option An option agreement in which the potential buyer has the right to renew the option one or more times upon the payment of a specified amount.

Sale The transfer from one entity to another entity, for a consideration, of the possession and right of use of some particular article of value to both parties.

Sales Contract An agreement by which a buyer and seller agree to the terms of a sale.

Salvage Value The amount realized at the final sale of an asset at the end of its useful life.

Sandwich Lease A lease that is held by a lessee who becomes a lessor upon the sublet of space.

Savings and Loan Association (S & L) A financial institution established to accept members' deposits and to make real estate loans.

Seasoned Loan A mortgage loan in which many payments have been collected.

Secondary Financing A loan secured by a second mortgage on real property.

Section of Land One square mile.

Securities Instruments that signify an ownership position in a corporation or a limited partnership.

Securities and Exchange Commission (SEC) The federal agency created by the Securities Exchange Act of 1934 that administers said act. The act outlaws misrepresentations in any securities offerings.

Security Deposit The amount of money required to be paid by a tenant at the start of the lease term to cover any damage to the property over and above normal wear and tear.

Security Interest An interest in property in which the real estate serves as collateral.

Seed Money Moneys that are needed to begin a real estate transaction.

Self-Amortizing Mortgage A mortgage loan that will retire itself through periodic payments of principal and interest.

Seller's Group The group of dealers appointed by the syndicate manager to underwrite the offering.

Seller's Market In a real estate marketplace, when there are more buyers than sellers, enabling the seller to obtain a higher sales price.

Selling Expenses Those expenses incurred by the seller on a particular piece of property during the money raising or resale period.

Sensitivity Analysis The multiple analyses of future cash flow, resale, and rates of return on an investment using different assumptions each time.

Shared Appreciation Mortgage (SAM) A mortgage in which the lender reduces the interest rate below market rate and then shares in the future appreciation of the property.

Shared Equity Mortgage (SEM) A mortgage in which an outside investor puts up all or part of the equity requirements and shares in the future appreciation of the property.

Shopping Center A collection of retail stores with a common parking area.

Short-Term Capital Gains A gain on the sale of a capital asset that was held under the prescribed time period to achieve a long term capital gain.

Sign Restriction Clause A lease restriction prohibiting the use of a particular type of signage.

Single-Family Housing A type of residential dwelling designed to house one family.

Sinking Fund A fund set aside which, when compounded, will equal a specified sum after a specified time period.

Site A plot of land.

Slum An area of a city in which the properties are deteriorating.

Social Obsolescence A loss in value brought about by the social conditions of an area.

Soft Dollars Money that does not improve the equity position of the payer, such as prepaid interest or fees paid to the seller.

Sole Proprietorship A form of ownership in which there is only one individual owner.

Sources and Applications of Funds The funding analysis of where the funds come from and how they are applied.

Special Purpose Building A structure that is designed for the particular needs of its occupant, such as a restaurant or bowling alley.

Special Warranty Deed A deed in which the grantor limits the title warranty given to the grantee to anyone claiming by, from, through, or under him, the grantor, the grantor does not warrant against any title defects.

Specific Performance An action that forces the performance of an agreement.

Specifications A list of instructions provided with working drawings detailing the material and how the property will be constructed.

Specified Fund A fund in which the properties to be purchased are already selected.

Speculation The acquisition of a property not for use but for resale at a high profit, often after only a short holding period.

Square Footage The area measured in square feet.

Standard Tenant Improvement Allowance An allowance for the building of tenant improvements at no extra cost to the tenant.

Standby Fee A fee paid by a borrower to a lender to provide a standby loan.

Standby Loan A loan made available to a borrower at a specified interest rate for a specified time period in the future.

Stepped-Up Basis An accounting term used to describe a change in the adjusted tax basis of a property, allowed for certain transactions.

Stick-Built A method of construction that uses wood frame construction.

Stipulations The terms and conditions outlined within a written contract.

Stop Clause A lease clause stipulating an amount of operating expenses above which the tenant must bear.

Straight-Line Depreciation Method The depreciation method allowed by the Internal Revenue Service (IRS), calculated by dividing the depreciable basis by its useful life as determined by the Internal Revenue Code.

Straw Man An individual who purchases property for another individual who wishes to conceal his or her identity.

Strip Center A retail shopping center that is a straight line of stores, usually narrow in proportion to its length.

Structure Any constructed improvements to a site.

Subchapter S Corporation A corporation with a limited number of stockholders that elects not to be taxed as a regular corporation. The tax benefits can be passed through to the individual stockholders. Corporate limited liability is still available.

Subdivision A tract of land that is surveyed and divided into smaller lots for the purpose of resale or development.

Subject To To acquire property with an existing mortgage, but not becoming personally liable for the debt.

Sublease A lease given to another by a tenant for a part of the leased premises or for a specified term.

Subordination In mortgage terms, being secondary, a mortgagee or lien holder is willing to accept payment after another creditor.

Subordination Clause A mortgage clause prohibiting a mortgage to be recorded at a later date which mortgage would have priority over an existing mortgage.

Subscription The signing of a binding contract to purchase an interest in a syndicated security.

Sum of the Years' Digits Depreciation Method A depreciation method that results in a higher depreciation than that of straight line depreciation, by allowing depreciation based on the inverted scale of the total of digits for the years of the useful life.

Super-Regional Center A shopping center that provides an extensive variety of general merchandise. It is usually built around three or more department stores with at least 100,000 square feet each. The total center consists of a minimum of 750,000 square feet.

Supply and Demand The principle stating that prices will increase as the supply of the product is decreased, or will decrease when there is an oversupply of the product.

Surety One who guarantees the performance of another.

Survey The measurement and description of a piece of land by a surveyor.

Surveyor An individual who prepares a survey.

Survivorship The right of a joint tenant or tenants to maintain ownership following the death of another joint tenant.

Sweat Equity The equity the investor creates by labor performed.

Syndicate Any general or limited partnership, joint venture or other type organization that is formed for the sole purpose of investing in a property for a profit.

Syndication The action taken by the syndicate to acquire a property.

Syndicator An individual whose business it is to sell investments in real estate partnerships.

Take-Out Mortgage Loan A mortgage loan that takes out a construction loan at a specified time.

Tax A government levy usually made on a regular basis and based on the relative value of the object being levied.

Tax Deductible An expense that may reduce the taxable income.

Tax Deferred Income The cash flow that is received in a given year, but in which no taxes are currently due because of tax shelter.

Tax-Free Exchange An exchange of property for other property of like kind, resulting in no immediate tax effect, because the taxes are deferred.

Tax Map A map showing the location and dimensions of parcels of property that are subject to property taxes.

Tax Preference Items Certain types of income or deductions that are added to the adjusted gross income to calculate the alternative minimum tax.

Tax Rate The ratio of tax assessed to the amount being taxed.

Tax Sale A sale of property held for the nonpayment of taxes.

Tax Sheltered Income that is not subject to a tax.

Taxable Income The portion of income, after all allowable deductions are taken, that is subject to tax.

Tenancy in Common Ownership by two or more individuals who have undivided interests in a particular piece of property without the right of survivorship. The undivided interests do not have to be equal.

Tenancy by the Entirety An estate that exists only between a husband and wife with equal rights of possession and enjoyment during their joint lives and with the right of survivorship.

Tenancy in Severalty The ownership of property by one person or one legal entity.

Tenancy at Sufferance A tenancy that is established when a lease has expired and the tenant remains on the property.

Tenancy at Will A license to use or occupy property at the will of the owner.

Tenancy for Years A lease for a fixed period of time.

Tenant One who pays rent to occupy real estate.

Tender To make an offer.

Term The time period within which a loan must be repaid.

Terms The conditions and arrangements specified in a contract.

Testament A will.

Testate Having made a valid will.

Testator A person who makes a will.

Theme/Specialty Center A shopping center that is diverse in format, size and market orientation. These centers usually have a common architectural design throughout the center. These centers are usually anchored by restaurants and entertainment facilities that appeal to tourists and the local market. The tenants usually offer unusual merchandise.

Time Is of the Essence A phrase used in a contract that requires that all references to specific dates and times of day noted in the contract be interpreted exactly.

Time Sharing A type of ownership in which a property is held by a number of individuals for a specified time period.

Title The legal evidence of an individual's right to ownership of real property.

Title Company A company that examines the title to property and then issues title insurance.

Title Insurance Insurance issued against the loss or damage from defects or failure of title to a particular piece of property.

Title Report A document that indicates the current state of the title.

Title Search An examination of the public records, laws and court decisions to discover the current facts regarding the ownership of property.

Topography The features of the land's surface, such as hills, valleys, etc.

Townhouse A type of single family housing built as an attached or semi-detached row house.

Township A six square mile parcel of land.

Tract In some states a unit of subdivided land that is numbered and recorded with the county recorder's office.

Traffic Report A record of the prospects who inquired about renting a property.

Transaction Costs The costs associated with the buying and selling of property.

Transfer Tax A tax that is charged on the transfer of an asset or mortgage.

Triple A Tenant A tenant that has a triple A credit rating, considered a prime tenant.

Triple Net Lease A lease in which the lessor receives a net amount, and the lessee pays the taxes, insurance, and all of the maintenance expenses.

Triplex Three dwellings that are connected under one roof.

Trust An arrangement whereby a property is transferred to or held by a third party or trustee.

Trust Deed A conveyance of property to a third party to be held for the benefit of another.

Trustee A person holding property in trust.

Trustor A grantor of property to a trustee.

Turnaround Property A property that with creative planning and hard work can be made to return a positive cash flow.

Turnkey Project A development in which a developer completes an entire project and then turns the property over to a buyer.

Underwriter An individual or corporation that coordinates the process of raising the investor money.

Undivided Interest An ownership right to use and possess a property with others.

Unencumbered Property Property with free and clear title.

Unilateral Contract An obligation given by one party that is contingent on the performance of another party, but without obligation of the second party to perform.

Unimproved Property Land that has no improvements.

Unit A prorated share of ownership in a limited partnership. A single dwelling.

Unleveraged Purchased for cash.

Unleveraged Program A limited partnership that invests in a property with 50 percent or less of the property mortgaged.

Unrealized Gain The excess of the current market value over the cost for the asset that is unsold.

Use Clause A lease provision indicating the purpose for which the leased space will be used.

Useful Life In appraisal for the purpose of sale, the true economic value of a structure in terms of years of use to the owner.

Usury Excessive interest charged by a lender as determined by state law.

Utilities Essential services, usually including electric, gas, water, sewer and telephone.

Utility Easement An easement for the use of laying the utilities.

Vacancy Factor A property's anticipated percentage of vacancy.

Vacant Land Land that is unimproved.

Vacate To move out.

Value The worth or usefulness of a good or service, expressed in terms of a specific sum of money.

Variable Rate Mortgage (VRM) A mortgage with interest that varies with a specified interest rate; an adjustable rate mortgage.

Vendee A purchaser of real property.

Vendor A seller of real property.

Veterans Administration (VA) A governmental agency that provides home loans for eligible veterans.

Void Having no legal force.

Voluntary Lien A lien placed on property with the full consent of the owner.

Warehousing a Loan The packaging of a number of mortgages with the intent to sell them in the secondary mortgage market.

Warranty A promise contained in a contract.

Warranty Deed An instrument of conveyance containing an agreement by the grantee to defend the premises against the lawful claims of a third party and an assurance that the grantee is the property owner and will defend the title given.

Wholesaler A middleman who coordinates the raising of equity.

Will The disposition of one's property that takes place after one's death.

Without Recourse A mortgage that secures a note without recourse, which allows the lender to look only to the property in the event of a default.

Working Capital The difference between the current assets and current liabilities.

Workout Loan A loan in which the lender has agreed to reduce the debt service payment to avoid foreclosure of the property.

Wraparound Mortgage A mortgage that secures a debt and also includes the balance due under the existing debt plus any new funds advanced.

Write-Off The excess deductions from an investment which may be used to offset income taxes on income from other sources.

Yield A rate of return as calculated by the profit earned on the investment over a specified time period.

Zoning The act of a governing authority that specifies the uses for which property may be used or developed in a specific area.

STEP-BY-STEP CHECKLIST FOR A SYSTEMIZED APPROACH TO INVESTING

The following checklists are designed to assist the investor in following a systematic approach to acquiring real estate. These checklists will take the investor from the start of the due diligence process to the ultimate resale of the property.

Property Submittal. During this period the investor will determine the type of property to be acquired and investment criteria, and then start the search process.

Contracting. During the contracting period the investor will make the offer and contract for the property.

Inspection Period. During the inspection period the investor will assemble the inspection team and make the "go" or "no go" decision.

Financing. During the financing period the investor will obtain any needed financing.

Equity. During this period the investor will determine the equity requirements and seek the necessary investment partners.

Closing. During this period the investor will coordinate the final details of the deal in order to have a smooth closing.

Postclosing. During the postclosing period the investor will follow up on the closing details.

Asset Management. This checklist details the asset management duties after closing.

Resale. This checklist details the steps necessary to resell the property.

Property Submittal Checklist

PROPERTY NAME _____
PREPARED BY _____
DATE _____
PAGE ___ OF ___

DESCRIPTION	DATE STARTED	DATE COMPLETED	RESPONSIBILITY	COMMENTS
DECIDE ON TYPE OF INVESTMENT				
DETERMINE INVESTMENT VEHICLE				
DETERMINE INVESTMENT CRITERIA				
CONTACT REAL ESTATE BROKERS				
CONTACT PROPERTY OWNERS				
REVIEW PROPERTIES SUBMITTALS				
PRELIMINARY ANALYSIS OF DEAL				
VISIT PROPERTY				

FORM A-2
Contracting Checklist

PROPERTY NAME _____
PREPARED BY _____
DATE _____
PAGE ___ OF ___

DESCRIPTION	DATE STARTED	DATE COMPLETED	RESPONSIBILITY	COMMENTS
SEND OUT LETTER OF INTENT				
NEGOTIATE DEAL STRUCTURE				
SIGN LETTER OF INTENT				
ATTORNEY PREPARES CONTRACT				
NEGOTIATE CONTRACT DOCUMENTS				
SIGN CONTRACT				
PUT UP EARNEST MONEY				

FORM A-3
Inspection Period Checklist

PROPERTY NAME _____
PREPARED BY _____
DATE _____
PAGE ___ OF ___

DESCRIPTION	DATE STARTED	DATE COMPLETED	RESPONSIBILITY	COMMENTS
START DUE DILIGENCE PROCESS				
ASSEMBLE INSPECTION TEAM				
MANAGEMENT:				
PREPARE PROPERTY INFORMATION PACKAGE				
INSPECT PROPERTY				
REVIEW LEASES				
REVIEW OPERATING BUDGET				
REVIEW CAPITAL IMPROVEMENTS				
REVIEW INSURANCE				
REVIEW REAL ESTATE TAXES				
REVIEW INVENTORY				
MARKETING:				
REVIEW MARKETING STRATEGY				
REVIEW MARKETING BUDGET				
REVIEW SIGNAGE				
REVIEW MODEL				
REVIEW RENTAL RATE STRUCTURE				
CONSTRUCTION MANAGEMENT:				
REVIEW CONSTRUCTION REPORT				
ATTORNEY:				
ORDER AND REVIEW AS-BUILT SURVEY				
ORDER AND REVIEW ESTOPPEL LETTER				
ORDER AND REVIEW ZONING LETTER				
ORDER AND REVIEW UTILITY LETTERS				
ORDER AND REVIEW TITLE POLICY				
ORDER AND REVIEW MORTGAGE DOCUMENTS				
REVIEW PROPERTY EASEMENTS				
REVIEW INSURANCE POLICY				
REVIEW PROPERTY LIENS				
REVIEW SELLER'S ATTORNEY OPINION LETTER				
REVIEW DEVELOPMENT AND BUILDING PERMITS				
ORDER AND REVIEW TITLE SEARCH				
ACCOUNTANT:				
REVIEW PROPERTY OPERATING STATEMENTS				
PREPARE INVESTMENT INFORMATION PACKAGE				
REVIEW FINANCIAL PROJECTIONS				
QUALIFY POTENTIAL INVESTORS				
QUALIFY POTENTIAL MORTGAGE LENDERS				
APPRAISAL:				
DETERMINE APPRAISER & NEGOTIATE FEE STRUCTURE				
REVIEW APPRAISAL				
FEASIBILITY STUDY:				
DETERMINE APPRAISER & NEGOTIATE FEE STRUCTURE				
REVIEW APPRAISAL				
REVIEW ALL INFORMATION WITH INSPECTION TEAM				
DECIDE "GO" OR "NO GO"				
IF "NO GO":				
SEND TERMINATION LETTER				
GET REFUND OF EARNEST MONEY				
IF "GO":				
PREPARE TO CLOSE DEAL				

636

FORM A-4
Financing Checklist

PROPERTY NAME _____
PREPARED BY _____
DATE _____
PAGE ___ OF ___

DESCRIPTION	DATE STARTED	DATE COMPLETED	RESPONSIBILITY	COMMENTS
IF FINANCING NEEDED:				
DETERMINE LOAN AMOUNT NEEDED				
CONTACT POTENTIAL LENDERS				
CONTACT MORTGAGE BROKERS				
PREPARE LENDER PACKAGE				
FINALIZE LOAN SOURCE				
NEGOTIATE LOAN TERMS AND CONDITIONS				
RECEIVE LOAN COMMITMENT				
REVIEW LOAN COMMITMENT				
FINE TUNE LOAN COMMITMENT				
SIGN LOAN COMMITMENT				
PAY LOAN COMMITMENT FEE				
ATTORNEY TO REVIEW LOAN DOCUMENTS				
NEGOTIATE LOAN DOCUMENTS				
PREPARE TO CLOSE LOAN				
REVIEW LOAN CLOSING STATEMENT				
SIGN LOAN DOCUMENTS				
FUND LOAN PROCEEDS				
IF INVESTOR NOTE LOAN NEEDED:				
DETERMINE LOAN AMOUNT NEEDED				
CONTACT POTENTIAL LENDERS				
CONTACT MORTGAGE BROKERS				
PREPARE LENDER PACKAGE				
FINALIZE LOAN SOURCE				
NEGOTIATE LOAN TERMS AND CONDITIONS				
RECEIVE LOAN COMMITMENT				
REVIEW LOAN COMMITMENT				
FINE TUNE LOAN COMMITMENT				
SIGN LOAN COMMITMENT				
PAY LOAN COMMITMENT FEE				
ATTORNEY TO REVIEW LOAN DOCUMENTS				
NEGOTIATE LOAN DOCUMENTS				
PREPARE TO CLOSE LOAN				
IF SURETY BOND NEEDED:				
CONTACT POTENTIAL INSURANCE COMPANIES				
CONTACT INSURANCE AGENTS				
SEND OUT DEAL INFORMATION AND MEMORANDUM				
FINALIZE SURETY SOURCE				
NEGOTIATE LOAN TERMS AND CONDITIONS				
RECEIVE SURETY COMMITMENT				
REVIEW SURETY COMMITMENT				
FINE TUNE SURETY COMMITMENT				
SIGN SURETY COMMITMENT				
PAY SURETY COMMITMENT FEE				
ATTORNEY TO REVIEW DOCUMENTS				
NEGOTIATE DOCUMENTS				
PREPARE TO CLOSE SURETY AND LOAN				

PROPERTY NAME _____
PREPARED BY _____
DATE _____
PAGE ___ OF ___

DESCRIPTION	DATE STARTED	DATE COMPLETED	RESPONSIBILITY	COMMENTS
IF EQUITY REQUIRED:				
DETERMINE EQUITY REQUIREMENTS				
DETERMINE OWNERSHIP VEHICLE				
DETERMINE EQUITY SOURCE				
CHECK OUT EQUITY REFERENCES				
IF LIMITED PARTNERSHIP:				
CONTACT WHOLESALERS				
CONTACT POTENTIAL MONEY RAISERS				
DETERMINE MONEY RAISER FEE STRUCTURE				
DETERMINE GENERAL PARTNER FEE STRUCTURE				
DETERMINE DEAL STRUCTURE				
REVIEW SELLING AGREEMENT				
PREPARE MEMORANDUM				
REVIEW FIRST DRAFT OF MEMORANDUM				
FINALIZE MEMORANDUM				
OBTAIN BLUE SKY STATES				
APPLY FOR BLUE SKY CLEARANCE				
OBTAIN BLUE SKY CLEARANCE				
START MARKETING PROCESS				
REVIEW INVESTOR SUBSCRIPTION PACKAGE				
SIGN OFF ON SUBSCRIPTION PACKAGE				
PUT INITIAL CONTRIBUTION IN ESCROW ACCOUNT				
LOG IN EACH INVESTOR				
IF INVESTOR NOTE FINANCING:				
SEND COPY OF SUBSCRIPTION PACKAGE TO LENDER				
SEND COPIES OF PROMISSORY NOTES TO LENDER				
IF JOINT VENTURE:				
DETERMINE JOINT VENTURE PARTNER				
STRUCTURE DEAL				
NEGOTIATE DOCUMENTS				
SIGN DOCUMENTS				
FUND DEAL				
PUT FUNDS IN ESCROW ACCOUNT				

638

PROPERTY NAME _____
PREPARED BY _____
DATE _____
PAGE ___ OF ___

DESCRIPTION	DATE STARTED	DATE COMPLETED	RESPONSIBILITY	COMMENTS
MANAGING PARTNER:				
COORDINATE ALL TEAM MEMBERS	———	———	———	———
ASK ATTORNEY FOR ITEMS TO BRING TO CLOSING	———	———	———	———
ASSET MANAGER:				
SET UP DEAL FILE	———	———	———	———
ORDER TAX I.D. NUMBER	———	———	———	———
SET UP PARTNERSHIP BANK ACCOUNTS	———	———	———	———
REVIEW THE CLOSING STATEMENT	———	———	———	———
ORDER THE INSURANCE BINDER	———	———	———	———
CONSTRUCTION MANAGEMENT:				
REVIEW CONSTRUCTION DOCUMENTS	———	———	———	———
MANAGEMENT:				
SET UP ACCOUNTING SYSTEMS	———	———	———	———
SET UP BANK ACCOUNTS	———	———	———	———
VERIFY RENT ROLL & SECURITY DEPOSITS	———	———	———	———
VERIFY VACANT SPACE AS "RENT-READY"	———	———	———	———
COMPLETE PRORATIONS	———	———	———	———
REVIEW ALL RECENT LEASES	———	———	———	———
MARKETING:				
PREPARE TO MARKET PROPERTY	———	———	———	———
ATTORNEY:				
SET UP CLOSING DATE AND PLACE	———	———	———	———
ATTORNEY TO REVIEW ALL CLOSING DOCUMENTS	———	———	———	———
REVIEW CLOSING STATEMENT	———	———	———	———
SIGN DOCUMENTS	———	———	———	———
DISBURSE FUNDS	———	———	———	———

639

PROPERTY NAME _____
PREPARED BY _____
DATE _____
PAGE ___ OF ___

DESCRIPTION	DATE STARTED	DATE COMPLETED	RESPONSIBILITY	COMMENTS
MANAGING PARTNER:				
COORDINATE ALL TEAM MEMBERS				
ASSET MANAGEMENT:				
PREPARE AND DISTRIBUTE POSTCLOSING MEMO				
FILE ALL CLOSING DOCUMENTS				
SEND OUT INVESTOR LETTER				
MAKE SURE FIRST MONTH DEBT SERVICE IS PAID				
SET UP TICKLER SYSTEM				
REIMBURSE FRONT MONEY				
PAY DOWN LINES OF CREDIT				
PAY ALL DEAL FEES AND BILLS				
MANAGEMENT:				
NOTIFY TENANTS OF NEW MANAGEMENT				
NOTIFY VENDORS OF NEW OWNERSHIP				
NOTIFY UTILITY COMPANIES TO CHANGE DEPOSITS				
SET UP EMPLOYEE INSURANCE				
START PROPERTY IMPROVEMENTS				
PRORATE ALL LATE INCOME AND EXPENSES				
IF NEW CONSTRUCTION:				
PUNCH OUT PROPERTY				
REVIEW TWELVE-MONTH WARRANTY				
MARKETING:				
START MARKETING PROGRAM				
ACCOUNTANT:				
RECONCILE CLOSING EXPENSES				
ATTORNEY:				
RECORD ALL DOCUMENTS				
MAKE SURE ALL FUNDS ARE DISBURSED				
BIND ALL CLOSING DOCUMENTS				
CONSTRUCTION MANAGEMENT:				
COORDINATE ANY PROPERTY IMPROVEMENTS				
IF NEW CONSTRUCTION:				
REVIEW WEEKLY PROGRESS				
REVIEW CONSTRUCTION DRAWS				
REVIEW LIEN WAIVERS				
REVIEW FINAL PUNCH OUT				
REVIEW GC'S COMPLETION LETTER				
REVIEW LENDER'S COMPLETION LETTER				
REVIEW TWELVE-MONTH WARRANTY				

640

FORM A-8
Asset Management Checklist

PROPERTY NAME _____
PREPARED BY _____
DATE _____
PAGE ___ OF ___

DESCRIPTION	DATE STARTED	DATE COMPLETED	RESPONSIBILITY	COMMENTS
OVERSEE MANAGEMENT COMPANY				
REVIEW WEEKLY REPORTS:				
SUMMARY OF OPERATIONS				
PROSPECT REPORTS				
REVIEW MONTHLY:				
MONTHLY PROPERTY TRACKING				
STATEMENT OF INCOME AND EXPENSES				
VARIANCE REPORTS				
RECEIPT OF PARTNERSHIP SERVICE FEES				
REVIEW QUARTERLY:				
MARKET COMPARABLE STUDY				
INVESTOR PARTNERSHIP LETTERS				
PROPERTY INSPECTION VISITS				
REVIEW YEARLY:				
BUDGET				
CAPITAL IMPROVEMENT BUDGET				
TAX RETURNS				
TAX AUDIT				
INVESTOR CALL FOR FUNDS				
IF PROPERTY IS SOLD WITH SELLER FINANCING:				
MONTHLY SELLER FINANCING TRACKING REPORT				

641

FORM A-9
Resale Checklist

PROPERTY NAME _____
PREPARED BY _____
DATE _____
PAGE ___ OF ___

DESCRIPTION	DATE STARTED	DATE COMPLETED	RESPONSIBILITY	COMMENTS
RESALE:				
MAKE DECISION TO SELL				
DECIDE ASKING PRICE AND TERMS				
PREPARE THE RESALE PACKAGE				
CONTACT REAL ESTATE BROKERS				
DETERMINE LIST OF POTENTIAL PURCHASERS				
SEND OUT RESALE PACKAGE				
COLLECT OFFERS				
REVIEW OFFERS				
NEGOTIATE COUNTEROFFERS				
FINALIZE DEAL				
ACCOUNTANT TO REVIEW DEAL				
PREPARE THE PURCHASE CONTRACT				
NEGOTIATE PURCHASE CONTRACT				
RECEIVE EARNEST MONEY				
SUPPLY PURCHASER WITH NEEDED DOCUMENTS				
BALLOT INVESTORS				
PREPARE TO CLOSE DEAL				
DISTRIBUTE PROFITS				
IF SELLER FINANCING:				
ADMINISTRATE MORTGAGE PROCEEDS				

642

DUE DILIGENCE CHECKLIST FOR APARTMENT PROPERTIES

Due Diligence Checklist for Apartment Properties

PROPERTY NAME: _____
ADDRESS: _____
CITY: _____ STATE: _____ COUNTY: _____
TEL. NO. (____) _____

PROPERTY HISTORY

DESCRIPTION	DATE SEND	DATE RECEIVED	REVIEWED BY	COMMENTS
Original Developer				
Year(s) Built				
Last sale price/date				
Land cost				

LEASING INFORMATION & POLICIES

DESCRIPTION	DATE SEND	DATE RECEIVED	REVIEWED BY	COMMENTS
I. LEASE INFORMATION				
Copy of standard lease/application forms				
Copies of all management forms				
Copies of all current leases				
Copy of current rent roll				
Copy of current security deposits				
Copy of rent concession schedule				
Copy of credit report				
Copy of resident profile				
II. RENTAL INFORMATION				
Current street rents per unit type				
Current rent concession policy				
Current list of free units				
III. TENANT RENTAL POLICY				
Rent qualification policy				
Application fee policy				
Security deposit policy				
Lease term policy				
Month-to-month rent policy				

Due Diligence Checklist for Apartment Properties (Cont'd)

PROPERTY NAME: _____

ADDRESS: _____

CITY: _____ STATE: _____ COUNTY: _____

TEL. NO. (____) _____

LEASING INFORMATION & POLICIES (CONT'D)

DESCRIPTION	DATE SEND	DATE RECEIVED	REVIEWED BY	COMMENTS
IV. PET POLICY				
List of all units with pets (type)				
Current pet pound limit				
Current pet deposit/fee policy				

MARKETING

DESCRIPTION	DATE SEND	DATE RECEIVED	REVIEWED BY	COMMENTS
Copy of current marketing plan				
Copies of all advertising				
Copy of current brochure/floor plans/site plan				
Pictures of property and comparables				
Copies of all market studies				

FINANCIAL & OPERATING REPORTS

DESCRIPTION	DATE SEND	DATE RECEIVED	REVIEWED BY	COMMENTS
I. OPERATING FINANCIAL STATEMENTS				
Detailed annual operating statements—last 3 years				
Monthly details for last 12 months with notes				
Current year's budget—month-to-month with notes				
Signed document all statements are accurate				
Audited financial statements last 2 years				
II. BOOKKEEPING REPORTS				
Current copy of delinquency report				
Copy of last 12 month delinquency report				
Current prepaid rent report				

Due Diligence Checklist for Apartment Properties (Cont'd)

PROPERTY NAME: _____

ADDRESS: _____

CITY: _____ STATE: _____ COUNTY: _____

TEL. NO. (___) _____

FINANCIAL & OPERATING REPORTS (CONT'D)

DESCRIPTION	DATE SEND	DATE RECEIVED	REVIEWED BY	COMMENTS
III. OCCUPANCY HISTORY				
Current vacancy report (per unit type)				
Last 3 year (month-month) vacancy history				
IV. LEASING REPORTS				
Current Property Status Report				
Lease Expiration Report (month-to-month)				
Month-month tenant Report				
V. MANAGEMENT REPORTS				
Traffic Reports				
Market Rent Devisation Report				
Days Vacant Report				
Pending Rent Change Report				
Rent Comparable Report—last 12 months (5-7 comparables)				
VI. MONTH-TO-DATE BOOKKEEPING REPORTS				
Month-to-Date Deposit Recap				
Cash Receipt Journal				
Month-to-Date Returned Items				
Charge/Adjustment Journal				
Automatic Charge Journal				
Month-to-Date Collections				
Security Deposit Control Report				
Activity Reconciliation Report (Detail)				
Activity Reconciliation Summary				
VII. BANK RECORDS				
Bank deposits for the last 12 months				
Bank statements for the last 12 months				
VIII. MISCELLANEOUS REPORTS				
Income Forecast Report				
Comprehensive Audit Report				

Due Diligence Checklist for Apartment Properties (Cont'd)

PROPERTY NAME: _____

ADDRESS: _____

CITY: _____ STATE: _____ COUNTY: _____

TEL. NO. ( ) _____

INCOME & EXPENSE INFORMATION

DESCRIPTION	DATE SEND	DATE RECEIVED	REVIEWED BY	COMMENTS
INCOME ITEMS				
List of Miscellaneous Income Items				
OPERATING EXPENSE ITEMS				
General & Administrative				
List of 12 month supplies required				
Copies of current office equipment leases				
List of local memberships				
Management Payroll				
List of staff—names, employment history/salaries/benefits				
Maintenance Payroll				
List of staff—names, employment history/salaries/benefits				
Marketing				
Copy of current marketing budget				
Copies of all current advertisements				
Utilities				
Utility logs/invoices—last 3 years by month/acct. #				
Utility names/telephone #, account #				
List of utility deposits/bonds				
Current utility rate charges/Potential utility increases				
Energy audit on all common area/vacant units—last 12 months				
Repairs & Maintenance				
Last 3 years work order history log				
List of recurring maintenance problems				
Real Estate Taxes				
Current Real Estate Tax Bill				
Past 2 years Real Estate Tax Bill				
Insurance				
Copy of current insurance policy & riders				
List of insurance claims—last 3 years				
Reserve Replacement				
List of current items replaced last 3 years				

647

Due Diligence Checklist for Apartment Properties (Cont'd)

PROPERTY NAME: _____

ADDRESS: _____

CITY: _____ STATE: _____ COUNTY: _____

TEL. NO. (___) _____

INVENTORY

DESCRIPTION	DATE SEND	DATE RECEIVED	REVIEWED BY	COMMENTS
Office Inventory				
Clubhouse Inventory				
Maintenance Shop Inventory—Tools/supplies				
Amenity Inventory				
Pool Inventory				
Unit Appliance Inventory/Model—Serial #'s				

STUDIES

DESCRIPTION	DATE SEND	DATE RECEIVED	REVIEWED BY	COMMENTS
Phase I Environmental Study				
Phase II Environmental Study				
Appraisal				
Soils Test				
Test/pest Inspection Report				
Structural Inspection Report				
Drainage Inspection Report				

FINANCING

DESCRIPTION	DATE SEND	DATE RECEIVED	REVIEWED BY	COMMENTS
Loan Documents				
Loan prepayment calculations				

LEGAL DOCUMENTS

DESCRIPTION	DATE SEND	DATE RECEIVED	REVIEWED BY	COMMENTS
Rent control ordinances				
Legal description				
Seller's certification that property meets all state/local codes				
Copies of zoning letter				
Copies of all utility letters				

648

Due Diligence Checklist for Apartment Properties (Cont'd)

PROPERTY NAME: _____

ADDRESS: _____

CITY: _____ STATE: _____ COUNTY: _____

TEL. NO. (___) _____

CONSTRUCTION DOCUMENTS

DESCRIPTION	DATE SEND	DATE RECEIVED	REVIEWED BY	COMMENTS
"As Built" survey				
Site plan				
Copy of original building plans and specifications				
List of subcontractors/telephone #/contact				
List of material suppliers/telephone #/contact				
Copies of all warranties				
Site diagram with unit numbers				
If new construction project				
List of change orders				
Copy of all construction manager reports				
Copy of all building/development permits				
Copies of certificates of occupancies				
Copy of general contractor's contract				
Copies of all soil compaction tests				
Copies of all concrete stress tests				
Copy of Architect's Certificate of Completion				
Copies of all mechanical approvals				
Copies of all plumbing approvals				
Copies of all electrical approvals				
Copies of all elevator approvals/inspection reports				
Certificate of total gross/net square footage				
Copy of fire marshall inspection reports				
Copy of truss calculations				
Copy of material safety data sheets for materials				
Copies of all operating manuals				

Due Diligence Checklist for Apartment Properties (Cont'd)

PROPERTY NAME: _____

ADDRESS: _____

CITY: _____ STATE: _____ COUNTY: _____

TEL. NO. (____) ____

CONTRACTS/SERVICE AGREEMENTS

DESCRIPTION	VENDOR	CONTRACT	TEL. NO.	MONTHLY COST	CONTRACT EXPIRATION
Landscaping					
Sweeping Service					
Snow Removal					
Chimney Cleaning					
Pest Control					
Lae Treatment					
Vending Machines					
Coin Operated Laundry					
In-unit W/D Rentals					
Security System					
Security Patrol					
Cable Television					
Pool Service					
Pager Service					
Answering Service					
Copier Service					
Fax Service					
Telephone Equipment Service					
Eviction Service					
Credit Bureau					
Chamber of Commerce					
Apartment Association Membership					
Interior Plant Maintenance Service					
PUD Association Fee					
Furniture Rental—Units					
Furniture Rental—Clubhouse					
Yellow Page Listing					
Offsite Billboard Rental					
Advertising Contracts					
Business Permits					
Rental Agency Agreements					
Apartment Guide Agreements					
Printing Contracts					
Apartment Turnkey Agreements					
Apartment Painting Agreements					
Apartment Carpet Agreements					
Maid Service Agreements					
Courier Agreements					

650

APARTMENT ACQUISITION TIME LINE

Apartment Acquisition Time Line

PROPERTY ______________________________

LOCATION ______________________________

DATE ____

DESCRIPTION/WEEK

RESPONSIBILTY

PRELIMINARY:
- REVIEW BROKER'S SALES PACKAGE
- PREPARE PRELIMINARY PROFORMA
- VISIT PROPERTY/DRIVE AREA
- PREPARE PRELIMINARY MARKET STUDY
- PREPARE LETTER OF INTENT
- PREPARE AND NEGOTIATE PURCHASE CONTRACT
- PUT UP EARNEST MONEY

DUE DILIGENCE:
- SITE INSPECTION—UNIT WALK THRU
- NEIGHBORHOOD SITE INSPECTION/POLICE REVIEW
- REVIEW THE LEASES/RENT ROLL
- REVIEW SERVICE CONTRACTS
- REVIEW ALL PROPERTY FINANCIAL STATEMENTS
- ORDER STRUCTURAL STUDY
- REVIEW STRUCTURAL STUDY
- ORDER PHASE I ENVIRONMENTAL STUDY
- REVIEW PHASE I ENVIRONMENTAL STUDY
- PREPARE FINAL PROPERTY BUDGET/CAP. EXPENDITURES
- PREPARE PROPERTY FINAL PROFORMA
- ORDER TITLE POLICY
- REVIEW TITLE POLICY
- REVIEW LOAN DOCUMENTS
- DETERMINE IF "GO" OR "NO GO"
  - IF "NO GO" TERMINATE CONTRACT
  - IF "NO GO" GET EARNEST MONEY REFUND

EQUITY:
- PREPARE LIST OF POTENTIAL INVESTORS
- CONTACT POTENTIAL INVESTORS
- MAKE INVESTOR PRESENTATION
- PREPARE INVESTOR DOCUMENTS
- COLLECT INVESTOR FUNDS

FINANCING:
- PREPARE LIST OF POTENTIAL LENDERS
- CONTACT POTENTIAL LENDERS
- REVIEW POTENTIAL DEALS
- MAKE LOAN APPLICATION
- REVIEW LOAN COMMITMENT
- OBTAIN APPRAISAL
- REVIEW APPRAISAL

POST RISK PERIOD:
- PREPARE CLOSING DOCUMENTS
- MONITOR PROPERTY PROGRESS

THE CLOSING DAY:
- PREPARE CLOSING STATEMENTS & PRORATIONS
- CONFIRM VACANT UNITS
- CONFIRM SECURITY DEPOSIT ACCOUNT
- CLOSE LOAN
- CLOSE PROPERTY

POST CLOSING:
- RECORD CLOSING DOCUMENTS
- PREPARE POST CLOSING MEMO
- TAKE OVER MANAGEMENT

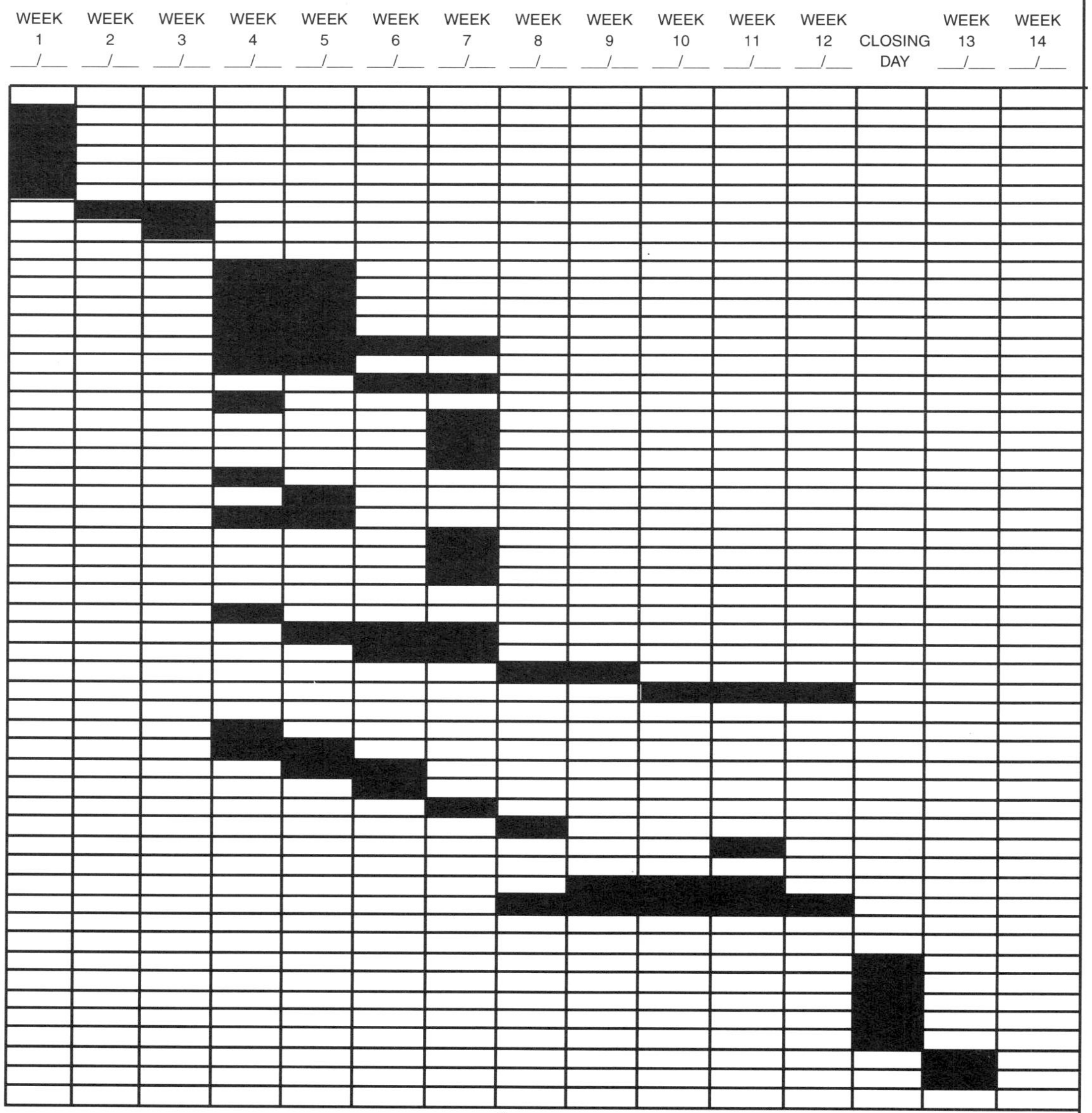

WEEK 1 ___/___
WEEK 2 ___/___
WEEK 3 ___/___
WEEK 4 ___/___
WEEK 5 ___/___
WEEK 6 ___/___
WEEK 7 ___/___
WEEK 8 ___/___
WEEK 9 ___/___
WEEK 10 ___/___
WEEK 11 ___/___
WEEK 12 ___/___
CLOSING DAY
WEEK 13 ___/___
WEEK 14 ___/___

ANNUAL MORTGAGE CONSTANT TABLES

The following tables are used to determine the annual mortgage constant for various types of loans. An annual constant is the sum of twelve monthly payments that are expressed in a percentage of a principal loan amount. The formula for this annual constant is as follows:

$$\text{Annual Constant} = \frac{1200 \times \text{Monthly Payment}}{\text{Loan Amount}}$$

$$\text{Monthly Payment} = \frac{\text{Annual Constant} \times \text{Loan Amount}}{1200}$$

Example: For a $200,000 loan amortized over thirty years at 10.0 percent interest, the monthly payment is $1,755.00.

MORTGAGE CONSTANT TABLE

Annual Percentage in Percent to Amortize a Principal Sum Assuming Monthly Payments

YEARS RATE	10	11	12	13	14	15	16	17	18	19	20	21
8%	14.56	13.70	12.99	12.40	11.90	11.47	11.10	10.78	10.50	10.25	10.04	9.85
8⅛%	14.64	13.78	13.07	12.48	11.98	11.55	11.19	10.87	10.59	10.35	10.13	9.94
8¼%	14.72	13.86	13.15	12.56	12.07	11.64	11.28	10.96	10.68	10.44	10.22	10.04
8⅜%	14.80	13.94	13.24	12.65	12.15	11.73	11.36	11.05	10.77	10.53	10.32	10.13
8½%	14.88	14.02	13.32	12.73	12.24	11.82	11.45	11.14	10.87	10.63	10.41	10.23
8⅝%	14.96	14.11	13.40	12.82	12.33	11.90	11.54	11.23	10.96	10.72	10.51	10.32
8¾%	15.04	14.19	13.49	12.90	12.41	11.99	11.63	11.32	11.05	10.81	10.60	10.42
8⅞%	15.12	14.27	13.57	12.99	12.50	12.08	11.72	11.41	11.14	10.91	10.70	10.52
9%	15.20	14.35	13.66	13.08	12.59	12.17	11.81	11.51	11.24	11.00	10.80	10.61
9⅛%	15.28	14.44	13.74	13.16	12.68	12.26	11.91	11.60	11.33	11.10	10.89	10.71
9¼%	15.36	14.52	13.83	13.25	12.76	12.35	12.00	11.69	11.43	11.19	10.99	10.81
9⅜%	15.45	14.60	13.91	13.34	12.85	12.44	12.09	11.78	11.52	11.29	11.09	10.91
9½%	15.53	14.69	14.00	13.42	12.94	12.53	12.18	11.88	11.61	11.39	11.19	11.01
9⅝%	15.61	14.77	14.08	13.51	13.03	12.62	12.27	11.97	11.71	11.48	11.28	11.11
9¾%	15.69	14.85	14.17	13.60	13.12	12.71	12.36	12.07	11.81	11.58	11.38	11.21
9⅞%	15.78	14.94	14.25	13.69	13.21	12.80	12.46	12.16	11.90	11.68	11.48	11.31
10%	15.86	15.02	14.34	13.77	13.30	12.90	12.55	12.25	12.00	11.78	11.58	11.41
10⅛%	15.94	15.11	14.43	13.86	13.39	12.99	12.64	12.35	12.09	11.87	11.68	11.51
10¼%	16.02	15.19	14.51	13.95	13.48	13.08	12.74	12.45	12.19	11.97	11.78	11.61
10⅜%	16.11	15.28	14.60	14.04	13.57	13.17	12.83	12.54	12.29	12.07	11.88	11.71
10½%	16.19	15.37	14.69	14.13	13.66	13.26	12.93	12.64	12.39	12.17	11.98	11.82
10⅝%	16.28	15.45	14.78	14.22	13.75	13.36	13.02	12.73	12.48	12.27	12.08	11.92
10¾%	16.36	15.54	14.87	14.31	13.84	13.45	13.12	12.83	12.58	12.37	12.18	12.02
10⅞%	16.45	15.62	14.95	14.40	13.94	13.55	13.21	12.93	12.68	12.47	12.28	12.12
11%	16.53	15.71	15.04	14.49	14.03	13.64	13.31	13.02	12.78	12.57	12.39	12.23
11⅛%	16.62	15.80	15.13	14.58	14.12	13.73	13.40	13.12	12.88	12.67	12.49	12.33
11¼%	16.70	15.89	15.22	14.67	14.21	13.83	13.50	13.22	12.98	12.77	12.59	12.43
11⅜%	16.79	15.97	15.31	14.76	14.31	13.92	13.60	13.32	13.08	12.87	12.69	12.54
11½%	16.87	16.06	15.40	14.86	14.40	14.02	13.69	13.42	13.18	12.97	12.80	12.64
11⅝%	16.96	16.15	15.49	14.95	14.49	14.11	13.79	13.52	13.28	13.08	12.90	12.75
11¾%	17.04	16.24	15.58	15.04	14.59	14.21	13.89	13.62	13.38	13.18	13.00	12.85
11⅞%	17.13	16.32	15.67	15.13	14.68	14.31	13.99	13.71	13.48	13.28	13.11	12.96
12%	17.22	16.41	15.76	15.22	14.78	14.40	14.08	13.81	13.58	13.38	13.21	13.06
12⅛%	17.30	16.50	15.85	15.32	14.87	14.50	14.18	13.91	13.69	13.49	13.32	13.17
12¼%	17.39	16.59	15.94	15.41	14.97	14.60	14.28	14.02	13.79	13.59	13.42	13.28
12⅜%	17.48	16.68	16.03	15.50	15.06	14.69	14.38	14.12	13.89	13.70	13.53	13.38
12½%	17.57	16.77	16.13	15.60	15.16	14.79	14.48	14.22	13.99	13.80	13.63	13.49
12⅝%	17.65	16.86	16.22	15.69	15.25	14.89	14.58	14.32	14.09	13.90	13.74	13.60
12¾%	17.74	16.95	16.31	15.79	15.35	14.99	14.68	14.42	14.20	14.01	13.85	13.71
12⅞%	17.83	17.04	16.40	15.88	15.45	15.08	14.78	14.52	14.30	14.11	13.95	13.81
13%	17.92	17.13	16.50	15.97	15.54	15.18	14.88	14.62	14.41	14.22	14.06	13.92
13⅛%	18.01	17.22	16.59	16.07	15.64	15.28	14.98	14.73	14.51	14.32	14.17	14.03
13¼%	18.09	17.31	16.68	16.16	15.74	15.38	15.08	14.83	14.61	14.43	14.27	14.14
13⅜%	18.18	17.40	16.77	16.26	15.83	15.48	15.18	14.93	14.72	14.54	14.38	14.25
13½%	18.27	17.50	16.87	16.36	15.93	15.58	15.28	15.03	14.82	14.64	14.49	14.36
13⅝%	18.36	17.59	16.96	16.45	16.03	15.68	15.39	15.14	14.93	14.75	14.60	14.47
13¾%	18.45	17.68	17.06	16.55	16.13	15.78	15.49	15.24	15.03	14.86	14.70	14.58
13⅞%	18.54	17.77	17.15	16.64	16.23	15.88	15.59	15.35	15.14	14.96	14.81	14.69
14%	18.63	17.86	17.25	16.74	16.33	15.98	15.69	15.45	15.24	15.07	14.92	14.80
14⅛%	18.72	17.96	17.34	16.84	16.42	16.08	15.80	15.55	15.35	15.18	15.03	14.91
14¼%	18.81	18.05	17.44	16.94	16.52	16.18	15.90	15.66	15.46	15.29	15.14	15.02
14⅜%	18.90	18.14	17.53	17.03	16.62	16.28	16.00	15.76	15.56	15.39	15.25	15.13
14½%	18.99	18.24	17.63	17.13	16.72	16.39	16.10	15.87	15.67	15.50	15.36	15.24
14⅝%	19.09	18.33	17.72	17.23	16.82	16.49	16.21	15.97	15.78	15.61	15.47	15.35
14¾%	19.18	18.42	17.82	17.33	16.92	16.59	16.31	16.08	15.88	15.72	15.58	15.46
14⅞%	19.27	18.52	17.91	17.42	17.02	16.69	16.42	16.19	15.99	15.83	15.69	15.57
15%	19.36	18.61	18.01	17.52	17.12	16.80	16.52	16.29	16.10	15.94	15.80	15.69
15⅛%	19.45	18.71	18.11	17.62	17.23	16.90	16.63	16.40	16.21	16.05	15.91	15.80
15¼%	19.54	18.80	18.20	17.72	17.33	17.00	16.73	16.51	16.32	16.16	16.02	15.91
15⅜%	19.64	18.89	18.30	17.82	17.43	17.10	16.84	16.61	16.43	16.27	16.13	16.02
15½%	19.73	18.99	18.40	17.92	17.53	17.21	16.94	16.72	16.53	16.38	16.25	16.14
15⅝%	19.82	19.08	18.50	18.02	17.63	17.31	17.05	16.83	16.64	16.49	16.36	16.25
15¾%	19.92	19.18	18.59	18.12	17.73	17.42	17.15	16.93	16.75	16.60	16.47	16.36
15⅞%	20.01	19.28	18.69	18.22	17.84	17.52	17.26	17.04	16.86	16.71	16.58	16.48

22	23	24	25	26	27	28	29	30	31	32	33	34	35
9.67	9.52	9.38	9.26	9.15	9.05	8.96	8.88	8.81	8.74	8.68	8.62	8.57	8.52
9.77	9.62	9.48	9.36	9.25	9.15	9.06	8.98	8.91	8.84	8.78	8.73	8.68	8.63
9.87	9.72	9.58	9.46	9.35	9.26	9.17	9.09	9.02	8.95	8.89	8.84	8.79	8.74
9.96	9.81	9.68	9.56	9.45	9.36	9.27	9.19	9.12	9.06	9.00	8.94	8.90	8.85
10.06	9.91	9.78	9.66	9.56	9.46	9.37	9.30	9.23	9.16	9.11	9.05	9.01	8.96
10.16	10.01	9.88	9.76	9.66	9.56	9.48	9.40	9.33	9.27	9.21	9.16	9.12	9.07
10.26	10.11	9.98	9.87	9.76	9.67	9.58	9.51	9.44	9.38	9.32	9.27	9.23	9.18
10.36	10.21	10.08	9.97	9.87	9.77	9.69	9.62	9.55	9.49	9.43	9.38	9.34	9.30
10.45	10.31	10.18	10.07	9.97	9.88	9.80	9.72	9.66	9.60	9.54	9.49	9.45	9.41
10.55	10.41	10.29	10.17	10.07	9.98	9.90	9.83	9.76	9.70	9.65	9.60	9.56	9.52
10.65	10.51	10.39	10.28	10.18	10.09	10.01	9.94	9.87	9.81	9.76	9.71	9.67	9.63
10.75	10.61	10.49	10.38	10.28	10.19	10.12	10.04	9.98	9.92	9.87	9.83	9.78	9.75
10.85	10.72	10.59	10.48	10.39	10.30	10.22	10.15	10.09	10.03	9.98	9.94	9.90	9.86
10.95	10.82	10.70	10.59	10.49	10.41	10.33	10.26	10.20	10.14	10.09	10.05	10.01	9.97
11.06	10.92	10.80	10.69	10.60	10.51	10.44	10.37	10.31	10.26	10.21	10.16	10.12	10.09
11.16	11.02	10.90	10.80	10.71	10.62	10.55	10.48	10.42	10.37	10.32	10.28	10.24	10.20
11.26	11.13	11.01	10.90	10.81	10.73	10.66	10.59	10.53	10.48	10.43	10.39	10.35	10.32
11.36	11.23	11.11	11.01	10.92	10.84	10.76	10.70	10.64	10.59	10.54	10.50	10.46	10.43
11.46	11.33	11.22	11.12	11.03	10.95	10.87	10.81	10.75	10.70	10.66	10.62	10.58	10.55
11.57	11.44	11.32	11.22	11.13	11.05	10.98	10.92	10.86	10.81	10.77	10.73	10.69	10.66
11.67	11.54	11.43	11.33	11.24	11.16	11.09	11.03	10.98	10.93	10.88	10.84	10.81	10.78
11.77	11.65	11.54	11.44	11.35	11.27	11.20	11.14	11.09	11.04	11.00	10.96	10.92	10.89
11.88	11.75	11.64	11.55	11.46	11.38	11.32	11.26	11.20	11.15	11.11	11.07	11.04	11.01
11.98	11.86	11.75	11.65	11.57	11.49	11.43	11.37	11.31	11.27	11.23	11.19	11.16	11.13
12.09	11.96	11.86	11.76	11.68	11.60	11.54	11.48	11.43	11.38	11.34	11.30	11.27	11.24
12.19	12.07	11.96	11.87	11.79	11.71	11.65	11.59	11.54	11.50	11.46	11.42	11.39	11.36
12.30	12.18	12.07	11.98	11.90	11.83	11.76	11.71	11.66	11.61	11.57	11.54	11.51	11.48
12.40	12.28	12.18	12.09	12.01	11.94	11.87	11.82	11.77	11.73	11.69	11.65	11.62	11.60
12.51	12.39	12.29	12.20	12.12	12.05	11.99	11.93	11.88	11.84	11.80	11.77	11.74	11.71
12.61	12.50	12.40	12.31	12.23	12.16	12.10	12.05	12.00	11.96	11.92	11.89	11.86	11.83
12.72	12.61	12.51	12.42	12.34	12.27	12.21	12.16	12.11	12.07	12.04	12.00	11.97	11.95
12.83	12.71	12.62	12.53	12.45	12.38	12.33	12.27	12.23	12.19	12.15	12.12	12.09	12.07
12.94	12.82	12.72	12.64	12.56	12.50	12.44	12.39	12.34	12.30	12.27	12.24	12.21	12.19
13.04	12.93	12.83	12.75	12.68	12.61	12.55	12.50	12.46	12.42	12.39	12.36	12.33	12.31
13.15	13.04	12.94	12.86	12.79	12.72	12.67	12.62	12.57	12.54	12.50	12.47	12.45	12.42
13.26	13.15	13.06	12.97	12.90	12.84	12.78	12.73	12.69	12.65	12.62	12.59	12.57	12.54
13.37	13.26	13.17	13.08	13.01	12.95	12.90	12.85	12.81	12.77	12.74	12.71	12.68	12.66
13.48	13.37	13.28	13.20	13.13	13.06	13.01	12.96	12.92	12.89	12.86	12.83	12.80	12.78
13.58	13.48	13.39	13.31	13.24	13.18	13.13	13.08	13.04	13.01	12.97	12.95	12.92	12.90
13.69	13.59	13.50	13.42	13.35	13.29	13.24	13.20	13.16	13.12	13.09	13.07	13.04	13.02
13.80	13.70	13.61	13.53	13.47	13.41	13.36	13.31	13.27	13.24	13.21	13.18	13.16	13.14
13.91	13.81	13.72	13.65	13.58	13.52	13.47	13.43	13.39	13.36	13.33	13.30	13.28	13.26
14.02	13.92	13.84	13.76	13.70	13.64	13.59	13.55	13.51	13.48	13.45	13.42	13.40	13.38
14.13	14.03	13.95	13.87	13.81	13.75	13.71	13.66	13.63	13.60	13.57	13.54	13.52	13.50
14.24	14.15	14.06	13.99	13.92	13.87	13.82	13.78	13.74	13.71	13.69	13.66	13.64	13.62
14.35	14.26	14.17	14.10	14.04	13.99	13.94	13.90	13.86	13.83	13.81	13.78	13.76	13.74
14.46	14.37	14.29	14.22	14.15	14.10	14.06	14.02	13.98	13.95	13.93	13.90	13.88	13.87
14.58	14.48	14.40	14.33	14.27	14.22	14.17	14.13	14.10	14.07	14.04	14.02	14.00	13.99
14.69	14.59	14.51	14.45	14.39	14.33	14.29	14.25	14.22	14.19	14.16	14.14	14.12	14.11
14.80	14.71	14.63	14.56	14.50	14.45	14.41	14.37	14.34	14.31	14.28	14.26	14.25	14.23
14.91	14.82	14.74	14.68	14.62	14.57	14.53	14.49	14.46	14.43	14.40	14.38	14.37	14.35
15.02	14.93	14.86	14.79	14.73	14.68	14.64	14.61	14.58	14.55	14.53	14.50	14.49	14.47
15.14	15.05	14.97	14.91	14.85	14.80	14.76	14.73	14.69	14.67	14.65	14.63	14.61	14.59
15.25	15.16	15.09	15.02	14.97	14.92	14.88	14.84	14.81	14.79	14.77	14.75	14.73	14.72
15.36	15.27	15.20	15.14	15.08	15.04	15.00	14.96	14.93	14.91	14.89	14.87	14.85	14.84
15.47	15.39	15.32	15.25	15.20	15.15	15.12	15.08	15.05	15.03	15.01	14.99	14.97	14.96
15.59	15.50	15.43	15.37	15.32	15.27	15.23	15.20	15.17	15.15	15.13	15.11	15.09	15.08
15.70	15.62	15.55	15.49	15.43	15.39	15.35	15.32	15.29	15.27	15.25	15.23	15.22	15.20
15.81	15.73	15.66	15.60	15.55	15.51	15.47	15.44	15.41	15.39	15.37	15.35	15.34	15.33
15.93	15.85	15.78	15.72	15.67	15.63	15.59	15.56	15.53	15.51	15.49	15.48	15.46	15.45
16.04	15.96	15.89	15.84	15.79	15.75	15.71	15.68	15.65	15.63	15.61	15.60	15.58	15.57
16.16	16.08	16.01	15.95	15.91	15.86	15.83	15.80	15.77	15.75	15.73	15.72	15.71	15.69
16.27	16.19	16.13	16.07	16.02	15.98	15.95	15.92	15.90	15.87	15.86	15.84	15.83	15.82
16.39	16.31	16.24	16.19	16.14	16.10	16.07	16.04	16.02	16.00	15.98	15.96	15.95	15.94

THE SIX MULTIPLIERS OF MONEY

The compounding of money is very significant when determining value in a real estate transaction. Money can be compounded either over time or value today for a payment that will not be received until sometime in the future. There are six factors in calculating these values. They are as follows:

TYPE OF TABLE	WHAT IT SHOWS	RELATIONS TO OTHER TABLES
Future Worth of 1 (FW1)	Growth at compound interest of a single initial deposit or investment	S = (1 = i)n
Future Worth of 1 per Period (FW1/P)	Growth at compound interest of a level series of periodic deposits	Sum of Preceding Future Worth of 1 Factors Plus 1
Sinking Fund (SF)	Amount of periodic deposit required which will grow at compound interest to a specified future amount	Reciprocal of Future Worth of 1 per Period (or Periodic Repayment less 1)
Present Worth of 1 (PW1)	Present worth of a single future income payment	Reciprocal of Future Worth of 1
Present Worth of 1 per Period (PW1/P)	Present worth of a series of future income payments	Sum of Present Worth of 1 factors
Periodic Repayment (Partial Payment) (PR)	Amount of periodic payment required to amortize a loan	Reciprocal of Present Worth of 1 per Period (or Sinking Fund Plus 1)

EXAMPLES

Future Worth of 1

What is the estimated value of a parcel of land purchased for $15,000 and held for five years, located in an area where land values are appreciating at 10 percent per year compounded?

$$\$15,000 \times 1.610510 = \$24,157.65$$

Future Worth of 1 per Period

A man deposits $100 per year into a savings account that pays 10 percent compounded annually. What will the value of this account be in five years?

$$\$100 \times 6.105100 = \$610.51$$

Sinking Fund

An investor plans to repave a driveway of an apartment property in ten years at an estimated cost of $25,000. How much money must be deposited annually for ten years into a sinking fund account paying 10 percent compounded annually?

$$\$25,000 \times .062745 = \$1,568.63$$

Present Worth of 1

An investor is looking at a piece of land that he feels will be worth $9,000 per acre in six years. At a yield rate of 10 percent per annum, what is its present worth today?

$$\$9,000 \times .564474 = \$5,080.27$$

Present Worth of 1 per Period

A ground lease runs for twenty years at an annual rental of $15,000 net. What is the present worth of the lease at a yield of 10 percent?

$$\$15,000 \times 8.513564 = \$127,703.46$$

Periodic Repayment

What yearly repayment would amortize a loan of $50,000 at 10 percent interest for thirty years?

$$\$50,000 \times .106079 = \$5,303.95$$

The following table should be used for these examples.

10%   **Annual Compound Interest Table**   **10%**

Effective Rate = 10%   **Base = 1.10**

YEARS	1 AMOUNT OF 1 AT COMPOUND INTEREST $S^n=(1+I)^n$	2 ACCUMULATION OF 1 PER PERIOD $S_{\overline{n}}=\frac{S^n-1}{I}$	3 SINKING FUND FACTOR $1/S_{\overline{n}}=\frac{I}{S^n-1}$	4 PRES. VALUE REVERSION OF 1 $V^n=\frac{1}{S^n}$	5 PRESENT VALUE ORD. ANNUITY 1 PER PERIOD $a_{\overline{n}}=\frac{1-V^n}{I}$	6 INSTALLMENT TO AMORTIZE 1 $1/a_{\overline{n}}=\frac{I}{1-V^n}$	n YEARS
1	1.100000	1.000000	1.000000	.909091	.909091	1.100000	1
2	1.210000	2.100000	.476190	.826446	1.735537	.576190	2
3	1.331000	3.310000	.302115	.751315	2.486852	.402115	3
4	1.464100	4.641000	.215471	.683013	3.169865	.315471	4
5	1.610510	6.105100	.163797	.620921	3.790787	.263797	5
6	1.771561	7.715610	.129607	.564474	4.355261	.229607	6
7	1.948717	9.487171	.105405	.513158	4.868419	.205405	7
8	2.143589	11.435888	.087444	.466507	5.334926	.187444	8
9	2.357948	13.579477	.073641	.424098	5.759024	.173641	9
10	2.593742	15.937425	.062745	.385543	6.144567	.162745	10
11	2.853117	18.531167	.053963	.350494	6.495061	.153963	11
12	3.138428	21.384284	.046763	.318631	6.813692	.146763	12
13	3.452271	24.522712	.040779	.289664	7.103356	.140779	13
14	3.797498	27.974983	.035746	.263331	7.366687	.135746	14
15	4.177248	31.772482	.031474	.239392	7.606080	.131474	15
16	4.594973	35.949730	.027817	.217629	7.823709	.127817	16
17	5.054470	40.544703	.024664	.197845	8.021553	.124664	17
18	5.559917	45.599173	.021930	.179859	8.201412	.121930	18
19	6.115909	51.159090	.019547	.163508	8.364920	.119547	19
20	6.727500	57.274999	.017460	.148644	8.513564	.117460	20
21	7.400250	64.002499	.015624	.135131	8.648694	.115624	21
22	8.140275	71.402749	.014005	.122846	8.771540	.114005	22
23	8.954302	79.543024	.012572	.111678	8.883218	.112572	23
24	9.849733	88.497327	.011300	.101526	8.984744	.111300	24
25	10.834706	98.347059	.010168	.092296	9.077040	.110168	25
26	11.918177	109.181765	.009159	.083905	9.160945	.109159	26
27	13.109994	121.099942	.008258	.076278	9.237223	.108258	27
28	14.420994	134.209936	.007451	.069343	9.306567	.107451	28
29	15.863093	148.630930	.006728	.063039	9.369606	.106728	29
30	17.449402	164.494023	.006079	.057309	9.426914	.106079	30
31	19.194342	181.943425	.005496	.052099	9.479013	.105496	31
32	21.113777	201.137767	.004972	.047362	9.526376	.104972	32
33	23.225154	222.251544	.004499	.043057	9.569432	.104499	33
34	25.547670	245.476699	.004074	.039143	9.608575	.104074	34
35	28.102437	271.024368	.003690	.035584	9.644159	.103690	35
36	30.912681	299.126805	.003343	.032349	9.676508	.103343	36
37	34.003949	330.039486	.003030	.029408	9.705917	.103030	37
38	37.404343	364.043434	.002747	.026735	9.732651	.102747	38
39	41.144778	401.447778	.002491	.024304	9.756956	.102491	39
40	45.259256	442.592556	.002259	.022095	9.779051	.102259	40
41	49.785181	487.851811	.002050	.020086	9.799137	.102050	41
42	54.763699	537.636992	.001860	.018260	9.817397	.101860	42
43	60.240069	592.400692	.001688	.016600	9.833998	.101688	43
44	66.264076	652.640761	.001532	.015091	9.849089	.101532	44
45	72.890484	718.904837	.001391	.013719	9.862808	.101391	45
46	80.179532	791.795321	.001263	.012472	9.875280	.101263	46
47	88.197485	871.974853	.001147	.011338	9.886618	.101147	47
48	97.017234	960.172338	.001041	.010307	9.896926	.101041	48
49	106.718957	1057.189572	.000946	.009370	9.906296	.100946	49
50	117.390853	1163.908529	.000859	.008519	9.914814	.100859	50
51	129.129938	1281.299382	.000780	.007744	9.922559	.100780	51
52	142.042932	1410.429320	.000709	.007040	9.929599	.100709	52
53	156.247225	1552.472252	.000644	.006400	9.935999	.100644	53
54	171.871948	1708.719477	.000585	.005818	9.941817	.100585	54
55	189.059142	1880.591425	.000532	.005289	9.947106	.100532	55
56	207.965057	2069.650567	.000483	.004809	9.951915	.100483	56
57	228.761562	2277.615624	.000439	.004371	9.956286	.100439	57
58	251.637719	2506.377186	.000399	.003974	9.960260	.100399	58
59	276.801490	2758.014905	.000363	.003613	9.963873	.100363	59
60	304.481640	3034.816395	.000330	.003284	9.967157	.100330	60

REMAINING LOAN BALANCE TABLES

This table illustrates the percentage of a loan balance that is unpaid based on a specified time period based on a 10 percent interest rate.

   Example: What is the loan balnce outstanding after five years, on a loan that was originally for $800,000 at a 10 percent interest rate with an amortization period of thirty years?

$$\$800,000 \times 96.6\% = \$772,800$$

Remaining Balance
in Percent or Original Loan Amount

10% | 10%

AGE OF LOAN	ORIGINAL TERM IN YEARS												AGE OF LOAN
	2.0	3.0	5.0	8.0	10.0	12.0	15.0	16.0	17.0	18.0	19.0	20.0	
1	52.5	69.9	83.8	91.4	93.9	95.5	97.0	97.3	97.6	97.9	98.1	98.3	1
2	0.0	36.7	65.8	81.9	87.1	90.4	93.6	94.4	95.0	95.6	96.1	96.5	2
3	0.0	0.0	46.0	71.4	79.6	84.9	89.9	91.1	92.1	93.0	93.8	94.5	3
4	0.0	0.0	24.2	59.8	71.3	78.8	85.8	87.5	89.0	90.2	91.3	92.3	4
5	0.0	0.0	0.0	47.0	62.2	72.0	81.3	83.5	85.5	87.1	88.5	89.8	5
6	0.0	0.0	0.0	32.9	52.1	64.5	76.3	79.1	81.6	83.7	85.5	87.1	6
7	0.0	0.0	0.0	17.3	41.0	56.2	70.8	74.3	77.3	79.9	82.1	84.1	7
8	0.0	0.0	0.0	0.0	28.6	47.1	64.7	68.9	72.5	75.7	78.4	80.7	8
9	0.0	0.0	0.0	0.0	15.0	37.0	58.0	63.0	67.3	71.0	74.3	77.1	9
10	0.0	0.0	0.0	0.0	0.0	25.9	50.6	56.5	61.5	65.9	69.7	73.0	10
11	0.0	0.0	0.0	0.0	0.0	13.6	42.4	49.2	55.1	60.2	64.7	68.5	11
12	0.0	0.0	0.0	0.0	0.0	0.0	33.3	41.2	48.1	54.0	59.1	63.6	12
13	0.0	0.0	0.0	0.0	0.0	0.0	23.3	32.4	40.3	47.1	53.0	58.1	13
14	0.0	0.0	0.0	0.0	0.0	0.0	12.2	22.7	31.6	39.4	46.2	52.1	14
15	0.0	0.0	0.0	0.0	0.0	0.0	0.0	11.9	22.1	31.0	38.7	45.4	15
16	0.0	0.0	0.0	0.0	0.0	0.0	0.0	0.0	11.6	21.7	30.4	38.0	16
17	0.0	0.0	0.0	0.0	0.0	0.0	0.0	0.0	0.0	11.4	21.3	29.9	17
18	0.0	0.0	0.0	0.0	0.0	0.0	0.0	0.0	0.0	0.0	11.2	20.9	18
19	0.0	0.0	0.0	0.0	0.0	0.0	0.0	0.0	0.0	0.0	0.0	11.0	19

AGE OF LOAN	ORIGINAL TERM IN YEARS												AGE OF LOAN
	21.0	22.0	23.0	24.0	25.0	26.0	27.0	28.0	29.0	30.0	35.0	40.0	
1	98.5	98.7	98.8	98.9	99.1	99.1	99.2	99.3	99.4	99.4	99.7	99.8	1
2	96.9	97.2	97.5	97.8	98.0	98.2	98.4	98.6	98.7	98.8	99.3	99.6	2
3	95.1	95.6	96.1	96.5	96.9	97.2	97.5	97.7	97.9	98.2	98.9	99.3	3
4	93.1	93.8	94.5	95.1	95.6	96.0	96.4	96.8	97.1	97.4	98.5	99.1	4
5	90.9	91.9	92.7	93.5	94.2	94.8	95.3	95.8	96.2	96.6	98.0	98.8	5
6	88.5	89.7	90.8	91.8	92.6	93.4	94.0	94.6	95.2	95.7	97.4	98.4	6
7	85.6	87.3	88.6	89.8	90.9	91.8	92.7	93.4	94.1	94.6	96.8	98.1	7
8	82.8	84.7	86.3	87.7	89.0	90.1	91.1	92.0	92.8	93.5	96.1	97.7	8
9	79.6	81.7	83.7	85.4	86.9	88.2	89.4	90.5	91.4	92.3	95.4	97.2	9
10	75.9	78.5	80.8	82.8	84.6	86.1	87.6	88.8	89.9	90.9	94.6	96.8	10
11	71.9	74.9	77.6	79.9	82.0	83.8	85.5	87.0	88.3	89.4	93.7	96.2	11
12	67.5	71.0	74.1	76.8	79.2	81.3	83.2	84.9	86.4	87.8	92.7	95.6	12
13	62.7	66.6	70.2	73.3	76.0	78.5	80.7	82.6	84.4	85.9	91.6	95.0	13
14	57.3	61.8	65.9	69.4	72.6	75.4	77.9	80.1	82.1	83.9	90.4	94.2	14
15	51.3	56.5	61.1	65.2	68.8	72.0	74.8	77.4	79.6	81.7	89.1	93.4	15
16	44.7	50.6	55.8	60.5	64.5	68.2	71.4	74.3	76.9	79.2	87.6	92.6	16
17	37.5	44.2	50.0	55.3	59.9	64.0	67.7	70.9	71.8	76.5	86.0	91.6	17
18	29.5	37.0	43.6	49.5	54.7	59.4	63.5	67.2	70.5	73.4	84.2	90.5	18
19	20.6	29.1	36.6	43.2	49.0	54.3	58.9	63.1	66.8	70.1	82.2	89.3	19
20	10.8	20.3	28.7	36.2	42.8	48.6	53.9	58.5	62.7	66.4	80.0	88.0	20
21	0.0	10.7	20.1	28.4	35.8	42.4	48.3	53.5	58.2	62.3	77.6	86.5	21
22	0.0	0.0	10.5	19.9	28.2	35.5	42.1	47.9	53.2	57.8	74.9	84.9	22
23	0.0	0.0	0.0	10.4	19.7	27.9	35.2	41.9	47.6	52.9	71.9	83.2	23
24	0.0	0.0	0.0	0.0	10.3	19.5	27.7	35.0	41.5	47.4	68.7	81.2	24
25	0.0	0.0	0.0	0.0	0.0	10.2	19.4	27.5	34.8	41.3	65.1	79.0	25
26	0.0	0.0	0.0	0.0	0.0	0.0	10.2	19.2	27.8	34.6	61.1	76.6	26
27	0.0	0.0	0.0	0.0	0.0	0.0	0.0	10.1	19.1	27.2	56.7	74.0	27
28	0.0	0.0	0.0	0.0	0.0	0.0	0.0	0.0	10.0	19.0	51.8	71.1	28
29	0.0	0.0	0.0	0.0	0.0	0.0	0.0	0.0	0.0	10.0	46.4	67.8	29
30	0.0	0.0	0.0	0.0	0.0	0.0	0.0	0.0	0.0	0.0	40.5	64.3	30
31	0.0	0.0	0.0	0.0	0.0	0.0	0.0	0.0	0.0	0.0	33.9	60.3	31
32	0.0	0.0	0.0	0.0	0.0	0.0	0.0	0.0	0.0	0.0	26.6	56.0	32
33	0.0	0.0	0.0	0.0	0.0	0.0	0.0	0.0	0.0	0.0	18.6	51.1	33
34	0.0	0.0	0.0	0.0	0.0	0.0	0.0	0.0	0.0	0.0	9.8	45.8	34
35	0.0	0.0	0.0	0.0	0.0	0.0	0.0	0.0	0.0	0.0	0.0	40.0	35
36	0.0	0.0	0.0	0.0	0.0	0.0	0.0	0.0	0.0	0.0	0.0	33.5	36
37	0.0	0.0	0.0	0.0	0.0	0.0	0.0	0.0	0.0	0.0	0.0	26.3	37
38	0.0	0.0	0.0	0.0	0.0	0.0	0.0	0.0	0.0	0.0	0.0	18.4	38
39	0.0	0.0	0.0	0.0	0.0	0.0	0.0	0.0	0.0	0.0	0.0	9.7	39

Appendix G

LOAN TO VALUE RATIO TABLES

This table illustrates the loans that are available based on various percentage ratios.

LOAN TO VALUE RATIO	VALUE	LOAN AMOUNT
25.00%	$1,000,000	$250,000
30.00%	$1,000,000	$300,000
35.00%	$1,000,000	$350,000
40.00%	$1,000,000	$400,000
45.00%	$1,000,000	$450,000
50.00%	$1,000.000	$500,000
55.00%	$1,000,000	$550,000
60.00%	$1,000,000	$600,000
65.00%	$1,000,000	$650,000
70.00%	$1,000,000	$700,000
75.00%	$1,000,000	$750,000
80.00%	$1,000,000	$800,000
85.00%	$1,000,000	$850,000
90.00%	$1,000,000	$900,000
95.00%	$1,000,000	$950,000

A p p e n d i x   H

RENT PRORATION TABLES

This table illustrates the proration of monthly rent on a 30-day and a 31-day monthly basis.

Rent Proration Tables

Rent Per Year	Rent Per Month	Rent Per Day (30 Days)	Rent Per Day (31 Days)	Rent Per Year	Rent Per Month	Rent Per Day (30 Days)	Rent Per Day (31 Days)
$100	$8.33	$0.28	$0.27	$825	$68.75	$2.29	$2.22
$125	$10.42	$0.35	$0.34	$850	$70.83	$2.36	$2.28
$150	$12.50	$0.42	$0.40	$875	$72.92	$2.43	$2.35
$175	$14.58	$0.49	$0.47	$900	$75.00	$2.50	$2.42
$200	$16.67	$0.56	$0.54	$925	$77.08	$2.57	$2.49
$225	$18.75	$0.63	$0.60	$950	$79.17	$2.64	$2.55
$250	$20.83	$0.69	$0.67	$975	$81.25	$2.71	$2.62
$275	$22.92	$0.76	$0.74	$1,000	$83.33	$2.78	$2.69
$300	$25.00	$0.83	$0.81	$1,025	$85.42	$2.85	$2.76
$325	$27.08	$0.90	$0.87	$1,050	$87.50	$2.92	$2.82
$350	$29.17	$0.97	$0.94	$1,075	$89.58	$2.99	$2.89
$375	$31.25	$1.04	$1.01	$1,100	$91.67	$3.06	$2.96
$400	$33.33	$1.11	$1.08	$1,125	$93.75	$3.13	$3.02
$425	$35.42	$1.18	$1.14	$1,150	$95.83	$3.19	$3.09
$450	$37.50	$1.25	$1.21	$1,175	$97.92	$3.26	$3.16
$475	$39.58	$1.32	$1.28	$1,200	$100.00	$3.33	$3.23
$500	$41.67	$1.39	$1.34	$1,225	$102.08	$3.40	$3.29
$525	$43.75	$1.46	$1.41	$1,250	$104.17	$3.47	$3.36
$550	$45.83	$1.53	$1.48	$1,275	$106.25	$3.54	$3.43
$575	$47.92	$1.60	$1.55	$1,300	$108.33	$3.61	$3.49
$600	$50.00	$1.67	$1.61	$1,325	$110.42	$3.68	$3.56
$625	$52.08	$1.74	$1.68	$1,350	$112.50	$3.75	$3.63
$650	$54.17	$1.81	$1.75	$1,375	$114.58	$3.82	$3.70
$675	$56.25	$1.88	$1.81	$1,400	$116.67	$3.89	$3.76
$700	$58.33	$1.94	$1.88	$1,425	$118.75	$3.96	$3.83
$725	$60.42	$2.01	$1.95	$1,450	$120.83	$4.03	$3.90
$750	$62.50	$2.08	$2.02	$1,475	$122.92	$4.10	$3.97
$775	$64.58	$2.15	$2.08	$1,500	$125.00	$4.17	$4.03

LAND MEASUREMENTS

The following tables illustrate the various measurements that pertain to real estate.

ENGLISH SYSTEM

Linear Measure

1 foot (ft)	= 12 inches (in)
3 feet	= 1 yard (yd)
40 rods	= 1 furlong (fur)
	= 220 yards
	= 660 feet
6,076.11549 feet	= 1 international nautical mile

Gunter's or Surveyor's Chain Measure

7.92 inches (in)	= 1 link
100 links	= 1 chain (ch)
	= 4 rods
	= 66 feet
80 chains	= 1 statute mile (mi)
	= 320 rods
	= 5,280 feet

Area Measure

144 square inches	= 1 square foot (ft^2)
9 square feet	= 1 square yard (yd^2)
	= 1,296 square inches
30¼ square yards	= 1 square rod (rd^2)
	= 272½ square feet
160 square rods	= 1 acre
	= 4,840 square yards
	= 43,560 square feet
640 acres	= 1 square mile (mi^2)
1 square mile	= 1 section (of land)
6 square miles	= 1 township
	= 36 sections
	= 36 square miles

METRIC SYSTEM

Linear Measure

10 millimeters (mm)	= 1 centimeter (cm)
10 centimeters	= 1 decimeter (dm)
	= 100 millimeters
10 decimeters	= 1 meter (m)
	= 1,000 millimeters
10 meters	= 1 dekameter (dam)
	= 100 meters
10 hectometers	= 1 kilometer (km)
	= 1,000 meters

Area Measure

100 sq. millimeters (mm^2)	= 1 square centimeter (cm^2)
10,000 sq. centimeters	= 1 square meter (m^2)
	= 1,000,000 square millimeters
100 square meters	= 1 are (a)
100 acres	= 1 hectare (ha)
	= 10,000 square meters
100 hectares	= 1 square kilometer (km^2)
	= 1,000,000 square meters

EQUIVALENTS BETWEEN ENGLISH AND METRIC SYSTEMS

Lengths

angstrom	= 0.1 nanometer (exactly)
	= 0.0001 micron (exactly)
	= 0.0000001 millimeter (exactly)
	= .000000004 inch
1 cable's length	= 120 fathoms
	= 720 feet
	= 219.456 meters (exactly)
1 centimeter (cm)	= .03937 inch
1 chain (ch.) (Gunter's	= 66 feet
or surveyor's)	= 20.1168 meters (exactly)
1 chain (engineer's)	= 100 feet
	= 30.48 meters (exactly)
1 decimeter (dm)	= 3.937 inches
1 dekameter (dam)	= 32.808 feet
1 fathom	= 6 feet
	= 1.8288 meters (exactly)

1 foot (ft)	= 0.3048 meters (exactly)
1 inch (in)	= 2.54 centimeters (exactly)
1 kilometer (km)	= 0.621 mile
	= 3,280.8 feet
1 league (land)	= 3 statute miles
	= 4.828 kilometers
1 link (Gunter's or surveyor's)	= 7.92 inches
	= 0.201 meter
1 link (engineer's)	= 1 foot
	= 0.305 meter
1 meter (m)	= 39.37 inches
	= 1.094 yards
1 mile (mi) statute or land)	= 5,280 feet
	= 1.609 kilometers
1 international nautical mile (INM)	= 1.852 kilometers (exactly)
	= 1.150779 statute miles
	= 6,076.11549 feet
1 rod (rd), pole, or perch	= 16½ feet
	= 5½ yards
	= 5.029 meters
1 yard (yd)	= 0.9144 meter (exactly)

Areas or Surfaces

1 acre	= 43,560 square feet
	= 4,840 square yards
1 are (a) (100 square meters)	= 119.599 square yards
	= 0.025 acre
1 hectare (ha) (10,000 square meters)	= 2.471 acres
1 square building	= 100 square feet
1 square centimeter (cm^2)	= 0.155 square inch
1 square decimeter (dm^2) .	= 15.500 square inches
1 square foot (ft^2)	= 929.030 square centimeters
1 square inch (in^2)	= 6.452 square centimeters
1 square kilometer (km^2)	= 247.105 acres
	= 0.386 square mile
	= 1,196 square yards
1 square meter (m^2)	= 10.764 square feet
1 square mile (mi^2)	= 640 acres 258.99 hectares
1 square rod (rd^2), sq. pole, or sq. perch	= 25.293 square meters
1 square yard (yd^2)	= 0.836 square meter

MATHEMATICAL FORMULAS

To find the circumference of a:

CIRCLE—Multiply the diameter by 3.14159265 (Pi)

To find the area of *a*:

CIRCLE—Multiply the square of a diameter by 0.785398.

RECTANGLE—Multiply the base by the height.

SQUARE—Multiply the length of one side by itself.

TRAPEZOID—Add the length of the parallel sides, multiply by the height and divide by 2.

TRIANGLE—Multiply the length of the base by the height and divide by 2.

The following table shows how a section is divided into acres.

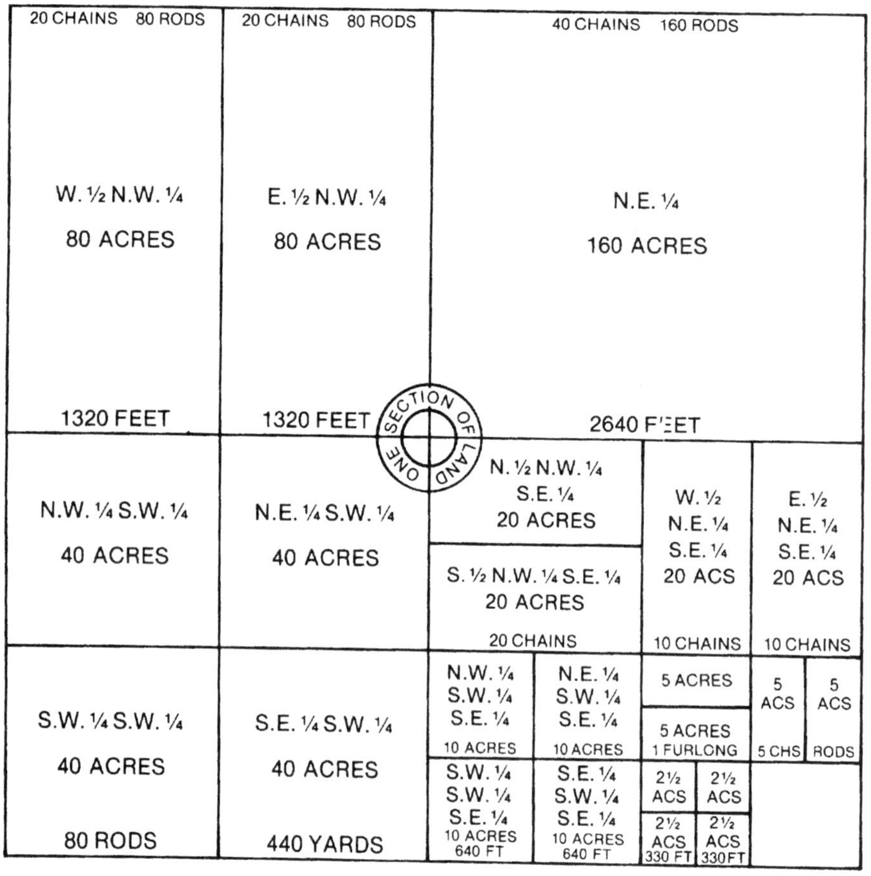

20 CHAINS 80 RODS	20 CHAINS 80 RODS	40 CHAINS 160 RODS			
W. ½ N.W. ¼ 80 ACRES	E. ½ N.W. ¼ 80 ACRES	N.E. ¼ 160 ACRES			
1320 FEET	1320 FEET	2640 FEET			
N.W. ¼ S.W. ¼ 40 ACRES	N.E. ¼ S.W. ¼ 40 ACRES	N. ½ N.W. ¼ S.E. ¼ 20 ACRES	W. ½ N.E. ¼ S.E. ¼ 20 ACS	E. ½ N.E. ¼ S.E. ¼ 20 ACS	
		S. ½ N.W. ¼ S.E. ¼ 20 ACRES			
		20 CHAINS	10 CHAINS	10 CHAINS	
S.W. ¼ S.W. ¼ 40 ACRES 80 RODS	S.E. ¼ S.W. ¼ 40 ACRES 440 YARDS	N.W. ¼ S.W. ¼ S.E. ¼ 10 ACRES S.W. ¼ S.W. ¼ S.E. ¼ 10 ACRES 640 FT	N.E. ¼ S.W. ¼ S.E. ¼ 10 ACRES S.E. ¼ S.W. ¼ S.E. ¼ 10 ACRES 640 FT	5 ACRES 5 ACRES 1 FURLONG 2½ ACS 2½ ACS 330 FT	5 ACS 5 ACS 5 CHS RODS 2½ ACS 2½ ACS 330 FT

INDEX